UFC®

ULTIMATE FIGHTING CHAMPIONSHIP®

HENDERSON
BEN

UFC®
ENCYCLOPEDIA

WRITTEN BY

THOMAS GERBASI

DK

BRADYGAMES

TABLE OF CONTENTS

EVENTS

FOREWORD

The premise was simple enough in 1993. What style of martial arts was most effective in a real fight? From there, the Ultimate Fighting Championship and the sport of mixed martial arts were born.

Of course, it wasn't that easy to go from those humble beginnings in Colorado to having a stadium show in Toronto with over 55,000 people. When you read this encyclopedia, you'll see the journey this organization took, not only in the Octagon® but also outside of it.

It was a rollercoaster ride to say the least, but as the years went by, you got to see this event evolve from a spectacle to a sport. You witnessed the sport itself grow from one where particular fighting styles would dominate for a few events at a time to one where you need to know all the main combat sports disciplines if you want to be the best of the best.

Whether you were a fan in the early days of Royce Gracie, Dan Severn, and Tank Abbott, or a fan today following Anderson Silva, Georges St-Pierre, and Cain Velasquez, if you're reading this book, you love fights. As I've said before, fighting is in our DNA—we get it, and we like it.

That's what this book is all about. It's a celebration of the athletes who have made this the fastest growing sport in the world, and the fights we will never forget. It's hard to believe we've come so far in less than two decades, but the best is still yet to come, and we can't wait to bring it to you.

Thank you for all your support over the years. Without you, none of this would be possible.

Enjoy the book,

Dana White
UFC President

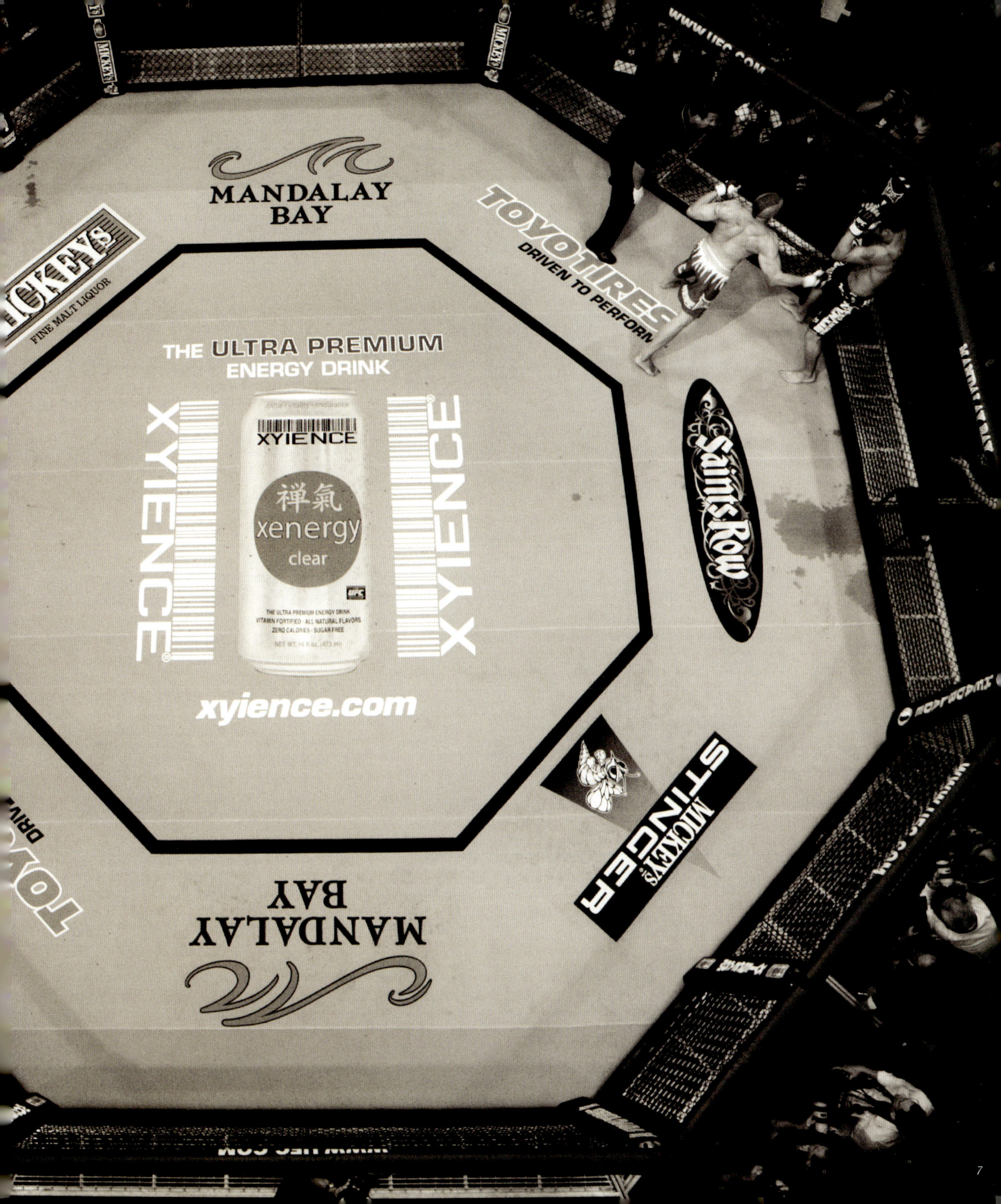
MANDALAY
BAY
MICKEYS
FINE MALT LIQUOR
TOYO TIRES
DRIVEN TO PERFORM
THE ULTRA PREMIUM
ENERGY DRINK
XYIENCE
XYIENCE
xenergy
clear
XYIENCE
xyience.com
Saints Row
MICKEY'S
STINGER
MANDALAY
BAY

DAVID ABBOTT *Tank*

HEIGHT: **6' 0" (183cm)** DATE OF BIRTH: **26 April 1965**
WEIGHT: **260-280 lbs (118-127 kg)** HOMETOWN: **Huntington Beach, CA**

PROFESSIONAL RECORD: 10-14 UFC RECORD: 8-10

"I'm going to be the most athletic person that's ever stepped into the Octagon." With those words, the UFC career of David "Tank" Abbott began. And while he wasn't going to live up to that statement, he established himself not only as one of the most popular figures in the UFC, but also as a legitimate knockout artist.

Entering the Octagon at UFC 6 in 1995 with a style described as "Pit Fighting," Abbott kept it quiet that he was an accomplished high school and junior college wrestler, and despite graduating from Long Beach State University with a degree in history, he was content to play the role of barroom brawler.

And it paid off, as his chilling 18-second knockout of John Matua set the stage for a career that—win or lose—saw him captivate fans for nearly 15 years.

On that first July night in the UFC, Abbott stopped Matua and Paul Varelans before being submitted by Oleg Taktarov, and the pattern of Abbot's career was set—if you let him be the bully, he would beat you; if you bullied him or got him to the canvas, the fight was over.

That didn't stop fans from tuning in whenever Abbott fought though, and through 1995-96, he was one of the organization's most reliable attractions. He would defeat the likes of Steve Jennum, Sam Adkins, Cal Worsham and Steve Nelmark, but when he would step up to world-class foes such as Dan Severn, Don Frye and Vitor Belfort, Abbott wasn't up to the task.

Even with back-to-back losses against Frye and Belfort, Abbott was awarded a heavyweight title shot against Maurice Smith at UFC 15 in October of 1997. Not surprisingly, Smith finished Abbott in 8:08.

After a knockout loss to Pedro Rizzo at UFC Brazil in 1998, Abbott took off from the sport for nearly five years, returning at UFC 41, where he was submitted by Frank Mir in 46 seconds. After two more Octagon defeats, Abbott left the UFC, but still remained a high-profile name for the resumes of Hidehiko Yoshida and Kimbo Slice.

YOSHIHIRO AKIYAMA *Sexyama*

HEIGHT: **5' 10" (178 cm)** DATE OF BIRTH: **29 July 1975**
WEIGHT: **185 lbs (84 kg)** HOMETOWN: **Osaka, Japan**

PROFESSIONAL RECORD: 13-3, 2 NC UFC RECORD: 1-2

A judo black belt who earned All-Asia and All-Japan titles, Yoshihiro Akiyama is a certified star in Japan, dubbed "Sexyama" for his appearances on television and on fashion show catwalks. How big is he at home? "Like Chuck Liddell in the U.S.," he said. Thankfully, he can fight too, and after a stellar stint in Asia, he brought his immense talents to the UFC in 2009. Though his Octagon record currently sits at just 1-2, with a decision win over Alan Belcher and losses to Chris Leben and Michael Bisping, Akiyama entered the record books as the first competitor to win Fight of the Night awards in each of his first three UFC bouts.

JOSE ALDO *Junior*

HEIGHT: **5' 7" (170 cm)** DATE OF BIRTH: **9 Sept. 1986**
WEIGHT: **145 lbs (66 kg)** HOMETOWN: **Rio de Janeiro, Brazil**

PROFESSIONAL RECORD: 19-1 UFC RECORD: 1-0
TITLES HELD: UFC AND WEC FEATHERWEIGHT CHAMPION

A dynamic fighter with myriad weapons to put opponents away, Jose Aldo has had a rapid rise up the mixed martial arts ranks. After winning 10 of his first 11 pro bouts on the local circuit (with his only loss coming via submission to Luciano Azevedo in 2005), he established himself as one of the sport's best, pound-for-pound. After arriving in the United States, he took the WEC featherweight title from Mike Brown in November of 2009 and then was named the first 145-pound champion in UFC history a year later.

What may have been more impressive is that despite holding a black belt in Brazilian jiu-jitsu, winning numerous grappling titles and learning his craft under world-renowned ground fighter André Pederneiras, Aldo made his name not with armbars or chokes, but with striking ability. He has seven KO victories in eight WEC bouts, three of which won "Knockout of the Night" honors.

"The thrill of knocking out an opponent is one of the best things in the world; your work is done," said the Manaus, Brazil native, who followed up his WEC debut win over Alexandre Nogueira with knockouts of Jonathan Brookins, Rolando Perez, Chris Mickle, Cub Swanson and Brown.

Aldo didn't rest on his laurels, and after scoring a lopsided five-round win over WEC superstar Urijah Faber (one dominated by Aldo's ferocious leg kicks) and knocking out durable contender Manny Gamburyan in his final two WEC bouts, he made his transition to the UFC. There he continued his reign of excellence at UFC 129 in April of 2011 by winning an exciting five-round battle over Canada's Mark Hominick that earned the two 145-pound warriors "Fight of the Night" honors.

Now it's on to face the rest of the featherweight division.

"I'm an employee and whoever the boss wants me to fight, that's who I've got to fight and take out," said Aldo. "I'm prepared to fight whoever they put in front of me anytime."

JOHN ALESSIO
The Natural

HEIGHT: **5' 10" (178 cm)**
WEIGHT: **170 lbs (77 kg)**
DATE OF BIRTH: **5 July 1979**
HOMETOWN: **Vancouver, BC, Canada**

PROFESSIONAL RECORD: 36-13
UFC RECORD: 0-3

With a 6-3 record and less than two years experience, John Alessio admits that he was "a deer caught in headlights" in his UFC debut—a 2000 clash with Pat Miletich for the welterweight championship. Alessio got submitted at UFC 26, and he wouldn't return to the Octagon for six years, when he lost a close decision to Diego Sanchez at UFC 60. In between, the Canadian competed in PRIDE and in other organizations. The loss to Sanchez, as well as one to Thiago Alves, forced his release from the UFC, but Alessio competed in the WEC, going 5-2, with his only losses coming to Brock Larson and in a title bout against Carlos Condit.

HOUSTON ALEXANDER
The Assassin

HEIGHT: **6' 0" (183 cm)**
WEIGHT: **205 lbs (93 kg)**
DATE OF BIRTH: **2 March 1972**
HOMETOWN: **Omaha, NE**

PROFESSIONAL RECORD: 11-6
UFC RECORD: 2-4

For a brief spell in 2007, the talk of the mixed martial arts world was Houston "The Assassin" Alexander, an exciting knockout artist with a heart of gold who went from obscurity to stardom thanks to a compelling back story and a 48-second finish of Keith Jardine at UFC 71. A single father raising six children, the Nebraskan even donated one of his kidneys to his daughter in 2000, and in the Octagon, Alexander's ferocious first-round knockout wins over Jardine and Alessio Sakara put him on the light heavyweight map. But a four-fight losing streak capped by a dismal decision loss to Kimbo Slice in 2009 prompted his release from the UFC.

RICARDO ALMEIDA
Big Dog

HEIGHT: **6' 0" (183 cm)**
WEIGHT: **170 lbs (77 kg)**
DATE OF BIRTH: **29 Nov. 1976**
HOMETOWN: **Hamilton, NJ**

PROFESSIONAL RECORD: 13-4
UFC RECORD: 6-4

One of the most gifted grapplers in MMA, black belt Ricardo Almeida has used his skills on the mat to befuddle some of the world's best fighters. His first time around in the Octagon wasn't a successful one though, as he lost two of three bouts. Undeterred, he went to Japan and defeated Nate Marquardt for the Pancrase Middleweight Title, one of six consecutive wins that he compiled there. Following a nearly four-year break from the sport to focus on his family and his growing academy, Almeida returned to MMA and the UFC in 2008, and has since won five of seven bouts.

THIAGO ALVES *Pitbull*

HEIGHT: **5' 9" (175 cm)** WEIGHT: **170 lbs (77 kg)** DATE OF BIRTH: **3 Oct. 1983** HOMETOWN: **Fortaleza, Brazil**

PROFESSIONAL RECORD: 23-6 UFC RECORD: 10-5

Given Thiago Alves' ever-present smile and laid-back demeanor, you wouldn't expect him to live up to his nickname "Pitbull" in the Octagon. But when the bell rings on fight night, you won't find any welterweight more feared than the native of Fortaleza, Brazil.

That's now. In the early stages of Alves' UFC career, which began with a submission loss to Spencer Fisher on October 3, 2005, his reputation was that of an ultra-talented rising star, but one who wasn't devoting the proper time to his chosen craft in the gym. That meant that when he was on, like in his knockouts of Ansar Chalangov and Derrick Noble, he would give anyone at 170 pounds fits. When he wasn't, as in his losses to Fisher and Jon Fitch, he was merely average.

After the loss to Fitch in June of 2006 though, Alves realized that he would never reach the next level if he didn't train as hard as he fought. The transformation was amazing, and from October of 2006 to October of 2008, he was unstoppable, winning seven fights in a row, including TKO victories over Chris Lytle and Karo Parisyan, a knockout of Matt Hughes and a decision win over Josh Koscheck.

The 7-0 run earned him a shot at Georges St-Pierre's welterweight title at UFC 100 on July 11, 2009, but he lost a lopsided five-round unanimous decision. That wasn't the worst of Alves' troubles though, as a UFC 111 rematch with Fitch in early 2010 was scratched due to an irregularity on his CT scan stemming from a pre-existing condition. A subsequent surgery separated an artery from a vein in his brain, and soon after he was given a clean bill of health and allowed back into the gym and into competition. He would lose the rematch to Fitch at UFC 117 in August 2010, but at UFC 124 four months later, the "Pitbull" was back in fearsome form in a three-round win over John "Doomsday" Howard and on his way back to the top. And this time around, he's got a reason to smile.

YOJI ANJO

HEIGHT: **5' 11" (180 cm)**
WEIGHT: **200 lbs (91 kg)**
DATE OF BIRTH: **31 Dec. 1969**
HOMETOWN: **Tokyo, Japan**

PROFESSIONAL RECORD: 0-5-1
UFC RECORD: 0-3

Though Yoji Anjo will be remembered as a fighter who never experienced the thrill of victory, the Suginami native was a pretty big deal in the world of pro wrestling where he played the "bad guy" role. That notoriety led him to MMA, and after debuting at home against Sean Alvarez in a bout that lasted over 34 minutes in 1996, he was a natural for a bout against Tank Abbott in the UFC's first visit to Japan in 1997. He lasted the distance against Abbott in a losing effort, but was finished by Murilo Bustamante and Matt Lindland in subsequent Octagon bouts. In 2004, he lost his final match to Ryan Gracie in PRIDE.

ANDREI ARLOVSKI *The Pit Bull*

HEIGHT: **6' 4" (193 cm)** DATE OF BIRTH: **4 Feb. 1979**

WEIGHT: **240 lbs (190 kg)** HOMETOWN: **Minsk, Belarus**

PROFESSIONAL RECORD: 15-8

UFC RECORD: 10-4

TITLES HELD: UFC HEAVYWEIGHT CHAMPION

It was as far away from the top of the mixed martial arts world as you could get, and frankly, Andrei "The Pit Bull" Arlovski had hit rock bottom in his professional fighting career. A native of Minsk, Belarus, Arlovski gave up a secure job as a police officer back home to roll the dice in a foreign country as a mixed martial artist, and after starting his career at 3-1 (including a UFC win over Aaron Brink), he would get stopped in back-to-back fights by Ricco Rodriguez and Pedro Rizzo.

The year was 2002, and everyone saw the potential of Arlovski, 6' 4", 240 pounds, with the speed and athleticism of a middleweight and the power of a heavyweight. Add in a solid ground game which dwarfed that of most of his peers, and stardom should have been a given.

But something was lost in the translation between Arlovski's talent and what showed up in the Octagon on fight night. It was nothing you could pinpoint by watching him fight, but it was obviously not there when he lost to the then-top contenders Rodriguez and Rizzo.

So he was at a crossroads. At 23, Andrei Arlovski had to decide whether he was going to be content with a .500 record and a paycheck here and there while being a step or two below the elite of the sport, or whether he was going to re-invent himself and go all-out in training and in fights in a quest to be the best.

Tough as nails Ian Freeman would be Arlovski's measuring stick at UFC 40 in November of 2002. Win, and he lives to fight another day; lose, and it's back to Belarus.

"If I wanted to stay in the United States and compete in the UFC, I was given one more opportunity to fight Ian Freeman," said Arlovski. "That was a breaking point for me."

Just 1:25 into the first round, with a blistering attack that left the Brit defenseless, the world then had its answer—Arlovski was not content to be mediocre; he wanted to be the best.

From there, Arlovski took over the heavyweight division, stopping Vladimir "The Janitor" Matyushenko and Wesley "Cabbage" Correira. Next he submitted Tim Sylvia with an Achilles lock in just 47 seconds at UFC 51 on February 5, 2005 to win the interim UFC heavyweight title. But don't tell him the win was an easy one.

UFC 66: Arlovski vs. Cruz

"I don't think I beat Tim Sylvia easily," said Arlovski. "For me it's not about the fight finishing in a few seconds or a few minutes—it's about the overall preparation process. When you put three months of your life into something like this and years before that, it's not easy."

It's this paradox that made Arlovski one of the most intriguing figures in the sport. Respectful and accessible outside the Octagon, inside of it he becomes a different person, right down to his fang-emblazoned mouthpiece. This Jekyll and Hyde persona hit home with fight fans as well, as they watched Arlovski declared undisputed champion after his title defense against Justin Eilers (TKO1) at UFC 53 and then saw him blast out dangerous Paul Buentello in just 15 seconds.

His reign would end at UFC 59 on April 15, 2006, as he was stopped in a single round by Sylvia in their rematch, and a third bout less than three months later saw Sylvia emerge victorious again, this time by five-round decision.

Following the Sylvia rubber match, Arlovski never seemed to recapture the fire that put him on top in the first place, and though he finished off his UFC contract with three wins over Marcio Cruz, Fabricio Werdum, and Jake O'Brien, he would not be re-signed.

Arlovski would go on to fight for the Affliction, Elite XC and Strikeforce promotions, losing three of five bouts. But he kept a level head throughout his career, noting before his rematch with Sylvia, "Fighters are only as good as their last fight, and after the last fight it's all from ground zero. I win the fight, yes, I'm on top. But the next time, if I don't win the fight, I'm not on top anymore."

UFC 61: Arlovski vs. Sylvia 3

RAPHAEL ASSUNCAO

HEIGHT: **5' 5" (165 cm)**
WEIGHT: **145 lbs (66 kg)**
DATE OF BIRTH: **19 July 1982**
HOMETOWN: **Recife, Brazil**

PROFESSIONAL RECORD: 15-4 UFC RECORD: 0-1

One of the most respected featherweight fighters in the world, Raphael Assuncao has won 15 of 19 pro bouts, with the only losses coming against big names Jeff Curran, Urijah Faber, Erik Koch and Diego Nunes. A Brazilian jiu-jitsu black belt from Recife, Brazil, Assuncao has been dazzling fight fans since his debut in 2004, defeating the likes of Joe Lauzon and Jorge Masvidal along the way. In the WEC, Assuncao—the brother of UFC vet Junior Assuncao—made his presence known by defeating Jameel Massouh, Yves Jabouin and L.C. Davis, and while he lost his UFC debut via knockout against Koch at UFC 128, he is using the setback as fuel to propel him even further in the future.

MARCUS AURELIO *Maximus*

HEIGHT: **5' 10" (175 cm)**
WEIGHT: **155 lbs (70 kg)**
DATE OF BIRTH: **18 Aug. 1973**
HOMETOWN: **Fortaleza, Brazil**

PROFESSIONAL RECORD: 20-9 UFC RECORD: 2-4

A pro fighter since 2002, Brazilian jiu-jitsu black belt Marcus Aurelio's ground game first made an international impact in April 2006, when he handed Japanese superstar Takanori Gomi his first defeat in the PRIDE organization. Seven months later, Gomi would get even via split decision, but following the bout, Aurelio received a UFC contract. Aurelio would struggle, with stellar finishes of Luke Caudillo and Ryan Roberts overshadowed by his losses, which included a decision defeat against his hometown rival Hermes Franca at UFC 90 that doubled as a Fortaleza turf war. After the loss to Franca, Aurelio was brought back one more time at UFC 102, but he dropped a close decision to Evan Dunham.

RYAN BADER *Darth*

HEIGHT: **6' 2" (188 cm)**
WEIGHT: **205 lbs (94 kg)**
DATE OF BIRTH: **7 June 1983**
HOMETOWN: **Tempe, AZ**

PROFESSIONAL RECORD: 13-0 UFC RECORD: 5-1
TITLES HELD: *THE ULTIMATE FIGHTER 8* LIGHT HEAVYWEIGHT WINNER

An imposing physical force with the size, strength, and athleticism to give any opponent a tough time in the Octagon, Ryan Bader is widely considered to be one of the top prospects for world title honors in the ultra-competitive 205-pound weight class.

A lifelong athlete, Bader was a two-time state high school champion in Nevada, and threw in recognition as the state's 2001 Defensive Player of the Year in football for good measure. In college, Bader's excellence continued, and by the time he graduated from Arizona State University, he had achieved All-American status twice and was a three-time Pac-10 champion.

Missing competition after college, Bader and college teammate CB Dollaway began training in mixed martial arts. In 2007, he made his pro debut, and after compiling a 7-0 record, he was brought to Las Vegas to compete as a member of *The Ultimate Fighter 8* cast.

Bader tore through his three opponents on the show before capping off his run with a TKO of Vinicius Magalhaes that earned him the season title. Bader's stellar wrestling carried him through decision wins against Carmelo Marrero and Eric Schafer in 2009, but it was in 2010 that he began showing the evolution of his all-around fight game as he knocked out Keith Jardine and decisioned veteran contender Minotauro Nogueira. At UFC 126, he kicked off 2011 with a highly-anticipated showdown against fellow hot prospect Jon Jones.

RENAN BARAO

HEIGHT: **5' 6" (168 cm)**
WEIGHT: **135 lbs (61 kg)**
DATE OF BIRTH: **27 Feb. 1987**
HOMETOWN: **Rio de Janeiro, Brazil**

PROFESSIONAL RECORD: 27-1, 1 NC UFC RECORD: 1-0

A training partner of UFC featherweight titleholder Jose Aldo, Brazil's Renan Barao is on a quest to join his teammate atop the championship ranks. Owner of a stellar 27-1 (1 NC) record, Barao lost his first pro bout in 2005 and has not lost since, submitting 11 opponents and knocking out five of his foes in the process.

In 2009, Barao won five times, and he kicked off 2010 with a decision win over Sergio Rodrigues in February. But it was his two submission wins against Anthony Leone and Chris Cariaso in his first two WEC bouts in 2010 that really turned heads, making his transition into the UFC a smooth one.

All it took was one look at 19-year-old Vitor Belfort back at UFC 12 in February 1997, and you were hooked. A black belt in jiu-jitsu under his adopted father, the legendary Carlson Gracie, Belfort instead used a blistering standup attack to stop Tra Telligman and Scott Ferrozzo in a combined two minutes, and with that one-night tournament victory, a star was born.

A native of Rio de Janeiro, Belfort said he turned to MMA simply because "I just liked the sport. It is challenging and I like to be challenged."

Vitor had little in the way of a challenge in the early UFC days. He easily won the UFC 12 tournament. Three months later at UFC 13, it took him only 52 seconds to dismantle Tank Abbott. Fans wondered if Belfort could be beaten.

However in this sport, all it takes is one bad night to overturn a perfect record, and at UFC 15 in October of 1997, Octagon newcomer Randy Couture taught Belfort a painful lesson as his ground and pound attack nullified the Brazilian's speed and power and issued Belfort his first pro loss via TKO.

"I was totally out of focus," said Belfort. "I wasn't training, I was thinking I was the greatest and that nobody could beat me."

The reality check appeared to work, as Belfort bounced back with a submission of Joe Charles and a 44-second knockout of Wanderlei Silva, but as soon as he was back on track, Belfort left the UFC to compete for Japan's PRIDE organization.

UFC Ultimate Brazil: Belfort vs. Silva

In PRIDE, Belfort enjoyed great success from 1999 to 2001 as he won four of five fights, defeating the likes of Heath Herring and Gilbert Yvel while only losing a decision to Kazushi Sakuraba.

UFC 37.5: Belfort vs. Liddell

This hot streak prompted a return to the UFC, and Belfort was immediately slotted for a light heavyweight championship fight against Tito Ortiz in the organization's debut in Las Vegas and return to Pay-Per-View television at UFC 33 in September of 2001. Yet an injury forced Belfort out of the high-profile bout and delayed his comeback.

In June of 2002, Belfort finally got back in the Octagon at UFC 37.5, but lost a three-round decision to the sport's newest star, Chuck Liddell. It would be nearly a year before Belfort returned to action, but when he did, he delivered in true "Phenom" form at UFC 43 as he knocked out Marvin Eastman in just 67 seconds.

UFC 43: Belfort vs. Eastman

VITOR BELFORT *The Phenom*

HEIGHT: **6' 0" (183 cm)**

DATE OF BIRTH: **1 April 1977**

WEIGHT: **185 lbs (84 kg)**

HOMETOWN: **Rio de Janeiro, Brazil**

PROFESSIONAL RECORD: 19-8

UFC RECORD: 8-4

TITLES HELD: UFC LIGHT HEAVYWEIGHT CHAMPION, UFC 12 HEAVYWEIGHT TOURNAMENT CHAMPION

Yet after his 2006 loss to Dan Henderson in PRIDE, a 30-year-old Belfort started to show the focus he had lacked consistently over the previous years. Three straight wins over Ivan Serati, James Zikic, and Terry Martin followed—two by knockout—and in January of 2009, the new middleweight knocked out former UFC title challenger Matt Lindland in just 37 seconds.

Back in the win column, Belfort was given a January 31, 2004 title shot against 205-pound champion Randy Couture. On January 9, just weeks before the bout, the joy of his December 2003 marriage to Joana Prado was shattered by the news that his sister, Priscila Vieira Belfort, had disappeared in Rio de Janiero.

At UFC 46, despite the emotional turmoil swirling around him, Belfort defeated Couture via first-round TKO due to a cut to win the UFC light heavyweight championship. Sadly, the win would not be followed by good news of his sister, as it was revealed in 2007 that she was murdered by her abductors.

From 2004 to 2006, Belfort went into a tailspin in his professional life, as he lost his championship to Couture via third-round TKO at UFC 49 in August of 2004, and went on to drop four of his next six bouts, including a decision to Ortiz at UFC 51, his last Octagon appearance for nearly five years.

UFC 46: Belfort vs. Couture

PRIDE 32: Belfort vs. Henderson

Belfort was back, and when he stopped former champion Rich Franklin in the first round in his victorious return to the Octagon at UFC 103 in September of 2009, the only thing remaining was for this more mature fighter to win another UFC title. On February 5, 2011, he got his chance against Anderson Silva.

UFC 103: Belfort vs. Franklin

JOSH BARNETT *The Baby-Faced Assassin*

HEIGHT: **6' 3" (191 cm)** WEIGHT: **250 lbs (113 kg)** DATE OF BIRTH: **10 Nov. 1977** HOMETOWN: **Seattle, WA**

PROFESSIONAL RECORD: **26-5** TITLES HELD: **UFC HEAVYWEIGHT CHAMPION**
UFC RECORD: **4-1**

When you look at the UFC career of Josh Barnett, it's the classic case of what might have been. An ultra-talented athlete who could handle himself on the ground or while standing, the Seattle product tore through his first six opponents, with a fourth-round submission win over Dan "The Beast" Severn in February of 2000 earning him an invite to the UFC.

While in the Octagon, Barnett didn't skip a beat, stopping Gan McGee at UFC 28 before suffering his pro defeat three months later against Brazilian contender Pedro Rizzo. Yet the bout was so well-received that even after getting knocked out, Barnett's stock remained high. After two comeback wins, Barnett was matched against Randy Couture at UFC 36 on March 22, 2002, and after stopping Couture in the second round, Barnett, at 24, became the youngest heavyweight champion in history, a record that still stands.

Four months later, Barnett was stripped of the title and suspended by the Nevada State Athletic Commission after testing positive for three anabolic agents. Barnett denied the charges, but ultimately, his time in the UFC was over.

Eventually, Barnett resurfaced in Japan, where he had great success in the Pancrase and PRIDE organizations, but when he returned to the United States for a 2009 Affliction bout against Fedor Emelianenko, he tested positive for anabolic steroids once again, canceling the match and the event. Barnett remains an active fighter.

PHIL BARONI

The New York Bad Ass

HEIGHT: **5' 9" (175 cm)**
WEIGHT: **185 lbs (84 kg)**
DATE OF BIRTH: **16 April 1976**
HOMETOWN: **Long Island, NY**

PROFESSIONAL RECORD: **13-13**
UFC RECORD: **3-7**

Ask Phil Baroni why he began fighting, and he'll tell you it's because he "can't sing or dance." The popular "New York Bad Ass" can scrap though, and despite his losing UFC record, he always came to fight. Baroni began his UFC career quietly with a decision win over Curtis Stout at UFC 30 in 2001, but by the end of that year, he was making plenty of noise thanks to his memorable loss to Matt Lindland. Baroni would bounce back with crushing knockouts of Dave Menne and Amar Suloev, and while the Menne win would be his last in the Octagon, Baroni will always have a place in the hearts of UFC fans worldwide.

PAT BARRY *HD*

HEIGHT: **5' 11" (180 cm)** DATE OF BIRTH: **7 July 1979**
WEIGHT: **235 lbs (107 kg)** HOMETOWN: **New Orleans, LA**

PROFESSIONAL RECORD: **6-2** UFC RECORD: **3-2**

Former K-1 kickboxer Pat Barry once said getting hit by one of his leg kicks was like "stepping on a land mine," and you won't get any arguments from Dan Evensen or Joey Beltran, two fighters who got chopped down by those kicks. Fellow kickboxer Antoni Hardonk also got finished by the big man from the Big Easy, and these devastating performances and a gregarious personality have made Barry a fan favorite in rapid fashion. Now the only thing left for Barry to do is to shore up the ground game that has led him to both of his submission defeats (to Tim Hague and Mirko Cro Cop), and it looks like smooth future sailing.

ALAN BELCHER *The Talent*

HEIGHT: **6' 2" (188 cm)** DATE OF BIRTH: **24 April 1984**
WEIGHT: **185 lbs (84 kg)** HOMETOWN: **Biloxi, MS**

PROFESSIONAL RECORD: **15-5** UFC RECORD: **7-4**

The moments before the opening bell can be the scariest for even the toughest fighters. Alan Belcher described it as "a bungee jump. Because you have to get yourself ready and there's no turning back." That's an accurate statement in the career of this middleweight, who has taken fans on an unpredictable but exciting ride since his UFC debut in 2006. From a front flip against Yushin Okami and a single-kick knockout of Jorge Santiago, to a three-round war with Yoshihiro Akiyama and a submission of Patrick Cote, "The Talent" has consistently brought excitement, and he has the two Fight of the Night and two Submission of the Night awards to prove it.

VITOR BELFORT PAGE 12

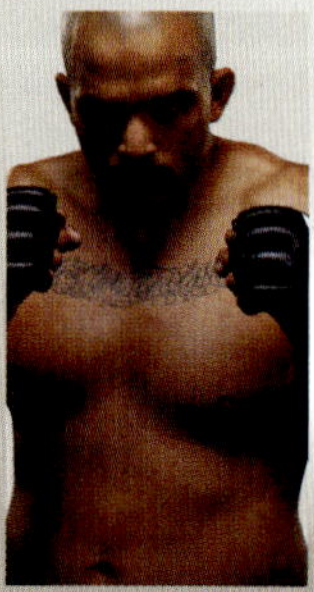

JOEY BELTRAN *The Mexicutioner*

HEIGHT: **6' 1" (185 cm)** DATE OF BIRTH: **8 Dec. 1981**
WEIGHT: **240 lbs (109 kg)** HOMETOWN: **Carlsbad, CA**

PROFESSIONAL RECORD: **12-5** UFC RECORD: **2-2**

Joey Beltran will never wow anyone with technique or athleticism, but when it comes to heart and a desire to fight, he's right up there with the best in the heavyweight division. A pro since 2007, Beltran parlayed TKO wins over UFC vets Sherman Pendergarst, Wes Combs and Houston Alexander into a 2010 shot in the Octagon, and he delivered in his first two bouts in the big show, stopping heavily favored Rolles Gracie at UFC 109 and decisioning hometown hero Tim Hague at UFC 113. Two unanimous decision defeats followed against Matt Mitrione and Pat Barry, but after both bouts, the victors certainly knew that they had been in a fight, a "Mexicutioner" trademark.

JOSEPH BENAVIDEZ

HEIGHT: **5' 4" (163 cm)**

WEIGHT: **135 lbs (61 kg)**

DATE OF BIRTH:

31 July 1984

HOMETOWN:

Las Cruces, NM

PROFESSIONAL RECORD: 14-2

UFC RECORD: 1-0

After talking to former WEC featherweight champion Urijah Faber for any length of time, the name Joseph Benavidez would inevitably come up, and he would rave about his training partner's talent and work ethic.

High praise. But would the former wrestler from San Antonio, Texas live up to his teammate's expectations? That question was answered affirmatively and impressively in December of 2008, as Benavidez pounded out a three-round decision win in his WEC debut over Danny Martinez to improve to 9-0 as a pro.

"I want to be the best, that's why I do this," said Benavidez, who has gone on to defeat Jeff Curran, Rani Yahya, Miguel Angel Torres and Ian Loveland, becoming one of the best bantamweights in the world in the process.

DAVE BENETEAU

Dangerous

HEIGHT: **6' 2" (188 cm)**

WEIGHT:

250 lbs (113 kg)

DATE OF BIRTH: **16 July 1968**

HOMETOWN:

Windsor, Ontario, Canada

PROFESSIONAL RECORD: 6-5-1

UFC RECORD: 3-3

He eventually became a criminal lawyer in his native Canada, but back in the early days of the UFC, Dave Beneteau laid down the law of a different sort. Scoring two quick wins in his UFC 5 debut over Asbel Cancio and Todd Medina that lasted a combined 2:33, Beneteau was considered to be a serious threat to future Hall of Famer Dan Severn, but "The Beast" emerged victorious in that night's tournament, submitting Beneteau in 3:01. Back-to-back losses to Oleg Taktarov and a nearly two-year break followed, but Beneteau finished his UFC career on a high note with a UFC 15 win over Carlos Barreto in 1997. Beneteau continued to fight until 2001.

STEVE BERGER

The Red Nose Pitbull

HEIGHT: **5' 11" (180 cm)**

WEIGHT: **170 lbs (77 kg)**

DATE OF BIRTH:

20 May 1973

HOMETOWN: **St. Louis, MO**

PROFESSIONAL RECORD: 21-21-2, 1 NC

UFC RECORD: 0-2, 1 NC

A journeyman in the best sense of the term, Steve Berger's talent isn't reflected in his winless UFC record or his overall mixed martial arts slate. But when you fight anyone at any time, even on short notice, it's a handicap that's hard to overcome. In the Octagon, Berger came up short in all three of his bouts, losing a decision to Tony DeSouza at UFC 31, getting a no contest against Benji Radach at UFC 37 when it was ruled that Radach's TKO win was stopped incorrectly, and then getting halted in two rounds by Robbie Lawler at UFC 37.5. Despite these setbacks, Berger remains active today, but has only gone 6-13 in the process.

MICHAEL BISPING

The Count

HEIGHT: **6' 2" (188 cm)**

WEIGHT: **185 lbs (84 kg)**

DATE OF BIRTH: **28 Feb. 1979**

HOMETOWN: **Manchester, England**

PROFESSIONAL RECORD: 21-3 UFC RECORD: 10-3

TITLES HELD: *TUF3* LIGHT HEAVYWEIGHT WINNER

Before Michael Bisping arrived, the track record of fighters from the United Kingdom in the UFC was spotty at best. Yet where fighters like Mark Weir and Ian Freeman only showed flashes of their potential, "The Count" established himself as one of the game's top 185-pounders, regardless of nationality.

A martial artist since the age of eight, Bisping turned to MMA in 2003, and with his kickboxing and jiu-jitsu background, he was a quick study, running through the local ranks to build an impressive unbeaten record. His obvious talent earned him a spot on *The Ultimate Fighter 3*, and to no one's surprise, he ran the table, winning three straight fights to take the season title.

Not skipping a beat, Bisping kept his winning streak going with a win against Eric Schafer and a UFC 70 stoppage of Elvis Sinosic in the organization's return to the UK. Those wins made Bisping a star in his home country, but after a controversial decision win over Matt Hamill at UFC 75, the outspoken Brit made few friends.

"I am who I am," he said. "I speak my mind, but a lot of what I say sometimes is tongue in cheek and I think sometimes people don't get that and they just think I'm being arrogant and cocky."

Embracing the attention, Bisping headlined UFC 78 in a losing effort against Rashad Evans, but then dropped to 185 pounds and started a new winning streak with victories over Charles McCarthy, Jason Day and Chris Leben. Next up was another stint on *The Ultimate Fighter*, this time as a coach against Dan Henderson on season nine. While his team won both season titles, coach Bisping got knocked out by Henderson at UFC 100.

Undeterred, Bisping showed what he was made of, bouncing back with a TKO of Denis Kang at UFC 105 in November of 2009. After a decision defeat to Wanderlei Silva three months later, he finished up 2010 with wins over Dan Miller and Yoshihiro Akiyama, proving that this UK standout is here to stay.

Bisping is one of the coaches of *TUF14* opposite Jason Miller.

AMAURY BITETTI

HEIGHT: **5' 9" (175 cm)**
WEIGHT: **185 lbs (84 kg)**
DATE OF BIRTH: **1971**
HOMETOWN: **Rio de Janeiro, Brazil**

PROFESSIONAL RECORD: 5-2
UFC RECORD: 1-1

When Amaury Bitetti was brought in to replace countryman Marco Ruas against United States superstar Don Frye at UFC 9 in 1996, many saw him as the second coming of Royce Gracie, and the Carlson Gracie jiu-jitsu black belt had the endless list of grappling titles to lend credence to such talk. But the unbeaten Frye was in top form, and despite a courageous effort, Bitetti was stopped via strikes. It would be four years until he returned to the Octagon, but his lone UFC victory at UFC 26 was anti-climactic, as Alex Andrade was disqualified for kicking with shoes on. Bitetti finished up his MMA career following a 2001 decision win over Dennis Hallman.

BRAD BLACKBURN

Bad

HEIGHT: **5' 10" (178 cm)**
WEIGHT: **170 lbs (77 kg)**
DATE OF BIRTH: **25 May 1977**
HOMETOWN: **Olympia, WA**

PROFESSIONAL RECORD: 15-12-1, 1 NC
UFC RECORD: 3-2

In the first four years of "Bad" Brad Blackburn's pro MMA career, the scouting report on him was simple: survive the first round, and opponents' odds of winning increased substantially. Yet after a rough start that saw him go 0-7-1 in fights that went past one round, Blackburn began dedicating his life to fighting full-time, and after defeating the likes of Chris Wilson and Jay Hieron, he eventually earned a UFC contract in 2008. There he used his hard-nosed determination and fight-ending power to win three Octagon bouts in a row against James Giboo (TKO2), Ryo Chonan (W3), and Edgar Garcia (W3) before consecutive losses to Amir Sadollah and DaMarques Johnson got him released in 2010.

MARK BOCEK

HEIGHT: **5' 8" (173 cm)**
WEIGHT: **155 lbs (70 kg)**
DATE OF BIRTH: **24 Oct. 1981**
HOMETOWN: **Toronto, Ontario, Canada**

PROFESSIONAL RECORD: 9-3
UFC RECORD: 5-3

In 1994, everything changed for 12-year-old Mark Bocek when he watched Royce Gracie submit foe after foe at UFC 2. "Once I started learning it (jiu-jitsu), it was this new profound experience. It was something you could feel was working." Bocek went on to became one of the world's finest practitioners of the art, a black belt who used his talent on the mat to win five UFC bouts thus far, including four by submission over Alvin Robinson, David Bielkheden, Joe Brammer and Dustin Hazelett. His only Octagon losses have come against fellow standouts Frankie Edgar, Mac Danzig and Jim Miller. Bocek dropped a hard-fought decision to Ben Henderson at UFC 129.

STEPHEN BONNAR PAGE 17

TIM BOETSCH

The Barbarian

HEIGHT: **6' 0" (183 cm)**
WEIGHT: **205 lbs (93 kg)**
DATE OF BIRTH: **28 Jan. 1981**
HOMETOWN: **Sunbury, PA**

PROFESSIONAL RECORD: 12-4
UFC RECORD: 4-3

A former wrestler for Lock Haven University, Tim Boetsch brought some different tricks to the table in his UFC debut against David Heath at UFC 81, as he threw his opponent to the mat and finished him off with strikes to become an overnight sensation in the Octagon. Boetsch wasn't able to keep that momentum going, as his UFC 88 win over Michael Patt was sandwiched between defeats to Matt Hamill and Jason Brilz. But the Jeet Kune Do practitioner ran off a three-fight winning streak that earned him a return call to the UFC in 2010. He has since gone 1-1 with a win over Todd Brown and a loss to Phil Davis.

JERRY BOHLANDER

HEIGHT: **5' 11" (180 cm)**
WEIGHT: **199 lbs (90 kg)**
DATE OF BIRTH: **12 Feb. 1974**
HOMETOWN: **Napa, CA**

PROFESSIONAL RECORD: 11-4
UFC RECORD: 5-2
TITLES HELD: UFC 12 LIGHTWEIGHT TOURNAMENT WINNER

A member of Ken Shamrock's Lion's Den team, Jerry Bohlander was one of the organization's first "Golden Boys" in the early years, a tenacious battler who specialized in submissions. Debuting in the UFC in 1996, Bohlander was outsized by his two opponents on the "David vs. Goliath" card, but he still submitted Scott Ferrozzo before getting stopped by Gary Goodridge. When he returned later that year, he would go 3-0, including two submission wins that earned him the UFC 12 lightweight tournament title. Bohlander's last UFC win would come via submission in an exciting UFC 16 bout against Kevin Jackson, with his 1999 cut-induced loss to Tito Ortiz being his last appearance in the Octagon.

BRIAN BOWLES

HEIGHT: **5' 7" (170 cm)**
WEIGHT: **135 lbs (61 kg)**
DATE OF BIRTH: **22 June 1980**
HOMETOWN: **Athens, GA**

PROFESSIONAL RECORD: 9-1
UFC RECORD: 1-0
TITLES HELD: WEC BANTAMWEIGHT CHAMPION

Anyone expecting Brian Bowles to rip off incendiary quotes to hype up a fight would be sorely disappointed. Instead, the soft-spoken West Virginia native prefers to let his fighting do the talking, and when his fists start flying, nothing speaks louder.

A pro since 2006, Bowles entered the WEC with little fanfare a year later, but after four consecutive finishes, he roared to the top of the 135-pound contenders list. In August of 2009, he stunned the MMA world with a first-round knockout of Miguel Angel Torres to win the WEC bantamweight title. He lost the belt in his first defense against Dominick Cruz, but in his UFC debut in March of 2011, he returned to form with a submission win over old rival Damacio Page.

STEPHAN BONNAR

The American Psycho

HEIGHT: **6' 4" (193 cm)** DATE OF BIRTH: **4 April 1977**
WEIGHT: **205 lbs (93 kg)** HOMETOWN: **Las Vegas, NV**

PROFESSIONAL RECORD: 16-7 UFC RECORD: 7-6

One half of what many believe to be the greatest UFC fight of all-time, Stephan Bonnar still remains humble after putting mixed martial arts on the map with Forrest Griffin in 2005. In fact, he admits that he just happened to stumble on the sport that became his vocation in life.

"It was a hobby," Bonnar explains. "I always loved fighting and I did wrestling and tae-kwondo growing up and got into jiu-jitsu and boxing. And I really just wanted to get better, so what's the best way to get better? Enter a competition and see where you're at. Then you enter another one; then with boxing it's like, let me enter the Golden Gloves and see how good I am. It just keeps escalating. Each time you win or each tournament you do, you get a little better. And then with the mixed martial arts, why not try it? I won some fights and got some bigger fights, and it pretty much just snowballed. And it wasn't something that I really planned on doing—it was something I always wanted to and I'm really thankful to find myself here."

A pro since 2001 whose only early loss came via cuts to Lyoto Machida in 2003, Bonnar was part of the grand experiment in 2005 known as *The Ultimate Fighter*.

"I remember (UFC President) Dana White being worried that the show wasn't even gonna make it to TV, and I could tell he was worried that it wouldn't be a success," Bonnar recalled. "For some reason, in my mind, I was like 'What, are you kidding me? This thing's gonna be a hit and we're gonna have a bunch of seasons like this.' I always thought it was gonna be the coolest show ever."

After beating Bobby Southworth and Mike Swick, Bonnar made it to the series finale against Griffin, and what happened next was nothing short of amazing. For three rounds, Bonnar and Griffin threw caution to the wind and engaged in a fight for the ages. When it was over though, Griffin had won the razor-thin unanimous decision.

Dana White was so impressed with Bonnar's effort that he awarded him a UFC contract on the spot, and after three straight wins over Sam Hoger, James Irvin and Keith Jardine, that decision was proven to be the correct one.

Two decision losses followed, one to Rashad Evans and the second to Griffin in their long-awaited rematch, but worse news was to come when he was suspended for nine months after a positive test for the banned substance boldenone metabolite following the Griffin bout.

After his suspension was up, Bonnar was back in form with finishes of Mike Nickels and Eric Schafer, but disaster would strike again in the form of a knee injury that required reconstructive surgery. When Bonnar returned 15 months later, he was decisioned by young phenom Jon Jones at UFC 94 and then by Hall of Famer Mark Coleman at UFC 100.

"When you're fighting a lot, you're not that worried about it because you know you're in shape," said Bonnar. "There were like six months when I just couldn't do anything in terms of training, and once I did start, it was a real gradual process, so in my mind I said 'I gotta keep pushing more, gotta keep training harder,' and looking back now, I see that it was a mistake."

Down but not out Bonnar entered 2010 with his career on the line, and while he lost an exciting war with Krzysztof Soszynski at UFC 110, he avenged the loss by TKO five months later in another instant classic, and then finished the year by decisioning Croatia's Igor Pokrajac, proving once and for all that "The American Psycho" was back.

"Every fighter has his ups and downs," said Bonnar. "That's just part of it. You get knocked out and the next day everybody's saying that you're done, but you can't really listen to that."

CHRIS BRENNAN *The Westside Strangler*

HEIGHT: **5' 8" (173 cm)** DATE OF BIRTH: **12 Oct. 1971**
WEIGHT: **155 lbs (70 kg)** HOMETOWN: **Compton, CA**

PROFESSIONAL RECORD: 19-12-1 UFC RECORD: 1-2

A respected Brazilian jiu-jitsu practitioner, Chris Brennan has also earned accolades for his mixed martial arts work in the early years of the sport, when he matched wits with some of the toughest fighters in the game including Joe Stevenson, Antonio McKee, Joe Hurley, Steve Berger and Pat Miletich. In fact, it was Miletich, who Brennan had already gone 0-1-1 against, who handed the Californian his first UFC loss at UFC 16 in March of 1998. Brennan, who had already beaten Courtney Turner earlier that night, went back to the local circuit, only to return once more at UFC 35 in January 2002, where he lost a decision to fellow grappler Gil Castillo.

JASON BRILZ *Hitman*

HEIGHT: **5' 11" (180 cm)** DATE OF BIRTH: **7 July 1975**
WEIGHT: **205 lbs (93 kg)** HOMETOWN: **Omaha, NE**

PROFESSIONAL RECORD: 18-3-1 UFC RECORD: 3-2

Fireman by day, MMA fighter by night, former University of Nebraska-Omaha wrestler Jason Brilz juggles both jobs—plus his life as a husband and father—with remarkable ease. A pro for over a decade, Brilz built a solid resume on the local circuit before getting the call to the UFC in 2008 and scoring a TKO of Brad Morris. Brilz went on to earn wins over Tim Boetsch and Eric Schafer (with a decision loss to Eliot Marshall thrown in) before a career-defining effort against Rogerio Nogueira at UFC 114. In that bout, Brilz was on top of his game, only to lose a controversial split decision that many observers believed he won.

MATT BROWN

The Immortal

HEIGHT: **6' 0" (183 cm)**

WEIGHT: **170 lbs (77 kg)**

DATE OF BIRTH: **10 Jan. 1981**

HOMETOWN: **Cincinnati, OH**

PROFESSIONAL RECORD: 13-10

UFC RECORD: 4-4

A gritty battler who is as tough as they come, Ohio's Matt Brown survived some rough years and a mediocre 7-6 start to his pro MMA career and was given a second chance when he was picked to compete on *The Ultimate Fighter 7* show. Brown wouldn't win a UFC contract, but he went on to earn one as he won four of his first five Octagon bouts, finishing Matt Arroyo, Ryan Thomas, Pete "Drago" Sell and James Wilks, with his only loss coming via split decision to Dong Hyun Kim. A recent three-fight losing skid has slowed Brown's momentum, but it would be unwise to ever count "The Immortal" out of this fight.

MIKE BROWN

HEIGHT: **5' 6" (168 cm)** WEIGHT: **145 lbs (66 kg)** DATE OF BIRTH: **8 Sept. 1975** HOMETOWN: **Coconut Creek, FL**

PROFESSIONAL RECORD: 24-8 UFC RECORD: 0-3 TITLES HELD: WEC FEATHERWEIGHT CHAMPION

It was the shot heard 'round the world, but from the man who threw it—Mike Brown—there are no flowery descriptions of the punch that separated the seemingly unbeatable Urijah Faber from his WEC featherweight title in November of 2008.

"I just saw him and I threw," said Brown of the right hand that dropped Faber and set in motion the finishing sequence of one of the biggest upsets in WEC history. "Whenever I get close enough I'm just gonna swing with all my might, and if I land, then it's gonna hurt."

For Brown, it was years of experience coming together at the perfect time. And when Faber hit the canvas, years of blood, sweat, and tears flashed before Brown's eyes as he saw himself becoming what he had worked for his entire career—a world champion.

Though his rise to the top was MMA's feel-good story of 2008, for Brown, the hard work was just beginning. He would lose his crown to Jose Aldo in November of 2009 after two successful title defenses over Faber and Leonard Garcia, but Brown remained one of the top featherweights on the planet. Now the only thing eluding the affable Brown is a UFC win, something he has been unable to secure in shots against Genki Sudo at UFC 47 and in 2011 bouts with Diego Nunes and Rani Yahya.

JUNIE BROWNING

The Lunatic

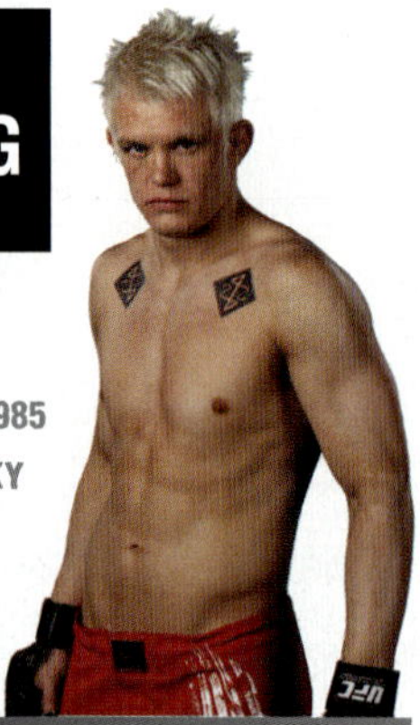

HEIGHT: **5' 9" (175 cm)**

WEIGHT: **155 lbs (70 kg)**

DATE OF BIRTH: **12 May 1985**

HOMETOWN: **Lexington, KY**

PROFESSIONAL RECORD: 4-5

UFC RECORD: 1-1

For a brief spell in 2008-09, there was no mixed martial artist who got more attention and who was more of a polarizing figure than a young man from Lexington, Kentucky named Junie Allen Browning. Perhaps the most controversial figure in *Ultimate Fighter* history, the brash Browning got into a number of incidents with his castmates during season eight before eventually getting submitted and eliminated by eventual winner Efrain Escudero. Following the show, Browning was brought back to the Octagon and he defeated Dave Kaplan, but in his second UFC bout he was submitted in less than two minutes by Cole Miller and released. He has since lost three of four bouts outside the organization.

PAUL BUENTELLO

The Headhunter

HEIGHT: **6' 2" (188 cm)**

WEIGHT: **235 lbs (107 kg)**

DATE OF BIRTH: **16 Jan. 1974**

HOMETOWN: **Amarillo, TX**

PROFESSIONAL RECORD: 27-13

UFC RECORD: 3-3

An old-school brawler with dynamite in his fists, Paul Buentello wasn't fancy, but he was effective. Winner of nearly 20 bouts before he even engaged in a UFC bout, Buentello finished off Justin Eilers and Kevin Jordan in back-to-back Octagon contests in 2005, earning him a shot at heavyweight champion Andrei Arlovski at UFC 55 on October 7, 2005. In this battle of gunslingers, Arlovski drew first, halting Buentello in 15 seconds. "The Headhunter" rebounded with a win over Gilbert Aldana, but then he wouldn't return to the UFC for nearly four years as he fought in other organizations. When he did come back, he lost consecutive bouts to Stefan Struve and Cheick Kongo.

JOSH BURKMAN

The People's Warrior

HEIGHT: **5' 10" (178 cm)**

WEIGHT: **170 lbs (77 kg)**

DATE OF BIRTH: **10 April 1980**

HOMETOWN: **Salt Lake City, UT**

PROFESSIONAL RECORD: 23-7

UFC RECORD: 5-5

Football was Josh Burkman's first love, but when the JUCO All-American running back discovered mixed martial arts, he turned down a scholarship to the University of Utah to pursue a career in the fight game. Two years into his new endeavor, he was chosen to compete on *The Ultimate Fighter 2*, but after defeating Melvin Guillard, a broken hand eliminated him from the show. From there, the well-rounded Burkman went on to win five of seven UFC bouts against the likes of Sam Morgan, Drew Fickett, Josh Neer and Forrest Petz before a three bout losing streak against Mike Swick, Dustin Hazelett and Pete Sell in 2008 forced his release from the organization.

MIKEY BURNETT *The Eastside Assassin*

HEIGHT: **5' 6" (168 cm)**
WEIGHT: **170 lbs (77 kg)**
DATE OF BIRTH: **12 April 1974**
HOMETOWN: **Tulsa, OK**

PROFESSIONAL RECORD: 5-2 UFC RECORD: 2-1

Though newer fans may remember Mikey Burnett for running into the wall when he was a member of *The Ultimate Fighter 4* cast, the Oklahoman's legacy starts with his work in the Octagon, where he was one of the top welterweights of the late 90s. A former Golden Gloves champion, Burnett was a tough opponent for anyone, a fact his foes found out the hard way. In March of 1998, he halted Eugenio Tadeu, earning a shot at Pat Miletich and the first-ever UFC 170-pound title. After 21 minutes, Miletich took a split decision win and the belt, and while Burnett would decision Townsend Saunders three months later, he would never get another title shot.

MURILO BUSTAMANTE

HEIGHT: **6' 1" (185 cm)**
WEIGHT: **185 lbs (84 kg)**
DATE OF BIRTH: **30 July 1966**
HOMETOWN: **Rio de Janeiro, Brazil**

PROFESSIONAL RECORD: 14-8-1 UFC RECORD: 3-1
TITLES HELD: UFC MIDDLEWEIGHT CHAMPION

You wouldn't know it by talking to the soft-spoken gentleman from Rio de Janeiro, but Murilo Bustamante was one of the most feared ground fighters on the planet during his heyday, a period that saw him briefly reign over the UFC middleweight division before leaving for Japan's PRIDE organization.

A fifth degree black belt in jiu-jitsu who earned his belt from Carlson Gracie, Bustamante used his ground skills in professional combat as early as 1991 in his native Brazil. But it was in 1996 that his mixed martial arts career truly kicked into gear. Unbeaten in his first six pro fights, including victories over Joe Charles, Chris Haseman and Jerry Bohlander, Bustamante made his UFC debut at UFC 25, submitting Yoji Anjo in the second round.

Two fights later, Bustamante was back, but he lost a close decision to Chuck Liddell at UFC 33. Bustamante wouldn't have to wait long to wear a championship belt though, as his next fight, at UFC 35 on January 11, 2002, saw him win the UFC middleweight title with a second-round TKO of Dave Menne.

The Brazilian grappling king didn't wait long to defend his title, and four months later he took on Matt Lindland at UFC 37 in May of 2002. What resulted was one of the most bizarre fights in organization history, as Bustamante appeared to submit Lindland with an armbar in the first round, only to have the challenger protest, leading referee John McCarthy to restart the fight. Bustamante did finish the fight for good in round three, this time with a guillotine choke.

Following the fight, Bustamante and the UFC were at an impasse when it came to contract negotiations, and the Brazilian vacated the title and would never fight in the Octagon again.

Bustamante would go on to compile mixed results in PRIDE, with defeats to Dan Henderson (twice) and Quinton "Rampage" Jackson getting more ink than his wins over Ikuhisa Minowa, Ryuta Sakurai and Dong Sik Yoon.

The Brazilian Top Team co-founder still has a connection to the UFC thanks to his work with middleweight contender Rousimar Palhares.

LUIZ CANE *Banha*

HEIGHT: **6' 2" (188 cm)**
WEIGHT: **205 lbs (93 kg)**
DATE OF BIRTH: **2 April 1981**
HOMETOWN: **Sao Paulo, Brazil**

PROFESSIONAL RECORD: 12-3, 1 NC UFC RECORD: 4-3

One look at Luiz Cane, and it's clear that he's one of the most intimidating figures in the UFC. But then you come to his nickname "Banha," which means "baby fat" in Portuguese, and you just have to smile. Fortunately, nicknames never won a fight, and the free-swinging Brazilian has made it clear that he's not the chubby kid who received that moniker anymore. After beginning his UFC stint with a DQ loss to James Irvin, Cane rebounded with knockouts of Jason Lambert and Sokoudjou and a decision win over Steve Cantwell. A two-fight losing streak ensued, but at UFC 128, he showed off his fearsome form again with a TKO of Eliot Marshall.

STEVE CANTWELL *The Robot*

HEIGHT: **6' 2" (188 cm)**
WEIGHT: **205 lbs (93 kg)**
DATE OF BIRTH: **12 Aug. 1986**
HOMETOWN: **Las Vegas, NV**

PROFESSIONAL RECORD: 7-4 TITLES HELD: WEC LIGHT HEAVYWEIGHT CHAMPION
UFC RECORD: 1-3

A well-rounded competitor who owns black belts in both kickboxing and Brazilian jiu-jitsu, Steve Cantwell first made his mark in MMA as a light heavyweight in the WEC organization. He had an auspicious debut, getting halted in 41 seconds by Brian Stann in March of 2007. Two wins later, he got his shot at redemption and made the most of it by stopping Stann in the second round to become the last 205-pound champion in WEC history. After retiring the belt, "The Robot" moved over to the UFC and impressively submitted Razak Al-Hassan, but his track record since then has been disappointing, as he has lost three straight bouts in the Octagon.

Mark Coleman was 31 years old. He had just finished a stellar amateur wrestling career that earned him an NCAA championship in 1988 for Ohio State University, All-American status two times, and also a spot representing the United States in the 1992 Olympics. But the competitive fires still burned, and he had no idea where his athletic career was going to lead him.

Then he turned on the television and saw the Ultimate Fighting Championship.

"I was definitely at a crossroads," said Coleman. "With wrestling, there wasn't a whole lot of pay involved; I was doing a lot for personal pride, and I was definitely not sure about what my future held. That's why it was so exciting when I saw the first UFC on TV. I was immediately attracted to it and I knew it was what I was gonna do. The first time I saw it I thought it was the greatest thing I had ever seen in my life. And I didn't think I was the only one thinking that way."

He still had to fight though, and while adding striking to his wrestling wasn't going to be the easiest thing to do, at least on paper, Coleman and his fellow wrestlers saw it as a mere formality—a minor detail on their way to greatness in the Octagon.

"Back in '96, me and a bunch of wrestlers may have been naïve, but we just really believed we were gonna get in there and win these things," he laughed. "I guess that was a good thing because confidence will take you a long way in this sport."

Talent, athleticism and unbelievable strength and technique don't hurt either, and in Coleman's UFC debut on July 12, 1996 in Birmingham, Alabama, he had it all in romping over Moti Horenstein, Gary Goodridge and Don Frye in one night to win the UFC 10 tournament and become an instant star in mixed martial arts. The Frye victory in particular was special to Coleman, who notes it as the highlight of his UFC career.

"My goal growing up as a little kid was always to be a professional athlete, and at that moment I really felt like I was a professional athlete," he said. "It was so overwhelming when I finally did beat him; it was surreal."

UFC 10: Coleman vs. Horenstein

UFC HALL OF FAME

- **Inducted March 1, 2008**
- **First UFC heavyweight champion**
- **Former NCAA Division I National Champion**
- **"The Godfather of Ground and Pound"**

MARK COLEMAN *The Hammer*

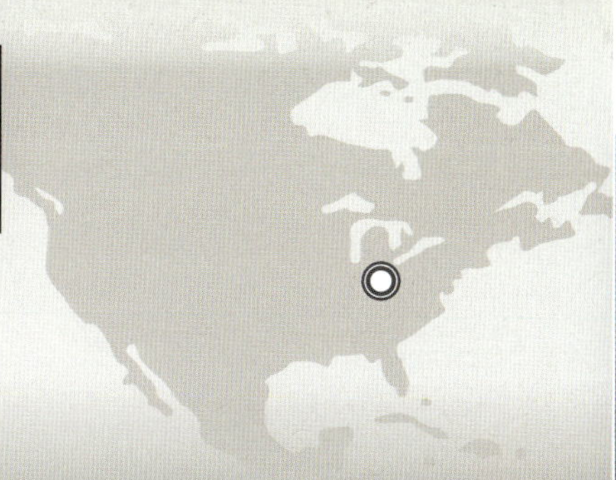

HEIGHT: **6' 1" (185 cm)**

DATE OF BIRTH: **20 Dec. 1964**

WEIGHT: **205 lbs (93 kg)**

HOMETOWN: **Columbus, OH**

PROFESSIONAL RECORD: 16-10

UFC RECORD: 7-5

TITLES HELD: UFC HEAVYWEIGHT CHAMPION, UFC 10 AND 11 TOURNAMENT WINNER, PRIDE 2000 GRAND PRIX WINNER, UFC HALL OF FAMER

Just two months later, Coleman was back in the Octagon and he was even more impressive, beating Julian Sanchez and Brian Johnston in a combined 3:05 to win the UFC 11 tournament in Augusta, Georgia. In February of 1997, he capped off his amazing run with a 2:57 win over UFC standout (and fellow Hall of Famer) Dan Severn to become the first UFC heavyweight champion. While the wins were impressive, Coleman was so dominant that many thought he would never be beaten.

"Growing up, I was a very shy kid and I didn't like getting picked on, so I knew I needed to get bigger and stronger because I didn't want anybody to bully me around," recalled Coleman. "So when I got the opportunity to get in the UFC, it was neat how everybody was representing their individual sports, and I definitely wanted to get in there and prove to the world what kind of fighter a wrestler could be and I did want to dominate, and I felt like I could dominate. Unfortunately, I started reading too many quotes and I paid the price. The reason I did so well in 10, 11, and 12, and in amateur wrestling, was because I outworked my opponents. I wasn't used to the exposure and the fanfare, and I got caught up in it and started believing what I was reading too much. It was a very humbling experience when I did finally lose."

UFC 10: Coleman vs. Frye

Coleman's winning streak came to an end at UFC 14 when he was decisioned by Maurice Smith, and while he left the organization after subsequent setbacks at the hands of Pete Williams and Pedro Rizzo, "The Hammer" couldn't be kept down, and after a brief break, he traveled to Japan to compete in the PRIDE organization, where he resurrected his career.

UFC 18: Coleman vs. Rizzo

In 2000, he defeated Masaaki Satake, Akira Shoji, Kazuyuki Fujita and Igor Vovchanchyn in succession to win the PRIDE Grand Prix finals in 2000, re-establishing himself as one of the best heavyweights in the world in the process. Bouts against the likes of Minotauro Nogueira, Fedor Emelianenko, Mirko Cro Cop and Mauricio "Shogun" Rua followed, captivating the MMA world.

PRIDE Grand Prix 2000 Opening Round: Coleman vs. Satake

Photography by: Susumu Nagao

Photography by: Susumu Nagao

PRIDE 13: Coleman vs. Goes

PRIDE 31: Coleman vs. Rua

PRIDE 26: Coleman vs. Frye

PRIDE Total Elimination 2004: Coleman vs. Emelianenko

Photography by: Susumu Nagao

PRIDE 16: Coleman vs. Minotauro

But his heart always stayed with the UFC.

"If I had my choice between being a Super Bowl champion, a World Series champion, an NBA titlist or a UFC champion, my personal choice would be UFC champion," said Coleman. "To me, that's the pinnacle of everything in the greatest sport there is, and I never gave up hoping that I was gonna be back in the UFC. I was gonna figure a way to get back in there somehow. It wasn't guaranteed that I was gonna do it, but I was gonna do whatever it took to get back in there."

At UFC 82 in March of 2008, Coleman had his chance when he was inducted into the UFC Hall of Fame, with the ceremony taking place in his beloved hometown of Columbus.

"My first question was to make sure it was actually true," he said. "I can't exaggerate how good a feeling it was to get that phone call. I was stunned and at a loss for words, and as far as my athletic career goes, other than actually competing, it was definitely the greatest day I ever had. A lot of times, life is about being in the right place at the right time and sometimes you have to get lucky."

Later on the night of his induction, he made the announcement that he was returning to active duty in the Octagon. His intentions were made clear from the start.

"I'm 'The Hammer' and I have been around a long time," said Coleman. "I said back in 1996 that I'm gonna be around for a long time and I'm still here. There are a lot of people that probably wish I wasn't still around, but that's too bad for them. I'll let them know when I'm ready to quit."

In his first bout back, at UFC 93 in January of 2009, he lost a Fight of the Night battle via third-round TKO to Rua in a rematch of the 2006 PRIDE fight won by Coleman. But less than six months later, Coleman returned and showed off the moves that earned him the title of "Godfather of Ground and Pound" as he won a three-round unanimous decision over Stephan Bonnar.

"No doubt about it, there was a lot of pressure on me for the Bonnar fight, but that's what being an athlete and a competitor is all about," he said. "You've got to be able to deal with the pressure and that's something I think I've been able to do pretty well over the years. I definitely knew how much was at stake against Bonnar."

UFC 93: Coleman vs. Rua 2

UFC 100: Coleman vs. Bonnar

UFC 109: Coleman vs. Couture

Coleman would lose his last UFC bout via submission to Randy Couture in February of 2010, but he will forever remain the prime "Hammer" in the eyes of his legion of fans.

"I have always fought for the fans and I appreciate anyone out there who wishes me well and who was pulling for me," said Coleman. "I hope I've treated the fans with respect."

As for the warriors of the Octagon, they all owe a debt to Coleman, one of the sport's true innovators for his ability to translate wrestling into mixed martial arts success.

"I'd like to think I've had some influence on some guys," he said. "I don't really sit back and think about it too much, but the response I've received from all the younger fighters makes me feel good and I'm just really glad I could be part of taking the whole sport to the level where it's at right now, which to me is just unbelievable."

ROAN CARNEIRO *Jucao*

HEIGHT: **5' 9" (175 cm)**
WEIGHT: **170 lbs (77 kg)**
DATE OF BIRTH: **6 Feb. 1978**
HOMETOWN: **Rio de Janeiro, Brazil**

PROFESSIONAL RECORD: 14-9 UFC RECORD: 2-3

How's this for a welcome to the world of professional fighting? After losing his debut in 2000 to Marcelo Belmiro, Roan Carneiro got matched up with none other than future UFC superstar Anderson Silva. "Nobody really wanted to fight him, but I decided I had nothing to lose so I stepped up and I'm glad I did," said Carneiro years later. Luckily, after losing to Silva, things got better for "Jucao," who went on to win 10 of his next 13 fights, earning him a shot in the UFC. Carneiro's UFC record was a spotty 2-3, but the Brazilian jiu-jitsu expert may still be considered one of the more underrated welterweights of the 2007-08 era.

SHONIE CARTER *Mr. International*

HEIGHT: **5' 9" (175 cm)**
WEIGHT: **170 lbs (77 kg)**
DATE OF BIRTH: **3 May 1972**
HOMETOWN: **Chicago, IL**

PROFESSIONAL RECORD: 91-28-8 UFC RECORD: 3-3

Shonie Carter was ahead of his time. Charismatic, flamboyant and able to fight with the best, "Mr. International" was networking socially before there was such a thing, and while he set the stage for the MMA explosion, he wasn't able to reap its benefits. "The new generation of fans don't know who I am," admitted Carter in 2005, when he returned to the Octagon to face Nate Quarry after four years away. He lost that fight and wasn't able to capitalize on a stint on *The Ultimate Fighter 4*, but diehards will always remember his spinning backfist finish of Matt Serra in 2001 and his philosophy that fighting isn't just a sport, it's entertainment.

SHANE CARWIN

HEIGHT: **6' 2" (188 cm)** WEIGHT: **265 lbs (120 kg)** DATE OF BIRTH: **4 Jan. 1975** HOMETOWN: **Denver, CO**

PROFESSIONAL RECORD: 12-1 UFC RECORD: 4-1
TITLES HELD: INTERIM UFC HEAVYWEIGHT CHAMPION

Shane Carwin has been an interim UFC heavyweight champion, an NCAA Division II Wrestling Champion, has earned recognition as a two-time All-American in football, garnered a tryout with the Philadelphia Eagles, has degrees in mechanical engineering and environmental technology and still works full-time as an engineer. That's enough of a résumé for anyone to settle into civilian life and breathe a satisfied sigh of accomplishment.

But not this heavyweight.

"Everybody has hobbies in their life, and competing just happens to be mine," said Carwin. "I enjoy it and I've been blessed with the gifts God has given me and I'll continue this stuff as long as it allows."

That's a good thing for fight fans, as Carwin has been a thrill-a-second knockout artist ever since entering the Octagon in 2008. He blitzed Christian Wellisch, Neil Wain and Gabriel Gonzaga, knocking each of them out in the first round, and when he did the same thing to Frank Mir at UFC 111 to win the interim heavyweight title, it looked like a long reign at the top was a done deal.

And it almost was, as Carwin battered Brock Lesnar for nearly five minutes in their 2010 bout for the undisputed heavyweight crown. But when the round was finished, so was Carwin's gas tank, and he was submitted in the second stanza.

Following an injury-induced layoff, Carwin returned in 2011.

GIL CASTILLO

HEIGHT: **5' 9" (175 cm)**
WEIGHT: **170-185 lbs (77-84 kg)**
DATE OF BIRTH: **21 Oct. 1965**
HOMETOWN: **Concord, CA**

PROFESSIONAL RECORD: 8-5
UFC RECORD: 1-2

His UFC record is far from memorable, but when you consider that Gil Castillo's two Octagon losses came against Matt Hughes and Dave Menne, it helps to explain such a number. And for a while, this Cesar Gracie jiu-jitsu brown belt was seen as one of the top fighters in the middleweight and welterweight divisions. After turning pro in 2000, Castillo ran off five wins without a loss, including back-to-back victories over Joe Hurley and Nate Marquardt, earning himself a shot at the UFC's newly created 185-pound title. Castillo would drop a five-round nod to Menne at UFC 33 in 2001, and a 2002 bout against Hughes finished via cuts, ending his championship dreams.

NICK CATONE *The Jersey Devil*

HEIGHT: **6' 0" (183 cm)**
WEIGHT: **185 lbs (84 kg)**
DATE OF BIRTH: **1 Sept. 1981**
HOMETOWN: **Brick, NJ**

PROFESSIONAL RECORD: 9-2 UFC RECORD: 3-2

The UFC career of Nick Catone has had more twists and turns than a Hollywood thriller, and most of them have taken place outside the Octagon. Signed in 2008, the Division I wrestling standout for Rider University saw his first two bouts with Amir Sadollah both get scrapped due to his opponent's injuries. Later, Catone would have his own injury ordeal, forcing him to sit out over a year. If that wasn't enough, his return included an opponent change with only a week's notice. It would be grounds for anyone to mentally break, but not the hard-nosed Catone, who used these setbacks as fuel to win three of his five UFC bouts.

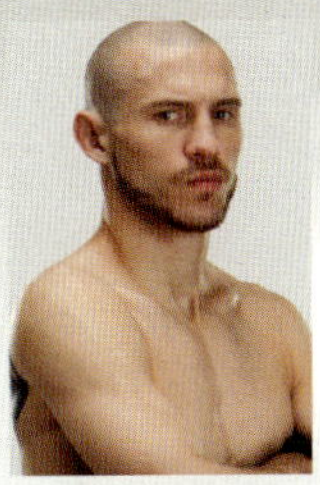

DONALD CERRONE *Cowboy*

PROFESSIONAL RECORD: 14-3, 1 NC   UFC RECORD: 1-0

HEIGHT: **6' 0" (183 cm)**   WEIGHT: **155 lbs (70 kg)**   DATE OF BIRTH: **29 March 1983**   HOMETOWN: **Denver, CO**

Whether he's sparring in the gym, in some small show like the ones where he first made his name, or in front of thousands of fight fans in packed arenas, the goal has always remained the same for Donald "Cowboy" Cerrone: finish the fight in as exciting a manner as possible. This has resulted in a 14-3 record with 1 no contest. The former WEC standout has only gone to a decision four times, and that was against Ben Henderson, Rob McCullough and twice against Jamie Varner. In his UFC debut, he added another bonus check to his bank account when he submitted Paul Kelly at UFC 126.

RYO CHONAN *Piranha*

PROFESSIONAL RECORD: 18-12   UFC RECORD: 1-3

HEIGHT: **5' 9" (175 cm)**   WEIGHT: **170 lbs (77 kg)**   DATE OF BIRTH: **8 Oct. 1976**   HOMETOWN: **Yamagata City, Japan**

You wouldn't know it by walking around Tokyo, but many of the buildings in the Japanese city bear the fingerprints of former construction worker Ryo Chonan. Similarly, you wouldn't know how good a fighter Chonan is by looking at his UFC record, but fans who followed him during his time in the PRIDE and DEEP organizations know that he has earned his place in MMA lore. The last man to finish Anderson Silva, Chonan did it in their 2004 PRIDE bout with one of the greatest submissions ever: a flying scissor heel hook. Chonan also defeated Carlos Newton and Hayato Sakurai, but he never seemed to catch a rhythm in his four-fight UFC stint.

LAVERNE CLARK

HEIGHT: **5' 11" (180 cm)**   DATE OF BIRTH: **2 Dec. 1973**
WEIGHT: **170 lbs (77 kg)**   HOMETOWN: **Davenport, IA**

PROFESSIONAL RECORD: 26-18
UFC RECORD: 3-1
TITLES HELD: WEC WELTERWEIGHT CHAMPION

Plain and simple, Laverne Clark was a fighter. With over 40 mixed martial arts bouts and 33 more in boxing's squared circle, Clark epitomized the "anywhere, anyone, any time" mantra many fighters claim to have but few actually adhere to. One of the Miletich Fighting System camp's early standouts, Clark fought a Who's Who on the Midwest circuit in the late '90s and early '00s, including Matt Hughes, Dave Menne and Shonie Carter. In between, he fit in UFC bouts, defeating Josh Stuart, Frank Caracci, Fabiano Iha and Koji Oishi before losing his rematch with Iha at UFC 27 in 2000. It was Clark's last UFC bout, but he continued to compete in MMA until 2008.

RICH CLEMENTI
No Love

HEIGHT: **5' 9" (175 cm)**   DATE OF BIRTH: **31 March 1976**
WEIGHT: **155 lbs (70 kg)**   HOMETOWN: **Slidell, LA**

PROFESSIONAL RECORD: 46-18-1
UFC RECORD: 5-5

Rich Clementi had reached a crossroads in his career in mid 2007. Despite a strong rep among his fans and peers, *The Ultimate Fighter 4* veteran had been unable to translate his talent into success in a UFC career that had him sitting with a 1-3 record. But then something funny happened, as Clementi went on a six-fight winning streak in 2007-08 that saw him dubbed "The Prospect Killer" as he defeated Anthony Johnson, Melvin Guillard, Sam Stout and Terry Etim. Clementi's streak would be snapped by back-to-back defeats to Gray Maynard and Gleison Tibau, but for a while there, "No Love" was one of the best lightweights on the UFC roster.

CARLOS CONDIT
The Natural Born Killer

HEIGHT: **6' 2" (188 cm)**   DATE OF BIRTH: **26 April 1984**
WEIGHT: **170 lbs (77 kg)**   HOMETOWN: **Albuquerque, NM**

PROFESSIONAL RECORD: 26-5
UFC RECORD: 3-1
TITLES HELD: WEC WELTERWEIGHT CHAMPION

One of the most versatile fighters in the world, Carlos Condit first made his name on the international scene with bouts everywhere from Mexico and Hawaii to Japan and his hometown of Albuquerque. But the son of Brian Condit (the Chief of Staff for New Mexico Governor Bill Richardson) took his game to the next level during his two years in the WEC, where he became the organization's 170-pound champion, going 5-0 with wins over John Alessio, Brock Larson and Hiromitsu Miura. When the WEC eliminated the welterweight class, Condit went crosstown to the UFC in 2009, and the victims list of "The Natural Born Killer" already includes Jake Ellenberger, Rory MacDonald and Dan Hardy.

WESLEY CORREIRA *Cabbage*

PROFESSIONAL RECORD: 19-14   UFC RECORD: 2-2

HEIGHT: **6' 3" (191 cm)**   WEIGHT: **260 lbs (118 kg)**   DATE OF BIRTH: **11 Nov. 1978**   HOMETOWN: **Hilo, HI**

His parents named him Wesley, but to fight fans around the world, he's only known as "Cabbage". And while "Cabbage" Correira will never go down in the annals of UFC history for his technique or mastery of any particular combat sports discipline, when it comes to toughness, few can match him. An unrepentant brawler, Correira was known for the granite chin he put on display in UFC bouts against the likes of power punchers Tim Sylvia, Andrei Arlovski and Tank Abbott, but "Cabbage" went one further, saying his whole head was filled "with concrete and stuff." In a game full of intriguing characters, Correira holds a prominent spot near the top.

PATRICK COTE *The Predator*

PROFESSIONAL RECORD: 14-7   UFC RECORD: 4-7

HEIGHT: **5' 11" (180 cm)**   WEIGHT: **185 lbs (84 kg)**   DATE OF BIRTH: **29 Feb. 1980**   HOMETOWN: **Montreal, Quebec, Canada**

Despite an impressive 5-0 start to his career, things could not have gone worse in Patrick Cote's early days in the UFC, as his first four fights in the Octagon against Tito Ortiz, Joe Doerksen, Chris Leben and Travis Lutter left *The Ultimate Fighter 4* finalist with an 0-4 record. "The Octagon was like a big monster for me in this sport," said Cote. With his back against the wall, he defeated Scott Smith at UFC 67, kicking off a four-fight UFC winning streak that earned him a shot at Anderson Silva's middleweight title. A knee injury cut Cote's effort short in the third round, and two subsequent losses forced his release in 2010.

MARK COLEMAN PAGE 20

RANDY COUTURE PAGE 26

"Not bad for an old man." The words from the mouth of 43-year-old Randy Couture came with a knowing smile just moments after he had shocked the world once again by soundly defeating 6' 8" Tim Sylvia to win his unprecedented third UFC world heavyweight title. It was the kind of victory that you expected to be the last time capsule moment in the career of this ageless wonder, but in keeping to the form he's shown since his debut in 1997, he's still not done thrilling fight fans.

A native of Everett, Washington, Randy Duane Couture served in the United States Army and then went on to become one of the nation's top wrestlers, counting among his accomplishments his three-time All-American status for Oklahoma State University, Pan Am Games champion, two-time runner-up at the NCAA National championship tournament and four-time U.S. Olympic Team alternate. But after seeing old college buddy Don Frye competing in a new venue called the Ultimate Fighting Championship, Couture was intrigued. Nine months later, he was stepping into the Octagon for the first time, defeating Tony Halme and Steven Graham in one night to win the UFC 13 heavyweight tournament. He was hooked.

"When I transitioned from wrestling to fighting, I had been wrestling for so long that the little teeny things I was learning and tweaking to improve my wrestling style and refine my technique seemed so minuscule in the grand scheme of things that it was almost frustrating," he said. "Then I started fighting and there was this whole new world where every time I worked out I learned some new technique or some new thing that seemed immense; it was exciting and fun."

Next up for the man dubbed "The Natural" was unbeaten phenom Vitor Belfort, who had obliterated his previous four opponents with extreme prejudice. The "old" Couture, at 34, was expected to fall like the rest at UFC 15 in October of 1997, but with a rock-solid game plan and execution, Couture delivered one of the biggest upsets the sport had seen at that time, stopping Belfort with strikes at the 8:17 mark.

Just two months later, Couture was thrust into a world title fight against Maurice Smith, and he stunned oddsmakers again by decisioning the kickboxing star to win the UFC heavyweight title. Couture didn't keep the honors for long, as a contract dispute prompted him to relinquish the belt and pursue a career in Japan, where he went 2-2 over the next three years, decisioning Jeremy Horn and Ryushi Yanagisawa and getting submitted by Enson Inoue and Mikhail Illoukhine.

By the tail end of 2000, Couture had mended fences with the UFC, and he picked up where he left off as he stopped Kevin Randleman in three rounds at UFC 28 to regain the heavyweight crown he never lost in the Octagon. Following two more fights in Japan, Couture returned to defend his title against Pedro Rizzo, one of the sport's top young guns and another fighter expected to send Couture packing.

UFC Ultimate Japan: Couture vs. Smith

UFC HALL OF FAME

- **Inducted June 24, 2006**
- **Three-time UFC heavyweight champion**
- **Two-time UFC light heavyweight champion**
- **One of two men to win titles in two weight classes**

RANDY COUTURE *The Natural*

HEIGHT: **6' 2" (187 cm)**

WEIGHT: **205 - 220 lbs (93 - 99 kg)**

DATE OF BIRTH: **22 June 1963**

HOMETOWN: **Las Vegas, NV**

PROFESSIONAL RECORD: 19-10

UFC RECORD: 16-7

TITLES HELD: THREE-TIME UFC HEAVYWEIGHT CHAMPION, TWO-TIME UFC LIGHT HEAVYWEIGHT CHAMPION, UFC HALL OF FAMER, UFC 13 HEAVYWEIGHT TOURNAMENT CHAMPION

UFC 28: Couture vs. Randleman

"I don't have anything to prove," said Couture before the bout. "I don't mind being the underdog. I operate well in that situation, and I like being in that situation. That makes it tougher on the other guy."

So do years of experience and a keen eye for figuring out an opponent's weaknesses, two traits Couture brought into the Octagon with him for his first fight with Rizzo at UFC 31 on May 4, 2001. What resulted was one of the greatest heavyweight title fights ever, as Couture weathered an early storm from Rizzo to roar back and finish the bout as the fresher of the two men. At the end of that five-round war of attrition, one in which he admits, "It was a good three weeks before I was walking right again," due to Rizzo's leg kicks, Couture emerged with a razor-thin decision. He knows what it would have been like to have come up on the other end of that verdict.

"I think it would have been real difficult to deal with having lost that decision, and I was fortunate to have won it," he said. "It was a very tough fight and I know it affected Pedro pretty significantly having been through that tough fight and losing the decision."

UFC 31: Couture vs. Rizzo

After beating a demoralized Rizzo much more easily in their rematch six months later, Couture would go on to lose his next two heavyweight fights to Josh Barnett and Ricco Rodriguez. Although he had to deal with defeat, both had extenuating circumstances that allowed him to deal with these setbacks.

UFC 39: Couture vs. Rodriguez

"Certainly the Barnett loss was a little bit different," said Couture of his 2002 stoppage loss to "The Baby-Faced Assassin". "It was still pretty early on and I really didn't feel like I was hurt. I felt I could have gone more, and I was ready to go more, but it didn't work out that way. The Ricco fight (in September of 2002) was a unique fight with the injury to the eye. Although the last two rounds were a struggle dealing with his size, I felt like I dominated the first three rounds. So psychologically it was frustrating losing that fight because of the injury. But I think if I had been able to finish the fight, I probably would have won it."

A man approaching his 40th birthday without a title, Couture announced his intention to drop to the 205-pound weight class to face knockout artist Chuck Liddell for the interim UFC light heavyweight title in June of 2003. Many saw it as a foolhardy decision, a last-ditch effort to stay relevant in a growing sport. Couture saw it as an opportunity to add another high-profile notch to his belt, and at UFC 43 he did just that, stopping Liddell in the third round. Three months later, he continued to leave mouths wide open as he unified the light heavyweight crown with a one-sided decision win over Tito Ortiz. Couture was not only back in the spotlight, he was a certified superstar now being dubbed "Captain America".

UFC 43: Couture vs. Liddell

UFC 44: Couture vs. Ortiz

UFC 49: Couture vs. Belfort

Two back-to-back fights against Belfort saw the pair of old rivals trade the light heavyweight title belt back and forth, but it was the rematch with Liddell at UFC 52 in April of 2005 that really captivated the MMA world. Coming just a week after Forrest Griffin and Stephan Bonnar helped introduce the UFC to the mainstream, their coaches on *The Ultimate Fighter 1*, Liddell and Couture, kept the momentum going. But in this rematch, Couture had no answer for the right hand of "The Iceman", and he was halted in the first round. A submission victory by Couture over Mike Van Arsdale put him back in the win column, but in the rubber match against Liddell at UFC 57 in February of 2006, the result was the same as the second bout, as he was knocked out again, this time in the second round.

Following the bout, an emotional Couture announced his retirement from the sport at the age of 42.

UFC 52: Couture vs. Liddell 2

UFC 54: Couture vs. Van Arsdale

On June 24, 2006, Couture became the fourth fighter inducted into the UFC Hall of Fame, but as 2006 turned to 2007, "The Natural" began to believe he still had some bullets left in his proverbial gun, and he announced that not only was he coming back, but that he was doing so at heavyweight to challenge the giant Tim Sylvia.

Many fans feared for Couture's safety in the UFC 68 bout, but they didn't have to worry, as he dominated from the first right hand he threw that knocked Sylvia down until the final bell, when he was once again crowned heavyweight champion.

Refusing to sit still, Couture defended his title with a TKO win over Gabriel Gonzaga, but then he hit the sidelines again after a contract dispute. Returning to defend his belt against upstart Brock Lesnar, Couture was stopped in the second round at UFC 91 in November of 2008.

UFC 68: Couture vs. Sylvia

UFC 91: Couture vs. Lesnar

UFC 102: Couture vs. Minotauro

Another defeat followed, this one in a Fight of the Year against Minotauro Nogueira, but since then, Couture has regained his mid-career form with consecutive wins over Brandon Vera, Mark Coleman and James Toney, the last one coming at the ripe old age of 47.

Not bad for an old man, indeed.

UFC 109: Couture vs. Coleman

UFC 118: Couture vs. Toney

TIM CREDEUR *Crazy*

HEIGHT: **6' 3" (191 cm)**
WEIGHT: **185 lbs (84 kg)**
DATE OF BIRTH: **9 July 1977**
HOMETOWN: **Breaux Bridge, LA**

PROFESSIONAL RECORD: 12-4 UFC RECORD: 3-1

A veteran of the United States Navy, Tim Credeur is the first Louisiana native to earn a Brazilian jiu-jitsu black belt, but it was his scrappy style that earned him praise from viewers of *The Ultimate Fighter 7*, where he made it to the semifinals twice but was unable to earn a berth in the finale. Undeterred, "Crazy" Tim made his name in the Octagon the old-fashioned way, finishing Cale Yarbrough, Nate Loughran, and Nick Catone in consecutive bouts before losing his first UFC fight in a crowd-pleasing slugfest with Nate Quarry in September of 2009 that gained him even more followers.

MIRKO CRO COP

Full Name: Mirko Filipovic

HEIGHT: **6' 2" (188 cm)**
WEIGHT: **220 lbs (100 kg)**
DATE OF BIRTH: **10 Sept. 1974**
HOMETOWN: **Zagreb, Croatia**

PROFESSIONAL RECORD: 27-9-2, 1 NC UFC RECORD: 4-5
TITLES HELD: 2006 PRIDE OPEN WEIGHT GRAND PRIX CHAMPION

"Right leg hospital, left leg cemetery." It's the line that made feared Croatian striker Mirko Cro Cop a legend, and when he landed one of his trademark kicks to the head or body, that was usually all she wrote for opponents.

A former kickboxer who began training to compete in the K-1 organization back in 1994, Cro Cop made his pro debut in 1996 at the age of 21. Over the next seven years he fought the elite of the sport, beating, among others, Jerome LeBanner, Peter Aerts, Mark Hunt and Remy Bonjasky. If that weren't impressive enough, when he wasn't training or fighting, he was a member of the Croatian anti-terrorist unit ATJ LUCKO and then later served on Croatia's Parliament.

In 2001, Cro Cop made his first inroads into MMA when he stopped Kazuyuki Fujita, and later that year he entered the PRIDE organization in Japan and started a reign of terror that saw him compile a 21-4-2 MMA record while knocking out, stopping, or submitting the likes of Heath Herring, Igor Vovchanchyn, Josh Barnett, Wanderlei Silva, Mark Coleman, and Kevin Randleman. And although Cro Cop would fall short of the PRIDE heavyweight title when he was decisioned by Fedor Emelianenko in 2005, his last stop in Japan netted him the organization's Open Weight Grand Prix tournament by walking through Ikuhisa Minowa, Hidehiko Yoshida, Silva and Barnett in successive bouts.

How do you top that? You come to the UFC and try to repeat your success. Time for Cro Cop in the Octagon in 2007 and then from 2009 to 2011 was epitomized by more stops than starts, as his victories over Eddie Sanchez, Mostapha Al-Turk, Anthony Perosh and Pat Barry were overshadowed by defeats at the hands of Gabriel Gonzaga, Cheick Kongo, Junior dos Santos, Frank Mir and Brendan Schaub, all but one (Kongo) coming by way of stoppage. But even a late-career slide won't overshadow the unforgettable wins and knockouts scored by the stone-faced and deadly Cro Cop in his fighting prime.

DOMINICK CRUZ

The Dominator

HEIGHT: **5' 8" (173 cm)**
WEIGHT: **135 lbs (61 kg)**
DATE OF BIRTH: **9 March 1985**
HOMETOWN: **San Diego, CA**

PROFESSIONAL RECORD: 17-1 UFC RECORD: 0-0
TITLES HELD: UFC AND WEC BANTAMWEIGHT CHAMPION

A high school wrestling standout, San Diego's Dominick Cruz wanted to keep competing after graduation, so he smoothly transitioned to mixed martial arts in 2005 and won his first nine professional fights, instantly stamping him as a fighter to watch as he showed a mix of ground fighting ability, aggressiveness, power and heart.

In fight number ten though, Cruz hit a wall when he lost his WEC debut in 2007 via submission to featherweight champion Urijah Faber.

Undeterred, Cruz went right back to the gym, and with a new attitude and a new weight class—bantamweight—he returned to the WEC and scored back-to-back wins over Charlie Valencia and Ian McCall. He had found his place. "Once I got here, I knew this is where I should have been," he said. "Everything fit just right for me at 135."

After the McCall fight, Cruz continued to impress fight fans and baffle opponents as he decisioned Ivan Lopez and previously-unbeaten Joseph Benavidez in consecutive bouts, and it was clear that he was on his way to the title.

He got his shot in March of 2010, and made the most of it, stopping Brian Bowles in two rounds. A title defense victory over Benavidez followed five months later, and on December 16, 2010, he closed out the year in the last WEC event ever, shutting out tough Scott Jorgensen over five rounds to retain his WEC belt and add a new one to his trophy case as the first ever UFC bantamweight champion.

"I think the most important parts about being champion are always becoming better and finding a way to look like a different fighter every single fight. Be a positive influence on everybody around you—setting the bar high. More than anything, you have to show people around you what it means to be a champion."

MARCIO CRUZ *Pe de Pano*

HEIGHT: **6' 4" (193 cm)**
WEIGHT: **246 lbs (112 kg)**
DATE OF BIRTH: **24 March 1978**
HOMETOWN: **Rio de Janeiro, Brazil**

PROFESSIONAL RECORD: 7-2 UFC RECORD: 2-2

One of the rare fighters to make his MMA debut inside the UFC Octagon, Marcio Cruz wasn't a mere rookie when he opened his career in October 2005 with a submission win over Keigo Kunihara. In fact, he was one of the game's most decorated grapplers, a six-time Brazilian jiu-jitsu world champion and five-time national champion. But it was his striking that garnered him his biggest win when he spoiled the comeback of former UFC champion Frank Mir at UFC 57, stopping him in the first round. It would be the highlight of "Pe de Pano's" UFC stay, which saw him drop his last two bouts in the organization to Jeff Monson and Andrei Arlovski.

LUKE CUMMO *The Silent Assassin*

HEIGHT: **6' 0" (183 cm)**
WEIGHT: **170 lbs (77 kg)**
DATE OF BIRTH:
27 April 1980
HOMETOWN:
Long Island, NY

PROFESSIONAL RECORD: 9-6
UFC RECORD: 3-4

If you were building the stereotype of a fighter, he wouldn't look like Luke Cummo, and that's just fine with the New Yorker. "I'm probably always going to be the underdog just because I'm skinny," he said. "I like proving people wrong." And beginning with his time on *The Ultimate Fighter 2*, he did just that, defeating Anthony Torres and Sam Morgan to shock the field and earn a place in the *TUF2* finals. On that night in 2005, Cummo would lose a hard-fought three-round decision to Joe Stevenson, but he would go on to defeat Jason Von Flue, Josh Haynes and Edilberto Crocota before a two-fight losing streak prompted his release.

MAC DANZIG

HEIGHT: **5' 8" (173 cm)**
WEIGHT: **155 lbs (70 kg)**
DATE OF BIRTH:
2 Jan. 1980
HOMETOWN:
Los Angeles, CA

PROFESSIONAL RECORD: 21-8-1
UFC RECORD: 4-4
TITLES HELD: *TUF6* WINNER

When it was announced that six-year MMA veteran Mac Danzig had been selected to compete on *The Ultimate Fighter 6* series, most assumed that the Ohio native was going to romp over his castmates on the way to the season title. They were right, as Danzig submitted all four of his foes in the first round to earn a UFC contract. Then things got tricky for the most notable vegan in the sport, as an opening post-*TUF* victory over Mark Bocek was followed by three consecutive losses. But after a change of scenery for training camp and wins over Justin Buchholz and Joe Stevenson, Danzig returned to fulfill his promise.

MARCUS DAVIS *The Irish Hand Grenade*

HEIGHT: **5' 10" (178 cm)**
WEIGHT:
155-170 lbs (70-77 kg)
DATE OF BIRTH:
24 Aug. 1973
HOMETOWN:
Bangor, ME

PROFESSIONAL RECORD: 22-9
UFC RECORD: 9-6

After a successful 17-1-2 boxing career, Marcus Davis believed the conventional wisdom that a legit pro boxer would have no problem knocking out anyone in his path in mixed martial arts. He was wrong, and he learned the hard way as he lost three of his first six bouts, including a TKO defeat against *Ultimate Fighter 2* castmate Melvin Guillard in 2005. But then Davis flipped the script, learned the ground game, and ran off an 11-fight winning streak that featured six submission wins and six UFC victories. The ultra-popular "Irish Hand Grenade" would eventually hit some landmines, though, losing four of his last five Octagon bouts before being released in 2011.

PHIL DAVIS *Mr. Wonderful*

HEIGHT: **6' 2" (188 cm)**
WEIGHT: **205 lbs (93 kg)**
DATE OF BIRTH: **25 Sept. 1984**
HOMETOWN: **Harrisburg, PA**

PROFESSIONAL RECORD: 9-0 UFC RECORD: 5-0

One of the new breed of mixed martial artists who combine athleticism, technique and a Spartan work ethic to dominate their opponents, Phil "Mr. Wonderful" Davis may be young in his pro career, but he has dazzled fans with his performances thus far. A four-time All-American wrestler for Penn State who won the 2008 NCAA National championship, Davis came to the UFC in 2010 after going 4-0 on the local circuit, and he's shown improvement in each contest, defeating Brian Stann, Alex Gustafsson, Rodney Wallace, Tim Boetsch and Rogerio Nogueira. And if that's not all, the Pennsylvania native's engaging personality has made him a fan favorite and a prime candidate for crossover success.

TONY DESOUZA

HEIGHT: **6' 1" (185 cm)**
WEIGHT: **170 lbs (77 kg)**
DATE OF BIRTH: **26 July 1974**
HOMETOWN: **Hilo, HI**

PROFESSIONAL RECORD: 10-4 UFC RECORD: 3-3

A native of Peru, Tony DeSouza grew up in Los Angeles, where he became a standout wrestler before discovering jiu-jitsu and learning under the wing of two of the game's best: Andre Pederneiras and John Lewis. In 2000, he moved to mixed martial arts, and by his third fight he was in the UFC, defeating Steve Berger via decision at UFC 31 in 2001. Over the next six years, the stablemate of BJ Penn would jump around in his fighting career, finding the time to fit in some UFC bouts against the likes of Jutaro Nakao, Dustin Hazelett and Thiago Alves. DeSouza's last match was a TKO loss to Roan Carneiro in 2007.

NATE DIAZ

HEIGHT: **6' 0" (183 cm)** WEIGHT: **170 lbs (77 kg)** DATE OF BIRTH: **16 April 1985** HOMETOWN: **Stockton, CA**

PROFESSIONAL RECORD: **13-6** UFC RECORD: **8-4**
TITLES HELD: ***THE ULTIMATE FIGHTER 5* WINNER**

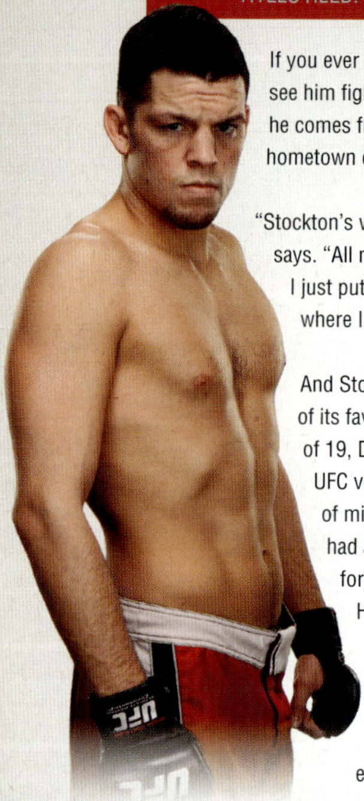

If you ever read an interview with Nate Diaz or see him fight, there is no question about where he comes from, as few athletes represent their hometown quite like Diaz does.

"Stockton's where I live, where I come from," he says. "All my family and friends are here, and I just put it out there because I remember where I came from."

And Stockton should be proud of one of its favorite sons. A pro since the age of 19, Diaz followed his older brother, UFC veteran Nick Diaz, into the world of mixed martial arts, and by 2006, he had already fought in Japan and battled for the WEC lightweight title held by Hermes Franca. But there were bigger things ahead, and in 2007 he made it through perhaps the most talent-rich cast in *Ultimate Fighter* history to win the *TUF5* title and earn a UFC contract.

Through his first four fights in the Octagon, the Cesar Gracie jiu-jitsu brown belt was unstoppable as he submitted Junior Assuncao, Alvin Robinson and Kurt Pellegrino, and decisioned Josh Neer. Razor-thin decision losses to Clay Guida, Joe Stevenson and Gray Maynard sandwiched a finish of Melvin Guillard in 2009 and slowed his progress, but a jump to welterweight kick-started his career again as he took out veterans Rory Markham and Marcus Davis and established himself as a threat to the 170-pound title.

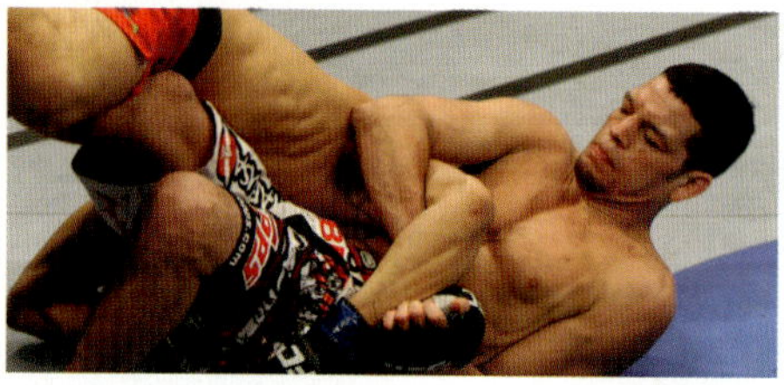

NICK DIAZ

HEIGHT: **6' 0" (183 cm)**

WEIGHT: **170 lbs (77 kg)**

DATE OF BIRTH:

2 Aug. 1983

HOMETOWN:

Stockton, CA

PROFESSIONAL RECORD: **25-7, 1 NC**
UFC RECORD: **6-4**

There are fighters, and then there's Nick Diaz, one of the most unique figures in UFC history. Competing professionally since he was a teenager, Diaz never went into the sport for the fame, but rather for the fights, and within two years of his debut, he was in the UFC, submitting California rival Jeremy Jackson at UFC 44 in 2003. Seven months later, Diaz scored a monumental upset when he knocked out highly touted Robbie Lawler, and while he had some peaks and valleys in the rest of his ten-fight UFC stint, his memorable scraps with Diego Sanchez and Joe Riggs live on. He found success in the Strikeforce organization. In recent developments, Diaz has vacated his Strikeforce welterweight title to fight GSP at UFC 137.

JOE DOERKSEN
El Dirte

HEIGHT: **6' 0" (183 cm)**

WEIGHT: **185 lbs (84 kg)**

DATE OF BIRTH:

9 Oct. 1977

HOMETOWN:

Winnipeg, Manitoba, Canada

PROFESSIONAL RECORD: **46-15**
UFC RECORD: **2-7**

Joe Doerksen was a throwback fighter who believed the best way to get better was by actually competing. His record in the UFC may not stand out, but he always came to fight. Owner of 33 submission wins, it's not surprising that Doerksen's two Octagon victories over Patrick Cote and Tom Lawlor both came via rear naked choke. Seven losses in the UFC kept him from ever getting into title contention in the sport's ultimate proving ground, but the black belt's 11-year career has included bouts against the likes of Matt Hughes, Paulo Filho, Chris Leben, David Loiseau and Denis Kang.

CB DOLLAWAY
The Doberman

HEIGHT: **6' 2" (188 cm)**

WEIGHT: **185 lbs (84 kg)**

DATE OF BIRTH:

10 Aug. 1983

HOMETOWN:

Tempe, AZ

PROFESSIONAL RECORD: **12-4**
UFC RECORD: **5-3**

An amateur wrestling standout who won a junior college national championship for Colby Community College and then earned All-American honors at Arizona State, CB Dollaway followed his college teammates Ryan Bader and Cain Velasquez into mixed martial arts. He has since become quite the submission artist, earning two Submission of the Night awards thus far in his UFC career while reintroducing fight fans to the deadly wonders of the "Peruvian Necktie" finishing hold. A finalist on *The Ultimate Fighter 7*, "The Doberman" has defeated Jesse Taylor, Mike Massenzio, Jay Silva, Goran Reljic and Joe Doerksen, with his only losses coming at the hands of Amir Sadollah, Tom Lawlor and Mark Munoz.

RAFAEL DOS ANJOS

HEIGHT: **5' 9" (175 cm)**

WEIGHT: **155 lbs (70kg)**

DATE OF BIRTH:

26 Oct. 1984

HOMETOWN:

Rio de Janeiro, Brazil

PROFESSIONAL RECORD: **14-5**
UFC RECORD: **3-3**

A Brazilian jiu-jitsu practitioner since he was a teenager, Rafael dos Anjos used his black belt to great effect in his early days as a mixed martial artist, finishing more than half of his opponents with submissions. But when he was knocked out by Jeremy Stephens in his Octagon debut at UFC 91 in 2008, he realized he needed to tighten up his standup game. He showed off his improvement in a close loss to Tyson Griffin five months later, but it was in a three-fight 2009-10 winning streak that fight fans saw the well-rounded nature of dos Anjos' game, and with all his weapons sharpened, big things are expected from him in the future.

JUNIOR dos SANTOS *Cigano*

HEIGHT: **6' 3" (191 cm)**
WEIGHT: **238 lbs (108 kg)**
DATE OF BIRTH: **30 Jan. 1984**
HOMETOWN: **Salvador, Bahia, Brazil**

PROFESSIONAL RECORD: 12-1 UFC RECORD: 6-0

As a stablemate of fighters such as Anderson Silva, Lyoto Machida and Minotauro Nogueira, heavyweight Junior dos Santos gets almost daily reminders of the tradition he will be expected to carry on if he reaches the heights of the sport. But instead of this being a daunting prospect, he embraces it.

"The great Brazilian fighters inspire me," said dos Santos. "I try to do my work as well as possible, because I believe I can follow the same path and one day become a great champion."

He's certainly on his way. Entering the Octagon at UFC 90 in 2008 as a virtual unknown, dos Santos stunned the MMA world with a one-punch knockout of top contender Fabricio Werdum. But this win was no fluke, as "Cigano" went on to finish Stefan Struve, Mirko Cro Cop, Gilbert Yvel, and Gabriel Gonzaga before scoring a punishing three-round decision win over Roy Nelson at UFC 117 in August of 2010.

Firmly established as the number one contender to the heavyweight crown, dos Santos opted to avoid waiting for a shot at champion Cain Velasquez.

"I am here to conquer a spot among the best of the best," he said. "I know it's a rough road, but I am not afraid and I will keep going forward."

TOMASZ DRWAL
Gorilla

HEIGHT: **6' 0" (183 cm)**
WEIGHT: **185 lbs (84 kg)**
DATE OF BIRTH: **22 Jan. 1982**
HOMETOWN: **Krakow, Poland**

PROFESSIONAL RECORD: 18-4
UFC RECORD: 3-3

Some people never figure out what they want to do with their lives. Tomasz Drwal knew his path when he was nine years old. "I discovered my inner passion for competitive sports at the tender age of nine," he said. "At this time I became involved in every sport and martial arts class I could possibly attend. Martial arts really felt like a glove and hand fit for me." Several years and 18 wins later, it's clear he made the right choice. A punishing striker with overpowering strength, Drwal bounced back from a debut UFC loss to Thiago Silva in 2007 to finish three consecutive opponents before back-to-back defeats led to his release in 2010.

EVAN DUNHAM

PROFESSIONAL RECORD: 11-2 UFC RECORD: 4-2

HEIGHT: **5' 10" (178 cm)** WEIGHT: **155 lbs (70 kg)** DATE OF BIRTH: **18 Dec. 1981** HOMETOWN: **Eugene, OR**

You will never hear an ounce of trash talk coming from the mouth of soft-spoken Evan Dunham, but when the Octagon door closes, you won't find a fiercer competitor. Quietly entering the UFC in early 2009, Dunham made his intentions known immediately with a TKO of Per Eklund. Then the Brazilian jiu-jitsu black belt continued to turn heads with upset wins over Marcus Aurelio, Efrain Escudero and Tyson Griffin. By the time he lost his first bout, a highly controversial split decision to former world champion Sean Sherk at UFC 119 in 2010, everyone knew Dunham's name. A KO loss to Melvin Guillard in 2011 slowed Dunham's progress, but he expects a quick return to prominence.

MARVIN EASTMAN *The Beastman*

PROFESSIONAL RECORD: 17-13-1 UFC RECORD: 1-4

HEIGHT: **5' 9" (175 cm)** WEIGHT: **185 lbs (84 kg)** DATE OF BIRTH: **28 June 1969** HOMETOWN: **Las Vegas, NV**

The first man to ever beat Quinton "Rampage" Jackson, Marvin Eastman was a hard-charging fighter who was a terror at times in his career, but when it came to his battles in the Octagon, he just couldn't win the big one.

Debuting with a win over Jackson in 2000, Eastman made it to the UFC in June of 2003, but a nasty cut on his forehead caused a halt to his bout with Vitor Belfort. Octagon losses to Travis Lutter and Jackson (in their 2007 rematch) followed before he scored his lone victory in the organization at UFC 81, a decision over Terry Martin.

After a first-round loss to Drew McFedries in 2008, Eastman was released.

FRANKIE EDGAR *The Answer*

HEIGHT: **5' 6" (168 cm)** DATE OF BIRTH: **16 Oct. 1981**

WEIGHT: **155 lbs (70 kg)** HOMETOWN: **Toms River, NJ**

PROFESSIONAL RECORD: 13-1-1

UFC RECORD: 8-1-1

TITLES HELD: UFC LIGHTWEIGHT CHAMPION

April 10, 2010. Frankie Edgar had been in this position before—on the wrestling mats for Toms River High School East and Clarion University, and now, thousands of miles away in Abu Dhabi.

UFC 112: Edgar vs. Penn

He had just given everything he had in 25 minutes against the best lightweight fighter ever, BJ Penn, and now he had to wait for Octagon announcer Bruce Buffer to render a decision that would determine whether he would have to settle for second as he did in high school and college, or if he would finally have the spotlight all to himself at the top.

The first score was 50-45, one met with oohs and aahs from Yas Island to Hilo and the Jersey shore, mainly because in a fight as close as this one was, it was shocking that someone saw it as a shutout.

"I talked to my friends back home, and they thought I was getting screwed when they heard that one," laughed Edgar. "But when I heard it, I just tried staying positive, and that was the best thing I had done through this whole camp. I thought, *'That's gotta be me, I know I won a bunch of rounds.'*"

Score number two—48-47.

"In wrestling in (high school) States competitions, my biggest goal was to win a state title: I took second," recalled Edgar. "Winning a national title in high school, I took second; to become an All-American, I lost in triple overtime in the All-American round."

Score number three—49-46.

"For the winner," bellowed Bruce Buffer, "annnnnnnnnnnnnnnnnnnnd NEW...!!!!"

For Frankie Edgar, UFC lightweight champion of the world, everything went blank.

"I've been there so many times that this was just unbelievable—I didn't know how to feel," he said. "I had been there so many times and disappointed so many times."

Not this time, and while Edgar's win over Penn was rightfully seen as an upset considering "The Prodigy" had dominated the division since 2008, it came as no surprise to Team Edgar, who approached the entire fight and the training camp leading up to it with a calm and confidence that made it look like Edgar had been in 10 championship fights before. That confidence showed in the fight, as Edgar utilized a stick-and-move strategy that kept Penn off balance all night and stunned the MMA world. Continually elevating his game has been Edgar's MO throughout his UFC career. He came into the UFC in 2007 as a scrappy wrestler with a lot of heart, which he showed in his wins over Tyson Griffin, Mark Bocek, Spencer Fisher, and Hermes Franca, and even in his lone defeat to Gray Maynard in 2008. By the time his 2009 bout with Sean Sherk arrived, he had developed a refined standup game that opened plenty of eyes around the MMA world. And as far as he's concerned, the victory over Sherk was the one that gave him the confidence to rely on his striking in the big fights.

UFC Fight Night 14: Edgar vs. Franca

Today, he's a world champion, with all the perks and perils that come with it. On the plus side, he's the talk of the fight game, and he's got a nice shiny belt on his couch; but on the other side, despite being the king overlooking his kingdom of contenders...

"Heavy lies the crown," he interjects with a chuckle. "I just got a nice bull's eye painted on my chest. But I wouldn't trade it for anything else."

Of course he wouldn't, and instead of resting on his laurels, he returned to the Octagon in August of 2010 to defeat Penn again. This time he made sure there were no questions, as he shut "The Prodigy" out over five rounds at UFC 118. If that weren't enough of an encore, in January of 2011, he faced off against his old nemesis Maynard again in the main event of UFC 125. After surviving a horrific first round, he roared back to earn a five-round draw with "The Bully," setting up a third bout in late 2011.

Heavy lies the crown? Frankie Edgar seems to be holding up under the weight just fine.

UFC 125: Edgar vs. Maynard 2

YVES EDWARDS

HEIGHT: **5' 9" (175 cm)**
WEIGHT: **155 lbs (70 kg)**
DATE OF BIRTH: **30 Sept. 1976**
HOMETOWN: **Austin, TX**

PROFESSIONAL RECORD: 40-16-1
UFC RECORD: 8-4

A dynamic lightweight pioneer, Yves Edwards is a pro who has never shied away from fighting the best. In the Octagon, he's compiled an 8-4 record, with wins over John Gunderson, Cody McKenzie, Joao Marcos, Rich Clementi, Eddie Ruiz, Nick Agallar, Hermes Franca and Josh Thomson. Still going strong, Edwards is reintroducing himself to a new generation of UFC fans.

JUSTIN EILERS

HEIGHT: **6' 2" (188 cm)**
WEIGHT: **235 lbs (107 kg)**
DATE OF BIRTH: **28 June 1978**
DATE OF DEATH: **25 Dec. 2008**
HOMETOWN: **Davenport, IA**

PROFESSIONAL RECORD: 19-7-1
UFC RECORD: 1-3

A former starting linebacker for Iowa State, Justin Eilers took off the pads and put on the gloves in 2002. Eagerly challenging the top fighters, Eilers knocked out Mike Kyle at UFC 49, but was victim of a first-round finish himself six months later against Paul Buentello. Eilers received a title shot in his next bout, but against Andrei Arlovski, his body gave out on him as he tore his ACL en route to a first-round loss. After recovering, Eilers would fight just once more in the Octagon, getting knocked out by Brandon Vera at UFC 57.

With a record of 10-2 in his final 12, Eilers was shot and killed by his stepfather during a domestic dispute on December 25, 2008. He was 30.

JAKE ELLENBERGER

The Juggernaut

HEIGHT: **6' 0" (183 cm)**
WEIGHT: **170 lbs (77 kg)**
DATE OF BIRTH: **28 March 1985**
HOMETOWN: **Omaha, NE**

PROFESSIONAL RECORD: 25-5
UFC RECORD: 4-1

Despite a solid early career that saw him take on and beat a series of established foes over his first four years, Nebraska native Jake Ellenberger wasn't going to make his move towards the UFC until he felt the time was right.

Well, "The Juggernaut" proved to the world that his attitude was correct in his UFC debut in September of 2009 as he engaged in a three-round war with Carlos Condit taking the former WEC welterweight champion to the brink of defeat before losing a controversial split decision. Ellenberger rebounded with emphatic wins over Mike Pyle, John Howard, Carlos Eduardo Rocha and Sean Pierson, establishing himself as a 170-pound title threat.

ROB EMERSON *The Saint*

HEIGHT: **5' 9" (175 cm)**
WEIGHT: **155 lbs (70 kg)**
DATE OF BIRTH: **30 July 1981**
HOMETOWN: **Orange County, CA**

PROFESSIONAL RECORD: 13-10, 1 NC UFC RECORD: 3-3, 1 NC

A pro since 2002, Emerson paid his dues and burst on the scene in 2007 with his stint on *The Ultimate Fighter 5*. He engaged in an exciting battle with Gray Maynard in the season finale before the bout was ruled a no contest. UFC wins over Keita Nakamura, Manny Gamburyan and Phillipe Nover followed, but losses against Rafael dos Anjos and Nik Lentz prompted his release in 2010.

EFRAIN ESCUDERO *Hecho en Mexico*

HEIGHT: **5' 9" (175 cm)**
WEIGHT: **155 lbs (70 kg)**
DATE OF BIRTH: **15 Jan. 1986**
HOMETOWN: **Tempe, AZ**

PROFESSIONAL RECORD: 17-3 UFC RECORD: 3-2
TITLES HELD: *THE ULTIMATE FIGHTER 8* LIGHTWEIGHT WINNER

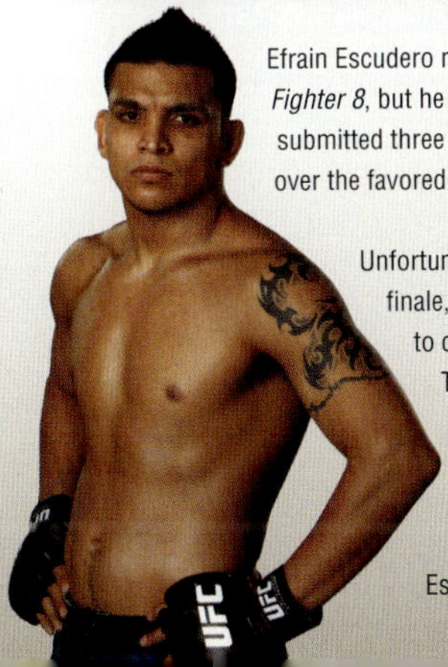

Efrain Escudero may not have been the loudest talker on *The Ultimate Fighter 8*, but he certainly proved he belonged in the Octagon as he submitted three opponents en route to the lightweight finals and a win over the favored Phillipe Nover.

Unfortunately, injuries kept Escudero sidelined after the *TUF8* finale, but in September of 2009, he finally got his chance to compete again, and he responded with a first-round TKO over Cole Miller. A back-and-forth war with Evan Dunham four months later ended via submission in his first pro defeat, and after a lackadaisical decision win over Dan Lauzon at UFC 114 and another third-round submission defeat, this one against Charles Oliveira, Escudero was released from his contract in late 2010.

TERRY ETIM

HEIGHT: **6' 1" (185 cm)**
WEIGHT: **155 lbs (70 kg)**
DATE OF BIRTH: **11 Jan. 1986**
HOMETOWN: **Liverpool, England**

PROFESSIONAL RECORD: 14-3 UFC RECORD: 5-3

One of the United Kingdom's top young talents, Terry Etim has impressed fight game insiders not only with his talent but with his poise when the bell rings. For evidence, look no further than his UFC debut in April of 2007, when he fought like an old pro in submitting Matt Grice in a single round, earning Submission of the Night honors in the process.

The Liverpool native would suffer some growing pains in losses to Gleison Tibau and Rich Clementi, but against Sam Stout at UFC 89, Etim showed what he was capable of once again as he pounded out an impressive decision win.

After three straight finishes over Brian Cobb, Justin Buchholz, and Shannon Gugerty, Etim was submitted by Rafael dos Anjos in the second round at UFC 112.

RASHAD EVANS *Suga*

HEIGHT: **5' 11" (180 cm)** DATE OF BIRTH: **25 Sept. 1979**

WEIGHT: **205 lbs (93 kg)** HOMETOWN: **Niagara Falls, NY**

PROFESSIONAL RECORD: 20-1-1

UFC RECORD: 10-1-1

TITLES HELD: UFC LIGHT HEAVYWEIGHT CHAMPION, *THE ULTIMATE FIGHTER 2* HEAVYWEIGHT WINNER

If you listened to the critics, Rashad Evans never should have been here. Supposedly too small for heavyweight and not dynamic enough for light heavyweight, the former Michigan State University wrestler instead went on to become a UFC superstar, winning *The Ultimate Fighter 2* title at heavyweight before winning the UFC world title at 205 pounds.

Not that he's going to say "I told you so."

"I surprised a lot of people, including (UFC President) Dana White," said Evans. "A lot of people thought I didn't have any talent at all. See, I always had confidence in myself, but the better I did, people would say 'wow' and they just couldn't believe it. I knew my own potential, but they didn't know, so it was a big surprise to them."

Following his graduation from MSU, Evans found a new calling in the sport of mixed martial arts, where his wrestling acumen served him well as he built an unbeaten record on the local circuit.

In 2005, he got his big break when he was selected to compete on *The Ultimate Fighter 2*, but at 5' 11", 220 pounds he was a significant underdog going up against a host of heavyweights. Four wins later though, he had a UFC contract in hand, the *TUF2* winner seemingly had a bright future aheadin his natural weight class of 205 pounds.

The road wasn't easy, as wins over Sam Hoger and Stephan Bonnar weren't exactly met with great fanfare. Undeterred, Evans began to show off the new elements of his game in subsequent bouts, namely, a frightening ability to mix speed and power to produce highlight-reel knockouts.

TUF2: Evans vs. Murphy

UFC 73: Evans vs. Ortiz

Jason Lambert and Sean Salmon were both victims of Evans' striking ability, and after a draw against Tito Ortiz and a decision win over Michael Bisping, "Suga" made his biggest statement at UFC 88 in 2008 with a one-punch right hand knockout of future Hall of Famer Chuck Liddell.

UFC 88: Evans vs. Liddell

"My intention when I threw the punch was to throw it as fast as I could. And I threw it, it went through, and I was gonna follow up with the left hook, but he was already going down. And after the left hook went by, I was like 'Oh no, he fell down. I've gotta hurry up and finish him.' But it seemed like it took forever for me to come out of that left hook to turn around and get on him. It was so quiet in there, I could hear a pin drop. The fight was over, (referee) Herb Dean had stopped it, and I was in shock because everybody was so quiet."

Next up after that defining win was a UFC light heavyweight championship bout against Forrest Griffin on December 27, 2008, and at 2:46 of the third round, Evans became only the third man to win a *TUF* and UFC title when he stopped the second man to do it, Griffin.

UFC 92: Evans vs. Griffin

Evans' reign and his unbeaten streak both came to a halt four months later when he was knocked out in the second round by Lyoto Machida, but a stint as a coach on the tenth season of *TUF* and back-to-back wins over Thiago Silva and Quinton "Rampage" Jackson in 2010 put him back in the number one contender's slot. He hopes that sooner rather than later he will be wearing the gold belt around his waist once again. But championship or not, he promises to keep pursuing his ultimate goal.

"I want fans to get that feeling you get when you're on the edge of your seat, you can't quite get up, and you've got the butterflies in your stomach, and you're not even out there," he said. "I want them to feel that, I want them to feel the passion from watching me fight. That's the most exciting thing I think we, as fighters, or anybody in the entertainment industry, can give to the fans. That feeling that they are there."

URIJAH FABER

The California Kid

HEIGHT: **5' 6" (168 cm)** DATE OF BIRTH: **14 May 1979**

WEIGHT: **135 lbs (61 kg)** HOMETOWN: **Sacramento, CA**

PROFESSIONAL RECORD: 25-4 UFC RECORD: 1-0

TITLES HELD: WEC FEATHERWEIGHT CHAMPION

One of the most amazing aspects of mixed martial arts is that no one is invincible. Somewhere, at some time, everyone's number eventually comes up. For a while though, it looked like no one was going to get close to former WEC featherweight champion Urijah Faber.

Just look at the facts: 13 straight wins, six in the WEC, with 12 of those wins not making it to the final bell…victories over Jens Pulver, Jeff Curran, Dominick Cruz and Charlie Valencia, among others.

On November 5, 2008, Mike Brown caught lightning in a bottle and upset Faber via a first-round TKO that earned him the 145-pound title and made "The California Kid" just a challenger again. What was most striking after the defeat was not only Faber's class, but his determination to get the belt back.

"It's one mistake and he capitalized on it," said Faber, who suffered just the second loss of his pro career that night. "Congratulations to Mike Brown. I love life and I'm a happy person and I'll be back to get that belt."

Two months later, Faber was back in action, and he needed just 94 seconds to submit Pulver with a guillotine choke in their rematch. The stage was set for 2009's Brown vs Faber II, and although he came up short a second time against the veteran champion, his gritty effort in going five rounds with a broken hand and a dislocated thumb earned him even more fans.

Following a comeback win over Raphael Assuncao in January of 2010, a second attempt at regaining the 145-pound belt was foiled by new champion Jose Aldo via five-round decision in the biggest WEC fight of all-time on April 24, 2010. Faber was at a crossroads in his career, so he decided to drop ten pounds to chase after the world title in the bantamweight division.

Thus far, that decision has been a wise one, as he's delivered victories over Takeya Mizugaki and Eddie Wineland, earning himself a July 2011 title shot against a man he defeated in 2007, Dominick Cruz.

SCOTT FERROZZO

The Pit Bull

HEIGHT: **5' 11" (180 cm)** DATE OF BIRTH: **26 April 1965**

WEIGHT: **320 lbs (145 kg)** HOMETOWN: **Shakopee, MN**

PROFESSIONAL RECORD: 4-2

UFC RECORD: 3-2

One of the appeals of the early UFC events was that there were just as many characters as there were fighters. Scott Ferrozzo had a little bit of both in him.

Managed by the future "Voice of The Octagon," Bruce Buffer, Ferrozzo was submitted in his first Octagon bout by Jerry Bohlander at UFC 8, but seven months later he earned an alternate spot in the UFC 11 tournament with a first-round win against Sam Fulton. When Bohlander ironically fell out due to injury, it was the 300-pounder who made the most of it, decisioning fellow brawler Tank Abbott in a bout the two still debate to this day. Ferrozzo would go on to retire after a 43-second loss to Vitor Belfort at UFC 12.

DREW FICKETT

The Master

HEIGHT: **5' 10" (178 cm)**

WEIGHT: **170 lbs (77 kg)**

DATE OF BIRTH:

14 Dec. 1979

HOMETOWN:

Tucson, AZ

PROFESSIONAL RECORD: 42-13

UFC RECORD: 4-3

A seasoned veteran whose reputation as a gifted gatekeeper for rising stars earned him respect from his peers and fans, Arizona-born Drew Fickett used submission wins over young guns Josh Koscheck, Kurt Pellegrino and Josh Neer, to cement his role as a tough out for anyone at 170 pounds.

"Once I get hit one time, I'm all about strategy," he exlained. "I'm all about how I can win. If I'm fighting, I'm going to fight until the very end. There's always a way to pull it out, and always a way to get that victory."

Fickett finished up his UFC career in 2007 with a decision win over Keita Nakamura, and he has since gone 11-8 on the regional fight circuit.

SPENCER FISHER

The King

HEIGHT: **5' 7" (170 cm)**

WEIGHT: **155 lbs (70 kg)**

DATE OF BIRTH:

9 May 1976

HOMETOWN:

Cashiers, NC

PROFESSIONAL RECORD: 25-7

UFC RECORD: 9-6

Owner of wins over highly-regarded contenders Thiago Alves and Matt Wiman, as well as a participant in two classics with Sam Stout, exciting slugger Spencer Fisher could walk away from the game today and still hold his head high. But the Cashiers, North Carolina native still has plenty to achieve in the fight game, and he's not resting on his laurels.

"I don't focus on anything else outside of my own fight," said Fisher. "Those guys were all tough and they deserve to be there, but my opinion is, you're only as good as your last fight."

Well, if his latest wins against Caol Uno, Jeremy Stephens, Shannon Gugerty, and Curt Warburton are any indication, "The King" has been pretty damn good.

JON FITCH

HEIGHT: **6' 0" (183 cm)** DATE OF BIRTH: **24 Feb. 1978**

WEIGHT: **170 lbs (77 kg)** HOMETOWN: **San Jose, CA**

PROFESSIONAL RECORD: 26-3, 1 NC UFC RECORD: 13-1

In the American Kickboxing Academy gym in San Jose, California, frequented by the likes of Cain Velasquez, Josh Koscheck and Mike Swick, there's only one man who has earned the title "Captain," and that's welterweight standout Jon Fitch.

"Jon wasn't the greatest athlete when he came here," said Javier Mendez, founder of AKA. "What he had was the greatest mind and determination."

Those traits carried the Fort Wayne, Indiana native through high school and college wrestling, and he capped off his amateur career as a four-year letterman and team captain for the Purdue Boilermakers.

With his assistant coach at Purdue, Tom Erikson, being a former PRIDE star, it wasn't surprising that Fitch decided to give MMA a go after graduation, yet his early days in the game saw him struggle to a 2-2 record that included losses to future UFC fighters Mike Pyle and Wilson Gouveia.

Undeterred, Fitch ran off a seven-fight winning streak and appeared to be on his way to a career-altering stint on *The Ultimate Fighter 1*, but at the last minute, he was scrapped from the final cast.

In October of 2005, he received his shot in the Octagon, and he made the most of it by decisioning Brock Larson. It would be the first of eight victories that tied Royce Gracie for most consecutive wins in UFC history (a record since broken by Anderson Silva). His defeats of Thiago Alves and Diego Sanchez earned him a shot at Georges St-Pierre's welterweight title at UFC 87 in August of 2008.

That night in Minnesota, Fitch showed the heart of a lion in what St-Pierre has called his toughest fight ever, and though he lost a five-round decision to the champion that night, he was back in action five months later with a decision win over Akihiro Gono at UFC 94. That victory began another winning streak for the well-conditioned and dominant wrestler, whose post-GSP victims include Alves (in their UFC 117 rematch), Ben Saunders, and Paulo Thiago.

KENNY FLORIAN

KenFlo

HEIGHT: **5' 10" (178 cm)** DATE OF BIRTH: **26 May 1976**

WEIGHT: **145 lbs (66 kg)** HOMETOWN: **Brookline, MA**

PROFESSIONAL RECORD: 15-5 UFC RECORD: 11-4

As a senior project manager for a translation firm following his graduation from Boston College, where he was a Division I soccer player, Kenny Florian's post-graduate life seemed pretty well set.

It wasn't, at least not in the eyes of the competitive Florian, who was soon testing his jiu-jitsu black belt in local mixed martial arts shows in Massachusetts. In one of those shows, he caught the eye of the UFC president, and by 2005 he was in America's living rooms as a member of *The Ultimate Fighter 1* cast.

Since then, his road to respect has taken him from the season finale of *The Ultimate Fighter 1* and the 185-pound weight class all the way down to the 145-pound featherweight division, where he hopes to win his first title.

"I'm definitely going to be a way more well-rounded guy," said Florian when asked what fans should expect from him at 145 pounds. "My wrestling's going to be much, much better and it's something I've been working on very diligently. I'm just going to be way more active, and you're going to see a lot of variety, a lot of excitement, and a guy with more weapons."

In between 185 and 145, Florian has been virtually unstoppable. Among his 15 Octagon wins are victories over Din Thomas, Joe Lauzon, Roger Huerta, Joe Stevenson, Clay Guida, Takanori Gomi, Sam Stout and Alex Karalexis, with his only losses coming against top contenders Diego Sanchez and Gray Maynard and in title bouts against Sean Sherk and BJ Penn.

But at this point, all that matters for "KenFlo" is making good on his potential by winning a world championship while still chasing that elusive goal of perfection.

"Every single day is to get better to the point where it's perfection. I know it's an impossibility, but that's my goal, to have flawless technique, and in everything I do, I want it to be perfect. If I have that in my mind but I never get down because it's not perfect, then I'll have the perfect mindset."

RICH FRANKLIN PAGE 40

BRIAN FOSTER

HEIGHT: **5' 10" (178 cm)**
WEIGHT: **170 lbs (77 kg)**
DATE OF BIRTH:
3 April 1984
HOMETOWN:
Sallisaw, OK

PROFESSIONAL RECORD: 17-5
UFC RECORD: 3-2

It took a tragedy to bring Brian Foster into the fight game, as the accidental death of his younger brother during a hiking trip prompted the Oklahoma native to begin training in MMA in 2006. What followed has been an unforgettable journey for the aggressive battler with dynamite in his gloves, as he's compiled a 3-2 UFC record while becoming a fan favorite.

Foster debuted in the Octagon at UFC 103 in 2009, winning Fight of the Night honors in his submission loss to Rick Story. He nabbed his first UFC win two months later as he steamrolled Brock Larson, and Foster has since knocked out Forrest Petz and submitted Matt Brown, with the Petz victory taking the Knockout of the Night award.

HERMES FRANCA

HEIGHT: **5' 6" (168 cm)**
WEIGHT: **155 lbs (70 kg)**
DATE OF BIRTH:
27 Aug. 1974
HOMETOWN:
Fortaleza, Brazil

PROFESSIONAL RECORD: 23-12, 1 NC
UFC RECORD: 6-5
TITLES HELD: WEC LIGHTWEIGHT CHAMPION

A charismatic competitor whose fight game was equally dangerous whether standing or on the ground, Hermes Franca's fighting career saw him take out the likes of Spencer Fisher, Nate Diaz and Jamie Varner with surgical precision, while exciting the fans with his energetic attack.In his lone shot at a UFC title, the former WEC champion lost a five-round unanimous decision to Sean Sherk at UFC 64 in 2007. After the bout, both tested positive for banned performance-enhancing substances and were suspended.

Following the suspension, Franca went 1-2 in the Octagon, defeating local rival Marcus Aurelio and losing to Frankie Edgar and Tyson Griffin. He was released from the organization in 2009.

IAN FREEMAN

The Machine

HEIGHT: **5' 11" (180 cm)**
WEIGHT: **205 lbs (93 kg)**
DATE OF BIRTH:
10 Oct. 1966
HOMETOWN:
Sunderland, England

PROFESSIONAL RECORD: 19-7-1
UFC RECORD: 3-2-1

The leading representative for British MMA long before the emergence of Michael Bisping, Ian Freeman was a tireless ambassador for the sport outside of competition and a fearless battler in it.

After a 2-1 start to his UFC career in 2000, a 2-6 run in his next eight bouts outside the Octagon marked Freeman as a heavy underdog when he took on undefeated rising star Frank Mir at UFC 38 in 2002.

But with his local fans cheering him on, and motivated by his seriously ill father, the 35-year-old delivered the performance of his career, stopping Mir at 4:35 of the first round. Tragically, it was later revealed that Freeman's father had passed away the day before from a battle with cancer, with the fighter not finding out until after the bout.

DON FRYE

The Predator

HEIGHT: **6' 1" (185 cm)**
WEIGHT: **219 lbs (100 kg)**
DATE OF BIRTH: **23 Nov. 1965**
HOMETOWN: **Sierra Vista, AZ**

PROFESSIONAL RECORD: 20-8-1, 1 NC
UFC RECORD: 10-1
TITLES HELD: UFC 8 AND ULTIMATE ULTIMATE 1996 TOURNAMENT WINNER

Don Frye looked like he came out of central casting when he first set foot in the Octagon at UFC 8 in 1996. Built like a truck, with a Tom Selleck-esque mustache and a swagger that immediately resonated among fans of the relatively new sport of mixed martial arts, Frye was the type of competitor no one wanted to meet in a dark alley. But at the same time, he was an instant star, a fighter with no quit in him and the power to back up any boasts.

The confidence came from a stellar amateur wrestling career (where he worked with UFC legends Dan Severn and Randy Couture), a black belt in judo, as well as some pro boxing experience. The rest, well, that was just part of the mystique of "The Predator".

His UFC debut didn't last long though, as he needed just eight seconds (a record at the time) to knock out Thomas Ramirez. Two more wins over Sam Adkins and Gary Goodridge followed on the same night in Puerto Rico, and in a little over three combined minutes, Frye had won the UFC 8 tournament.

After a UFC 9 TKO of highly-touted Amaury Bitetti, Frye competed in the July 1996 UFC 10 tournament in Alabama and romped over Mark Hall and Brian Johnston before getting upset in the night's final by newcomer Mark Coleman.

Frye's perfect record was gone, but it would be the last time he lost in the Octagon.

To cap off a hectic year of action, Frye got back to business in 1996's Ultimate Ultimate tournament, submitting Goodridge, Mark Hall, and Tank Abbott to earn his second UFC tourney title.

Unfortunately, it was his last UFC appearance. After leaving on top with the victory over Abbott, Frye mainly made his money as a pro wrestler in Japan before returning to full-time MMA in 2001, where he notched a series of victories, including a win over Ken Shamrock and a classic TKO of Yoshihiro Takayama in a fight dubbed one of PRIDE's greatest.

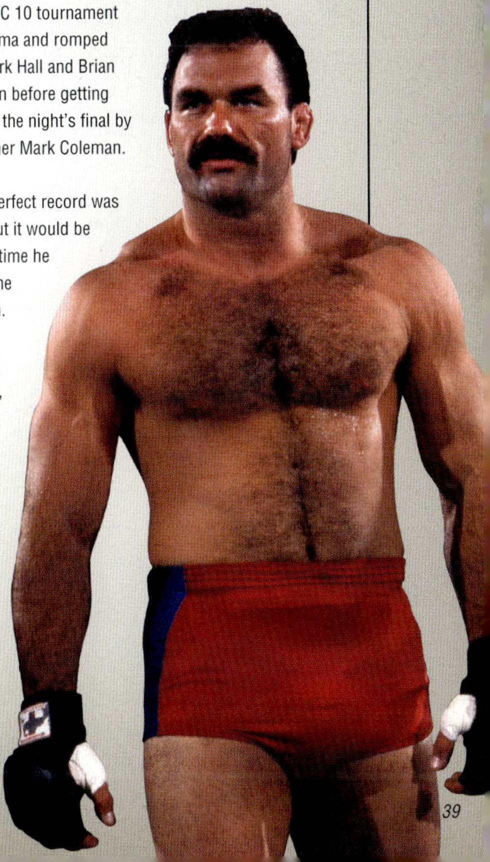

This was it for Rich Franklin. He had given it a good shot, but by the midway point of 2004, he just assumed that his career as a professional fighter was nearing its end. He was respected in the sport and considered one of the top young prospects in the game, but the wisest course of action for him seemed to be to go back to his full-time gig as a high school math teacher.

"I had given some serious consideration to quitting," admitted Franklin. "I was going to go back to my job and teaching, and I wasn't making bad money, but I wasn't making great money, and I thought if I can make 'x' number of dollars a year teaching and make the same amount of dollars fighting, it makes no sense to me if teaching is more of a secure environment. So with my degree and everything, I really thought about going back to teaching and just hanging the hat up here."

He would give it one more shot, though, and following wins over Jorge Rivera and Curtis Stout in 2004, he was matched with UFC Hall of Famer Ken Shamrock on an April 2005 card that wound up being the first UFC event on live cable television. He defeated Shamrock that night, and as the cliché goes, the rest is history. Franklin went on to win the UFC middleweight title and to become a beloved fan favorite and one of the Octagon's true superstars.

And to think, it all began in a 12x15 shed in Cincinnati, where he trained with his friend and future *Ultimate Fighter* competitor Josh Rafferty. Franklin had studied karate from the age of 12, but during college at the University of Cincinnati, he was exposed to a new sport: mixed martial arts.

TUF1 Finale: Franklin vs. Shamrock

UFC 50: Franklin vs. Rivera

"As soon as classes were over I left campus, went to the gym, lifted, trained, and did my thing. I was a UFC fan, and as the UFC was evolving, so was my training. I was doing a lot of learning off of video tapes, I went to a local jiu-jitsu school, and I kept doing all this training, but it was strictly as a hobby. I never intended to take a fight."

RICH FRANKLIN *Ace*

HEIGHT: **6' 1" (185 cm)**

DATE OF BIRTH: **5 Oct. 1974**

WEIGHT: **185-205 lbs (84-93 kg)**

HOMETOWN: **Cincinnati, OH**

PROFESSIONAL RECORD: 28-6, 1 NC

UFC RECORD: 13-5

TITLES HELD: UFC MIDDLEWEIGHT CHAMPION

UFC 42: Franklin vs. Tanner

Eventually, he did want to see how his training was panning out, so he took an amateur fight, then another, and another. Soon, Franklin—who was now working full-time as a teacher—cleaned out the local amateur circuit, prompting an inquiry from a local promoter about the possibility of his turning pro.

"He offered me 200 bucks and I thought, 'Wow, I can make money fighting?' It never dawned on me. So I started fighting and I was one of those guys where my paydays went from 200 to 400 to 800 to 1000, and I thought it was a nice bonus for Christmas money or to help pay my taxes at the end of the year. I was never really thinking beyond the next fight, and I wasn't thinking of it as a career."

By 2001 though, Franklin was 5-0 and getting positive notices from fight game insiders. One of those insiders was top manager Monte Cox, who signed Franklin to a deal and began getting him bigger fights. In April of 2003, Franklin made his UFC debut with a first-round TKO of Evan Tanner. A second Octagon victory followed five months later when he stopped Edwin Dewees, but a December 2003 loss in Japan to future champion Lyoto Machida jeopardized his standing in the UFC.

Some soul-searching followed, but when he was given another chance to make good on his potential in the Octagon, he made the most of it, with the Shamrock fight taking his career and life to a whole other level.

Just two months after the defining victory of his career to that point, Franklin was given a shot at the UFC middleweight title held by former foe Evan Tanner. "Ace" fired on all cylinders that night in New Jersey, and at 3:25 of the fourth round, he was crowned 185-pound champion after a punishing TKO win.

UFC 53: Franklin vs. Tanner 2

UFC 56: Franklin vs. Quarry

By the end of that year to remember, Franklin defended his title with a one-punch knockout of Nate Quarry at UFC 56, and he then kicked off 2006 in March with a bout against a man many expected to give him his toughest test ever—David Loiseau. As the second round concluded against his Canadian challenger, Franklin sat in his corner and told his trainer Jorge Gurgel matter-of-factly, "The left hand's broken."

Gurgel only hesitated for a millisecond before blurting out, "Then use the elbow."

He knew Franklin wouldn't quit. He also knew that despite what happened in the previous two rounds, Loiseau was still dangerous. So he had to get his fighter ready to fight again.

"Keep throwing punches," said Gurgel. "It'll go numb."

Franklin nodded, and continued to defend his title, winning a lopsided five-round decision. It wouldn't be Franklin's last bout with injuries suffered during a fight, but the result was always the same—he kept battling without complaint.

This type of courage made the results of the fights almost irrelevant, so when he lost his middleweight crown to Anderson Silva in his next bout in October of 2006, Franklin didn't lose any prestige among his fans, and he bounced back with wins over Jason MacDonald and Yushin Okami to earn a second shot at defeating "The Spider".

UFC 64: Franklin vs. A. Silva

UFC 68: Franklin vs. MacDonald

UFC 72: Franklin vs. Okami

In their UFC 77 rematch, the result was the same, a KO win for Silva, so after getting back in the win column with a UFC 83 stoppage of Travis Lutter in April of 2008, Franklin moved back to the division where he first made his mark—light heavyweight.

UFC 77: Franklin vs. A. Silva 2

UFC 88: Franklin vs. Hamill

"Ace" made an immediate impression in September of 2008 with a third-round finish of Matt Hamill, and then began a string of bouts that could only be described as "dream fights," as Franklin began matching wits and fists with fellow superstars Dan Henderson, Wanderlei Silva, Vitor Belfort, Chuck Liddell, and Forrest Griffin.

Along the way, he also became one of mixed martial arts' most visible ambassadors, the lead voice when it came to explaining his sport to the uninformed.

F

"I'm an educated fighter, so for me to speak publicly about the sport's safety record, the standardized rules, and the way they take care of the athletes in the UFC, I have no problem with that," Franklin, who holds a bachelor's degree in mathematics and a master's in education, said. "I get tired of the misconceptions. I honestly get tired of doing interviews that constantly use words like 'barbaric' and 'bloody,' and just those kinds of adjectives to describe what you do. In reality, I feel much safer doing what I do than I would riding a bull or driving NASCAR or doing flips on a motorcycle at a motocross event. That's just my choice. I have a good referee in the ring at all times to keep watch on me and I have the ability, if I want to, to tap out of a fight. That keeps me safe and I know it."

UFC 93: Franklin vs. Henderson

UFC 99: Franklin vs. W. Silva

UFC 115: Franklin vs. Liddell

In the Octagon, Franklin would defeat the aforementioned Wanderlei Silva and Chuck Liddell, the latter victory coming by knockout at UFC 115 in June of 2010. Yet what made that win even more remarkable is that he knocked out Liddell after getting his arm broken by a kick just moments before the finish.

"You're standing in the cage and you've got two options: you can quit or you can continue going, and I'm not a quitter," said Franklin. "At the end of the day, if I had turned around and looked at the ref and said, 'my arm is broken, I can't continue,' I think I really would have been kicking myself for something like that in the long run. So basically, you keep going and keep going until you can't go anymore."

That's Rich Franklin's career in a nutshell. He's a warrior, a fighter, and a money player.

"I think individual athletes and fighters like myself, these are the guys who would be the playmakers on teams," he said. "You're the guy who wants the ball in a pressure situation. You're the guy who can say, 'You know what, I can make the difference between winning and losing in a game.'"

UFC 126: Franklin vs. Griffin

HEIGHT: **6' 0" (183 cm)**
WEIGHT: **185 lbs (84 kg)**
DATE OF BIRTH: **26 March 1971**
HOMETOWN: **Boston, MA**

ANTHONY FRYKLUND *The Freak*

PROFESSIONAL RECORD: 14-9 UFC RECORD: 2-2

One of the stalwarts of the Miletich Fighting Systems camp during their prime years, Tony Fryklund made a career out of testing himself against big name opposition, competing in not only the UFC, but in the WEC and Strikeforce as well. In July of 1997, "The Freak" made his mixed martial arts debut with two fights in the UFC 14 tournament in Alabama. Both ended in under two minutes, with Fryklund submitting Donnie Chappell and then getting submitted by Kevin Jackson. He only fought twice more in the Octagon, going 1-1.

HEIGHT: **6' 0" (183 cm)**
WEIGHT: **240 lbs (109 kg)**
DATE OF BIRTH: **29 May 1977**
HOMETOWN: **Waterloo, IA**

TRAVIS FULTON *The Ironman*

PROFESSIONAL RECORD: 246-48-10, 1 NC UFC RECORD: 1-1

Travis Fulton's UFC stint only consisted of two fights, with an armbar loss to Pete Williams at UFC 20 in 1999 evened up by a decision victory over David Dodd two months later at UFC 21. Both were mere blips on a career that began in 1996 and has since run for over 300 fights. The Midwest staple was never in the title hunt or a serious contender, but his record does include names like Rich Franklin, Forrest Griffin, Evan Tanner, Ben Rothwell, Ricco Rodriguez, and Heath Herring, making him a memorable participant in the history of mixed martial arts.

HEIGHT: **5' 5" (165 cm)**
WEIGHT: **145 lbs (66 kg)**
DATE OF BIRTH: **8 May 1981**
HOMETOWN: **Hollywood, CA**

MANVEL GAMBURYAN *The Anvil*

PROFESSIONAL RECORD: 13-6 UFC RECORD: 2-3

Manny Gamburyan has made a career of upsetting the odds. Just 5' 5", the man dubbed "The Anvil" has battled the best in the world over the course of his 12-year career. In 2009, Gamburyan found a place to call home in the 145-pound featherweight division, and after WEC wins over John Franchi, Leonard Garcia, Mike Brown, with his only loss coming against Jose Aldo, his form is better than ever.

TIKI GHOSN

HEIGHT: **5' 10" (178 cm)**
WEIGHT: **170 lbs (77 kg)**
DATE OF BIRTH:
9 Feb. 1977
HOMETOWN:
Huntington Beach, CA

PROFESSIONAL RECORD: 10-8
UFC RECORD: 0-4

A longtime member of the fight community whose association with former UFC champions Tito Ortiz and Quinton "Rampage" Jackson has kept him in the spotlight, Tiki Ghosn gave up a possible college football career to chase after glory in mixed martial arts.

Turning pro in 1998 with a bout against Japanese star Genki Sudo, Tiki made it to the Octagon for UFC 24 in 2000. While he eventually lost his four bouts there to Bob Cook, Sean Sherk, Robbie Lawler, and Chris Lytle, outside the organization he defeated Kit Cope and Ronald Jhun and ended his career in 2009 on a two-fight winning streak.

TAKANORI GOMI *The Fireball Kid*

HEIGHT: **5' 8" (173 cm)** WEIGHT: **155 lbs (70 kg)** DATE OF BIRTH: **22 Sept. 1978** HOMETOWN: **Kanagawa, Japan**

PROFESSIONAL RECORD: 32-7, 1 NC
UFC RECORD: 1-2
TITLES HELD: PRIDE LIGHTWEIGHT CHAMPION, 2005 PRIDE GRAND PRIX CHAMPION

A former PRIDE lightweight and Shooto welterweight champion, Kanagawa, Japan's Takanori Gomi has competed with the top international competition for over 11 years, first making an impact in mixed martial arts circles when he defeated the legendary Rumina Sato for the Shooto title in 2001.

From there, it was practically one big fight after another for Gomi, whose stellar wrestling ability and two-fisted knockout power thrilled fight fans. In 2004, he made his debut in PRIDE with a first-round TKO of Jadson Costa that kicked off one of the greatest runs in the organization's history. From 2004 to 2007, Gomi went 13-1 with 1 NC, defeating Ralph Gracie (with a PRIDE record six-second KO), Jens Pulver, Tatsuya Kawajiri, Luiz Azeredo, and David Baron, among others, while winning the 2005 Lightweight Grand Prix that earned him the first PRIDE lightweight championship.

A 2007 no contest against Nick Diaz ended his PRIDE run, and Gomi went on to win four of his next six bouts before deciding that the time was right to test himself in the UFC.

"I didn't want my career to end before fighting in the most prestigious competition in the world," he said.

Gomi stumbled in UFC bouts against Kenny Florian and Clay Guida, but a one-punch knockout of Tyson Griffin in August of 2010 reminded fight fans why The Fireball Kid is still one of the most dangerous lightweights in the sport.

HEIGHT: **5' 9" (175 cm)**
WEIGHT: **170 lbs (77 kg)**
DATE OF BIRTH: **7 Oct. 1974**
HOMETOWN: **Niiza, Saitama, Japan**

AKIHIRO GONO *The Japanese Sensation*

PROFESSIONAL RECORD: 31-16-7 UFC RECORD: 1-2

Charismatic Akihiro Gono has been competing in mixed martial arts since 1994, compiling over 30 wins. Along the way, he faced a big names from welterweight to light heavyweight, (such as former UFC champions Matt Hughes and Mauricio "Shogun" Rua, UFC and PRIDE vet Yuki Kondo, and two division PRIDE champion Dan Henderson) while making a name for himself in the PRIDE, Pancrase, and Shooto organizations for his aggressive style and well-rounded attack. In the UFC, Gono's resume included a win over Tamdan McCrory in his UFC debut in November of 2007 and hard-fought decision losses against Dan Hardy and Jon Fitch.

GABRIEL GONZAGA *Napao*

HEIGHT: **6' 2" (188 cm)**
WEIGHT: **242 lbs (110 kg)**
DATE OF BIRTH: **18 May 1979**
HOMETOWN: **Rio de Janeiro, Brazil**

PROFESSIONAL RECORD: 11-6
UFC RECORD: 7-5

Gabriel "Napao" Gonzaga's rise up the heavyweight ranks in 2005-07 was nothing short of spectacular. His wins over Kevin Jordan, Fabiano Scherner, Carmelo Marrero, along with an unforgettable highlight reel knockout of Mirko Cro Cop at UFC 70, put the Brazilian jiu-jitsu black belt on the world map as a top contender.

In August of 2007, his well-deserved title shot arrived, but he was halted in three rounds by Randy Couture at UFC 74. A 3-4 slate in his final seven UFC bouts followed, with Gonzaga able to dominate Justin McCully, Josh Hendricks, and Chris Tuchscherer, but unable to get over the hump against top-level big men like Shane Carwin and Junior dos Santos.

GARY GOODRIDGE *Big Daddy*

HEIGHT: **6' 3" (191 cm)**
WEIGHT: **240 lbs (110 kg)**
DATE OF BIRTH: **17 Jan. 1966**
HOMETOWN: **Barrie, Ontario, Canada**

PROFESSIONAL RECORD: 23-23-1 UFC RECORD: 4-4

Gary Goodridge has always been a fighter's fighter. He doesn't ask who, he doesn't ask how much. He just asks where. A mixed martial artist since UFC 8 in 1996, the Trinidad and Tobago native's record reads like a Who's Who of the sport. Mark Coleman, Marco Ruas, Don Frye, Alistair Overeem, Igor Vovchanchyn, Taktarov, and Fedor Emelianenko have all been in with Goodridge, and one of the still-active competitor's strengths is his willingness to fight anyone.

"It's just a warrior attitude," said Goodridge in 2001. "If you're going to war, you've got to be able to go to war with anybody. The sport is not big enough for people to start pointing and choosing whom they will and will not fight. Every fight I turn down, I will not get that fight back. I'm a professional athlete, so therefore, rather than sitting at home on my thumbs and saying I'll only fight him for a million dollars, pay me what I'm worth, or sometimes pay me whatever you want, and I'll go fight."

His debut match with Paul Herrera was quick and brutal. And as a barrage of elbows rendered Herrera unconscious, a star—and a career—was born. 4-4 in the Octagon, with wins over Herrera, Jerry Bohlander, John Campatella, and Andre Roberts, "Big Daddy" went on to become an even bigger attraction in Japan, where he fought in PRIDE rings from 1997 to 2003.

GERARD GORDEAU

HEIGHT: **6' 5" (195 cm)**
WEIGHT: **216 lbs (99 kg)**
DATE OF BIRTH: **30 March 1959**
HOMETOWN: **Den Haag, the Netherlands**

PROFESSIONAL RECORD: 3-4 UFC RECORD: 2-1

Gerard Gordeau made his name in Europe as a premier Savate and Kyokushin karate practitioner, but Stateside, he will always be remembered as the man who introduced mixed martial arts to the world as the opening bout on the UFC 1 broadcast. Said future UFC lightweight Dale Hartt, "I watched the first UFC, and I thought it was gonna be like pro wrestling and be fake. Then Gerard Gordeau kicks Teila Tuli in the face. All of a sudden I see that tooth flying out. I was sold."

Gordeau won two bouts that night in 1993 before being submitted by Royce Gracie in the tournament final. He only fought once more, in Japan in 1995, before retiring.

JONATHAN GOULET *The Road Warrior*

HEIGHT: **6' 1" (185 cm)**
WEIGHT: **170 lbs (77 kg)**
DATE OF BIRTH: **13 July 1979**
HOMETOWN: **Victoriaville, Quebec, Canada**

PROFESSIONAL RECORD: 23-12, 1 NC UFC RECORD: 4-5

A martial artist for most of his life, Victoriaville, Quebec's Jonathan Goulet was an erratic fighter who had the well-rounded ability to look brilliant on some nights, like he did in victories over Luke Cummo, Paul Georgieff, and Kuniyoshi Hironaka, with the Hironaka win earning him Fight of the Night honors. But on others, he would lose in equally spectacular fashion, getting knocked out by hard-hitting strikers Marcus Davis, Mike Swick, and Duane "Bang" Ludwig. Yet no matter whether he was on the winning or losing end of things, the man known as "The Road Warrior" could always be relied on to deliver exciting fights in the consistently talent-rich welterweight division.

"This is my house," Royce Gracie said in 2006. "I built it."

A bold statement indeed, but as boxing great Muhammad Ali once said, "It ain't bragging if you're telling the truth."

And Gracie was unquestionably telling the truth.

The standard bearer for Gracie jiu-jitsu since his UFC debut in 1993, the Rio de Janeiro native always had the confidence to step into competition and the skills to succeed. Maybe even more importantly, he had broad enough shoulders to carry the Gracie name into each fight, knowing that a loss could cripple the mystique of fighting's first family. He never saw it as an issue, though.

"There's no pressure if you believe in what you're doing, and you grow up in an environment that's been competitive for the last 80 years," he said. "If I put you in the middle of the war in Iraq, you're gonna freak out. But if you spent 10 years in there, you'd be like, 'Okay, the grenade just blew up, it's not a problem.' This has been in my family for 80 years and we grew up with that, so there's pressure to be a Gracie every day, not just to walk into a fight. You do seminars and everybody wants to challenge you, so it's not a problem."

Photography by: Susumu Nagao

UFC 1: Gracie vs. Jimmerson

The son of the legendary Helio Gracie, who, along with his brother Carlos, founded the art that eventually became known internationally as Brazilian jiu-jitsu, Royce and his own brothers—Rickson, Royler, Relson, and Rorion—practically grew up on the mats in their father's academy in Brazil. But as he points out, there was never any pressure to pursue the family business.

"My father never forced me to do anything," said Gracie of his father, who passed away in 2009 at the age of 95. "He just said, 'Learn it, and if you want to use it, use it, and if you don't, don't.' When the time came, I stepped into the Octagon and that's what I chose to do. I've been doing it since I was a kid and it's just a part of my life, it's part of my family, and it's just what I do."

UFC HALL OF FAME

- **Inducted November 21, 2003**
- **Won three UFC tournaments**
- **Won eight consecutive UFC bouts**
- **Most UFC submission wins of all-time with 11**

ROYCE GRACIE

HEIGHT: **6' 1" (185 cm)** DATE OF BIRTH: **12 Dec. 1966**

WEIGHT: **175 lbs (81 kg)** HOMETOWN: **Rio de Janeiro, Brazil**

PROFESSIONAL RECORD: 13-2-3, 2 NC

UFC RECORD: 11-1-1, 1 NC

TITLES HELD: UFC 1, 2, AND 4 TOURNAMENT WINNER

But on the night of November 12, 1993, few in the United States knew who the Gracies were, and even fewer knew what to expect from an event called the Ultimate Fighting Championship, which, ironically, was created in part by Royce's older brother Rorion to show the world which style of martial arts would be most effective in a real fight. Rorion Gracie obviously believed his family's art form, jiu-jitsu, was the most effective, and it had been proven so over the years in countless challenge matches in Brazil. Now it was time to take Gracie jiu-jitsu worldwide, and the McNichols Sports Arena in Denver, Colorado was the first stop.

Photography by: Susumu Nagao

UFC 1: Gracie vs. Gordeau

UFC 2: Royce Gracie

Photography by: Susumu Nagao

Who would represent the family in this first competition though? It was Royce, a skinny and unassuming 26-year-old. Many shielded their eyes, fearing for his safety against his more visually imposing opposition.

"It was just the right time," said Gracie when asked why he was chosen to be the family's rep in the UFC. "I was the right size. I wasn't bulked up and big and I didn't look very scary, so to speak. It was just the right timing for me."

UFC 1: Gracie vs. Shamrock

Photography by: Susumu Nagao

And the wrong timing for everyone he faced. Art Jimmerson, future UFC Hall of Famer Ken Shamrock, and Gerard Gordeau all went down to defeat on that single night, and even though fighters from the first UFC are now seen as crude compared to today's Octagon athletes, the fact is that Gracie was the lesser man up and down the tale of the tape in everything but technique and smarts, and he used those to pull out the victories. Add in that Gracie was forced to prepare for an entire tournament's worth of styles, and his accomplishments back then are even more impressive.

"It was very different from the way it is now," said Gracie. "You draw the fighter right before the fight and your strategy is done right there on the spot. You train for everybody. When you're in training camp you train for a big guy, little guy, fast guy, slow guy, heavy guy, strong guy, everybody. So when you get an opponent, you say, 'Okay, that's the guy—here's the strategy for him. He's a boxer, so I'm gonna shoot.' It was a lot more on the fly. You have to be prepared for everybody. Now, you get an opponent, you know who he is, you have the footage, and you train for him. It's different."

Gracie's style amazed viewers and his ease in defeating three opponents in one night shocked them. But it was no fluke. Four months after his first tournament victory, he did it again at UFC 2, submitting four opponents (Minoki Ichihara, Jason DeLucia, Remco Pardoel, and Pat Smith) in one night to take home a second tournament title.

On September 9, 1994, Gracie finally ran into a test via imposing Kimo Leopoldo, but despite being pushed to his limits, he submitted his foe with an armlock 4:40 into the fight. Forced due to exhaustion to withdraw from his next UFC 3 tournament fight that night against Harold Howard, Gracie rebounded in the UFC 4 tourney, scoring three more submission wins over Ron Van Clief, Keith Hackney, and Dan Severn to take his third title.

Following a 36-minute draw in his April 1995 rematch with Ken Shamrock at UFC 5, Gracie disappeared from the fight game for close to five years before returning to the ring in Japan for three PRIDE fights in 2000, which included his first loss after a 90-minute epic with Kazushi Sakuraba. Two more bouts in Japan followed before he made the stunning 2006 announcement that he was returning to the UFC to face longtime welterweight champion Matt Hughes in a non-title bout.

Photography by: Susumu Nagao

PRIDE Grand Prix 2000 Opening Round: Gracie vs. Takada

PRIDE Grand Prix 2000 Finals: Gracie vs. Sakuraba

Photography by: Susumu Nagao

"He is a very tough opponent," Gracie said of Hughes. "I'm coming to fight; I hope he does the same, and I hope we can decide this in the ring, just the two of us, without the judges. It's gonna be a good fight."

It proved to be an uphill climb. The athletes had gotten better in mixed martial arts, the rules were different from when Gracie last competed in the UFC 10 years prior, and at 39, he was giving up seven years to his opponent. Gracie acknowledged the changes in the sport.

UFC 60: Gracie vs. Hughes

"In the beginning there were no time limits, no weight divisions…and today we've got time limits, the boxing commission got involved, and that's the way to do it to make it legal all over Las Vegas and all over the world. I just have to adapt to the new rules, to the new game. But I've been fighting. It's not like I had stopped," he said. "(Also) in the beginning it was style versus style, but today it's the person who can study the other one's game better, who can practice more, who can decode the other one's game and pull him out of his game, and be able to put your own game on the table. It's not just being a strong athlete; it's who's better prepared, who does their homework better."

UFC 60: Gracie vs. Hughes

At UFC 60 in May of 2006, Gracie made the walk to the Octagon once again. And while he fell short of victory, getting stopped via strikes at 4:39 of the first round, during the bout he displayed what was perhaps his greatest attribute—heart—in refusing to tap out to a tight submission locked in by the longtime welterweight champion. When it was all over, he was given a rousing ovation by the appreciative crowd, a fitting tribute for a man who meant so much to so many.

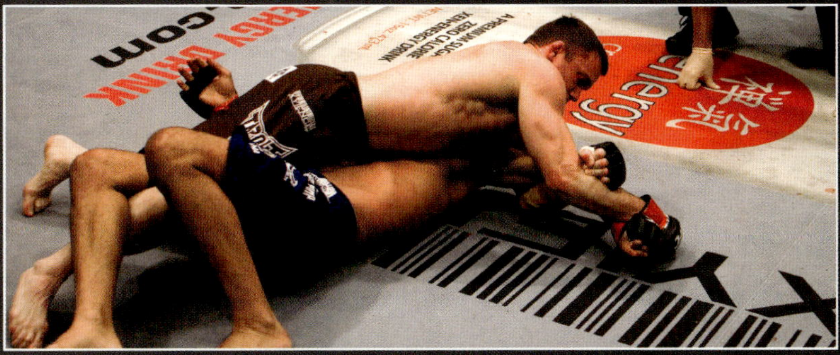

Helio Gracie

Gracie, along with old rival Ken Shamrock, was inducted into the UFC Hall of Fame on November 21, 2003. Just don't call the humble man from Rio de Janeiro a legend.

"The legend is my father," said Gracie. "He's the man who created this whole no-holds-barred deal, who came up with the concepts. I'm just a fighter; I'm just doing my job."

ROYCE GRACIE PAGE 46

FORREST GRIFFIN PAGE 52

WILSON GOUVEIA

HEIGHT: **6' 1" (185 cm)**

WEIGHT: **185 lbs (84 kg)**

DATE OF BIRTH: **3 Oct. 1978**

HOMETOWN: **Fortaleza, Brazil**

PROFESSIONAL RECORD: 12-8

UFC RECORD: 6-4

Wilson Gouveia came into the UFC with a spotty 6-3 record and few expectations from fight fans. But then came a hard fought loss to Keith Jardine at *The Ultimate Fighter 3* finale in 2006, and the MMA world started to pay attention to the exciting jiu-jitsu black belt.

Three consecutive wins continued building Gouveia's reputation, but it was after a fourth straight victory over Jason Lambert via knockout that he became a player in the Octagon. A move to middleweight after a UFC 84 loss to Goran Reljic followed, but victories over Ryan Jensen and Jason MacDonald were tempered by back-to-back KO defeats against Nate Marquardt and Alan Belcher that forced his release after UFC 107.

RENZO GRACIE

HEIGHT: **5' 10" (178 cm)**

WEIGHT: **170 lbs (77 kg)**

DATE OF BIRTH: **11 March 1967**

HOMETOWN: **Rio de Janeiro, Brazil**

PROFESSIONAL RECORD: 13-7-1, 1 NC   UFC RECORD: 0-1

With a lifetime of memories in and out of the ring, including victories over four former UFC champions, Renzo Gracie could have chosen just about any snapshot to frame and post in his New York jiu-jitsu academy.

But the one picture adorning the walls, the one he sees every time he walks through the door is of perhaps his most notable loss—the technical submission defeat to Kazushi Sakuraba in their 2000 PRIDE bout in Japan.

"Technical" is the key word here, because Gracie didn't tap out that night, despite a severely dislocated elbow. In a nutshell, that's who Renzo Gracie is, a warrior.

Seven months later, Gracie was back in action against Dan Henderson, and for the jiu-jitsu black belt and owner of wins over Oleg Taktarov and Maurice Smith, it was just another fight, and that's what fighters do.

By 2007 though, Gracie was ready to move on to another chapter in his life after competing as a mixed martial artist since the early Vale Tudo days in 1992. He was coming off a three-fight winning streak that saw him turn back former UFC titleholders Pat Miletich, Carlos Newton, and Frank Shamrock, and the time was right for him to focus on his academies.

In 2010, he returned, making his long-awaited UFC debut against Matt Hughes. And though he lost that night at UFC 112 in Abu Dhabi, the ultra-popular Gracie still is, and will always remain, a fighter.

TJ GRANT

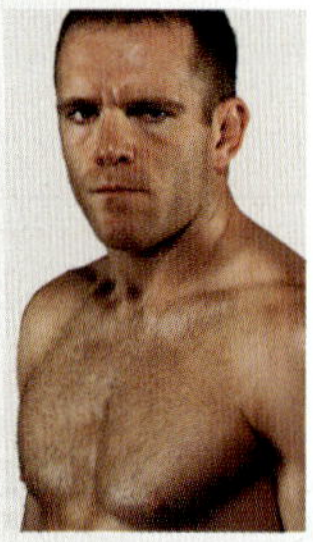

HEIGHT: **5' 10" (178 cm)**

WEIGHT: **170 lbs (77 kg)**

DATE OF BIRTH: **26 Feb. 1984**

HOMETOWN: **Cole Harbour, Nova Scotia, Canada**

PROFESSIONAL RECORD: 16-5   UFC RECORD: 3-3

One of Canada's top imports, Nova Scotia's TJ Grant made a loud statement to the 170-pound division in 2009 with his wins over veteran competitors Ryo Chonan and Kevin Burns, the latter victory earning him UFC 107's Knockout of the Night award. But the Brazilian jiu-jitsu brown belt and underrated striker is far from done when it comes to making an impact in the Octagon, "This (being in the UFC) is awesome, but I'm gonna take it one fight at a time," he said. "And I've got to take it to the next level because there are no easy fights in the UFC."

TYSON GRIFFIN

HEIGHT: **5' 6" (168 cm)**

WEIGHT: **145 lbs (66 kg)**

DATE OF BIRTH: **20 April 1984**

HOMETOWN: **Las Vegas, NV**

PROFESSIONAL RECORD: 14-5   UFC RECORD: 7-5

A relentless force who took down the likes of Urijah Faber, Clay Guida, Thiago Tavares, and Marcus Aurelio, Las Vegas' Tyson Griffin was on the fast track to a world championship fight. His skill was evident when he took on former lightweight title challenger Hermes Franca at UFC 103 and put on a spectacular performance that resulted in a second-round knockout win, his first knockout or submission win since he tapped out David Lee in his Octagon debut in September of 2006.

A trio of losses against Evan Dunham, Takanori Gomi, and Nik Lentz sent the talented Griffin back to the drawing board, and in 2011 he was set to return as a featherweight to test himself at 145 pounds.

JOSH GRISPI *The Fluke*

HEIGHT: **5' 11" (180 cm)**

WEIGHT: **145 lbs (66 kg)**

DATE OF BIRTH: **14 Oct. 1988**

HOMETOWN: **Rockland, MA**

PROFESSIONAL RECORD: 14-2   UFC RECORD: 0-1

In his first 22 years, Josh Grispi fought professionally 16 times, was the youngest fighter to ever fight in both Massachusetts and New Hampshire, and put WEC victories over Mark Hominick, LC Davis, Micah Miller and Jens Pulver under his belt. That's quite a start.

"I didn't think I'd go this far this fast," said Grispi, a quick finisher in the Octagon. "I just love to fight. Of course it was my goal to get to the big shows, but I didn't think it was gonna happen this fast."

It did though, and after a tough decision loss against Dustin Poirier in his UFC debut in January of 2011, Grispi will restart his pursuit of the featherweight title.

KENDALL GROVE *Da Spyder*

HEIGHT: **6' 6" (198 cm)** WEIGHT: **185 lbs (84 kg)** DATE OF BIRTH: **12 Nov. 1982** HOMETOWN: **Maui, HI**

PROFESSIONAL RECORD: 14-8, 1 NC UFC RECORD: 7-6 TITLES HELD: *THE ULTIMATE FIGHTER 3* MIDDLEWEIGHT WINNER

Confidence is a necessary element in any top level fighter's arsenal. Overconfidence can be a killer. Despite his success at the height of the sport, he remains humble and honest.

"My honesty came from Joe Riggs, from Hector Ramirez, from Savant Young, Patrick Cote and Jorge Rivera," said Grove, referring to five of the fighters who have put losses on his 14-8, 1 NC pro record. "Those guys beat humbleness into me. Plus, my parents always tell me to be humble, pray to God, and that even the best fall down. The true champions stand up and roll with the punches."

The middleweight winner of *The Ultimate Fighter 3*, Hawaii's Grove started his UFC career off with a nice winning streak as he won a classic battle with Ed Herman to win *TUF3* before submitting Chris Price and Alan Belcher.

From there, big wins over former UFC middleweight champion Evan Tanner, Canadian standout Jason Day, and top prospects Jake Rosholt and Goran Reljic were evened out by a host of losses against 185-pound standouts Patrick Cote, Jorge Rivera, Mark Munoz, Ricardo Almeida, and Demian Maia. But when his back is against the wall, the 6' 6" Grove is always at his best, and his resilience makes him a favorite among fans who respect his talent, style, and will to win.

CLAY GUIDA
The Carpenter

HEIGHT: **5' 7" (170 cm)** DATE OF BIRTH: **8 Dec. 1981**
WEIGHT: **155 lbs (70 kg)** HOMETOWN: **Johnburg, IL**

PROFESSIONAL RECORD: 28-8 UFC RECORD: 8-5

It's hard to believe you can fit such unbelievable amounts of energy into a 155-pound body, but with each UFC fight, Clay Guida showed it's not only possible, but that he could put on action-packed bouts night in and night out. "I kinda put pressure on myself almost, in that my teammates and my brother tell me, 'you have all this energy; I want to see you look like you just fought two title fights back to back. Use all that energy and don't save anything for the judges, don't save anything for the next fight, leave it all out there,'" said Guida. "Sometimes I feel so good after a fight and between rounds that I wonder if I'm doing enough in that round."

After a solid career on the Midwest circuit, Guida debuted in the UFC with a win over Justin James at UFC 64, followed by razor-thin decision defeats to Din Thomas and Tyson Griffin in 2007. Each fight had fans on their feet, and he went on to become one half of the best fight of 2007 when he faced Roger Huerta in December of that year. But after the heartbreaking third-round defeat, Guida did some soul-searching and realized that being exciting wasn't enough in the UFC.

In 2008, Guida upped his game in a big way, defeating Samy Schiavo and Mac Danzig as he made himself as effective in the Octagon as he is entertaining. Today, "The Carpenter" is one dangerous man at 155 pounds, as evidenced by his wins over Nate Diaz, Shannon Gugerty, Rafael dos Anjos, and Takanori Gomi, and his 2009 war with Diego Sanchez. So what's the secret to being a UFC action hero?

"There is no secret," he admits. "I don't think about it while I'm out there, and it's mostly reaction and leaving it all out there. I think that's what true athletes are made of, leaving everything in the ring, on the field, on the track, on the diamond, or wherever you're at, and not holding anything back."

MELVIN GUILLARD *The Young Assassin*

HEIGHT: **5' 9" (175 cm)** DATE OF BIRTH: **30 March 1983**
WEIGHT: **155 lbs (70 kg)** HOMETOWN: **New Orleans, LA**

PROFESSIONAL RECORD: 45-9-3 UFC RECORD: 9-4

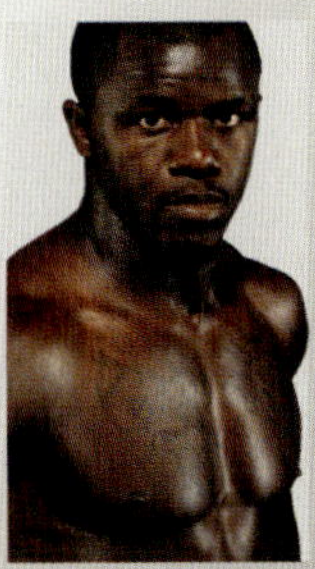

The life of Melvin Guillard has seen its share of ups and downs, from surviving Hurricane Katrina and the death of his father a couple years later, to out-of-the-ring issues that threatened his career. But the resilient veteran of *The Ultimate Fighter 2* was not about to let his talent go to waste.

So after a 3-3 start to his UFC career, Guillard bounced back, and with a renewed focus on his ground game, he has won seven of eight recent bouts. His maturing game was evident in his two victories over jiu-jitsu black belts Gleison Tibau and Ronys Torres, but to make sure opponents didn't sleep on his power, he took out Waylon Lowe and Evan Dunham with frightening glimpses of his finishing ability.

In 2005, shortly after winning *The Ultimate Fighter 1*, the idea of stardom hadn't set in for Forrest Griffin.

Forget that he almost single-handedly put mixed martial arts on the mainstream map with his stirring three-round victory over Stephan Bonnar on April 16, 2005 and captivated a nation with his self-effacing humor and ability to smile through a mask of blood. He was just another guy taking out his stitches with the aid of an X-ACTO knife nine days after the biggest fight of his life.

TUF 1 Finale: Griffin vs. Bonnar

"I still do it," he deadpanned three years later. "It's convenient."

He's still pretty much the same guy. Celebrity sits unsteadily on his head. He'd rather have a good book—particularly one of the two *New York Times* bestsellers he's written—in his hands than doing the rounds of the hottest clubs, and life is fairly simple: train, eat, train, sleep, train, fight. Throw in the usual media obligations and you've got the picture.

But as the years have gone by, the Georgia product is no longer an unknown brawler looking to make a name for himself while trying to earn a spot in the UFC. He's a former world champion on his way back to the top and one of the seminal figures in the elevation of the sport.

Yet by staying humble and grounded, he's able to keep himself on an even keel because in this game, more than in any other, there are no guarantees, and Griffin's career is a case study. On top of the world after beating Bonnar in April of 2005, Griffin would win his next two bouts over Bill Mahood and Elvis Sinosic before a high-profile clash with former UFC light heavyweight boss Tito Ortiz in April of 2006. On a UFC 59 card aptly titled "Reality Check", Griffin survived a frightful first-round beating to come back and arguably win the next two rounds. He would lose a close decision to Ortiz, but his stock may have risen even higher in defeat.

UFC 66: Griffin vs. Jardine

That wasn't the case two fights later, when Keith Jardine halted him in the first round in December of 2006. Unable to accept simply getting caught and stopped, Griffin questioned himself incessantly after the bout's conclusion, wondering if he could compete with the best in the division.

In his return against Hector Ramirez at UFC 72, Griffin showed a different side of his fight game as he picked his foe apart methodically and with a discipline he sorely needed. No longer was it "hit Forrest and watch him put his head down and swing away." He looked like a contender.

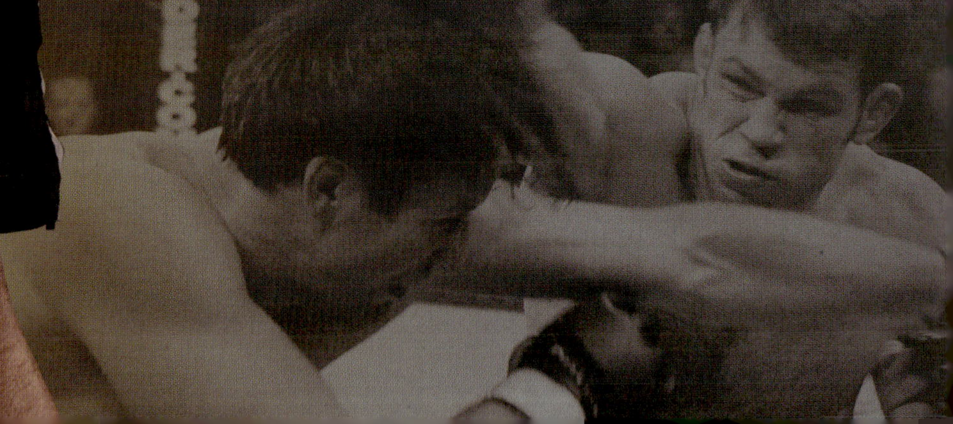

FORREST GRIFFIN

HEIGHT: **6' 3" (190 cm)** DATE OF BIRTH: **16 March 1979**

WEIGHT: **205 lbs (93 kg)** HOMETOWN: **Las Vegas, NV**

PROFESSIONAL RECORD: 18-6

UFC RECORD: 9-4

TITLES HELD: UFC LIGHT HEAVYWEIGHT CHAMPION, *THE ULTIMATE FIGHTER 1* LIGHT HEAVYWEIGHT WINNER

On September 22, 2007, most questions about Forrest Griffin disappeared in 14 minutes and 45 seconds, the time it took him to dominate and then submit Mauricio "Shogun" Rua, the PRIDE star with the reputation as one of the top 205-pounders in the world. Griffin made him look like he shouldn't even have shown up for the fight, and when it was over, the idea of Griffin as light heavyweight champion wasn't so far-fetched anymore.

UFC 76: Griffin vs. Rua

UFC 86: Griffin vs. Jackson

It was on July 5, 2008 that he fulfilled all his promise with a fight for the ages against Quinton "Rampage" Jackson. For five rounds, the two battled tooth and nail in search of victory, and it was Griffin who got it with a unanimous decision.

UFC 92: Griffin vs. Evans

UFC 101: Griffin vs. Silva

UFC 106: Griffin vs. Ortiz 2

UFC 126: Griffin vs. Franklin

He would lose his crown five months later to Rashad Evans, and at UFC 101 in August of 2009 he got knocked out by Anderson Silva. After dealing with myriad injuries, Griffin won two in a row over Ortiz and Rich Franklin, and as he moves forward, his fighting philosophy has not changed a bit.

"It's one of those things where when you're training and fighting, you can't worry about your bills, your mortgage, did you get your girlfriend pregnant, your pet's cancer, or anything," he said. "Nothing else matters but that dude trying to kick you in the face or throw you on your head or trying to rip your arm out of the socket. It becomes a singularity of purpose, which an ADD kid like me rarely gets. I like that moment of clarity in fights, and I truly have that. I lose myself in the details of those 15 minutes and you don't worry about what people think of you."

JORGE GURGEL *JG*

HEIGHT: **5' 9" (175 cm)** DATE OF BIRTH: **25 Jan. 1977**
WEIGHT: **155 lbs (70 kg)** HOMETOWN: **Fortaleza, Brazil**

PROFESSIONAL RECORD: 17-7 UFC RECORD: 3-4

It was a long wait for *The Ultimate Fighter 2's* Jorge Gurgel to make his way to the Octagon, but the exciting Brazilian certainly made up for lost time, fighting seven times during his two-year UFC stint from 2006 to 2008. A gifted jiu-jitsu black belt, Gurgel surprisingly opted for an all-guns-blazing standup style when the bell rang. This led him to three wins over Danny Abbadi, Diego Saraiva, and John Halverson, but cost him when he stepped up his level of competition against the likes of Cole Miller and Aaron Riley. After the loss to Riley at UFC 91 in 2008, Gurgel was released, but he has since gone on to success in the Strikeforce organization.

ALEXANDER GUSTAFSSON *The Mauler*

HEIGHT: **6' 5" (195 cm)** DATE OF BIRTH: **15 Jan. 1987**
WEIGHT: **205 lbs (93 kg)** HOMETOWN: **Gothenburg, Sweden**

PROFESSIONAL RECORD: 11-1 UFC RECORD: 3-1

In 2006, 19-year-old Alexander Gustafsson decided that he wasn't going to follow the conventional path chosen by his friends when it came to a career. Instead, he was going to blaze his own trail as a professional mixed martial artist.

Winner of 11 out of 12 pro fights with 10 early finishes, and long seen as one of Europe's top light heavyweight prospects, Gustafsson made his highly-anticipated UFC debut in November of 2009 and impressed fight fans with a blistering 41-second knockout of Jared Hamman. He would lose his next bout to Phil Davis at UFC 112, but he got back on track with submission victories over Cyrille Diabate and James Te Huna.

KEITH HACKNEY

HEIGHT: **5' 11" (180 cm)** DATE OF BIRTH: **Unknown**
WEIGHT: **200 lbs (91 kg)** HOMETOWN: **Roselle, IL**

PROFESSIONAL RECORD: 2-2 UFC RECORD: 2-2

Poor Keith Hackney. At just 200 pounds, the black belt in taekwondo and Kenpo karate was about to get wiped out by 600 pound Emmanuel Yarborough at UFC 3 in 1994. But then the bell rang, and Hackney exploded with a right hand that sent Yarborough to the canvas. The sumo wrestler would shake off the shot, but he couldn't weather the next attack of flying fists, as Hackney stunned onlookers with a 1:59 TKO win.

Unable to continue in that night's tournament due to a broken hand, Hackney defeated Joe Son three months later at UFC 4 before losing to Royce Gracie the same night. In his final bout, the cult hero was submitted by Marco Ruas on the Ultimate Ultimate 1995 show.

MARK HALL *The Cobra*

HEIGHT: **6' 0" (180 cm)** DATE OF BIRTH: **Unknown**
WEIGHT: **190 lbs (86 kg)** HOMETOWN: **Murrieta, CA**

PROFESSIONAL RECORD: 5-6 UFC RECORD: 4-3

A taekwondo specialist, Mark Hall was one of the early UFC fighters who was able to stick around for a bit thanks to a mix of power and stubbornness. He had an interesting first night in the Octagon, getting Harold Howard to submit via strikes in less than two minutes before getting submitted himself by Paul Varelans in the next round of the UFC 7 tournament.

From there, Hall scored three more UFC wins which were mixed in with three bouts against early UFC star Don Frye (one outside of the UFC in Japan). He lost all three fights against "The Predator", and would go 1-2 in his final three bouts before leaving MMA in 2001.

DENNIS HALLMAN *Superman*

HEIGHT: **5' 9" (175 cm)** DATE OF BIRTH: **2 Dec. 1975**
WEIGHT: **170 lbs (77 kg)** HOMETOWN: **Yelm, WA**

PROFESSIONAL RECORD: 66-13-2, 1 NC UFC RECORD: 3-4

It's a bold move to take the nickname "Superman", but considering that Dennis Hallman's career includes 66 wins, two submission victories over UFC Hall of Famer Matt Hughes, fights against Frank Trigg (twice), Denis Kang, Dave Menne, Caol Uno, and wins in seven of his last eight bouts, it's clear that the ground fighting wizard has earned his moniker.

The only thing missing for the Washington native thus far is a world championship belt, and with wins against Ben Saunders and Karo Parisyan in his latest stint the UFC, he will fight in the Octagon again.

MATT HAMILL

The Hammer

HEIGHT: **6' 1" (185 cm)** DATE OF BIRTH: **5 Oct. 1976**

WEIGHT: **205 lbs (93 kg)** HOMETOWN: **Loveland, OH**

PROFESSIONAL RECORD: 11-2 UFC RECORD: 9-3

As one of the contenders in the UFC's most high-profile division, light heavyweight star Matt Hamill has proven that being deaf isn't a handicap, but instead, a mere obstacle to be overcome on the way to bigger and better things. And in Hamill's case, bigger and better means a UFC championship belt.

This was never more evident than in his 2008 wins over Tim Boetsch and Reese Andy, in which he took out each of his foes with strikes in the second round. But this was just a taste of what "The Hammer" could do in the Octagon.

A two-time world champion wrestler, Hamill first made his mark in the UFC on *The Ultimate Fighter 3*. He has since shown off his improving MMA game, bouncing back from defeats to Michael Bisping (via controversial decision) and Rich Franklin (via knockout), to finish Mark Munoz with a highlight-reel head kick knockout. He also outlasted longtime contender Keith Jardine in a classic three-round battle that earned "Fight of the Night" honors back in June of 2010.

But it was his three-round unanimous decision victory over his former *Ultimate Fighter* coach, UFC superstar Tito Ortiz, at UFC 121 in October of 2010, where Hamill showed just how far he had come in the sport as he dominated his mentor for 15 minutes en route to the most important win of his career.

"I learned my lesson when I lost to Rich Franklin," said Hamill. "But facing Tito, I had learned my lesson and I didn't want it to happen again. So I got a killer instinct. I was going to do my job and my job is to win the fight."

"I'm starting to climb the ladder," he said. "But I'm getting better. I'm more of a well-rounded mixed martial artist now and every day I learn something new. I'm ready to go to that next level of competition."

ANTONI HARDONK

HEIGHT: **6' 4" (193 cm)**

WEIGHT: **245 lbs (110 kg)**

DATE OF BIRTH: **5 Feb. 1976**

HOMETOWN: **Weesp, Holland**

PROFESSIONAL RECORD: 8-6

UFC RECORD: 4-4

Having learned kickboxing from K-1 champion Ernesto Hoost and Brazilian jiu-jitsu from the legendary Rickson Gracie, former pro kickboxer Antoni Hardonk had a schooling most fighters could only dream of. But he didn't squander such knowledge, as he used it to compile an 8-6 record in a ten-year MMA career that ended with his retirement in 2011.

A UFC vet since 2006, when he debuted at UFC 65 with a knockout of Sherman Pendergarst, Hardonk finished up with a 4-4 slate in the Octagon. Even though he left on a losing note with a TKO loss against Pat Barry at UFC 104 in October of 2009, it was a Fight of the Night performance that saw him go out with guns blazing.

DAN HARDY

The Outlaw

HEIGHT: **6' 0" (183 cm)**

WEIGHT: **170 lbs (77 kg)**

DATE OF BIRTH: **17 May 1982**

HOMETOWN: **Nottingham, England**

PROFESSIONAL RECORD: 23-9, 1 NC

UFC RECORD: 4-3

Part of the United Kingdom's first wave of contenders making their mark in the world of MMA, Nottingham's Dan "The Outlaw" Hardy has been training in martial arts since the age of six, even spending time with the famed Shaolin monks in China. In October of 2008, this exciting battler with the red Mohawk and confident manner began his journey in the Octagon with a three-round win over Akihiro Gono. And following a knockout of Rory Markham and upset victories over Marcus Davis and Mike Swick, he became the first British fighter to contend for a UFC title when he fought Georges St-Pierre in 2010. His gritty five-round loss to GSP kicked off a three-fight losing streak that he hopes to reverse as soon as possible.

GERALD HARRIS

Hurricane

HEIGHT: **5' 11" (180 cm)**

WEIGHT: **185 lbs (84 kg)**

DATE OF BIRTH: **19 Nov. 1979**

HOMETOWN: **Tulsa, OK**

PROFESSIONAL RECORD: 17-4

UFC RECORD: 3-1

Despite being known for his wrestling abilities, *The Ultimate Fighter 7* alumnus Gerald Harris showed plenty of heat on his fastball in three UFC fights in 2010 that saw him knock out John Salter, Mario Miranda, and David Branch in succession.

"I love competition," said the former Cleveland State standout. "It's the closest thing I can get to wrestling, and I can't explain what a victory feels like. A knockout is like a game-winning shot or touchdown and I'm addicted to that feeling."

The hot streak of the "Hurricane" ended at UFC 123 though, and was released from the UFC.

JOHN HATHAWAY
The Hitman

HEIGHT: **6' 1" (185 cm)**
WEIGHT: **170 lbs (77 kg)**
DATE OF BIRTH: **23 July 1987**
HOMETOWN: **Brighton, Sussex, England**

PROFESSIONAL RECORD: 15-1
UFC RECORD: 5-1

One of the UK's brightest young prospects, Brighton's John Hathaway won his pro with a first-round submission victory over Jim Morris in June of 2006.

From there, he has continued to dominate his opposition, including his UFC debut against Tom Egan in January of 2009. He delivered subsequent wins over Rick Story, Paul Taylor, Kris McCray and Diego Sanchez, with his only defeat coming against Mike Pyle at UFC 120.

DUSTIN HAZELETT

HEIGHT: **6' 1" (185 cm)**
WEIGHT: **170 lbs (77 kg)**
DATE OF BIRTH: **29 April 1986**
HOMETOWN: **Cincinnati, OH**

PROFESSIONAL RECORD: 14-7
UFC RECORD: 5-5

When the bell rings, Dustin Hazelett pulls off amazing submissions, "I'm doing a lot of really unorthodox, wild stuff that could be potentially dangerous, but I'm not afraid to try things that others may shy away from."

Hazelett scored wins over Jonathan Goulet, Josh Burkman and Tamdan McCrory, but in pivotal bouts against Josh Koscheck, Paul Daley, Rick Story and Mark Bocek, he couldn't take it to the next level.

DAVID HEATH

HEIGHT: **5' 11" (180 cm)**
WEIGHT: **205 lbs (93 kg)**
DATE OF BIRTH: **10 Feb. 1976**
HOMETOWN: **Tulsa, OK**

PROFESSIONAL RECORD: 16-7
UFC RECORD: 2-3

David Heath was always a fan of mixed martial arts, "I don't want to have a good time and put a show on for everybody; I want to go in there and put my fist, knee, foot, or shin through his face and go on with my career."

In his first Octagon bout, at UFC 62, Heath submitted Cory Walmsley. Then in December of 2006, he scored a decision win over Victor Valimaki. After three consecutive Octagon losses David was sent packing.

BEN HENDERSON *Smooth*

PROFESSIONAL RECORD: 13-2
UFC RECORD: 1-0
TITLES HELD: WEC LIGHTWEIGHT CHAMPION

HEIGHT: **5' 9" (175 cm)** WEIGHT: **155 lbs (70 kg)** DATE OF BIRTH: **16 Nov. 1983** HOMETOWN: **Glendale, AZ**

Former WEC lightweight champion Ben Henderson earned plenty of accolades in his college career, but it was in MMA competition that fans really got a look at what "Smooth" could do. But he was just getting started, and in his first two fights of 2010, he unified the 155-pound belt with a win over Jamie Varner and submitted Donald Cerrone in their rematch. And even though he lost his crown via close decision to Anthony Pettis in the WEC's final event in December of 2010, he has a clean slate in the UFC, where he outpointed Mark Bocek at UFC 129.

DAN HENDERSON
Hendo

HEIGHT: **6' 1" (185 cm)**
WEIGHT: **205 lbs (93 kg)**
DATE OF BIRTH: **24 Aug. 1970**
HOMETOWN: **Temecula, CA**

PROFESSIONAL RECORD: 27-8
UFC RECORD: 5-2
TITLES HELD: PRIDE MIDDLEWEIGHT AND WELTERWEIGHT CHAMPION

A native of Temecula, California, Dan Henderson turned to mixed martial arts in 1997 after a stellar Greco-Roman wrestling career that saw him represent the United States in the 1992 and 1996 Olympics.

Henderson made his pro debut with two fights in one night on June 15, 1997, and from there, the train just kept on rolling.

On May 15, 1998, he would make his Octagon debut, scoring consecutive victories over Carlos Newton and Allen Goes on the same night at UFC 17. For the next nine years, he took his solid wrestling attack and devastating right hand overseas to compete, most notably in the PRIDE organization, where he defeated Renzo Gracie, Murilo "Ninja" Rua, Murilo Bustamante (twice), Yuki Kondo, Vitor Belfort, and Kazuhiro Nakamura.

By early 2007, the Team Quest standout had established himself as one of the best fighters, pound for pound, in the world and taken home the PRIDE 183-pound championship for his efforts. He wasn't satisfied though, and in February, he moved up to the 205-pound class to face old rival Wanderlei Silva.

In that fight, Henderson was on top of his game, knocking out Silva in the third round to add the PRIDE middleweight title to his welterweight crown, the only fighter in history to own both titles simultaneously.

Following the bout, Henderson returned to the UFC in search of another set of gold belts. He would fall short of that goal in back-to-back losses against Quinton Jackson and Anderson Silva, but three consecutive wins over Rousimar Palhares, Rich Franklin and Michael Bisping showed that he had his mojo back.

After his highlight-reel knockout of Bisping at UFC 100 in July of 2011, Henderson took himself to the Strikeforce organization, where he shook off a decision loss to Jake Shields and won the promotion's light heavyweight title in 2011 with a TKO of Rafael Cavalcante.

JOHNY HENDRICKS

HEIGHT: **5' 9" (175 cm)** DATE OF BIRTH: **12 Sept. 1983**
WEIGHT: **170 lbs (77 kg)** HOMETOWN: **Ada, OK**

PROFESSIONAL RECORD: 10-1 UFC RECORD: 5-1

Charismatic and talented, Johny Hendricks is seen by many fight insiders as a future star in the UFC's welterweight division. The Ada, Oklahoma native agrees, claiming that the only reason he began training in mixed martial arts in June of 2007 was a simple, but definitive one—to be the world champion.

So far he's on the right track, using a mix of stellar wrestling and knockout power to win all but one of his 11 professional bouts, including two in the WEC. There's more on the agenda for the two-time Division I National Champion and four-time Oklahoma State All-American in wrestling following his UFC wins over Amir Sadollah, Ricardo Funch, TJ Waldburger and TJ Grant.

ED HERMAN *Short Fuse*

HEIGHT: **6' 2" (188 cm)** DATE OF BIRTH: **2 Oct. 1980**
WEIGHT: **185 lbs (84 kg)** HOMETOWN: **Vancouver, WA**

PROFESSIONAL RECORD: 17-7 UFC RECORD: 4-5

If history has proven anything in the career of Ed Herman, it's that he's most dangerous when his back's against the wall. For proof of that, look at the three-fight unbeaten streak that saw *The Ultimate Fighter 3* finalist submit Chris Price and Scott Smith and knock out Joe Doerksen after he dropped a 2006 bout to Jason MacDonald.

Hard times would hit again though when he lost back-to-back bouts to Demian Maia and Alan Belcher in 2008. And after spoiling the return of former world title challenger David "The Crow" Loiseau at UFC 97, Herman would injure his knee in a defeat to Aaron Simpson and get forced to the sidelines for nearly two years before making his return in 2011.

HEATH HERRING *The Texas Crazy Horse*

HEIGHT: **6' 4" (193 cm)** DATE OF BIRTH: **2 March 1978**
WEIGHT: **250 lbs (113 kg)** HOMETOWN: **Waco, TX**

PROFESSIONAL RECORD: 28-14, 1 NC UFC RECORD: 2-3

A true Texan from the top of his ten-gallon hat to the bottom of his cowboy boots, Waco-born Heath Herring made his state proud with his aggressive style and world-class MMA game. And while that was good news for people in the Lone Star State, it was even better for fight fans around the globe, because when "The Texas Crazy Horse" was on his game and matched with a fighter as eager to throw down as he is, it made for a memorable night.

Herring, a PRIDE vet, is the owner of standout wins over Mark Kerr, Igor Vovchanchyn, Gary Goodridge, and most recently Cheick Kongo, but his rocky ascension up the UFC ranks hit a roadblock when he lost to Brock Lesnar in August of 2008.

BOBBY HOFFMAN *The Truth*

HEIGHT: **6' 2" (188 cm)** DATE OF BIRTH: **28 Oct. 1966**
WEIGHT: **245 lbs (110 kg)** HOMETOWN: **Bettendorf, IA**

PROFESSIONAL RECORD: 36-10-1, 2 NC UFC RECORD: 0-2, 1 NC

Bobby Hoffman had the power and aggressive style to become a star in mixed martial arts, but his inability to control himself in everyday life made him a cautionary tale and not a champion. Winner of 36 of his 49 pro bouts, 15 by knockout and 14 by submission, Hoffman extended former UFC heavyweight champion Maurice Smith the distance before losing a decision, and knocked out Mark Robinson at UFC 30 but failed a post-fight drug test, rendering the bout a no contest. In November of 2001, he made his last Octagon appearance, getting knocked out by Josh Barnett, but he continued to fight until 2006, going 8-5 with 1 no contest in his post-UFC years.

SAM HOGER *The Alaskan Assassin*

HEIGHT: **6' 3" (191 cm)** DATE OF BIRTH: **28 June 1980**
WEIGHT: **205 lbs (93 kg)** HOMETOWN: **Baton Rouge, LA**

PROFESSIONAL RECORD: 10-4 UFC RECORD: 2-3

Mixed martial arts can be a game of inches. Just ask Sam Hoger, who could have conceivably been 4-1 in the UFC instead of 2-3 if not for some bad breaks and questionable scoring in his fights against Rashad Evans and Stephan Bonnar.

But the "Alaskan Assassin", who first jumped into the spotlight during his stay on *The Ultimate Fighter 1* and then defeated Bobby Southworth and Jeff Newton in the Octagon, didn't cry over the past, especially when he got a chance to score the biggest win of his career against international star Lyoto Machida at UFC 67 in 2007, only to fall short via unanimous decision in what was ultimately his last UFC bout.

Matt Hughes was probably tired of hearing about the topic, but as the two-time welterweight champion celebrated his induction into the UFC Hall of Fame on May 28, 2010, it was tough not to remember his words before his Extreme Challenge bout against Chatt Lavender in 2001.

At that point, Hughes was 27 years old and already three years into his career. At 2-1 in the UFC, he was probably headed back there, but the former All-American wrestler from Eastern Illinois University had no problem keeping active in other promotions. In fact, the Lavender fight was his sixth of the year, and he would have nine bouts in total by the end of 2001. So the question at the time was, how long did he see himself competing in mixed martial arts?

"Two or three years maybe," said Hughes. "That's it. I was born and raised on a farm, and I want to go back there. I prefer my hometown because it's the people I've been around my whole life. I'm not trying to make an impact on the sport. I'm just doing what I love. I would like to win a UFC championship. It will be funny. If I've saved my money, and in 2-3 years, if it takes me that long to win that belt, it may very well be that I'll retire on the spot."

Well, things changed significantly in the years after that 2001 bout.

UFC 22: Hughes vs. Ignatov

"I remember the fight," said Hughes. "Stars and Stripes (Nightclub), he almost went all three rounds with me. Tough kid."

As for his earlier statement?

"I'm gonna give you the exact same answer, but I think I'm really gonna mean it this time," he laughed. "But seriously, we're looking at around 12 months. We have a 5-month-old girl, and she's now getting a personality where she can move around in her crib and this and that, and in 12 months I want to be able to raise my kids, all of them. In 12 months she's gonna be needing someone to keep her out of the refrigerator. (Laughs) So that's my goal, but you know what, the last fight against Renzo (Gracie at UFC 112), I had a fun time in there. I like Renzo; he's always been respectful to me and he's just a nice guy. But I had a fun time, and if they keep going like that, who knows when I'm gonna stop, to be honest."

UFC HALL OF FAME

- **Inducted May 28, 2010**
- **Two-time UFC welterweight champion**
- **Defended title seven times over two reigns**
- **Defeated six men who held UFC titles**

MATT HUGHES

HEIGHT: **5' 9" (175 cm)** DATE OF BIRTH: **13 Oct. 1973**

WEIGHT: **170 lbs (77 kg)** HOMETOWN: **Hillsboro, IL**

PROFESSIONAL RECORD: 45-8
UFC RECORD: 18-6
TITLES HELD: TWO-TIME UFC WELTERWEIGHT CHAMPION

A decade after the Lavender fight, Hughes is not only still fighting, but with wins over Matt Serra, Gracie, and Almeida in 2009-10, and just one loss to BJ Penn in November of 2010, he's still relevant in the UFC welterweight division he practically put on the map during two title reigns that saw him defend his title a combined seven times.

But there are even more numbers that made Hughes' induction into the UFC Hall of Fame a no-brainer:

- **45 pro wins**
- **18 UFC wins (most all time)**
- **2 welterweight championship reigns**
- **7 successful welterweight title defenses (most ever)**
- **9 championship fight wins (tied with Randy Couture and Anderson Silva for most ever)**
- **5 knockout wins in championship fights (tied with Couture, Silva and Chuck Liddell for most ever)**
- **5 successful consecutive welterweight title defenses (tied with Georges St-Pierre for first all-time)**
- **12 welterweight championship fights (first all-time)**
- **3 submission wins in welterweight championship fights (first all-time)**
- **6 former or current UFC champions defeated by Hughes (St-Pierre, Serra, Penn, Dave Menne, Sean Sherk, Carlos Newton)**

Even though this honor is no surprise, it did come as a shock to Hughes when he got the call from UFC President Dana White.

"I just never thought about it, to be honest, so yeah, it came out of the blue," said Hughes. "I really thought a lot about it the first couple of days after Dana told me, and I really didn't know what to think about it. I've always been the type of guy who thought that somebody who gets inducted into the Hall of Fame needs to be a retired individual. That's just my train of thought. But I'm very privileged and I thank the UFC."

UFC 36: Hughes vs. Sakurai

And if you know anything about Matt Hughes, you know that joining Liddell, Couture, Mark Coleman, Ken Shamrock, Dan Severn, and Charles "Mask" Lewis in the Hall isn't going to prompt Hughes to start sitting on the back porch and waxing poetic about his accomplishments.

"I hate looking at myself and telling people what I've done," said Hughes, who also coached two seasons of *The Ultimate Fighter* reality show. "I do know that if you look at a piece of paper and if you compare me with other people in the UFC on that piece of paper, yes, I would have more wins than anybody else and defended the title more, so I see why, but I'm just a Midwest guy kinda living the dream."

It has been a dream run for Hughes, and after defeating Lavender via third-round submission, he put together two more wins and then was invited back to the UFC to take on welterweight champion Carlos Newton at UFC 34 in November of 2001. Hughes defeated Newton that night and began a title reign that saw him defeat Mach Sakurai, Newton in a rematch, Gil Castillo, Sean Sherk, and Frank Trigg.

UFC 34: Hughes vs. Newton

Photography by: Susumu Nagao

Hughes would lose his crown to Penn at UFC 46 in 2004, but nine months later he was back on top after beating soon-to-be welterweight great Georges St-Pierre. In Hughes' first defense of his second reign, he was pitted against Trigg again, and what resulted was not only one of the greatest fights in UFC history, but the one fight Hughes said he would pick if forced to choose one fight that represents what he's all about.

UFC 42: Hughes vs. Sherk

UFC 50: Hughes vs. St-Pierre

"I do a lot of things with the military and I always tell them that no matter what type of bad spot you're in, whether pinned down in the gunfight in Afghanistan or if you're in the States doing something silly—no matter what's going on, there's always a way out," he said. "You've just got to calm down, relax, and think about it. Never give up. The second Frank Trigg fight was one of those things where I kinda woke up and he was mounted on me and I was able to think of a way out and end up winning the fight."

UFC 52: Hughes vs. Trigg 2

UFC 60: Hughes vs. Royce Gracie

The first-round submission win over Trigg could have been enough for Hughes to hang his hat on and walk into the sunset, but the pride of Hillsboro, Illinois wasn't done yet. Since that win, he has defeated Joe Riggs, Royce Gracie, BJ Penn, Chris Lytle, Matt Serra, Ricardo Almeida, and Renzo Gracie, with his only losses coming to St-Pierre (twice), Penn, and Thiago Alves. Along the way he's built a diehard fan following that has stuck with him for over a decade.

UFC 63: Hughes vs. Penn 2

UFC 68: Hughes vs. Lytle

UFC 85: Hughes vs. Alves

UFC 98: Hughes vs. Serra

"I'm a pretty straight shooter," said Hughes when asked to explain his appeal. "I'm not a politician when it comes to what I'm thinking in my head and I communicate with my people. I do a blog every week, and if you go to my website, it's family-friendly. You can take your kids there and there's nothing I have to hide from my kids or anybody else's kids."

UFC 112: Hughes vs. Renzo Gracie

UFC 117: Hughes vs. Almeida

UFC 123: Hughes vs. Penn 3

And at the ripe old age of 36, Matt Hughes became a Hall of Famer.

"I took this up as just a hobby, something to occupy my time and to vent some aggressiveness and be competitive," he said. "I never thought that I would be in the position I'm in today. If I want a new car, I can trade my truck in and get a new car. My kids have got shoes and clothes and we don't worry about food on the table. Shaking hands, signing autographs, being a world titleholder and being inducted into the Hall of Fame, this is beyond what I ever would have pictured my life being. I'm supposed to be that guy that's got a shovel or a hammer in his hands, and he's working hard. That's just who I am."

MARK HOMINICK *The Machine*

HEIGHT: **5' 8" (173 cm)**
WEIGHT: **145 lbs (66 kg)**
DATE OF BIRTH: **22 July 1982**
HOMETOWN: **Thamesford, Ontario, Canada**

PROFESSIONAL RECORD: 20-9 UFC RECORD: 3-1

Ontario's Mark Hominick is known as one of the best-conditioned fighters in the game, hence his nickname "The Machine". But in addition to his limitless gas tank, he has also made his mark in the fight game with ferocious striking attacks, that have seen him end nine of his pro fights via knockout.

In March of 2006, the Canadian standout made his UFC debut, shocking fight fans with a submission win over top lightweight contender Yves Edwards. A victory over Jorge Gurgel would follow, but then Hominick walked away from the UFC.

"I was a 145-pound fighter, and that's what I looked at," he said when asked about his mindset at the time. "I thought Yves Edwards was a great matchup, the same with Gurgel, and I knew I could beat those guys, but my goal in this sport is to be the best in the world, and my opportunity to do that was at 145."

In recent years in the featherweight division, Hominick has been nearly unstoppable, as he defeated Savant Young, Bryan Caraway, Yves Jabouin, and Leonard Garcia before the WEC and UFC merge in late 2010 brought him back to the Octagon. In January of 2011, he earned a title shot with a blistering first-round stoppage of George Roop, and though he fell short of victory in his challenge for Jose Aldo's 145-pound crown, his gritty effort earned him Fight of the Night honors at UFC 129 in April of 2011.

JEREMY HORN

HEIGHT: **6' 2" (188 cm)**
WEIGHT: **185 lbs (84 kg)**
DATE OF BIRTH: **25 Sept. 1975**
HOMETOWN: **Salt Lake City, UT**

PROFESSIONAL RECORD: 95-21-5
UFC RECORD: 6-7

What more can you say about Jeremy Horn other than to give him his respect as one of the most experienced and talented fighters in the game? With over 100 professional fights to his name, he earned his accolades the hard way, and he's still standing and still relevant in the fight game today.

"I was never really that gifted of an athlete or that physical, but I could look, see, and think my way through a lot of things," says Horn, whose biggest UFC win was a finish of Chuck Liddell at UFC 19, a result "The Iceman" avenged in a title bout in 2005. "If I couldn't do it physically, I could find a way around it just by thinking. It got to be the way I fought too."

HAROLD HOWARD

HEIGHT: **6' 2" (188 cm)**
WEIGHT: **248 lbs (113 kg)**
DATE OF BIRTH: **1958**
HOMETOWN: **Niagara Falls, Ontario, Canada**

PROFESSIONAL RECORD: 1-3 UFC RECORD: 1-2

Whether it was his ever-present mullet, missing teeth, or the immortal line, "We have a saying back home that if you're coming on, COME ON," odds are that you didn't forget Canada's Harold Howard once you saw him in the Octagon.

That's impressive considering that he only had four MMA fights in a career that lasted from 1994 to 1996. And two of those fights came at UFC 3, where he knocked out Roland Payne in 46 seconds and was submitted due to strikes by Steve Jennum. In between, he gained most of his notoriety for a bout he didn't fight, the UFC 3 tournament semifinal against Royce Gracie, which the UFC legend withdrew from due to exhaustion before a single blow was thrown.

JOHN HOWARD *Doomsday*

HEIGHT: **5' 7" (170 cm)**
WEIGHT: **170 lbs (77 kg)**
DATE OF BIRTH: **1 March 1983**
HOMETOWN: **Boston, MA**

PROFESSIONAL RECORD: 14-6 UFC RECORD: 4-2

John Howard came to the UFC in 2009 from the mixed martial arts hotbed of New England with a reputation as a well-rounded competitor who also had the heart to have come back from the brink of defeat to win on a number of occasions. This dramatic style garnered Howard a sizeable fan following back home, and it grew worldwide after he pounded out a decision win over Chris Wilson at UFC 94.

Two more nailbiting wins against Tamdan McCrory and Dennis Hallman followed before an emphatic KO of the Night over Daniel Roberts in March of 2010. Since then, Howard has dropped two in a row to Jake Ellenberger and Thiago Alves.

MATT HUGHES PAGE 58

ROGER HUERTA *El Matador*

HEIGHT: **5' 9" (175 cm)** WEIGHT: **155 lbs (70 kg)** DATE OF BIRTH: **20 May 1983** HOMETOWN: **Austin, TX**

PROFESSIONAL RECORD: 23-5-1, 1 NC UFC RECORD: 6-2

One of the most charismatic young stars in the UFC during an eight-fight stint from 2006 to 2009, Roger Huerta announced his arrival as a serious threat to the lightweight title with an unforgettable win over Leonard Garcia in April of 2007. In fact, it landed him on the cover of Sports Illustrated, the first MMA fighter to ever be so honored.

Huerta refused to rest on his laurels, jumping right back into the Octagon to stop tough newcomers Doug Evans and Alberto Crane. But none of those victories compared to his stirring come-from-behind win in December of 2007 over Clay Guida in what was widely acknowledged as one of the best fights of the year. It was the perfect end to an amazing year.

"A lot of people were very emotional," he recalled. "I was emotional as well. It was my last fight of the year and I had nothing left going into that fight. By the time it was all said and done, at the very end of that fight, I left it all in there. I can literally say that I left everything I had in there, physically and emotionally."

That raw honesty captivated fans around the world, especially when they heard the story of his harrowing childhood and his struggles to make a life for himself in the most unforgiving of environments.

Huerta's UFC career would end after consecutive losses against Kenny Florian and Gray Maynard, but "El Matador" remains an active fighter and an inspiration to others.

FABIANO IHA *The King of The Armbar*

HEIGHT: **5' 8" (173 cm)**
WEIGHT: **155 lbs (70 kg)**
DATE OF BIRTH: **28 July 1970**
HOMETOWN: **Florianopolis, Brazil**

PROFESSIONAL RECORD: 9-5
UFC RECORD: 3-4

When your nickname is "The King of The Armbar", you had better be prepared to back up such a boast in the Octagon. Brazilian jiu-jitsu black belt Fabiano Iha certainly did, as he finished all nine of his mixed martial arts wins, six by way of—you guessed it—armbar.

"I know for sure that my armbar is better than anybody else's," said Iha in 2001. "It doesn't matter if he escapes from somebody else; I know I'll be able to get him anyway."

3-4 in the UFC from 1999 to 2001, Iha finished Laverne Clark (in a rematch), Daiju Takase, and Phil Johns, but fell short against big names like Caol Uno and Dave Menne.

BRAD IMES *Hillbilly Heartthrob*

HEIGHT: **6' 7" (201 cm)** DATE OF BIRTH: **16 March 1977**
WEIGHT: **260 lbs (118 kg)** HOMETOWN: **Springfield, MO**

PROFESSIONAL RECORD: 13-7 UFC RECORD: 0-3

A former Division I football player for Missouri, Brad Imes moved from the obscurity of the offensive line to the bright spotlight of the UFC with his stint on *The Ultimate Fighter 2*, where he made it to the finals against Rashad Evans. Imes' UFC career was epitomized by classic toe-to-toe scraps with Evans, Dan Christison, and Heath Herring, and that willingness to engage in fan-friendly fights made "The Hillbilly Heartthrob" a favorite among MMA followers. Now retired from the sport, Imes' post-UFC career included two victories via the ultra-rare gogoplata submission.

JAMES IRVIN *The Sandman*

HEIGHT: **6' 2" (188 cm)** DATE OF BIRTH: **12 Sept. 1978**
WEIGHT: **205 lbs (84 kg)** HOMETOWN: **Huntington Beach, CA**

PROFESSIONAL RECORD: 15-9, 2 NC TITLES HELD: WEC HEAVYWEIGHT CHAMPION
UFC RECORD: 4-6

Owner of some of the heaviest hands and most devastating knees in the light heavyweight division, James Irvin tried to live up to his nickname of "The Sandman" with every trip to the Octagon. It worked for him against knockout victims Terry Martin, Hector Ramirez, and Houston Alexander, with the single-knee KO of Martin and the eight-second finish of Alexander being particularly memorable.

Unfortunately for Irvin, key losses to Anderson Silva, Alessio Sakara, Thiago Silva, and Stephan Bonnar, along with a series of injuries, weight class jumps and out-of-the-ring issues kept the Californian from ever realizing his true potential on the world stage in the UFC.

EUGENE JACKSON *The Wolf*

HEIGHT: **5' 8" (173 cm)** DATE OF BIRTH: **31 Dec. 1969**
WEIGHT: **185 lbs (93 kg)** HOMETOWN: **Palo Alto, CA**

PROFESSIONAL RECORD: 15-8-1 UFC RECORD: 3-4

If you wanted to sum up the mixed martial arts career of Eugene Jackson, you could say that he was always game, always had difficulty with submission artists, and always could end your night in a split second if he caught you with his lethal left hand.

One of the sport's most exciting fighters during the "Dark Ages" of the UFC in the late '90s, Jackson's back-to-back knockouts of Royce Alger and Keiichiro Yamamiya got fight fans buzzing. But when paired up with tapout artists Sanae Kikuta, Jeremy Horn and Ricardo Almeida, things ended poorly. Ironically, Jackson's last win in the Octagon was via submission, as he tapped out Keith Rockel at UFC 35.

QUINTON JACKSON PAGE 66

KEITH JARDINE
The Dean of Mean

HEIGHT: **6' 2" (188 cm)**
WEIGHT: **205 lbs (93 kg)**
DATE OF BIRTH: **31 Oct. 1975**
HOMETOWN: **Albuquerque, NM**

PROFESSIONAL RECORD: 16-10-2
UFC RECORD: 6-7

Make no mistake about it, Keith Jardine likes the underdog role. There's a fine line between being the underdog and being underestimated, and despite the ups and downs, Jardine wants to make it clear that the man now showing up to fights is the one who scored monumental wins over Forrest Griffin, Brandon Vera and Chuck Liddell, not the one who fell short against Wanderlei Silva and Thiago Silva. Win or lose though, Jardine is respected by his peers, and loved by his fans.

STEVE JENNUM

HEIGHT: **5' 10" (178 cm)**
WEIGHT: **215 lbs (98 kg)**
DATE OF BIRTH: **1961**
HOMETOWN: **Omaha, NE**

PROFESSIONAL RECORD: 2-3
UFC RECORD: 2-1
TITLES HELD: UFC 3 TOURNAMENT CHAMPION

Ninjitsu fighter Steve Jennum sat back and watched the UFC 3 tournament in 1994 unfold as an alternate, not really expecting to get called into action. But when Ken Shamrock couldn't continue in his final match, the Nebraska police officer got the opportunity of a lifetime and he made the most of it, defeating Harold Howard in 87 seconds to win the tourney with just one fight.

UFC tournament rules were changed after the bout, and while Jennum submitted Melton Bowen in his first bout at UFC 4, an injury kept him from advancing, and he would go on to lose the three remaining fights in his MMA career before retiring in 1997.

RYAN JENSEN

HEIGHT: **6' 1" (185 cm)**
WEIGHT: **185 lbs (84 kg)**
DATE OF BIRTH: **20 Sept. 1977**
HOMETOWN: **Omaha, NE**

PROFESSIONAL RECORD: 16-7
UFC RECORD: 2-6

Ryan Jensen's journey through the middleweight division was a rollercoaster ride. But despite the ups and downs, the talented native of Omaha, Nebraska never lost sight of his UFC goals. In September of 2009, his patience and persistence paid off when he submitted Steve Steinbeiss for his first UFC win.

Jensen went on to win Submission of the Night honors at UFC 114, but back-to-back losses at the hands of Court McGee and Jason MacDonald brought his stint in the organization to a halt.

ANTHONY JOHNSON *Rumble*

HEIGHT: **6' 2" (188 cm)**
WEIGHT: **170 lbs (77 kg)**
DATE OF BIRTH: **6 March 1984**
HOMETOWN: **Dublin, GA**

PROFESSIONAL RECORD: 9-3
UFC RECORD: 6-3

Anthony "Rumble" Johnson is one of those 'can't miss' prospects, the kind of fighter that gets better with each passing win. Despite knocking out his first five UFC opponents, Johnson remained grounded, "The numbers and experience can play a factor, but in my opinion, as long as you go out there and lay everything on the line, you've got nothing to worry about."

This attitude helped him deal with losses to Rich Clementi, Burns, and Josh Koscheck, and when he returned from an injury-induced layoff to dominate Dan Hardy with his wrestling in March of 2011, he looked better than ever.

DAMARQUES JOHNSON *Darkness*

HEIGHT: **6' 1" (185 cm)**
WEIGHT: **170 lbs (77 kg)**
DATE OF BIRTH: **28 June 1982**
HOMETOWN: **Salt Lake City, UT**

PROFESSIONAL RECORD: 17-9
UFC RECORD: 3-3

DaMarques Johnson first made waves on *The Ultimate Fighter 9* for his trash talk of Team UK coach Michael Bisping. But it was his fighting that got him to the season's final match, and though he fell short in his attempt to add James Wilks to the names of opponents he's sent packing, there was no question that we had not heard the last of Johnson in the Octagon.

That fact was evident in wins over Edgar Garcia and Brad Blackburn that both earned him post-fight bonus awards. Whether he's beating vets like Mike Guymon or falling short of victory against Matthew Riddle and Amir Sadollah, you can always expect a fight out of the Utah native.

DEMETRIOUS JOHNSON *Mighty Mouse*

HEIGHT: **5' 3" (160 cm)**
WEIGHT: **135 lbs (61 kg)**
DATE OF BIRTH: **13 Aug. 1986**
HOMETOWN: **Parkland, WA**

PROFESSIONAL RECORD: 14-1
UFC RECORD: 2-0

Inspired by *The Ultimate Fighter 1*, multi-sport high school athlete Demetrious Johnson took his talents and work ethic to MMA in 2005 and never looked back, winning 14 of 15 fights and earning a reputation as one of the sport's top prospects.

In 2011 "Mighty Mouse" was put to the test in the world's toughest proving ground—the UFC Octagon—and he's adapted nicely, defeating Japanese star "Kid" Yamamoto and former WEC bantamweight champ Miguel Angel Torres in his first two bouts.

BRIAN JOHNSTON *Fury*

HEIGHT: **6' 4" (193 cm)**
WEIGHT: **222 lbs (100 kg)**
DATE OF BIRTH: **Unknown**
HOMETOWN: **San Jose, CA**

PROFESSIONAL RECORD: 5-6
UFC RECORD: 2-4

One of the first hybrid fighters to enter the Octagon in the early days of the UFC, Brian Johnston could handle himself standing or on the mat, and he would shine in victories over Scott Fiedler and Reza Nasri in 1996. Unfortunately for the Californian, most of his bouts came against the early UFC elite. Losing to Don Frye and future Hall of Famers Mark Coleman and Ken Shamrock. He returned for UFC 14 in 1997, but was stopped by Dan Bobish. A stroke cut his career short, but he has since made a solid recovery.

JON JONES *Bones*

HEIGHT: **6' 4" (193 cm)**
DATE OF BIRTH: **19 July 1987**
WEIGHT: **205 lbs (93 kg)**
HOMETOWN: **Endicott, NY**

PROFESSIONAL RECORD: 13-1
UFC RECORD: 7-1
TITLES HELD: UFC LIGHT HEAVYWEIGHT CHAMPION

Before he was called NBT (Next Big Thing) or UFC light heavyweight champion, Jon Jones was a 21-year-old armed with talent, desire, and the dreams of every young fighter in MMA—to be in the UFC.

And despite a spotless 6-0 record, when he set foot inside the Octagon for the first time to face Andre Gusmao in 2008, it was more than just another fight.

UFC 87: Jones vs. Gusmao

"Being an MMA fighter, you put the UFC on such a high pedestal and you look at these guys like they're superheroes and unbeatable," said Jones, who since that night in Minnesota has been either blessed or cursed with the words 'superhero' and 'unbeatable' in many circles.

Jones scored a unanimous decision win over Gusmao that night, showing glimpses of the unorthodox and dynamic techniques that have become his trademark, and when his hand was raised, he knew his time had come.

"Once I got my very first win and I hear 'the winner is, Jonny "Bones" Jones,' a level of 'Yes, I can' came across me and it made me believe from that point on," said the New Yorker.

UFC 128: Jones vs. Rua

UFC 92: Jones vs. Bonnar

Five months later he defeated Stephan Bonnar at UFC 100, and victories over Jake O'Brien, Brandon Vera, Vladimir Matyushenko, and Ryan Bader (which were sandwiched around a controversial disqualification defeat to Matt Hamill) came in a fast and furious fashion after that, earning him a shot at the light heavyweight crown held by Mauricio "Shogun" Rua after his then-teammate, Rashad Evans, got injured.

On March 19th, at UFC 128, Jones took the belt, tearing through Rua in less than three rounds. And what made the feat—which catapulted him into the record books as the youngest UFC champion ever—even more amazing, is that the fight was the capper on a day that began with Jones and coaches Greg Jackson and Mike Winklejohn foiling a robbery in a Paterson, New Jersey park.

How do you top that? He's got a few ideas.

"Being great is one thing, but being remembered is another. To be great, magnificent and remembered, you have to stand for something and change the world in a way. I want to change the world."

What's in a nickname? Well, if you go by the moniker "Rampage", you'd better not lay and pray, jab and grab, or practice any other less-than-scintillating technique in search of victory in the mixed martial arts arena. Luckily, Quinton "Rampage" Jackson has only one speed in competition and life.

PRIDE Shockwave 2003: Jackson vs. Minowa

From the first interview to the final bell, Jackson has always made it a point to entertain. Whether it's with his self-effacing and sometimes outrageous humor outside the Octagon or with his trademark slams inside of it, this is a fighter who doesn't let the fight come to him—he's going after it. He's not looking to do anything calmly or with technical brilliance, he wants to smash, slam, and pound his way to victory; he wants to punch a hole through the man on the other side of the Octagon.

That's entertainment.

"It's a fight: you win some and you lose some, but you have to give the fans what they want, what they paid for," said Jackson. "They're the most important ones in the sport, and there's no sport without them. I love my fans, and I really try to give them what they want. And I really don't call them fans, I call them friends."

Yet while Jackson seemingly goes through life with an unbridled joy, he's escaped a rough past and rollercoaster professional career to make it to this point.

Born and raised in Memphis, Tennessee, Jackson came up hard in life, and to get past the fact that he didn't have the same clothes and things that more fortunate kids had in school, he quickly learned how to use his fists. But eventually the young Rampage got a talking-to from an uncle, and coupled with his own mental fortitude and a move to a more stable environment, Jackson suddenly had reason to leave the dead-end life behind.

PRIDE Critical Countdown 2004: Jackson vs. Arona

"One of my uncles sat me down and told me that if I didn't change the way I was living and the way I was acting, I wasn't going to live long," remembered Jackson in 2003. "I saw a lot of my friends disappearing, either going to prison or getting killed, and I didn't want that type of life. Strangely, something changed when we moved out of the neighborhood and we moved to a place where they had better things. They had wrestling in school and a lot of other things."

A few years after his first exposure to organized wrestling, his friend and former wrestling rival Dave Roberts exposed him to MMA. Jackson fell in love, and after a loss to Marvin Eastman in his pro debut in June of 2000, he would go on to win eight in a row before getting the call to be the sacrificial lamb to Japanese superstar Kazushi Sakuraba in the PRIDE organization.

Jackson would get submitted by Sakuraba in that July 2001 bout, but he made enough of an impression that he kept getting called back and soon became a fan favorite known for his charisma and the trademark heavy chain he wore around his neck. Over the next two years in PRIDE, he would only lose once (via a controversial disqualification to Daijiro Matsui) while beating the likes of Ricardo Arona, Igor Vovchanchyn, Kevin Randleman, Murilo Bustamante, and UFC star Chuck Liddell.

QUINTON JACKSON *Rampage*

HEIGHT: **6' 1" (185 cm)** DATE OF BIRTH: **20 June 1978**

WEIGHT: **205 lbs (93 kg)** HOMETOWN: **Memphis, TN**

PROFESSIONAL RECORD: 31-8
UFC RECORD: 7-2
TITLES HELD: UFC LIGHT HEAVYWEIGHT CHAMPION

But from the tail end of 2003, Jackson started to get a bit disillusioned with fighting in Japan, and coupled with disappointing losses to Wanderlei Silva and Mauricio Rua, a conversion to Christianity in 2004, and the explosion in popularity of the UFC in 2005, the idea of coming home to the States to reap the rewards of his hard work began to take shape.

UFC 75: Jackson vs. Henderson

Jackson left PRIDE after his February 2006 win over Yoon Dong Sik, and after a brief stay in the now-defunct WFA for a win over Matt Lindland, Rampage finally arrived in the world-famous Octagon in 2007. After avenging his loss to Eastman at UFC 67, he won the UFC light heavyweight championship in May of that year by knocking out Liddell a second time.

PRIDE 28: Jackson vs. Silva 2

UFC 67: Jackson vs. Eastman

Now a star in his own country, Jackson became the first man to unify the UFC and PRIDE titles when he decisioned Dan Henderson at UFC 75, but he would lose his belt in July of 2008 via a razor-thin decision to Forrest Griffin.

UFC 86: Jackson vs. Griffin

Undeterred, Jackson settled some unfinished business with Wanderlei Silva, knocking him out in the first round, and then went on to defeat Keith Jardine. Jackson's star went on to shine even brighter with his stint as a coach on *The Ultimate Fighter 10* and as one of the stars of the hit action film *The A-Team*. But his heart was still in fighting, and despite a disappointing loss to his rival Rashad Evans at UFC 114, Rampage roared back with a decision victory over Lyoto Machida to put himself squarely in the title picture at the tail end of 2010. In fact, Quinton faces Jon Jones in September 2011.

UFC 71: Jackson vs. Liddell 2

UFC 92: Jackson vs. Silva 3

SCOTT JORGENSEN *Young Guns*

HEIGHT: **5' 4" (163 cm)** WEIGHT: **135 lbs (61 kg)** DATE OF BIRTH: **17 Sept. 1982** HOMETOWN: **Boise, ID**

PROFESSIONAL RECORD: 11-4 UFC RECORD: 0-0

An aggressive battler whose greatest attribute may be his determination to always find a way to win in the cage, Scott "Young Guns" Jorgensen has generated some serious buzz in just over five years as a pro, nearly three of which came in the WEC.

"The WEC gave me a home and a payoff I will soon be able to see, hold and spend for all my hard work. I will take full advantage of my opportunity and rise to be the best."

After an impressive win over Kenji Osawa in August of 2008, Jorgensen made it two WEC victories in January of 2009 when he submitted Frank Gomez with a guillotine choke in just 69 seconds.

Far from content, Jorgensen followed up these bouts with consecutive victories over Noah Thomas, Takeya Mizugaki and Chad George, and then he made his case for a title shot when he decisioned the last man to beat him—Antonio Banuelos—in April of 2010.

There would still be one more hurdle to get over though, and in August of 2010, Jorgensen pounded out an impressive win over Brad Pickett in a bout awarded Fight of the Night honors. All that was left for the three-time Pac-10 wrestling champion for Boise State was a world title, but he wasn't able to figure out the puzzle of Dominick Cruz, losing via decision.

MARTIN KAMPMANN *Hitman*

HEIGHT: **6' 0" (183 cm)**
WEIGHT: **170 lbs (77 kg)**
DATE OF BIRTH: **17 April 1982**
HOMETOWN: **Aarhus, Denmark**

PROFESSIONAL RECORD: 17-5
UFC RECORD: 8-4

Martin Kampmann came to the UFC in 2006 with a reputation as a fierce standup fighter. But in his first Octagon bout against Crafton Wallace, Kampmann displayed his all-around MMA game as he quickly took Wallace down and submitted him in the first round with a rear naked choke.

Unfortunately, after a submission of Drew McFedries at UFC 68, a knee injury put him on the shelf. But after a year away, he returned with a win over Jorge Rivera, and after dropping to 170 pounds, "The Hitman" made an impact at welterweight with victories over Alexandre Barros, Carlos Condit, Jacob Volkmann, and Paulo Thiago, consistently showing the effortless cool that has become his trademark, even in controversial decision defeats against Jake Shields and Diego Sanchez.

PAUL KELLY *Tellys*

HEIGHT: **5' 9" (175 cm)** DATE OF BIRTH: **9 Dec. 1984**
WEIGHT: **155 lbs (70 kg)** HOMETOWN: **Liverpool, England**

PROFESSIONAL RECORD: 12-4 UFC RECORD: 5-4

Paul "Tellys" Kelly came to the UFC in 2008 with an unbeaten record and a stellar reputation as one of the most exciting fighters in the UK.

Both aspects of his rep were left intact after a hard-fought win over veteran Paul Taylor in an action-packed war that kicked off a nine-fight UFC stint.

And though he fell short in his next Octagon outing against Marcus Davis, he roared back to form with a win over Troy Mandaloniz and then dropped to the lightweight division, where he defeated Rolando Delgado, Matt Veach, and TJ O'Brien before a Fight of the Night loss at UFC 126 in February of 2011 to Donald Cerrone.

MARK KERR *The Smashing Machine*

HEIGHT: **6' 3" (191 cm)** DATE OF BIRTH: **21 Dec. 1968**
WEIGHT: **263 lbs (119 kg)** HOMETOWN: **Toledo, OH**

PROFESSIONAL RECORD: 15-11, 1 NC TITLES HELD: UFC 14 AND 15 HEAVYWEIGHT TOURNAMENT WINNER
UFC RECORD: 4-0

Known at various times in his career as "The Specimen", "The Titan", and "The Smashing Machine", Mark Kerr was all of those things in the Octagon, where he dominated his opponents over a four-fight stint in 1997.

Winning the UFC 14 and UFC 15 heavyweight tournaments in a little over five combined minutes, Kerr was seemingly destined for greatness, but it was not to be. Chasing glory in Japan's PRIDE organization, Kerr pounded his way to five wins and one no contest, but after a loss to Kazuyki Fujita, the wheels came off for Kerr, who only managed a 3-10 record over the next nine years.

DONG HYUN KIM *Stun Gun*

HEIGHT: **6' 1" (185 cm)** DATE OF BIRTH: **17 Nov. 1981**
WEIGHT: **170 lbs (77 kg)** HOMETOWN: **Busan, South Korea**

PROFESSIONAL RECORD: 14-0-1, 1 NC UFC RECORD: 5-0, 1 NC

One of South Korea's fighting pioneers, Dong Hyun Kim became only the second fighter from his country to compete in the UFC. "It's an honor me to fight in the UFC, the world's best fight event," he said before his bout with Jason Tan. "It will be a big opportunity for me to show my fighting style to MMA fans around the world."

Just showing up wasn't enough for this talented judo black belt, and he scored a stirring TKO victory over Tan, and followed it up with wins over Matt Brown, TJ Grant, Amir Sadollah and, most recently, Nate Diaz, marking him as a contender in the 170-pound shark tank.

ROB KIMMONS *The Rosedale Reaper*

HEIGHT: **5' 1" (178 cm)**
WEIGHT: **185 lbs (84 kg)**
DATE OF BIRTH: **30 Jan. 1981**
HOMETOWN: **Liberty, MO**

PROFESSIONAL RECORD: 23-7 UFC RECORD: 3-4

A submission specialist who wasn't afraid to scrap, Rob Kimmons achieved a career long dream in June of 2008 when he made his UFC debut with a win over Rob Yundt. "I said I was going to do this when I was 14," he recalled. "I feel blessed because only a small percentage of people get to make a living doing what they dreamed of doing." Kimmons hung on longer than most in the Octagon, balancing losses against Dan Miller and Jorge Rivera with wins over Joe Vedepo and Steve Steinbeiss in the competitive middleweight division. But after getting finished by Kyle Noke and Dongi Yang, he was released in 2011.

KYLE KINGSBURY *KingsBu*

HEIGHT: **6' 4" (193 cm)**
WEIGHT: **205 lbs (93 kg)**
DATE OF BIRTH: **22 March 1982**
HOMETOWN: **San Jose, CA**

PROFESSIONAL RECORD: 10-2, 1 NC UFC RECORD: 3-1

Having survived grueling training sessions with UFC heavyweight champion Cain Velasquez ever since he traded in his shoulder pads for mixed martial arts gloves, Kyle Kingsbury expects that nothing he will ever encounter in the Octagon can be more difficult than what he sees on a regular basis in the gym. That's good news for the former Arizona State University football player, who has shown in consecutive UFC wins over Razak Al-Hassan, Jared Hamman, and Ricardo Romero just how much he's evolved since his stint on *The Ultimate Fighter 8* in 2008. Now the quest for "KingsBu" is to make a run at the UFC light heavyweight title.

ERIK KOCH *New Breed*

HEIGHT: **5' 10" (178 cm)**
WEIGHT: **145 lbs (66 kg)**
DATE OF BIRTH: **4 Oct. 1988**
HOMETOWN: **Milwaukee, WI**

PROFESSIONAL RECORD: 12-1 UFC RECORD: 1-0

Milwaukee featherweight Erik Koch might be one of the youngest current fighters in the UFC, but don't think that he's in over his head in the world of mixed martial arts. Winner of 12 out of 13 pro contests, Koch takes a no-nonsense approach to the sport, an attitude which has made him a fan favorite. Included on his slate is a submission win over Bendy Casimir and highlight-reel knockout victories over Francisco Rivera and Raphael Assuncao. Along with his roommate and training partner Anthony Pettis, he's seen as one of the game's top up-and-comers.

YUKI KONDO

HEIGHT: **5' 11" (180 cm)**
WEIGHT: **205 lbs (93 kg)**
DATE OF BIRTH: **17 July 1975**
HOMETOWN: **Niigata, Japan**

PROFESSIONAL RECORD: 52-26-8
UFC RECORD: 1-2

A 1-2 UFC record really doesn't tell the whole story when it comes to the 15-year career of Yuki Kondo. In fact, his UFC 27 win over Alexandre Dantas and Octagon losses to Tito Ortiz and Vladimir Matyushenko barely touch the surface when it comes to one of the most underrated fighters of his time. A King of Pancrase who defeated Frank Shamrock, Semmy Schilt, and Guy Mezger among others, Kondo also starred in PRIDE, where his dance card included Wanderlei Silva, Dan Henderson, and Igor Vovchanchyn. Still active at 36 years old, Kondo's impact will always be felt at home, even if he wasn't able to break out on the UFC scene.

CHEICK KONGO

HEIGHT: **6' 4" (193 cm)**
WEIGHT: **240 lbs (109 kg)**
DATE OF BIRTH: **17 May 1975**
HOMETOWN: **Paris, France**

PROFESSIONAL RECORD: 25-6-2
UFC RECORD: 8-4-1

Not much was known of France's Cheick Kongo when he made his UFC debut in July of 2006 against Gilbert Aldana. Fans quickly and emphatically learned who he was as he halted his rugged foe in a little over four minutes of the first round.

Not everyone was sold on the dynamic striker, so Kongo jumped back in the Octagon a month later to defeat Christian Wellisch, and after a temporary setback against Carmelo Marrero, he impressively defeated Assuerio Silva and PRIDE superstar Mirko Cro Cop in successive bouts.

A three-fight winning streak that began in 2008 inched him closer to a title shots, but a 1-2-1 string with losses against Cain Velasquez and Frank Mir has put him back in rebuilding mode.

TSUYOSHI KOSAKA *TK*

HEIGHT: **5' 11" (180 cm)**
WEIGHT: **225 lbs (102 kg)**
DATE OF BIRTH: **6 March 1970**
HOMETOWN: **Kusatsu, Japan**

PROFESSIONAL RECORD: 26-18-2
UFC RECORD: 3-3

A staple of the UFC's heavyweight division in the late '90s, Tsuyoshi "TK" Kosaka—like his countryman Yuki Kondo—suffered from being in the Octagon during the organization's "Dark Ages," almost guaranteeing that he wouldn't get the respect he deserved from later generations of fight fans.

But for those who never saw him, rest assured that he was the real deal, a courageous fighter with legitimate skills who never backed down. The first man to beat Fedor Emelianenko, Kosaka was a long-time training partner of Maurice Smith and Frank Shamrock, and his UFC resume included wins over Kimo Leopoldo, Pete Williams and Tim Lajcik. In his final Octagon bout in 2002, he was stopped by Ricco Rodriguez, one of seven UFC or PRIDE champions he faced in his career.

When news hit the street that former WWE superstar Brock Lesnar was about to embark on a career in mixed martial arts, many snickered. Sure, he had legit physical talent that saw him win an NCAA Division I National Championship in wrestling for the University of Minnesota and then earn a tryout with the NFL's Minnesota Vikings, but this was different.

Over the next few months though, some of the sport's biggest names, who actually trained with Lesnar, started chiming in with their thoughts on him and his potential.

First there was UFC great Pat Miletich, who raved about Lesnar's raw talent. Next was former UFC lightweight champ Sean Sherk, who dubbed him a phenom.

Now he just needed to show it for real in a fight. Originally set to take on seven-foot-two Hong Man Choi at a K-1 event in Los Angeles in June of 2007, Lesnar was instead matched up with late replacement Min Soo Kim, an Olympic silver medalist in judo.

The fight was a blowout for Lesnar, who took Kim to the mat and pounded on him, forcing a tapout due to strikes in just one minute and nine seconds.

"I was just so happy to put my fist in some other guy's face," said Lesnar of his pro debut. "I felt like I was in heaven. It did go fast, 69 seconds, and it felt like it was five seconds."

Of course, after such an explosive first performance, the question everyone had was, "What's next?" In Lesnar's eyes, the next step had to take place in the UFC, and he wasn't shy about calling out the top heavyweights in the organization.

He got his wish, and in his first Octagon bout at UFC 81 in February of 2008, Lesnar got paired with none other than former world champion Frank Mir. Just seven seconds in, it looked like all the pre-fight hype around Lesnar was going to be justified as he took Mir to the canvas and began to open fire. But just as soon as the assault began, it was halted due to a point deduction from referee Steve Mazzagatti for an inadvertent blow to the back of the head. To most, it seemed like a hasty call, especially since a warning before the deduction wasn't audible on the television broadcast, and Lesnar's momentum was admittedly thrown off.

When the action resumed, Lesnar scored with a right hand, putting Mir back on the mat. But in his haste to finish the fight, Lesnar was caught in a kneebar. Though he won the first 1:20 of the fight, the last ten seconds and the victory went to Mir.

UFC 81: Lesnar vs. Mir

BROCK LESNAR

HEIGHT: **6' 3" (190 cm)**

DATE OF BIRTH: **12 July 1977**

WEIGHT: **265 lbs (210 kg)**

HOMETOWN: **Alexandria, MN**

PROFESSIONAL RECORD: 5-2

UFC RECORD: 4-2

TITLES HELD: UFC HEAVYWEIGHT CHAMPION

UFC 87: Lesnar vs. Herring

Picking himself up and dusting himself off, Lesnar's next bout went a lot better as he dominated former PRIDE star Heath Herring over three rounds at UFC 87. Three months after that bout, on November 15, 2008, he became only the second man in history to win a UFC title in just his fourth professional fight as he stopped the first man to do it, Hall of Famer Randy Couture, in the second round at UFC 91.

UFC 91: Lesnar vs. Couture

The Lesnar story was far from finished. After he got his revenge on Mir at UFC 100 in July of 2009, halting him in the second round, the big man from Minnesota was stricken in October of that year with the intestinal ailment diverticulitis. Put on antibiotics and pain medication, Lesnar was able to avoid initial surgery as his body began to heal itself, but after 11 days in the hospital, he had lost 40 pounds.

After a visit to the Mayo Clinic where surgery to remove his colon was recommended, Lesnar still held out hope to avoid the procedure. After returning to the gym and putting 30 pounds back on, a January 2010 checkup and CT scan revealed that amazingly, the champion was back to full strength.

UFC 100: Lesnar vs. Mir 2

To top this news, Lesnar put on the performance of his career in his return against Shane Carwin at UFC 116 in July of 2010, surviving a hellacious first-round beating to roar back and submit Carwin with an arm triangle in the second round.

UFC 116: Lesnar vs. Carwin

Lesnar would lose his crown later in 2010, as he was TKO'd by Cain Velasquez at UFC 121 in October. After a stint as a coach *The Ultimate Fighter 13*, Lesnar was prepared to face number-one contender Junior dos Santos in mid-2011 and shock the world one more time. Unfortunately, Lesnar had to pull out after his diverticulitis became symptomatic again.

UFC 121: Lesnar vs. Velasquez

BROCK LESNAR PAGE 72

CHRIS LEBEN *The Crippler*

HEIGHT: **5' 11" (180 cm)** WEIGHT: **185 lbs (84 kg)** DATE OF BIRTH: **21 July 1980** HOMETOWN: **Oahu, HI**

PROFESSIONAL RECORD: 21-7
UFC RECORD: 11-6

A season one sparkplug from *The Ultimate Fighter* series who used his aggressive style and brash personality to gain a legion of fans, built an unbeaten 5-0 Octagon record. This stretch included wins over Patrick Cote, Edwin Dewees, Jorge Rivera and Luigi Fioravanti. Chris Leben hit hard times over a 12-month period in 2006-2007 as he was beaten by soon-to-be UFC middleweight champion Anderson Silva, Jason MacDonald and Kalib Starnes.

But "The Crippler" was not one to give up on his dream of a world championship though, and he got back to business in September of 2007 with a spectacular knockout of Terry Martin. He followed that win up with an even more impressive victory over Alessio Sakara.

After two losses against Michael Bisping and Jake Rosholt, the Portland native truly showed that he was back in middleweight title contention with a trifecta of 2010 wins over Jay Silva, Aaron Simpson and Yoshihiro Akiyama, the latter two victories coming just two weeks apart.

Despite a subsequent loss to Brian Stann at UFC 125, a July 2011 fight against the legendary Wanderlei Silva was just the kind of matchup to get his blood flowing. Win or lose, Leben has come a long way since his days on reality television.

"My career's definitely been through a lot of ups and downs since then and I'd like to think I've improved quite a bit and gained a lot of experience both inside and outside the ring."

THALES LEITES

HEIGHT: **6' 1" (185 cm)**
WEIGHT: **185 lbs (84 kg)**
DATE OF BIRTH: **6 Sept. 1981**
HOMETOWN: **Rio de Janeiro, Brazil**

PROFESSIONAL RECORD: 19-4
UFC RECORD: 5-3

A fighter who made his bones as a professional on the tough Brazilian fight circuit, Thales Leites' grappling pedigree was in evidence as he built an impressive unbeaten record against standouts like Ronald Jhun and Jose Landi-Jons.

In his UFC debut against Martin Kampmann in 2006, Leites faced defeat for the first time, losing a three-round decision. Yet in that defeat, he displayed the qualities of heart and determination that all elite fighters possess.

Leites rebounded with a five-fight winning streak (including wins over Nate Marquardt and Drew McFedries) that led to a title shot in 2009. Though he fell short against Anderson Silva, he became the first man to extend "The Spider" five rounds.

NIK LENTZ *The Carny*

HEIGHT: **5' 8" (173 cm)** DATE OF BIRTH: **13 Aug. 1984**
WEIGHT: **155 lbs (70 kg)** HOMETOWN: **Eden Prairie, MN**

PROFESSIONAL RECORD: 23-3-2 UFC RECORD: 5-0-1

Former University of Minnesota wrestler Nik Lentz has been one of the most active young fighters in the lightweight division, with 27 pro fights since he turned pro in 2005, an average of more than five per year. But he isn't just showing up for these bouts, he's winning them, most notably UFC victories over Tyson Griffin, Rafaello Oliveira, Rob Emerson and Andre Winner that justified all his hard work.

"Even though it took a while, it's been for the best because now when I go to the UFC, I feel I can really compete, and I'll be at the same level as everyone else," said Lentz, a native of Eden Prairie, Minnesota who is currently unbeaten in his last 13 fights.

KIMO LEOPOLDO

HEIGHT: **6' 1" (185 cm)** DATE OF BIRTH: **4 Jan. 1968**
WEIGHT: **244 lbs (110 kg)** HOMETOWN: **Waikiki, HI**

PROFESSIONAL RECORD: 9-7-1 UFC RECORD: 3-4

Kimo Leopoldo was one of the most recognizable fighters from the early days of the UFC, and that's not much of a surprise considering he entered the Octagon for the first time at UFC with a cross on his back. Once in the cage, Kimo's battering of the up-to-then untouchable Royce Gracie earned him instant acclaim, and he was able to parlay that first bout into six more in the organization, including two bouts with Ken Shamrock (both of which he lost). At UFC 43 in 2003, Leopoldo earned his biggest victory when he submitted Tank Abbott in less than two minutes, and despite 2009 rumors to the contrary, he is still alive and well.

JOHN LEWIS

HEIGHT: **6' 0" (183 cm)** DATE OF BIRTH: **8 Feb. 1968**
WEIGHT: **180 lbs (80 kg)** HOMETOWN: **Las Vegas, NV**

PROFESSIONAL RECORD: 3-4-3 UFC RECORD: 1-1

A pioneering jiu-jitsu black belt whose impact stretched way beyond the Octagon or ring, John Lewis could be considered one of the most important figures in MMA history for being the man who introduced UFC owners Dana White and Lorenzo and Frank Fertitta to the wonders of the ground game. In competition, Lewis was fearless, facing off with the likes of Jens Pulver, Laverne Clark, Rumina Sato (twice), Johil de Oliveira and Carlson Gracie Jr.. It was after his active career ended in 2000 that he began to really influence the fight scene due to his coaching of the likes of Chuck Liddell, Tito Ortiz, BJ Penn, Marc Laimon and the Inoue brothers.

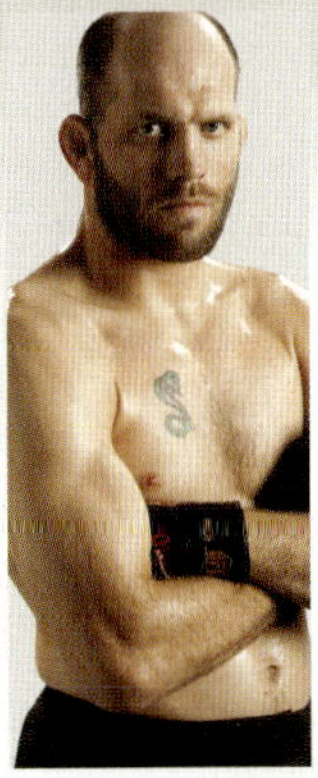

MATT LINDLAND *The Law*

HEIGHT: **6' 0" (183 cm)**
WEIGHT: **185 lbs (84 kg)**
DATE OF BIRTH: **17 May 1970**
HOMETOWN: **Portland, OR**

PROFESSIONAL RECORD: 22-9 UFC RECORD: 9-3

2000 US Olympic Silver medalist Matt Lindland was a top middleweight contender in the early days of the UFC, a swarming wrestler who could nullify practically any opponent's gameplan. A native of Oregon who came up in the sport with Randy Couture and Dan Henderson, Lindland debuted in the UFC in 2000. After winning four in a row, including bouts against Phil Baroni and Pat Miletich, he got a title shot against Murilo Bustamante at UFC 37, where he actually got submitted twice, with the second one sticking. He would go 5-2 over his next seven UFC bouts before being released in 2005, but he remains active both in the US and abroad.

DEAN LISTER

The Boogeyman

HEIGHT: **6' 1" (185 cm)**
WEIGHT: **185 lbs (84 kg)**
DATE OF BIRTH:
13 March 1976
HOMETOWN:
San Diego, CA

PROFESSIONAL RECORD: 11-7
UFC RECORD: 4-2

A true wizard on the mat, he could make anyone a fan of groundfighting. Dean Lister's technique gave any middleweight in the world a tough night. He proved that by turning back the challenge of Jordan Radev at UFC 79 and by avenging a 2003 loss to Jeremy Horn by submitting the seasoned vet in less than a round in June of 2008.

Lister's run at the elite was derailed by Yushin Okami at UFC 92, and though his UFC career ended, he still has his life on the mat to keep him satisfied.

"As far as grappling is concerned, a grappler is truly what I am deep down inside, and for me, it would be difficult for me to stray from that."

DAVID LOISEAU

The Crow

HEIGHT: **6' 0" (183 cm)**
WEIGHT: **185 lbs (84 kg)**
DATE OF BIRTH:
17 Dec. 1979
HOMETOWN: **Montreal, Quebec, Canada**

PROFESSIONAL RECORD: 20-10
UFC RECORD: 4-5

One of the most popular middleweights in the world during his prime in the Octagon, Montreal's David Loiseau was one of the earliest Canadian fighters to make an impact in the UFC.

That's no shock, considering the memorable battles he had with the likes of Rich Franklin, Evan Tanner and Charles McCarthy, and it's hard to picture anything else but highlight-reel performances from "The Crow", whose elbows are some of the deadliest ever seen in the sport.

"It's just consistency and hard work," said Loiseau. "I work them (the elbows) on a regular basis and I train 12 months a year. I don't take any off seasons or anything like that, so I'm always trying to improve."

DUANE LUDWIG

Bang

HEIGHT: **5' 10" (178 cm)**
WEIGHT: **170 lbs (77 kg)**
DATE OF BIRTH:
4 Aug. 1978
HOMETOWN:
Denver, CO

PROFESSIONAL RECORD: 28-11
UFC RECORD: 3-2

One of the most feared strikers in the sport of mixed martial arts, former kickboxer Duane Ludwig's precision strikes have turned out the lights on the likes of Jens Pulver, Jonathan Goulet and Sam Morgan.

"I've been fighting since I was 15, doing amateur fights and I never stepped into this for the fame," he said. "I just love training and fighting is in my blood."

And after UFC 122 win over British prospect Nick Osipczak, Ludwig may be hitting his prime at the perfect moment.

"It's a 24-hour job, but this is something I love and something I signed up for, so there are no complaints. I'm a fighter and I'll step up to fight whoever it is."

TRAVIS LUTTER *The Serial Killer*

HEIGHT: **5' 11" (180 cm)**
WEIGHT: **185 lbs (84 kg)**
DATE OF BIRTH: **12 May 1973**
HOMETOWN: **Fort Worth, TX**

PROFESSIONAL RECORD: 13-6 UFC RECORD: 2-4 TITLES HELD: *THE ULTIMATE FIGHTER 4* MIDDLEWEIGHT WINNER

After his first-round dismantling of dangerous striker Patrick Cote in November of 2006 to win *The Ultimate Fighter 4* series finale and earn a world title shot, soft-spoken Travis Lutter was confident about his chances against world champion Anderson Silva,. The Brazilian jiu-jitsu black belt backed up those words by giving "The Spider" one of his toughest fights ever despite not making weight for the championship bout.

In the end, Silva would prevail via submission in the second round, but after an injury-induced layoff, Lutter—who holds victories over Marvin Eastman, Jose Landi-Jons, and Pete Sell—got back in the saddle against middleweight star Rich Franklin at UFC 83, only to lose that bout and his UFC contract.

CHUCK LIDDELL PAGE 76

When you think of the UFC, odds are that the first name to pop in your head will be that of Chuck Liddell. Whether it's his trademark Mohawk, knockout power, always-exciting fights or his post-fight scream, "The Iceman" is the one fighter who took mixed martial arts from fringe sport to mainstream phenomenon.

Yet you'll never hear him admit to that. Instead, when asked in 2006 how he would like to be remembered, his response was as succinct as one of his right crosses.

"As a fighter, I love to fight. I love the fight game, and I went out there and performed."

Born and raised in Santa Barbara, California, Liddell never shied away from a fight, even as a youngster. But he put his combative nature to work for him in his teenage years, as he started training in karate, as well as nabbing the captainship of both the football and wrestling teams at San Marcos High School.

A good student, Liddell graduated and then earned a degree in Business / Accounting at Cal Poly University. He was also a four-year starter on the school's Division I wrestling team, where he admitted, "I won about half my matches, and lost about half."

It was in college that Liddell first saw the UFC. It was a moment he still remembers vividly, not realizing that one day he would be among the best in the game. "I've been a fighter since I was a kid and I thought that I'd love to do that one day. At that point I never thought I would because I was going to school, wrestling and doing that stuff."

Once he left college, Liddell was hit with the inevitable decision of pursuing his fighting career (which he started in the form of kickboxing) or getting a "real job" by putting his degree to use. Training with John Hackleman, Liddell compiled a 20-2 (16 KOs) record in kickboxing, grabbing two national, the USMPA and WKA titles along the way.

Through it all, his biggest fans were the ones at home. "My grandpa was my greatest influence and so was my mom," said Liddell in 2003. "They always supported me, no matter what I did. My grandpa told me that I could beat anybody in the world back when I started kickboxing. I wish he were here to see me now."

UFC 22: Liddell vs. Jones

Inspired by his kickboxing prowess and his budding jiu-jitsu training with John Lewis, Liddell threw his hat into the MMA ring, making his UFC debut with a decision win over Noe Hernandez at UFC 17 in May of 1998.

UFC HALL OF FAME

- **Inducted July 10, 2009**
- **UFC light heavyweight champion**
- **MMA's first crossover superstar**
- **Devastating right hand**

CHUCK LIDDELL *The Iceman*

HEIGHT: **6' 2" (187 cm)** DATE OF BIRTH: **17 Dec. 1969**

WEIGHT: **205 lbs (93 kg)** HOMETOWN: **San Luis Obispo, CA**

PROFESSIONAL RECORD: 21-8

UFC RECORD: 16-7

TITLES HELD: UFC LIGHT HEAVYWEIGHT CHAMPION, UFC HALL OF FAMER

UFC 35: Liddell vs. Suloev

Liddell followed up with a victory over Jose Landi-Jons three months later in the IVC before being invited back to the UFC on March 5, 1999, to tackle Jeremy Horn. In a battle between two of the best up-and-comers in the sport, Liddell was choked out by Horn. It was his first pro MMA defeat, but he wouldn't lose again for over four years.

Undaunted by the loss, Liddell got back on track by stopping Paul Jones and Steve Heath and decisioning Jeff Monson. But some critics were unconvinced, and when he stepped into the cage with former UFC heavyweight champion Kevin Randleman at UFC 31 on May 4, 2001, Liddell was a huge underdog.

UFC 31: Liddell vs. Randleman

Seventy-eight seconds and a big right hand by Liddell later, Randleman was stopped, and the UFC had a new star. But the road to a championship still had some bumps to navigate along the way. Following a brief visit to Japan's PRIDE organization in May of 2001 to defeat former UFC fighter Guy Mezger, Liddell had to turn back the challenges of Murilo Bustamante, Amar Suloev, Vitor Belfort and Renato "Babalu" Sobral before putting himself firmly in line for a shot at the light heavyweight crown held by Tito Ortiz.

The only problem was that Ortiz was having contract issues with the organization at the time while also claiming that his friendship with Liddell made him unwilling to fight "The Iceman". Liddell begged to differ.

"We knew that sooner or later, if we kept winning, that we were both gonna have to fight," said Liddell in 2003.

Unwilling to wait for Ortiz, Liddell was pitted against former heavyweight champion Randy Couture for the interim 205-pound crown at UFC 43 in June of 2003. A heavy favorite, Liddell was upset by Couture and TKO'd in the third round.

UFC 43: Liddell vs. Couture

Forced to regroup, Liddell was sent to Japan by the UFC to represent the organization in the 2003 PRIDE Middleweight Grand Prix tournament. After a quarterfinal knockout of Alistair Overeem in August of 2003, Liddell went back three months later with the hope of winning his semifinal match to meet PRIDE standout Wanderlei Silva in the finals. It was not to be, as fellow American Quinton "Rampage" Jackson stopped "The Iceman" in the second round.

Returning to the US and the UFC, Liddell got the one match he had been waiting for when he headlined UFC 47 in April of 2004 against Ortiz. All the frustration of the previous years was released in five minutes and 38 seconds as he stopped his rival and finished up with a post-fight scream that was in stark contrast to his usual soft-spoken demeanor.

PRIDE Total Elimination 2003: Liddell vs. Overeem

UFC 47: Liddell vs. Ortiz

"I don't get very excited very often about too many things, but that's one of the things I do," he said of his now-iconic victory yelp. "I prepare for two to three months for a guy, and you end it quickly like that or you have a good fight and you win. I'm excited."

There would be a lot more excitement over the next three years, as the win over Ortiz kicked off a reign of terror over the light heavyweight division that saw Liddell win seven fights in a row, all by knockout.

After defeating Vernon White at UFC 49 in August of 2004, Liddell got a shot at redemption against Couture. The bout followed Liddell's stint as a coach on a new reality show, *The Ultimate Fighter*, which put him in the nation's living rooms on a weekly basis.

"My manager at the time quit because I wouldn't take his advice to hold out for more money and not do the show," recalled Liddell. "I said, 'I gotta be part of it, this is gonna big, this is what we need, and we need for people to see this on free TV, to see what kind of product we have, what great style of fighting this is, and how exciting this could be.'"

And in the UFC 52 rematch against "The Natural", Liddell not only became a champion for the first time, but his first-round knockout of Couture made him the face of mixed martial arts. Over the next few years, Liddell would become the first UFC fighter to appear on the cover of *ESPN The Magazine*, release a best-selling autobiography and make numerous movie and television cameos, including a memorable appearance on HBO's *Entourage*. His appeal to fans, peers and the media was clear.

UFC 52: Liddell vs. Couture 2

UFC 62: Liddell vs. Sobral 2

UFC 71: Liddell vs. Jackson 2

"I think the reason people like me is because I'll fight anybody, anywhere, I don't talk bad about people that don't deserve it, and I'm not a guy who's out there trying to trash talk and make a name for myself," said Liddell. "I earned the name that I have—I went out and fought for it. And I go out there, I fight hard, and I fight to win."

And despite his growing fame, his focus always remained on his fighting. After defeating Couture, he would defend his title with finishes of the first man to beat him, Jeremy Horn, Couture (in their 2006 rubber match), Sobral, and Ortiz.

In May of 2007, Liddell's reign ended at the hands of a familiar foe, Rampage Jackson, who knocked him out in the first round at UFC 71. The defeat kicked off a stint where Liddell, now in his late 30s, lost five of his last six bouts, albeit against top-notch competition like Jackson, Keith Jardine, Rashad Evans, Mauricio "Shogun" Rua and Rich Franklin.

UFC 79: Liddell vs. Silva

UFC 115: Liddell vs. Franklin

Yet sandwiched between these losses was a stirring three-round victory over Wanderlei Silva at UFC 79 in December of 2007. It was the dream fight fans had been talking about for years, and the win was vintage Liddell, as he gave as good as he got while showing the heart and determination only possessed by champions. As far as final victories go, this was one to be proud of.

In July of 2009, Liddell was inducted into the UFC Hall of Fame. He would fight once more, getting stopped in the first round by Franklin at UFC 115 in June 2010 after a second stint as coach on *The Ultimate Fighter*. He announced his retirement on December 29, 2010.

He is currently the UFC's Executive Vice President of Business Development.

CHRIS LYTLE

Lights Out

HEIGHT: **5' 11" (180 cm)**
WEIGHT: **170 lbs (77 kg)**
DATE OF BIRTH: **18 Aug. 1974**
HOMETOWN: **Indianapolis, IN**

PROFESSIONAL RECORD: 40-18-4 UFC RECORD: 9-10

For over 12 years, if a young fighter had aspirations of getting to the next level in the sport of mixed martial arts, he had to get by seasoned veteran Chris Lytle. More often than not, that meant "Lights Out" for prospects like Kevin Burns, Paul Taylor, Kyle Bradley, Brian Foster and Matt Brown.

For Lytle, a former pro boxer who has also been in with the likes of Matt Hughes, Thiago Alves and Josh Koscheck, fighting is just a way of life.

"I don't know if the word is that I'm addicted to it, but I just love to compete, and there's nothing I've ever found to equal the overall feeling you get after you've struggled so much and put so much into something and then come out on top and achieve something," he said.

A pro since 1999, the Indianapolis native has seen the good, the bad and the ugly in the fight game, and he fought his way to the big show the hard way as he competed consistently on the Midwest circuit before getting called to the UFC in 2000. Lytle lost his debut to Ben Earwood, but he remained persistent, winning a call-back three years later.

Again, Lytle would fall short of victory against Robbie Lawler at UFC 45, and after going 2-2 in the Octagon in his next four fights, he was able to use *The Ultimate Fighter 4* to catapult himself back into the sport's largest promotion.

Losing a controversial decision to Matt Serra in the *TUF4* final, Lytle slowly worked his way back into the win column, and as the fights wore on, something was evident: Lytle wasn't just fighting to win, he was fighting to give the fans something to cheer about. And they cheered as he won two Submission of the Night, one Knockout of the Night and five Fight of the Night awards. As far as he's concerned, that's a great legacy to leave.

"It can't be all about winning and losing. The best fight of my life is what I'm looking for right now. We'll see if it happens."

JASON MacDONALD

The Athlete

HEIGHT: **6' 3" (191 cm)**
WEIGHT: **185 lbs (84 kg)**
DATE OF BIRTH: **3 June 1975**
HOMETOWN: **Edmonton, Alberta, Canada**

PROFESSIONAL RECORD: 26-14
UFC RECORD: 6-6

It took Jason MacDonald close to seven years to get to the UFC, but once he got there with a first-round win over Ed Herman in 2006, he made it clear that he belonged in the world's premier mixed martial arts organization.

Since then, "The Athlete" has weathered some rocky moments, but he has also won more fights in the Octagon than any Canadian fighter not named Georges St-Pierre, defeating Chris Leben, Rory Singer, Jason Lambert and old nemesis Joe Doerksen.

At UFC 129, he was expected to be pushed by fellow vet Ryan Jensen, but he instead he kept the fireworks all to himself as he submitted his foe in the first round.

RORY MacDONALD

Ares

HEIGHT: **6' 0" (183 cm)**
WEIGHT: **170 lbs (77 kg)**
DATE OF BIRTH: **22 July 1989**
HOMETOWN: **Kelowna, BC, Canada**

PROFESSIONAL RECORD: 11-1
UFC RECORD: 2-1

Rory MacDonald entered the UFC at 21 with plenty of hype behind him, and he kept the buzz going with a first-round submission victory against veteran Mike Guymon in January of 2010.

But the kid from Kelowna made believers out of the staunchest skeptics in June of 2010 when he battled tooth and nail with Carlos Condit, a legit and longtime contender with whom no 21-year-old should be holding his own. But MacDonald is far from your typical youngster, and though he got stopped in the third round of UFC 115's Fight of the Night, he returned from his first pro loss better than ever at UFC 129, where he decisioned Nate Diaz.

ANTHONY MACIAS

Mad Dog

HEIGHT: **5' 10" (178 cm)**
WEIGHT: **170 lbs (77 kg)**
DATE OF BIRTH: **9 Feb. 1969**
HOMETOWN: **Oklahoma City, OK**

PROFESSIONAL RECORD: 26-15
UFC RECORD: 1-2

The unfortunate recipient of repeated suplexes from Dan "The Beast" Severn in both fighters' UFC debut in 1994, Anthony Macias was more than just a foil for the future Hall of Famer, even if his UFC record didn't reflect it. A hard-nosed Oklahoma native who fought like he was double-parked, it was feast or famine for the "Mad Dog", who only saw three of his 41 pro fights go the distance. In the Octagon, Macias dusted himself off from the UFC 4 loss to Severn to defeat "He-Man" Gipson via submission due to strikes at UFC 6, but he lost his next tournament match that night to Oleg Taktarov in just nine seconds.

LYOTO MACHIDA *The Dragon*

HEIGHT: **6' 1" (185 cm)** WEIGHT: **205 lbs (93 kg)** DATE OF BIRTH: **30 June 1978** HOMETOWN: **Belem, Brazil**

PROFESSIONAL RECORD: 17-2
UFC RECORD: 9-2
TITLES HELD: UFC LIGHT HEAVYWEIGHT CHAMPION

The son never had a chance.

There would be no soccer fields or jiu-jitsu mats for Lyoto Machida…not if his father had a say in the matter. As the head of the family, Yoshizo Machida did have the last word, so when his son was three, he began training in the family business—not as a banker, a farmer, a storekeeper, or a craftsman—but as a martial artist.

Studying Shotokan karate under his father, a renowned Master who had left Japan for a new life in Salvador, Brazil, young Lyoto was a quick study in the art of combat. What he was being taught went far beyond blocks, kicks, and katas.

"My father always taught me to be an honest man with integrity," said the younger Machida. "He also showed me the path of being a true fighter through oriental philosophy."

As he grew older, Machida would find time for the usual pursuits of youth, but he never strayed far from a gym or dojo, whether it was to study and compete in karate, sumo wrestling or the art usually associated with Brazil, jiu-jitsu. There was no doubt—young Machida was going to be a fighter.

"Fighting has been in my blood since I was born," he admits, and at 15, when he first walked into the gym to start training in jiu-jitsu with Master Alexei Cruz, he began putting all the pieces of the mixed martial arts puzzle together.

Preparing to fight for a living would be anything but easy though, and his true graduation day wouldn't come until May 2, 2003, when the 24-year-old Machida made his professional MMA debut with a decision over Kengo Watanabe. Four months later, Machida would take 4:21 to stop a young American fighter who was on the verge of becoming a star in the States, Stephan Bonnar. Suddenly, fight-industry insiders started to take notice of the son of the karate master.

Fight fans soon jumped on the bandwagon that New Years' Eve in Japan, when unbeaten rising star Rich Franklin—fresh off impressive first-round wins over Evan Tanner and Edwin Dewees—stepped into battle with Machida and left with his first loss via a second-round TKO.

UFC 70: Machida vs. Heath

Machida began fighting for the K-1 organization in 2004, and added two more wins to his ledger as he submitted Michael "The Black Sniper" McDonald and decisioned Sam Greco. 2005 saw another high-profile name fall to defeat at Machida's hands as BJ Penn rose up in weight to fight the then-heavyweight and lose a three-round decision.

Machida then stopped Dimitri Wanderley back home in Brazil and outpointed Vernon White in his US MMA debut for the now-defunct WFA in 2006. With the demise of that organization, he migrated to the UFC, where he debuted in 2007 with a three-round decision win over Sam Hoger at UFC 67.

In his early days in the organization, Machida was criticized for his methodical and unorthodox style, but you couldn't argue with the results: two more victories over David Heath and Kazuhiro Nakamura.

When he submitted Rameau Sokoudjou, decisioned Tito Ortiz and knocked out Thiago Silva, he made believers out of the harshest critics. Next up was a world title shot, and with a second-round knockout of Rashad Evans at UFC 98 in May of 2009, he announced to the world that "karate is back."

UFC 98: Machida vs. Evans

A two-fight series with countryman Mauricio "Shogun" Rua was the first order of business for the new champion. After winning the first bout via controversial decision, he was knocked out in the rematch at UFC 113 in 2010, costing him his belt and his unbeaten record. A second consecutive loss followed, as he lost a close decision to Quinton "Rampage" Jackson. However, at UFC 129 in April of 2011, "The Dragon" was back in top form as he knocked out Randy Couture in the second round.

As for his father's reaction to all his success?

"My father is very proud of my accomplishments," said Machida, "and he is very happy that I am able to spread the family name throughout the world." Yeah, the son never had a chance; but then again, he's not complaining either. "I love what I do," he said.

JON MADSEN

HEIGHT: **6' 0" (183 cm)**
WEIGHT: **245 lbs (110 kg)**
DATE OF BIRTH: **12 Feb. 1980**
HOMETOWN: **Orange County, CA**

PROFESSIONAL RECORD: 7-1 UFC RECORD: 4-1

Former Division II national wrestling champion Jon Madsen first came to the attention of the fight world during his 2009 stint on *The Ultimate Fighter 10*, but it was on the season finale card that the ground and pound specialist announced his arrival to the UFC with a three-round win over castmate Justin Wren.

Following subsequent wins over Mostapha Al-Turk and Karlos Vemola that upped his record to 6-0, Madsen—a training partner of former UFC heavyweight champion Brock Lesnar—made it seven in a row with an impressive first-round stoppage of Gilbert Yvel before a 2011 loss to Mike Russow led to his release from the UFC.

DEMIAN MAIA

HEIGHT: **6' 0" (183 cm)**
WEIGHT: **185 lbs (84 kg)**
DATE OF BIRTH:
6 Nov. 1977
HOMETOWN:
Sao Paulo, Brazil

PROFESSIONAL RECORD: 14-2
UFC RECORD: 8-2

When a world-class grappler enters the MMA world, there is always a little skepticism. But Demian Maia—winner of a seemingly endless array of grappling tournaments, including the world championships, Abu Dhabi and Pan Ams—has impressed from the moment he put on the gloves.

In 2007, he made his UFC debut with a first-round submission win over Ryan Jensen, and in subsequent bouts he submitted Ed Herman, Jason MacDonald, Nate Quarry and Chael Sonnen before a knockout loss to Nate Marquardt.

At UFC 112, Maia fought Anderson Silva for the middleweight title. Despite losing a five-round decision, he was praised for his toughness, which he showed again in comeback wins over Mario Miranda and Kendall Grove.

NATE MARQUARDT *The Great*

HEIGHT: **6' 0" (183 cm)** WEIGHT: **170 - 185 lbs (77 - 84 kg)** DATE OF BIRTH: **20 April 1979** HOMETOWN: **Denver, CO**

PROFESSIONAL RECORD: 34-10-2 UFC RECORD: 10-4

There are plenty of class acts in the world of MMA, and one of those people you will never hear a bad word about is middleweight contender Nate Marquardt.

That type of class is a great attribute to have, but when you're a fighter in a business where the squeaky wheel is often the one that gets oiled, it can be a problem. It's been a particular issue with Marquardt, whose talent in the sport is matched by his previous accomplishments, which include recognition as a seven-time King of Pancrase while competing in Japan.

Beginning with his UFC debut in 2005, Marquardt still brought the "nice guy" into the Octagon with him, and while he won his first four fights, he lost the fifth, a UFC title fight against Anderson Silva in 2007. So in 2008, he added a new mindset to his arsenal—strike first, ask questions later. The results have amazed fight fans, as four of his last five wins—over Martin Kampmann, Wilson Gouveia, Demian Maia and Rousimar Palhares—have come by knockout.

"I think I've always had that mean streak in me, and I kinda lost it there for a little while just because certain things changed in the way I was fighting," he said. "Then the loss to Anderson (Silva) gave me it back."

So he's still a nice guy and a class act, just not when the bell rings.

ELIOT MARSHALL *The Fire*

HEIGHT: **6' 3" (191 cm)**
WEIGHT: **205 lbs (93 kg)**
DATE OF BIRTH: **7 July 1980**
HOMETOWN: **Boulder, CO**

PROFESSIONAL RECORD: 11-4 UFC RECORD: 3-2

After an impressive run on season eight of *The Ultimate Fighter* that saw him earn the praise of his teammates as well as coach Frank Mir, Eliot "The Fire" Marshall finished off his stint with a dominant first-round submission win over Jules Bruchez.

"What I took away most from the six weeks is that I can do anything," he said. "And it's more mental stuff than physical stuff. Just dealing with that whole situation in the house, that was tough."

After beating Bruchez, Marshall defeated Vinny Magalhaes and Jason Brilz in the Octagon, but losses to Vladimir Matyushenko and Luiz Cane have slowed the progress of the Colorado submission specialist.

TERRY MARTIN

HEIGHT: **5' 9" (175 cm)**
WEIGHT: **185 lbs (84 kg)**
DATE OF BIRTH: **10 Oct. 1980**
HOMETOWN: **Chicago, IL**

PROFESSIONAL RECORD: 22-9 UFC RECORD: 2-4

With a master's degree in psychology to go with his knockout punch, Terry Martin was one of the UFC's most intriguing fighters. But after losses to James Irvin and Jason Lambert in the light heavyweight division, the Chicago native was in danger of never reaching a mainstream audience.

So with his career on the line, Martin dropped down to 185 pounds and took on Jorge Rivera at UFC 67. The change couldn't have been more dramatic, as Martin knocked Rivera out in just 14 spectacular seconds, proving that he had found a new home. The glory was short-lived though, as a knockout of Ivan Salaverry came before consecutive defeats to Chris Leben and Marvin Eastman. Martin was released in 2008.

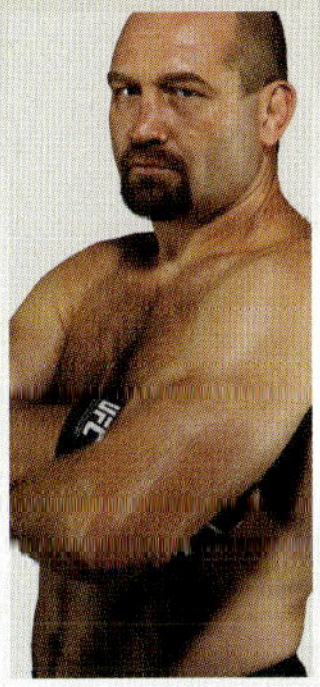

VLADIMIR MATYUSHENKO *The Janitor*

HEIGHT: **6' 0" (183 cm)**
WEIGHT: **205 lbs (93 kg)**

DATE OF BIRTH: **4 Jan. 1971**
HOMETOWN: **El Segundo, CA**

PROFESSIONAL RECORD: 26-5 UFC RECORD: 7-3

A native of Belarus, Vladimir Matyushenko made his mark in the sports world in the United States, first as a two-time national junior college wrestling champion, then as one of the premier mixed martial artists in the game. A former world title challenger who owns wins over Yuki Kondo, Pedro Rizzo and Travis Wiuff, Matyushenko enjoyed great success in the six years between his UFC stints, winning nine of ten bouts before returning to the Octagon in 2009 with victories against Igor Pokrajac and Eliot Marshall.

In August of 2010, Matyushenko saw his winning streak snapped at the hands of future light heavyweight champion Jon Jones, but after knockouts of Alexandre Ferreira and Jason Brilz, "The Janitor" is showing that for him, life begins at 40.

GRAY MAYNARD

The Bully

HEIGHT: **5' 8" (173 cm)**
WEIGHT: **155 lbs (70 kg)**

DATE OF BIRTH: **9 May 1979**
HOMETOWN: **Las Vegas, NV**

PROFESSIONAL RECORD: 11-0-1, 1 NC UFC RECORD: 8-0-1, 1 NC

An undefeated record can be a burden for many fighters. It can make them cautious or paranoid, or make them fight not to lose as opposed to fighting to win, Gray Maynard, unbeaten in 13 pro mixed martial arts bouts (11 wins, 1 draw and 1 no contest), is not one of those fighters.

"I don't really keep up with that stuff," he says with a laugh. "I get asked what my record is and I couldn't even tell you. I don't know how many wins I had in college, I don't know how many wins I had in high school, but I can tell you every one that I lost because that eats me up. I expect to win, so I'm not counting them. I'm not here to have a chance to win or to hope I win, I'm going into fights expecting to win."

And that's when things get serious. Maynard—one of the most affable fighters in the game—becomes "The Bully". If you agree to compete against him in anything—fighting, wrestling, checkers, etc.—it's on.

"I really love to win and that's the time that I don't care who you are," he said. "We can be close as hell, but when it's time to train, I'm coming after you. I take that stuff personally. I'm a competitor. Whatever I have to do, I want to win, no matter what it takes."

And while he was once just known for his world-class wrestling and amazing strength, Maynard—an *Ultimate Fighter 5* alumnus and former NCAA Division I All-American from Michigan State—showed his ever-improving MMA game in wins over seasoned vets Kenny Florian and Rich Clementi, then-unbeaten Frankie Edgar, and rising stars Jim Miller, Roger Huerta and Nate Diaz.

The winning streak earned him a shot at Edgar's title in January of 2011, and the top two lightweights in the world went to war for five rounds before a draw verdict was rendered. There will be a third match between the two though, and this time, Maynard promises to bring his own judges in the form of his fists.

SEAN McCORKLE *Big Sexy*

HEIGHT: **6' 7" (201 cm)**
WEIGHT: **265 lbs (120 kg)**

DATE OF BIRTH: **17 July 1976**
HOMETOWN: **Indianapolis, IN**

PROFESSIONAL RECORD: 10-2 UFC RECORD: 1-2

Standing at 6' 7", Indianapolis' Sean McCorkle entered the UFC for the first time as one of the heavyweight division's most physically intimidating figures, one who had to cut from over 300 pounds to make the 265-pound limit. And with an unbeaten record, it was clear that he brought more to the table than just size.

When he submitted PRIDE and K-1 superstar Mark Hunt in just 67 seconds at UFC 119 in September of 2010, he made a statement that he had arrived. Unfortunately, the division was waiting for the charismatic "Big Sexy". McCorkle and Struve talked trash over the internet which led to their fight being promoted as the co-main event at UFC 124. After losses against Stefan Struve and Christian Morecraft, he was released in 2011.

TAMDAN McCRORY *The Barn Cat*

HEIGHT: **6' 4" (193 cm)**
WEIGHT: **170 lbs (77 kg)**

DATE OF BIRTH: **5 Nov. 1986**
HOMETOWN: **Cortland, NY**

PROFESSIONAL RECORD: 12-3 UFC RECORD: 3-3

A young man who has worn his glasses all the way through his ring walk, Tamdan McCrory may not look like your stereotypical fighter, but when the bell rings, all bets are off. The 6' 4" banger immediately garners respect from his opponents for his size, power and underrated ground game.

Winner of his first UFC fight over Pete Spratt in June of 2007, the "Barn Cat" may have fallen short of victory in three fights against Akihiro Gono, Dustin Hazelett and John Howard. In his wins over Spratt, Luke Cummo and Ryan Madigan, he showed the potential to one day become a serious player in the talent-rich UFC.

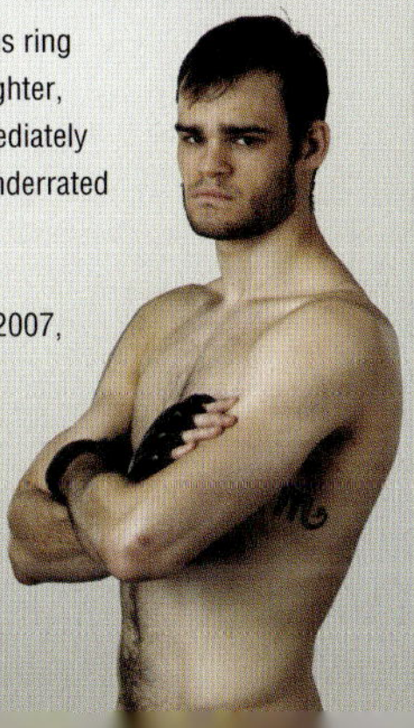

JUSTIN McCULLY *The Nsane1*

HEIGHT: **6' 2" (188 cm)**
WEIGHT: **240 lbs (109 kg)**
DATE OF BIRTH: **18 Feb. 1976**
HOMETOWN: **Washington, DC**

PROFESSIONAL RECORD: 9-5-2 UFC RECORD: 2-2

After his dominant three-round victory over Antoni Hardonk in April of 2007, bright things were forecast for heavyweight Justin McCully, despite it being only his third fight following a three-year layoff. Unfortunately, injuries sidelined the Brazilian jiu-jitsu black belt for much of the next year, but when "The Nsane1" returned to the Octagon in December of 2008 against Eddie Sanchez, it was like he never left, as he pounded a three-round unanimous decision win. He lost his next bout against Mike Russow at UFC 102 and was released, but he remains active in the game, most recently serving as a coach for UFC star BJ Penn.

MICHAEL McDONALD
Mayday

HEIGHT: **5' 9" (175 cm)**
WEIGHT: **135 lbs (61 kg)**
DATE OF BIRTH: **15 Jan. 1991**
HOMETOWN: **Modesto, CA**

PROFESSIONAL RECORD: 13-1
UFC RECORD: 2-0

Currently the youngest fighter in the UFC, 20-year-old Michael "Mayday" McDonald amazed veteran observers in 2010 with three finishes of fellow bantamweight standouts Manny Tapia, Cole Escovedo and Clint Godfrey that made him a hardcore fan favorite.

It was his UFC debut in March of 2011 that got people really talking, as he pounded out a three-round win over Edwin Figueroa that earned him well-deserved Fight of the Night honors.

Just two months later at UFC 130 in Las Vegas, he made it 2-0 in the Octagon with a three-round split decision win over fellow Californian Chris Cariaso that once again showed off his amazing talent and grace under pressure.

DREW McFEDRIES
The Massacre

HEIGHT: **6' 0" (183 cm)**
WEIGHT: **185 lbs (84 kg)**
DATE OF BIRTH: **27 July 1978**
HOMETOWN: **Davenport, IA**

PROFESSIONAL RECORD: 9-6
UFC RECORD: 4-5

Breaking down the fighting style of Iowa's Drew McFedries is simple—if he hits you on the chin, you're going down.

"I throw hammers like I expect this guy's gonna drop, and I commit to punches. A lot of guys don't commit and I think that's a big deal, because if you commit, you could miss. I'm fairly accurate, but I've had my misses and my mishaps."

Want more proof? Just ask UFC victims Xavier Foupa-Pokam, Marvin Eastman, Jordan Radev and Alessio Sakara. Yet despite the jaw-dropping wins delivered by "The Massacre", his deficiencies on the ground led to submission defeats against Martin Kampmann, Mike Massenzio, Thales Leites and Tomasz Drwal and his release in 2009.

COURT McGEE *The Crusher*

HEIGHT: **5' 11" (180 cm)**
WEIGHT: **185 lbs (84 kg)**
DATE OF BIRTH: **12 Dec. 1984**
HOMETOWN: **Orem, UT**

PROFESSIONAL RECORD: 12-1 UFC RECORD: 2-0 TITLES HELD: *THE ULTIMATE FIGHTER 11* WINNER

An inspiration to fans for rebounding from the ravages of drug addiction, Court McGee got a second chance in fighting as well when he was brought back to *The Ultimate Fighter 11* after losing a controversial decision to Nick Ring. In response, McGee won three in a row, finishing all of his opponents. To top everything off, he defeated Kris McCray via second-round submission in the season finale to earn a UFC contract, proving that fighters are made, not born.

"I didn't do it because I wanted people to think of me as an MMA fighter; I did it because I loved the sport," said McGee, who has since added a win over Ryan Jensen.

GAN McGEE *The Giant*

HEIGHT: **6' 10" (208 cm)**
WEIGHT: **265 lbs (120 kg)**
DATE OF BIRTH: **20 Nov. 1976**
HOMETOWN: **San Luis Obispo, CA**

PROFESSIONAL RECORD: 13-5 UFC RECORD: 2-2

Trained by John Hackleman and a stablemate of Chuck Liddell, 6' 10" Gan McGee seemingly had all the tools to win a heavyweight title, and as a finisher, he had the fan support that can lift a fighter to the next level as well. But things never clicked for "The Giant", and after shaking off a UFC 28 loss to Josh Barnett with back-to-back stoppages of Pedro Rizzo and Alexandre Dantas, he lost his lone title shot to Tim Sylvia via knockout at UFC 44 in 2003. He endured two PRIDE defeats to Heath Herring and Semmy Schilt in his post-UFC career, and took four years off from the game before returning in 2008, going 1-1.

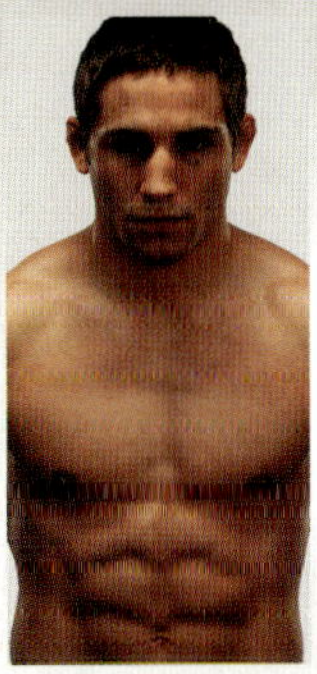

CHAD MENDES *Money*

HEIGHT: **5' 6" (168 cm)**
WEIGHT: **145 lbs (66 kg)**
DATE OF BIRTH: **1 May 1985**
HOMETOWN: **Sacramento, CA**

PROFESSIONAL RECORD: 10-0 UFC RECORD: 1-0

With 10 wins in 10 pro bouts and the endorsement of his training partner and former WEC featherweight champ Urijah Faber, Chad Mendes has gotten a lot of people excited about his UFC career. But no one is more excited about competing against the best featherweights in the world than the Hanford, California native himself.

"This is a huge accomplishment for me considering I've only been fighting for about two and a half years now," said Mendes, a two-time Division I All-American and Pac-10 champion for Cal Poly who owns wins over Cub Swanson, Javier Vazquez and Michihiro Omigawa. "I remember watching the UFC when I was a kid and thought it was the coolest thing ever and now I'm a part of it."

DAVE MENNE
The Warrior

HEIGHT: **5' 10" (178 cm)**
WEIGHT: **170 lbs (77 kg)**
DATE OF BIRTH: **29 July 1974**
HOMETOWN: **Minneapolis, MN**

PROFESSIONAL RECORD: 43-16-2
UFC RECORD: 2-4
TITLES HELD: UFC MIDDLEWEIGHT CHAMPION

Dave Menne once held the UFC middleweight title. In fact, he was the first 185-pound belt holder in the organization's history, but in terms of loudly proclaiming himself as the baddest man on the planet, he even admitted back in 2001 that, "I guess I'm an unlikely champion."

Inside of the Octagon, though, Menne was always one of MMA's fiercest competitors. A tireless worker, he came up the hard way, fighting close to 40 times en route to his title-winning effort over Gil Castillo at UFC 33 in September of 2001.

On his way up the ranks, Menne was a regular in places like Indiana, Iowa, Wisconsin and his native Minnesota, fighting against the likes of Matt Hughes, Shonie Carter, Chris Lytle and Jose "Pele" Landi-Jons. What may have been even more impressive is that he did it all while training himself.

"It's an advantage in that I can tailor things where I know I need to work," he said. "It wouldn't be for everybody though. I have a good overview of the sport, my weaknesses and other guys' strengths. And it's always been a catalyst for me to push myself. So I think that being on my own helps me to strive a little harder and prove that you can do it."

In March of 2000, Menne got his first taste of the UFC, decisioning Fabiano Iha at UFC 24. He wouldn't return for over a year, but when he did, he was competing for the UFC middleweight title against Castillo. Five rounds later, he was a world champion, and it was vindication for years of hard work.

In his first defense at UFC 35, Menne lost his title via TKO to Murilo Bustamante, and then was KO'd in 18 seconds by Phil Baroni. He returned in 2006 following a four-year break from the Octagon, but lost to Josh Koscheck and Luigi Fioravanti. Regardless, Menne holds a place in UFC lore as someone who may have been an unlikely champion, but who was still a top-level fighter.

GUY MEZGER

HEIGHT: **6' 1" (185 cm)**
WEIGHT: **205 lbs (93 kg)**
DATE OF BIRTH: **1 Jan. 1968**
HOMETOWN: **Dallas, TX**

PROFESSIONAL RECORD: 30-14-2 UFC RECORD: 4-1 TITLES HELD: UFC 13 LIGHTWEIGHT TOURNAMENT WINNER

At one time in the late 90s and early part of the new millennium, Guy Mezger was perhaps the most visible mixed martial arts fighter in the United States, appearing on VH1 and Fox television and writing a book on kickboxing. He could fight too, as evidenced by his four wins in the UFC, including one over Tito Ortiz at UFC 13 in 1997. But after losing to Ortiz in their 1999 rematch, the former Pancrase star returned to Japan, the place where he fought much of his early career, to star in PRIDE from 1999 to 2002. In 2004, Mezger was scheduled to face Ortiz a third time at UFC 50, but he withdrew from the bout due to stroke-like symptoms. He retired shortly afterward.

PAT MILETICH

The Croatian Sensation

HEIGHT: **5' 10" (178 cm)** DATE OF BIRTH: **9 March 1968**

WEIGHT: **170 lbs (77 kg)** HOMETOWN: **Davenport, IA**

PROFESSIONAL RECORD: 29-7-2

UFC RECORD: 8-2

TITLES HELD: UFC WELTERWEIGHT CHAMPION

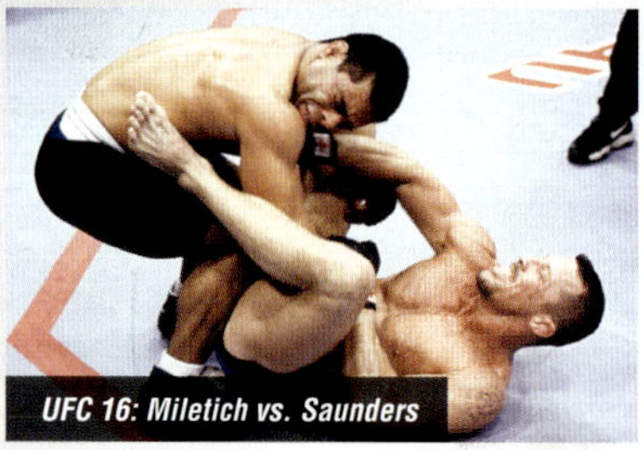

UFC 16: Miletich vs. Saunders

There's no denying the impact Pat Miletich has had on the sport of mixed martial arts. A former UFC welterweight champion who also led Matt Hughes, Jens Pulver and Tim Sylvia to world titles as a trainer, he is one of the sport's pioneers, in and out of the Octagon. He always believed that his success could be boiled down to one thing: hard work.

"If you're not willing to make your training harder than your fight ever could be, then you're not going to end up at the top," said Miletich. "There's a lot of times in my training when I'm ready to puke, and I'm ready to walk right out of the room, but you've just got to keep going. I think that makes a difference, so you don't mentally fold."

Involved in combat sports since he was a child, first in wrestling, then boxing and kickboxing, Miletich had the work ethic to outperform more naturally gifted competitors, and he also had a keen eye for what was happening on the mat or in the ring.

"I wrestled from the time I was in kindergarten through college and I watched how different coaches had coached in all those different aspects of sports. I took the good aspects of coaching that I liked, because there were coaches that couldn't convey to me correctly the information that they were trying to get through my head, and there were other coaches that were really good at it. I just kind of modeled myself after them, and tried to explain myself (to my own fighters) so that they could understand."

Eventually, Miletich sought an opportunity to put his wits and his fists to use in the budding sport of mixed martial arts and teamed up with Mark Hansen to get started in the gym.

"He was ranked in the top ten among heavyweights in the world, and was a Davenport police officer," said Miletich of Hansen. "He and I were training partners for two, three years at least by ourselves before things got rolling. That was actually the first guy. He was a very dominant fighter and a really powerful guy, an All-American lineman at Northern Iowa."

On October 28, 1995, Miletich made his pro MMA debut with three wins in one night in a Chicago tournament. He continued to build his resume and his fight game on the midwest circuit, going 17-1-1 with the only loss coming against fellow MMA mastermind Matt Hume.

Then the UFC called, and on March 13, 1998, he defeated Townsend Saunders and old rival Chris Brennan (they had fought twice previously) to win the UFC 16 tournament. Seven months later, Miletich was back, this time to fight for the UFC's first lightweight (later converted to welterweight) title. In the opposite corner was scrappy Mikey Burnett, and though anticipation was high for the matchup, the reality didn't live up to the hype. Regardless of the lack of sustained action in the bout, Miletich eked out a 21-minute split decision to earn the championship belt.

UFC 18: Miletich vs. Patino

Miletich successfully defended his belt four times over the next two years, defeating Jorge Patino, Andre Pederneiras, John Alessio and Kenichi Yamamoto, while battling an even tougher foe in the gym—a laundry list of mounting injuries.

UFC 32: Miletich vs. Carter

Finally, in May of 2001, the longtime champion surrendered his belt to Carlos Newton via submission in what was a shocking upset at the time. Less than two months later though, Miletich was back, knocking out Shonie Carter with a head kick at UFC 32. A rematch with Newton would not be in the cards though, as Miletich's charge Hughes seized the belt from "The Ronin" at UFC 34.

"The Croatian Sensation" moved up to middleweight for his next bout, at UFC 36 in 2002, but he was stopped by Matt Lindland. He then took a break from the game to heal his injuries and focus on his gym, which was occupied at one time or another by such standouts as Hughes, Pulver, Sylvia, Jeremy Horn, Robbie Lawler, Drew McFedries, Rory Markham, Tony Fryklund and Jason Black.

Miletich attempted comebacks in 2006 and 2008, losing to Renzo Gracie and then knocking out Thomas Denny. Currently, he provides expert commentary for various outlets including Showtime and ESPN.

FRANK MIR PAGE 88

COLE MILLER
Magrinho

HEIGHT: **6' 1" (185 cm)**
WEIGHT: **155 lbs (70 kg)**
DATE OF BIRTH: **26 April 1984**
HOMETOWN: **Macon, GA**

PROFESSIONAL RECORD: 17-5
UFC RECORD: 6-3

A talented ground fighter and submission artist with a finisher's mentality, Georgia native Cole Miller first burst onto the national scene during his stint on *The Ultimate Fighter 5*, where he made it to the show's quarterfinals. But it was after notching impressive post-show wins over Andy Wang and Leonard Garcia that "Magrinho" furthered his reputation as one of the lightweight division's top up-and-comers. He would hit bumps in the road in losses to Jeremy Stephens, Efrain Escudero and Matt Wiman, but his victories over Jorge Gurgel, Junie Browning, Dan Lauzon and Ross Pearson have kept him in the hunt for world title honors.

DAN MILLER

HEIGHT: **6' 1" (185 cm)**
WEIGHT: **185 lbs (84 kg)**
DATE OF BIRTH: **30 June 1981**
HOMETOWN: **Whippany, NJ**

PROFESSIONAL RECORD: 13-5, 1 NC
UFC RECORD: 5-4

Dan Miller has accomplished a lot in his short fighting career. This accelerated development is no problem for the New Jersey native, who parlayed a win over Ryan McGivern in May of 2008 into a shot in the world-renowned Octagon. Once the bell rang for his bout against Rob Kimmons, he made a smooth transition to the UFC by submitting his foe in just 87 seconds.

Since then, the hard-charging Miller has added four wins and a black belt in Brazilian jiu-jitsu to his resume, but what really impresses is his resilience in bouncing back from a three-fight losing streak in 2009-10.

JIM MILLER

HEIGHT: **5' 8" (173 cm)**
WEIGHT: **155 lbs (70 kg)**
DATE OF BIRTH: **30 Aug. 1983**
HOMETOWN: **Whippany, NJ**

PROFESSIONAL RECORD: 20-2
UFC RECORD: 9-1

A former Virginia Tech wrestler who turned to MMA in 2005, Jim Miller came to the Octagon in 2008 with a stellar reputation. Winner of 15 of his last 16 bouts, the Brazilian jiu-jitsu black belt's last three victories have come over Kamal Shalorus, Charles Oliveira and Mark Bocek.

"I go out there and just try to let it all out. I'm not one of those guys that can sit there and say that they fight because of the money. I fight because I love to fight and I love to win. I get a rush from submitting guys, and if there's time on the clock, I'm trying to finish the fight."

PHILLIP MILLER

HEIGHT: **5' 11" (180 cm)**
WEIGHT: **185 lbs (84 kg)**
DATE OF BIRTH: **20 July 1979**
HOMETOWN: **Hesperia, CA**

PROFESSIONAL RECORD: 16-0 UFC RECORD: 2-0

What can you say about the mysterious case of Phillip Miller? One of the fight game's most talented prospects during his run in the sport from 2000 to 2003, the California middleweight opted to walk away from the sport in his prime with an unbeaten record, and he never came back.

While competing, Miller handed an early defeat to current welterweight star Jake Shields, and in the UFC, he made two appearances, decisioning James Zikic at UFC 38 and submitting Mark Weir at UFC 40. He never fought in the Octagon again, and only fought once more, decisioning Moacir Oliveira in 2003. He now works as a Los Angeles police officer.

MATT MITRIONE

HEIGHT: **6' 3" (191 cm)**
WEIGHT: **265 lbs (120 kg)**
DATE OF BIRTH: **15 July 1978**
HOMETOWN: **Indianapolis, IN**

PROFESSIONAL RECORD: 4-0 UFC RECORD: 4-0

A four-year NFL veteran, Matt Mitrione turned to mixed martial arts as a way to keep his competitive spirit satisfied. With his win over UFC vet Scott Junk on the tenth season of *The Ultimate Fighter*, the entertaining heavyweight made it clear that he was going to keep his name in the sports pages for a long time. It was his performance on the *TUF10* season finale card that really turned heads though, as he showed that he could deliver big hits even without his helmet and pads on by knocking out Marcus Jones in devastating fashion. Then he topped that victory with wins over Kimbo Slice, Joey Beltran and Tim Hague, confirming him as one of the most unlikely heavyweight contenders ever.

JEFF MONSON *The Snowman*

HEIGHT: **5' 9" (175 cm)**
WEIGHT: **230 lbs (104 kg)**
DATE OF BIRTH: **18 Jan. 1971**
HOMETOWN: **St. Paul, MN**

PROFESSIONAL RECORD: 42-11
UFC RECORD: 4-3

If you're good enough to win the Abu Dhabi submission wrestling world championship, you're a pretty special athlete. If you've done it twice, like Jeff Monson has, you're on a whole other level. Instead of being content with his elite status in the grappling world, Monson has chased after glory in the Octagon as well. After some ups and downs while facing the likes of Chuck Liddell, Forrest Griffin, and Ricco Rodriguez during his MMA career, "The Snowman" hit his stride in the UFC in 2006, as he defeated Brandon Lee Hinkle, Marcio Cruz and Anthony Perosh in succession to earn a shot at the heavyweight title. Tim Sylvia ended Monson's year on a down note though, decisioning the challenger over five rounds.

The win was quick, decisive and career-altering for Frank Mir, a talent-laden mixed martial artist who had proved more than once that he needed a little adversity to truly show what he could do in the Octagon.

On February 2, 2008, Mir, 2-2 in his previous four fights after a serious motorcycle accident broke his leg and stole almost two years from his career, revived his MMA life again with a 90-second submission of a man who would be crowned the UFC heavyweight champion just two fights later, Brock Lesnar.

It was the latest chapter in the storied career of Las Vegas' Mir, who went from "next big thing" to "damaged goods" to finally starting to realize the potential he had to become the best heavyweight on the planet.

That's the short version.

Seen as the future of the UFC division after two Octagon wins built his record to 4-0, Mir was upset in July of 2002 by veteran Ian Freeman. His next bout was against the comebacking Tank Abbott, a one-dimensional but entertaining sort who had been out of the Octagon for the previous five years. His return met with snickers from the hardcore fans, but enough casual followers came on board to ensure that UFC 41 was going to be a big event for the Tank. And Mir was the foil.

UFC 36: Mir vs. Williams

UFC 41: Mir vs. Abbott

46 seconds later, Mir wasn't just Abbott's foil, he was his conqueror, with a toe hold ending the Californian's night in emphatic fashion. Mir would go on to win his next three bouts, including an arm-breaking victory over Tim Sylvia in June of 2004 that earned him the UFC heavyweight title.

Three months later, a motorcycle accident almost ended his career and his life. Luckily, Mir survived. The career resurrection would take a little longer though.

UFC 48: Mir vs. Sylvia

"The first few times I went back to the gym, I'm walking around limping," he remembers. "I was learning how to protect certain sides of my body, I couldn't do certain moves because I was still healing, and I had to find a way to beat people."

FRANK MIR

HEIGHT: **6' 3" (191 cm)** DATE OF BIRTH: **24 May 1979**

WEIGHT: **260 lbs (118 kg)** HOMETOWN: **Las Vegas, NV**

PROFESSIONAL RECORD: 15-5

UFC RECORD: 10-6

TITLES HELD: UFC HEAVYWEIGHT CHAMPION, INTERIM UFC HEAVYWEIGHT CHAMPION

UFC 61: Mir vs. Christison

Mir finally returned to the Octagon almost two years later, and he would lose two bouts (to Marcio Cruz and Brandon Vera) sandwiched around a lackluster decision win over Dan Christison. The losses were just the latest low points he had to fight through.

"I guess like anything else, there are highs and lows," said Mir. "But your family and friends get you through the low points, and you just ride it out. You keep pushing forward no matter how discouraging this all can be."

Just when it appeared that all Frank Mir's promise had truly ended on that Las Vegas road in September of 2004 and that he was finished as a heavyweight contender, he rebounded, submitting Antoni Hardonk in 77 seconds in August of 2007, his first submission win since beating Sylvia three years earlier. The win over the massive Lesnar was the true icing on the cake though, the victory that put him back in the title picture.

UFC 100: Mir vs. Lesnar 2

UFC 111: Mir vs. Carwin

UFC 107: Mir vs. Kongo

UFC 92: Mir vs. Minotauro

A stirring knockout of Antonio Rodrigo "Minotauro" Nogueira in December of 2008 to win the interim UFC heavyweight championship was next. Though he lost his rematch with Lesnar at UFC 100 and an interim title bout against Shane Carwin in March of 2010, recent wins over Mirko Cro Cop and Roy Nelson have kept him relevant in the division, something no one would have expected after those dark days of 2004.

UFC 119: Mir vs. Cro Cop

"I think my career's been a pretty interesting one as far as some really good highs and some really good lows, and it really hasn't been a consistent increase in any one direction," he said. "The reason why my life is different than someone's in the same situation is that I never stopped trying to move forward. It's not that I've got anything different going for me than anybody else. I think we all have our strengths and weaknesses, and I'm not inhuman. I obviously have my shortcomings like anybody else; I just don't give up. I just keep looking for a way to succeed, regardless of whether I do or not. That's not a guarantee for success, but the only way you guarantee failure is by giving up."

MARK MUNOZ
The Filipino Wrecking Machine

HEIGHT: **6' 0" (183 cm)**
WEIGHT: **185 lbs (84 kg)**
DATE OF BIRTH: **9 Feb. 1978**
HOMETOWN: **Vallejo, CA**

PROFESSIONAL RECORD: 10-2
UFC RECORD: 5-2

Winner of the 2001 NCAA Division I national wrestling championship for Oklahoma State, two-time All-American Mark Munoz finally listened to the prodding of former WEC featherweight champ Urijah Faber in 2007 and began training in mixed martial arts.

Since then, the Filipino sensation has thrilled fans and struck fear into opponents. In August of 2009 at UFC 102, he added another accolade to his resume as he bounced back from a knockout loss to Matt Hamill to pound out a decision over Nick Catone for his first UFC win.

Following stoppages of CB Dollaway, Ryan Jensen and Kendall Grove, a hard-fought scrap with Yushin Okami, and a decision win over Aaron Simpson, Munoz is firmly entrenched as a middleweight contender.

JOSH NEER
The Dentist

HEIGHT: **5' 11" (180 cm)**
WEIGHT: **155 lbs (70 kg)**
DATE OF BIRTH: **24 March 1983**
HOMETOWN: **Des Moines, IA**

PROFESSIONAL RECORD: 29-10-1
UFC RECORD: 4-6

A three-sport athlete in high school, Josh Neer found his true calling in the sport of mixed martial arts, where he has compiled a 29-10-1 record that included four wins in the UFC.

"I just love going in there and getting in a war," he said. "It's the best thing in the world; it's just me against the other guy and I don't want to be the guy who falls first."

Known as "The Dentist" for his tendency to re-arrange his opponents' teeth, Neer has long been one of the sport's most rugged warriors, and he used that attribute to good use in his Octagon victories against Din Thomas, Mac Danzig, Melvin Guillard and Joe Stevenson.

LEE MURRAY *Lightning*

HEIGHT: **6' 3" (191 cm)**
WEIGHT: **185 lbs (84 kg)**
DATE OF BIRTH: **12 Nov. 1977**
HOMETOWN: **London, England**

PROFESSIONAL RECORD: 8-2-1, 1 NC
UFC RECORD: 1-0

In normal circumstances, a fighter with one UFC appearance wouldn't warrant a mention in a UFC Encyclopedia, even if that one bout was a win. For all the wrong reasons, Lee Murray remains one of the most fascinating characters to ever set foot in the organization and it has nothing to do with his upset submission win over Jorge Rivera at UFC 46 in 2004. A brawler who once extended Anderson Silva the full distance, Murray first came to the attention of fans for a post-UFC 38 brawl with then-champion Tito Ortiz. His later notoriety was more ominous though, as he participated in a 2006 robbery that netted over 86 million dollars (53 million pounds), making it the largest cash robbery in British history. He is currently incarcerated in Morocco.

ROY NELSON *Big Country*

HEIGHT: **6' 0" (183 cm)** WEIGHT: **263 lbs (119 kg)** DATE OF BIRTH: **20 June 1976** HOMETOWN: **Las Vegas, NV**

PROFESSIONAL RECORD: 16-6
UFC RECORD: 2-2
TITLES HELD: *THE ULTIMATE FIGHTER 10* WINNER

A favorite of hardcore fight fans, Roy Nelson may not have a typical fighter's physique, but it's hard to argue with the success of the bellied big man known as "Big Country".

Owner of a black belt in Brazilian jiu-jitsu from Renzo Gracie, Nelson competed successfully in a number of grappling tournaments before turning his eye to MMA in 2004. Winner of his first six bouts, Nelson soon signed with the now-defunct IFL in 2007 and within five fights, he was the promotion's heavyweight champion.

Following two successful title defenses and then two non-IFL losses to Andrei Arlovski and Jeff Monson, Nelson finally hit the big time in 2009 when he defeated Kimbo Slice, Justin Wren and James McSweeney on season ten of *The Ultimate Fighter*. He closed out the series in spectacular fashion by closing out Brendan Schaub to join the ranks of *TUF* winners.

"I know how the UFC is as a PR machine and what kind of things they can do for you, so going this route is like fighting seven or eight fights in the UFC," he said, explaining his reasoning for going on *TUF*.

But Nelson's journey was just beginning. In the UFC, he scored an impressive 39-second knockout over Stefan Struve in 2010, but punishing back-to-back losses against Junior dos Santos and two-time heavyweight champion Frank Mir have forced the Las Vegan to regroup and get recharged if he wants to earn a world title shot.

CARLOS NEWTON

The Ronin

HEIGHT: **5' 9" (175 cm)** DATE OF BIRTH: **17 Aug. 1976**

WEIGHT: **170 lbs (77 kg)** HOMETOWN: **Newmarket, Ontario, Canada**

PROFESSIONAL RECORD: 15-14
UFC RECORD: 3-4
TITLES HELD: UFC WELTERWEIGHT CHAMPION

UFC 17: Newton vs. Gilstrap

When the sport of mixed martial arts was going through its years of growing pains, fighters were routinely stereotyped as barroom brawlers with little going on in their lives outside of punching their opponents in the face.

Then came Carlos Newton, and suddenly, all the negative connotations that went along with fighting went out the window. In fact, you could have called him the anti-brawler, because "The Ronin" is all about technique, planning and training. He has fun but carries himself as a professional outside of the Octagon.

"It used to bother me a lot when I was younger," said Newton of the stereotypes in 2001. "I think the reason it bothered me was that when I was younger, I couldn't quite explain myself and the feelings I had. But now that I'm capable of explaining myself much better, conveying my feelings and helping people understand my sport, myself, and the people who participate in it, I've become more comfortable about it."

A martial artist for much of his life, Newton was a quick study in the art of combat.

"It's the sport I chose," he said. "It's something I'm skilled at. I've been doing martial arts since I was six years old and I just have a predisposition for it. It's something I found that I'm good at and that I enjoy. It's my hobby, my everyday activity as I go through life."

Taught by his stepfather in karate, Newton developed into a well-rounded martial artist as he grew up, eventually becoming a three-time Canadian jiu-jitsu champion and a two-time Canadian Pankration titlist. He also made his mark in mixed martial arts, with his acrobatic style gaining him a legion of fans.

A veteran of fighting in Japan, Newton notched three victories out of four fights in PRIDE from 1998 to 2000, with his only loss coming to renowned superstar Kazushi Sakuraba. Newton also fell in love with Japanese culture, learning the language and becoming a huge fan of the anime series *Dragonball Z*, even going as far as naming his fighting style "Dragonball jiu-jitsu".

UFC 31: Newton vs. Miletich

"I just love that stuff," said Newton of the series. "Its philosophy pertaining to the martial arts is so consistent with a fighter's philosophy and so many other principles of life. If God were to have a fighter, it would be Goku (the series' main character). I feel that sincerely."

In the UFC, Newton lost to Dan Henderson via a controversial decision at UFC 17, and after a February 2001 loss to future middleweight champion Dave Menne in a local event, little chance was given to the Canadian when he took on longtime 170-pound champion Pat Miletich for the UFC title in May of 2001.

But a chokeout of Miletich changed everyone's opinion fast, and Newton rapidly shot to the top of the charts in the welterweight division. There would be little rest for the new champion, and six months after winning the belt, he was pitted again Miletich's teammate, powerhouse wrestler Matt Hughes.

UFC 34: Newton vs. Hughes

Hughes was the underdog against the new welterweight star, but in a foreshadowing of things to come, Newton was asked if he was worried about the slams of Hughes.

"Let's see me slam him," he bristled. "I wouldn't give him the option of slamming me. I wouldn't stay on my feet. I wouldn't resist his slam; I would just go with it. Dan Henderson tried to slam me and we ended doing some crazy acrobatic swirl. That's what happens."

Not on November 2, 2001. On that night, Newton caught Hughes in a triangle choke, and the challenger proceeded to lift the champion over his head and prop him on the fence. After a few tense moments, Hughes slammed Newton to the mat, knocking him out. There were some who believed Hughes was out first from the choke, but the result stood and the title changed hands.

Following a PRIDE win over Jose Landi-Jons three months later, Newton got a rematch with Hughes at UFC 38 but was pounded into defeat in four rounds.

It would be the charismatic and dynamic Newton's final UFC title shot, and while he stayed busy against top-level competition around the world over the next eight years, including bouts with Anderson Silva, Renzo Gracie, Matt Lindland and Shonie Carter, "The Ronin" never again reached the heights he touched as a rising star in 2001.

ANTONIO RODRIGO NOGUEIRA

Minotauro

HEIGHT: **6' 3" (191 cm)** DATE OF BIRTH: **2 June 1976**

WEIGHT: **240 lbs (109 kg)** HOMETOWN: **Rio de Janeiro, Brazil**

PROFESSIONAL RECORD: 32-6-1, 1 NC

UFC RECORD: 3-2

TITLES HELD: INTERIM UFC HEAVYWEIGHT CHAMPION, PRIDE HEAVYWEIGHT CHAMPION

November 9, 2003. For almost ten minutes at the Tokyo Dome, Minotauro Nogueira went through hell. In a battle for the PRIDE heavyweight championship, the Brazilian was battered by feared striker Mirko Cro Cop. When the round was over, Minotauro may have thought about what just happened. Most likely though, he thought about Bahia, the city where, at ten years old, his life almost ended.

At a neighborhood party, Minotauro and his friends played in the street. Everything changed when a truck began to move and backed up and over him.

He would stay in a coma for four days and in the hospital for almost 11 months with broken legs and internal injuries. After finally being released from the hospital, Minotauro still couldn't walk for two more months, and if anyone one would have told his family that this child would one day be one of the greatest heavyweights of all-time, they would have been smacked for telling such a cruel joke. But they would have been right.

"I think that time makes me strong. I feel when I fight that nothing's gonna be worse than that."

By the age of 19, he was making his professional debut. From there, he established himself as the best heavyweight in the business, a fact borne from his reign as PRIDE heavyweight champion and his victories over the likes of Dan Henderson, Jeremy Horn, Ricco Rodriguez, Josh Barnett, Mark Coleman, Heath Herring…

…And Mirko Cro Cop.

When the bell rang for round two, Minotauro showed his unbreakable spirit by taking Cro Cop to the mat and securing an armbar for the submission victory.

It was the sweetest and most memorable win of his PRIDE career, but there would be new mountains to climb in the UFC.

At UFC 73 in July of 2007, he faced a familiar foe in Herring, and in typical Minotauro style, he rose from the canvas to decision his opponent over three rounds.

UFC 73: Minotauro vs. Herring

UFC 81: Minotauro vs. Sylvia

There was more of the same in his next bout at UFC 81 in 2008, as he took a horrific pounding from Tim Sylvia for two rounds before winning the interim UFC heavyweight title with a guillotine choke in round three. As Minotauro said after becoming the first man to win UFC and PRIDE heavyweight titles, "I played his game for almost three rounds. He played my game for two minutes and I won the fight."

Following the victory, Minotauro and former UFC heavyweight champion Frank Mir squared off as coaches on *The Ultimate Fighter 8*. The two met in the Octagon at UFC 92. But there would be no miracles this time, as Minotauro Nogueira was knocked out for the first time in his career by Mir.

Many believed that Minotauro, despite entering the Mir bout with a knee injury and after healing from a staph infection, was done as a top level heavyweight. But the great ones don't fade away that easily, and he would get a shot at redemption at UFC 102 in August of 2009.

Facing Randy Couture in Oregon, a place "The Natural" called home for years, Minotauro was going to be fighting a Hall of Famer, the crowd, and the doubts coming from scores of fight fans. But he liked those odds.

"I loved that," said Minotauro. "I was fighting in his hometown, all the crowd was against me, and it was an amazing experience. My mental game was strong, and all my concentration was on that fight."

What resulted that night was a vintage Minotauro performance. For three action-packed rounds, he went to war with Couture, but despite the competitive nature of the bout, when it was all over, there was no doubt who the winner was. Minotauro Nogueira was back.

In February of 2010, Minotauro Nogueira returned against unbeaten star on the rise Cain Velasquez, but there was no stopping the man who would soon be heavyweight champion, as he knocked Minotauro out in the first round.

The loss prompted Minotauro to take a break to finally have surgery on his ailing knee and hips in an attempt to show the world once again that there is no more resilient fighter on the planet than Antonio Rodrigo "Minotauro" Nogueira.

ANTONIO ROGERIO NOGUEIRA

Minotoro

HEIGHT: **6' 2" (188 cm)**

WEIGHT: **205 lbs (93 kg)**

DATE OF BIRTH: **2 June 1976**

HOMETOWN:

Rio de Janeiro, Brazil

PROFESSIONAL RECORD: 19-5

UFC RECORD: 2-2

The twin brother of heavyweight legend Minotauro Nogueira, Antonio Rogerio Nogueira remains on a quest to join his sibling in the history books as a world champion.

A Brazilian jiu-jitsu black belt whose boxing talent earned him a Bronze medal in the 2007 Pan-American Games, Nogueira entered the world of MMA in 2001 and made his mark with wins over Kazushi Sakuraba, Dan Henderson, Vladimir Matyushenko and Alistair Overeem, as well as in a classic war with Mauricio "Shogun" Rua in 2005.

In November of 2009, Nogueira made a spectacular UFC debut against Luiz Cane, earning Knockout of the Night honors. He followed up that win with a victory over Jason Brilz, but has dropped his last two bouts against Ryan Bader and Phil Davis.

KYLE NOKE

HEIGHT: **6' 2" (188 cm)**

WEIGHT: **185 lbs (84 kg)**

DATE OF BIRTH:

18 March 1980

HOMETOWN: **Dubbo,**

New South Wales,

Australia

PROFESSIONAL RECORD: 19-4-1

UFC RECORD: 3-0

A former member of the security team of "The Crocodile Hunter" Steve Irwin, as well as a rugby player, Australia's Kyle Noke began training in mixed martial arts simply as a way to keep busy in the off-season.

Eight years later, after fighting his way up the ranks on the local scene at home and abroad, he finally earned a spot in the Octagon with a strong effort on *The Ultimate Fighter 11* that culminated in an impressive TKO victory over Josh Bryant in June of 2010.

Two submission wins against Rob Kimmons and Chris Camozzi have followed for the well-rounded 185-pounder, making Noke one of the middleweight division's top prospects.

DIEGO NUNES

The Gun

HEIGHT: **5' 6" (168 cm)**

WEIGHT: **145 lbs (66 kg)**

DATE OF BIRTH:

30 May 1982

HOMETOWN:

Rio de Janeiro, Brazil

PROFESSIONAL RECORD: 16-1

UFC RECORD: 1-0

Despite all the physical gifts that allowed Rio De Janeiro's Diego Nunes to sail to an ultra-impressive record of 16-1 as a mixed martial artist, his greatest joy while competing is using his mind to achieve victory.

"I love MMA more than any other sport," said Nunes, who began his Zuffa career with a 4-1 run in the WEC. "You use your intelligence more than your muscles, so even a big and strong guy can lose to a much smaller guy."

Following a debut UFC win over former WEC champion Mike Brown at UFC 125, the banger known as "The Gun" looked to secure his biggest victory yet against Kenny Florian at UFC 131.

JAKE O'BRIEN

Irish

HEIGHT: **6' 3" (191 cm)**

WEIGHT: **205 lbs (93 kg)**

DATE OF BIRTH:

25 Sept. 1984

HOMETOWN:

Indianapolis, IN

PROFESSIONAL RECORD: 13-4

UFC RECORD: 4-3

When former Purdue wrestler Jake O'Brien defeated perennial heavyweight contender Heath Herring in 2007, it was the result heard 'round the MMA world and pegged O'Brien as a future contender. But then surgery sidelined the Indiana native for over a year, and many wondered if he would ever be the fighter he was that night.

O'Brien returned in March of 2008, and though he fell short in bouts against former UFC heavyweight champ Andrei Arlovski and future titleholder Cain Velasquez, a move to the light heavyweight division had "Irish" Jake confident once again. After a decision win over Christian Wellisch and a submission defeat against Jon Jones, O'Brien was released in 2009.

YUSHIN OKAMI *Thunder*

HEIGHT: **6' 2" (188 cm)** WEIGHT: **185 lbs (84 kg)** DATE OF BIRTH: **21 July 1981** HOMETOWN: **Kanagawa, Japan**

PROFESSIONAL RECORD: 27-5 UFC RECORD: 10-2

Yushin Okami has ripped through the middleweight ranks since arriving in the UFC in 2006, defeating Mike Swick, Alan Belcher, Kalib Starnes and Rory Singer along the way.

It was in a close decision loss to Rich Franklin in June of 2007 that Okami truly showed that he belongs among the elite at 185 pounds as he pushed the former UFC champion to the limit and almost submitted him in the final round of a closely-contested bout.

The powerful Okami then got back in the win column with consecutive victories over Jason MacDonald, former middleweight champ Evan Tanner and Dean Lister. While he lost a decision to Chael Sonnen at UFC 104 in October of 2009, Okami showed off his "Thunder" in 2010 with an ultra-impressive TKO of Lucio Linhares in March of 2010 and a hard-fought three-round win over Mark Munoz five months later.

Next up was a pivotal battle against Nate Marquardt at UFC 122, and with a title shot on the line, Okami was at his best as he pounded out a three-round decision win to achieve his longtime goal, an August 2011 rematch with UFC middleweight champion Anderson Silva, the man Okami holds a 2006 disqualification win over.

"The records say I won but I really lost the match," said Okami of his first bout with Silva. "But I believe because of this fight I've grown stronger. The next time I fight him things will be different. I am confident of that."

Before Forrest Griffin and Stephan Bonnar kicked off the mixed martial arts explosion in 2005, there was Tito Ortiz, "The Huntington Beach Bad Boy", who was the face of the UFC after Zuffa bought the company in 2001.

He was brash, charismatic, and he could fight, too—a triple threat that helped change the perception of what was once perceived to be an outlaw sport.

A two-time state junior college wrestling champion in California, Ortiz got his chance at the big time when he was enlisted as a sparring partner for the UFC's original bad boy, David "Tank" Abbott.

"I was a wrestler in high school, I wrestled in college, and then I started training with Tank Abbott," said Ortiz. "When Ultimate Fighting first came out, it caught my eye right off the bat. Plus, I watched a movie called *Bloodsport*. There was always a dream in the back of my mind of being somebody, and being one of the best martial artists in the world really intrigued me into doing something about it."

But to be competitive in the UFC, Ortiz needed more than wrestling. "I noticed that people need a lot of technique," he said. "In Ultimate Fighting, you need to be an ultimate fighter by putting everything together. All of a sudden I started seeing guys who were winning belts and becoming champions, and they had everything in their game. They had the ground game, the standup, the cardio…and so I said, 'I've got to take this sport seriously.'"

Ortiz made his debut at UFC 13, and as an alternate, he defeated Wes Albritton in under a minute. An injury gave Ortiz a shot at Guy Mezger in the main draw that night, and though a controversial submission loss followed, the California native was hooked.

UFC 18: Ortiz vs. Bohlander

UFC 19: Ortiz vs. Mezger

He went on to score victories over Jerry Bohlander and Mezger (in a rematch), and at UFC 22 on September 24, 1999, he was pitted against Frank Shamrock for the UFC's 205-pound title. In one of the most memorable fights from the early UFC era, Ortiz and Shamrock went to war for three rounds, and it was safe to say that either man had a good chance of eventually pulling the fight out. By the fourth round, Ortiz was winded. Shamrock, whose conditioning has never been questioned, pressed the attack and stopped him. Ortiz learned a valuable lesson that day though, and never again would conditioning be an issue for "The Huntington Beach Bad Boy", who instead adopted a Spartan philosophy when it comes to preparing for a fight.

UFC 22: Ortiz vs. F. Shamrock

TITO ORTIZ *The Huntington Beach Bad Boy*

HEIGHT: 6' 3" (190 cm) DATE OF BIRTH: 23 Jan. 1975

WEIGHT: 205 lbs (93 kg) HOMETOWN: Huntington Beach, CA

PROFESSIONAL RECORD: 16-8-1

UFC RECORD: 14-0-1

TITLES HELD: UFC LIGHT HEAVYWEIGHT CHAMPION

In April of 2000, that conditioning paid off as he won a five-round decision over Wanderlei Silva at UFC 25 in Tokyo to capture the 205-pound title. Ortiz would go on to hold the belt longer than any fighter in UFC history.

UFC 25: Ortiz vs. Silva

The media coverage for the UFC 40 main event in Las Vegas was unprecedented, and Ortiz cemented his spot as the best in the game with a one-sided three-round stoppage of the UFC pioneer.

From 2000 to 2001, Ortiz successfully defended his title against Yuki Kondo, Evan Tanner, Elvis Sinosic and Vladimir Matyushenko, all the while promoting the sport at every turn. Soon, Ortiz was a star in the new UFC, but there was an old lion waiting to reclaim that title—Ken Shamrock—and the two were matched up in the biggest UFC fight to date on November 22, 2002.

UFC 40: Ortiz vs. K. Shamrock

After the bout, every fight fan wanted to see Ortiz matched up with his former training partner, number-one contender Chuck Liddell. At the same time, Ortiz was embroiled in a contract dispute with the UFC, and combined with his initial reluctance to face Liddell, a nearly year-long layoff ensued.

In the meantime, Liddell lost a bout to Randy Couture for the interim light heavyweight belt, and Ortiz followed suit, getting decisioned by "The Natural" in his September 2003 return. Backed into a corner, and without his title belt, Ortiz had to go through Liddell to get another title shot, so finally, the two met in a huge event at UFC 47 on April 2, 2004.

Liddell dominated from the outset, eventually knocking Ortiz out in the second round. The feud was apparently over, with both men going their separate ways both personally and professionally. Ortiz was upset by the way everything went down.

UFC 44: Ortiz vs. Couture

UFC 47: Ortiz vs. Liddell

"It bothers me a whole bunch, but it shows you what money can do to people," said Ortiz. "It changes them. Liddell's his own man now and for him to say that we were never friends, that's just BS, and he knows the truth. And the first time we fought, that was one of the reasons why I couldn't compete on the level that I usually did. It really hurt me a lot at that time, but now it's all hard feelings."

Following comeback wins over Patrick Cote and Vitor Belfort, Ortiz left the UFC at the end of his contract in 2005 and went through a 14-month layoff before returning to re-establish himself as one of the best light heavyweights in the world in 2006. Included in that year was a coaching stint on *The Ultimate Fighter 3* and after he decisioned Forrest Griffin at UFC 59, he scored back-to-back first-round TKOs of his *TUF3* coaching rival and old nemesis Ken Shamrock.

UFC 50: Ortiz vs. Cote

UFC 51: Ortiz vs. Belfort

Ortiz vs. K. Shamrock 3

The three consecutive wins earned Ortiz a shot at redemption against Liddell in a world title fight on December 30, 2006. This time the bout was more competitive, but the end result in the main event of UFC 66 remained the same, as the champion stopped Ortiz in the third round.

UFC 66: Ortiz vs. Liddell 2

Following a draw with Rashad Evans at UFC 73 in July of 2007 and a loss to Lyoto Machida in May of 2008, Ortiz again ran into contractual issues with the UFC and particularly company President Dana White. The two waged a war of words through the press, and it was believed throughout the fight world that this time, we had seen the last of Ortiz in the Octagon.

Ortiz had more pressing issues to deal with though, and they all centered on his back, which had been ailing him for years. Now, in 2008, it was giving out on him.

Finally, the realization that his fighting career and the quality of his life were going downhill made him decide that the only option for him was a complex surgery that did have a successful precedent in middleweight Nate Quarry, who had the procedure done in 2007. Ortiz spoke to Quarry, which calmed his nerves somewhat.

UFC 73: Ortiz vs. Evans

UFC 84: Ortiz vs. Machida

"Getting the surgery done was scary for me. I wasn't really sure what was gonna happen, but seeing Nate Quarry get it done, and him bouncing back, really solidified what I was gonna do with my back surgery. He told me about it and how much better it feels to wrestle with no pain, and I said 'God, I wish I could have that.'"

On October 6, 2008, Ortiz' wish came true, and he went through the three-and-a-half-hour surgery. Rehab was an arduous process, but he survived and was able to train again. But he had no home to fight in until a mutual friend, Wayne Harriman, got Ortiz and White talking again. UFC co-owner Lorenzo Fertitta got involved as well, and soon, Ortiz was back in the UFC family.

"I'm still a force to be reckoned with," he said after re-signing. "I read on blogs and forums that I'm a has-been, my career is done, but people have to understand that I'm only 34 years old. Randy Couture started his career at 33 years old. Now that I have a new back and am able to wrestle the way I used to wrestle, I'm gonna be a force."

UFC 106: Ortiz vs. Griffin 2

UFC 121: Ortiz vs. Hamill

His ensuing bouts with Forrest Griffin and Matt Hamill in 2009 and 2010, respectively, have resulted in decision defeats. An expected third bout with Liddell (which was set up by another coaching stint on *The Ultimate Fighter*, this time against "The Iceman") hit the skids due to an Ortiz injury, but with a July bout with Ryan Bader approaching, "The Huntington Beach Bad Boy" would get another chance to show that he still belongs with the top guns in the division he helped put on the map.

TITO ORTIZ PAGE 94

HEIGHT: **5' 10" (178 cm)**
WEIGHT: **155 lbs (70 kg)**
DATE OF BIRTH: **17 Oct. 1989**
HOMETOWN: **Sao Paulo, Brazil**

CHARLES OLIVEIRA *Do Bronx*

PROFESSIONAL RECORD: 14-1 UFC RECORD: 2-1

Charles Oliveira entered the UFC in 2010 as one of the organization's youngest fighters, and he turned into one of its most charismatic when it comes to delivering exciting fights. Whether slamming opponents, submitting them or knocking them out, Oliveira always brings the heat, and in his first two years as a pro, he compiled a stellar 14-0 record.

That record includeed one of the most spectacular UFC debuts seen in a long time, as he scored a 41-second submission win over Darren Elkins in August of 2010. Then he followed up that victory with an equally memorable finish of Efrain Escudero. At UFC 124, Oliveira suffered his first pro loss when he was submitted by Jim Miller.

ROUSIMAR PALHARES

Toquinho

HEIGHT: **5' 8" (173 cm)**
WEIGHT: **185 lbs (84 kg)**
DATE OF BIRTH:
26 Feb. 1980
HOMETOWN:
Rio de Janeiro, Brazil

PROFESSIONAL RECORD: 21-3
UFC RECORD: 5-2

Rousimar "Toquinho" Palhares entered the UFC's Octagon in May of 2008 with a well-deserved reputation as one of the premier submission artists in the game, having won his previous four bouts via first-round tapouts.

Virtually no one expected the decorated jiu-jitsu black belt to submit seasoned veteran Ivan Salaverry in just over two minutes the way he did at UFC 84 in May of 2008.

The heel hook master (a protégé of former middleweight champ Murilo Bustamante) has since scored four more UFC wins over Jeremy Horn, Lucio Linhares, Tomasz Drwal and Dave Branch, with his only losses coming against Dan Henderson and Nate Marquardt. In August of 2011, he will fight at home for the first time since 2007 at UFC 134.

REMCO PARDOEL

Grizzly

HEIGHT: **6' 2" (188 cm)**
WEIGHT: **250 lbs (113 kg)**
DATE OF BIRTH: **Unknown**
HOMETOWN: **Oss, Holland**

PROFESSIONAL RECORD: 9-6-1, 2 NC
UFC RECORD: 3-2

Despite hailing from the kickboxing capital of the world, Holland's Remco Pardoel instead focused on Brazilian jiu-jitsu, which he parlayed into a visit to the UFC in 1994.

On that first night, Pardoel submitted Alberta Cerra Leon, then delivered one of the most frightening knockouts in UFC history as he elbowed Orlando Welt into defeat in just 89 seconds. Next was his true test, a UFC 2 tournament final bout against Royce Gracie, but Pardoel wasn't ready, as he was submitted in 91 seconds. Pardoel would return for UFC 7 a year later, losing a semifinal bout to Marco Ruas. It was his last Octagon bout, but he continued to compete until 2003 and has recently worked with UFC heavyweight Stefan Struve.

KARO PARISYAN

The Heat

HEIGHT: **5' 10" (178 cm)**
WEIGHT: **170 lbs (77 kg)**
DATE OF BIRTH:
28 Aug. 1982
HOMETOWN:
North Hollywood, CA

PROFESSIONAL RECORD: 26-7, 1 NC
UFC RECORD: 8-4, 1 NC

World-class judoka Karo Parisyan was fighting professionally from the time he was 16, and while he bounced around the MMA circuit over the next few years, it wasn't until 2003 and a spectacular submission win over Dave Strasser at UFC 44 that he truly arrived as a fighter to watch.

Over the next two years, Parisyan would win four out of five bouts, losing only to Georges St-Pierre while beating the likes of Matt Serra, Nick Diaz and Chris Lytle. A title shot was secured for Parisyan against then-champion Matt Hughes at UFC 56, but a hamstring tear shelved him from the bout. He has only gone 4-4 with 1 NC since then, but he remains a compelling figure in the fight game.

HEIGHT: **5' 11" (180 cm)**
WEIGHT: **170 lbs (77 kg)**
DATE OF BIRTH: **14 June 1980**
HOMETOWN: **Toronto, Ontario, Canada**

CLAUDE PATRICK *The Prince*

PROFESSIONAL RECORD: 14-1 UFC RECORD: 3-0

Toronto submission specialist Claude Patrick has been one of Canada's best-kept secrets over the last few years, forcing nine opponents to tap out since he turned pro. Included among his victims is Ray Steinbeiss, and after that 2006 IFL victory and a short break from the fight game, Patrick returned in 2008 and has since finished off six of eight opponents, including Ricardo Funch in his UFC debut in June of 2010. Patrick remains unbeaten in the Octagon, with victories over James Wilks and Daniel "Ninja" Roberts.

"I'm honored to be able to compete at the highest level of the sport. It's what I dedicated my time towards, so I wouldn't say it's vindication, but it definitely feels good to see that I was right."

BJ PENN PAGE 100

ROSS PEARSON *The Real Deal*

HEIGHT: **5' 8" (173 cm)** WEIGHT: **155 lbs (70 kg)** DATE OF BIRTH: **26 Sept. 1984** HOMETOWN: **Sunderland, England**

PROFESSIONAL RECORD: 14-4 UFC RECORD: 4-1 TITLES HELD: *THE ULTIMATE FIGHTER 9* LIGHTWEIGHT WINNER

Sunderland, England's Ross Pearson was an early favorite on *The Ultimate Fighter 9*, and he lived up to all expectations with his wins over Richie Whitson and Jason Dent. But there was still one more mountain to climb for Pearson, and in June of 2009, he reached the summit when he defeated his UK teammate Andre Winner to earn *TUF9*'s lightweight title. It was a dream win for "The Real Deal", who, despite his star status, may still be the UFC's ultimate fan.

"I'm a crazy fan myself," he said. "I get excited before each UFC fight comes on and I still watch all of them. I watch so many fights that I pick up other guys' stuff because I'm a fan and I try things out. I think that's why I'm improving so much, because I still am a fan of the sport. I love going to the UFC events, I love cornering my teammates, and I just love it."

The journey's not over yet for Pearson. After winning three of his four post-*TUF* bouts (against Aaron Riley, Dennis Siver and Spencer Fisher) in impressive fashion, the former bricklayer will need to get ready the coming years for a world title shot.

KURT PELLEGRINO
Batman

HEIGHT: **5' 8" (173 cm)** DATE OF BIRTH: **7 May 1979**
WEIGHT: **155 lbs (70 kg)** HOMETOWN: **Point Pleasant, NJ**

PROFESSIONAL RECORD: 21-6
UFC RECORD: 7-5

An energetic fighter who participated in some of the most exciting lightweight bouts of the current era, Kurt Pellegrino is someone who always gave fans their money's worth. His reasoning is simple, "I'm not fighting because I think it's cool. I'm fighting because this is what I want to do with my life."

7-5 in the UFC from 2006 to 2011, Pellegrino won a Fight of the Night award for his 2008 victory over Thiago Tavares and a Submission of the Night award for his finish of Fabricio Camoes in 2010.

ANTHONY PETTIS
Showtime

HEIGHT: **5' 10" (178 cm)** DATE OF BIRTH: **27 Jan. 1987**
WEIGHT: **155 lbs (70 kg)** HOMETOWN: **Milwaukee, WI**

PROFESSIONAL RECORD: 11-1
UFC RECORD: 0-0
TITLES HELD: WEC LIGHTWEIGHT CHAMPION

When the bell rings, Anthony Pettis knows that it's time for him to perform, and so far he has lived up to his nickname of "Showtime" as he has won all but one of his pro fights, with only two victories going the distance.

It was his fight against Shane Roller that really turned heads and put him on the fast-track to the WEC lightweight title, which he won in December of 2010 via five-round decision over Ben Henderson in a bout featuring a now-infamous *Matrix*-style kick off the cage.

FORREST PETZ
The Meat Cleaver

HEIGHT: **5' 10" (178 cm)** DATE OF BIRTH: **22 Sept. 1975**
WEIGHT: **170 lbs (70 kg)** HOMETOWN: **Cleveland, OH**

PROFESSIONAL RECORD: 26-9
UFC RECORD: 2-5

With a nickname like "The Meat Cleaver", you'd better be ready to fight. Sure enough, Forrest Petz is a hard-hitting competitor with knockout power in both hands and a fearsome body attack.

Petz got his UFC shot in 2006 and drubbed Sam Morgan over three rounds. He lost three of his next four in the Octagon, with the only win coming against Luigi Fioravanti, but a four-fight winning streak that began in 2009 brought him back in 2010. He subsequently lost to Daniel Roberts and Brian Foster, resulting in his second release.

BRAD PICKETT *One Punch*

PROFESSIONAL RECORD: 21-5 UFC RECORD: 0-0

HEIGHT: **5' 6" (168 cm)** WEIGHT: **135 lbs (61 kg)** DATE OF BIRTH: **24 Sept. 1978** HOMETOWN: **East London, England**

Long considered to be one of England's top mixed martial artists, Brad Pickett took his game to the United States and the WEC in 2009, debuting with a win over Kyle Dietz that the submission expert ended with the rarely-used Peruvian Necktie maneuver. The victory upped his pro record to 19-4, and after splitting fights with Demetrious Johnson (win) and Scott Jorgensen (loss), he was able to secure victory number 21 against Ivan Menjivar in an entertaining scrap on the WEC's last card in December of 2010. Next for Pickett will be his UFC debut in 2011.

MIKE PIERCE

PROFESSIONAL RECORD: 12-3 UFC RECORD: 4-1

HEIGHT: **5' 8" (173 cm)** WEIGHT: **170 lbs (70 kg)** DATE OF BIRTH: **1 Sept. 1980** HOMETOWN: **Vancouver, WA**

A standout wrestler for Portland State University, Mike Pierce isn't used to doing anything at half-speed. "I hope people see that I've got heart and that I'm ready to throw down with anybody."

A tenacious battler who is always looking for the spectacular finish, the only man to beat him in the Octagon is longtime contender Jon Fitch. In his two most recent bouts, Pierce has turned up the heat, finishing both Amilcar Alves and Kenny Robertson.

In 2006, BJ Penn was asked why, after all his ups and downs in the fight game, he still had the most diehard of fan followings. He paused only for a moment before responding.

"There's just something about BJ Penn that gets people amped up," he said. "You don't know what's gonna happen, but something's gonna happen. He might disappoint you, he might make you happy, he might make you cry, he might make you jump out of your chair, but he'll do something to you."

That, in a nutshell, describes the unforgettable odyssey of the fighter known to the world as "The Prodigy".

When Penn made his MMA debut in 2001 (in the UFC no less), he was 22 years old, just a year removed from becoming the first non-Brazilian to win a gold medal in the black belt division of the Mundial World Jiu-Jitsu Championships, and in every way, shape, and form, he was a prodigy. Fighting was something to do and something he was good at—nothing more, nothing less.

UFC 31: Penn vs. Gilbert

He went on to walk through Joey Gilbert in his UFC debut, and he was even more impressive in stopping Din Thomas in the first round and knocking out Caol Uno in just 11 seconds. A lightweight title shot against then-champion Jens Pulver was a given, and he was expected to similarly blow through Pulver at UFC 35 in January of 2002. But as he admitted later, he wasn't ready.

UFC 34: Penn vs. Uno

Photography by: Susumu Nagao

BJ PENN *The Prodigy*

HEIGHT: **5' 9" (175 cm)**

DATE OF BIRTH: **13 Dec. 1978**

WEIGHT: **155-170 lbs (70-77 kg)**

HOMETOWN: **Hilo, HI**

PROFESSIONAL RECORD: 16-7-2

UFC RECORD: 12-6-2

TITLES HELD: UFC WELTERWEIGHT CHAMPION, UFC LIGHTWEIGHT CHAMPION

UFC 32: Penn vs. Thomas

"The Din Thomas fight and the Caol Uno fight, those were probably two of the best things for my career, to blow me up and to get me a bigger fan base, but they were also the worst things for my career as far as getting me experience to get ready for that title fight," said Penn. "And I was scared going out there and being the main event. I think I was more afraid of everything else—I was afraid to have that lightweight title, I was afraid to be the main event—but don't do something great if you can't take the congratulations, and I wasn't ready to get congratulated. I was just a kid."

Pulver went on to upset Penn over five rounds and retain his title. "Lil' Evil" would leave the UFC over a contract dispute after the bout, and after Penn bounced back with wins over Paul Creighton and Matt Serra, he was again matched with Uno at UFC 41 in 2003, this time with the vacant belt on the line. Five rounds couldn't determine a winner that night, and a draw verdict was rendered.

UFC 35: Penn vs. Pulver

In a lot of ways, that draw sent Penn into a period of his career where his focus was scattered. Sure, he would submit Takanori Gomi in a non-UFC bout and then come back to the organization to win the welterweight title from Matt Hughes in 2004. Whether it was leaving the UFC and his belt to fight elsewhere, or jumping to heavyweight to battle Lyoto Machida in 2005, Penn's career resembled that of a kid in a candy store who wanted to try everything but at the end of the day wound up with a toothache.

UFC 46: Penn vs. Hughes

UFC 46: Penn vs. Hughes

Eventually, Penn would mend fences with UFC management and return in 2006 with a razor-thin split decision loss to Georges St-Pierre. A rematch with Hughes at UFC 63 served him with another defeat, and some wondered whether Penn was destined to be a shooting star who fizzled out after a short reign at the top. But when he dropped back to 155 pounds to coach against Pulver on *The Ultimate Fighter 5* and then fight him again (winning via second-round submission), Penn found his center again by going back to where he started.

UFC 63: Penn vs. Hughes 2

The Ultimate Fighter 5 Finale: Penn vs. Pulver 2

"Something just awoke inside of me where I thought, 'What are you doing?'" Penn said at the time. "'You can beat every one of these people. You've been doing it half-assed all this time and it's time to finally step up and let's see it.' If you can't, you can't, but at least you know you tried. Words can't explain how pumped I am about fighting right now. It's what I am, it's who I am, and it's what I want to be."

At UFC 80 on January 19, 2008, Penn finally won his lightweight title, submitting Joe Stevenson in the second round. A one-sided TKO of former champion Sean Sherk followed in Penn's first title defense, but then he got the itch to test the waters at 170 pounds again, and a January 2009 Superfight was scheduled between him and old rival St-Pierre.

UFC 80: Penn vs. Stevenson

"Jiu-jitsu was created where the small man can beat the big man, and I've been doing jiu-jitsu since I was 17 years old, and that has always stuck in my head throughout all the time and all the way until now," said Penn. "It's ingrained in me that I believe I have a chance. I know that something's gonna happen, the guy's gonna make a mistake and I'm gonna get that armlock or get that choke."

It was not to be against GSP though, and Penn was thrashed for four rounds before his corner decided he had taken enough punishment, and they pulled the plug on the bout.

UFC 84: Penn vs. Sherk

"I trained, I did my roadwork, I did my sparring, I did all those things, but as far as my mistake, I think I started too early and I got too excited for the fight."

Luckily for Penn, his faithful lightweight title belt was waiting at home for him, and despite pre-GSP talk that hinted at retirement, in his mind, there was no question that he was coming back to the Octagon to defend that belt.

UFC 94: Penn vs. St-Pierre 2

"I knew that wouldn't have been the last one," he said. "There's no way. What would I have done? Sit home and twiddle my thumbs? There's no way that could have been the end. I'm not gonna say it never crossed my mind, but I just don't know what else I'd be doing."

Simply put, Penn's a fighter, and fighters fight, especially when they're only 30 years old and at the height of their powers. So when number-one contender Kenny Florian was brought to the table, Penn signed on the dotted line and silenced any doubts with a fourth-round submission victory at UFC 101 in August of 2009. Four months later, he shattered all lightweight title records with a fifth-round TKO of Diego Sanchez, and was seemingly unstoppable again.

UFC 101: Penn vs. Florian

Enter unheralded Frankie Edgar, who beat Penn not once but twice by decision in 2010, taking his lightweight crown in the process.

"The first thing that came to me was 'I don't know if I want to do this,' and that comes to every fighter after some losses," said Penn. "I thought that maybe I didn't have the motivation anymore."

UFC 118: Penn vs. Edgar 2

He was crushed by the back-to-back defeats, yet Penn opted to make one last stand at welterweight, and in November of 2010, he was pitted against Matt Hughes in a highly anticipated rubber match.

Before the UFC 123 bout, Penn had a one-on-one chat with his brother JD in the locker room.

"JD, you know what, times have been tough lately for us, but I don't care if I win or lose, I just want to show everybody why I started doing this," said Penn to his older brother.

"BJ, I could care less if you win or lose, too," JD responded. "Go show everybody who you are."

UFC 123: Penn vs. Hughes 3

UFC 127: Penn vs. Fitch

He did, ending his trilogy with Hughes with a 21-second knockout win. A hard-fought draw with top contender Jon Fitch would kick off Penn's 2011 campaign at UFC 127 in Australia, and through it all, the pride of Hilo, Hawaii remains one of the game's most popular fighters.

"I've just been so blessed with these fans that always have my back," said Penn. "When I've lost and I've come back, I think they know my story so well and they relate to it in their lives. Nobody's on top always. We're up one day, we're down one day, and that's just the nature of life. And when they see me, they can really relate. People like to follow that storyline and sometimes they like to see people fall but climb back up again."

JENS PULVER *Lil' Evil*

HEIGHT: **5' 7" (170 cm)**

DATE OF BIRTH: **6 Dec. 1974**

WEIGHT: **145-155 lbs (66-70 kg)**

HOMETOWN: **Bettendorf, IA**

PROFESSIONAL RECORD: 24-14-1

UFC RECORD: 6-2-1

TITLES HELD: UFC LIGHTWEIGHT CHAMPION

Jens Pulver arrived in the fight game after battling through an abusive childhood and not only surviving but thriving, graduating from Boise State University with a degree in Criminal Justice/Sociology. But the 9-to-5 world was not for him, and the former college wrestler sought out a new life as a mixed martial artist. Then, after a trip to California to train with the late Bob Shamrock didn't pan out, he was at a crossroads.

"I thought I had completely ruined my life," said Pulver. "I got really scared, I was really paranoid, and then I got the opportunity to come out to Iowa. That's when I said, 'You know what, this is my second chance. I'm going to go out and give it 150 percent.'"

In Iowa, training with the Miletich Fighting Systems team, Pulver found his home. He turned pro in April of 1999 with a TKO win over Curtis Hill, and he was off and running. Five months later he was making his UFC debut, battling to a draw with Alfonso Alcarez.

UFC 30: Pulver vs. Uno

By March of 2000, he got his first Octagon victory, stopping David Velasquez in two rounds. After victories over Joao Roque and John Lewis, he had earned a shot to become the first-ever UFC 155-pound champion when he took on Japanese star Caol Uno at UFC 30 on February 23, 2001.

Pulver did it, earning a unanimous decision over Uno. He was a world champion.

UFC 35: Pulver vs. Penn

There would be no rest for the new champion. Media tours and appearances filled his days between training sessions, and six months after winning the belt, he was back in the Octagon to defend it against rival Dennis Hallman. After defeating Hallman via five-round decision, Pulver was matched up with unbeaten Hawaiian wunderkind BJ Penn. This one wasn't going to be pretty, and Pulver's Cinderella story was going to end in spectacular fashion in Connecticut on January 11, 2002.

At least that's what most believed.

Pulver wasn't among that crowd though, and he took it as a personal insult that he—as a legitimate world champion—was being written off by fans and media in the lead-up to the Penn bout. What ensued over the next five rounds turned into one of the best fights of all-time. The UFC 35 bout contained drama, talent, heart, twists and turns and a shocking final result, as Pulver shut up the critics and took home a well-deserved five-round majority decision.

It would be his last bout in the UFC for over four years due to a contract dispute. Over those four years, Pulver continued to fight, but there was always something missing for him, so in 2006, he came full circle when it was announced that he was coming back to the UFC.

Fights against Joe Lauzon and Penn followed, along with a stint as a coach on *The Ultimate Fighter 5* that introduced him to a new generation of fans. Next up was a debut in the WEC's featherweight division, where he submitted Cub Swanson in 35 seconds in December of 2007.

WEC 31: Pulver vs. Swanson

Despite a subsequent five-fight losing streak that ended his WEC career, no true fan cared, because who cared about Willie Mays in a New York Mets uniform, or Joe Namath taking the field as a member of the Los Angeles Rams? You remember "The Say Hey Kid" roaming the outfield with grace while striking fear into opposing pitchers, and Namath pulling off the impossible as he led the Jets to a victory over the Colts in Super Bowl III. For fight fans, Jens Pulver will always be the kid knocking out John Lewis, defeating BJ Penn and going to war with Takanori Gomi. He is a pioneer for the lighter weight classes in mixed martial arts, and an inspiration to a generation of fighters 155 pounds and below, and that's just based on what he did in competition.

Outside the cage or ring, Pulver continues to inspire, and will do so long after his gloves are hung up. Surviving what he has over the years is impressive enough; being open and talking about it lifts it to a new level, and despite all the great things he's done as a fighter, that may be his greatest legacy.

TREVOR PRANGLEY

HEIGHT: **6' 1" (185 cm)** DATE OF BIRTH: **24 Aug. 1972**
WEIGHT: **205 lbs (93 kg)** HOMETOWN: **Cape Town, South Africa**

PROFESSIONAL RECORD: 23-7-1
UFC RECORD: 2-2

An ultra-tough warrior who relocated to the United States from South Africa, Trevor Prangley was the type of fighter opponents never wanted to see across from them on fight night because they may be able to submit him on the mat, but if they couldn't, odds were that his foes were in for a long grueling battle.

Only knocked out once (and that was from a body shot courtesy of Jorge Santiago), Prangley's toughness served him well as a two-time All-American wrestler for North Idaho. As a mixed martial artist as he scored 23 wins, including UFC victories over Curtis Stout and Travis Lutter during a four fight stint from 2004 to 2006. Still active, Prangley competes for the Strikeforce promotion.

MIKE PYLE *Quicksand*

HEIGHT: **6' 1" (185 cm)** DATE OF BIRTH: **18 Sept. 1975**
WEIGHT: **170 lbs (77 kg)** HOMETOWN: **Las Vegas, NV**

PROFESSIONAL RECORD: 21-7-1
UFC RECORD: 4-2

A brown belt in Brazilian jiu-jitsu, Mike Pyle was one of those fighters who fans would always talk about and say, "I can't wait until he comes to the UFC."

The Tennessee native felt the same way as he battled up the ranks, defeating UFC vets such as Jon Fitch, Brian Gassaway and Shonie Carter, and even making his pro debut against former light heavyweight champion Quinton "Rampage" Jackson.

In 2009, Pyle finally got the call to the Octagon. After ending 17 of his 21 victories by submission, it looks like "Quicksand" won't be leaving the UFC's welterweight division anytime soon.

NATE QUARRY *Rock*

HEIGHT: **6' 0" (183 cm)** DATE OF BIRTH: **18 March 1972**
WEIGHT: **185 lbs (84 kg)** HOMETOWN: **Gresham, OR**

PROFESSIONAL RECORD: 10-1
UFC RECORD: 7-3

A member of *The Ultimate Fighter*'s first season cast, Nate Quarry roared up the middleweight ranks with unbelievable speed, scoring knockouts of Lodune Sincaid, Shonie Carter, and Pete Sell to earn a 185-pound title shot in 2005 against Rich Franklin. Franklin would turn him back that night via first-round knockout. After surgery for a serious back injury, some thought Quarry would never fight again.

Fighters like the "Rock" don't quit that easily. After an exhaustive rehab, he came back with wins over Pete Sell, Kalib Starnes, Jason MacDonald and Tim Credeur.

BENJI RADACH

PROFESSIONAL RECORD: 21-6 UFC RECORD: 1-1, 1 NC

HEIGHT: **5' 10" (178 cm)** WEIGHT: **185 lbs (84 kg)** DATE OF BIRTH: **5 April 1980** HOMETOWN: **Castle Rock, WA**

Benji Radach's brief three-fight UFC stint in 2002 was characterized by bad luck. First, the former high school wrestler's TKO win over Steve Berger was overturned to a no contest because the fight was stopped too early and Radach was throwing "illegal punches". After a decision win over Nick Serra a month later, Radach's third Octagon bout against Sean Sherk was stopped via cuts in the first round. Radach ran off a 5-1 stint in the IFL that saw him defeat Brian Foster and Gerald Harris. He also gained notoriety for foiling an armed robbery attempt in 2006.

KEVIN RANDLEMAN
The Monster

HEIGHT: **5' 10" (178 cm)** DATE OF BIRTH: **10 Aug. 1971**
WEIGHT: **205 lbs (93 kg)** HOMETOWN: **Sandusky, OH**

PROFESSIONAL RECORD: 17-16
UFC RECORD: 4-3
TITLES HELD: UFC HEAVYWEIGHT CHAMPION

Full of charisma, power, and fury, Kevin Randleman was a shock to the system in the UFC from 1999 to 2002. While his performances didn't always match his incendiary interviews, there was no denying his athleticism and wrestling ability in the Octagon.

A two-time Division I national wrestling champion for Ohio State University, Randleman followed his close friend and training partner Mark Coleman into mixed martial arts. He debuted in 1996 in Brazil, where he fought his first eight fights, going 6-2.

By March of 1999, "The Monster" was in the UFC, where he grounded and pounded his way to a decision victory over Maurice Smith. Just two months later at UFC 20, he was doing the same thing to Bas Rutten, but in one of the most controversial verdicts in UFC history, Rutten was awarded a split decision win and the vacant UFC heavyweight title after 21 minutes.

Said Randleman in 2002, "I beat Bas Rutten and everyone knows it. That's why they changed the rules. That's why they went to rounds. I made them go to rounds."

At the UFC's next event, a rounds system and the 10-point must scoring system, were implemented, and when Rutten retired, Randleman was tabbed to compete for the vacant crown against Pete Williams at UFC 23. This time Randleman was awarded the decision and the UFC belt. In June of 2000 he defended his title successfully against Pedro Rizzo in what was widely considered a top-10 winner when it came to horrible fights in the UFC.

Randleman lost his title to Randy Couture in his next fight at UFC 28, and a drop to light heavyweight didn't help, as he was knocked out by Chuck Liddell at UFC 31. Randleman would only fight once more in the UFC, but he left on a winning note, decisioning Renato Sobral at UFC 35.

In need of some new scenery, his next step would be Japan's PRIDE organization, where, like his friend Coleman, he resurrected his career in 12 fights over the next four years.

MATTHEW RIDDLE

HEIGHT: **6' 1" (185 cm)**
WEIGHT: **170 lbs (77 kg)**
DATE OF BIRTH: **14 Jan. 1986**
HOMETOWN: **Las Vegas, NV**

PROFESSIONAL RECORD: 5-2
UFC RECORD: 5-2

Before *The Ultimate Fighter 7*, practically no one in the fight game knew who Matthew Riddle was, and with good reason, considering that his career consisted of one amateur fight. After a devastating knockout of Dan Simmler on the show and a good effort against Tim Credeur, Riddle's name was on everyone's lips, and seven fights into his pro mixed martial arts career (with all fights taking place in the UFC), Riddle continues to turn heads with his solid wrestling ability and willingness to go to war if necessary. A winner against Dante Rivera, Steve Bruno, Dan Cramer and DaMarques Johnson, this is one young man with a bright future in the sport of mixed martial arts.

JOE RIGGS *Diesel*

HEIGHT: **6' 0" (183 cm)**
WEIGHT: **170 lbs (77 kg)**
DATE OF BIRTH: **23 Sept. 1982**
HOMETOWN: **Phoenix, AZ**

PROFESSIONAL RECORD: 37-14, 1 NC
UFC RECORD: 4-4

Owner of some of the heaviest hands in all of mixed martial arts, Joe "Diesel" Riggs had quite a journey through the sport after his debut in 2001.

Starting off his career as a 300-pound heavyweight, Riggs fought anyone and everyone, and along the way kept shedding the pounds as he looked for his true weight class. Four years later, he found himself as a 170-pound contender. In November of 2005, he was submitted by Matt Hughes, but bounced back with a win over Nick Diaz. He lost two of his next three fights, forcing him to fight elsewhere.

AARON RILEY

HEIGHT: **5' 8" (173 cm)**
WEIGHT: **155 lbs (70 kg)**
DATE OF BIRTH: **9 Dec. 1980**
HOMETOWN: **Tell City, IN**

PROFESSIONAL RECORD: 29-12-1 UFC RECORD: 3-4

A 14-year MMA veteran whose fights against Robbie Lawler, Steve Berger and Yves Edwards are ones for the time capsule, Aaron Riley made a welcome return to the UFC in November of 2008 after two years away from the Octagon. "The UFC is the premier organization, the biggest and best, and it's an honor to be fighting and displaying my skills here," said Riley, an iron-chinned warrior who never backed down from a fight. "It's really exciting."

It was exciting for fight fans too, as the Indiana native reintroduced himself to old fans and made new ones with a memorable war and subsequent decision win over Jorge Gurgel and victories over Shane Nelson and Joe Brammer.

PEDRO RIZZO PAGE 107

JORGE RIVERA *El Conquistador*

HEIGHT: **6' 1" (185 cm)**
WEIGHT: **185 lbs (84 kg)**
DATE OF BIRTH:
28 Feb. 1972
HOMETOWN: **Milford, MA**

PROFESSIONAL RECORD: 18-8
UFC RECORD: 7-6

Despite a spotty record, Jorge Rivera has always been a blue collar worker who thrives on challenges. Facing the best is what the *Ultimate Fighter 4* competitor has done his entire career against the likes of Anderson Silva, Rich Franklin, Travis Lutter, David Loiseau, Dennis Hallman, Chris Leben, Kendall Grove and Martin Kampmann.

After wins in three of his last four bouts, he's not content just to to be in a fight, he expects to win.

"You do take your youth for granted," he admits. "I was happy just being there and saying I fight in the UFC. Now I don't want to just say that—I want to say I'm one of the best there."

ANDRE ROBERTS *The Chief*

HEIGHT: **6' 2" (188 cm)**
WEIGHT: **345 lbs (156 kg)**
DATE OF BIRTH: **24 Feb. 1965**
HOMETOWN: **Tama, IA**

PROFESSIONAL RECORD: 14-2-1
UFC RECORD: 2-1

With his ever-present Mohawk, Andre "The Chief" Roberts wasn't someone you would forget once you saw him for the first time, and he certainly wasn't a fighter to be taken lightly by any opponent. Clocking in at nearly 350 pounds, Roberts had a deceptive ground game, as evidenced by his nine wins via submission. It was his power that got him noticed, especially in his three-fight UFC stint, where he went 1-1 before enaging in a classic bout against Ron Waterman at UFC 21 in 1999. Battered for much of the early going, Roberts roared back, knocking his opponent out at 2:51 of the opening round. After the bout, "The Chief" went 4-1-1 before retiring in 2005.

DANIEL ROBERTS *Ninja*

HEIGHT: **5' 10" (178 cm)**
WEIGHT: **170 lbs (77 kg)**
DATE OF BIRTH: **5 Aug. 1980**
HOMETOWN: **Tulsa, OK**

PROFESSIONAL RECORD: 12-2
UFC RECORD: 3-2

Former college wrestler Daniel "Ninja" Roberts has transitioned smoothly into mixed martial arts, posting a stellar 12-2 record that has seen him submit most of his opponents.

In March of 2010, it took just two minutes and one second for him to make an impression on UFC fans, and while he fell short of victory against John Howard, his tenacious and exciting style guaranteed him another shot in the Octagon, which he made the most of as he decisioned Forrest Petz at UFC 116.

Next up were back-to-back submission victories over Mike Guymon and Greg Soto before he saw his winning streak snapped at UFC 129 in 2011 by Toronto standout Claude "The Prince" Patrick.

PEDRO RIZZO *The Rock*

HEIGHT: **6' 1" (185 cm)**
DATE OF BIRTH: **3 May 1974**
WEIGHT: **244 lbs (110 kg)**
HOMETOWN: **Rio de Janeiro, Brazil**

PROFESSIONAL RECORD: **19-9**
UFC RECORD: **9-5**

Pedro Rizzo should have been one of the greats. A skilled striker whose brutal leg kicks could make any fighter reconsider his vocation in life, the Rio de Janeiro native showed flashes of brilliance throughout his 14-fight UFC career, but in three shots at the heavyweight title, he came up empty. It wasn't because he wasn't good enough to win, it was because he just couldn't pull the trigger when the stakes were at their highest.

A protégé of "The King of the Streets", Marco Ruas, Rizzo turned pro in 1996 and ran off a 5-0 record to start his career. Included was a one-night, three-fight tournament in which he finished his first two opponents in a combined 2:07 before ending the night with a soccer kick knockout of Vernon White.

By 1998, he was in the UFC, and in the organization's first Brazil event, he sent his local fans home happy with a blistering knockout of Tank Abbott. Looking to keep the momentum going, Rizzo was matched up with former heavyweight champ Mark Coleman at UFC 18, and he won a disputed split decision. A win's a win though, and he left the judges out of it in his next two victories, knockouts of Tra Telligman and Tsuyoshi Kosaka.

Now all he had to do was win the title against Kevin Randleman, and after an initial postponement of the bout, the two met up at UFC 26 in 2000. What followed was one of the worst fights in UFC history, a 25-minute study in tedium "won" by Randleman.

Vowing to show the "real" Pedro Rizzo, the Brazilian knocked out Dan Severn and Josh Barnett in successive bouts and was a heavy favorite when he took on Randy Couture in his second world title fight. Early on, he made the oddsmakers smile as he battered the champion, but Couture rebounded in the late rounds and retained the title. The loss seemed to take the life out of Rizzo's career, and he was blown out in three rounds by Couture in their rematch.

There would be no more title shots for Rizzo, only "what ifs" for a fighter whose 11-3 career start has turned into an 8-6 slate in the ensuing years.

RICCO RODRIGUEZ *Suave*

HEIGHT: **6' 4" (193 cm)**
DATE OF BIRTH: **19 Aug. 1977**
WEIGHT: **240 lbs (109 kg)**
HOMETOWN: **Staten Island, NY**

PROFESSIONAL RECORD: **46-11**
UFC RECORD: **5-2**
TITLES HELD: **UFC HEAVYWEIGHT CHAMPION**

Ricco Rodriguez' career was on the line when he squared off against Andrei Arlovski at UFC 32 in 2001. But for him, it was no cliche; it was true. "If I would have lost that fight," he said at the time, "I pretty much would have been blackballed from the industry." It had all happened so quickly for him. Blessed with good looks, charisma and a brutally effective ground game, Rodriguez won the Abu Dhabi submission title at the ripe old age of 19, and soon he duplicated his success in mixed martial arts, winning three straight PRIDE matches and the King of the Cage heavyweight title.

With a daughter to feed, a girlfriend in the hospital recuperating from a serious accident and bridges burned with the aforementioned organizations, Rodriguez had a one-fight UFC deal to face Arlovski. Win, and he could rebuild his life with the biggest MMA organization in the United States.

Lose, and he may have had to look for another line of work.

He won, stopping Arlovski in the third round.

From there, it was your typical rags-to-riches tale, with Rodriguez' next four fights all ending early, culminating with a gutsy fifth-round TKO win over Randy Couture at UFC 39 that made him a world heavyweight champion on September 27, 2002.

The belt didn't prove to be the cure-all for Rodriguez' ills, however. He let complacency and outside affairs enter through the cage door with him against Tim Sylvia, and he lost the title in his first defense, getting stopped by "The Maine-iac" in the first round at UFC 41.

Two more consecutive losses would follow, a controversial decision defeat to Minotauro Nogueira in a PRIDE bout and a listless three-round points loss to Pedro Rizzo in what proved to be his final UFC bout in November of 2003.

Rodriguez continued to fight, going 32-7 over the next seven-plus years. Rodriguez has battled his demons (even appearing on the VH1 reality series *Celebrity Rehab*), but when he's on and in shape, he can still provide glimpses of the talent that once brought him a world championship.

GEORGE ROOP

HEIGHT: **6' 1" (185 cm)**
WEIGHT: **145 lbs (66 kg)**
DATE OF BIRTH: **11 Nov. 1981**
HOMETOWN: **Tucson, AZ**

PROFESSIONAL RECORD: 11-8-1
UFC RECORD: 1-3

Former high school quarterback George Roop first came to the attention of the fight world in 2008 as a member of *The Ultimate Fighter 8* cast. It was a necessary step for the Arizona native to take at the time if he wanted to compete on the world stage.

With two wins on the show and four more since taping ended, including an unforgettable head kick knockout of the "Korean Zombie", Chan Sung Jung, the veteran of the UFC and WEC certainly proved that he belongs. And finally at his optimum weight of 145 pounds, Roop is prepared to show even more of his arsenal in the coming years.

BEN ROTHWELL

HEIGHT: **6' 4" (193 cm)**
WEIGHT: **265 lbs (120 kg)**
DATE OF BIRTH: **17 Oct. 1981**
HOMETOWN: **Kenosha, WI**

PROFESSIONAL RECORD: 31-7
UFC RECORD: 1-1

Despite a decade in the fight game and 30 professional mixed martial arts wins, Ben Rothwell looked at his UFC debut in October of 2009 against Cain Velasquez like it was the beginning of his career, "I've been doing this for ten years, and it's always been about being in the UFC. It sounds like I've done some things, but to me, it's all been training for this."

Though Rothwell fell short of victory against Velasquez, he got back in the win column at UFC 115 with a win over Gilbert Yvel, showing fans the mixture of technique and tenacity that led him to wins in 15 of his last 17 bouts.

MARCO RUAS

The King of the Streets

HEIGHT: **6' 1" (185 cm)**
WEIGHT: **210 lbs (95 kg)**
DATE OF BIRTH: **23 Jan. 1961**
HOMETOWN: **Rio de Janeiro, Brazil**

PROFESSIONAL RECORD: 9-4-2
UFC RECORD: 4-2
TITLES HELD: UFC 7 TOURNAMENT WINNER

Rio de Janeiro's Marco Ruas could have lost every one of his 15 professional mixed martial arts fights, and you probably still would have remembered him, if only for what was one of the best nicknames in the history of the game, "The King of the Streets". It wasn't "Rocky" or "Monster" or anything like that; it was a statement saying "Hey, if you have a problem and I get you outside, it's game over."

In the Octagon, Ruas fought with a cool confidence that could easily unnerve an opponent. That ease in competition came from years of training and the development of a style he titled "Ruas Vale Tudo". Vale Tudo mea ns "anything goes," and despite being stereotyped initially as strictly a jiu-jitsu fighter merely because he came from Brazil, Ruas' well-rounded attack gave fits to his foes because they didn't know what was coming next.

Debuting in the UFC at the age of 34 in 1995, he submitted Larry Cureton and Remco Pardoel in his first two bouts before finishing up his night by chopping down "The Polar Bear" Paul Varelans in 13:17 to win the UFC 7 tournament.

Three months later he was back for the Ultimate Ultimate event, but after submitting Keith Hackney, he lost the first bout of his career via decision to Oleg Taktarov. Having a decision in a match was foreign to Ruas given his background, but those were the rules he signed up for, so he accepted them.

After the Taktarov bout, Ruas fought three times in the World Vale Tudo Championship event, defeating UFC vets Steve Jennum and Pat Smith and engaging in another scrap with Taktarov, this one being declared a draw after 31 minutes and 12 seconds.

Still a big name in the sport despite age and injuries creeping up on him, Ruas returned to the UFC to face Maurice Smith in 1999 following two PRIDE fights, but he was forced to retire in his corner due to a knee injury. He would face Smith one more time, in an IFL event in 2007, but the 46-year-old was halted in the fourth round of what was his last pro fight.

MIKE RUSSOW

HEIGHT: **6' 1" (185 cm)**
WEIGHT: **255 lbs (116 kg)**
DATE OF BIRTH: **11 Aug. 1976**
HOMETOWN: **Chicago, IL**

PROFESSIONAL RECORD: 14-1, 1 NC
UFC RECORD: 3-0

The moment Mike Russow first saw the UFC when he was in high school, he decided that he had to become a fighter. Though he took a slight detour to become a Chicago police officer, he never lost sight of his dream.

Fourteen pro wins have followed—including submission victories over Roman Zentsov and Jason Guida, UFC decisions over Justin McCully and Jon Madsen, and the granddaddy of them all, a come-from-behind one-punch knockout of unbeaten Todd Duffee at UFC 114 in May of 2010. Needless to say, that's more than enough strong evidence to show that this submission expert and PRIDE veteran is ready for anything.

MAURICIO RUA *Shogun*

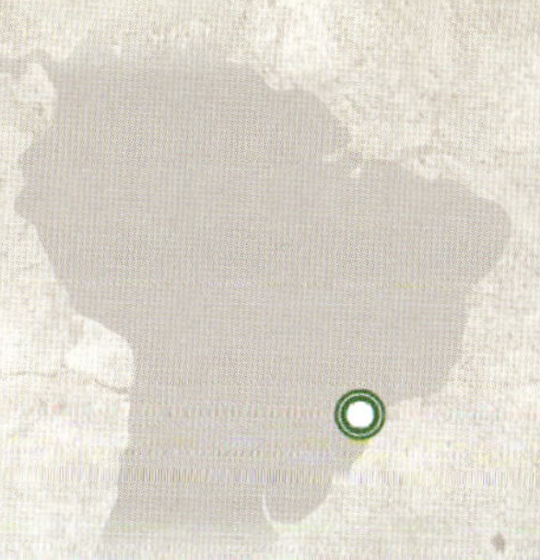

HEIGHT: **6' 1" (185 cm)** DATE OF BIRTH: **25 Nov. 1981**

WEIGHT: **205 lbs (93 kg)** HOMETOWN: **Curitiba, Brazil**

PROFESSIONAL RECORD: 19-5
UFC RECORD: 3-3
TITLES HELD: UFC LIGHT HEAVYWEIGHT CHAMPION, 2005 PRIDE MIDDLEWEIGHT (205 POUND) GRAND PRIX CHAMPION

When he was a child just getting into combat sports, one of Mauricio Rua's first heroes was former heavyweight boxing champion Mike Tyson. As he got older and began his own journey through the world of mixed martial arts, his idols were not only his older brother Murilo, but his Chute Boxe teammate Wanderlei Silva. Silva was obviously the PRIDE wrecking machine and MMA's most feared competitor, while "Ninja", just by virtue of being Mauricio's brother, could do no wrong in or out of the ring.

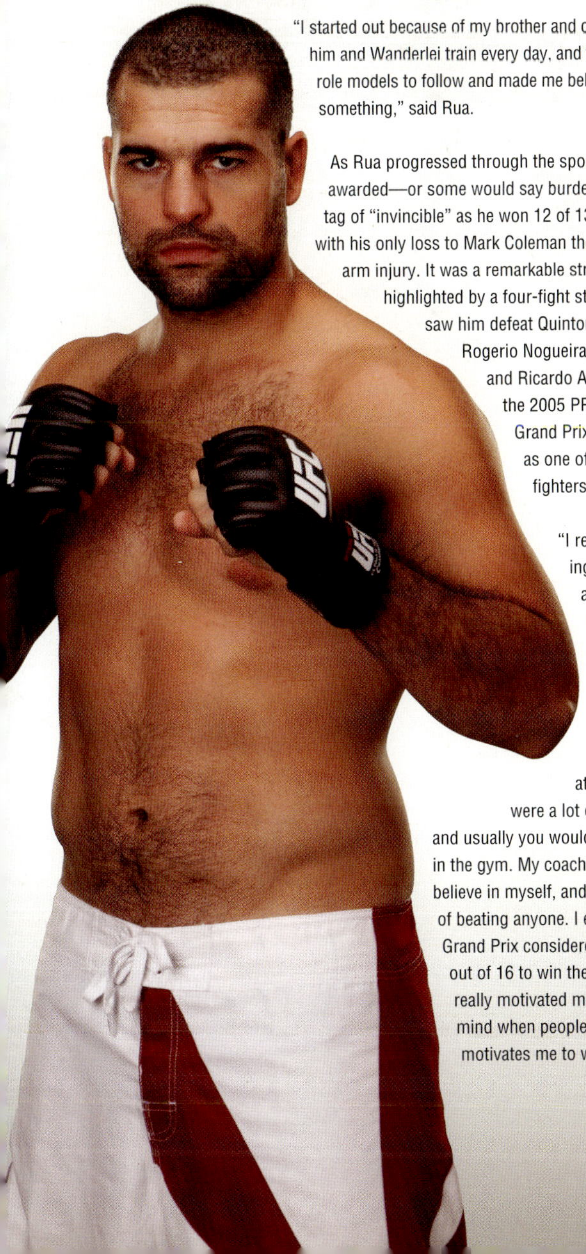

"I started out because of my brother and could train and watch him and Wanderlei train every day, and this gave me great role models to follow and made me believe I could achieve something," said Rua.

As Rua progressed through the sport, he was soon awarded—or some would say burdened with—the tag of "invincible" as he won 12 of 13 fights in PRIDE, with his only loss to Mark Coleman the result of a freak arm injury. It was a remarkable string of excellence highlighted by a four-fight streak in 2005 that saw him defeat Quinton Jackson, Antonio Rogerio Nogueira, Alistair Overeem and Ricardo Arona that earned him the 2005 PRIDE middleweight Grand Prix title and recognition as one of the top 205-pound fighters on the planet.

"I remember that training every day at my academy was tougher than anything else," he said when asked about winning the prestigious Grand Prix. "Back in those days at Chute Boxe there were a lot of tough fighters, and usually you would get a tougher time in the gym. My coaches always made me believe in myself, and I felt I was capable of beating anyone. I entered the PRIDE Grand Prix considered the least favorite out of 16 to win the whole thing. That really motivated me a lot, as I don't mind when people doubt me; it just motivates me to work harder."

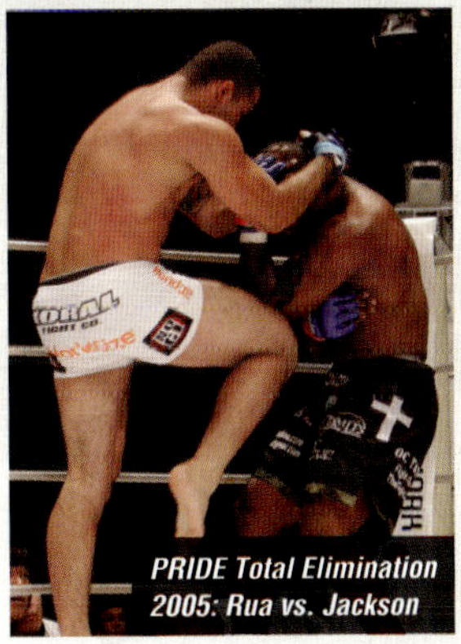

PRIDE Total Elimination 2005: Rua vs. Jackson

Rua's hard work allowed him to skyrocket to the top, and his eventual arrival to the UFC in September of 2007 was greeted with great fanfare, as Shogun would finally have the opportunity to address all the questions fans wanted answered. It didn't work out as planned though, as Rua lost his Octagon debut to Forrest Griffin and subsequently underwent the first of multiple knee surgeries.

Following his second surgery and the entire rehabilitation process, Rua returned to the Octagon in January of 2009 against his old nemesis, Mark Coleman, at UFC 93. Although the bout was awarded Fight of the Night honors, it was far from a stellar performance from Rua, who nonetheless stopped "The Hammer" with 24 seconds left in the fight. Again, many wondered whether Rua's best days were behind him, and Shogun heard all the criticism.

Three months later, at UFC 97 in April 2009, a lot of mouths were closed when Rua finally delivered the UFC performance fans were waiting to see as he knocked out Chuck Liddell in the first round. It was the victory that propelled him into a title shot against UFC light heavyweight champion Lyoto Machida, and after their 25-minute war of attrition at UFC 104, most observers believed that a new king was about to be crowned. The three judges disagreed, awarding the controversial verdict to Machida.

UFC 104: Rua vs. Machida

Disappointed but undeterred, Rua went back to the gym to devise a strategy to crack the Machida riddle in their May 2010 rematch, and at UFC 113 he did just that, knocking out the previously unbeaten "Dragon" in the first round to win the UFC 205-pound title.

While Rua's reign would last less than a year, as he was stopped in the third round by Jon Jones at UFC 128 on March 19, 2011, Shogun and his team expect a return to prominence sooner rather than later.

"I love fighting," he said. "This is my job and something I love to do. When I decided I wanted to try to be a fighter, like my brother, I always dreamed of fighting in the big shows and becoming world champion, so being able to live my dreams is plenty of motivation enough for me to keep training hard and pushing myself."

UFC 113: Rua vs. Machida 2

BAS RUTTEN *El Guapo*

HEIGHT: **6' 1" (185 cm)** DATE OF BIRTH: **24 Feb. 1965**

WEIGHT: **205 lbs (93 kg)** HOMETOWN: **Eindhoven, Holland**

PROFESSIONAL RECORD: 28-4-1 UFC RECORD: 2-0

TITLES HELD: UFC HEAVYWEIGHT CHAMPION

One of the most popular figures in mixed martial arts today, Bas Rutten has garnered a huge fan base among a new generation of fans for his commentary work for the PRIDE organization and for various other outlets. That in itself is fascinating, considering that these new fans may not know that the witty and gregarious Holland native was once one of the most feared fighters in the world.

Known for his devastating striking, Rutten wasn't a points fighter. Each shot he threw, whether with his fists or feet, was designed to knock an opponent out. During a 16-fight Muay Thai kickboxing career, all 14 of the taekwondo and Kyokushin karate black belt's wins ended via KO.

The next challenge for Rutten was mixed martial arts, and he took to it like he took to kickboxing, adding groundfighting along the way to become a standout in Japan's Pancrase organization. Rutten would fight 30 times in Pancrase, going 25-4-1 with victories over the likes of Vernon White, Maurice Smith, Frank Shamrock, Guy Mezger and Masakatsu Funaki.

The only person he couldn't seem to beat was Ken Shamrock, to whom he lost to twice.

Firmly established in Japan, Rutten finally made the leap to America in 1999, and a month shy of his 34th birthday, he battled Tsuyoshi Kosaka at UFC 18. Far behind on points, Rutten was looking at a decision loss as he began the overtime period, but he wasn't done yet.

At the 14:15 mark of the bout, Rutten finished Kosaka, earning a shot at the vacant heavyweight title against Kevin Randleman. This time, the bout went the full 21-minute distance, and despite a strong late surge from Rutten, it was assumed that Randleman would get the nod. He didn't, and with the split decision victory, Rutten was now the UFC heavyweight champion.

It was a short-lived reign. Rutten vacated his title, initially to chase Frank Shamrock in the middleweight division, but then he retired due to an accumulation of injuries. His post-fighting life has been a rich one though, with acting and commentating gigs keeping him busy and in the public eye.

AMIR SADOLLAH

HEIGHT: **5' 11" (180 cm)** WEIGHT: **170 lbs (77 kg)** DATE OF BIRTH: **27 Aug. 1980** HOMETOWN: **Las Vegas, NV**

PROFESSIONAL RECORD: 6-2 TITLES HELD: *THE ULTIMATE FIGHTER 7* WINNER

UFC RECORD: 5-2

Amir Sadollah's emergence on the mixed martial arts scene in 2008 as the winner of *The Ultimate Fighter 7* was one of the year's great stories. But there are more chapters to be written in a pro career that has seen him develop into a welterweight talent after arriving simply as a raw and gutsy prospect.

"One thing I took from the show is that I saw it as a microcosm of everything that's hard about fighting and I looked at it as my grad school," he said. "All the little things and little pressures—interviews, seeing your opponent, not seeing your opponent, injuries, last minute fights. Every little scenario that happens on the show, whether it was purposely built or not, I think prepares you to be a fighter."

On *The Ultimate Fighter*, Sadollah stunned Steve Byrnes, Gerald Harris, Matt Brown and CB Dollaway (twice). Yet even after going from unknown to star at breakneck speed, he remained refreshingly humble.

"The only thing I've got figured out is that I'll never have it figured out," he said.

In his first post-*TUF* bout, Sadollah was the victim of a controversial TKO at the hands of Johny Hendricks at UFC 101, but he went on to win four of his next five bouts, defeating Phil Baroni, Brad Blackburn, Peter Sobotta and DaMarques Johnson, with his only loss to Dong Hyun Kim.

ALESSIO SAKARA *Legionarius*

HEIGHT: **6' 0" (183 cm)** DATE OF BIRTH: **2 Sept. 1981**
WEIGHT: **185 lbs (84 kg)** HOMETOWN: **Rome, Italy**

PROFESSIONAL RECORD: 19-8, 1 NC UFC RECORD: 6-5, 1 NC

After building a reputation as a fighter to watch in the UFC with his scraps against Ron Faircloth and Elvis Sinosic, Alessio Sakara hit a wall in his MMA career with losses to Dean Lister, Drew McFedries and Houston Alexander. But beginning with UFC 80 in January of 2008, this former pro boxer showed his resilience in style as he stopped James Lee in the first round, engaged in a memorable brawl with Chris Leben, and then added a highlight-reel knockout to his resume with his KO of Joe Vedepo in September of 2009. "Legionarius" wasn't through yet though, and he defeated Thales Leites and James Irvin before seeing his winning streak end in 2011 at the hands of Chris Weidman.

IVAN SALAVERRY

HEIGHT: **6' 0" (183 cm)** DATE OF BIRTH: **11 Jan. 1971**
WEIGHT: **185 lbs (77 kg)** HOMETOWN: **Seattle, WA**

PROFESSIONAL RECORD: 12-7-1 UFC RECORD: 3-4

Given his ground knowledge, and a solid standup attack, Toronto native Ivan Salaverry—who has trained in the martial arts since the age of 13—always proved to be a rough night out for anyone at 185 pounds. Just ask the people who he has defeated in the Octagon, such as Andrei Semenov, Tony Fryklund and Joe Riggs, and they'll tell you that beating Salaverry is no easy task, even in the best of circumstances. But key losses at the wrong times against Matt Lindland and Nate Marquardt kept him from moving into title contention, and back-to-back defeats in 2007-08 to Terry Martin and Rousimar Palhares forced his release from the UFC.

DIEGO SANCHEZ

The Dream

HEIGHT: **5' 10" (178 cm)** DATE OF BIRTH: **31 Dec. 1981**
WEIGHT: **170 lbs (77 kg)** HOMETOWN: **Albuquerque, NM**

PROFESSIONAL RECORD: 25-4 UFC RECORD: 12-4
TITLES HELD: *THE ULTIMATE FIGHTER 1* MIDDLEWEIGHT WINNER

Diego Sanchez is one of the brightest young stars in mixed martial arts, but he hasn't been handed anything on his way to the top.

A native of Albuquerque, New Mexico, Sanchez first rose to prominence when he won the first season of the reality show *The Ultimate Fighter* by defeating Kenny Florian. He subsequently built a stellar pro record of 19-0 that included UFC wins over Karo Parisyan, Nick Diaz and Joe Riggs.

In 2007, Sanchez hit a wall, losing back-to-back decisions to Josh Koscheck and Jon Fitch while also going through the transition of changing his training team and relocating to California.

"Even though I had good fights and great wins, slowly, the fame was changing me," said Sanchez. "I wasn't that same tiger that I was whenever I started getting into this game. I was going through the motions and I wasn't focused. I just need to be me and not think about anything else. I have to be that same hungry fighter that was at the bottom of the barrel."

In 2008, Sanchez returned with an unyielding vengeance, scoring a submission win over David Bielkheden and then stopping Luigi Fioravanti to improve to 21-2. The win over Fioravanti was particularly revealing for the groundfighting ace as he showed off an ever-improving standup game.

It was in 2009 that he made his move, dropping to the 155-pound weight class and quickly defeating respected contenders Joe Stevenson and Clay Guida to earn a title shot against 155-pound champion BJ Penn. But in their UFC 107 bout, "The Prodigy" was too much for Sanchez, and Penn stopped him in the fifth round.

After a return to welterweight in 2010, Sanchez suffered a second consecutive loss when he was upset by John Hathaway, but this time, he knew what was missing: a return to his roots and his original trainer, Greg Jackson. The reunion was a success, as Sanchez has since thrilled fans with back-to-back Fight of the Night wins over Paulo Thiago and Martin Kampmann, turning "The Nightmare" into "The Dream".

EDDIE SANCHEZ *The Manic Hispanic*

HEIGHT: **6' 2" (188 cm)** DATE OF BIRTH: **14 Nov. 1982**
WEIGHT: **230 lbs (104 kg)** HOMETOWN: **Temecula, CA**

PROFESSIONAL RECORD: 14-5 UFC RECORD: 3-3

A gutsy competitor whose heart was only matched by the fight-ending power in his right hand, Eddie "The Manic Hispanic" Sanchez may have been a fairly one-dimensional brawler, but he always came to fight, giving fans some memorable battles along the way.

A pro since 2005, Sanchez debuted in the UFC in 2006 with a knockout of Mario Neto, but was then given the unenviable task of being Mirko's first UFC opponent at UFC 67. Sanchez was stopped by the PRIDE legend, but he came back with two knockouts of Colin Robinson and Soa Palelei before being released after losses against Antoni Hardonk and Justin McCully. He has won four of six bouts outside of the organization.

HEIGHT: **6' 3" (191 cm)**
WEIGHT: **170 lbs (77 kg)**
DATE OF BIRTH: **13 April 1983**
HOMETOWN: **Orlando, FL**

BEN SAUNDERS *Killa B*

PROFESSIONAL RECORD: 10-3-2 UFC RECORD: 4-3

Winner of 10 pro bouts, four in the UFC, Jeet Kune Do specialist Ben Saunders first established himself as a fighter to watch with his stint on *The Ultimate Fighter 6*. But Saunders wasn't done impressing fight fans with his stellar all-around game, as he went on to beat Dan Barrera, submit Ryan Thomas and knock out Brandon Wolff. Saunders delivered a career-best performance at UFC 106 when he became the first man to knock out veteran contender Marcus Davis. Losses to Mike Swick, Jon Fitch and Dennis Hallman got him released from his UFC contract, but he expects to one day get back to the Octagon.

ERIC SCHAFER *Ravishing Red*

HEIGHT: **6' 3" (191 cm)**
WEIGHT: **205 lbs (93 kg)**
DATE OF BIRTH: **20 Sept. 1977**
HOMETOWN: **Milwaukee, WI**

PROFESSIONAL RECORD: 13-5-2
UFC RECORD: 3-4

Eric Schafer graduated magna cum laude from the University of Wisconsin-Oshkosh with a BS in Biology/Chemistry. His true passion was jiu-jitsu, where he earned a black belt under Henry Matamoros and Pedro Sauer, and mixed martial arts, where he battled his way into the UFC in 2006.

Unfortunately, he was only able to show glimpses of his substantial talent due to injuries that plagued him since his December 2006 bout with Michael Bisping. But in September of 2008, a healthy Schafer showed what he could do when firing on all cylinders when he submitted heavy-handed Houston Alexander via arm triangle in his Nebraska hometown. Next came a TKO win over Antonio Mendes, but he was released after losses to Ryan Bader and Jason Brilz.

BRENDAN SCHAUB *The Hybrid*

HEIGHT: **6' 4" (193 cm)**
WEIGHT: **245 lbs (110 kg)**
DATE OF BIRTH: **18 March 1983**
HOMETOWN: **Denver, CO**

PROFESSIONAL RECORD: 9-1
UFC RECORD: 4-1

With size, speed and a Spartan work ethic, former college football standout Brendan "The Hybrid" Schaub joined the talent-rich UFC heavyweight division after making it to the finals of *The Ultimate Fighter 10* with wins over Demico Rogers, Jon Madsen and Marcus Jones.

It was the Colorado native's impressive first-round knockouts of Chase Gormley and Chris Tuchscherer that really opened eyes, and after he decisioned former world title challenger Gabriel Gonzaga and knocked out PRIDE legend Mirko Cro Cop, a star was born in one of the sport's most talent-rich weight classes.

"I'm doing what I love, and it's easy for me to get up in the mornings," he said. "I can't wait to go to work and become a better fighter."

HEIGHT: **6' 11" (210 cm)**
WEIGHT: **265 lbs (120 kg)**
DATE OF BIRTH: **27 Oct. 1973**
HOMETOWN: **Rotterdam, Netherlands**

SEMMY SCHILT *Hightower*

PROFESSIONAL RECORD: 26-14-1 UFC RECORD: 1-1

Semmy Schilt made his Pancrase debut in 1996 with a victory over Manabu Yamada. Over the next three years, he took on quality opponents like Masakatsu Funaki, Guy Mezger and Yuki Kondo, winning more than losing, and quickly gaining a following. In 2001 he had a brief stay in the UFC, and the 6' 11" giant quickly became a fan favorite. His brutal KO of Pete Williams at UFC 31 and his bloody loss to Josh Barnett at UFC 32 proved his worth as not only a tough competitor, but also an action fighter. A seven-fight stint in PRIDE and a record four K-1 World Grand Prix titles would follow, cementing his place as one of the best fighters of his era.

HEIGHT: **5' 11" (180 kg)**
WEIGHT: **170 lbs (77 kg)**
DATE OF BIRTH: **25 Aug. 1982**
HOMETOWN: **Westbury, NY**

PETE SELL *Drago*

PROFESSIONAL RECORD: 12-7-1 UFC RECORD: 3-4

Hard-hitting New Yorker Pete Sell first introduced himself to the MMA world with his win over Phil Baroni in 2005. Since then, he has dealt with the ups and downs most young fighters encounter. With the guidance of his mentor, former UFC welterweight champion Matt Serra, he emerged as a better and more focused fighter whose fights against Scott Smith and Nate Quarry were instant classics. In October of 2008, Sell (who also competed on *The Ultimate Fighter 4*) scored his second UFC win by upsetting welterweight contender Josh Burkman, but "Drago" was released from the organization after a first-round TKO loss to Matt Brown five months later.

MATT SERRA *The Terror*

HEIGHT. **5' 6" (168 cm)** DATE OF BIRTH: **2 June 1974**

WEIGHT: **170 lbs (77 kg)** HOMETOWN. **East Meadow, NY**

PROFESSIONAL RECORD: 17-7
UFC RECORD: 7-7
TITLES HELD: UFC WELTERWEIGHT CHAMPION, *THE ULTIMATE FIGHTER 4* WELTERWEIGHT WINNER

Following his decision loss to Karo Parisyan in June of 2005, Matt Serra was at a crossroads in his career. As a veteran of the sport, he was coming off a defeat and starting to see a new generation of fighters make their way into the UFC courtesy of a new TV series called *The Ultimate Fighter*. He could stay home and run his two jiu-jitsu schools, but the fighter inside of him couldn't bear to give up the competition.

Then he got a call about becoming a member of the cast for *The Ultimate Fighter 4*, titled "The Comeback". It was perfect. He could fight, and at the same time get national television exposure for himself and his schools.

That wasn't even the best part though. The Renzo Gracie black belt not only won the show, but in his guaranteed welterweight title shot, he showed off his underrated power by stunning Georges St-Pierre via first-round TKO in April of 2007. The popular New Yorker was a world champion.

UFC 83: Serra vs. St-Pierre 2

Injuries kept him from a UFC 79 grudge match with Matt Hughes after their stint as coaches on *TUF6*, but after Serra lost his belt in the rematch to St-Pierre at UFC 83, they did meet, with Hughes winning a close decision. Following the bout, Serra has gone 1-1, knocking out Frank Trigg and dropping a decision to the man he beat in the *TUF4* finale, Chris Lytle. But whether he's winning or losing, you won't ever hear anyone complain about seeing "The Terror" in the Octagon.

UFC 69: Serra vs. St-Pierre

UFC 98: Serra vs. Hughes

TUF4 Finale: Serra vs. Lytle

If you ask Dan "The Beast" Severn his first impression of the Ultimate Fighting Championship, he doesn't hesitate in his response.

"'Awe' might be one of the best words to sum it up," he said. "To do this type of competition in the United States, I was almost flabbergasted. I knew if it survived, it would gather a great deal of attention."

And while Coldwater, Michigan didn't have Pay-Per-View back in 1993, a buddy of Severn's in Detroit did, and when he brought the VHS tape over, the die was cast.

"He showed it to me and said 'You ever think about doing this stuff?' The rest is history."

At the time, Severn, a two-time All-American wrestler at Arizona State University and a competitor in the 1984 and 1988 Olympic trials, was 35 years old, and as far as he was concerned, his best days had passed him by.

"If anybody wants to call me "The Beast" now, then their sights were not all that high in the first place," he said. "If they wanted to see a real animal, they should have seen me from 1984 to 1986 because I ruled the world, hands down."

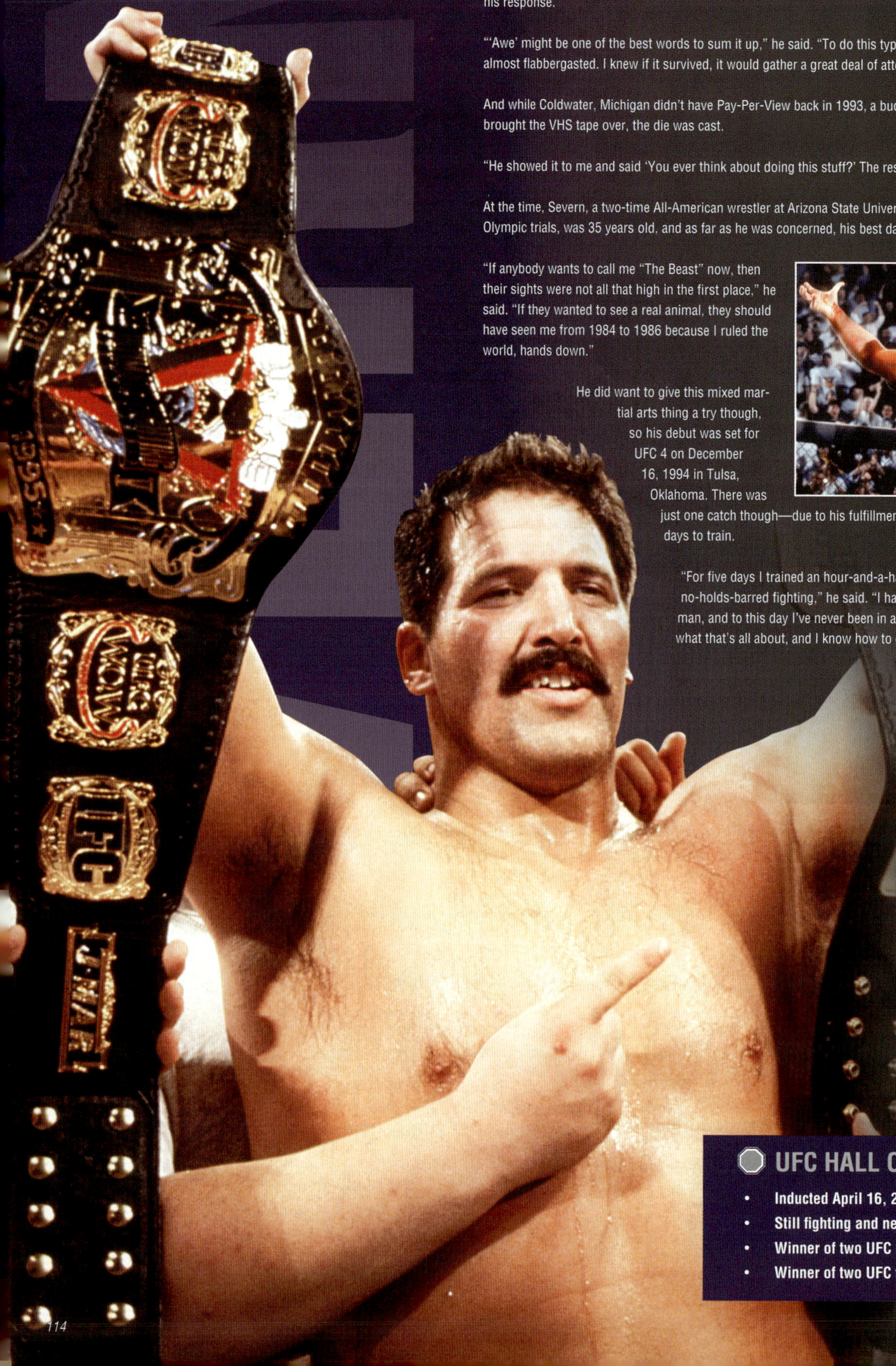

He did want to give this mixed martial arts thing a try though, so his debut was set for UFC 4 on December 16, 1994 in Tulsa, Oklahoma. There was just one catch though—due to his fulfillment of previous commitments, he only had five days to train.

"For five days I trained an hour-and-a-half a day and I walked into the world of no-holds-barred fighting," he said. "I had never balled my fist up against my fellow man, and to this day I've never been in a fight my entire life. But competition, I know what that's all about, and I know how to exploit the rules."

UFC HALL OF FAME

- **Inducted April 16, 2005**
- **Still fighting and nearing 100 wins**
- **Winner of two UFC Superfights**
- **Winner of two UFC tournaments**

DAN SEVERN *The Beast*

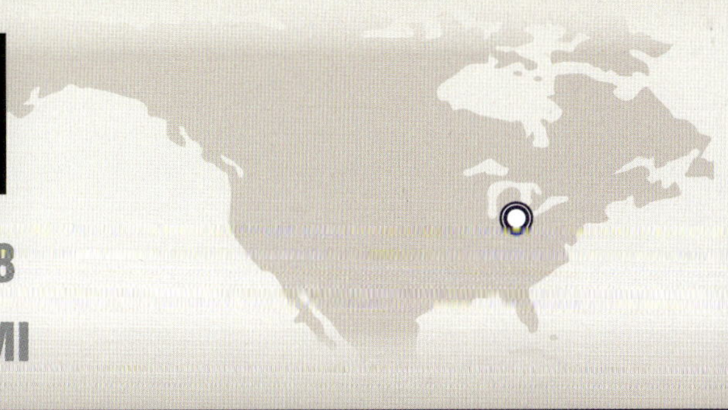

HEIGHT: **6' 2" (188 cm)**
DATE OF BIRTH: **8 June 1958**
WEIGHT: **250 lbs (113 kg)**
HOMETOWN: **Coldwater, MI**

PROFESSIONAL RECORD: 99-18-7
UFC RECORD: 0 1
TITLES HELD: UFC 5 AND ULTIMATE ULTIMATE 95 TOURNAMENT WINNER, UFC SUPERFIGHT CHAMPION

UFC 4: Severn vs. Macias

In his first match against Anthony Macias, he suplexed his opponent like a rag doll before submitting Macias with a read naked choke in 1:45. Marcus Bossett didn't get that far, lasting just 52 seconds. Then, he would face the UFC's undisputed superstar, Royce Gracie, in the night's tournament final. Early on, things went according to plan as he took the jiu-jitsu expert to the mat and kept him there.

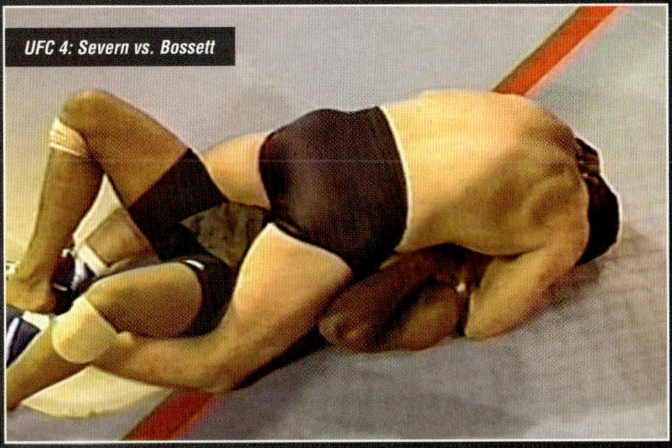
UFC 4: Severn vs. Bossett

UFC 4: Severn vs. Gracie

"If you watch the match from my perspective, it was just going fine my way," said Severn. "I took the man down, and I would rather rain down any day than rain up. It wasn't until several minutes into the match before I realized, you know, I may have to hit this guy. But I had to think about it because it was not in my repertoire, I had never practiced it before, and I was going against 26 years of rules, regulations, and sportsmanlike conduct. So that was difficult for me. I struggled more with my conscience than I ever did with an opponent. I'm out there as a sportsman; I don't have to create any anger issues or things of that nature. I'll shake his hand before, I'll shake it after, there's no hard feelings."

Eventually, Severn started firing off some strikes, and as the bout went from five minutes, to 10, to nearly 15, it looked like just a matter of time until Gracie would be forced to give in.

"They say the eyes are a window to a man's soul, and I'm staring through this man's soul," said Severn. "And he's looking at his dad (Helio Gracie) outside the cage, and I could read exactly what was going through his mind. It's kinda like 'dad, I'm hangin' in there, but if you would throw that towel in, I wouldn't hold it against you.' So my eyes go from Royce's to the old man, and he's got the towel in his hand, and he raises the towel and crosses his arms and shakes his head no. In my mind I'm thinking, 'You'd let me kill your kid out here for Gracie jiu-jitsu, wouldn't ya?'"

At the 15:49 mark, Gracie found his opening and forced Severn to tap out to a triangle choke.

"I'd like to find another human, either living or deceased, that could have done what I did on the limited amount of preparation time that I had, and without ever training a single strike or a single submission," said Severn, and he's right when it comes to the incredible nature of his feat.

Today, he admits with a laugh that, "When I walked out there in 1994, I was looking at this and going, 'just one event.'"

After losing to Gracie, the competitor in him wouldn't let him stop. He signed on for UFC 5, but this time he wouldn't train for just five days.

"I took a 32- to 35-day block of time and I actually trained for no-holds-barred," he said. "The only two rules I had to be concerned about were no biting and no eye gouging. And I'm a very creative person, even in my training camp."

UFC 5: Severn vs. Taktarov 2

UFC 5: Severn vs. Taktarov 1

UFC 5: Severn vs. Beneteau

When he returned in April of 1995, there was no stopping him, as he tore through Joe Charles, Oleg Taktarov and Dave Beneteau to win the UFC 5 tournament. After a submission loss to Ken Shamrock at UFC 6, three more victories against Paul Varelans, Tank Abbott and Taktarov earned him the Ultimate Ultimate 1995 tournament. Five months later he avenged the loss to Shamrock with a 30-minute split decision that was dreadful to watch, but that added a Superfight championship belt to his trophy case.

UFC 6: Severn vs. Shamrock

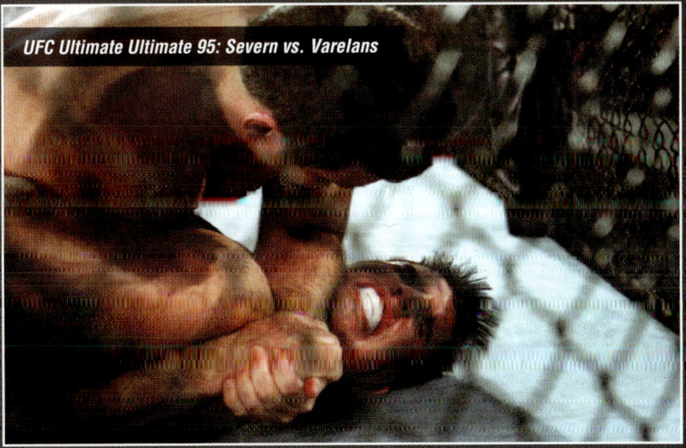

UFC Ultimate Ultimate 95: Severn vs. Varelans

UFC Ultimate Ultimate 95: Severn vs. Abbott

UFC Ultimate Ultimate 95: Severn vs. Taktarov

Before and after the Rizzo bout, Severn stayed active, fighting anyone and everyone whenever asked. His record currently stands at 99-18-7, and if you want a list of impressive names, look no further than a record that includes Cal Worsham, Victor Valimaki, James Thompson, Seth Petruzelli, Forrest Griffin, Marcus Silveira, Josh Barnett, Kimo Leopoldo, Paul Buentello, Jeremy Horn and Pat Miletich.

At 53, he's still competing, looking for that elusive 100th win, but he says "By the end of 2012, I will be done." He won't be gone though; instead, he will continue to run his training facility in Michigan as well as work with local schools as a strong advocate of education. As for the sport of MMA, he doesn't think about his influence too much, but he does appreciate when it's brought to his attention that he was the one who made it safe for wrestlers to make their move into the sport.

"It makes you feel good that you're recognized as a guy who opened the floodgates for all these wrestlers," he said. "And what a lot of people may not realize is that for amateur wrestling, there is no real profession for amateur wrestlers to move on to. The mixed martial arts has become that new profession for them to move into."

They can thank Dan Severn for that.

Following the Shamrock fight, Severn would only fight twice more in the Octagon, losing a heavyweight title fight to Mark Coleman in 1997 and then getting stopped on leg kicks by Pedro Rizzo at UFC 27 in 2000.

UFC 9: Severn vs. Shamrock

Severn was inducted into the UFC Hall of Fame on April 16, 2005.

FRANK SHAMROCK

HEIGHT: **5' 10" (178 cm)** DATE OF BIRTH: **8 Dec. 1972**
WEIGHT: **185 lbs (84 kg)** HOMETOWN: **San Jose, CA**

PROFESSIONAL RECORD: **23-10-2** UFC RECORD: **5-0**
TITLES HELD: **UFC LIGHT HEAVYWEIGHT CHAMPION (THEN CALLED MIDDLEWEIGHT)**

Frank Juarez Shamrock began his fighting career in the shadow of his older adopted brother Ken, but that didn't last long. In fact, by the time he ended his five-fight string in the UFC from 1997 to 1999, he was not only the king of the 205-pound weight class, but he was considered by many to be the best fighter in the sport, pound-for-pound.

Shamrock began his career in Japan's Pancrase organization in 1994, when, amazingly, he debuted against—and beat—future UFC heavyweight champion Bas Rutten. Over the next two years, he competed solely in Japan, winning most but losing some against the best fighters in the organization.

By 1997 he began to explore other options, and after a memorable war with Enson Inoue in a Vale Tudo Japan bout that included a post-fight brawl with Inoue's brother Egan, Shamrock made his UFC debut on December 21, 1997. There he needed just 16 seconds to submit world-class wrestler Kevin Jackson to win the UFC's first middleweight (later changed to light heavyweight) title.

For an encore, Shamrock slammed Igor Zinoviev into defeat in just 22 seconds at UFC 16 to move to 2-0 in the Octagon, and now fans and pundits wondered not when someone would beat the champion, but if. Jeremy Horn and John Lober couldn't pull it off, but at UFC 22 in September of 1999, rising star Tito Ortiz almost did, as he pushed Shamrock harder than he had been pushed in the Octagon over the first three rounds of their bout. But in round four, Shamrock turned up the heat, forcing the challenger to tap out due to strikes.

It was Shamrock's finest hour, but also his last in the UFC, as he retired immediately after the bout.

Like with many fighters, retirement didn't last long. While he didn't return to the UFC when he came back, he did stay active in the Strikeforce organization, falling short in two of his last three bouts against Cung Le and Nick Diaz. Age may have caught up to Frank Shamrock, but when he was at his best, he was something to see.

KEN SHAMROCK

The World's Most Dangerous Man

HEIGHT: **6' 0" (183 cm)** DATE OF BIRTH: **11 Feb. 1964**
WEIGHT: **245 lbs (111 kg)** HOMETOWN: **Susanville, CA**

PROFESSIONAL RECORD: **28-15-2** UFC RECORD: **6-6-2**
TITLES HELD: **UFC SUPERFIGHT CHAMPION**

In the early days of the UFC, if you were going to build a prototype of a fighter, you probably would have come up with someone who looked like Ken Shamrock. Skilled in all aspects of MMA, Shamrock made a hybrid style of fighting essential to success in the sport. His impact went far beyond a win-loss record. Because while fighters like Royce Gracie and Randy Couture went about their business in a low-key fashion, Shamrock built a base of fans who either loved him or hated him, as he was the master of promoting a fight and getting fans to have a reaction towards him.

From his first UFC bout in 1993, when he submitted Pat Smith with a heel hook in just a minute and 49 seconds, Shamrock was not only a world class fighter, but he looked and acted the part. Scowl on his face, shoulders barely able to fit through doors, Shamrock's swagger was one of the earliest memories for tons of UFC fans, and it rubbed plenty of his peers the wrong way. Then again, that was the idea, as Shamrock's bad blood matchups both here and abroad lifted his profile to a level of stardom few fighters enjoyed.

UFC HALL OF FAME

- **Inducted November 21, 2003**
- **Won UFC Superfight championship**
- **UFC 1 veteran**
- **Engaged in memorable trilogy with Tito Ortiz**

The biggest feud of them all was Ortiz-Shamrock, and though they buried the hatchet after Ortiz' second consecutive first-round win (his third stoppage victory in as many fights against his rival) publicly, the animosity between them was real.

Beyond the bluster, Shamrock was a fighter, one who scored wins over the likes of Bas Rutten, Matt Hume, Dan Severn, Kimo Leopoldo (twice), and Maurice Smith. He also fought Gracie to a draw after losing to him in their first bout. That's not even touching on his influential role as the leader of the Lion's Den fight team that launched the careers of his adopted brother Frank, Guy Mezger, Vernon White, Jerry Bohlander and Tra Telligman, among others.

While age and injuries eventually caught up to Shamrock, there's no questioning his influence on the sport, so it was no surprise when he joined Gracie as the first two fighters inducted in the UFC Hall of Fame in 2003.

SEAN SHERK *The Muscle Shark*

HEIGHT: **5' 6" (168 cm)** WEIGHT: **155 lbs (70 kg)** DATE OF BIRTH: **5 Aug. 1973** HOMETOWN: **Oak Grove, MN**

PROFESSIONAL RECORD: 38-4-1 UFC RECORD: 8-4
TITLES HELD: UFC LIGHTWEIGHT CHAMPION

With over 40 fights and 12 years in the sport of mixed martial arts, there's little that Sean Sherk hasn't figured out when it comes to professional fighting. He's a pro's pro, a stellar wrestler who, through fight experience and hard work, became a true mixed martial artist. But one thing had always eluded him—a world championship.

"The thought of winning that title belt and being the best in the world is what gets me up in the morning and makes me train three, four times a day," said Sherk, who lost a grueling five-rounder to Matt Hughes in a 2003 bout for the UFC welterweight title.

On October 14, 2006, Sherk's dream finally became a reality when he scored a unanimous five-round decision over Kenny Florian to win the UFC lightweight championship. But when he was stripped of the belt after failing a post-fight test for the banned substance nandrolone following his first title defense against Hermes Franca, the dream became a nightmare. Sherk protested his innocence, and after returning in 2008, he was hungrier than ever to regain his belt, despite a UFC 84 loss to BJ Penn.

Injuries and a 2009 loss to Frankie Edgar slowed Sherk down, but a UFC 119 win over hot prospect Evan Dunham got "The Muscle Shark" back on track for what he hopes is the addition of some new hardware to his collection.

"I think it (winning the title again) will definitely be sweeter the second time around," he said.

JAKE SHIELDS

HEIGHT: **6' 0" (183 cm)**
WEIGHT: **170 lbs (77 kg)**
DATE OF BIRTH:
9 Jan. 1979
HOMETOWN:
San Francisco, CA

PROFESSIONAL RECORD: 26-5-1
UFC RECORD: 1-1

The talent-rich UFC welterweight division got richer in 2010 when Jake Shields—whose grappling prowess places him among the best in the world—made his Octagon debut with a three-round win over Martin Kampmann. A standout high school wrestler, Shields began his fighting career in 1999, and has gone on to compile a stellar record that includes wins over a Who's Who of modern MMA, including Hayato "Mach" Sakurai, Carlos Condit, Mike Pyle and Jason Miller. Shields has also defeated middleweight standouts Dan Henderson, Robbie Lawler, Dave Menne and Yushin Okami. In his first UFC title shot, Shields couldn't add Georges St-Pierre's name to his list, as he lost a five-round decision at UFC 129.

THIAGO SILVA

HEIGHT: **6' 1" (185 cm)** DATE OF BIRTH: **12 Nov. 1982**
WEIGHT: **205 lbs (93 kg)** HOMETOWN: **Sao Paulo, Brazil**

PROFESSIONAL RECORD: 14-2, 1 NC UFC RECORD: 5-2, 1 NC

Houston Alexander was everywhere in the weeks leading up to his UFC 78 bout against Thiago Silva, with newspapers and websites telling his story with a fervor. When the two 205-pounders stepped into the Octagon, it was Silva who carved his own name into the headlines as he stopped the knockout artist in the first round.

Now everyone knows the Brazilian, who has scored UFC victories over Houston Alexander, Chad Mendes, Tomasz Drwal, James Irvin and Keith Jardine, losing only to Lyoto Machida and Rashad Evans. In January of 2011, Silva battled Brandon Vera, and though he won a decision, the verdict was later changed to a no contest when Silva was found to have falsified a urine sample to hide the use of banned substance. He is serving a one-year suspension.

ANDERSON SILVA PAGE 120

Anderson Silva sat quietly in his locker room at the Hard Rock Hotel and Casino in Las Vegas. Just a few minutes earlier he had made an earth-shattering statement to the mixed martial arts world in his UFC debut, knocking out granite-chinned Chris Leben in just 49 seconds. But you wouldn't know it by the calm the native of Curitiba, Brazil showed as he humbly and politely answered questions.

One query centered on his otherworldly striking attack, but he was not about to pat himself on the back, chalking his talent simply up to hard work. The interview done, a reporter turned to walk away. Silva patted him on his shoulder and proceeded to tell his manager and translator, Ed Soares, something in Portuguese. Then the true secret of power and accuracy of "The Spider" was revealed.

"I'm one of the X-Men," said Silva, before breaking out into a hearty laugh.

This was vintage Anderson Silva, deadly in the Octagon, light-hearted and quick with a smile or a joke outside of it. And as the years progressed, he went from talented Octagon newcomer to the best fighter in the world, pound for pound.

But there was work to be done before he ruled the UFC. A taekwondo practitioner from the age of 14, the lanky, graceful Silva came up the hard way in life and in the fight game.

"I came from very humble beginnings, but I received a lot of love and support from my family," said Silva. At the time that he discovered taekwondo, he was a typical teenager, a fan of comic books who was quick to play practical jokes—two aspects of his personality he's kept with him to this day. Just look at his official UFC bio, where he lists Spider-Man as his hero.

"I love comic books and I have every Spider-Man comic book series since 1984," said Silva. "I listed him as my hero because he was the only superhero that had bills to pay. Batman was rich, and Superman was from another planet."

After getting a taste of combat sports, Silva became a more serious young man, one who loved testing himself in a one-on-one competition where his fists, feet, and mind were the only weapons he needed. From taekwondo, Silva would move to Muay Thai, and it was there that he truly found his calling in life—as a professional fighter.

"After my first professional Muay Thai bout, I realized this isn't bad, and I'm pretty good," said Silva, adding that his transition into pro fighting "happened kind of naturally."

Photography by: Susumu Nagao

PRIDE 21: Silva vs. Stiebling

Of course, his family, like any family, was concerned about Silva's new vocation.

"At first they didn't want me to become a fighter, but eventually they realized it was something I loved to do, and that I was actually pretty good," said Silva, who eventually turned to mixed martial arts, making his debut at home in Curitiba in 2000.

"I was very nervous," said Silva of that first fight, "but I was excited to get in there and do what I came to do."

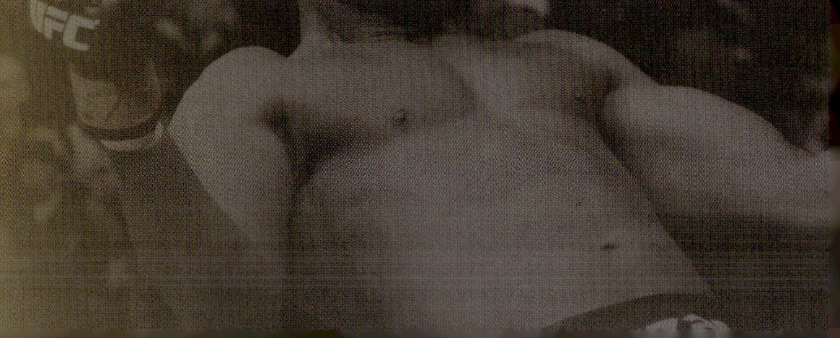

ANDERSON SILVA *The Spider*

HEIGHT: **6' 2" (187 cm)** DATE OF BIRTH: **14 April 1975**

WEIGHT: **185 lbs (84 kg)** HOMETOWN: **Curitiba, Brazil**

PROFESSIONAL RECORD: 28-4
UFC RECORD: 13-0
TITLES HELD: UFC MIDDLEWEIGHT CHAMPION

In 2001, after introducing himself on the vicious Vale Tudo circuit, he began making inroads in Japan, and a year later he began what turned into a five-fight stint in PRIDE. While in the Land of the Rising Sun's premier organization, he defeated Alex Stiebling, Alexander Otuska and Carlos Newton, but got submitted by Daiju Takase and Ryo Chonan.

PRIDE 22: Silva vs. Otsuka

PRIDE 25: Silva vs. Newton

PRIDE Shockwave 2004: Silva vs. Chonan

The still-raw talent also became a world traveler of sorts, defeating Jeremy Horn in South Korea; Lee Murray, Jorge Rivera, Curtis Stout and Tony Fryklund in England; and losing via disqualification due to an illegal upkick to Yushin Okami in Hawaii.

The Okami defeat would prove to be his last, and after he knocked Fryklund out with a spectacular elbow to the head in April of 2006, he got the call to compete in the UFC.

"I have fought in Japan, England, and all over Brazil, and I've always wanted to fight in the U.S.," said Silva shortly after his signing. "I felt the UFC was the most well-known organization in the world and has some of the best middleweights. I want to fight the best."

At the time, the UFC was just taking off with mainstream sports fans, and many fans of this fast-growing sport had no exposure to the mysterious young man known as "The Spider". To diehard aficionados, he was not only the real deal, but a fighter entering his prime who was about to shake up the UFC's middleweight division.

And he made an immediate impression, blitzing and finishing Leben in less than a minute. But the real shock was to come on October 14, 2006.

UFC Fight Night 5: Silva vs. Leben

Given an immediate title shot after the win over Leben, Silva was pitted against popular champion Rich Franklin in the main event of UFC 64 in Las Vegas. The card was dubbed "Unstoppable", and Silva was, as he caught the champion in a Thai clinch from which Franklin couldn't break free. What followed was a series of knees that broke Franklin's nose and sent him to the canvas. At two minutes and 59 seconds of the first round, a new champion was crowned and his name was Anderson Silva.

UFC 64: Silva vs. Franklin

The early days of Silva's reign at 185 pounds were filled with spectacular win after spectacular win. He showed off his Brazilian jiu-jitsu game when he submitted fellow black belt Travis Lutter at UFC 67, easily crushed Nate Marquardt in the first round five months later and knocked out Franklin a second time when they met in October of 2007.

It was his second-round submission of Dan Henderson in a UFC/PRIDE middleweight unification bout at UFC 82 in March 2008 that prompted people to put Silva on top of the mythical pound-for-pound list and start talking about him reigning for as long as he wanted to. No one would hear such lofty comments coming from Silva's mouth, though.

UFC 67: Silva vs. Lutter

UFC 73: Silva vs. Marquardt

UFC 82: Silva vs. Henderson

"I don't think I am the best," he said in mid-2008. "I'm far from being the best in the world. People can say what they want, but I don't believe I am yet. I can only say that when I stop fighting. I still have a lot to go through, and there are still many great fighters out there."

UFC Fight Night 14: Silva vs. Irvin

Silva's performances said otherwise. In July of 2008 he moved up to the light heavyweight division for a one-shot bout against knockout artist James Irvin, and he needed just 61 seconds to end the night of "The Sandman".

UFC 101: Silva vs. Griffin

Yet as he defended his crown with wins over Patrick Cote (TKO3) and Thales Leites (W5), the latter victory breaking the record for most consecutive UFC victories (9) and tying the record for most title defenses (5), Silva appeared bored at 185 pounds, and his lackluster, yet dominating, performances showed it.

In response, UFC President Dana White decided to test his champion at 205 pounds again, setting up an August 2009 bout against former UFC light heavyweight titleholder Forrest Griffin. If Silva wanted a fight, Griffin was undoubtedly going to give him one. But this UFC 101 bout got ugly quick for Griffin, and Silva, showing off amazing offensive and defensive wizardry, knocked him out in just 3:23.

UFC 117: Silva vs. Sonnen

Another disappointing showing, this one a lopsided five-round decision win against Demian Maia at UFC 112, followed though, and after a prolonged trash-talking attack from Chael Sonnen, Silva was on the receiving end of a thrashing from the number-one contender in their August 2010 bout.

Just as he was on the verge of losing his title to Sonnen, Silva—nursing a pre-fight rib injury—sprung into action in the fifth round, submitting his foe at the 3:10 mark to cap off perhaps the most spectacular comeback in UFC history.

UFC 126: Silva vs. Belfort

"The Spider" was back, and if there were any doubters, he silenced them at UFC 126 in February of 2011 with a first-round knockout of Vitor Belfort that began with an indescribably devastating front kick to the jaw. It was vintage Anderson Silva, the champion of cool who never seems to get rattled, even in the seconds before he's called to battle.

"At that moment there's nowhere to run," he smiled. "If you trained, you trained; if you didn't, you're screwed."

WANDERLEI SILVA *The Axe Murderer*

HEIGHT: **5' 11" (180 cm)** DATE OF BIRTH: **3 July 1976**

WEIGHT: **185 lbs (84 kg)** HOMETOWN: **Las Vegas, NV**

PROFESSIONAL RECORD: 33-10-1, 1 NC
UFC RECORD: 3-5
TITLES HELD: PRIDE MIDDLEWEIGHT (205 POUND) CHAMPION

With all due respect to the 1986-89 version of Mike Tyson, from August of 2000 to October of 2004, Wanderlei Silva was the baddest man on the planet.

15-0-1 with 1 no contest during that period, the man dubbed "The Axe Murderer" was a tornado of terror in Japanese rings for the PRIDE organization, defeating the likes of Kazushi Sakuraba (three times), Quinton Jackson (twice), Dan Henderson, Ikuhisa Minowa and Guy Mezger.

Those four years cemented Silva in the history books as PRIDE's greatest 205-pounder ever, but strangely enough, if you look back at his early career, Silva's eventual ascension wasn't necessarily a foregone conclusion. A Muay Thai ace who tore through the Vale Tudo circuit back home in Brazil after making his pro debut in 1996, with his only loss coming due to a cut, Silva was brought to the UFC in 1998 to battle "The Phenom", countryman Vitor Belfort.

The still-explosive Belfort stopped Silva in just 44 seconds. Even though he would rebound with a UFC win over Tony Petarra and put together three wins in PRIDE, Silva rolled the dice by going back to the UFC. Silva lost via decision in a title bout against Tito Ortiz, putting the 11-3 fighter's future in question.

After a 39-second knockout of Todd Medina in a Meca Vale Tudo show in his hometown of Curitiba, Brazil—less than four months after the Ortiz fight—Silva was welcomed back into PRIDE. There he began a reign of terror that saw him go on his 17-fight unbeaten streak with the only hiccups being a draw with Mirko Cro Cop and a no contest with Gilbert Yvel.

It was as if a new fighter was born in the Land of the Rising Sun, but for Silva, the explanation for his MMA rebirth was a simple one.

"In PRIDE, I went step by step," he said. "In UFC, they gave me the big names to fight and there was a lot of pressure. And before, I was also working another job and training. I didn't have the money to only train. Now I was a professional fighter."

In other words, fights against the Dan Hendersons and Kazushi Sakurabas of the world were mixed with bouts against lesser names like Shungo Oyama and Tatsuya Iwasaki, allowing Silva to build his confidence and his game at a pace that was hectic but wise for the time as he became a superstar in Japan, something helped by his three stoppages of national icon Sakuraba.

And at the same time, Silva slowly added more wrinkles to his fight game, making him even more dangerous.

PRIDE 28: Silva vs. Jackson 2

Silva's confidence was at its peak when he battled current UFC light heavyweight champion Quinton Jackson in 2003 and 2004, walking away with a TKO win in the first bout and a devastating knee-induced knockout in the rematch.

That second win over Jackson may have been Silva's finest moment in PRIDE, but over the next two and a half years, the pace of fighting against some of the best fighters in the world started to catch up to him. He would lose to heavyweight Mark Hunt in his next fight, and also get decisioned by Ricardo Arona (a loss later avenged). The key defeats though would be knockouts in 2006 and February of 2007 to Cro Cop and Henderson. After the losses, some questioned whether Silva's best days were behind him. But all he really needed was some time off.

In 2007, Silva made the decision to move to the United States to live and train, and shortly thereafter, he re-signed with the UFC, with his first fight being one for the ages as he engaged in a classic hard-fought decision loss to Chuck Liddell at UFC 79. A 36-second knockout win over Keith Jardine at UFC 84 in 2008 followed, but after back-to-back losses to Jackson and Rich Franklin, Silva decided to test the waters at 185 pounds, where his most recent fight was a decision victory over England's Michael Bisping.

The win reminded UFC fans that when you talk about exciting fights, the conversation begins and ends with Wanderlei Silva.

UFC 79: Silva vs. Liddell

AARON SIMPSON *A-Train*

HEIGHT: **6' 0" (183 cm)**
WEIGHT: **185 lbs (84 kg)**
DATE OF BIRTH: **20 July 1974**
HOMETOWN: **Phoenix, AZ**

PROFESSIONAL RECORD: 8-2 UFC RECORD: 4-2

Though most will immediately gravitate towards Aaron Simpson's six knockout victories, it was in his win over Tom Lawlor in January of 2010 that he showed a world-class chin and heart as he soared to a victory that kept him unbeaten.

"I was glad I was in that type of fight," said the former Arizona State All-American wrestler. "It was a good test to see where I was at."

WES SIMS *The Project*

HEIGHT: **6' 10" (208 cm)**
WEIGHT: **260 lbs (118 kg)**
DATE OF BIRTH: **12 Sept. 1979**
HOMETOWN: **Lancaster, OH**

PROFESSIONAL RECORD: 22-13-1, 2 NC
UFC RECORD: 0-3

A member of Mark Coleman and Kevin Randleman's Hammer House, Wes Sims went 6-1 with 1 no contest in the first eight bouts of a career that began in 2001, and some thought he had the potential to become the third member of his team to win a UFC heavyweight title. It wasn't going to happen though, as Sims went 0-3 in the Octagon, a stint that included a disqualification for stomping a downed Frank Mir in the head, a knockout loss to Mir in their rematch and a KO loss to Mike Kyle in which Sims claimed that he was bit. This never-a-dull-moment personality brought him back in the form of *The Ultimate Fighter 10*, but Sims was eliminated in his first bout.

RORY SINGER *Outburst*

HEIGHT: **6' 2" (188 cm)**
WEIGHT: **185 lbs (84 kg)**
DATE OF BIRTH: **28 May 1976**
HOMETOWN: **Athens, GA**

PROFESSIONAL RECORD: 12-10
UFC RECORD: 2-2

A member of the cast of *The Ultimate Fighter 3*, Rory Singer crashed the UFC party in 2006 by submitting Ross Pointon at the season finale with a triangle choke in 44 seconds. It was a bout that included some of the most furious action seen in the Octagon in 2006, and four months later, he made it two in a row with a brutal three-round decision win over good friend Josh Haynes in another war. His string of victories came to a close with a submission defeat against Yushin Okami at UFC 66 and a TKO loss to Jason MacDonald in 2007, but for a brief moment, there was no more exciting middleweight than Rory Singer.

ELVIS SINOSIC *The King of Rock and Rumble*

HEIGHT: **6' 3" (191 cm)**
WEIGHT: **205 lbs (93 kg)**
DATE OF BIRTH: **13 Feb. 1971**
HOMETOWN: **Sydney, Australia**

PROFESSIONAL RECORD: 8-11-2
UFC RECORD: 1-6

If you ever get a chance to talk to Elvis Sinosic, you will undoubtedly walk away knowing that he is one of the most accessible and classy athletes you could ever meet in professional sports.

A black belt in Brazilian jiu-jitsu, Shootfighting, taekwondo, and Kai Shin, the Canberra native debuted in the Octagon with a stunning upset victory over Jeremy Horn at UFC 30. He remained winless throughout his subsequent six, despite delivering a supreme effort each time out and a Fight of the Night battle with Michael Bisping in 2007.

DENNIS SIVER

HEIGHT: **5' 7" (170 cm)**
WEIGHT: **155 lbs (70 kg)**
DATE OF BIRTH: **13 Jan. 1979**
HOMETOWN: **Mannheim, Germany**

PROFESSIONAL RECORD: 18-7 UFC RECORD: 7-4

With victories like his recent ones over rising stars George Sotiropoulos and Andre Winner, Russia native Dennis Siver has been gathering more and more fans with each bout. But if you ask him about his crowd-pleasing style, he smiles, saying that it's just luck that he happens to be in more than his share of exciting bouts.

Since debuting in the Octagon in 2007, Siver has earned two Knockout of the Night, one Fight of the Night and one Submission of the Night award, only losing four bouts against standouts like Gray Maynard, Melvin Guillard and Ross Pearson. Currently sporting a three-fight winning streak, the master of the spinning back kick never disappoints when the bell rings.

KIMBO SLICE

HEIGHT: **6' 2" (188 cm)**
WEIGHT: **225 lbs (102 kg)**
DATE OF BIRTH: **8 Feb. 1974**
HOMETOWN: **Miami, FL**

PROFESSIONAL RECORD: 4-2 UFC RECORD: 1-1

One of the most unlikely sports success stories of recent years was that of Kimbo Slice, a former streetfighter turned MMA athlete and worldwide sensation who set viewing records during his stint on *The Ultimate Fighter 10*. In the Octagon, Slice outpointed Houston Alexander in December of 2009 before getting cut after a UFC 113 loss to his *TUF10* castmate, Matt Mitrione. So what was it about the Miami resident that has captivated millions around the world?

"I'm the same guy as the guy that shops at K-Mart," he said, "and they feel like they can relate to that. I'm one of theirs."

MAURICE SMITH

HEIGHT: **6' 2" (188 cm)** DATE OF BIRTH: **13 Dec. 1961**
WEIGHT: **220 lbs (100 kg)** HOMETOWN: **Seattle, WA**

PROFESSIONAL RECORD: 12-13 UFC RECORD: 4-3
TITLES HELD: UFC HEAVYWEIGHT CHAMPION

When talking about the kickboxing prowess of former UFC heavyweight champion Maurice Smith, the term "legendary" is usually attached at the front. These days, when the word is thrown out routinely, it doesn't hold much weight, but in the case of the Seattle standout, consider that in a sport where one kick or punch can end your night, he went unbeaten against the best in the game for nearly 10 years.

That was kickboxing though. Mixed martial arts is a whole different animal, and when Smith began dabbling in the sport as a competitor in Japan's Pancrase organization, he got bit by that animal as he learned the ropes. If he hit you, odds are you were getting knocked out; if you survived and got him to the mat, you would submit him.

It was a war of nerves, but Smith made an effort to push the odds in his favor, and against Marcus Silveira in 1996, he began to show off his takedown defense. Then he showed off his power, stopping his foe in the third round.

In the summer of 1997, he was brought to the UFC to face heavyweight champion Mark Coleman. Wrestlers like Coleman had made the Octagon a no man's land for strikers, just like Royce Gracie had done in the early UFCs. But then Smith went and shocked the world at UFC 14, showing off his takedown defense, his solid ground game when the bout hit the mat and, of course, his striking to win a unanimous decision and the title.

The victory was a high water mark for strikers in the Octagon, and though he would lose his title to Randy Couture at UFC Japan after just one successful defense (against Tank Abbott), the die had been cast. Strikers could survive in the Octagon, and Mo Smith had just given them the blueprint.

Smith would never rise to championship heights again in the UFC, going 2-2 in his final four bouts, with wins over Marco Ruas and Bobby Hoffman and losses to Kevn Randleman and Renato "Babalu" Sobral. He remained active in MMA until 2008.

PATRICK SMITH

HEIGHT: **6' 2" (188 cm)** DATE OF BIRTH: **28 Aug. 1963**
WEIGHT: **225 lbs (102 kg)** HOMETOWN: **Denver, CO**

PROFESSIONAL RECORD: 18-14 UFC RECORD: 4-2

In six early UFC fights, Pat Smith only lost twice—to future Hall of Famers Ken Shamrock and Royce Gracie. That's pretty impressive in and of itself, but what may have gotten lost in the shuffle was that Smith, a black belt in a number of martial arts, including taekwondo and Kenpo karate, made a concerted effort to learn the ground game *after* his UFC 1 loss to Shamrock. By the time he returned to the Octagon, he was able to submit two of three foes in the UFC 2 tournament before losing in his fourth bout of the night to Gracie. Following a submission of Rudyard Moncayo at UFC 6, Smith continued to fight until 2009 as a mixed martial artist, boxer and kickboxer.

SCOTT SMITH *Hands of Steel*

HEIGHT: **6' 0" (183 cm)** DATE OF BIRTH: **21 May 1979**
WEIGHT: **185 lbs (84 kg)** HOMETOWN: **Elk Grove, CA**

PROFESSIONAL RECORD: 18-8, 1 NC UFC RECORD: 1-3

The Ultimate Fighter 4's Scott Smith knew he only had one punch left in him after getting badly hurt with a body shot from Pete Sell in their November 2006 fight in Las Vegas. If he landed, he had a chance—if he didn't, he was probably going to get knocked out. Sell rushed in, Smith timed his delivery, and BOOM, fight over, as he knocked his opponent out in one of the most spectacular finishes ever seen in mixed martial arts history.

But for the exciting Californian, it was just another day at the office in a career that has seen his "Hands of Steel" produce a lot of memorable endings, even though losses against David Terrell, Patrick Cote and Ed Herman shortened his UFC career.

RENATO SOBRAL *Babalu*

HEIGHT: **6' 1" (185 cm)** DATE OF BIRTH: **7 Aug. 1975**
WEIGHT: **205 lbs (93 kg)** HOMETOWN: **Rio de Janeiro, Brazil**

PROFESSIONAL RECORD: 33-9 UFC RECORD: 6-4

When you ask Renato Sobral what he learned from his 2002 loss to Chuck "The Iceman" Liddell, the answer comes as fast as one of Sobral's triangle chokes.

"The most important thing I learned is that if you don't want to fight, stay home," said Sobral, who went on to reel off wins in 11 of 13 bouts after that defeat, losing only to Liddell (in their 2006 rematch) and Jason Lambert. He was released from the UFC after his win over David Heath at UFC 74, but Sobral's overall career has been an impressive one, with wins against Jeremy Horn, Mauricio "Shogun" Rua, Chael Sonnen and Trevor Prangley.

The Brazilian currently competes in the Strikeforce organization.

CHAEL SONNEN

HEIGHT: **6' 1" (185 cm)**
WEIGHT: **185 lbs (84 kg)**
DATE OF BIRTH: **3 April 1977**
HOMETOWN: **West Linn, OR**

PROFESSIONAL RECORD: 26-11-1
UFC RECORD: 4-4

Chael Sonnen, a former Olympic alternate and All-American wrestler was always a good fighter, a solid contender who showed up and gave his best every time out. It wasn't until 2009 that Sonnen started breaking through on the elite level in the UFC, and by the time he pulled off wins over Dan Miller, Yushin Okami, and Nate Marquardt, he had catapulted into the number-one middleweight contender's spot. He wasn't done yet though, as he battered champion Anderson Silva for nearly five rounds in their UFC 117 title fight before getting submitted in the final stanza.

KRZYSZTOF SOSZYNSKI

The Polish Experiment

HEIGHT: **6' 1" (185 cm)**
WEIGHT: **205 lbs (93 kg)**
DATE OF BIRTH: **2 Aug. 1977**
HOMETOWN: **Winnipeg, Manitoba, Canada**

PROFESSIONAL RECORD: 22-11-1
UFC RECORD: 5-2

One of *The Ultimate Fighter 8*'s most successful veterans, Krzysztof Soszynski has logged a slew of UFC wins, and after a heated two-fight series against Stephan Bonnar and a win against Goran Reljic, he has added "most exciting" to his list of accolades despite 11 pro losses.

"Those losses made me the fighter I am today, and if it wasn't for those losses, I wouldn't be here because I wouldn't know how to fight."

GEORGE SOTIROPOULOS

HEIGHT: **5' 10" (178 cm)**
WEIGHT: **155 lbs (70 kg)**
DATE OF BIRTH: **9 July 1977**
HOMETOWN: **Geelong, Victoria, Australia**

PROFESSIONAL RECORD: 14-3
UFC RECORD: 7-1

George Sotiropoulos came to *The Ultimate Fighter* in 2007 as a virtual unknown despite his solid 7-2 record. A Brazilian jiu-jitsu black belt with an impressive standup game as well, Sotiropoulos has been honing his game in the United States. His progress was never more evident than when he defeated lightweight contenders Joe Stevenson, Kurt Pellegrino and Joe Lauzon in succession before a 2011 loss to Dennis Siver at UFC 127.

PETE SPRATT *The Secret Weapon*

HEIGHT: **5' 9" (175 cm)**
WEIGHT: **170 lbs (77 kg)**
DATE OF BIRTH: **9 Jan. 1971**
HOMETOWN: **San Antonio, TX**

PROFESSIONAL RECORD: 23-16
UFC RECORD: 3-4

Actor, musician, former college football star—the question isn't why Pete Spratt fights; it's how does he find time for it?

"Fighting is first and foremost," he laughs. "That pays all the bills. It's when do I find time to do all the other stuff."

A 12-year MMA veteran, Spratt made a splash on the UFC scene in 2003 with an upset victory over previously unbeaten Robbie Lawler at UFC 42. Unable to capitalize, Spratt went back to the local circuit, but resurfaced in a 2005 bout with Josh Koscheck and on *The Ultimate Fighter 4*. He was released after losses to Marcus Davis and Tamdan McCrory in 2007, but he remains active in the sport today at 40.

BRIAN STANN *All-American*

HEIGHT: **6' 1" (185 cm)**
WEIGHT: **185 lbs (84 kg)**
DATE OF BIRTH: **24 Sept. 1980**
HOMETOWN: **Scranton, PA**

PROFESSIONAL RECORD: 11-3
UFC RECORD: 5-2
TITLES HELD: WEC LIGHT HEAVYWEIGHT CHAMPION

As a former WEC light heavyweight champion, Brian Stann knows how to handle himself in a fight—it's a trait he picked up as a Captain in the United States Marine Corps who was awarded the prestigious Silver Star for his valor in combat.

After completing his active duty, Stann began focusing on his fight career and after compiling a 2-2 record in the UFC at 205 pounds, he decided to try his hand at competing in the middleweight division.

The positive results were immediate, as he scored the first submission win of his career, finishing Mike Massenzio with a triangle choke, and followed that up with 2011 knockout victories over steel-chinned Chris Leben and top contender Jorge Santiago.

KALIB STARNES

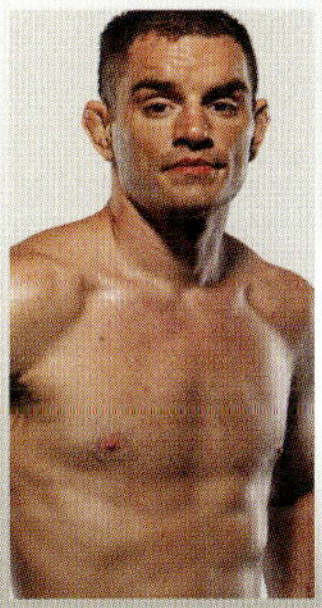

HEIGHT: **6' 3" (191 cm)**
WEIGHT: **185 lbs (84 kg)**
DATE OF BIRTH: **6 Jan. 1975**
HOMETOWN: **Surrey, British Columbia, Canada**

PROFESSIONAL RECORD: 14-7-1
UFC RECORD: 2-3

A well-rounded fighter from British Colombia, Kalib Starnes was a member of *The Ultimate Fighter 3* cast who quietly made his way into the UFC with a first-round submission of Danny Abbadi on the season finale card in 2006. A TKO loss to Yushin Okami followed four months later, but after an exciting win over Chris Leben and an equally compelling loss via cuts to Alan Belcher, he was marked as a fighter to watch. That made his bizarre defensive-minded performance against Nate Quarry at UFC 83 in April of 2008 even more baffling. Having proved his skill, it was strange to see Starnes turn tail and run for three rounds. But what wasn't surprising was that he was released from his contract after the unanimous decision defeat.

If not for his parents' intervention, we might be talking about Georges St-Pierre as the best right wing or center to ever play for the Montreal Canadiens. But when the native of St. Isidore wanted to play hockey and begin studying karate at the age of six, he was forced to choose one or the other.

"Everybody growing up here in Montreal plays hockey; it's the national sport," said St-Pierre. "I was playing hockey, but I wanted to do karate. My parents told me I needed to choose one sport because it was a lot of money and I would not be able to do both—so I chose karate."

In a lot of ways, St-Pierre's choice of karate was one of self-preservation as he was dealing with bullies in school. Eventually, that problem went away as St-Pierre developed mentally and physically under the tutelage of his Kyokushin karate teacher, Jean Couture.

"He told me to always respect my opponent," said St-Pierre of the late Couture. "When somebody in my school tried to be arrogant, he got kicked out. He also influenced me to always work hard, to never give up, and to always work to do what I want to do."

St-Pierre's parents and Couture laid the groundwork for the humble warrior whom fight fans have admired for years. But the mixed martial artist fighters have come to fear was just getting started on his road to the welterweight championship.

After Couture's passing, St-Pierre began looking toward mixed martial arts. He won his first amateur bout at 16, and then began supplementing his knowledge of karate by studying jiu-jitsu and wrestling. He was a quick study in both disciplines, as well as boxing, and he supplemented his education and combat sports studies with various odd jobs. Soon, St-Pierre was wrestling with the Canadian national team and training Brazilian jiu-jitsu with the renowned Nova Uniao team, and by 2002, the 20-year-old was scheduled to face unbeaten Ivan Menjivar in his first pro MMA bout on January 25 of that year.

"I was really nervous," said St-Pierre of the lead-up to the bout, which was held at the Verdun Auditorium in Montreal. "It was my first experience and I had a hard time sleeping a couple of weeks before."

Once the opening bell rang, though, it was obvious St-Pierre had the basic foundation of the fight game that would one day lead him to a championship.

"It finished in a controversy, but it was a pretty cool fight," said St-Pierre of the bout, which he won via TKO late in the first-round when the referee misunderstood Menjivar and believed he was verbally submitting while weathering a ground and pound assault from the Montreal native.

UFC 46: St-Pierre vs. Parisyan

The result stood, and thus began the mixed martial arts journey of St-Pierre.

"I thought I would be able to do this as a career, but I didn't know the sport was going to explode as much as it has right now," he said. "I thought it was going to get big, but not this fast."

GEORGES ST-PIERRE *Rush*

HEIGHT: **5' 11" (180 cm)**
DATE OF BIRTH: **19 May 1981**
WEIGHT: **170 lbs (77 kg)**
HOMETOWN: **Montreal, Quebec, Canada**

PROFESSIONAL RECORD: 21-2
UFC RECORD: 15-2
TITLES HELD: TWO-TIME UFC WELTERWEIGHT CHAMPION

UFC 48: St-Pierre vs. Hieron

It did, and St-Pierre was smack dab in the middle of the sport's emergence on the world scene. In January of 2004 he made his UFC debut with a three-round decision win over Karo Parisyan, and after a first-round TKO of Jay Hieron in the Octagon less than five months later, he was tabbed to face Matt Hughes for the vacant UFC welterweight belt in October of 2004. St-Pierre's year would end on a sour note with a first-round submission loss to Hughes, a fight that left more questions than answers. Sure, St-Pierre was young and talented, but did he have the mental toughness to become a world champion?

UFC 52: St-Pierre vs. Miller

Those answers would come soon enough. In 2005 St-Pierre tore through the division with extreme prejudice as he defeated Dave Strasser and Jason Miller, simply destroyed Frank Trigg, and stopped soon-to-be light-weight king Sean Sherk. It would be his 2006 fight with BJ Penn that truly showed his progression from talent-rich athlete to true mixed martial artist, as he rebounded from a horrific first round to win the next two stanzas and gut out a three-round decision. All that was left was to beat Hughes, and on November 18, 2006, he accomplished that feat with little effort as he dominated the longtime champion en route to a second-round TKO that allowed him to claim the UFC welterweight title.

UFC 65: St-Pierre vs. Hughes 2

UFC 50: St-Pierre vs. Hughes

But the fall, like all great falls in hindsight, seemed to be inevitable. Matt Serra, a veteran fighter whose shining attribute may be his tenacity, was waiting in the wings. While the New Yorker was loved by all, including opponents, when the bell rang, it was all business for Serra, a true believer in the adage that old age and treachery will overcome youth and skill. Translated to MMA terms, Serra's experience and gameplan on April 7, 2007 took apart a St-Pierre who found out in Houston, Texas that he was human just like everyone else. Maybe he was even more human than most of us, as a maelstrom of personal issues leading up to the fight took his focus off what most believed to be a routine first title defense.

UFC 69: St-Pierre vs. Serra

"After my loss with Serra I've been accused of not being mentally tough, but a lot of things happened to me, and it's really personal stuff," said St-Pierre, who was the victim of perhaps the biggest upset in UFC history when Serra knocked him out in the first round at UFC 69. "People read some stuff, but they have no idea what happened to me. The reason why I don't want to talk about it is because a lot of it concerns people in my family. I have a public life because I'm a professional fighter and I accept the fact that people talk about my personal life. But I don't want people to talk about the personal lives of people in my family who don't have a public life, who don't ask to have their personal lives written about. I think if any person went through what I went through last time, it would affect them. But I will never let that happen again."

UFC 79: St-Pierre vs. Hughes 3

Suddenly, Georges St-Pierre had to begin on the road back, and following what could be deemed the dark days of his fighting career, St-Pierre cleaned house in his personal and professional life. Having survived the slings and arrows of his detractors, from both in and out of the fight game, he has become a different, and maybe even better, fighter. A dominant decision win over Josh Koscheck in August of 2007 and a submission win over Hughes in their UFC 79 rubber match served to make St-Pierre a favorite over Serra leading into their rematch at UFC 83.

UFC 83: St-Pierre vs. Serra 2

On that night in his hometown of Montreal, St-Pierre destroyed Serra, regaining his title via second-round TKO at the Bell Centre. This time, he vowed not to let the belt go.

UFC welterwight champion Georges St-Pierre, April 19, 2008

"It (the second title reign) will be way more important because I know what it takes to be champion and I know what it takes to stay champion, and I'm going to stick to it."

Since that emotional victory, St-Pierre has shut the door on all challengers at 170 pounds, defeating Jon Fitch, BJ Penn, Thiago Alves, Dan Hardy, Josh Koscheck and Jake Shields in successive bouts. The next fighter to test St-Pierre's aura of invincibility is Nick Diaz.

UFC 100: St-Pierre vs. Alves

UFC 111: St-Pierre vs. Hardy

UFC 87: St-Pierre vs. Fitch

UFC 94: St-Pierre vs. Penn 2

UFC 124: St-Pierre vs. Koscheck 2

It's an unmatched reign of dominance over top-level opposition, yet St-Pierre—who coached on *The Ultimate Fighter 12* in 2010—remains unchanged by his place in the mixed martial arts world. He's still the same kid from St. Isidore, and one you expect would have done well in whatever he chose to dedicate his life to.

Maybe even the NHL?

"I don't know," he laughed. "I've got a lot of friends who play in the NHL, but it's one thing to say it, and one thing to do it, so I can't tell. But one thing I do know is that I made the right choice (becoming a fighter)."

Absolutely.

JEREMY STEPHENS

Lil' Heathen

HEIGHT: **5' 9" (175 cm)**
WEIGHT: **155 lbs (70 kg)**
DATE OF BIRTH:
25 May 1986
HOMETOWN:
Des Moines, IA

PROFESSIONAL RECORD: 19-6
UFC RECORD: 6-5

A stellar example of the kind of fighters that the state of Iowa produces, Jeremy Stephens is as tough as they come.

"I've been a fighter all my life," said the lightweight prospect. "I fought through some difficult times in my life and I feel like fighting's just for me. I was born a fighter and I want to be made into a champion."

Besides toughness, Stephens also has the skill and power to succeed in the Octagon, and that's garnered him a reputation as a top prospect. Winner of UFC bouts over Diego Saraiva, Cole Miller, Rafael dos Anjos, Justin Buchholz and Sam Stout, the hard-hitting Stephens scored another big victory when he knocked out Marcus Davis at UFC 125.

JOE STEVENSON *Daddy*

HEIGHT: **5' 7" (170 cm)** WEIGHT: **155 lbs (70 kg)** DATE OF BIRTH: **15 June 1982** HOMETOWN: **Victorville, CA**

PROFESSIONAL RECORD: 36-13 UFC RECORD: 8-7
TITLES HELD: *THE ULTIMATE FIGHTER 2* WELTERWEIGHT WINNER

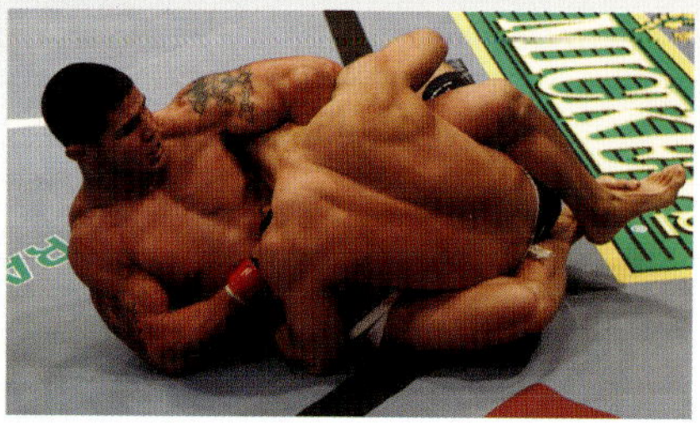

Joe Stevenson was done. After fighting professionally since the age of 16, compiling an impressive mixed martial arts record in over 30 fights, and basically doing whatever was asked of him as a fighter without reaping the benefits of such dedication, it was time to move on, time to think about doing something else for a living.

Then he got a phone call that would change his life, as he was asked to compete Spike TV's *The Ultimate Fighter*. The reality series saved the career of Forrest Griffin in its first season, and in its second, Stevenson got a new lease on his career after he beat Luke Cummo in the welterweight finale in 2006.

From there, the popular "Joe Daddy" dropped down to the lightweight division, squared off with the best in the game, and after a four-fight winning streak in 2006-07, he was pegged to face BJ Penn for the vacant UFC lightweight title.

Sometimes you learn more about a fighter in defeat than you do in victory, and that was the case when Stevenson fell short Penn at UFC 80, as he showed not only his prodigious talent, but the heart of a champion as he battled through a bad cut.

After that bout he dealt with a rollercoaster ride that led him to a 3-5 record, but in the summer of 2011, he began a new journey as a featherweight, one he hopes will eventually bring him his first title.

GEORGES ST-PIERRE PAGE 128

RICK STORY

The Horror

HEIGHT: **5' 10" (178 cm)**
WEIGHT: **170 lbs (77 kg)**
DATE OF BIRTH:
28 Aug. 1984
HOMETOWN:
Vancouver, WA

PROFESSIONAL RECORD: 13-3
UFC RECORD: 6-1

The rise of Washington's Rick Story up the welterweight ranks is happening with the speed of a runaway train. That's not surprising, given the fact that Story's intention every time out is to keep moving forward until he's broken his opponent's will.

Though he has only been training in mixed martial arts since 2004, he has come a long way in a short time. In 2009, Story made his UFC debut, and he has since defeated Brian Foster, Jesse Lennox, Nick Osipczak, Dustin Hazelett, Johny Hendricks and Thiago Alves in consecutive bouts.

SAM STOUT

Hands of Stone

HEIGHT: **5' 9" (175 cm)**
WEIGHT: **155 lbs (70 kg)**
DATE OF BIRTH:
23 April 1984
HOMETOWN:
London, Ontario, Canada

PROFESSIONAL RECORD: 17-6-1
UFC RECORD: 5-5

A striker who lives up to his "Hands of Stone" nickname, Sam Stout wasn't affected by the bright lights of the UFC in his debut against Spencer Fisher in 2006 as he pounded out a decision win.

In June of 2007, Stout got reacquainted with Fisher in a three-round war, and though Stout lost a three-round decision, he got back in the win column with victories over Per Eklund, Matt Wiman, Joe Lauzon and Paul Taylor that have pushed him back to the forefront in the lightweight division. With six "of the Night" bonuses, fans know a fight with "Hands of Stone" is going to be exciting.

STEFAN STRUVE

Skyscraper

HEIGHT: **6' 11" (210 cm)**
WEIGHT: **238 lbs (108 kg)**
DATE OF BIRTH:
18 Feb. 1988
HOMETOWN:
Beverwijk, Netherlands

PROFESSIONAL RECORD: 25-5
UFC RECORD: 5-3

With his only UFC losses coming to Junior dos Santos, Roy Nelson and Travis Browne, Struve is confident of his future, but also patient about getting there. Struve's ferocious attack has seen him defeat UFC veterans Colin Robinson, Mario Neto, Paul Buentello, Denis Stojnic and Chase Gormley.

"I've got a lot of growing to do and I need to get a lot better at everything, but I don't really consider myself a prospect anymore. We set a goal and in six or seven years I want to have the belt."

TIM SYLVIA PAGE 134

GENKI SUDO *Neo-Samurai*

HEIGHT: **5' 9" (175 cm)**
WEIGHT: **155 lbs (70 kg)**
DATE OF BIRTH: **8 March 1978**
HOMETOWN: **Hokkaido, Japan**

PROFESSIONAL RECORD: 16-4-1
UFC RECORD: 2-1

A free spirit in the best sense of the word, Genki Sudo built a stellar reputation among hardcore fans both at home and Japan as a true showman who could still deliver the goods when the bell rang. He even submitted Butterbean in a Japanese show in 2003. That bizarre victory aside, Sudo earned his keep in MMA because he always fought not only to win but to entertain, something lost on many fighters. Whether it's a flying triangle, his quirky movements or a quick flurry of fight-ending blows, Sudo always brought it, and as victories over Royler Gracie, Nate Marquardt and Mike Brown showed, the "Neo-Samurai" could fight at the top levels of the lightweight division as well.

MIKE SWICK *Quick*

HEIGHT: **6' 1" (185 cm)**
WEIGHT: **170 lbs (77 kg)**
DATE OF BIRTH: **19 June 1979**
HOMETOWN: **San Jose, CA**

PROFESSIONAL RECORD: 14-4
UFC RECORD: 9-3

A member of *The Ultimate Fighter 1* cast, Houston native Mike Swick certainly lived up to his nickname "Quick" in his first four UFC bouts. It only took him a combined five minutes and 10 seconds to take out Alex Schoenauer, Gideon Ray, Steve Vigneault and Joe Riggs in spectacular fashion. After defeating David Loiseau, Swick hit the middleweight wall in April of 2007 as he lost to Yushin Okami.

The defeat gave him the opening he needed to make a move down to welterweight, and he has since scored victories over Josh Burkman, Marcus Davis, Jonathan Goulet and Ben Saunders. While a couple of losses held him back, he expects to make a return to the top 10 in 2011.

DAIJU TAKASE

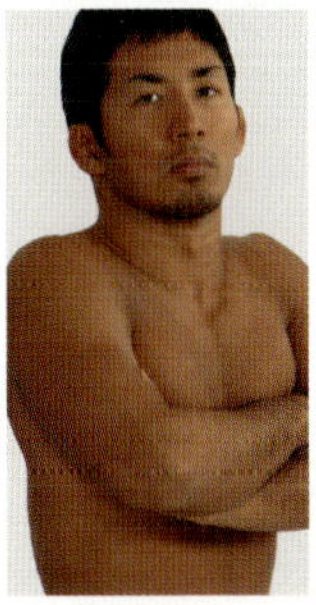

HEIGHT: **6' 0" (183 cm)**
WEIGHT: **183 lbs (83 kg)**
DATE OF BIRTH: **20 April 1978**
HOMETOWN: **Tokyo, Japan**

PROFESSIONAL RECORD: 9-13-2
UFC RECORD: 0-3

One of the hard luck stories in UFC history, Tokyo jiu-jitsu fighter Daiju Takase was a solid competitor who suffered from a case of poor career management, leading him into match after match against a killer series of opponents. Winless in three UFC bouts against Jeremy Horn, Kenichi Yamamoto and Fabiano Iha, Takase was nonetheless able to make a decent living fighting at home for the PRIDE and Pancrase organizations. His 9-13-2 record was obviously nothing to brag about, but he will always have one thing to brag about, and that's his 2003 triangle choke submission win over future UFC superstar Anderson Silva in PRIDE, a stunning upset that no one can ever take away.

OLEG TAKTAROV
The Russian Bear

HEIGHT: **6' 0" (183 cm)**
WEIGHT: **209 lbs (95 kg)**
DATE OF BIRTH: **26 Aug. 1967**
HOMETOWN: **Gorky, Russia**

PROFESSIONAL RECORD: 17-5-2
UFC RECORD: 6-2-1
TITLES HELD: UFC 6 TOURNAMENT WINNER

Calm, cool, and collected, Russia's Oleg Taktarov wasn't one to engage in any trash talk, but if you were courageous enough to step into an Octagon or ring with him, he would do whatever it took within the rules to get the victory.

A native of Siberia's Arzamas who moved with his family to Gorky, the young Taktarov was immediately smitten by the martial arts of judo and sambo, and he became a combat sports natural. After serving as a self-defense instructor in the Russian army, he went on to win numerous jiu-jitsu and sambo championships, and then traveled to America to chase a dream of becoming an actor.

That dream would have to wait, as he became a professional fighter competing in the UFC. At UFC 5 in April of 1995, he made his Octagon debut with a submission of Ernie Verdicia. Later that night he would lose a bloody battle to Dan Severn, but three months later he was back, and this time he ran the table, defeating Dave Beneteau, Anthony Macias and Tank Abbott to win the UFC 6 tournament.

Following a 33-minute draw with Ken Shamrock in a UFC 7 Superfight, Taktarov returned to the Octagon one more time in December of 1995, for the Ultimate Ultimate tournament. After two victories over Beneteau and Marco Ruas, he would lose a second time to Severn in his last UFC bout.

Still competitive in MMA up until 2008, when he defeated former UFC star Mark Kerr via kneebar, the leg lock master fought the likes of Renzo Gracie and Gary Goodridge (in the first PRIDE show) before finally hitting the big screen as an actor. Seen in such hits as *Bad Boys II*, *We Own The Night*, *Air Force One*, and *Predators*, Taktarov's dream may have been deferred, but he certainly had a heck of a tale to tell once he got there.

TIM SYLVIA *The Maine-iac*

HEIGHT: **6' 8" (203 cm)** DATE OF BIRTH: **5 March 1976**

WEIGHT: **255 lbs (116 kg)** HOMETOWN: **Davenport, IA**

PROFESSIONAL RECORD: 30-7
UFC RECORD: 9-4
TITLES HELD: TWO-TIME UFC HEAVYWEIGHT CHAMPION

All you really need to know about Tim Sylvia can be found in his second pro fight back in 2001. Long before "The Maine-iac" became only the second fighter in history to win the UFC heavyweight championship twice, he was pitted against Gabe Beauperthy in a small show in Friant, California.

UFC 41: Sylvia vs. Rodriguez

Just months into his pro MMA career, Sylvia was taken down and pounded unmercifully for two-plus rounds by Beauperthy. But with the seconds ticking away in the final round, Sylvia amazingly turned the tables on his more experienced opponent and was able to find the strength to submit Beauperthy late in the third.

"You can't teach heart," he said, still with a tinge of Maine in his voice. "Heart is something that you're born with and blessed with. Some guys take an ass whipping and just want to lay down. I don't lay down for no one."

One of the most underrated champions in UFC history, Sylvia was initially seen as simply an imposing figure with the power that came with being 6' 8" and nearly 265 pounds. And by his own admission, he didn't exactly take the hard road to the title when he first held it in 2003.

He had built up a gaudy unbeaten record with just one victory in the Octagon—over Wesley "Cabbage" Correira—and was seen as just another faceless up-and-comer with potential when the call came for him to face Ricco Rodriguez, then the organization's heavyweight champion and potential Golden Boy, at UFC 41.

"I had a 15-0 record, I came to the UFC and put on a good performance against Cabbage and all of a sudden they were like 'Hey, you want to fight for the title?'" remembered Sylvia, who quickly agreed to the championship match.

"It was a win-win situation," he explains. "You lose, and you're losing to the guy who's already the champ; and if you win, you become the champ. I didn't really have to work hard at it. It kinda flopped in my lap, we took it, and we capitalized on it."

Did he ever. After surviving an early triangle choke attempt by Rodriguez, Sylvia dominated, stopping the heavily-favored champion with strikes at 3:09 of the first round.

UFC 48: Sylvia vs. Mir

A new star was born, or so it seemed.

After Sylvia tested positive for an anabolic agent following a title defense win over Gan McGee in September of 2003 and relinquished his belt, it was like starting over. And starting from the bottom when you know what it's like at the top is anything but easy. Subsequent losses to Frank Mir and Andrei Arlovski didn't help matters either.

"I've overcome a lot of obstacles my whole life, so hard work is something I'm used to," he said.

He was going to need every ounce of it to not only get back in the heavyweight title mix. After putting aside the demons of doubt, he came back, starting with a first-round TKO of Mike Block in an IFC show in May of 2005, and then he returned to the Octagon with wins over Tra Telligman and Assuerio Silva.

UFC 68: Sylvia vs. Couture

The only thing left was to get his redemption against the seemingly unstoppable Arlovski at UFC 59, but seconds into the bout, Sylvia was knocked down by Arlovski, and it appeared that the second match would end up with the same result as the first. Sylvia bounced back up though, and as Arlovski moved in for the kill, it was the Maine native who landed first, with a short right hand that sent the soon to be ex-champion to the canvas face first. Moments later, the fight was halted, and once again Tim Sylvia was the UFC heavyweight champion, and in the process became only the second fighter in the organization's history to wear the belt twice (Randy Couture being the first).

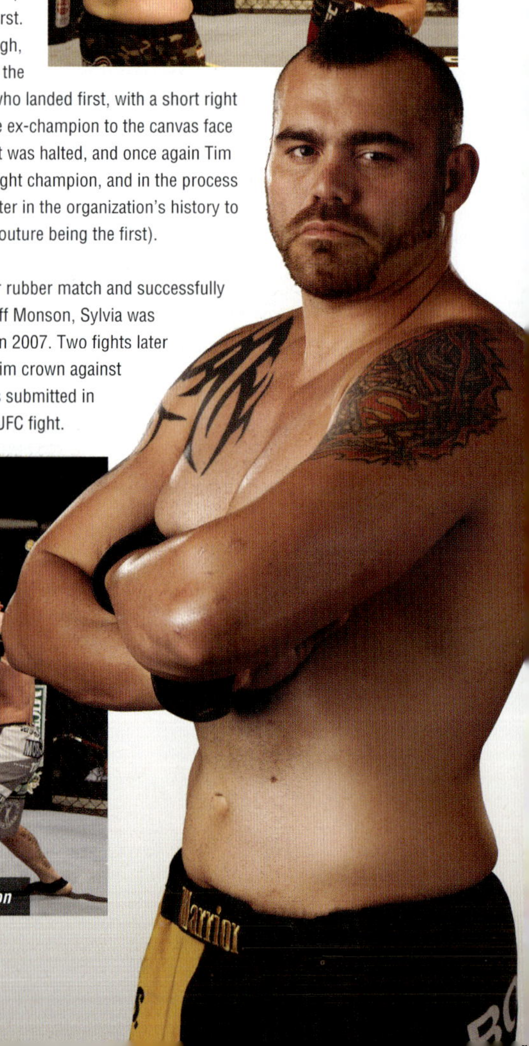

After beating Arlovski in their rubber match and successfully defending the belt against Jeff Monson, Sylvia was upset by Couture at UFC 68 in 2007. Two fights later he attempted to win the interim crown against Minotauro Nogueira, but was submitted in what was ultimately his last UFC fight.

UFC 65: Sylvia vs. Monson

EVAN TANNER

HEIGHT: **6' 0" (183 cm)**
WEIGHT: **185 lbs (84 kg)**
DATE OF BIRTH: **11 Feb. 1971**
DATE OF DEATH: **8 Sept. 2008**
HOMETOWN: **Amarillo, TX**

PROFESSIONAL RECORD: 34-8 UFC RECORD: 11-6
TITLES HELD: UFC MIDDLEWEIGHT CHAMPION

A native of Amarillo, Texas, Evan Tanner worked various jobs as a bouncer, a cable TV contractor, a framer building beach houses, a dishwasher, a baker, a ditch digger and a slaughterhouse worker before stumbling on to mixed martial arts in 1997.

Over the next 11 years, fighting would be a major part of his life, to the tune of 42 professional bouts, but he never considered himself a fighter.

"I always thought of myself as the poet, the writer or the philosopher—I never thought of myself as a fighter," he chuckled. "But here I am. I always had an idea of the flow of my life, but not exactly what I would be doing day to day. And fighting definitely wasn't something I thought I'd be doing."

He was good at it—very good, in fact. Over the course of his career, Tanner scored wins over Paul Buentello, Heath Herring, Ikuhisa Minowa, Justin McCully, Elvis Sinosic, Phil Baroni (twice) and Robbie Lawler. His biggest win, however, came at UFC 51 on February 5, 2005, when he stopped David Terrell in the first round to win the UFC middleweight championship.

Tanner would lose the belt to Rich Franklin in his first defense four months later, but the fans never abandoned him, and he returned that admiration, both in person and through his internet blogs.

"I wanted to give something back to the fans and let them know that I'm just a regular guy," said Tanner in early 2008. "Some of the guys forget that and get caught up in the lights, and I never want to forget that and that I'm one of the lucky ones that got a chance to get out there and do this."

He fell short in his final two bouts against Okami and Grove, but there was no keeping him down, and his off-time after the Grove bout in June of 2008 was filled with his typical adventures. Unfortunately, a camping trip turned tragic when his dirt bike ran out of gas and he got stranded in the desert. His body was found on September 8, 2008. He was only 37.

THIAGO TAVARES

HEIGHT: **5' 7" (170 cm)**
WEIGHT: **155 lbs (70 kg)**
DATE OF BIRTH: **8 Nov. 1984**
HOMETOWN: **Florianopolis, Brazil**

PROFESSIONAL RECORD: 19-4-1
UFC RECORD: 5-4-1

A proud native of Florianopolis, Brazil, Thiago Tavares was first exposed to mixed martial arts while watching the UFC exploits of the legendary Royce Gracie on television.

Aiming to emulate the success of his countryman, Tavares—one of the brightest prospects to emerge from Brazil in recent years—earned black belts in jiu-jitsu and judo, and showed flashes of brilliance in his UFC wins over Naoyuki Kotani, Jason Black, Michihiro Omigawa and Manny Gamburyan, and in spectacular yet losing efforts against Matt Wiman and Kurt Pellegrino.

In recent bouts in 2010-11, he has been erratic, fighting to a draw with Nik Lentz, submitting Pat Audinwood and getting knocked out by Shane Roller.

PAUL TAYLOR

Relentless

HEIGHT: **6' 0" (183 cm)**
WEIGHT: **155 lbs (70 kg)**
DATE OF BIRTH: **15 Dec. 1979**
HOMETOWN: **Walsall, England**

PROFESSIONAL RECORD: 11-6-1, 1 NC
UFC RECORD: 4-5

Paul Taylor may not make a lot of noise in pre-fight interviews, but when the Octagon door closes, the pride of Walsall, England lives up to his nickname "Relentless" with all-out attacks that have made him one of the UFC's most exciting fighters.

Despite UFC wins over Edilberto Crocota, Jess Liaudin, Gabe Ruediger and Peter Sobotta, this perfectionist isn't satisfied with his game yet.

"If you want to stay in the UFC you've really got to master everything and become an all-round fighter because guys will find your Achilles' heel in an instant."

TRA TELLIGMAN

Trauma

HEIGHT: **6' 2" (188 cm)**
WEIGHT: **233 lbs (106 kg)**
DATE OF BIRTH: **7 Feb. 1965**
HOMETOWN: **Dallas, TX**

PROFESSIONAL RECORD: 7-5
UFC RECORD: 1-4

Tra Telligman was another of a long line of Lion's Den fighters to make their way through the UFC, and with athleticism and standup power, it looked like he had potential to go a long way. It didn't happen, as he only managed one win in the Octagon, a 1997 submission of Brad Kohler, with losses coming against Vitor Belfort, Tim Sylvia and Pedro Rizzo (twice). Telligman, who also dabbled in pro boxing, did score a huge win in the PRIDE organization in 2001, decisioning top contender Igor Vovchanchyn in what was a personal milestone.

"When I started MMA, my goal was to beat the best," said Telligman in 2001. "To me, Igor Vovchanchyn was the best for a couple of years. He was my goal."

DAVID TERRELL *The Soul Assassin*

HEIGHT: **6' 0" (183 cm)**
WEIGHT: **185 lbs (84 kg)**
DATE OF BIRTH: **9 Jan. 1978**
HOMETOWN: **Santa Rosa, CA**

PROFESSIONAL RECORD: 10-2 UFC RECORD: 2-1

A gifted jiu-jitsu fighter who was pegged for greatness, Cesar Gracie black belt David Terrell instead saw his mixed martial arts career fall short of expectations due to repeated bouts with debilitating injuries.

An IFC and Grappler's Quest champion, Terrell debuted in the Octagon at UFC 49 with a stunning 24-second knockout of top contender Matt Lindland in August of 2004. That victory propelled him into a title shot against Evan Tanner at UFC 51, but the veteran Tanner pulled off the victory in a significant upset. After being sidelined for over a year, Terrell returned at UFC 59 with a first-round submission of Scott Smith in 2006, but injuries would again keep him from competition. He has not fought since.

PAULO THIAGO

HEIGHT: **5' 11" (180 cm)**
WEIGHT: **170 lbs (77 kg)**
DATE OF BIRTH: **25 Jan. 1981**
HOMETOWN: **Brasilia, Brazil**

PROFESSIONAL RECORD: 13-3 UFC RECORD: 3-3

As a member of the Brazilian police's Special Operations team, it's amazing that Brasilia's Paulo Thiago has found time for combat sports. Even still, he has been even more impressive in his time in mixed martial arts, compiling a stellar 13-3 pro record.

An intense and focused fighter with an iron jaw, Thiago is a six-time jiu-jitsu champion in Brasilia, and he has also earned five state championships. Yet it was his UFC debut, a first-round knockout of Josh Koscheck at UFC 95 that earned Upset of the Year honors, that made the world sit up and take notice. Wins over Jacob Volkmann and Mike Swick followed, with his only losses coming against Jon Fitch, Martin Kampmann and Diego Sanchez.

DIN THOMAS

HEIGHT: **5' 10" (178 cm)**
WEIGHT: **155 lbs (70 kg)**
DATE OF BIRTH: **28 Sept. 1976**
HOMETOWN: **Port St. Lucie, FL**

PROFESSIONAL RECORD: 26-9 UFC RECORD: 5-4

Din Thomas was one of a select group of fighters who helped put the lightweight division on the map in the United States in the late 90s and in the early part of the new millennium. Along the way he scored wins over Matt Serra, Jens Pulver and Fabiano Iha, losing only to elite fighters, like Caol Uno and BJ Penn.

It's a track record few fighters can claim, and in contrast to most of those who have been around as long as he has, the well-rounded Thomas is still relevant, as evidenced by his 6-2 record (3-2 in the UFC) since appearing on *The Ultimate Fighter 4* in 2006.

JOSH THOMSON *The Punk*

HEIGHT: **5' 10" (178 cm)**
WEIGHT: **155 lbs (70 kg)**
DATE OF BIRTH: **21 Sept. 1978**
HOMETOWN: **San Jose, CA**

PROFESSIONAL RECORD: 18-4, 1 NC UFC RECORD: 2-1

Josh Thomson is a fighter whose UFC career turned into a case of poor timing, as his three-bout run in the organization coincided with the temporary hiatus of the lightweight division from 2004 to 2006.

While in the UFC, "The Punk" impressed with his wins over Gerald Strebendt and Hermes Franca, and even though he got knocked out by Yves Edwards at UFC 49 in what turned out to be the last 155-pound fight in the UFC for nearly two years, his future was bright. Only it wasn't going to be in the Octagon. Instead, Thomson became a staple for the Strikeforce promotion, where he was lightweight champion from 2008 to 2009.

GLEISON TIBAU

HEIGHT: **5' 10" (178 cm)**
WEIGHT: **155 lbs (70 kg)**
DATE OF BIRTH: **7 Oct. 1983**
HOMETOWN: **Rio Grande Norte, Brazil**

PROFESSIONAL RECORD: 33-7 UFC RECORD: 9-5

Gleison Tibau showed he belonged in the UFC in 2006 as he put forth a courageous effort against Nick Diaz at UFC 65. Displaying stellar jiu-jitsu techniques that had Diaz in trouble, Tibau was eventually overpowered by the bigger fighter and stopped in the second round.

With the knowledge gained from the loss and a drop to the 155-pound weight class, Tibau got back in the Octagon and showed what he could truly do when he was on a level playing field as he scored notable victories over Kurt Pellegrino, Josh Neer, Terry Etim, Rich Clementi, Caol Uno and Jeremy Stephens while only suffering a handful of defeats against elite-level opponents.

MIGUEL ANGEL TORRES

HEIGHT: **5' 9" (175 cm)** WEIGHT: **135 lbs (61 kg)** DATE OF BIRTH: **18 Jan. 1981** HOMETOWN: **East Chicago, IN**

PROFESSIONAL RECORD: 38-4 UFC RECORD: 1-1 TITLES HELD: WEC BANTAMWEIGHT CHAMPION

For years, former WEC bantamweight champion Miguel Angel Torres toiled on the small show circuit, watching patiently as fighters with more size but less talent got television exposure and media attention while all he did was win fights. In 2007, Torres got his shot in the WEC, and finally had a chance to show fight fans what state-of-the-art bantamweight fighting looked like.

"When I was fighting at 135 and there was no place to go, everybody was like 'Dude, you gotta put on weight and get big,' but I always had faith in my size," said the protégé of the legendary Carlson Gracie. "I started seeing (former WEC featherweight champion) Urijah (Faber) fight at 145, the weight class started getting big, and I knew one day someone was gonna step up and put us in the spotlight."

He won the title from Chase Beebe in 2008, but that didn't mean the work was over. Torres' life got more intense as he became the target for all the world's top bantamweights. He embraced the pressure though, defeating Yoshiro Maeda, Manny Tapia and Takeya Mizugaki.

Shockingly, Torres' reign came to an end in 2009 when he was stopped by Brian Bowles, but after another tough defeat against Joseph Benavidez, he returned better than ever in defeating Charlie Valencia and Antonio Banuelos before losing a controversial decision to Demetrious Johnson at UFC 130.

ROBERTO TRAVEN

Spider

HEIGHT: **6' 3" 191 cm)**

WEIGHT: **227 lbs (103 kg)**

DATE OF BIRTH: **16 Sept. 1968**

HOMETOWN: **Rio de Janeiro, Brazil**

PROFESSIONAL RECORD: 6-4-1

UFC RECORD: 1-1

Roberto Traven was a gifted jiu-jitsu prodigy who earned his black belt in just four years, and as one of the top grapplers in the world, he won numerous titles including two world championships and an Abu Dhabi title.

In MMA, he tore out of the gate as well, winning his first five pro fights, including an 83-second finish of Dave Berry in his pro debut at UFC 11 in 1996. An injury kept Traven from continuing on in that night's tournament, and it would prove to be his final moment of glory in the Octagon, as he wouldn't be back until 2001, when he was shockingly submitted by rookie (and future world champion) Frank Mir at UFC 34.

FRANK TRIGG

Twinkle Toes

HEIGHT: **5' 10" (178 cm)**

WEIGHT: **170 lbs (77 kg)**

DATE OF BIRTH:

7 May 1972

HOMETOWN:

Las Vegas, NV

PROFESSIONAL RECORD: 21-8

UFC RECORD: 2-5

A graduate of the University of Oklahoma, Frank Trigg was a world-class collegiate wrestler, but it was in MMA where he truly made his mark.

A pro since 1997, Trigg made appearances in PRIDE and Shooto before debuting in the UFC in 2003 against welterweight champion Matt Hughes. Trigg fell short in that bout, but after wins over Dennis Hallman and Renato Verissimo, he engaged in a rematch with Hughes at UFC 52 in 2005 that is considered one of the greatest bouts in UFC history, despite his submission defeat to the future Hall of Famer.

Trigg's first stint in the UFC ended shortly thereafter, but he returned in 2009, losing consecutive fights against Josh Koscheck and Matt Serra.

CAOL UNO

HEIGHT: **5' 7" (170 cm)** WEIGHT: **155 lbs (70 kg)** DATE OF BIRTH: **8 May 1975** HOMETOWN: **Kanagawa, Japan**

PROFESSIONAL RECORD: 26-14-5 UFC RECORD: 3-5-2

One of the UFC lightweight division's first stars, Kanagawa, Japan's Caol Uno fought the elite during his first stint in the Octagon from 2001 to 2003, including BJ Penn (twice), Jens Pulver, Din Thomas, Yves Edwards and Hermes Franca. He would come perilously close to winning the lightweight crown twice, losing a five-round decision to Pulver in 2001 and battling to a five-round draw with Penn in 2003.

Following his departure from the UFC, he continued to face off against top-notch fighters like Joachim Hansen, Kid Yamamoto, JZ Cavalcante and Shinya Aoki in Japan, prompting a return to the organization after nearly six years away in 2009.

"I wanted to challenge in the UFC again," said Uno. "This is the category where the best fighters meet and I missed the unique atmosphere, which is very different from Japanese events."

This time around, Uno was unable to recapture the magic of his first go-round, as he could only manage an 0-2-1 record with losses against Spencer Fisher and Gleison Tibau.

The proud warrior is not through yet though, as he continues to compete in high-profile shows in his native Japan following his 2010 release from the UFC.

"I will keep winning one by one till I challenge the champion," said Uno. "The fans will always see my spirit in my fights."

A member of the world-renowned AKA camp that has produced such UFC standouts as Jon Fitch, Mike Swick, and Josh Koscheck, Cain Velasquez came to the Octagon in April of 2008 with only two pro fights, but the buzz around the two-time All-American wrestler from Arizona State University was deafening. His approach to fighting was just one reason.

"I'm non-stop, I don't get tired out there, my game is good all-around, and I want people to see that I'm gonna be the next big thing. That's what I want people to keep thinking about, that they can't wait to see me fight again."

The other reason was that Velasquez' respected coach, Javier Mendez, told anyone and everyone who would listen that the young man training at his gym was going to be the next world champion of the UFC. That could have been unbearable pressure on Velasquez, but there was a method to the madness.

"He (Mendez) said 'I'm saying this kind of stuff now to get you prepared so when it all comes down to it, you'll be ready,'" recalled Velasquez. "He's prepared me ever since I got here and he's talked me up."

It wasn't mere talk though, and Velasquez proved his mentor right as soon as the bell rang for his first UFC fight. After wins over Brad Morris and Jake O'Brien in 2008, Velasquez blazed through 2009 with TKOs of Denis Stojnic and Ben Rothwell and a stirring three-round decision win over Cheick Kongo that showed off even more of his ever-improving fight game. And while his fan base continued to grow as he upped his stellar pro record to 7-0, Velasquez wasn't letting the attention get to his head.

UFC 83: Velasquez vs. Morris

UFC Fight Night 14: Velasquez vs. O'Brien

"I'm a perfectionist in the gym," he said. "I know my skills all aren't where they're supposed to be or where I want them to be. I need everything to be perfect."

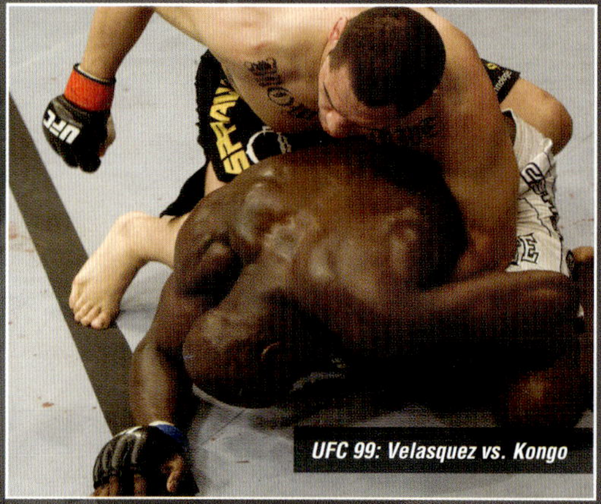

UFC 99: Velasquez vs. Kongo

CAIN VELASQUEZ

HEIGHT: **6' 1" (185 cm)** DATE OF BIRTH: **20 July 1982**

WEIGHT: **240 lbs (109 kg)** HOMETOWN: **San Jose, CA**

PROFESSIONAL RECORD: 9-0
UFC RECORD: 7-0
TITLES HELD: UFC HEAVYWEIGHT CHAMPION

UFC 104: Velasquez vs. Rothwell

UFC 121: Velasquez vs. Lesnar

They were at UFC 110 in Australia, as Velasquez made himself the number-one contender to Brock Lesnar's title with a first-round knockout of heavyweight superstar Minotauro Nogueira in the biggest fight of his young career.

UFC 110: Velasquez vs. Minotauro

The stage was now set for Velasquez to not only win his first title at UFC 121 in October of 2010, but to also become the first fighter of Mexican descent to win a major combat sports heavyweight title. Again, he took the pressure and attention in stride, and when fight night arrived in Anaheim, he wasn't intimidated; he was ready to take his belt home.

At the sound of the bell, Lesnar—a nearly 300-pound Mack truck with no brakes—charged at Velasquez, intent on taking out his most dangerous challenger before he could even get a shot off. It certainly wasn't what Velasquez and his coaches expected.

"We knew he was gonna come out with a lot of pressure, but we didn't think he was gonna come out that hard," recalled Velasquez. "It definitely did surprise me and I got into that brawl mode after that, but I just had to tell myself to relax and get back into the fight."

He got back into it in a big way, rising quickly from two Lesnar takedowns to score his own before finishing off the big man with a crushing series of ground strikes that brought a halt to the bout at 4:12 of the opening round.

Cain Velasquez was the new UFC heavyweight champion, and now he belonged to the world.

Yet despite his quiet nature, he embraced his newfound fame, and to celebrate his win and introduce him to the world that hasn't met him already, Velasquez went coast to coast and to Mexico to greet the media and fans.

It was a well-deserved victory tour. Now that it's over and he's recovered from surgery for a torn rotator cuff, Velasquez is ready to get back to work.

"I have the belt, but I have to go into every fight thinking that neither of us have a belt and I'm fighting for it," he said. "I have to stay hungry. And not just to win, but to go to the gym every day, give a hundred percent in every practice, to improve, and to evolve. If you don't, then you get left behind."

MIKE VAN ARSDALE

PROFESSIONAL RECORD: 10-5 UFC RECORD: 2-2

HEIGHT: **6' 2" (188 cm)** WEIGHT: **205 lbs (93 kg)** DATE OF BIRTH: **20 June 1965** HOMETOWN: **Waterloo, IA**

A 1998 NCAA wrestling champion for Iowa State, as well as a US Olympic alternate, Mike Van Arsdale has been a competitor his entire life. "Any athlete is going to compete to win," he said. "With proper training and with the right attitude, of course I'm going to be thinking, 'I'm gonna win this.'"

More often than not, in the world of mixed martial arts, he did.

PAUL VARELANS *The Polar Bear*

PROFESSIONAL RECORD: 9-9 UFC RECORD: 4-4

HEIGHT: **6' 8" (203 cm)** WEIGHT: **300 lbs (136 kg)** DATE OF BIRTH: **Unknown** HOMETOWN: **Sunnyvale, CA**

Few nicknames are as apt as the one given to Paul Varelans. Simply put, Varelans looks like a bear. Varelans was a staple of the early UFC broadcasts, a powerful and effective fighter who was resilient in the face of danger and who was able to beat fighters like Cal Worsham, Mark Hall and Joe Moreira consistently. Yet when he stepped up against the next level of competition, UFC standouts like Tank Abbott, Marco Ruas, Dan Severn and Kimo Leopoldo always prevailed. This pattern continued in his post-UFC career (which lasted until 1998), with losses against Igor Vovchanchyn and Mark Kerr.

JAMIE VARNER

PROFESSIONAL RECORD: 17-5-1, 2 NC TITLES HELD: WEC LIGHTWEIGHT CHAMPION
UFC RECORD: 1-1

HEIGHT: **5' 8" (173 cm)** WEIGHT: **155 lbs (70 kg)** DATE OF BIRTH: **12 Oct. 1984** HOMETOWN: **Phoenix, AZ**

Jamie Varner burst on the world scene with two exciting UFC fights in 2006-2007, defeating Jason Gilliam and losing to Hermes Franca. His success attracted the WEC, which brought him to the organization in 2007. By February of 2008, Varner had become the WEC lightweight champion after his third-round TKO of Rob McCullough. It looked like Varner was settling in for a long reign at the top. After a long layoff due to a hand injury, Varner fell short of victory against Ben Henderson in 2010, and then suffered a controversial draw against Kamal Shalorus and losses against Shane Roller and old rival Donald Cerrone.

CAIN VELASQUEZ PAGE 138

BRANDON VERA

The Truth

HEIGHT: **6' 3" (191 cm)** DATE OF BIRTH: **10 Oct. 1977**
WEIGHT: **205 lbs (93 kg)** HOMETOWN: **San Diego, CA**

PROFESSIONAL RECORD: 11-6 UFC RECORD: 7-6

Things were going pretty smoothly for Brandon Vera in his first year as a UFC fighter. Four fights, four wins, and four finishes, including a 69-second blitz of former heavyweight champion Frank Mir.

Then he hit a wall. A contract dispute with his now-former manager put "The Truth" on the shelf for nearly a year, and when he came back in 2007, a broken hand led to a decision loss to Tim Sylvia. A 2008 stoppage against Fabricio Werdum was deemed one of the most controversial in recent history.

You can't keep a good man down, and in order to get back on track, Vera decided to drop down to the 205-pound light heavyweight division to take on an even more formidable cast of characters. In July of 2008, he defeated Reese Andy, and after a tough decision loss to Keith Jardine, he was even more impressive in his stoppage of Michael Patt. In August of 2009, he turned back Krzysztof Soszynski at UFC 102, then faced his biggest test in Hall of Famer Randy Couture, but dropped a controversial three-round decision.

Discouraged, Vera was stopped in his next fight by future world champion Jon Jones in March of 2010 and engaged in a no-contest with Thiago Silva 10 months later. Yet as he prepares for his latest comeback, Vera is energized to use the ups and downs of his past to finally allow him to fulfill his potential.

"It's been a blessing in disguise," he said. "I've grown so much as a person growing up in the public eye. Fans have been able to see me at my highs and at my lows, and they're about to see me back on my highs again and they'll be able to understand that I'm a real person and not this super phenom that seems inhuman. I'm just like everybody else and I've had to go through my trials and tribulations to overcome my own demons and make this happen. I think that the fans will be able to appreciate me as a fighter and as a human being more because of this."

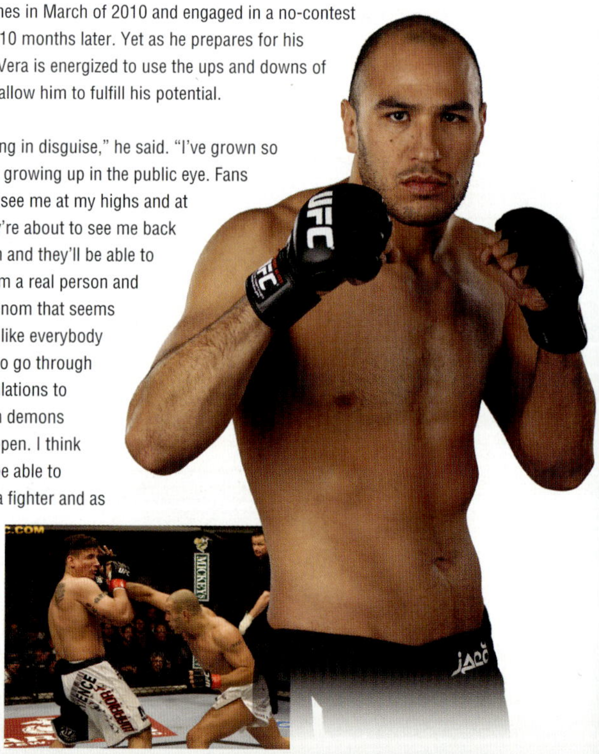

RENATO VERISSIMO *Charuto*

PROFESSIONAL RECORD: 8-5 UFC RECORD: 1-2

HEIGHT: **6' 1" (185 cm)** WEIGHT: **170 lbs (77 kg)** DATE OF BIRTH: **3 Aug. 1973** HOMETOWN: **Rio de Janeiro, Brazil**

If you take a glance at Renato Verissimo's UFC record of 1-2, you will undoubtedly wonder what the big deal was about "Charuto". During 2004 in the UFC, he was one of the welterweight division's toughest contenders, one who might have challenged for world title honors if not for a close decision loss to Matt Hughes at UFC 48. That defeat, and a subsequent one to Frank Trigg forced his release from the organization, but hardcore fans will always refer to his dominant win over Carlos Newton at UFC 46 and his pre-UFC victory over Gil Castillo, as well as his long association with BJ Penn in Hawaii.

JACOB VOLKMANN *Christmas*

HEIGHT: **5' 9" (175 cm)**
WEIGHT: **155 lbs (70 kg)**
DATE OF BIRTH: **5 Sept. 1980**
HOMETOWN: **White Bear Lake, MN**

PROFESSIONAL RECORD: 12-2 UFC RECORD: 3-2

Owner of one of the UFC's most unique nicknames, welterweight prospect Jacob "Christmas" Volkmann isn't likely to be spreading any holiday cheer when the bell rings, as he's won all but two of his 14 pro mixed martial arts bouts, including six by submission.

3-2 in the UFC, Volkmann—a three-time Division I All-American wrestler for the University of Minnesota who is also a practicing chiropractor—is coming off three consecutive wins over Ronys Torres, Paul Kelly and Antonio McKee. It's a nice rebound from the start of the swarming wrestler's UFC career, when he lost back-to-back bouts to Paulo Thiago and Martin Kampmann.

RON WATERMAN *H2O Man*

HEIGHT: **6' 2" (188 cm)**
WEIGHT: **260 lbs (118 kg)**
DATE OF BIRTH: **23 Nov. 1965**
HOMETOWN: **Greeley, CO**

PROFESSIONAL RECORD: 16-6-2 UFC RECORD: 2-1-1 TITLES HELD: WEC SUPER HEAVYWEIGHT CHAMPION

One of the more underrated heavyweights of the late '90s, Ron Waterman was a hulking presence in the Octagon who parlayed his wrestling ability and strength into victories over Chris Condo and Satoshi Honma.

It wasn't until after he left the organization after UFC 25 in 2000 that his career really took off, and he counted PRIDE wins over Valentijn Overeem and Kevin Randleman, both by keylock submission, among his biggest. In 2003 he became the first and only WEC super heavyweight champion, a title he defended against a former UFC titleholder Ricco Rodriguez in 2005. In recent years, he's stayed in the news for his work with current UFC heavyweight contender Shane Carwin, who he also coached in high school.

MARK WEIR *The Wizard*

HEIGHT: **6' 2" (188 cm)**
WEIGHT: **185 lbs (84 kg)**
DATE OF BIRTH: **19 Sept. 1967**
HOMETOWN: **Gloucester, England**

PROFESSIONAL RECORD: 20-17-1
UFC RECORD: 1-2

There were a host of memorable moments on the UFC's first UK card in 2002, but one that definitely rose to the top was Mark Weir's 10-second knockout of Eugene Jackson.

Weir, who ran off eight wins after a loss in his first pro fight, was an underdog, but he was the one who delivered a spectacular finish of the veteran.

Four months later, Weir was back to face Phillip Miller, and before the fight, he said, "I want to be the first British fighter to get a title shot and then actually win the UFC middleweight title." It was not to be, as he lost to Miller and to David Loiseau, but no one can ever take away his night of UFC glory.

CHRISTIAN WELLISCH *The Hungarian Nightmare*

HEIGHT: **6' 3" (191 cm)**
WEIGHT: **205 lbs (93 kg)**
DATE OF BIRTH:
13 Sept. 1975
HOMETOWN:
Sacramento, CA

PROFESSIONAL RECORD: 9-4
UFC RECORD: 2-3

A native of Hungary who now makes his home in Sacramento, California, multi-faceted Christian Wellisch had a short UFC career, but he delivered some memorable moments during his 2006-2009 run at heavyweight and light heavyweight.

Standing at an imposing 6' 3", Wellisch scored a solid three-round win over Australia's Anthony Perosh after a UFC 62 loss to Cheick Kongo in his Octagon debut. He was even more impressive in his first-round submission of Scott Junk. Losses to Shane Carwin and Jake O'Brien prompted Wellisch's release in 2009, but after retiring from the sport, the McGeorge School of Law graduate now runs his own law practice in California.

FABRICIO WERDUM *Vai Cavalo*

HEIGHT: **6' 4" (193 cm)**
WEIGHT: **231 lbs (105 kg)**
DATE OF BIRTH:
30 July 1977
HOMETOWN:
Porto Alegre, Brazil

PROFESSIONAL RECORD: 14-4-1
UFC RECORD: 2-2

As legend has it, Fabricio Werdum turned to Brazilian jiu-jitsu after falling victim to a triangle choke in a fight with his girlfriend's ex-boyfriend. Embarrassed by this turn of events, he began training fanatically, eventually earning his black belt and becoming one of the world's top jiu-jitsu practitioners.

In 2002, Werdum looked for a new challenge and found it in MMA, where he established himself as a top heavyweight contender in PRIDE and the UFC by beating the likes of Tom Erikson, Alistair Overeem, Gabriel Gonzaga and Brandon Vera.

Following a UFC 90 loss to Junior dos Santos, Werdum moved on to Strikeforce, where he stunned the world in June of 2010 with a 69-second submission win over former PRIDE heavyweight champion Fedor Emelianenko.

VERNON WHITE *Tiger*

HEIGHT: **6' 0" (183 cm)**
WEIGHT: **205 lbs (93 kg)**
DATE OF BIRTH: **3 Dec. 1971**
HOMETOWN: **Palo Alto, CA**

PROFESSIONAL RECORD: 26-34-2 UFC RECORD: 0-1-1

A quick look at the record of Vernon "Tiger" White, and you may be inclined to dismiss him as a mere opponent, but this original member of Ken Shamrock's famed Lion's Den was no pushover. Instead, he was an honest competitor who always came to fight, and though he would lose bouts against the elite of the game—like Chuck Liddell, Frank Shamrock and Lyoto Machida—when he was on he could pull off wins over Vladimir Matyushenko, David Terrell, Sam Hoger and Marvin Eastman.

In UFC action, the Pancrase vet fought to a draw against Ian Freeman at UFC 43 and slugged it out with Liddell at UFC 49 before being knocked out late in the first round.

JAMES WILKS *Lightning*

HEIGHT: **6' 1" (185 cm)** WEIGHT: **170 lbs (77 kg)** DATE OF BIRTH: **5 April 1978** HOMETOWN: **Laguna Hills, CA**

PROFESSIONAL RECORD: 8-4 TITLES HELD: *THE ULTIMATE FIGHTER 9* WELTERWEIGHT WINNER
UFC RECORD: 2-2

At 31 years old, James Wilks was one of *The Ultimate Fighter 9*'s elder statesmen, and it was clear during the season that the mature native of Leicester, England had come to the show to win a UFC contract, not get TV time.

"I've definitely gone up and down over the years—I want to fight, I don't want to fight—and you could see that by the sporadic nature of my fights," said Wilks at the time. "But this time I really thought, 'I don't want to regret anything.

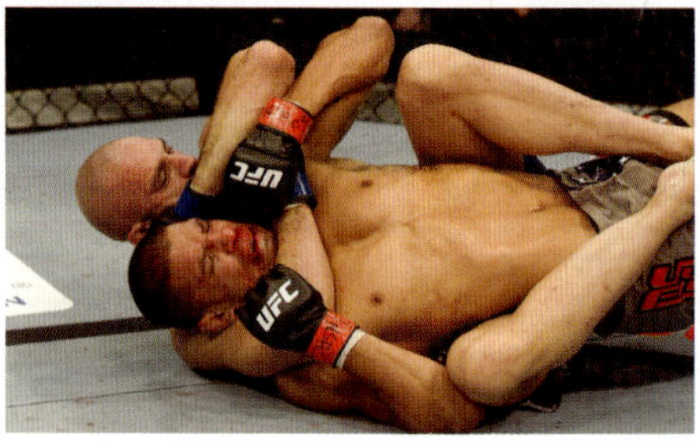

Now is the time, the UFC is the place to be, and I really want to make a go of it, test myself and see how far I can go.'"

In the end, he accomplished his mission, scoring three big wins on the show and then finishing off DaMarques Johnson to claim the season nine crown. A series of injuries has slowed his post-*TUF* progress down, but he has still managed to get in three fights, decisioning Peter Sobotta at UFC 115 and losing bouts to Matt Brown and Claude Patrick.

PETE WILLIAMS *El Duro*

HEIGHT: **6' 3" (191 cm)**
WEIGHT: **235 lbs (106 kg)**
DATE OF BIRTH: **10 July 1975**
HOMETOWN: **Dallas, TX**

PROFESSIONAL RECORD: 12-6
UFC RECORD: 3-5

A high school wrestling teammate of UFC vet Jerry Bohlander, Pete Williams followed his friend into mixed martial arts. As a member of Ken Shamrock's Lion's Den team, he won seven of his first eight bouts, competing both in the United States and in Japan's Pancrase and Rings organization.

The success earned him a call from the UFC, and in his first Octagon bout, he delivered the defining moment of his career as he knocked out Mark Coleman with a head kick at UFC 17 in 1998. A decision loss to former training partner Tsuyoshi Kosaka halted his momentum, but back-to-back wins against Jason Godsey and Travis Fulton earned him a UFC 23 title shot, which he lost via decision to Kevin Randleman. Williams retired after three UFC losses in 2001-02.

MATT WIMAN *Handsome*

HEIGHT: **5' 10" (78 cm)**
WEIGHT: **155 lbs (70 kg)**
DATE OF BIRTH: **19 Sept. 1983**
HOMETOWN: **Arvada, CO**

PROFESSIONAL RECORD: 13-5 UFC RECORD: 7-3

After battling through ups and downs for much of his career, *The Ultimate Fighter 5*'s Matt Wiman had the breakthrough year he was looking for in 2008, as he submitted Justin Buchholz and knocked out Thiago Tavares before finishing up in December with a Fight of the Night against Jim Miller.

Now 13-5 as a pro with seven UFC victories, the always-exciting Wiman (who made his Octagon debut before his stint on *TUF5*, losing a memorable UFC 60 bout to Spencer Fisher in 2006) has won three fights in a row over Shane Nelson, Mac Danzig and Cole Miller, allowing him to move from prospect to contender in the crowded 155-pound weight class.

EDDIE WINELAND

HEIGHT: **5' 7" (170 cm)**
WEIGHT: **135 lbs (61 kg)**
DATE OF BIRTH: **26 June 1984**
HOMETOWN: **Chesterton, IN**

PROFESSIONAL RECORD: 18-7-1
UFC RECORD: 0-1
TITLES HELD: WEC BANTAMWEIGHT CHAMPION

Eddie Wineland earned his stripes on the local mixed martial arts level for three years before making an impact in the WEC with a first-round knockout of Antonio Banuelos in May of 2006 that earned him the first-ever WEC bantamweight crown.

Though he lost that title to Chase Beebe 10 months later, he put together two impressive finishing victories and returned to the WEC in April of 2009. And though he was submitted in his first return bout by Rani Yahya, he bounced back with four consecutive wins, including two knockouts, earning him a call to the UFC, where he lost a competitive decision to Urijah Faber at UFC 128.

ANDRE WINNER

HEIGHT: **5' 11" (180 cm)**
WEIGHT: **155 lbs (70 kg)**
DATE OF BIRTH: **11 Sept. 1981**
HOMETOWN: **Leicester, England**

PROFESSIONAL RECORD: 12-5-1
UFC RECORD: 2-3

Andre Winner studied martial arts from the time he was a teenager, but it was at his first MMA training session that he saw UK star Dan "The Outlaw" Hardy and decided that he was going to make his mark in the sport as well. Nine wins on the local circuit followed until he got the call to compete on *The Ultimate Fighter 9*. While there, the Leicester standout continued his run of success, and while he wasn't able to pull off the victory in the finals against Ross Pearson, Winner's potential kept him fighting in the Octagon, where he scored wins over Rolando Delgado and Rafaello Oliveira and engaged in tough losses against Nik Lentz and Dennis Siver.

CAL WORSHAM

HEIGHT: **5' 10" (178 cm)**
WEIGHT: **230 lbs (104 kg)**
DATE OF BIRTH: **11 June 1963**
HOMETOWN: **Folsom, CA**

PROFESSIONAL RECORD: 11-10
UFC RECORD: 1-2

One of the first fighters to bring a taekwondo background into the Octagon, Cal Worsham showed no fear when the bell rang. That was never more evident than in his debut against 300-pounder Paul Varelans at UFC 6, where he took the fight to the "Polar Bear" before being knocked out by an elbow.

In his next two UFC bouts, Worsham stopped Zane Frazier and was halted by Tank Abbott, but he continued fighting after his days in the promotion were done.

In recent years, Worsham has stayed active, doing some matchmaking and even competing on the same card as his son Hunter. In his last bout, he lost a decision to UFC Hall of Famer Dan Severn in February of 2011.

NORIFUMI YAMAMOTO

Kid

HEIGHT: **5' 4" (163 cm)**
WEIGHT: **135 lbs (61 kg)**
DATE OF BIRTH: **15 March 1977**
HOMETOWN: **Kanagawa, Japan**

PROFESSIONAL RECORD: 18-4, 1 NC
UFC RECORD: 0-1

A Japanese superstar who has thrilled fight fans for nearly a decade, Norifumi "Kid" Yamamoto finally made his UFC debut in 2011 against Demetrious Johnson, but fell short via decision in their UFC 126 bout.

Despite this setback, Yamamoto's fan base has not waned, and for good reason. A charismatic fighter in and out of the Octagon, Yamamoto (a former high school wrestling champion in the United States) possesses world-class wrestling as well as knockout power, and after headline-making wins over Royler Gracie, Caol Uno and Genki Sudo, he was long rumored for Superfights with Urijah Faber and Miguel Angel Torres before finally making his move Stateside in 2011. Now he pursues a UFC bantamweight crown.

YOSHIYUKI YOSHIDA

Zenko

HEIGHT: **5' 11" (180 cm)**
WEIGHT: **170 lbs (77 kg)**
DATE OF BIRTH: **10 May 1974**
HOMETOWN: **Tokyo, Japan**

PROFESSIONAL RECORD: 11-6
UFC RECORD: 2-3

Owner of a fourth-degree black belt in judo and numerous titles in the art, Yoshiyuki Yoshida made a smooth transition to the world of MMA.

Since his debut in 2005, he has won 11 of 17 pro fights, and though he was a relative unknown in the United States when he entered the Octagon for the first time against *The Ultimate Fighter*'s Jon Koppenhaver in May of 2008, less than a minute later, a packed house in Las Vegas knew who he was after his impressive submission win. Losses in three of his next four UFC bouts followed against Josh Koscheck, Anthony Johnson and Mike Guymon, leading to his 2010 release.

BEST OF A NATION

BRAZIL

JOSE ALDO

UFC Debut: *UFC 129 – W5 Mark Hominick*
Key UFC Win: *UFC 129 – W5 Mark Hominick*

MANAUS

Kicking off his Zuffa career in the WEC organization in June of 2008, Jose Aldo quickly established himself as one of the best—and most feared—featherweights on the planet with his devastating finishes of Alexandre Nogueira, Jonathan Brookins and Cub Swanson, among others. In November of 2009, he became the 145-pound champ of the WEC with a TKO of Mike Brown, and after subsequent victories against Urijah Faber and Manny Gamburyan, he was crowned UFC champ after the merge of the two organizations. In his first defense, he decisioned Mark Hominick at UFC 129.

VITOR BELFORT

UFC Debut: *UFC 12 – TKO1 Tra Telligman*
Key UFC Win: *Ultimate Brazil – TKO1 Wanderlei Silva*

RIO DE JANEIRO

No one will ever forget their first look at Vitor Belfort back in 1997, as the 19-year-old lived up to his nickname "The Phenom" at UFC 12 with a blistering striking attack that saw him finish Tra Telligman and Scott Ferrozzo in a combined two minutes. And though he would go on to win the UFC light heavyweight title and also put together a notable run in PRIDE, it has always seemed like fans have kept Belfort in a time capsule, remembering him only as a teenager with blazing hand speed and fight ending power.

MURILO BUSTAMANTE

UFC Debut: *UFC 25 – Wsub2 Yoji Anjo*
Key UFC Win: *UFC 37 – Wsub3 Matt Lindland*

RIO DE JANEIRO

Before Demian Maia dazzled UFC fans with his otherworldly ground game, the gold standard for Brazilian ground wizardry in the Octagon was the equally soft-spoken Murilo Bustamante, who became the second UFC middleweight champion in 2002 when he stopped Dave Menne in two rounds. But even more impressive was his first title defense and last UFC bout, when he submitted contender Matt Lindland not once but twice in the same match. Now that's a jiu-jitsu black belt.

ROYCE GRACIE

UFC Debut: *UFC 1 – Wsub1 Art Jimmerson*
Key UFC Win: *UFC 3 – Wsub1 – Kimo Leopoldo*

RIO DE JANEIRO

He's the man who started it all in 1993, and it may be safe to say that if not for Royce Gracie submitting three consecutive opponents in one night to win the UFC 1 tournament—in the process introducing the United States to Gracie jiu-jitsu—there would be no UFC today. That's how amazing it was for the skinny kid from Brazil to defeat bigger and stronger athletes night in and night out, and every active fighter today owes him a debt of gratitude for his contributions to the sport of mixed martial arts.

LYOTO MACHIDA

UFC Debut: *UFC 67 – W3 Sam Hoger*
Key UFC Win: *UFC 98 – KO2 Rashad Evans*

SALVADOR

Taught karate by his father Yoshizo since he was a child, Lyoto Machida eventually brought his family's art into MMA and the UFC Octagon, where he immediately and consistently baffled opponents who had no idea how to defend against his unorthodox attacks. By mid-2009, Machida held victories over BJ Penn, Tito Ortiz, Stephan Bonnar and Rashad Evans, and although he would suffer the first two losses of his career in back-to-back bouts against Shogun Rua and Rampage Jackson, he bounced back with a spectacular knockout of Hall of Famer Randy Couture at UFC 129.

MINOTAURO NOGUEIRA

UFC Debut: *UFC 73 – W3 Heath Herring*
Key UFC Win: *UFC 102 – W3 Randy Couture*

BAHIA

A PRIDE legend whose reign as the organization's first heavyweight champion lasted nearly two years, Antonio Rodrigo "Minotauro" Nogueira survived a horrific childhood accident to become one of the greatest heavyweights of all-time. In 2007, he made his way to the UFC, and he earned the interim heavyweight crown with a submission win over Tim Sylvia in 2008. He lost that belt to Frank Mir after their stint as coaches on *The Ultimate Fighter 8*, but an unforgettable three-round win over fellow legend Randy Couture reminded fight fans just who "Minotauro" was.

PEDRO RIZZO

UFC Debut: *Ultimate Brazil – KO1 Tank Abbott*
Key UFC Win: *UFC 30 – KO2 Josh Barnett*

RIO DE JANEIRO

Clearly one of the best fighters to never be crowned champion in the UFC, Pedro "The Rock" Rizzo had finishing power, a solid chin and some of the sport's most devastating leg kicks. Unfortunately, he could never match his big wins over Josh Barnett, Dan Severn, Mark Coleman and Tank Abbott in three championship bouts against Randy Couture (twice) and Kevin Randleman.

SHOGUN RUA

UFC Debut: *UFC 76 – Lsub3 Forrest Griffin*
Key UFC Win: *UFC 113 – KO1 Lyoto Machida*

CURITIBA

An aggressive Muay Thai standout whose 12-1 run through PRIDE resulted in a 2005 Grand Prix championship and recognition as a premier light heavyweight, Mauricio "Shogun" Rua struggled in his early UFC run, which began with a submission loss to Forrest Griffin in 2007. But after multiple knee surgeries, knockouts of Hall of Famers Mark Coleman and Chuck Liddell and a controversial loss to Lyoto Machida, Rua found his stride with a first-round knockout of Lyoto Machida that earned him the UFC light heavyweight title in 2010. He lost the belt less than a year later to Jon Jones, but he planned a quick return to the Octagon in 2011.

ANDERSON SILVA

UFC Debut: *UFN5 – KO1 Chris Leben*
Key UFC Win: *UFC 101 – KO1 Forrest Griffin*

CURITIBA

One of mixed martial arts' all-time greats, Anderson Silva burst onto the UFC scene in 2006 with a 49-second blitz of Chris Leben. He never looked back, becoming a record-shattering middleweight titleholder, an equally devastating light heavyweight and a dynamic role model for fighters who want to see what happens when you mix technique, athleticism, speed, power and a world-class ground game. Yes, Anderson Silva has it all, and he's showing no signs of slowing down yet.

WANDERLEI SILVA

UFC Debut: *Ultimate Brazil – TKO by 1 Vitor Belfort*
Key UFC Win: *UFC 84 – KO1 Keith Jardine*

CURITIBA

It's hard to call someone nicknamed "The Axe Murderer" a beloved figure, but that's just the way fight fans feel about Wanderlei Silva. Part of that loyalty is due to his accessibility outside of competition, but when it comes down to it, fighters and fans love Silva because of his ferocious attack when the bell rings, a style perfected during a 22-4-1, 1 NC run in Japan's PRIDE organization. And while his two stints in the Octagon haven't matched that success, his wins over Keith Jardine and Michael Bisping have shown Silva to still be a threat to anyone he faces.

CANADA

JONATHAN GOULET

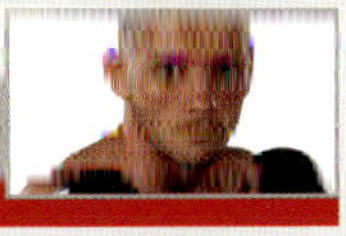

UFC Debut: *UFC Fight Night 2 – TKO3 Jay Hieron*
Key UFC Win: *UFC 83 – TKO2 Kuniyoshi Hironaka*
VICTORIAVILLE

Unfortunately for Jonathan "The Road Warrior" Goulet, fight fans more readily remember his losses to fighters like Mike Swick and Duane Ludwig than his stirring wins over Kuniyoshi Hironaka, Jay Hieron and Luke Cummo. [illegible] performances in victory and defeat.

SAM STOUT

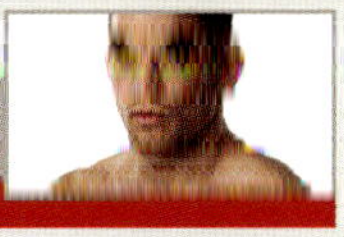

UFC Debut: *UFC 58 – W3 Spencer Fisher*
Key UFC Win: *UFC 108 – W3 Joe Lauzon*
LONDON

It would have been easy to put Sam Stout's 2007 loss to Spencer Fisher as his key fight because it remains one of the greatest fights ever witnessed in the Octagon. And for a while, that was Stout's MO—win or lose, he was going to bring it and put on a great fight. But at the same time, if a contender could get him to the mat, Stout's odds of losing [illegible] greatly. In January of 2010 though, Stout put on a career-defining performance in his victory over Joe Lauzon. He followed up with a jaw-shattering knockout of Yves Edwards. This marked Stout's first stoppage in the UFC.

MARK BOCEK

UFC Debut: *UFC 73 – TKO by 1 Frankie Edgar*
Key UFC Win: *UFC 124 – Wsub1 Dustin Hazelett*
TORONTO

After a slow start to his UFC career that saw him lose two of his first three fights (albeit to Frankie Edgar and Mac Danzig), Bocek started to warm up in late 2008 with a win over Alvin Robinson. And once he settled in with the American Top Team squad, Bocek's game really took off. Now the Brazilian jiu-jitsu black belt is firmly established as one of those rare fighters who can finish anyone off in seconds if he gets his opponent to the mat.

JASON MACDONALD

UFC Debut: *Ortiz vs Shamrock 3 – Wsub1 Ed Herman*
Key UFC Win: *Ortiz vs Shamrock 3 – Wsub1 Ed Herman*
NEW GLASGOW

Despite his status as one of the Canadian fight scene's top veterans, few expected MacDonald to defeat *TUF3* finalist Ed Herman in Herman's first post-*TUF* fight. MacDonald did it though, and he went on to beat two more *TUF* alumni (Chris Leben and Rory Singer), earning him the nickname "The *TUF* Killer". But MacDonald also performed against non-*TUF* fighters, defeating Joe Doerksen and Jason Lambert and giving Demian Maia hell for nearly three rounds in an entertaining ground war. MacDonald's only issue in the UFC was beating that next level of competition, like Rich Frankin, Maia and Yushin Okami, and his up-and-down performances kept him from moving into true contender status.

GARY GOODRIDGE

UFC Debut: *UFC 8 – KO1 Paul Herrera*
Key UFC Win: *UFC 8 – KO1 Paul Herrera*
BARRIE

Few will ever forget the devastating barrage of elbows that produced Goodridge's first-round knockout of Paul Herrera, and as one of the UFC's early pioneers, he battled it out with a Who's Who of early standouts like Jerry Bohlander, Don Frye (twice) and Mark Coleman. Goodridge actually went on to more acclaim in Japan's PRIDE organization, where he was a mainstay for years, but to early UFC fans, "Big Daddy" will always be associated with the Octagon.

PATRICK COTE

UFC Debut: *UFC 50 – L3 Tito Ortiz*
Key UFC Win: *UFC Fight Night 12 – TKO1 Drew McFedries*
RIMOUSKI

After an 0-4 start to his UFC career, no one would have expected to see Cote on this list. But the hard-nosed Cote was not about to go away that easily, and after he fought his way into the final of *The Ultimate Fighter 4*, he made a run at the title with consecutive Octagon victories over Scott Smith, Kendall Grove, Drew McFedries and Ricardo Almeida. In his shot at the belt at UFC 90 in 2008, Cote became the first man to extend Anderson Silva into the third round of a UFC fight before a knee injury sent Cote down to defeat.

KRZYSZTOF SOSZYNSKI

UFC Debut: *TUF8 Finale – Wsub2 Shane Primm*
Key UFC Win: *UFC 110 – TKO3 Stephan Bonnar*
WINNIPEG

Once seen as a journeyman whose erratic performances kept him from getting to the next level, Soszynski hit his stride after a stint on *The Ultimate Fighter 8*, and has since won five of his six UFC fights. His only loss being via decision to Brandon Vera. In February of 2010, he stopped Stephan Bonnar in an exciting three-rounder that was revisited months later, and those two bouts lifted Soszynski from journeyman to contender.

CARLOS NEWTON

UFC Debut: *UFC 17 – Wsub1 Bob Gilstrap*
Key UFC Win: *UFC 31 – Wsub3 Pat Miletich*
NEWMARKET

With a 3-4 record, you may wonder how Newton gets such a lofty ranking. But the talented and charismatic "Ronin" is a former UFC champion, and three of those four Octagon losses came to Matt Hughes (twice) and Dan Henderson. More importantly, while we're judging Octagon performances here, guys like Newton were handicapped a bit by the fact that the UFC wasn't running shows at the rate it is now. If a prime Carlos Newton was able to compete in the Octagon three or four times a year, his record might be a little different. Newton's prime was from 2000 to 2003. During that time, he went 2-2 in the UFC, beating Pat Miletich and Pete Spratt and losing twice to Hughes. Outside of the Octagon during that period, he went 5-2, beating the likes of Jose Landi-Jons, Johil de Oliveira and Renzo Gracie, losing only to future middleweight champs Dave Menne and Anderson Silva. Newton was the real deal.

DAVID LOISEAU

UFC Debut: *UFC 42 – KO1 Mark Weir*
Key UFC Win: *UFC 53 – TKO2 Charles McCarthy*
MONTREAL

Go to any UFC event, and you will see David Loiseau's amazing spinning back kick of Charles McCarthy during the pre-fight highlight reel that plays in the arena. That fight is an apt one when it comes to the career of "The Crow", as the victory came in the middle of a three-fight run (Gideon Ray and Evan Tanner were the others) that saw Loiseau tearing through all comers. That trio of victories earned the elbow strike master a shot at the middleweight crown held by Rich Franklin, and though Loiseau would lose to the champ that night in 2006, his display of heart and determination throughout the five-rounder won't be soon forgotten.

GEORGES ST-PIERRE

UFC Debut: *UFC 46 – W3 Karo Parisyan*
Key UFC Win: *UFC 65 – TKO2 Matt Hughes*
MONTREAL

The no-brainer of no-brainers: with 15 UFC wins (ten more than his closest competitor on the all-time Canadian UFC win list, Jason MacDonald), two UFC welterweight titles and a cemented place in the upper reaches of the mythical pound for pound list, St-Pierre is the best of the best when it comes to Canadian MMA. Owner of victories over Hughes (twice), BJ Penn (twice), Matt Serra, Jon Fitch, Josh Koscheck (twice), and Thiago Alves, St-Pierre already has a stellar resume, and if his December 2010 win over Koscheck is any indication, he's showing no signs of slowing down either.

JAPAN

YOSHIHIRO AKIYAMA

UFC Debut: UFC 100 – W3 Alan Belcher
Key UFC Win: UFC 100 – W3 Alan Belcher
OSAKA

A skilled judo black belt who has no qualms about standing and trading with anyone, Yoshihiro Akiyama made his UFC debut to much fanfare in 2009, and he didn't disappoint as he decisioned Alan Belcher over three exciting rounds. The bout earned Akiyama Fight of the Night honors, and he went on to win the award in his next two bouts as well—tough losses against Chris Leben and Michael Bisping.

TAKANORI GOMI

UFC Debut: UFN21 – Lsub3 Kenny Florian
Key UFC Win: UFC Live 2 – KO1 Tyson Griffin
KANAGAWA

The only man to hold the PRIDE lightweight title, Takanori Gomi ruled the Japanese organization with an iron fist, going 13-1 with 1 NC from 2004 to 2007. In 2010, he arrived in the Octagon, and he struggled in losses to Kenny Florian and Clay Guida, but in August of 2010 he showed off that "Fireball Kid" style with an impressive knockout of Tyson Griffin.

YUSHIN OKAMI

UFC Debut: UFC 62 – W3 Alan Belcher
Key UFC Win: UFC 122 – W3 Nate Marquardt
KANAGAWA

The most successful Japanese fighter in UFC history, Yushin Okami is a powerhouse in the Octagon who is a tough win for anyone at 185 pounds. Winner of 10 of 12 bouts, including victories over Nate Marquardt, Mark Munoz, Mike Swick and Evan Tanner, Okami is the last man to defeat Anderson Silva (albeit via disqualification in a non-UFC bout), and in August of 2011, he saw his long-awaited shot at the middleweight crown.

KAZUSHI SAKURABA

UFC Debut: UFC Japan – NC1 Marcus Silveira
Key UFC Win: UFC Japan – Wsub1 Marcus Silveira
AKITA

Kazushi Sakuraba's UFC career lasted all of one night, but he was unbeaten with one win and one no contest that night, earning him the Ultimate Japan heavyweight tournament title. A true legend of the game, it is the rest of Sakuraba's career that earns him a mention here though, as he became a PRIDE superstar dubbed "The Gracie Hunter" for his wins over four of MMA's first family.

CAOL UNO

UFC Debut: UFC 30 – L5 Jens Pulver
Key UFC Win: UFC 32 – KO1 Fabiano Iha
KANAGAWA

A two-time title challenger in the UFC, Caol Uno gave Jens Pulver and BJ Penn fits in those championship fights but was unable to secure the victory and become the first UFC champion from Japan. As for the rest of his two UFC stints, he defeated solid contenders like Yves Edwards and Din Thomas, but the big win always eluded him.

ENGLAND

MICHAEL BISPING

UFC Debut: TUF3 Finale – TKO2 Josh Haynes
Key UFC Win: UFC 105 – TKO2 Denis Kang
MANCHESTER

Bold and brash, but willing to back it up in the Octagon, "The Count" became the great hope of UK MMA as soon as he won *The Ultimate Fighter 3* in 2006, and his star kept rising with each passing fight. Starting in the Octagon as a light heavyweight, Bisping moved to 185 pounds after suffering his first pro loss to Rashad Evans, and he has since won seven of nine fights, defeating Chris Leben, Dan Miller, Jorge Rivera and Yoshihiro Akiyama. His only losses have come against former PRIDE champions Dan Henderson and Wanderlei Silva.

IAN FREEMAN

UFC Debut: UFC 24 – Lsub1 Scott Adams
Key UFC Win: UFC 38 – TKO1 Frank Mir
SUNDERLAND

The first Brit to have any significant success in the Octagon, Ian "The Machine" Freeman bounced back from a debut loss against Scott Adams in 2000 to win his next three UFC bouts. The most notable was his 2002 win over previously unbeaten Frank Mir, a victory made even more poignant because it came on the heels of his father's death the day before, a passing he wasn't made aware of until after the bout.

DAN HARDY

UFC Debut: UFC 89 – W3 Akihiro Gono
Key UFC Win: UFC 99 – W3 Marcus Davis
NOTTINGHAM

With a bright red Mohawk, a willingness to bang it out on the feet, and no qualms about engaging in smack talk to promote a fight, Dan Hardy soared up the welterweight ranks, winning four in a row to become the first British fighter to earn a shot at a UFC title. A five-round decision loss to Georges St-Pierre followed in March of 2010, sending "The Outlaw" on a three-fight skid.

ROSS PEARSON

UFC Debut: TUF9 Finale – W3 Andre Winner
Key UFC Win: UFC 127 – W3 Spencer Fisher
SUNDERLAND

A gritty battler who won *The Ultimate Fighter 9*, Ross Pearson's blue collar work ethic in the Octagon has won him scores of fights and fans. Owner of victories over veterans Spencer Fisher, Aaron Riley and Dennis Siver, Pearson may end up being the UK's greatest hope for world title honors in the coming years.

MARK WEIR

UFC Debut: UFC 38 – KO1 Eugene Jackson
Key UFC Win: UFC 38 – KO1 Eugene Jackson
GLOUCESTER

When you blast out an opponent in 10 seconds, like Mark Weir did to Eugene Jackson at UFC 38 in July of 2002, expectations suddenly shoot through the roof. But the dynamic striker was unable to capitalize on that first Octagon win, and by mid-2003 he was out of the organization after back-to-back losses to Phillip Miller and David Loiseau.

USA

MARK COLEMAN

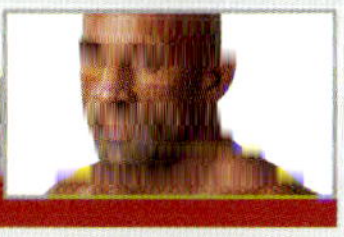

UFC Debut: UFC 10 – Wsub1 Moti Horenstein
Key UFC Win: UFC 12 – Wsub1 Dan Severn

COLUMBUS

The "Godfather of Ground and Pound," Mark Coleman went from national wrestling champion to Octagon superstar in the space of three wins on one night in 1996. As he trounced Moti Horenstein, Gary Goodridge and Don Frye to win the UFC 10 tournament, he introduced a new technique into the mixed martial arts lexicon. After three more wins that included a UFC heavyweight championship victory over Dan Severn, it would be 12 more years before he tasted victory again in the UFC (against Stephan Bonnar), but no one will ever forget the accomplishments of "The Hammer".

RANDY COUTURE

UFC Debut: UFC 13 – Wsub1 Tony Halme
Key UFC Win: UFC 43 – TKO3 Chuck Liddell

LAS VEGAS

Would a guy many called "Captain America" not find a place on this list? That would be blasphemy. And thankfully, UFC Hall of Famer Randy Couture earned every one of the accolades he received over the course of his nearly 14-year pro career. A three-time heavyweight and two-time light heavyweight champion, Couture fought and beat some of the best of all-time, including Chuck Liddell, Tito Ortiz, Vitor Belfort and Mark Coleman, cementing a legacy that stands head and shoulders above the rest.

RICH FRANKLIN

UFC Debut: UFC 42 – TKO1 Evan Tanner
Key UFC Win: UFC 115 – KO1 Chuck Liddell

CINCINNATI

Before Anderson Silva took his title belt in 2006, there was little question that the best UFC middleweight to ever hold the championship was Rich Franklin. A former high school teacher who sailed to the top of the mixed martial arts world, "Ace" didn't fade away after the UFC 64 loss to Silva. Instead, he became a regular main eventer in Superfights against fellow stars like Dan Henderson, Forrest Griffin, Chuck Liddell, Vitor Belfort and Wanderlei Silva. While he has won some and lost some, his exciting style and humble demeanor keeps him at the head of the class when it comes to fan favorites.

DAN HENDERSON

UFC Debut: UFC 17 – W3 Allan Goes
Key UFC Win: UFC 100 – KO2 Michael Bisping

TEMECULA

A world-class wrestler with concussive power in his right hand, Dan Henderson made his name in the PRIDE organization after a brief one-night / two-fight stint in the Octagon at UFC 17 in 1998. After his PRIDE days, Henderson returned to the UFC, but lost two consecutive title fights to Quinton Jackson and Anderson Silva. He did finish off his run in style though, winning three bouts, including a decision win over Rich Franklin and a highlight-reel knockout of Michael Bisping.

MATT HUGHES

UFC Debut: UFC 22 – W3 Valeri Ignatov
Key UFC Win: UFC 63 – TKO3 BJ Penn

HILLSBORO

He may humbly call himself just a country boy, but Hillsboro, Illinois' Matt Hughes is also a fighter. He took a hobby that he was engaging in just to keep his competitive juices flowing and made it into a legendary career. He won the welterweight title twice, beat the best in the game, including Georges St-Pierre and BJ Penn, and eventually end up in the Hall of Fame. And even with his legacy secure, Hughes still fights and competes on a high level with the UFC elite.

CHUCK LIDDELL

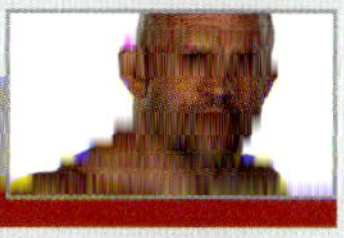

UFC Debut: UFC 17 – W3 Noe Hernandez
Key UFC Win: UFC 47 – KO2 Tito Ortiz

SAN LUIS OBISPO

Any newer fan of the sport who didn't see a prime Chuck Liddell KO'ing seven consecutive opponents from 2004 to 2006, including Randy Couture (twice), Tito Ortiz (twice), Renato Sobral and Jeremy Horn, would need to dig out those DVDs and relive why Liddell was the most feared knockout artist in the game. And while anyone could almost dismiss the final five losses of his career from 2007 to 2010, he did give us one last night of greatness when he defeated Wanderlei Silva in a memorable UFC 79 war.

TITO ORTIZ

UFC Debut: UFC 13 - TKO1 Wes Albritton
Key UFC Win: UFC 51 - W3 Vitor Belfort

HUNTINGTON BEACH

Even though Tito Ortiz has received more attention at times for his out-of-the-Octagon antics and contract squabbles, "The Huntington Beach Bad Boy" has earned his place in the UFC history books as the longest-reigning light heavyweight champion in history. And that's not even mentioning the fact that in the early days of the Zuffa era, Ortiz was the face of the organization, a tireless promoter of the sport when it needed all the positive attention it could get. And today, he still has a significant fanbase that has his back, win or lose.

BJ PENN

UFC Debut: UFC 31 – TKO1 Joey Gilbert
Key UFC Win: UFC 46 – Wsub1 Matt Hughes

HILO

BJ Penn first arrived on the map when he became the first non-Brazilian to win the black belt division of the jiu-jitsu Mundials in 2000, and he hasn't left the headlines since. A gifted athlete with the heart of a lion, Penn is only one of two fighters to win UFC titles in two different weight classes, and while he has had his share of erratic performances, when he's on and focused, he's a joy to watch in the Octagon.

DAN SEVERN

UFC Debut: UFC 4 – Wsub1 Anthony Macias
Key UFC Win: UFC 5 – Wsub1 Dave Beneteau

COLD WATER

Along with Mark Coleman, Dan "The Beast" Severn was one of the first wrestlers to make a major impact in MMA, and his aggressive style made him an instant fan favorite. Probably best remembered for his fight with Royce Gracie, which he dominated for over 15 minutes until getting submitted, Severn's Hall of Fame legacy includes wins over Oleg Taktarov, Dave Beneteau, Tank Abbott and Ken Shamrock, and at the age of 52, he's amazingly still competing.

FRANK SHAMROCK

UFC Debut: UFC Japan – Wsub1 Kevin Jackson
Key UFC Win: UFC 22 – Wsub4 Tito Ortiz

SUSANVILLE

From submissions to striking to everything in between, Frank Shamrock did it all in the Octagon from 1997 to 1999, submitting a world-class wrestler in Kevin Jackson, slamming Igor Zinoviev into unconsciousness and also earning an epic victory over future champion Tito Ortiz. One of the former champ's biggest accomplishments though was that he showed the value of a non-heavyweight division in the sport.

UFC 1 *The Beginning*

12
Nov.
1993

McNichols Sports Arena, Denver, CO

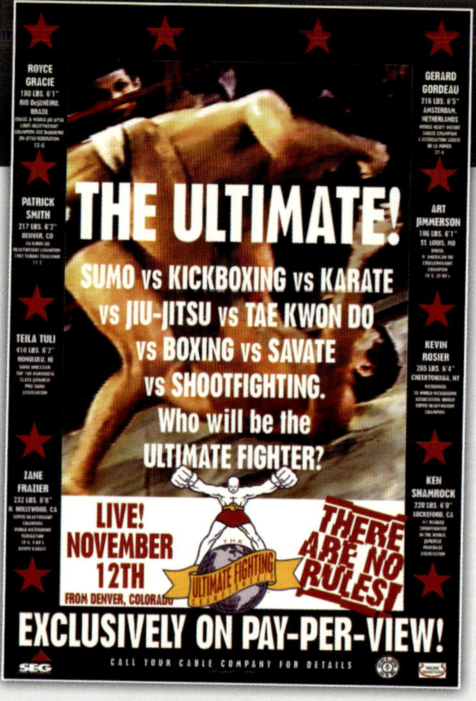

Debuts: Jason DeLucia, Trent Jenkins, Gerard Gordeau, Teila Tuli, Kevin Rosier, Zane Frazier, Royce Gracie, Art Jimmerson, Ken Shamrock, Patrick Smith

Fighters			Division	Method	Time	Round
Alternate Bout						
Jason DeLucia	def.	Trent Jenkins	N/A	Submission	0:52	1
Quarter Finals						
Gerard Gordeau	def.	Teila Tuli	N/A	Technical Knockout	0:26	1
Kevin Rosier	def.	Zane Frazier	N/A	Technical Knockout	4:20	1
Royce Gracie	def.	Art Jimmerson	N/A	Submission - Position	2:18	1
Ken Shamrock	def.	Patrick Smith	N/A	Submission - Heel Hook	1:49	1
Semi-Finals						
Gerard Gordeau	def.	Kevin Rosier	N/A	Technical Knockout	0:59	1
Royce Gracie	def.	Ken Shamrock	N/A	Submission - Choke	0:57	1
Final						
Royce Gracie	def.	Gerard Gordeau	N/A	Submission - Rear Naked Choke	1:44	1

Commentator and kickboxing legend Bill "Superfoot" Wallace may have gotten it wrong in the televised intro, calling it the Ultimate Fighting Challenge, but thankfully the fighters got it right in the Octagon during the first Ultimate Fighting Championship event at McNichols Arena in Denver, as they all played a key role in giving the world their first dose of the sport of mixed martial arts.

The undisputed star of UFC 1 was 26-year-old Brazilian jiu-jitsu black belt Royce Gracie, whose introduction of "the gentle art" to the world stunned three bigger, stronger, and faster opponents who had no defense for his submission wizardry.

In the final of the eight man, one-night tournament, which was created to see which martial arts style would fare best in a real fight, Gracie forced Savate specialist Gerard Gordeau to submit to a rear naked choke in one minute and 44 seconds.

Submission of the Night (unofficial):
Gracie vs. Gordeau

The victory capped off a night that began with Gordeau's frightening soccer kick knockout of 400-pound Teila Tuli, who lost a tooth in the 26-second bout thanks to the Dutchman.

Knockout of the Night (unofficial):
Gordeau vs. Tuli

The next quarterfinal bout was a back-and-forth affair, as Kevin Rosier shook off some rough moments in the early going against Zane Frazier to roar back and halt his opponent with two stomps to the head at the 4:20 mark that caused Frazier's corner to throw in the towel.

Following this bout, the world got its first glimpse of the gi-wearing Gracie, a member of what would eventually be known as fighting's first family. Standing across the cage from him was pro boxer Art Jimmerson, who bizarrely prepared for battle with one boxing glove on. Shortly after the opening bell, Gracie closed the distance with a kick and then took Jimmerson to the mat. Jimmerson baffled and unable to escape, tapped out 2:18 into the match.

Joining the final four in the semifinals was Ken Shamrock, who was already a veteran of Japan's Pancrase organization. He needed just 1:49 to submit Pat Smith with a heel hook, and if anyone had a chance at figuring out the mysterious style of Gracie, it was Shamrock. He was not only physically imposing, but he had submission experience.

Fight of the Night (unofficial):
Gracie vs. Shamrock

Gracie was not about to be figured out, though, and in his semifinal bout with his fellow future Hall of Famer, he took Shamrock down, popped in a choke and tapped out his opponent at the 57-second mark.

The two would meet again, but there was other business to be taken care of first. After Gordeau won his semifinal bout with a 59-second technical knockout of Rosier, Gracie squared off against the lanky European in the final bout of the tournament.

Again, fans wondered what Gracie would do with the devastating striker, but the Brazilian had the answer, and it was the one he had all night—takedown, choke, game over. This time, he used a rear naked choke to end his opponent's evening, and at 1:44 of the bout, Royce Gracie was 3-0, was holding a check for $50,000 and had just started a revolution.

An alternate bout between Jason DeLucia and Trent Jenkins saw DeLucia take just 52 seconds to finish off his opponent via rear naked choke.

One Hit Wonders: Teila Tuli, Art Jimmerson, Trent Jenkins, Gerard Gordeau

Art Jimmerson fared better in combat sports with two gloves, compiling a 33-18 record as a pro boxer from 1985 to 2002. And though he never won a world title, he did face off against future champions Jeff Harding, Dennis Andries, Orlin Norris, Vassiliy Jirov, and Arthur Williams. Jimmerson was never going to morph into a mixed martial artist, but Gerard Gordeau may have had a future in the game. Yet after one more post-UFC 1 bout, he called it quits.

UFC 2 *No Way Out*

11 March 1994

Mammoth Gardens, Denver, CO

Debuts: Remco Pardoel, Johnny Rhodes, Orlando Wiet, Fred Ettish, Scott Morris, Minoki Ichihara, Scott Baker, Alberta Cerra Leon, Robert Lucarelli, Thaddeus Luster, Frank Hamaker, David Levicki, Ray Wizard, Sean Daugherty

Fighters			Division	Method	Time	Round
Opening Round						
Scott Morris	def.	Sean Daugherty	N/A	Submission - Guillotine Choke	0:20	1
Patrick Smith	def.	Ray Wizard	N/A	Submission - Guillotine Choke	0:58	1
Johnny Rhodes	def.	David Levicki	N/A	Submission - Strikes	12:13	1
Frank Hamaker	def.	Thaddeus Luster	N/A	Technical Knockout	4:52	1
Orlando Wiet	def.	Robert Lucarelli	N/A	Technical Knockout	2:50	1
Remco Pardoel	def.	Alberta Cerra Leon	N/A	Submission - Armlock	9:51	1
Jason DeLucia	def.	Scott Baker	N/A	Submission - Strikes	6:41	1
Royce Gracie	def.	Minoki Ichihara	N/A	Submission - Choke	5:08	1
Quarter Finals						
Patrick Smith	def.	Scott Morris	N/A	Knockout	0:30	1
Johnny Rhodes	def.	Fred Ettish	N/A	Submission - Rear Naked Choke	3:07	1
Remco Pardoel	def.	Orlando Wiet	N/A	Knockout	1:29	1
Royce Gracie	def.	Jason DeLucia	N/A	Submission - Armlock	1:07	1
Semi-Finals						
Patrick Smith	def.	Johnny Rhodes	N/A	Submission - Guillotine Choke	1:07	1
Royce Gracie	def.	Remco Pardoel	N/A	Submission - Choke	1:31	1
Final						
Royce Gracie	def.	Patrick Smith	N/A	Submission - Strikes	1:17	1

Four months. That's the amount of time 15 competitors in the Ultimate Fighting Championship 2 tournament had to figure out the 16th man, jiu-jitsu phenom Royce Gracie. It wasn't enough time, as Gracie continued to dazzle at Mammoth Gardens in Denver with a ground game no one had found an antidote for, winning the 16-man tourney in the process.

The four wins lifted Gracie's UFC record to 7-0 and he received $60,000 for his efforts.

In the final, the Rio de Janeiro standout submitted Pat Smith in 77 seconds, but he didn't do it with his jiu-jitsu game, as punches from the mount earned him his second consecutive tournament championship.

Yet even though Gracie remained unstoppable, early action showed that the idea of using jiu-jitsu to finish fights was starting to catch on, as Smith, Scott Morris, and Remco Pardoel all advanced using submissions. Gracie was the leader though, finishing Minoki Ichihara in his longest fight to date, 5:08.

Knockout of the Night (unofficial): Smith vs. Morris

Also moving on in first-round bouts were UFC 1 vet Jason DeLucia, vicious striker Orlando Wiet, Frank Hamaker, and Johnny Rhodes.

In the quarterfinals, the fun really began, but only for the fighters advancing, because some of their victims were on the receiving end of some of the most brutal UFC knockouts ever. Gracie was Gracie, submitting DeLucia in 67 seconds, and Rhodes moved on with a submission of Fred Ettish, an alternate brought in to replace the injured Hamaker. Morris and Weit didn't get off that easily, as Smith and Pardoel delivered early technical knockout wins that stunned onlookers with their ferocity.

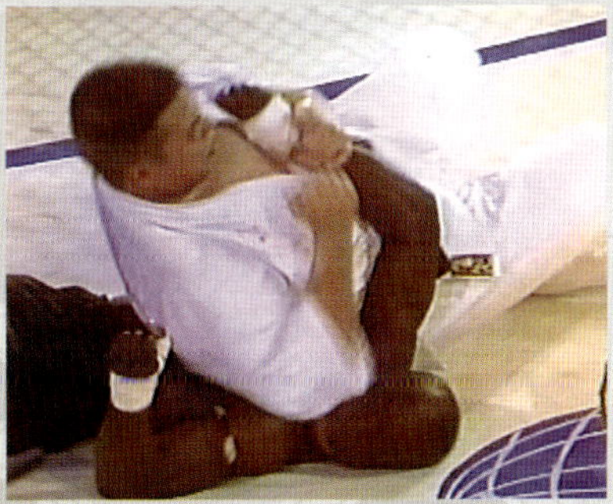

Smith and Pardoel were so impressive that both were now seen as threats to the man at the top of the bracket, and Holland's Pardoel, all 6' 2", 250 pounds of him, was up first. Matching wits on the mat, the gi-wearing combatants looked to be settling in for an interesting scrap until Gracie took the drama out of it with a lapel choke at the 91-second mark. Smith, who made short work of Rhodes with a head butt followed by a guillotine choke in 67 seconds, didn't fare any better in his final match, but no man is unbeatable, and most knew that eventually, Gracie would be pushed to the limit.

Submission of the Night (unofficial): Gracie vs. Pardoel

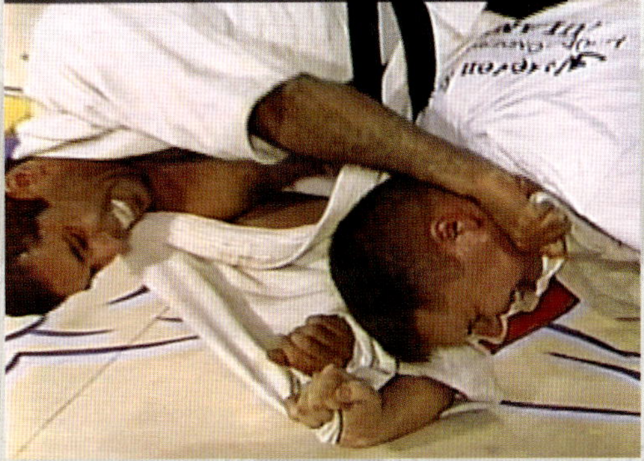

One Hit Wonders: Johnny Rhodes, Orlando Wiet, Fred Ettish, Scott Morris, Minoki Ichihara, Scott Baker, Alberta Cerra Leon, Robert Lucarelli, Thaddeus Luster, Frank Hamaker, David Levicki, Ray Wizard, Sean Daugherty

UFC 3 *The American Dream*

09 Sept. 1994

Grady Cole Center, Charlotte, NC

Debuts: Steve Jennum, Felix Mitchell, Kimo Leopoldo, Roland Payne, Christophe Leninger, Emmanuel Yarborough, Keith Hackney, Harold Howard

Fighters			Division	Method	Time	Round
Quarter Finals						
Keith Hackney	def.	Emmanuel Yarborough	N/A	Technical Knockout	1:59	1
Ken Shamrock	def.	Christophe Leninger	N/A	Submission - Strikes	4:49	1
Harold Howard	def.	Roland Payne	N/A	Knockout	0:46	1
Royce Gracie	def.	Kimo Leopoldo	N/A	Submission - Armbar	4:40	1
Semi-Finals						
Ken Shamrock	def.	Felix Mitchell	N/A	Submission - Rear Naked Choke	4:34	1
Harold Howard	def.	N/A	N/A	Bye*	—	—
Final						
Steve Jennum	def.	Harold Howard	N/A	Submission - Strikes	1:31	1

*Gets bye to finals when Gracie could not continue due to exhaustion.

The famous Robert Burns poem reads that the best laid plans of mice and men often go awry. That would be the perfect description for UFC 3 at the Grady Cole Center in Charlotte, as expectations for a rematch of the UFC 1 battle between Royce Gracie and Ken Shamrock went up in smoke, allowing an unknown alternate, Nebraska police officer Steve Jennum, to make his way to the finals of the eight-man tournament and win it.

It was a stunning turn of events, especially considering that Jennum hadn't even fought earlier in the evening before he forced Canada's Harold Howard to submit due to strikes 1:31 into their final match. Perhaps even more shocking was that fight fans got to see that the seemingly unbeatable Royce Gracie was human.

Not that it's a bad thing, as the jiu-jitsu wizard, who went 7-0 in winning the first two UFC tournaments, showed in his grueling 4:40 battle with Octagon rookie Kimo Leopoldo that he didn't just have technique, but the heart of a lion as well.

Fight and Submission of the Night (unofficial):
Gracie vs. Kimo

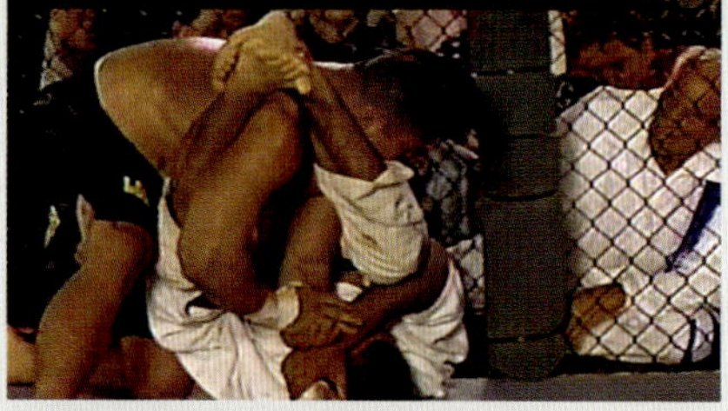

Expected to romp through his side of the tournament bracket to meet Shamrock who was expected to do the same on the other end), Gracie instead ran into a bull named Kimo. Using his 60 pound weight advantage to impose his will on the UFC star, Kimo pushed the Brazilian to the limit for over four minutes until Gracie found an opening and finished his foe with an armbar. The end arrived at 4:40, but it was also the end of Gracie in the tournament, as he couldn't continue due to exhaustion.

Howard's road to glory took only 46 seconds, as he knocked out fellow newcomer Roland Payne to advance to the Gracie bout and then to the finals. It wouldn't be Shamrock waiting for him, as a night that began well for the "The World's Most Dangerous Man" with submission wins over Christophe Leninger (strikes) and Felix Mitchell (rear naked choke) ended in the locker room as he was unable to continue in the tournament due to injury.

Also getting hit with the injury bug was newcomer Keith Hackney who delivered the "shot heard 'round the world" in his bout with 600-pound sumo wrestler Emmannuel Yarborough. Giving up unbelievable amounts of size to his foe, the 200 pound Hackney understandably looked tentative at the bell to start the match, but once he cracked Yarborough with a right hand and dropped him, the nerves disappeared and Hackney went on to stop his opponent with a series of unanswered punches. It was an amazing victory, but those punches also caused Hackney to break his hand and remove himself from the tournament (he was replaced by Mitchell).

Knockout of the Night (unofficial):
Hackney vs. Yarborough

Yet despite the craziness, it's safe to say that no one left the arena complaining. Who knows, it looks like this UFC stuff may stick around for a while.

One Hit Wonders: Roland Payne, Emmanuel Yarborough

Despite only competing in one UFC match, Emmanuel Yarborough remains one of the figures fight fans just can't forget, and they probably never will. Despite outweighing Keith Hackney by upward of 400 pounds, the sumo specialist from Rahway, NJ wasn't able to secure a victory, and he only fought twice more, most notably losing to Daiju Takase at PRIDE 3 in 1998.

UFC 4 *Revenge of the Warriors*

16 Dec. 1994

Expo Square Pavilion, Tulsa, OK

Debuts: Dan Severn, Marcus Bossett, Anthony Macias, Melton Bowen, Joe Son, Ron Van Clief, Jason Fairn, Guy Mezger, Eldo Dias Xavier, Joe Charles

Fighters			Division	Method	Time	Round
Alternate Bouts						
Joe Charles	def.	Kevin Rosier	N/A	Submission - Armbar	0.14	1
Marcus Bossett	def.	Eldo Dias Xavier	N/A	Knockout	4:55	1
Guy Mezger	def.	Jason Fairn	N/A	Technical Knockout	2:13	1
Quarter Finals						
Royce Gracie	def.	Ron Van Clief	N/A	Submission - Rear Naked Choke	3:59	1
Keith Hackney	def.	Joe Son	N/A	Submission - Choke	2:44	1
Steve Jennum	def.	Melton Bowen	N/A	Submission - Armlock	4:47	1
Dan Severn	def.	Anthony Macias	N/A	Submission - Rear Naked Choke	1:45	1
Semi-Finals						
Royce Gracie	def.	Keith Hackney	N/A	Submission - Armlock	5:32	1
Dan Severn	def.	Marcus Bossett	N/A	Submission - Rear Naked Choke	0:52	1
Final						
Royce Gracie	def.	Dan Severn	N/A	Submission - Triangle Choke	15:49	1

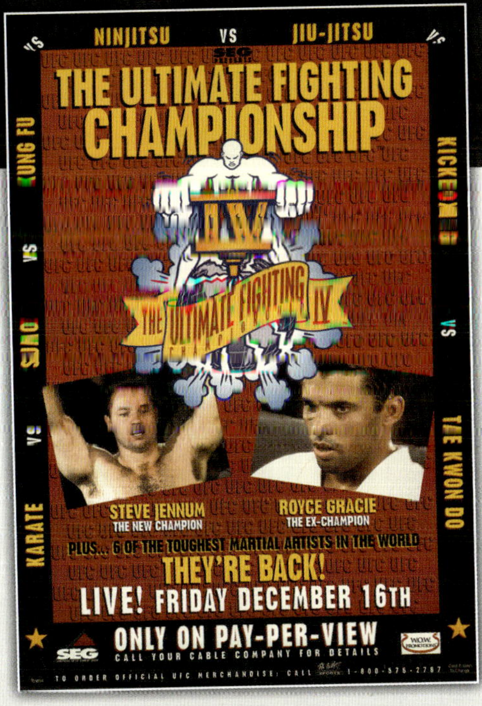

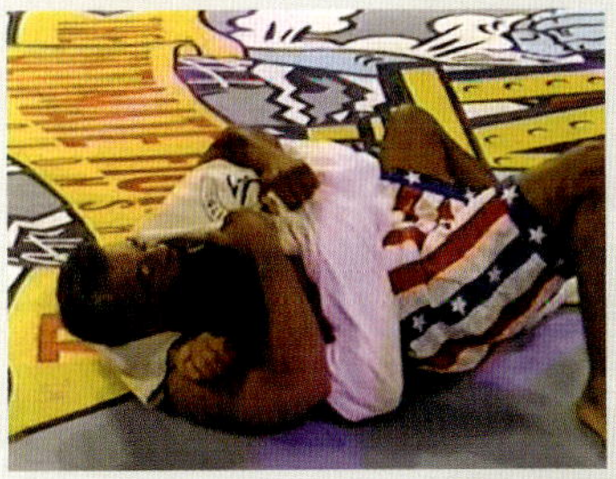

Following his grueling win over Kimo Leopoldo at UFC 3, a bout which prevented him from adding a third tournament title to his trophy case, Royce Gracie returned to the Octagon three months later to not only win an unprecedented third crown at the Expo Square Pavilion in Tulsa, but to prove once and for all that no matter who you throw at him, the Brazilian jiu-jitsu master will find a way to win.

Gracie's most formidable foe in the eight-man tournament wasn't defending champion Steve Jennum, who pulled out of the tournament due to exhaustion after one bout, or giant killer Keith Hackney, who Gracie defeated in the semis, but amateur wrestling star Dan "The Beast" Severn, who made his UFC debut in spectacular fashion, defeating two overmatched foes before meeting up with the unbeaten young man from Rio de Janeiro in the finals.

And what a final match it was, as Gracie was once again forced to dig deep to secure victory, going over 15 minutes against the Michigan powerhouse before submitting him with a triangle choke.

A newcomer to UFC fans before the tournament began, Severn made introductions with a several spectacular suplexes of Anthony Macias before submitting him with a rear naked choke 1:45 into their quarterfinal match. Next up was replacement opponent Marcus Bossett, and he didn't fare much better, as he was taken down and finished with a head and arm choke in less than a minute. Now less than three minutes into his UFC career, Severn had become an instant fan favorite and a threat to Gracie, whose journey to the showdown with "The Beast" followed a familiar path, as he submitted 51-year-old Ron Van Clief, the oldest competitor in UFC history, and Keith Hackney in his own inimitable style.

Severn would prove to be a tougher mountain to climb, especially when he took the smaller Gracie to the canvas with relative ease. From there, both grappled for position, looking for fight-ending submissions. None would come though, and this stalemate became a war of nerves. Eventually, as time wore on, it was Gracie looking to turn things around from the bottom as he tried to submit Severn, and in the bout's 16th minute, he found the opening he was looking for, and Severn was forced to tap out to the triangle choke at the 15:49 mark.

Fight and Submission of the Night (unofficial): Gracie vs. Severn

Let the legend continue.

In other quarterfinal action, Jennum, who made headlines by winning the UFC 3 tournament with only having to fight once, remained unbeaten in the Octagon with a 4:47 submission of pro boxer Melton Bowen, but the bout took a toll on the Nebraska policeman as he withdrew from the tourney following the fight.

Hackney, who shocked fight fans with his victory over 600-pound Emmanuel Yarborough, added to his string of unique victories as he submitted Joe Son at 2:44 after weakening his foe with a string of punches to the groin.

Knockout of the Night (unofficial): Bossett vs. Xavier

Bossett earned a shot replacing Jennum in the semifinals when he knocked out Eldo Dias Xavier in 4:55 of their alternate bouts. Also winning their alternate encounters were the Lion's Den's Guy Mezger (a technical knockout of Jason Fairn) and Joe Charles (a 14-second submission of UFC 1's Kevin Rosier).

One Hit Wonders: Melton Bowen, Joe Son, Ron Van Clief, Jason Fairn, Eldo Dias Xavier

UFC 5 *The Return of The Beast*

07 April 1995

Independence Arena, Charlotte, NC

Debuts: Dave Beneteau, Asbel Cancio, Oleg Taktarov, Todd Medina, Ernie Verdecia, Larry Cureton, Jon Hess, Andy Anderson, John Dowdy

Fighters			Division	Method	Time	Round
Alternate Bouts						
Dave Beneteau	def.	Asbel Cancio	N/A	Technical Knockout	0:21	1
Guy Mezger	def.	John Dowdy	N/A	Technical Knockout	2:02	1
Quarter Finals						
Dan Severn	def.	Joe Charles	N/A	Submission - Rear Naked Choke	1:39	1
Oleg Taktarov	def.	Ernie Verdecia	N/A	Submission - Choke	2:24	1
Todd Medina	def.	Larry Cureton	N/A	Submission - Choke	2:55	1
Jon Hess	def.	Andy Anderson	N/A	Technical Knockout	1:23	1
Semi-Finals						
Dan Severn	def.	Oleg Taktarov	N/A	Technical Knockout - Cuts	4:21	1
Dave Beneteau	def.	Todd Medina	N/A	Technical Knockout	2:12	1
Final						
Dan Severn	def.	Dave Beneteau	N/A	Submission - Keylock	3:00	1
Superfight						
Royce Gracie	vs.	Ken Shamrock	N/A	Draw	—	—

It was the rematch UFC fans had waited for, but the "Superfight" between UFC 1 rivals Royce Grace and Ken Shamrock didn't live up to expectations. Instead of settling the score, the UFC 5 main event turned into a war of attrition that ended up in a draw.

Gracie attacked with leg kicks early, with Shamrock shooting for and getting a takedown. Gracie waited for an opening for submissions from the bottom, but Shamrock stayed close, even as the Brazilian chopped away with kicks to the back. This went on for quite some time, with periodic bursts of action as Shamrock and Gracie traded shots on the mat. As the 30-minute time limit bout approached the 16-minute mark, Gracie began making his move, but Shamrock kept him pinned to the canvas and the pattern continued as neither was willing to take the risks necessary to break the fight open.

At the 30-minute mark, the bout surprisingly kept going, and at the 31:06 mark, referee John McCarthy restarted the bout in the standing position and implemented a five-minute overtime period. But after a hard right from Shamrock, the two hit the mat again and remained there until the five minutes were done, drawing boos from the crowd, which had just witnessed—at 36:06—the longest fight in UFC history.

In the UFC 5 tournament final, Dan "The Beast" Severn made good on his second tourney appearance, submitting newcomer Dave Beneteau with a keylock at the three-minute mark.

The two wrestlers locked up immediately, with Beneteau landing some good shots at close range. Severn shook off the shots and bulled his foe into the fence, looking for the takedown. After a long stalemate, Severn got the trip and Beneteau was on his back. Seconds later, Severn secured the Canadian's arm, and it was game over, as Beneteau tapped, giving the Michigan native his first UFC belt.

There was final-like anticipation for the semifinal bout between Severn and Taktarov, but Severn dominated, putting a bloody pounding on his foe that forced a stoppage and sent "The Beast" to the finals.

Not surprisingly, Severn got the takedown to open the bout, and his active attack kept Taktarov from getting his bearings. Taktarov eventually settled in and looked for submissions from the bottom, but Severn defended well, and his knees to the head opened cuts on the Russian's face that forced a halt to the bout by referee John McCarthy at the 4:21 mark.

Canada's Dave Beneteau made the most of his promotion from alternate to semifinalist, stopping Todd Medina via strikes.

Severn got his second UFC started in impressive style, choking out Joe Charles. Severn got Charles to the mat within seconds, and after pinning his foe to the fence, he unleashed a series of punches and knees. Charles gamely tried to lock up Severn's arm, but after "The Beast" broke loose, he took Charles' back and forced a tap out via rear naked choke.

Fight and Submission of the Night (unofficial): Taktarov vs. Verdecia

Russian sambo champion Taktarov made his highly-anticipated Octagon debut, submitting Kenpo karate expert Ernie Verdecia.

Verdecia started strong as he engaged with Taktarov and got him to the canvas, and after a brief stall, Verdecia's strikes, which included a headbutt, gave him an early lead. Out of nowhere, Taktarov sprung into action and reversed position, locking in a choke that forced the Floridian to tap out.

Knockout of the Night (unofficial): Hess vs. Anderson

Jeet Kune Do specialist Medina showed off his ground game against Larry "Thunderfoot" Cureton as he submitted the striker in less than three minutes.

6' 7", 290-pound "Giant with an Attitude" Jon Hess certainly lived up to his nickname in the opener, as he thrashed 5' 9", 238-pound Texan Andy "The Hammer" Anderson in 83 seconds. Unfortunately, a broken hand kept Hess from continuing in the competition.

One Hit Wonders: Asbel Cancio, Todd Medina, Ernie Verdecia, Jon Hess, Andy Anderson, John Dowdy

UFC 6 *Clash of the Titans*

14 July 1995

Casper Events Center, Casper, WY

Debuts: Joel Sutton, Jack McGlaughlin, He-Man Ali Gipson, Rudyard Moncayo

Fighters			Division	Method	Time	Round
Alternate Bouts						
Joel Sutton	def.	Jack McGlaughlin	N/A	Submission - Strikes	2:01	1
Anthony Macias	def.	He-Man Ali Gipson	N/A	Submission - Strikes	3:06	1
Quarter Finals						
Tank Abbott	def.	John Matua	N/A	Knockout	0:18	1
Paul Varelans	def.	Cal Worsham	N/A	Knockout	1:04	1
Patrick Smith	def.	Rudyard Moncayo	N/A	Submission - Rear Naked Choke	1:08	1
Oleg Taktarov	def.	Dave Beneteau	N/A	Submission - Choke	0:57	1
Semi-Finals						
Tank Abbott	def.	Paul Varelans	N/A	Technical Knockout	1:53	1
Oleg Taktarov	def.	Anthony Macias	N/A	Submission - Guillotine Choke	0:09	1
Final						
Oleg Taktarov	def.	Tank Abbott	N/A	Submission - Rear Naked Choke	17:47	1
Superfight						
Ken Shamrock	def.	Dan Severn	N/A	Submission - Guillotine Choke	2:14	1

After a disappointing draw with Royce Gracie at UFC 5 three months earlier in the UFC's first Superfight Championship bout, Ken Shamrock got a second crack at the crown against ferocious wrestler Dan "The Beast" Severn, fresh off his first tournament title on the same event as Shamrock-Gracie 2. This time, "The World's Most Dangerous Man" made the most of his opportunity, submitting Severn in a little over two minutes at the Casper Events Center in Wyoming.

Submission of the Night (unofficial): Shamrock vs. Severn

The victory lifted Shamrock's UFC record to 4-1-1. He would next defend his title against the winner of the UFC 6 tournament, promising Russian battler Oleg Taktarov, who defeated Dave Beneteau, Anthony Macias, and Tank Abbott to earn the title.

Yet given Shamrock's form against Severn, Taktarov and the rest of the UFC warriors would have a tough time knocking him off the Superfight throne anytime soon.

Looking to remove the memory of his 36-minute stalemate with Gracie, Shamrock used crisp striking and most importantly, stellar takedown defense, to keep Severn guessing. After a failed guillotine attempt, Shamrock was able to catch his opponent's neck a second time, this one producing a tap out 2:14 into the bout.

His future foe, Taktarov, was bloodied into defeat in his semifinal bout against Severn at UFC 5, but this time, he ran the table, kicking things off by surviving some rough early moments to submit Dave Beneteau with a guillotine choke in less than a minute in their quarterfinal bout.

Knockout of the Night (unofficial): Abbott vs. Matua

Also earning spots in the semifinals were veteran Pat Smith, a rear naked choke winner over Rudyard Moncayo in 68 seconds, monstrous 6' 8", 300-pounder Paul "The Polar Bear" Varelans, who crushed Cal Worsham with elbows in 64 seconds, and newcomer David "Tank" Abbott, whose scary 18-second destruction of John Matua was one of the most impressive UFC debuts to date.

The 280-pound Abbott, described as a pit fighter, was an unrepentant brawler who had the power and wrestling skills to give anyone fits, and in the first semifinal bout, he eliminated Varleans' height advantage almost immediately by taking him down and forcing a stoppage by referee John McCarthy when his opponent couldn't intelligently defend himself.

Taktarov had an even easier road to the final, as Smith withdrew from the tournament due to stomach cramps, leading alternate Anthony Macias to step into the Octagon and get submitted in just nine seconds, a result that didn't please the crowd.

The finish by Taktarov did set up an interesting final with Abbott though, and while the eventual bout didn't live up to expectations from an action standpoint, strategically Taktarov was able to nullify the brawler's attack throughout the bout. Extreme fatigue on the part of both men didn't help matters as the bout strayed past the 17-minute mark, but Taktarov proved to have a little more gas in the tank than Abbott did, and he finally ended things with a rear naked choke 17:47 into the match.

In alternate bouts, Macias submitted He-Man Ali Gipson due to strikes at the 3:06 mark, and Joel Sutton achieved a similar result over Jack McGlaughlin in 2:01.

Fight of the Night (unofficial): Taktarov vs. Abbott

UFC 7 *The Brawl in Buffalo*

08 Sept. 1995

Memorial Auditorium, Buffalo, NY

Debuts: Geza Kalman, Onassis Parungao, Francesco Maturi, Scott Bessac, David Hood, Gerry Harris, Larry Cureton

Fighters			Division	Method	Time	Round
Alternate Bouts						
Joel Sutton	def.	Geza Kalman	N/A	Technical Knockout - Cuts	0:48	1
Onassis Parungao	def.	Francesco Maturi	N/A	Submission - Strikes	5:26	1
Scott Bessac	def.	David Hood	N/A	Submission - Guillotine Choke	0:31	1
Quarter Finals						
Paul Varelans	def.	Gerry Harris	N/A	Submission - Strikes	1:07	1
Mark Hall	def.	Harold Howard	N/A	Submission - Strikes	1:41	1
Remco Pardoel	def.	Ryan Parker	N/A	Submission - Choke	3:05	1
Marco Ruas	def.	Larry Cureton	N/A	Submission - Heel Hook	3:23	1
Semi-Finals						
Paul Varelans	def.	Mark Hall	N/A	Submission - Keylock	1:01	1
Marco Ruas	def.	Remco Pardoel	N/A	Submission - Position	12:27	1
Final						
Marco Ruas	def.	Paul Varelans	N/A	Technical Knockout	13:17	1
Superfight						
Ken Shamrock	vs.	Oleg Taktarov	N/A	Draw	—	—

Bad luck seemed to follow Ken Shamrock. After being forced out of tournaments due to injury and drawing with Royce Gracie in a bout many believed he won, the UFC Superfight champion was forced down the road of black cats and upraised ladders once again at UFC 7 in Buffalo, New York as what would have been ruled a victory over Russia's Oleg Taktarov if judges were involved was instead ruled a draw when the Russian was able to make it to the final bell after 33 minutes.

The bout itself lacked any sustained or compelling action, with Shamrock content to do just enough while standing and on the mat to keep Taktarov at bay. Taktarov's offense was virtually non-existent, as he was unable to find an opening from his back for a submission against the defensively sound Shamrock. While he was able to land some shots while standing, it wasn't enough to get Shamrock in trouble.

With the draw, Shamrock retained his Superfight title for the first time.

Joining the ranks of UFC tournament winners at the Memorial Auditorium was Brazil's debuting Marco Ruas, who not only entered the Octagon with a memorable nickname "The King of The Streets", but who showed a well-rounded mixed martial arts game that was likely to keep him in the win column for a long time.

Starting off with a win via heel hook submission over competitive Larry Cureton in the quarterfinals, Ruas moved on to battle veteran Remco Pardoel in the semis, and despite some solid work by Pardoel, Ruas adjusted his game plan and used leg kicks and foot stomps to weaken his foe and eventually force him to tap at the 12:27 mark when he got caught in the mounted position.

The Rio de Janeiro native was at his best when it counted though, as he chopped down "The Polar Bear", 6' 8" Paul Varelans, in the finals with leg kicks that eventually dropped the giant and allowed Ruas to finish him off with strikes 13:17 into their bout.

Not a bad night's work for Ruas, who fought for over 29 minutes to earn his first UFC tournament title.

In the other quarterfinal matchups, Varelans forced a tapout due to strikes from Gerry Harris, Mark Hall did the same to Harold Howard, and Pardoel submitted Ryan Parker with a forearm choke.

Varelans went on to earn a spot in the final when he submitted Mark Hall with a keylock in just 61 seconds.

In the three alternate bouts, Scott Bessac submitted David Hood in 31 seconds, Onassis Parungao forced Francesco Maturi to tap out due to strikes, and Joel Sutton toppled Geza Kalman via cuts, but none were needed to step up as replacements in the tournament.

Submission of the Night (unofficial): Ruas vs. Cureton

Fight of the Night (unofficial): Ruas vs. Varelans

Ultimate Ultimate 1995

16 Dec. 1995

Mammoth Gardens, Denver, CO

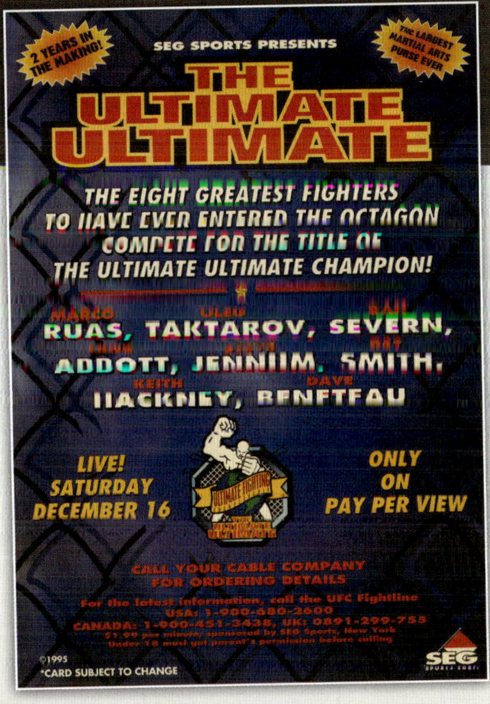

Debuts: Joe Charles, Trent Jenkins

Fighters			Division	Method	Time	Round
Alternate Bouts						
Joe Charles	def.	Scott Bessac	N/A	Submission - Armlock	4:38	1
Mark Hall	def.	Trent Jenkins	N/A	Submission - Armlock	5:29	1
Quarter Finals						
Tank Abbott	def.	Steve Jennum	N/A	Submission - Neck Crank	1:14	1
Dan Severn	def.	Paul Varelans	N/A	Submission - Arm Triangle Choke	1:01	1
Marco Ruas	def.	Keith Hackney	N/A	Submission - Rear Naked Choke	2:39	1
Oleg Taktarov	def.	Dave Beneteau	N/A	Submission - Achilles Lock	1:15	1
Semi-Finals						
Dan Severn	def.	Tank Abbott	N/A	Unanimous Decision	—	—
Oleg Taktarov	def.	Marco Ruas	N/A	Unanimous Decision	—	—
Final						
Dan Severn	def.	Oleg Taktarov	N/A	Unanimous Decision	—	—

With seven events under its belt, the Ultimate Fighting Championship had cemented its place among fans of combat sports, but after some bizarre mismatches, tedious bouts, and the idea that a fighter could earn a draw just by surviving, it was time for the organization to begin the process of growing up. What better place to start than with an event entitled The Ultimate Ultimate?

Consisting of an eight-man tournament featuring four previous tournament winners Steve Jennum, Marco Ruas, Dan Severn, Oleg Taktarov), three finalists Tank Abbott, Dave Beneteau, Paul Varelans), and perennial contender Keith Hackney, the only thing missing was an appearance from Octagon superstar Royce Gracie, but fans would not see him in action again for nearly five years, when he resumed his career in Japan.

The absence of Gracie and Superfight champion Ken Shamrock opened up the field considerably, making it anyone's tournament to win. But in the end, it was "The Beast" Severn locking up his second title with another display of his world-class wrestling.

Meeting Taktarov for the second time, Severn, who stopped "The Russian Bear" via cuts at UFC 5, earned a 30-minute unanimous decision over his foe in the final bout, using his ground control to keep Taktarov on the mat for the majority of the bout. A bloodied Taktarov had a few openings to look for a leg lock on Severn, but they all came up empty, dropping his UFC record to 6-2-1.

Severn's semifinal victory over Abbott was a harbinger of things to come, as he survived an early knee from the hard-hitting brawler to control him everywhere the bout went, mainly the mat, en route to an 18-minute unanimous decision victory.

Matching the result in his own semifinal bout was Taktarov, who was the slightly more aggressive fighter over the 18-minute time limit against Ruas, earning him a trip to the finals.

In the quarterfinals, all four favorites advanced via submission, showing just how far the new sport had come in just two years.

First up was Abbott, who used his underrated wrestling ability to take Jennum to the mat, prop him against the fence, and produce a tap out via neck crank when the Nebraskan's head got stuck against the side of the Octagon.

Fight of the Night (unofficial): Severn vs. Varelans

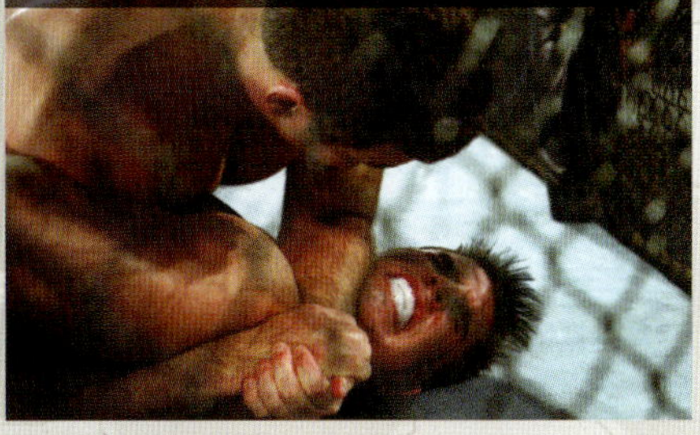

Severn impressively finished off Paul Varelans in just 61 seconds, taking him down and causing "The Polar Bear" to submit via arm triangle.

The UFC 6 bout between Taktarov and Beneteau was competitive for the 57 seconds it lasted. In their quarterfinal rematch, Taktarov needed a little more time, 18 more seconds to be exact, to finish the Canadian, this time via Achilles lock.

Ruas had little difficulty in his quarterfinal bout, submitting Hackney via rear naked choke.

Joe Charles submitted Scott Bessac via armbar submission in the opening alternate bout, and also taking an early victory was Mark Hall, who submitted Trent Jenkins.

UFC 8 *David vs. Goliath*

16 Feb. 1996

Ruben Rodriguez Coliseum, Bayamon, Puerto Rico

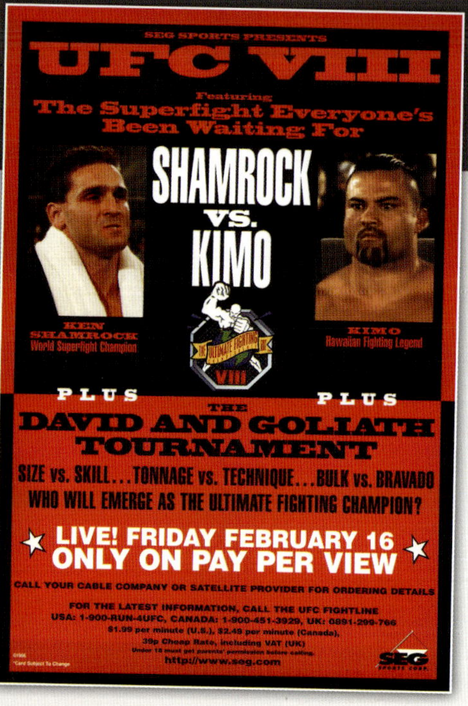

Debuts: Gary Goodridge, Paul Herrera, Scott Ferrozzo, Don Frye, Jerry Bohlander, Sam Adkins, Paul Herrera, Joe Moreira, Thomas Ramirez, Keith Mielke

Fighters			Division	Method	Time	Round
Alternate Bouts						
Sam Adkins	def.	Keith Mielke	N/A	Submission - Strikes	0:50	1
Quarter Finals						
Don Frye	def.	Thomas Ramirez	N/A	Knockout	0:08	1
Paul Varelans	def.	Joe Moreira	N/A	Unanimous Decision	—	—
Jerry Bohlander	def.	Scott Ferrozzo	N/A	Submission - Guillotine Choke	9:05	1
Gary Goodridge	def.	Paul Herrera	N/A	Knockout	0:13	1
Semi-Finals						
Don Frye	def.	Sam Adkins	N/A	Technical Knockout	0:48	1
Gary Goodridge	def.	Jerry Bohlander	N/A	Technical Knockout	5:32	1
Final						
Don Frye	def.	Gary Goodridge	N/A	Submission - Position	2:14	1
Superfight						
Ken Shamrock	def.	Kimo Leopoldo	N/A	Submission - Kneebar	4:24	1

Kimo Leopoldo made quite an impression in his Octagon debut against Royce Gracie back at UFC 3, but it was veteran Ken Shamrock who emerged victorious in his bout against Leopoldo at the Ruben Rodriguez Coliseum in Bayamon, Puerto Rico, as "The World's Most Dangerous Man" retained his UFC Superfight title with an ankle lock submission.

Giving up 65 pounds to Leopoldo, Shamrock used his superior MMA experience to take his foe down to the mat, leveling the playing field. Shamrock kept himself in the dominant top position for much of the bout, but Kimo was able to reverse things and briefly take control before Shamrock found his opening to force the tap out at the 4:24 mark.

In the night's "David vs. Goliath" tournament, former college wrestling standout Don Frye burst onto the UFC scene with three wins to take the one-night event in impressive fashion.

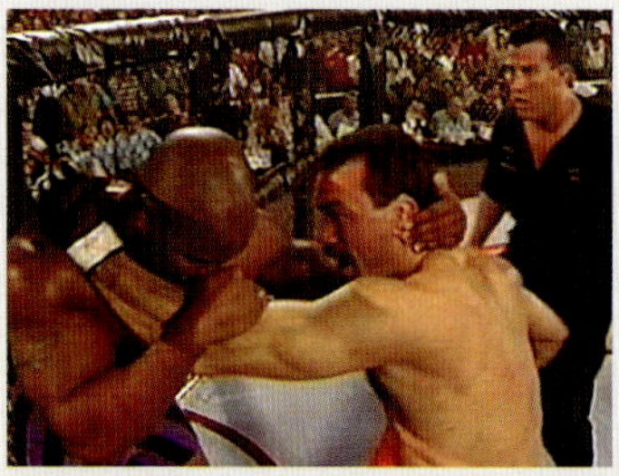

The final saw two Octagon debutants, Frye and Gary "Big Daddy" Goodridge collide, with Frye emerging victorious in a competitive bout due to submission.

After a tentative start, the two engaged, with Frye and Goodridge both trading control on the feet and the mat. Frye's superior striking accuracy and stamina eventually won out though, as he mounted an exhausted Goodridge on the mat and forced him to tap out after a series of unanswered punches to the head.

Frye had little difficulty with alternate Sam Adkins who was replacing the injured Paul Varelans in his semifinal bout, taking him down and finishing him with strikes in 48 seconds.

Fight of the Night (unofficial): Goodridge vs. Bohlander

Goodridge got a lot more resistance in his bout with the much smaller rookie Jerry Bohlander, but the Canadian's strength and power proved to be too much for the submission fighter from the Lion's Den team, and he stopped Bohlander via strikes at the 5:32 mark.

"Big Daddy" Goodridge made a frightening impression on fight fans in his Octagon debut, as he took opponent Paul Herrera down immediately, locked him in a crucifix position, and proceeded to knock him out with a series of elbows. It was without question the most startling UFC debut to date.

Knockout of the Night (unofficial): Goodridge vs. Herrera

The 21-year-old Bohlander didn't get any favors in his first tournament draw against 330-pound Scott Ferrozzo, but after surviving a series of hellacious throws to the mat, he was able to cut "The Pit Bull" and eventually submit him with a choke at 9:05 of the fight.

Submission of the Night (unofficial): Bohlander vs. Ferrozzo

Paul Varelans was expected to roll over newcomer Joe Moreira in their bout, but instead he was forced to go the 10-minute distance before being awarded a unanimous decision victory in a less-than-scintillating contest.

The only local Puerto Rican fighter on the card, 410-pound Thomas Ramirez, was advertised as being 200-0. Frye made that 200-1 with an eight-second knockout that stood until 2009 as the fastest in UFC history.

One Hit Wonders: Paul Herrera, Thomas Ramirez, Keith Mielke

UFC 9 *Motor City Madness*

17 May 1996

Cobo Arena, Detroit, MI

Debuts: Amaury Bitetti, Koji Kitao, Mark Schultz, Matt Andersen, Rafael Carino, Steve Nelmark, Tai Bowden

Fighters			Division	Method	Time	Round
Superfight						
Dan Severn	def.	Ken Shamrock	N/A	Split Decision	—	—
Main Bouts						
Don Frye	def.	Amaury Bitetti	N/A	Technical Knockout	9:30	1
Mark Hall	def.	Koji Kitao	N/A	Technical Knockout	0:47	1
Mark Schultz	def.	Gary Goodridge	N/A	Technical Knockout - Cuts	12:00	1
Rafael Carino	def.	Matt Andersen	N/A	Technical Knockout	5:33	1
Cal Worsham	def.	Zane Frazier	N/A	Technical Knockout	3:17	1
Alternate Bout						
Steve Nelmark	def.	Tai Bowden	N/A	Technical Knockout	7:23	1

Legal troubles plagued the Ultimate Fighting Championship as it rolled into Detroit's Cobo Hall, with local officials threatening to close the event down before it even began. A court battle ensued, with the UFC eventually getting the green light to proceed hours before the opening bell, but only without the use of headbutts and closed-fist strikes to the head.

Luckily, the fights went off without a hitch (and with closed-fist strikes), but someone forgot to tell Superfight stars Dan Severn and Ken Shamrock, who engaged in perhaps the worst bout in organization and maybe even MMA history. They rarely engaged in their highly-anticipated rematch, opting instead to circle each other for 30 minutes before the judges awarded "The Beast" the bout via split decision, allowing him to even the score with Shamrock, who had submitted him at UFC 6.

The crowd was restless almost from the start, and rightfully so with the lack of action. At the bout's halfway point, Severn hit a takedown, but was unable to keep Shamrock on the mat. A second attempt later was more successful, at least until Shamrock and Severn changed controlling positions on the mat. Eventually, Severn landed some shots on the mat that cut his opponent, but that was the extent of the compelling action, as the rest of regulation time and two overtime periods were unable to decisively settle anything.

With no tournament and a horrific main event, it was up to the rest of the card to save UFC 9, and while saving it might have been a lost cause, there were some solid bouts on tap that kept the fans happy.

In a featured bout, the star of UFC 8, tournament winner Don Frye, took on a late replacement for Marco Ruas, Amaury Bitetti, but he didn't miss a beat, fighting off an early charge from the Brazilian to deliver a hellacious beating that finally brought an end to the bout at the 9:30 mark.

Fight of the Night (unofficial): Frye vs. Bitetti

The United States' Mark Hall spoiled the debut of Japanese sumo wrestling standout Koji Kitao, breaking his nose en route to a stoppage 47 seconds into the fight.

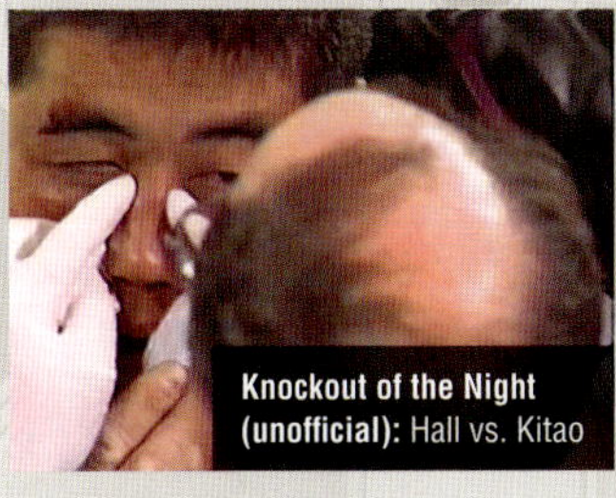

Knockout of the Night (unofficial): Hall vs. Kitao

1984 US Olympic Gold medal winner Mark Schultz was dominant in his first Octagon debut, taking down up-and-comer Gary Goodridge and keeping him there with ground control and punishing strikes. After 12 minutes of regulation, referee John McCarthy had seen enough, calling a stop to the fight due to cuts suffered by "Big Daddy".

Brazilian giant 6' 8", 245-pound Rafael Carino was workmanlike in his effort against fellow debutant Matt Andersen, eventually scoring a technical knockout at the 5:33 mark.

Cal Worsham and Zane Frazier met in the Motor City, and Worsham kept his opponent winless as he nabbed his first UFC victory 3:17 into the bout via submission due to strikes.

In the opener, Steve Nelmark brought a stop to his bout with Tai Bowden at the 7:23 mark due to cuts.

One Hit Wonders: Koji Kitao, Mark Schultz, Matt Andersen, Rafael Carino

Some interesting one-timers on this event: Japan's Koji Kitao was a top-level sumo wrestler, the sport's 60th Yokozuna. He would only fight three times in MMA, losing his first two bouts before a submission win over Nathan Jones at PRIDE 1 in 1997. Mark Schultz was a 1984 Olympic Gold medal winner in freestyle wrestling, as well as a two-time world champion on the mat. Though he was victorious at UFC 9 and probably would have been successful in MMA, he only fought once more, losing a bout in Brazil in 2003. Finally, there's Matt Andersen, a Midwest MMA veteran who didn't match the success of his half-brother, Jeremy Horn.

UFC 10 *The Tournament*

12 July 1996

Fairgrounds Arena, Birmingham, AL

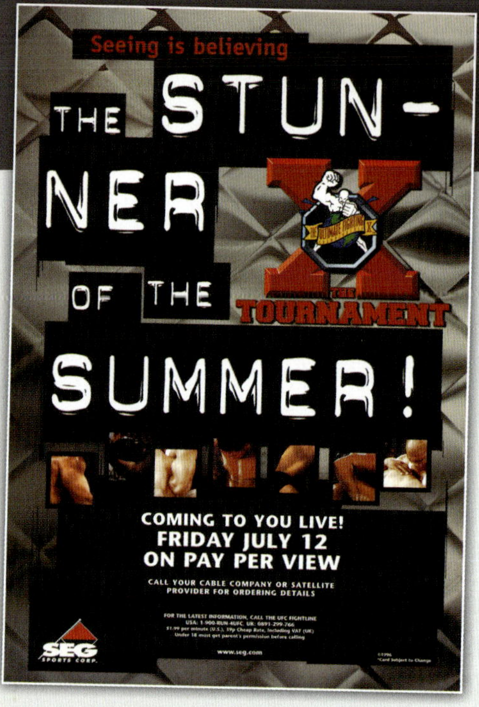

Debuts: Mark Coleman, Brian Johnston, John Campetella, Moti Horenstein, Scott Fiedler

Fighters			Division	Method	Time	Round
Alternate Bouts						
Sam Adkins	def.	Felix Lee Mitchell	N/A	Unanimous Decision	—	3
Geza Kalman	def.	Dieusel Berto	N/A	Technical Knockout	5:56	1
Quarter Finals						
Gary Goodridge	def.	John Campetella	N/A	Technical Knockout	1:27	1
Mark Coleman	def.	Moti Horenstein	N/A	Technical Knockout	2:43	1
Brian Johnson	def.	Scott Fiedler	N/A	Technical Knockout	2:25	1
Don Frye	def.	Mark Hall	N/A	Submission - Strikes	10:23	1
Semi-Finals						
Mark Coleman	def.	Gary Goodridge	N/A	Submission - Dominant Position	7:00	1
Don Frye	def.	Brian Johnston	N/A	Submission - Strikes	4:37	1
Final						
Mark Coleman	def.	Don Frye	N/A	Technical Knockout	11:30	1

Fight of the Night (unofficial):
Coleman vs. Frye

The Ultimate Fighting Championship brought the tournament format back for UFC 10, and a star was born in former Ohio State wrestling standout Mark Coleman, who romped over three foes, including favorite Don Frye, who suffered his first pro loss in the final against "The Hammer".

Both Coleman and Frye were coming off extended semifinal bouts, but Coleman seemed to be the fresher of the two as he took his opponent's back quickly when they first hit the mat. As Frye scrambled to a more favorable position, he would up eating plenty of leather as Coleman fired away from the top, bloodying his foe in the process. Surprisingly, Frye survived this initial onslaught, and with a little over four minutes gone he used a headlock attempt by Coleman to get back to his feet.

Now both fighters looked winded, but Coleman used Frye's subsequent striking attack to score another takedown. Again, Coleman delivered thudding blows to the face, and referee John McCarthy called a halt to the bout to have the doctor check Frye's cuts. "You've got to do something, son," said McCarthy to Frye, but when the bout resumed, Coleman wouldn't be denied, as he fought off fatigue and finished matters on the mat with more punishing ground strikes at 11:30 into the bout.

Coleman's swarming attack on the mat and against the fence made life miserable for Gary "Big Daddy" Goodridge in their semifinal match, with "The Hammer" eventually ending things via tapout as Goodridge was unable to escape when Coleman took his back seven minutes into the bout.

Frye got the toughest test of his UFC career in the first semifinal, but eventually, first-timer Brian Johnston succumbed to strikes at the 4:37 mark.

Johnston showed little fear of Frye, swinging for the fences from the outset and even holding his own when the two locked up at close range. Frye's toughness kept him in the fight though, and once he was able to get Johnston to the mat, he began pounding away. The game Johnston almost broke loose, but as Frye got into side control a couple of hard strikes forced the Octagon rookie to tap out.

Octagon veteran Goodridge spoiled the debut of John Campetella, beating the Staten Island, New York product in 87 seconds. Campetella started strong as he locked up with "Big Daddy" and landed some good shots, but when the bout hit the mat, Goodridge was able to force the stoppage with a couple of unanswered blows, prompting boos from the crowd for the seemingly quick hook.

Knockout of the Night (unofficial):
Coleman vs. Horenstein

Israel's Moti Horenstein listed his martial arts discipline as "survival," but Coleman wasn't about to let that happen, as he took his opponent to the mat almost immediately and kept the pressure on until a couple of big right hands forced a referee stoppage at the 2:43 mark.

A battle of newcomers saw Johnston make short work of Scott Feidler. The Californian used two throws to start things off before he fought off some solid wrestling from Fiedler and then ended things with strikes on his downed foe.

In the first quarterfinal bout, Frye took an early kick from Mark Hall before slamming his foe to the mat and keeping him there until referee John McCarthy halted the bout at the 10:23 mark to rescue the overmatched fighter from further punishment.

In alternate bouts, Sam Adkins decisioned Felix Lee Mitchell, and Geza Kalman halted Dieusel Berto in a little less than six minutes.

One Hit Wonders: John Campetella, Dieusel Berto

The Haiti-born Berto, whose MMA career finished at 0-3, may not have had the most distinguished run in the sport, but he did a fine job of producing fighters, as his sons Andre and James Edson both had combat sports success: Andre as the welterweight boxing champion of the world, and James Edson as a mixed martial artist who fought for the EliteXC and Strikeforce organizations.

UFC 11 *The Proving Ground*

20 Sept. 1996

Augusta Civic Center, Augusta, GA

[illegible]: Fabio Gurgel, Reza Nasri, Julian Sanchez, Dave Berry, Roberto Traven, Sam Fulton

Fighters			Division	Method	Time	Round
Alternate Bouts						
Scott Ferrozzo	def.	Sam Fulton	N/A	Submission - Strikes	1:45	1
Roberto Traven	def.	Dave Berry	N/A	Submission - Strikes	1:33	1
Quarter Finals						
Mark Coleman	def.	Julian Sanchez	N/A	Submission - Choke	0.44	1
Brian Johnston	def.	Reza Nasri	N/A	Technical Knockout	0:30	1
Tank Abbott	def.	Sam Adkins	N/A	Submission - Neck Crank	2:06	1
Jerry Bohlander	def.	Fabio Gurgel	N/A	Unanimous Decision	—	—
Semi-Finals						
Mark Coleman	def.	Brian Johnston	N/A	Submission	2:20	1
Scott Ferrozzo	def.	Tank Abbott	N/A	Unanimous Decision	—	—
Final						
Mark Coleman	def.	N/A	N/A	Forfeit	—	—

It was a bizarre night in the UFC 11 tournament at the Augusta Civic Center, and while the expected favorite Mark Coleman emerged victorious, he did it without having to compete in a final match, as injuries and exhaustion left "The Hammer" with no one left to fight.

Semifinalist Jerry Bohlander and alternates Scott Ferrozzo and Roberto Traven were all forced out of the tourney, leaving Coleman the victor via default.

In what proved to be his final bout of the evening, Coleman took the drama out of an intriguing semifinal matchup with Brian Johnston early, taking Johnston down, and then out, in slightly over two minutes.

After a tentative opening, Johnston started landing leg kicks, and the stalking Coleman suddenly struck with a double leg takedown. Johnston held on, hoping to defuse the attack of "The Hammer", but even Coleman's short shots did damage, and after a series of headbutts and right hands, referee John McCarthy had seen enough, halting the bout at the 2:20 mark.

Fight of the Night (unofficial): Ferrozzo vs. Abbott

The other semifinal saw alternate Scott Ferrozzo upset crowd favorite Tank Abbott via 18-minute decision.

The brawlers engaged immediately, with Abbott landing some good shots but Ferrozzo answering right back as the fans roared. A little over a minute in, Ferrozzo was cut over the right eye as Abbott pinned him to the fence. The two engaged in some trash talk between punches, and knees by Ferrozzo drew even more of a reaction before the two proceeded to throw more wild shots.

Following a quick break for the Octagonside physician to check Ferrozzo's cut, it was more of the same, with each having their moments. Despite being held against the fence, Ferrozzo's knees were scoring and taking their toll, and "The Pit Bull" kept imploring Abbott to let him loose, but to no avail.

After the 15-minute time limit expired, the overtime period started with some fury, as Abbott tried to turn things around, but he soon resorted to pushing the fight back to the fence, where Ferrozzo continued to pound away and secure the decision win.

The grueling win came with a price, as Ferrozzo was unable to continue in the tournament due to exhaustion and the cut over his eye.

Rising star Jerry Bohlander fought his route into the semifinals the hard way, with a solid, but fairly uneventful 15-minute decision win over newcomer Fabio Gurgel, but the bout took its toll, as the Lion's Den team member was unable to continue in the tournament.

Revered brawler Abbott returned from his suspension for an out-of-the-Octagon brawl at UFC 8 in impressive style, submitting Sam Adkins in a little over two minutes. Taking Adkins to the mat immediately, Abbott patiently sought an opening until he pinned his foe's head against the fence, forcing a tapout at the 2:06 mark.

Knockout of the Night (unofficial): Johnston vs. Nasri

Johnston kept the momentum from his impressive UFC 10 effort going, as he earned a semifinal berth with a 30-second KO of Iran's Reza Nasri. After a quick tie-up, Johnston slammed his foe to the mat and then ended the bout via strikes. Johnston actually received more damage from John McCarthy than his foe, as his nose was bloodied when the referee halted the bout.

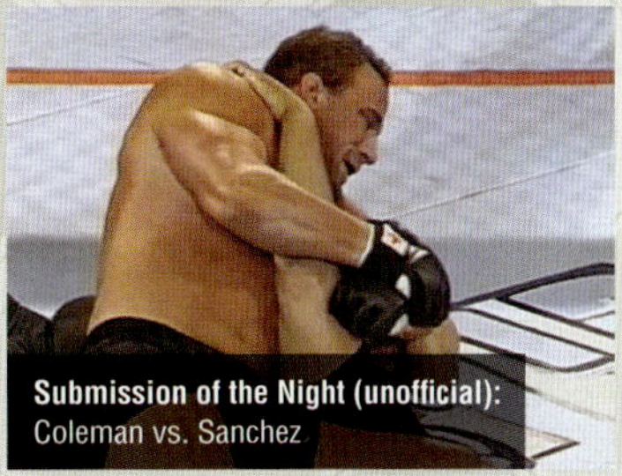

Submission of the Night (unofficial): Coleman vs. Sanchez

Coleman emerged unscathed in his first bout of the night, taking an overmatched Julian Sanchez to the mat and then finishing him off with a choke in 44 seconds.

In alternate bouts, Ferrozzo finished Sam Fulton via strikes in 1:45, and Roberto Traven did the same just 1:33 into their bout. Ferrozzo continued on in the tournament, but a broken hand kept Traven from returning to the Octagon as a replacement opponent.

One Hit Wonders: Fabio Gurgel, Reza Nasri, Julian Sanchez, Dave Berry

Ultimate Ultimate 1996

07 Dec. 1996

Fair Park Arena, Birmingham, AL

Debut: Jack Nilson

Fighters			Division	Method	Time	Round
Alternate Bouts						
Mark Hall	def.	Felix Mitchell	N/A	Technical Knockout	1:45	1
Steve Nelmark	def.	Marcus Bossett	N/A	Submission - Choke	1:37	1
Tai Bowden	def.	Jack Nilson	N/A	Submission - Headbutts	4:46	1
Quarter Finals						
Don Frye	def.	Gary Goodridge	N/A	Submission - Fatigue	11:19	1
Tank Abbott	def.	Cal Worsham	N/A	Submission - Strikes	2:51	1
Kimo Leopoldo	def.	Paul Varelans	N/A	Technical Knockout	9:08	1
Ken Shamrock	def.	Brian Johnston	N/A	Submission - Choke	5:48	1
Semi-Finals						
Don Frye	def.	Mark Hall	N/A	Submission - Achilles Lock	0:20	1
Tank Abbott	def.	Steve Nelmark	N/A	Knockout	1:05	1
Final						
Don Frye	def.	Tank Abbott	N/A	Submission - Rear Naked Choke	1:23	1

The stars of the UFC were out in force for the organization's second Ultimate Ultimate tournament, in a field including Ken Shamrock, Tank Abbott, and Kimo Leopoldo. It was "The Predator", Don Frye, earning his second Octagon title with three consecutive wins.

Fight of the Night (unofficial): Frye vs. Abbott

In the final, Frye survived an early knockdown against Abbott to roar back and submit the popular brawler in a war that packed plenty of action into just 83 seconds.

Seconds after the opening bell, a left jab by Abbott sent Frye sprawling to the mat. Frye immediately got to this feet, but was swarmed by Abbott, who continued to rock him with the left hand. Frye, bloodied, instinctively fired back, but after a quick clinch, Abbott looked to be on the verge of finishing his foe. Moments later though, Abbott lost his footing and was pushed to the mat. Frye, seeing his opening, took Abbott's back, eventually sinking in a rear naked choke that forced Abbott to tap out at the 1:23 mark.

The road to the finals was a quick one for both Frye and Abbott, who needed just a combined 1:25 to earn their spots.

Frye's bout against alternate Mark Hall, who replaced the fatigued Kimo Leopoldo, was the third between the two, and the result remained the same—a victory for "The Predator". This time though, he finished his rival in 20 seconds, taking him down immediately and forcing him to submit to an ankle lock.

Abbott was just as efficient in his semifinal match, as he defeated alternate Steve Nelmark, a replacement for the injured Ken Shamrock, in 65 seconds. A slam by Abbott began the carnage, with a final battage of power punches eventually finishing off "The Sandman" in frightening fashion.

The popular Kimo Leopoldo secured his first UFC win by stopping tough Paul Varelans, but the technical knockout victory was so grueling that he removed himself from the tournament semifinals due to fatigue.

Giving up over a hundred pounds to Varelans, Kimo survived the onslaught of "The Polar Bear", and after finally turning the tables on his bigger foe on the mat, a series of unanswered strikes produced a stoppage at the 9:08 mark of the bout.

Knockout of the Night (unofficial): Leopoldo vs. Varelans

Abbott's first bout of the night was a bizarre one, but he took the win, a submission due to strikes against Cal Worsham that came 2:51 into the fight.

Landing early with his power shots, Abbott proceeded to close the distance, and he attempted to lift Worsham for a slam. Worsham grabbed the top of the fence, and Abbott's response was to try to throw him out of the Octagon. Eventually, Worsham broke free, but the two ended up on the canvas. From there, Abbott was in control, and after Worsham took a couple shots, he surprisingly tapped out.

Frye met Gary "Big Daddy" Goodridge for a second time, and once again Frye emerged victorious, forcing the Canadian to submit due to fatigue.

Goodridge was aggressive early, but Frye used solid inside work while standing and on the mat to wear his opponent down. By the 11:19 mark, Goodridge was spent, and he tapped out to avoid further punishment.

Ken Shamrock opened up the quarterfinals with a submission victory over Brian Johnston. Using his superior ground game, Shamrock pinned Johnston to the mat and used his ground strikes to open up a forearm choke that ended matters at the 5:48 mark. In the fight though, Shamrock broke his hand and was unable to continue in the tournament.

Alternate bout action didn't last long, as Hall stopped Felix Lee Mitchell in 1:45, Nelmark submitted Marcus Bossett in 1:37, and Tai Bowden finished Jack Nilson with headbutts in 4:46.

UFC 12 *Judgement Day*

07 Feb. 1997

Dothan Civic Center, Dothan, AL

Debuts: Nick Sanzo, Jackie Lee, Justin Martin, Eric Martin, Kazou Takahashi, Wallid Ismail, Rainy Martinez, Vitor Belfort, Tra Telligman

Fighters			Division	Method	Time	Round
Alternate Bouts						
Nick Sanzo	def.	Jackie Lee	Lightweight	Technical Knockout	0:48	1
Justin Martin	def.	Eric Martin	Heavyweight	Submission - Heel Hook	0:14	1
Lightweight Tournament						
Jerry Bohlander	def.	Nick Sanzo	Lightweight	Submission - Choke	0:39	1
Kazuo Takahashi	def.	Wallid Ismail	Lightweight	Unanimous Decision	—	—
Jerry Bohlander	def.	Rainy Martinez	Lightweight	Submission - Choke	1:24	1
Heavyweight Tournament						
Vitor Belfort	def.	Scott Ferrozzo	Heavyweight	Technical Knockout	0:43	1
Vitor Belfort	def.	Tra Telligman	Heavyweight	Technical Knockout - Cuts	1:17	1
Scott Ferrozzo	def.	Jim Mullen	Heavyweight	Technical Knockout	8:02	1
Superfight						
Mark Coleman	def.	Dan Severn	Heavyweight	Submission - Choke	2:57	1

Before a little over 3,000 fans at the Dothan Civic Center in Alabama, Ultimate Fighting Championship history was made as the organization crowned its first heavyweight champion, Mark Coleman, who defeated Dan Severn in a battle of wrestlers that also passed the UFC torch from "The Beast" to "The Hammer".

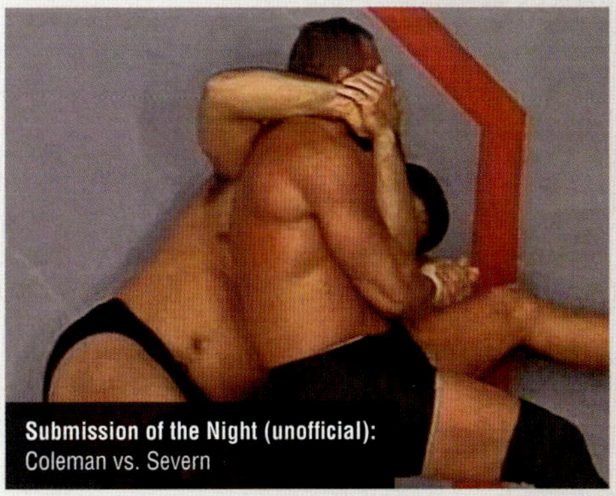
Submission of the Night (unofficial): Coleman vs. Severn

The unbeaten Coleman was now 6-0 in the Octagon, with none of his opponents managing to hear the final bell.

That wasn't the forecast going in, as most believed that Severn's experience and size would nullify the explosive ground and pound strategy of the former Ohio State star. From the moment Coleman turned away Severn's first takedown attempt, you got the impression that things weren't going to turn out well for the Michigan native.

Coleman got the bout to the mat and imposed his will from the top position. Soon, he got into the mount, and after locking Severn up, he forced a tapout via choke 2:57 into the match. The UFC now had its first champion.

Also notable from a history-making standpoint was that the UFC introduced weight classes for the first time, with fighters over 200 pounds competing at heavyweight, and those under 200 pounds competing in the newly-created lightweight division.

First appearance of commentator Joe Rogan

To inaugurate the two weight classes, UFC 12 contained two four-man tournaments, with Brazilian newcomer Vitor Belfort (heavyweight) and rising star Jerry Bohlander (lightweight) both emerging victorious.

At heavyweight, the 19-year-old Belfort became the youngest fighter to compete in the UFC to date, but he mixed the fiery aggression and athleticism of youth with the skills of a veteran in tearing through fellow newcomer Tra Telligman and veteran Scott Ferrozzo in a combined two minutes. Belfort's power and hand speed led him to victory in both bouts, and his charismatic star power was evident.

In the case of Bohlander, UFC fans already knew what the Lion's Den product could do in the Octagon, but that was fighting opponents who dwarfed him in size. Now competing on a level playing field physically, he got to display his game at its best, and he did in Dothan, submitting Rainy Martinez and replacement opponent Nick Sanzo in 1:24 and 0:39, respectively. The wins came five days before his 23rd birthday, and with Belfort and Bohlander both making bold statements in the Octagon, the stage had been set for the next generation to start moving into the UFC.

Knockout of the Night (unofficial): Belfort vs. Ferrozzo

Other semifinal bouts saw Ferrozzo halt Jim Mullen via strikes, and Kazuo Takahashi decision Wallid Ismail before being forced to withdraw from the final due to a broken hand.

Sanzo earned a spot in the lightweight tournament in place of the injured Takahashi, stopping Jackie Lee via strikes in 48 seconds. In the heavyweight alternate bout, Justin Martin defeated Eric Martin (no relation) via heel hook submission in 14 seconds.

UFC 13 *The Ultimate Force*

30 May 1997

Augusta Civic Center, Augusta, GA

Debuts: Tito Ortiz, Wes Albritton, Saeed Hosseini, Enson Inoue, Royce Alger, Christophe Leninger, Randy Couture, Steven Graham, Tony Halme, Dmitri Stepanov

Fighters			Division	Method	Time	Round
Alternate Bouts						
Tito Ortiz	def.	Wes Albritton	Lightweight	Technical Knockout	0:31	1
Jack Nilson	def.	Saeed Hosseini	Heavyweight	Technical Knockout	1:24	1
Lightweight Tournament						
Guy Mezger	def.	Tito Ortiz	Lightweight	Submission - Guillotine Choke	2:00	1
Enson Inoue	def.	Royce Alger	Lightweight	Submission - Armlock	1:37	1
Guy Mezger	def.	Christophe Leninger	Lightweight	Unanimous Decision	—	—
Heavyweight Tournament						
Randy Couture	def.	Steven Graham	Heavyweight	Technical Knockout	3:13	1
Randy Couture	def.	Tony Halme	Heavyweight	Submission - Rear Naked Choke	0:56	1
Steven Graham	def.	Dmitri Stepanov	Heavyweight	Submission - Armlock	1:30	1
Superfight						
Vitor Belfort	def.	Tank Abbott	Heavyweight	Technical Knockout	0:53	1

Could 20-year-old Brazilian phenom Vitor Belfort be stopped? Because if his 53-second blowout of UFC veteran David "Tank" Abbott in the UFC 13 Superfight at the Augusta Civic Center was any indication the pride of Rio de Janeiro might be staying on top for a long time.

Knockout of the Night (unofficial): Belfort vs. Abbott

"I was really focused," he said. "I respect my opponents a lot, and a fight is a fight. You never know what's gonna happen."

At least not until the bell rang, and Belfort began the delivery of his third consecutive UFC win.

Looking intense as he paced back and forth during the introductions, Abbott stalked Belfort at the opening bell, but after missing a looping right, Belfort grabbed him and tossed him to the mat. Belfort attempted to lock up Abbott's arm, but Tank powered free. Back standing, the two locked up and traded body shots, but when Belfort suddenly moved his attack upstairs, Abbott couldn't cope with the youngster's hand speed. A left dropped Abbott, and after some sloppy attempts to escape the ensuing barrage, he gave up his back and forced referee John McCarthy to halt the bout at the 53-second mark.

On the other end of the age spectrum from the 20-year-old Belfort was 33-year-old debutant Randy Couture, but the wrestling star was no less impressive in his first trip to the UFC, as he won the evening's heavyweight tournament with back-to-back wins over Tony Halme and Steven Graham.

"I wanted to represent my sport of wrestling really well and I think my years of wrestling experience paid off," he said. "I look forward to the next fight."

Not surprisingly, it was Couture's stellar mat work that brought him to victory, as he used takedowns, superior positioning and transitioning, along with well-placed strikes to submit Halme and stop Graham.

The Lion's Den's Guy Mezger won the UFC 13 lightweight tourney, following up a 15-minute decision win over Christophe Leninger in the semifinals with a two-minute submission victory against newcomer Tito Ortiz, who replaced the injured Enson Inoue.

Fight of the Night (unofficial): Mezger vs. Ortiz

Submission of the Night (unofficial): Mezger vs. Ortiz

Ortiz aggressively pursued Mezger as the final began, firing off punches before stuffing a takedown and beginning a ground assault that included thudding knees to the head. With 1:08 gone, referee McCarthy halted the bout to have the Octagonside physician check a cut on Mezger's head, but the bout was allowed to continue. When it resumed, Mezger had his bearings back, and when Ortiz shot in, he sunk in a guillotine choke that forced "The Huntington Beach Bad Boy" to tap out.

"I was tired, but I was ready for this," said Mezger. "Tito is a really, really tough guy. I give him a lot of credit. He made a mistake and I capitalized on it."

Ortiz earned his tournament final spot when Inoue was forced out of the tournament, but Hawaii native Inoue certainly left a lasting impression in his semifinal match as he spoiled the debut of highly touted wrestling star Royce Alger via submission. Easily avoiding Alger's first takedown attempt, Inoue almost locked his foe up within seconds, but the Iowan powered free. After Alger got the top position, he appeared to relax, but Inoue kept moving, avoiding a series of strikes to lock in the armbar and end the bout at 1:37 of the round.

The other heavyweight semifinal bout pitted Graham against Dmitri Stepanov, with Graham emerging victorious via submission in 1:30.

Ortiz made his Octagon debut in an alternate bout, stopping Wes Albritton in 31 seconds. The heavyweight alternate bout saw Jack Nilson delivered a technical knockout to Saeed Hosseini in 84 seconds.

UFC 14 *Showdown*

27 July 1997

Boutwell Auditorium, Birmingham, AL

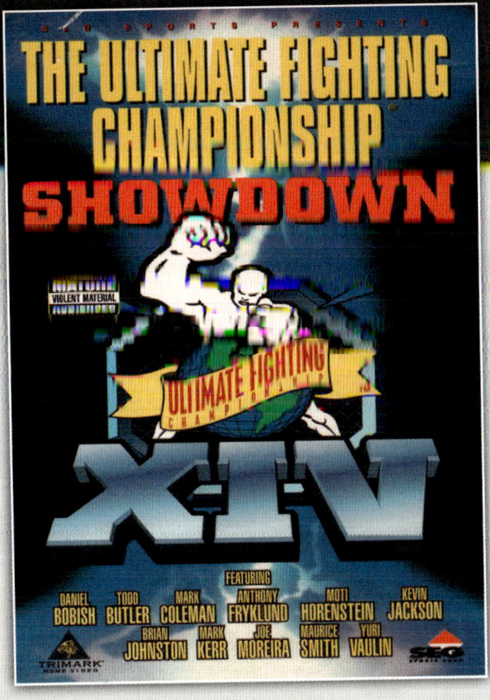

Debuts: Tony Fryklund, Donnie Chappell, Alex Hunter, Sam Fulton, Kevin Jackson, Todd Butler, Joe Moreira, Yuri Vaulin, Mark Kerr, Dan Bobish, Moti Horenstein

Fighters			Division	Method	Time	Round
Alternate Bouts						
Tony Fryklund	def.	Donnie Chappell	Middleweight	Submission - Choke	1:01	1
Alex Hunter	def.	Sam Fulton	Heavyweight	Technical Knockout	2:22	1
Middleweight Tournament						
Kevin Jackson	def.	Tony Fryklund	Middleweight	Submission - Rear Naked Choke	0:44	1
Kevin Jackson	def.	Todd Butler	Middleweight	Submission - Strikes	1:28	1
Joe Moreira	def.	Yuri Vaulin	Middleweight	Unanimous Decision	—	—
Heavyweight Tournament						
Mark Kerr	def.	Dan Bobish	Heavyweight	Submission - Chin to Eye	1:38	1
Dan Bobish	def.	Brian Johnston	Heavyweight	Technical Knockout	2:10	1
Mark Kerr	def.	Moti Horenstein	Heavyweight	Technical Knockout	2:22	1
Superfight						
Maurice Smith	def.	Mark Coleman	Heavyweight	Unanimous Decision	—	—

If recent history had proven anything, the evolution of the Ultimate Fighting Championship had moved from the dominance of Gracie jiu-jitsu to the dominance of the wrestler. At the Boutwell Auditorium in Birmingham, Alabama, Maurice Smith showed that a kickboxer can not only survive in the Octagon, but he can become a champion, as he stunned previously unbeaten Mark Coleman via unanimous decision to win the UFC heavyweight title.

It was a stirring victory for Smith, who showed great defensive and offensive work on the canvas to exhaust his foe and then take over on the feet for the latter stages of regulation time, as well as in two overtime periods.

Fight of the Night (unofficial):
Smith vs. Coleman

Coleman shot for, and got, his first takedown of the night 20 seconds in, and "The Hammer" immediately began raining down punches and headbutts on his foe. After surviving the initial barrage, Smith was calm, and he began delivering his own strikes from his back. Nearly three minutes in, Coleman worked for a neck crank briefly, but Smith wasn't having it, and he wasn't allowing the champion to improve his position either. Smith's vicious elbows from the bottom weren't helping matters for Coleman, but as the five-minute mark arrived, Coleman got Smith's back, worked for a choke, and then took the mount position. It looked like game over as Coleman began firing away, but Smith's defense was solid, and finally, with a little over nine minutes left, he scrambled to his feet and the crowd roared.

Now it was Smith's turn to attack the tired Coleman, but a kick to the head of the downed champion drew a warning from referee John McCarthy. After a brief break, Smith began his scoring with kicks to the leg, but a missed kick upstairs led to Coleman getting the fight back to the mat. This time though, Smith was doing most of the damage from the bottom as Coleman looked for any kind of breather he could get. With less than a minute left in regulation, Smith reversed position and then stood, and he finished the opening period with a flourish as Coleman looked to be close to collapse due to fatigue.

Now in control, Smith pecked at Coleman with his kicks from long-range, with the champion's weakened takedown attempts getting pushed away with ease. A flurry of punches jarred Coleman a little over two minutes in, and there was no question who had pulled ahead. In the second overtime, Smith maintained his lead, and when the final horn sounded, the kickboxer had shocked the world.

Despite Coleman's defeat, don't expect the parade of top-notch wrestlers into the UFC to end though, as 1992 US Olympic Gold medalist Kevin Jackson and former NCAA national champion Mark Kerr both made their Octagon debuts in impressive style by winning the night's middleweight (under 200 pounds) and heavyweight (over 200 pounds) tournaments.

Jackson made his presence known immediately, forcing Todd Butler to tap out due to strikes at 1:28 of their semifinal bout. In the middleweight final, Jackson submitted alternate Tony Fryklund via rear naked choke in 44 seconds.

Submission of the Night (unofficial):
Jackson vs. Fryklund

Kerr was just as impressive in his two wins as he romped over Moti Horenstein (technical knockout) and Dan Bobish (submission) in rapid-fire fashion.

Bobish had submitted UFC vet Brian Johnston to earn his heavyweight final berth Joe Moreira earned a spot in the middleweight finals by decisioning Yuri Vaulin over 15 minutes, but was removed from the tournament due to a concussion.

In UFC 14's alternate bouts, Fryklund submitted Donnie Chappell and heavyweight Alex Hunter TKO'd Sam Fulton.

Knockout of the Night (unofficial):
Kerr vs. Horenstein

UFC 15 *Collision Course*

17 Oct. 1997

Casino Magic, Bay St. Louis, MS

Debuts: Harry Moskowitz, Dwayne Cason, Houston Dorr, Dave Beneteau, Carlos Barreto, Greg Scott

Fighters			Division	Method	Time	Round
Alternate Bouts						
Alex Hunter	def.	Harry Moskowitz	Heavyweight	Unanimous Decision	—	—
Dwayne Cason	def.	Houston Dorr	Heavyweight	Technical Knockout	3:43	1
Heavyweight Tournament						
Mark Kerr	def.	Dwayne Cason	Heavyweight	Submission - Rear Naked Choke	0:53	1
Dave Beneteau	def.	Carlos Barreto	Heavyweight	Unanimous Decision	—	—
Mark Kerr	def.	Greg Stott	Heavyweight	Knockout	0:17	1
Superfight						
Randy Couture	def.	Vitor Belfort	Heavyweight	Technical Knockout	8:17	1
Maurice Smith	def.	Tank Abbott	Heavyweight	Submission - Strikes	8:08	1

The big men of mixed martial arts took center stage again at UFC 15 in Bay St. Louis, Mississippi, and when the dust settled, UFC heavyweight champion Maurice Smith and new contenders Randy Couture and Mark Kerr had all made statements to the fight world in various ways.

In the main event, kickboxing legend Smith was expected to engage in an all-out striking war with brawler Tank Abbott, but with Abbott coming in on short notice to replace the injured Dan Severn, the war didn't materialize. Instead, Smith fought a patient fight, pushing the challenger's already low gas tank to empty, and Abbott submitted due to fatigue at the eight-minute mark.

Abbott, as usual, began stalking at the opening bell, with Smith opting to use all of the Octagon real estate to wear his foe down. Smith scored with kicks to the leg while rebuffing Abbott's takedown attempts, but eventually, a short right a little over two minutes in produced the trip to the canvas Tank was looking for. While on the mat, Abbott did solid work, but not enough to avoid a restart from referee John McCarthy. Now the die had been cast, and Smith moved in for the kill on his exhausted foe. After two leg kicks, Abbott had enough, and the bout was waved off. The win was Smith's first successful title defense of the crown he won from Mark Coleman at UFC 14.

More emphatic in his victory was wrestling great Couture, who pulled off one of the sport's biggest upsets by halting the rise of the seemingly unbeatable Brazilian wunderkind Vitor Belfort via technical knockout in the UFC 15 heavyweight Superfight.

Fight of the Night (unofficial): Couture vs. Belfort

Couture was super from the outset, shaking off Belfort's opening burst of energy to practically manhandle the youngster at close range in the clinch and on the mat. While it was on the canvas that Couture really showed his dominance, his ability to stand fearlessly with Belfort was what really sucked the confidence out of the feared knockout artist. Finally, battered and tired, Belfort was taken to the mat, where a seemingly endless series of blows rained down on him until McCarthy halted the bout at the 8:17 mark. The defeat was Belfort's first as a pro.

Former Syracuse wrestling standout Mark Kerr made it 4-0 in the Octagon, and amazingly, he looked to be even better than he was at UFC 14, as it took "The Smashing Machine" only 70 seconds combined to knock out Greg Stott and submit Dwayne Cason to take his second consecutive heavyweight tournament title.

Knockout of the Night (unofficial): Kerr vs. Stott

Submission of the Night (unofficial): Kerr vs. Cason

In the other tournament semifinal bout, Canadian vet Dave Beneteau eked out a close but unanimous, decision win over Brazilian newcomer Carlos Barreto in a hard fought and entertaining 15-minute battle.

Opening the show were two alternate bouts for the heavyweight tournament, with Alex Hunter taking a split decision over Harry Moskowitz and the 20-year-old Cason stopping Houston Dorr via strikes.

UFC Ultimate Japan 1

21 Dec. 1997

Yokohama Arena, Yokohama, Japan

Debuts: Tra Telligman, Brad Kohler, Kazushi Sakuraba, Marcus Silveira, Yoji Anjo

Fighters			Division	Method	Time	Round
Alternate Bout						
Tra Telligman	def.	Brad Kohler	Heavyweight	Submission - Armbar	10:05	1
Heavyweight Tournament						
Kazushi Sakuraba	def.	Marcus Silveira	Heavyweight	Submission - Armbar	3:45	1
Tank Abbott	def.	Yoji Anjo	Heavyweight	Unanimous Decision	—	—
Kazushi Sakuraba	def.	Marcus Silveira	Heavyweight	No Contest	1:51	1
Superfight						
Randy Couture	def.	Maurice Smith	Heavyweight	Unanimous Decision	—	—
Frank Shamrock	def.	Kevin Jackson	Middleweight	Submission - Armbar	0:16	1
Vitor Belfort	def.	Joe Charles	Heavyweight	Submission - Armbar	4:03	1

It took him only four fights, but Randy Couture earned the UFC heavyweight championship at the Yokohama Arena in Japan, taking a close majority decision over Maurice Smith in the main event of the organization's first foray to the Land of the Rising Sun.

The 21-minute bout was far from a barnburner, with Couture using the gameplan many believed should have worked for Mark Coleman in his title-losing effort to Smith: score the takedown and control the bout from the top, using just enough activity to keep the fight there. The difference in this bout was that the supremely conditioned Couture showed the patience and pace necessary to get the job done.

"I knew it was gonna be a very close fight," said the new champion. "A lot of guys come out and try to devastate Maurice right off and he's too composed and too conditioned to do that. I knew it was gonna be a matter of being able to take him down and control him. I expected it to go long."

"All Randy did was hold me down really good," said a disappointed Smith. "That's all he did. He got a couple shots, I got a couple shots. A draw seemed about right."

Two judges declared Couture the winner, while the third had it a draw.

UFC Japan's other championship fight certainly brought the heat as far as excitement goes, as debuting 24-year-old Frank Shamrock, the adopted younger brother of Ken, became the UFC's first middleweight champion, taking just 16 seconds to submit Olympic Gold medal wrestler Kevin Jackson.

Submission of the Night (unofficial):
Shamrock vs. Jackson

Things looked to be going well initially for Jackson as he got Shamrock to the mat in the opening seconds, but in an ensuing scramble, Shamrock locked up Jackson's arm and ended the bout.

"I studied his fights, I studied his tape, he's an awesome wrestler and an elite athlete," said Shamrock. "I just saw a few holes in his wrestling ability and in his fighting style and I capitalized on it. I think I got lucky, but I was prepared."

Brazil's Vitor Belfort shook off the disappointment of his first pro loss against Couture at UFC 15, as he spoiled the return of "The Ghetto Man", Joe Charles, with a submission at 4:03 of the bout.

The fight showed off Belfort's ground game, as he eschewed his lethal striking attack for a quick takedown and some excellent grappling that led to the armbar that finished Charles' night.

It was a bizarre heavyweight tournament, yet it started out normally enough with veteran Tank Abbott breaking a three-fight losing streak with a decision win over Yoji Anjo. A broken hand would force Abbott from the tournament though, seemingly opening a spot for the Lion's Den's Tra Telligman, who won the alternate bout with an armbar submission of Brad Kohler.

The other semifinal bout, featuring Japan's Kazushi Sakuraba against Brazil's Marcus "Conan" Silveira, ended in controversial fashion. After some entertaining early action, Silveira got off some solid standup strikes as Sakuraba covered up against the fence. Looking to turn the tide, Sakuraba dropped to the mat for a takedown, with referee John McCarthy calling the bout, mistakenly thinking Sakuraba had been knocked out by Silveira's punches. Sakuraba and his corner were bewildered, but the verdict was later overruled and judged a no contest. The solution? Sakuraba and Silveira would meet again in the heavyweight final with Abbott eliminated due to injury.

Fight of the Night (unofficial):
Sakuraba vs. Silveira

This time, Sakuraba made sure he took matters into his own hands, working his submissions from the start until he found the finisher, an armbar that produced a tapout 3:45 into the bout.

UFC 16 *Battle in the Bayou*

13 March 1998

Pontchartrain Center, New Orleans, LA

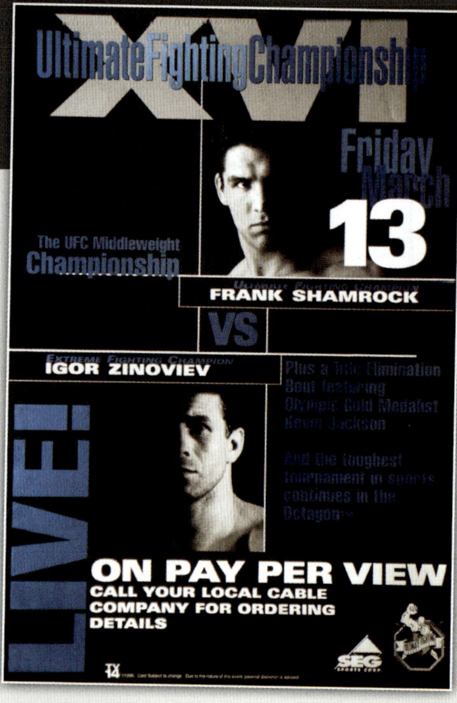

Debuts: Igor Zinoviev, Tsuyoshi Kosaka, Chris Brennan, Pat Miletich, Townsend Saunders, Eugenio Tadeu, Mikey Burnett, Courtney Turner, Laverne Clark, Josh Stuart

Fighters			Division	Method	Time	Round
Alternate Bouts						
Laverne Clark	def.	Josh Stuart	Lightweight	Technical Knockout	1:15	1
Chris Brennan	def.	Courtney Turner	Lightweight	Submission - Armbar	1:20	1
Lightweight Tournament						
Pat Miletich	def.	Chris Brennan	Lightweight	Submission - Choke	9:01	1
Mikey Burnett	def.	Eugenio Tadeu	Lightweight	Technical Knockout	9:46	1
Pat Miletich	def.	Townsend Saunders	Lightweight	Split Decision	—	1
Superfights						
Frank Shamrock	def.	Igor Zinoviev	Middleweight	Knockout	0:22	1
Tsuyoshi Kosaka	def.	Kimo Leopoldo	Heavyweight	Unanimous Decision	—	1
Jerry Bohlander	def.	Kevin Jackson	Middleweight	Submission - Armbar	10:21	1

UFC middleweight champion Frank Shamrock made it look easy in "The Big Easy", as he defended his title for the first time with a devastating 22-second finish of previously unbeaten Igor Zinoviev in the main event of UFC 16 at the Pontchartrain Center in New Orleans.

After Shamrock opened up with some leg kicks and feints, Zinoviev engaged with his foe but was immediately picked up and slammed. Zinoviev was out on impact as he hit the canvas, bringing referee John McCarthy in to stop the fight immediately.

Knockout of the Night (unofficial):
Shamrock vs. Zinoviev

"I train hard, I come prepared, and I've got luck and skill," said the 24-year-old Shamrock. "Igor is an awesome competitor, he's a friend of mine. The best man won tonight, but he'll be back and I'm here to stay."

After nearly two years away, Kimo Leopoldo came back to the Octagon to compete in a heavyweight superfight, but UFC rookie Tsuyoshi Kosaka spoiled his return with a unanimous decision victory.

Kimo shot out fast, even securing an ankle lock in the early going. Kosaka pulled loose, but Kimo continued to press the action on the mat. Kosaka remained calm, and he even looked for his own leg lock before the two stood. The standup action didn't last long, and on the mat, the two traded hard shots and submission attempts periodically. As the fighters rose again in the ninth minute, Kosaka began tagging the tiring Kimo with shot after shot, drawing roars from the crowd as regulation time ticked away. In overtime, Kosaka opened up with a hard knee, but Kimo kept coming, eventually getting the Japanese fighter to the canvas. After a brief time in the mount position, Kimo got reversed, and Kosaka ended the bout by feeding his opponent a steady diet of ground strikes, sealing the victory.

Submission of the Night (unofficial):
Bohlander vs. Jackson

Fight of the Night (unofficial):
Kosaka vs. Leopoldo

1992 Olympic Gold medal winning wrestler Kevin Jackson took on Jerry Bohlander in the evening's middleweight superfight, and it was California's Bohlander taking home the win by submission. Jackson looked to be on his way to victory as he controlled much of the bout on the canvas, but Bohlander's continued submission attempts finally paid off when he caught his opponent's arm and prompted referee McCarthy to stop the fight, much to Jackson's protests. The end came at 10:21.

Iowa's Pat Miletich won the UFC's first lightweight 170 pounds and under tournament, submitting California's Chris Brennan at the 9:01 mark. Brennan replaced Mikey Burnett, who withdrew from the bout due to a broken finger. It was the third bout between the Octagon newcomers, with Miletich now holding a 2-0-1 edge.

Both men's striking was sharp in the opening minute, but then Brennan switched things up and decided to take matters south. Brennan started out in control on top, but soon Miletich got into the dominant position and began firing off strikes. Brennan stayed busy from the bottom, but eventually Miletich wore him down and forced him to submit to a choke.

Midwest standout Miletich upset Olympic Silver medalist Townsend Saunders in their semifinal bout, scoring a close split decision win over the world-class wrestler.

In the second semifinal, Burnett's punching power proved to be too much for Eugenio Tadeu, as he stopped him via strikes 9:46 into their match.

In alternate lightweight tournament bouts, Brennan used an armbar to submit Courtney Turner in 80 seconds, and Laverne Clark used his striking skills to halt Josh Stewart even quicker, needing just 75 ticks of the clock.

One Hit Wonders: Igor Zinoviev, Eugenio Tadeu, Courtney Turner, Josh Stuart

A talented mixed martial artist from Russia, Igor "Houdini" Zinoviev broke into the sport in 1995, winning his first four bouts and even stopping Enson Inoue in a 1996 bout. After two draws in his next two contests, he got the call to the UFC, but a broken collarbone suffered in the loss to Shamrock ended his career abruptly.

UFC 17 *Redemption*

15
May
1998

Mobile Civic Center, Mobile, AL

Debuts: Pete Williams, Jeremy Horn, Carlos Newton, Dan Henderson, Hugo Duarte, Joe Pardo, Mike Van Arsdale, Bob Gilstrap, Allan Goes, Andre Roberts, Chuck Liddell, Noe Hernandez

Fighters			Division	Method	Time	Round
Alternate Bouts						
Chuck Liddell	def.	Noe Hernandez	Middleweight	Unanimous Decision		1
Andre Roberts	def.	Harry Moskowitz	Heavyweight	Knockout	3:15	1
Middleweight Tournament						
Dan Henderson	def.	Carlos Newton	Middleweight	Split Decision	—	1
Carlos Newton	def.	Bob Gilstrap	Middleweight	Submission - Triangle Choke	0:52	1
Dan Henderson	def.	Allan Goes	Middleweight	Unanimous Decision	—	3
Superfights						
Frank Shamrock	def.	Jeremy Horn	Middleweight	Submission - Kneebar	16:28	1
Pete Williams	def.	Mark Coleman	Heavyweight	Knockout	12:39	1
Tank Abbott	def.	Hugo Duarte	Heavyweight	Technical Knockout	0:44	1
Mike Van Arsdale	def.	Joe Pardo	Heavyweight	Submission - Keylock	11:02	1

Knockout of the Night (unofficial): Williams vs. Coleman

The title of UFC 17 was "Redemption", but former UFC heavyweight champion Mark Coleman was unable to get any in his first bout since losing the belt to Maurice Smith 10 months earlier, as he was knocked out by a head kick from unheralded Octagon rookie Pete Williams.

"I'm on top of the world right now. I knew I could do it, I trained hard for this, and I just hung in there and got that kick to the head," said the 22-year-old Williams.

Coleman looked to be in Hammer-esque form early as he took the Lion's Den fighter to the mat for some ground and pound action. Williams showed poise from the bottom though, almost catching Coleman in an armbar. With 5:34 gone, referee John McCarthy restarted the action, and Coleman looked winded despite knocking his foe back with two hard right hands. Williams was content to peck away at the former champion from long range, and Coleman was clearly out of gas. Finally, after eating a series of leg kicks, Coleman got the energy to score a takedown at the 8:30 mark. Williams rose, but he ate some shots on the way up as Coleman pinned him to the fence. Coleman was able to get the bout back to the mat late in regulation, but there was still the overtime to contend with. And in the overtime, Williams stalked and caught Coleman with a right kick to the head, knocking him down and out, ending matters at the 39-second mark.

Frank Shamrock defended his 205-pound championship for the second time in a bout not aired on May 15's Pay-Per-View broadcast, submitting Jeremy Horn via kneebar at the 16:28 mark.

In the final of the UFC 17 middleweight tournament, world-class wrestler Dan Henderson eked out a split decision win over Carlos Newton in an exciting 15 minute bout.

Fight of the Night (unofficial): Henderson vs. Newton

Newton came blazing out of the corner to start the bout, using his speed and striking to tag Henderson. Less than 30 seconds in, Newton rocked Henderson with a right hand, and moments later jumped guard with his opponent in a guillotine choke. Henderson broke loose and began working his ground and pound game. At the 2:40 mark, the bout was momentarily halted to fix Newton's glove and give him his mouthpiece, and when it resumed, it was Newton slamming the wrestler. Henderson got back to his feet and began firing away with his right hand before unleashing a series of hard knees at close range. After some more solid ground work from Henderson, the two stood eight minutes in, and midway through the tenth minute, Newton dropped Henderson. The wrestler quickly got his bearings back and finished up regulation with a slam that got a rise out of the crowd. In the overtime period, the two continued to battle, but it was Henderson who finished strong to take the close decision win.

After nearly six months away, David "Tank" Abbott made his return to the Octagon, and in the process won his second consecutive bout, finishing off Hugo Duarte in the first round. After avoiding a choke and an armbar in the opening stages of the bout, Abbott unleashed a series of furious ground strikes, bringing in referee John McCarthy to rescue the Brazilian 44 seconds in.

The first of three heavyweight superfights saw world-class wrestler Mike Van Arsdale add a UFC win to his resume as he forced Joe Pardo to tap out to a keylock 11:02 into their bout.

Kicking off the night's card were two semifinal bouts in the UFC 17 middleweight tournament, and debutants Henderson and Newton both moved on with wins over Allan Goes (unanimous decision) and Bob Gilstrap (submission).

Submission of the Night (unofficial): Newton vs. Gilstrap

In undercard bouts, Andre Roberts won a unanimous decision over Harry Moskowitz, and kickboxer Chuck Liddell made a victorious professional MMA debut in the same manner as he outpointed Noe Hernandez.

One Hit Wonders: Hugo Duarte, Joe Pardo, Bob Gilstrap, Allan Goes, Noe Hernandez

BROADCASTERS

MIKE GOLDBERG

Fresh out of a job doing play-by-play for the Detroit Red Wings, Mike Goldberg needed some good news late in 1997. Little did he know an encounter would turn out to actually be one of his producers at ESPN and former teammate with the Wings, Bruce Connal.

"Goldie, you got a raw deal with the Wings, but I got a gig for you," said Connal. "You need to take a jiu-jitsu class; it's in Japan, but they'll pay you."

Goldberg, who was broadcasting anything and everything—even women's soccer—to get back on his feet, immediately accepted the job to do play-by-play for something called the Ultimate Fighting Championship.

"I had no idea what the UFC was," he recalled. "But it was a gig, it was in Japan, and it seemed pretty cool. I thought that maybe I'd get a second one [event] out of the whole deal."

It's gone on a bit longer than that, and after calling nearly 150 events, Mike Goldberg has become synonymous with the sport of mixed martial arts in general and the UFC in particular. Goldberg with the UFC is like Vin Scully with baseball, Keith Jackson with college football or Marv Albert with NBA basketball—you can't have one without the other. Goldberg has taken his immersion in MMA even further than just showing up on fight night. His work in the gym started in the days after the 9/11 attacks in 2001, when UFC President Dana White brought his play-by-play man down to the Zuffa Gym to get a taste of how fighters prepared for their bouts. And after four days of hitting the pads and working out with Bobby Stellm, Goldberg was hooked. Since then, Muay Thai has been an integral part of his daily regimen.

"It has helped me to see the sport the way I was able to see hockey when I was a hockey broadcaster because I had played hockey since I was seven years old," said Goldberg, who admits he's still learning all the intricate details of the sport. It doesn't hurt having Joe Rogan by his side either, considering the color commentator's history in jiu-jitsu and taekwondo.

"I look at it like I'm Al Michaels and Joe's John Madden," said Goldberg of his broadcast partner. "I didn't coach the game, I didn't play the game, so I see Joe as John Madden. That being said, it's still important for me to bring more than a fork and a knife to the table, and I've been able to achieve that because of my training and because of the time I've spent with the guys who have helped train me and helped me really understand the sport. But I still have a long way until I'm done because I'll always try to get better."

Whether it's show 1, 150 or 1000 for Mike Goldberg, the feeling is always the same when the lights in the arena go down.

"That's when the work ends and the fun begins," he said. "At that point I can't prep anymore, and the minute we call the first prelim, I get this sense of calm. Then we play that Who song, and I start jumping around like a little kid. That is truly when it's the highest of highs."

"The thing that makes the Ultimate Fighting Championship unique and, to me, the best gig in broadcasting today, is that every show is 'game seven,'" he continues. "I was the sideline guy with Michael Jordan and the Bulls during their first three titles, and every game watching Michael play was a privilege, but there was still game 44 against a bad Charlotte team and game 62 against a bad Sacramento team. We don't have those games. Every UFC event is the Super Bowl, Game Seven of the World Series or the NCAA Championship. That, to me, as a broadcaster, is what everybody dreams of. You want to play in a game seven or broadcast a game seven; I get to do about 25 game sevens a year, and that's why I've got the greatest job in the world."

JOE ROGAN

Joe Rogan has met plenty of success in the entertainment business, not only with his popular standup act and the television series *Fear Factor*, but also as a member of the cast of *News Radio*. However, it's the role he's had as the UFC's color commentator that may have garnered the black belt in taekwondo and brown belt in jiu-jitsu the most acclaim.

It's not something he expected when he first began working as an interviewer for previous UFC owners SEG beginning with UFC 12 in Dothan, Alabama.

"The old SEG, we were in weird little s**t holes in the middle of nowhere," he recalled. "You're in a 10,000-seat arena and there are like 2,000 people in there, scattered. That was the real dark ages."

The gig didn't last for too long, but when Zuffa took over the UFC in 2001 and got Rogan and some buddies tickets for an event, one conversation with the diehard MMA fan convinced President Dana White that Rogan was the man for the commentator's chair.

"He (White) was talking to me about fights and I was just going off about this and that, and he asked me if I ever thought about doing commentary," said Rogan. "I told him that I just wanted to watch. He said 'Just do it once for me, as a favor.' I said 'sure', I did it once, I did it again, and then I wound up doing all of them."

Rogan's commentary mixes the enthusiasm of a fan with the knowledge of someone well versed in combat sports. And many media members can say without a hint of shame that his knowledge of the ground game has saved them on more than one occasion when they looked at a submission and said "what the heck is that?"

"When I do the UFC," said Rogan, "my preparation is that I'm a huge MMA fan and I watch all of them and pay attention to everything, and there are a lot of matchups that really interest me 100 percent. That's my preparation—it's my life. It's not like a job to me, where it's something I have to sit down and do. I would have done it anyway—I did it anyway. It's really crazy, but I never set out to be a sports broadcaster. That was the criticism I got a lot in the beginning—'well, he doesn't sound like a sports broadcaster.' Well, I'm not; I don't even know how I got the job."

This self-effacing honesty is a hallmark of Rogan's first love—comedy—and to him, it's a key to good comedy in general.

"Honesty and insight, two things that most people don't really have a whole lot of, make good comedy," he said. "What's really funny is stuff that you can relate to; the stuff someone points out that really makes sense to you. That's what's really funny. But in order to really do that correctly, you've got to be honest with yourself. And that's something that very few people really are, which is why there's so much bad comedy and why there are so many boring people. These people aren't really honest and they're not figuring life out; they're just pretending they figured life out. The best comedy is 'here's the world through my eyes and I happen to have an unusual or unique point of view.' There's other kinds of comedy, like Carrot Top stuff and other silly stuff—and I'm not knocking any of it. It's all fun and makes people feel better and enjoy the show, but there's a huge difference between a great standup comedian like Dave Chappelle and the boring kind of comedy. The boring kind of comedy is like point karate, and the kind of comedy I do is like MMA."

It's his personality on stage and how he calls the action in the Octagon that makes him the perfect choice to man the UFC broadcast booth.

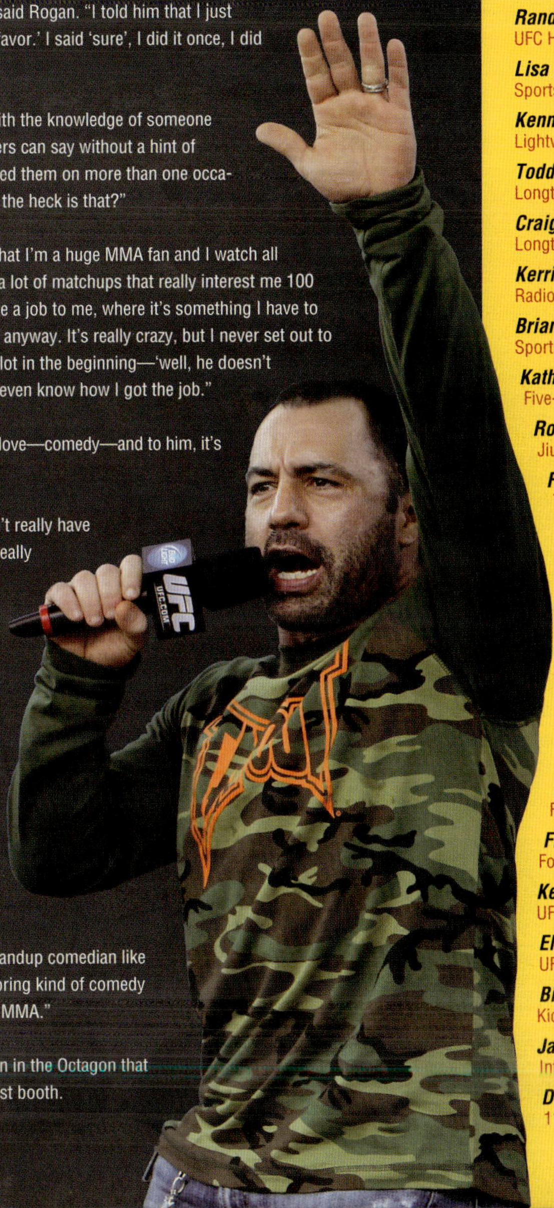

OTHER OCTAGONSIDE COMMENTATORS

In addition to mainstays Mike Goldberg and Joe Rogan, 28 men and women have grabbed the microphone as either play-by-play announcers, color commentators, or interviewers. And like the competitors in the Octagon, the ones calling the action come from a wide array of backgrounds, making their addition to UFC broadcasts as diverse as the sport itself.

Phil Baroni
Former UFC middleweight contender

Bruce Beck
Longtime sportscaster

Ryan Bennett
Longtime sportscaster

Jeff Blatnick
1984 US Olympic Gold medalist in Greco-Roman wrestling

Eddie Bravo
Jiu-jitsu black belt, best remembered for submitting Royler Gracie

Jim Brown
NFL Hall of Famer for the Cleveland Browns

Randy Couture
UFC Hall of Famer and five-time UFC champion

Lisa Dergan
Sportscaster / former *Playboy* Playmate of the Month

Kenny Florian
Lightweight and featherweight contender

Todd Harris
Longtime sportscaster

Craig Hummer
Longtime sportscaster

Kerri Kasem
Radio and television host

Brian Kilmeade
Sportscaster and Fox News Channel host

Kathy Long
Five-time world kickboxing champion

Rod Machado
Jiu-jitsu practitioner and analyst

Frank Mir
Two-time UFC heavyweight champion

Jeff Osborne
Expert MMA analyst

Herb Perez
1992 US Olympic Gold medalist in taekwondo

Ben Perry
Hollywood stuntman

Jens Pulver
First-ever UFC lightweight champion

Ricco Rodriguez
Former UFC heavyweight champion

Bas Rutten
Former UFC heavyweight champion

Frank Shamrock
Former UFC light heavyweight champion

Ken Shamrock
UFC Hall of Famer

Elvis Sinosic
UFC veteran and Australian MMA pioneer

Bill "Superfoot" Wallace
Kickboxing legend

James Werme
Interviewer

Don "The Dragon" Wilson
11-time world kickboxing champion

Ultimate Brazil

16 Oct. 1998

Ginasio da Portuguesa, Sao Paulo, Brazil

Debuts: Cesar Marcussi, Paulo Santos, Tulio Palhares, Adriano Santos, Ebenezer Fontes Braga, Pedro Rizzo, Wanderlei Silva, John Lober

Fighters			Division	Method	Time	Round
Main Card						
Frank Shamrock	def.	John Lober	Middleweight	Submission - Strikes	7:40	1
Pat Miletich	def.	Mikey Burnett	Lightweight	Split Decision	—	—
Vitor Belfort	def.	Wanderlei Silva	Middleweight	Technical Knockout	0:44	1
Pedro Rizzo	def.	Tank Abbott	Heavyweight	Knockout	8:07	1
Tsuyoshi Kosaka	def.	Pete Williams	Heavyweight	Unanimous Decision	—	—
Ebenezer Fontes Braga	def.	Jeremy Horn	Middleweight	Submission - Guillotine Choke	3:28	1
Preliminary Card						
Tulio Palhares	def.	Adriano Santos	Middleweight	Technical Knockout	9:00	1
Cesar Marcussi	def.	Paulo Santos	Lightweight	Technical Knockout	—	1

After three fights in the UFC that saw him debut with a 16-second win over Kevin Jackson to win the middleweight title, knock out Igor Zinoviev in 22 seconds to retain the belt, and submit Jeremy Horn in a 16-plus minute scrap to show that he had the gas tank to push himself to the limit, what was next for Frank Shamrock as the UFC visited Brazil for the first time in its history?

Fight of the Night (unofficial): Shamrock vs. Lober

A little revenge, and it was sweet for Shamrock, who defended his title for the third time by using his strikes to force a submission from the last man to beat him by decision back in January of 1997, John Lober.

It looked like Shamrock was going to make it another short night as he sunk in a guillotine choke on his foe and then used it to slam Lober to the ground. Lober went into defensive mode on his back, and as he rose, he got caught in another guillotine. Again, Lober survived and even tried to sink in a submission of his own—an arm triangle—but Shamrock escaped.

Six minutes in, the two stood, and Shamrock began teeing off with leg kicks. A right hand upstairs dropped Lober, but Shamrock refused to follow. Lober got back up, only to be sent back down by a barrage of strikes. Now Shamrock moved in for the kill, and Lober—cut, battered, and fatigued—decided that he had enough and the bout was called at the 7:40 mark.

The Brazilian turf war between Rio de Janeiro's Vitor Belfort and Curitiba's Wanderlei Silva instead turned into a one-sided beatdown, as "The Phenom" showed off his blazing hand speed and concussive power in his middleweight debut.

Knockout of the Night (unofficial): Belfort vs. Silva

The 21-year-old Belfort was stalked by the 22-year-old Muay Thai machine, but after eating a leg kick, Belfort began to walk forward, and when he found his opening, he struck, ripping off a furious barrage of straight punches that sent Silva across the Octagon. By the time they reached the fence, Silva was hurt and defenseless and referee John McCarthy had no choice but to call off the fight at the 44 second mark.

The UFC's first ever lightweight championship fight was a highly-anticipated one, as skilled battlers Pat Miletich and Mikey Burnett met up for the vacant belt. Unfortunately, the fight didn't perform up to expectations, as Miletich's defensive gameplan and effective guard work nullified Burnett's more aggressive attack, allowing the Iowan to escape with a split decision and the title in the 21-minute match.

"The main thing I wanted to do was hit him with some leg kicks, close the gap, grapple with him, and try to get him into a submission," said Miletich. "The guy's got great balance and he's very powerful. It's unbelievable how strong he is. Very few guys I've ever rolled around with are that strong. That fight was too close for one of us to deserve the belt. He's a champ, that's all there is to it."

Octagon rookie Pedro Rizzo threw his name into the heavyweight title mix, ripping off a series of leg kicks taught to him by his trainer Marco Ruas before wearing out Tank Abbott and finishing him with strikes 8:07 into their bout.

In other bouts, Tsuyoshi Kosaka decisioned Pete Williams unanimously over 15 minutes, and Ebenezer Fontes Braga submitted Jeremy Horn via guillotine choke in 3:28.

One Hit Wonders: Cesar Marcussi, Paulo Santos, Adriano Santos, Tulio Palhares, Ebenezer Fontes Braga, John Lober

UFC 18 *Road to the Heavyweight Title*

08 Jan. 1999

Pontchartrain Center, New Orleans, LA

Debuts: Bas Rutten, Evan Tanner

Fighters			Division	Method	Time	Round
Main Card						
Pat Miletich	def.	Jorge Patino	Lightweight	Unanimous Decision	—	—
Bas Rutten	def.	Tsuyoshi Kosaka	Heavyweight	Technical Knockout	14:15	1
Pedro Rizzo	def.	Mark Coleman	Heavyweight	Split Decision	—	—
Tito Ortiz	def.	Jerry Bohlander	Middleweight	Technical Knockout - Cuts	14:31	1
Mikey Burnett	def.	Townsend Saunders	Lightweight	Unanimous Decision	—	—
Evan Tanner	def.	Darrel Gholar	Middleweight	Submission - Rear Naked Choke	7:57	1
Laverne Clark	def.	Frank Caracci	Lightweight	Submission - Strikes	6:52	1

With the UFC heavyweight division thrown into disarray with the vacating of the title by champion Randy Couture, the hunt was on for a new star to rise to the top and claim the belt. That star may have been found in the form of Holland's Bas Rutten, who made his Octagon debut after a long career in Japan's Pancrase organization with a hard-fought technical knockout win of Tsuyoshi Kosaka in the main event of UFC 18 at the Pontchartrain Center in New Orleans.

Fight of the Night (unofficial): Rutten vs. Kosaka

Rutten showed off some impressive takedown defense initially as he peppered Kosaka with strikes before finally getting brought to the mat. Rutten had some success getting back to his feet, but Kosaka was relentless about putting him on the canvas again. Nearing the six-minute mark, referee John McCarthy stood the fighters, and Rutten got off some shots before the inevitable trip to the mat. After another standup, Rutten finished the regulation period strong, but he would need even more to pull ahead on the scorecards.

And he got it, as he battered the tiring Kosaka with strikes, eventually adding a knee to his arsenal that rocked the Japanese fighter. A series of straight punches finished the job, with McCarthy stopping the fight at the 14:15 mark.

"My corner said he's not gonna shoot anymore, he's gonna be too tired," said Rutten, who scored wins over Maurice Smith, Frank Shamrock, and Guy Mezger in Japan. "So in this overtime I said give me the sign of one minute and I will explode on him. So that's what I did."

In the championship co-feature, UFC lightweight champion Pat Miletich continued to shut down all opposition, scoring a relatively uneventful unanimous decision over newcomer Jorge Patino in a 21-minute contest that, like the Miletich-Burnett title bout, didn't sit too well with fans in attendance that were craving action. It does take two to fight though, and Patino didn't exactly conduct himself like a fighter trying to win a world championship. Outside of a tight guillotine choke in overtime, Miletich was in little trouble as he waltzed to another victory.

The slide of former heavyweight champion Mark Coleman continued, as rising star Pedro Rizzo moved closer to a shot at the belt with a split-decision victory. The defeat was the third in a row for "The Hammer", but this was one many viewers believed should have gone Coleman's way.

Not surprisingly, Coleman was able to get the bout to the mat in the opening stages, and he kept Rizzo there effectively before a McCarthy restart. Looking winded already, Coleman was not forced to deal with his Achilles heel—his cardio—against a hard-hitting striker eager to make a name for himself. Rizzo began landing his devastating leg kicks, and Coleman was feeling the effects, but he was able to hit another takedown to catch a breather and score some more points before a final standup just before the end of regulation.

The overtime period was marked by Rizzo's lack of aggression, even though he tagged Coleman almost at will, and it was apparently enough for the judges to award him the verdict.

Middleweight up-and-comer Tito Ortiz got a measure of revenge on Ken Shamrock's Lion's Den, using a well-rounded attack to dominate Jerry Bohlander before the bout was stopped in the overtime period due to a cut. (Ortiz had lost a UFC 13 match to Guy Mezger via submission.)

Submission of the Night (unofficial): Tanner vs. Gholar

In other bouts, lightweight Laverne Clark defeated Frank Carraci via submission due to strikes, newcomer Evan Tanner submitted Darrel Gholar via rear naked choke, and Mikey Burnett bounced back from his disappointing loss to Miletich by decisioning Townsend Saunders.

UFC 19 *Ultimate Young Guns*

05 March 1999

Casino Magic Bay St. Louis, Bay St. Louis, MS

Debuts: Kevin Randleman, Sione Latu

Fighters			Division	Method	Time	Round
Main Card						
Tito Ortiz	def.	Guy Mezger	Middleweight	Technical Knockout	9:55	1
Gary Goodridge	def.	Andre Roberts	Heavyweight	Submission - Strikes	0:43	1
Jeremy Horn	def.	Chuck Liddell	Middleweight	Technical Knockout - Arm Triangle Choke	12:00	1
Kevin Randleman	def.	Maurice Smith	Heavyweight	Unanimous Decision	—	—
Evan Tanner	def.	Valeri Ignatov	Middleweight	Technical Knockout	2:57	1
Pete Williams	def.	Jason Godsey	Heavyweight	Submission - Kneebar	1:54	1
Preliminary Card						
Sione Latu	def.	Joey Roberts	Middleweight	Technical Knockout - Cuts	—	1

Knockout of the Night (unofficial): Ortiz vs. Mezger

Rising star Tito Ortiz evened his score with veteran Guy Mezger in the main event of UFC 19 at Casino Magic in Bay St. Louis, Mississippi, halting the man who beat him nearly two years earlier via technical knockout.

Taking the bout on late notice to replace the injured Vitor Belfort, Ortiz eagerly stepped in for a shot at some payback against Mezger. He shot for a takedown and got it to begin the bout, and Mezger held his foe close in order to force a restart. Ortiz was undeterred, bulling his foe to the fence. Mezger found an opening and got back up to his feet, but Ortiz' pace was unforgiving, and he smothered the Lion's Den product at every turn.

On an ensuing submission attempt, Mezger almost secured a kimura, but when it failed, it left Ortiz in control from the top. Ortiz tried to stay busy, and after rocking Mezger with a strike, the Texan gave up his back momentarily. Around two minutes later, Mezger briefly tried a triangle choke and a kimura from his back, but Ortiz again powered out.

The action began to stall, and after a quick standing period, Ortiz took the tired Mezger down again. A series of peppering ground strikes followed, and with Mezger not responding, referee John McCarthy stopped the fight at the 9:55 mark.

The feud wasn't over yet though, as Ortiz' post-fight gloating incensed Mezger's trainer, UFC pioneer Ken Shamrock, setting the stage for some more grudge matches in the coming years.

Returning to the Octagon for the first time in over two and a half years, "Big Daddy" Gary Goodridge gave UFC fans something to cheer about as he forced Andre Roberts to submit due to strikes 43 seconds into their bout. The end was a bit anti-climactic as Roberts waved the fight off after taking a couple shots to the head, but it was a good win nonetheless for Goodridge, whose last appearance in the UFC was at the Ultimate Ultimate 96.

Former middleweight title challenger Jeremy Horn secured his first UFC win in three tries, engaging in an entertaining scrap with California kickboxer Chuck Liddell before sinking in an arm triangle choke in the closing seconds of regulation time that put his opponent to sleep as time ran out, ending the bout in his favor.

Two-time Division I national wrestling champion Kevin Randleman followed his teammate Mark Coleman into the Octagon, and the Ohio State standout made an immediate statement to the MMA world in his debut with a 15-minute unanimous decision win over former heavyweight champion Maurice Smith.

Evan Tanner was impressive in middleweight action, stopping Valeri Ignatov via strikes at the 2:57 mark.

Heavyweight prospect Pete Williams got back in the win column after his upset loss to Tsuyoshi Kosaka, submitting Jason Godsey via kneebar in 1:54.

In the middleweight opener, Sione Latu stopped Joey Roberts via cuts.

Fight and Submission of the Night (unofficial): Horn vs. Liddell

UFC 20 *Battle for the Gold*

07 May 1999

Boutwell Auditorium, Birmingham, AL

Debuts: Ron Waterman, Chris Condo

Fighters			Division	Method	Time	Round
Main Card						
Bas Rutten	def.	Kevin Randleman	Heavyweight	Split Decision	—	1
Pedro Rizzo	def.	Tra Telligman	Heavyweight	Knockout	4:30	1
Pete Williams	def.	Travis Fulton	Heavyweight	Submission - Arm Lock	6:28	1
Wanderlei Silva	def.	Tony Petarra	Middleweight	Knockout	2:53	1
Marcelo Mello	def.	David Roberts	Lightweight	Technical Knockout	1:23	1
Laverne Clark	def.	Fabiano Iha	Lightweight	Technical Knockout	1:31	1
Preliminary Card						
Ron Waterman	def.	Chris Condo	Heavyweight	Technical Knockout	0:28	1

Kevin Randleman seemingly did everything he needed to do to fill the vacancy at the top of the heavyweight division in the main event of UFC 20 at the Boutwell Auditorium in Birmingham, Alabama, but the judges didn't agree, awarding Bas Rutten a split decision and the UFC heavyweight title vacated by Randy Couture.

"Randleman did real good in the first round, then he broke my nose and I was considering quitting, but I said these last two rounds are gonna be my rounds," said Rutten. "Even when he takes me down, I'm gonna fight him. And I just unloaded."

Randleman tore out of his corner at the bell, but didn't immediately engage. Instead, he waited for Rutten to make a move. When he did, the Ohio State wrestler took him down and fired away with strikes. Less than two minutes in, Rutten was bleeding from the bridge of his nose, and he had no route of escape. 2:57 in, Rutten tried for a quick armbar, but Randleman escaped and landed more strikes, totally controlling the action.

At 4:51 into the bout, referee John McCarthy halted the bout momentarily to have Rutten's nose checked, but the battler insisted on continuing. Unfortunately, his next kick led to another takedown and at the 10-minute mark, another break was taken to inspect Rutten's nose.

After being green lit again, Rutten tried to turn the tide, but Randleman pinned the former King of Pancrase to the fence for a spell until nailing another takedown. Rutten finally got his offense in gear with strikes from the bottom in the closing stages of regulation time, but at the horn, Randleman was clearly the fresher fighter.

Rutten came out firing to start the first overtime, but was taken down before he could do any damage. Rutten tried to sink an armbar again, only to have it come up empty a second time. The two traded shots on the mat for the remainder of the period, with neither taking a decided edge before the bell.

Needing a big finish, Rutten stalked and landed a kick and punch on his foe, but the end result was the same as it was throughout the bout—a Randleman takedown. The two tired heavyweights peppered each other with strikes in order to score points, but again, neither was able to truly pull away, leaving it in the hands of the judges.

Fight of the Night (unofficial): Rizzo vs. Telligman

Knockout of the Night (unofficial): Silva vs. Petarra

Submission of the Night (unofficial): Williams vs. Fulton

Brazilian bomber Pedro Rizzo continued to impress, surviving a vicious early barrage by Tra Telligman before ending matters with his own concussive strikes.

Telligman and Rizzo immediately exchanged, with Telligman rocking his foe with a flurry of flush shots. Rizzo took each shot and kept firing back, igniting the crowd. After the furious start, the pace dipped momentarily until Rizzo, his nose bloody, began working his way back into the bout. A takedown by Telligman came up empty, and Rizzo, sensing that his foe was tired, moved in with more aggression, and a right hand to the jaw knocked Telligman down, prompting McCarthy to stop the bout at the 4:30 mark.

Rizzo's countryman, free swinging Wanderlei Silva, erased the memory of his first-round loss to Vitor Belfort with a single knee knockout of Tony Petarra. The end came 2:53 into the bout.

Pete Williams made it three out of four in the Octagon, submitting Travis Fulton in 6:28.

In a lightweight matchup, Marcello Mello ended his bout with David Roberts via elbows in 83 seconds, and Laverne Clark got a fortunate technical knockout via cuts in his bout with Fabiano Iha, as the stoppage came just as the jiu-jitsu specialist had locked in a kneebar.

Ron Waterman opened up the event with a 28-second submission due to strikes win over Chris Condo.

UFC 21 *Return of the Champions*

16 July 1999

Five Seasons Events Center, Cedar Rapids, IA

Debuts: Flavio Luiz Moura, Tim Lajcik, Andre Roberts, Travis Fulton, David Dodd

Fighters			Division	Method	Time	Round
Main Card						
Maurice Smith	def.	Marco Ruas	Heavyweight	Technical Knockout	5:00	1
Pat Miletich	def.	Andre Pederneiras	Lightweight	Technical Knockout	2:20	2
Jeremy Horn	def.	Daiju Takase	Middleweight	Technical Knockout	4:41	1
Paul Jones	def.	Flavio Luiz Moura	Middleweight	Submission - Rear Naked Choke	4:20	1
Tsuyoshi Kosaka	def.	Tim Lajcik	Heavyweight	Technical Knockout	5:00	2
Eugene Jackson	def.	Royce Alger	Middleweight	Knockout	1:19	2
Preliminary Card						
Andre Roberts	def.	Ron Waterman	Heavyweight	Knockout	2:51	1
Travis Fulton	def.	David Dodd	Heavyweight	Unanimous Decision	—	2

Using the 10-point must scoring system for the first time, as well as a five-minute round system (five for title bouts, three for non-title main card bouts, and two for preliminary fights), UFC 21 was a pivotal card for the present and future of the Ultimate Fighting Championship. For the main event at the Five Seasons Events Center in Cedar Rapids, Iowa, the organization dug into its past as it brought back early Octagon vet Marco Ruas to take on former heavyweight champion Maurice Smith.

There would be no pleasant trip down memory lane for the Brazilian though, as a knee injury forced him to withdraw from the bout after the first round, giving Smith his first win since he defeated Tank Abbott in October of 1997.

Smith and Ruas traded leg kicks to open up the bout, with Smith's second attempt at going low getting met with a takedown from "The King of the Streets". The two traded guillotine choke attempts on the mat, with neither being sunk in too tight, and the action stalled considerably. With two minutes left, Ruas tried to pass Smith's guard, but Smith's defense was solid, and again, there was a depressing lack of activity until Ruas sought a heel hook with a minute left. Smith punched his way out of trouble, and though Ruas tried again before the bell, he came up empty.

That would be the end of the bout though, as Ruas injured his left knee and retired in his corner after the round, rendering Smith the winner via technical knockout.

Hometown hero Pat Miletich defended his lightweight title for the second time, halting Brazil's Andre Pederneiras via cuts in the second round.

The Iowan's standup was sharp in round one, as he landed hard knees at close range and then got loose, keeping the bout from the mat. Quick strikes followed, and Miletich was showing a complete mastery of the in-and-out game with his striking.

The champion's confidence was evident as he strode out for round two, and in the opening minute, a vicious right hand opened a nasty cut over Pederneiras' left eye. As he closed in for the kill, Pederneiras pulled guard, but Miletich easily stood back up, and referee John McCarthy stepped in to check out the Brazilian's cut. And that was all she wrote, as the fight was stopped at the 2:20 mark.

Knockout of the Night (unofficial): Jackson vs. Alger

Middleweight Jeremy Horn extended his overall win streak to 16 and his Octagon successes to two with a dominant first round technical knockout of Daiju Takase. Also in the middleweight division, Paul Jones submitted Flavio Luiz Moura via rear naked choke, and Eugene Jackson made sure former college wrestling star Royce Alger stayed winless in the UFC with a single left hook that ended the bout via knockout in round two.

Heavyweight contender Tsuyoshi Kosaka started slow against newcomer Tim Lajcik, but he finished strong, using a barrage of late ground strikes to rock his foe and force him to retire in his corner when the doctor didn't allow him out for round three.

Submission of the Night (unofficial): Jones vs. Moura

Andre Roberts was on the receiving end for much of his heavyweight bout with Ron Waterman. It's who finishes stronger that counts, and Roberts did just that with a memorable come from behind first-round knockout win.

Fight of the Night (unofficial): Roberts vs. Waterman

After a touch of gloves, Waterman locked up and fired off knees at Roberts, bloodying his face. Roberts gamely weathered the storm, but he looked overmatched as McCarthy had the doctor check out his cut. When the bout resumed, Roberts looked to regroup, but it was more of the same as the faster Waterman kept teeing off. McCarthy looked close to stopping, but out of nowhere, a left by Roberts dropped Waterman. Roberts pounced and took control briefly on the mat, but when they stood, Waterman was still wobbly. This time when Roberts' left sent his opponent to the mat, McCarthy called a stop to the bout, completing an amazing comeback for "The Chief".

Travis Fulton scored a unanimous decision win over David Dodd in the heavyweight opener.

UFC 22 *Only One Can Be Champion*

24 Sept. 1999

Lake Charles Civic Center, Lake Charles, LA

Debuts: John Lewis, Lowell Anderson, Brad Kohler, Steve Judson, Jens Pulver, Alfonso Alcarez

Fighters			Division	Method	Time	Round
Main Card						
Frank Shamrock	def.	Tito Ortiz	Middleweight	Submission - Strikes	4:42	4
Tim Lajcik	vs.	Ron Waterman	Heavyweight	Draw	—	3
Jeremy Horn	def.	Jason Godsey	Heavyweight	Submission - Armbar	2:00	1
Chuck Liddell	def.	Paul Jones	Middleweight	Technical Knockout	3:53	1
Matt Hughes	def.	Valeri Ignatov	Lightweight	Unanimous Decision	—	3
John Lewis	def.	Lowell Anderson	Middleweight	Technical Knockout	0:13	3
Preliminary Card						
Brad Kohler	def.	Steve Judson	Heavyweight	Knockout	0:30	1
Jens Pulver	vs.	Alfonso Alcarez	Lightweight	Draw	—	2

It was a short-lived return for UFC middleweight champion Frank Shamrock, back in the Octagon for the first time in nearly a year, but what a memorable 19 minutes and 42 seconds he gave fight fans at the Lake Charles Civic Center, as he held off a furious challenge from Tito Ortiz to retain his title via fourth-round submission.

Fight of the Night (unofficial): Shamrock vs. Ortiz

After the stirring victory, Shamrock retired.

"I came here to challenge myself, to fight all comers, and I feel like I've done that," said the long-reigning titleholder. "Who's left? I'm good right now just retiring my belt and concentrating on my marriage and doing a few other things. I think I'm gonna leave this belt in the ring here for the next crew to pick up, and retire my title tonight."

Shamrock didn't get any gimme in his final Octagon bout though, as Ortiz' sole intent was to leave Louisiana with the title, and he made that known immediately as he slammed the champion to the mat in the opening 30 seconds and threw a quick flurry of strikes before standing up. When the bout went back to the mat, the two scrambled for positioning, with Ortiz settling into his opponent's guard. Ortiz pushed Shamrock to the fence, and he powered out of any submission attempts. Shamrock landed open-handed strikes to the side of Ortiz' head and tried to get back to his feet. Ortiz kept him grounded with the exception of a brief stand in the final minute, wrapping up an impressive first round.

The champion began round two with some hard kicks, but Ortiz dumped him on his back again. Shamrock's defense was solid, and he wasn't allowing the challenger to get too big of an advantage. Ortiz was expending a lot of energy though, as he tried to dominate the round while deflecting Shamrock's peppering strikes from the bottom.

Mixing up his strikes nicely, Shamrock began the third round well before he suffered the now routine trip to the mat. In the second minute, Ortiz got into side control and then he took Shamrock's back, but the champion scrambled and brought his opponent back into the guard. With two minutes left, Shamrock got back to his feet and the two traded. Shamrock held the edge, but when he got too close, Ortiz landed the takedown and kept the fight grounded until the bell.

After some hard kicks downstairs and punches upstairs by Shamrock to start the championship rounds, the tiring Ortiz looked to catch a breather when he took the bout to the mat with a little over three minutes to go in the fourth. Still, Shamrock was the busier fighter from the bottom, and with less than a minute left, he reversed Ortiz, got to his feet and emptied his clip on the challenger. Ortiz desperately sought a takedown, and Shamrock locked in a guillotine choke in response. Not getting a tap, Shamrock turned his foe over and fired off a few unanswered strikes and Ortiz finally tapped with just seconds left in the round.

"He's got 20-plus pounds on me, so the whole thing was just beat him down and wear him out," said Shamrock. "It's my game past 15 minutes. I knew once I got him there I just had to light him up, and I got it going."

That he did.

Three heavyweight bouts were on tap in Lake Charles, and after a 30-second knockout by Brad Kohler over Steve Judson and a first-round submission of Jason Godsey by Jeremy Horn, Tim Lajcik and Ron Waterman fought to a three-round draw.

Knockout of the Night (unofficial): Kohler vs. Judson

Three future UFC champions also took to the Octagon on the UFC 22 card. Chuck Liddell stopped Paul Jones via strikes in the first round, Matt Hughes made his UFC debut with a three-round unanimous decision over Valeri Ignatov, and Jens "Lil' Evil" Pulver fought to a two-round draw with Alfonso Alcarez.

In a middleweight contest, John Lewis halted Lowell Anderson in the third round.

THE EVOLUTION OF A SPORT

When the Ultimate Fighting Championship began in 1993, there were probably no concerns that viewers would have difficulty with the rules. This was because there were barely any to deal with. Just no groin shots, no eye gouging and no biting. That was it.

It made for the possibility of some exciting action, but it would eventually lead to controversy that almost crippled the sport permanently when politicians called for its banishment.

UFC 1 PENALTIES

1. Groin attacks of any kind
2. Eye gouging of any kind
3. Biting

Getting knocked off Pay-Per-View television and being called "human cockfighting" were the issues that hit the mainstream media. Behind the scenes, the new sport of mixed martial arts had to go through an almost endless stream of changes to make the sport safer for its competitors, exciting for its fans and on the same level as other combat sports. If MMA was ever going to break the chains holding it back, the change had to come from within.

So while the idea of no-holds-barred fights with no time limits was sexy in theory, in reality, a bout like the one between Ken Shamrock and Dan Severn could try even the most die-hard fan's patience. The early days of the UFC didn't feature judges either, so when time limits were instituted for Superfights and Shamrock clearly defeated Oleg Taktarov at UFC 7, he was only able to receive a draw verdict.

By UFC 8, a fight going the distance (10 minutes) was voted on by three judges who simply held up a card with the name of who they thought won the bout. It wasn't perfect, but at least it was a start.

At UFC 12, a heavyweight champion (Mark Coleman) was crowned for the first time, and a lightweight (under 200 pounds) division was instituted. No longer would 600-pounders like Emmanuel Yarborough be matched with a 200-pound Keith Hackney.

There was still work to be done though and one of the biggest rule implementations came at UFC 21 in 1999, when five-minute rounds and a 10-point must scoring system was adopted.

A year later, in September of 2000, the Unified Rules of Mixed Martial Arts were accepted by the prestigious New Jersey State Athletic Control Board, and UFC 28 in November of 2000 was the first event held under the rules that still govern the sport today.

Currently containing nine weight classes, judging criteria, ways to win a fight, safety regulations and over 30 fouls, these rules are the bible by which the most exciting sport in the world is run. While focusing on fighter safety and fair play, the rules provide the level playing field all athletes want. These days, it's not about style vs. style. It's about who is the more skilled, better conditioned and more determined athlete when the bell rings. It may have taken nearly 20 years, but now it's clear that mixed martial arts is here to stay and only getting bigger.

CURRENT UFC PENALTIES

The following acts constitute fouls in a contest or exhibition of mixed martial arts and may result in penalties, at the discretion of the referee, if committed:

1. Butting with the head
2. Eye gouging of any kind
3. Biting
4. Spitting at an opponent
5. Hair pulling
6. Fish hooking
7. Groin attacks of any kind
8. Putting a finger into any orifice or any cut or laceration of an opponent
9. Small joint manipulation
10. Striking downward using the point of the elbow
11. Striking to the spine or the back of the head
12. Kicking to the kidney with a heel
13. Throat strikes of any kind, including (without limitation) grabbing the trachea
14. Clawing, pinching or twisting the flesh
15. Grabbing the clavicle
16. Kicking the head of a grounded opponent
17. Kneeing the head of a grounded opponent
18. Stomping a grounded opponent
19. Holding the fence
20. Holding the shorts or gloves of an opponent
21. Using abusive language in fenced ring/fighting area
22. Engaging in any unsportsmanlike conduct that causes injury to an opponent
23. Attacking an opponent on or during the break
24. Attacking an opponent who is under the care of the referee
25. Attacking an opponent after the bell has sounded the end of the round
26. Timidity, including (without limitation) avoiding contact with an opponent, intentionally or consistently dropping the mouthpiece or faking an injury
27. Throwing opponent out of ring/fighting area
28. Flagrantly disregarding the instructions of the referee
29. Spiking an opponent to the canvas on his head or neck
30. Interference by the corner
31. Applying any foreign substance to the hair or body to gain an advantage

UFC 23 *Ultimate Japan 2*

19 Nov. 1999

Tokyo Bay NK Hall, Tokyo, Japan

Debuts: Keiichiro Yamamiya, Katsuhisa Fujii, Kenichi Yamamoto

Fighters			Division	Method	Time	Round
Main Card						
Kevin Randleman	def.	Pete Williams	Heavyweight	Unanimous Decision	—	5
Pedro Rizzo	def.	Tsuyoshi Kosaka	Heavyweight	Technical Knockout	1:17	3
Middleweight Tournament						
Joe Slick	def.	Jason DeLucia	Middleweight	Technical Knockout - Injury	1:12	1
Eugene Jackson	def.	Keiichiro Yamamiya	Middleweight	Knockout	3:12	3
Kenichi Yamamoto	def.	Katsuhisa Fujii	Middleweight	Submission - Kneebar	4:15	1
Kenichi Yamamoto	def.	Daiju Takase	Middleweight	Unanimous Decision	—	3
Katsuhisa Fujii	def.	Masutatsu Yano	Middleweight	Technical Knockout	3:12	2

After a controversial decision loss to Bas Rutten at UFC 20 in May of 2009, Kevin Randleman was understandably disappointed and discouraged, but six months later, he would call himself UFC heavyweight champion, as he scored a five-round unanimous decision win over Pete Williams to earn the title vacated by Rutten's expected move to the middleweight division.

Things went according to plan for Randleman for much of the first round, until a late surge by Williams allowed him to get the mount and score some much needed strikes. As the bell rang, Randleman remained on the canvas. Eventually, the former Ohio State wrestler rose to his feet and came out on time for round two.

The pace slowed a bit in the second frame, but Randleman was able to get the takedown after a little work. With a little over two minutes left, Williams almost sunk in an armbar, but Randleman muscled loose and kept his opponent pinned to the mat.

The pattern continued in rounds three through five, with Randleman keeping Williams on the canvas, unable to mount a sustained offensive. It proved to be enough to win for "The Monster".

"That punch he hit me with stunned me and I was very surprised, but I came back and did what I had to do," said the new champion.

There would be little rest for Randleman though, as his next opponent emerged in the night's co-main event, and it was Brazilian bomber Pedro Rizzo, who halted Japanese contender Tsuyoshi Kosaka at the 1:17 mark of the third round.

The two combatants fought at a measured pace for much of the bout, with Rizzo eventually taking control behind his devastating leg kicks. In round three, Rizzo dropped Kosaka with a left hand. While "TK" rose immediately, he was stunned, and after a takedown attempt failed, Rizzo landed a right uppercut on his downed foe and referee John McCarthy stepped in and stopped the fight.

In the first ever UFC Japan tournament, Kenichi Yamamoto decisioned Daiju Takase in the semifinals and then submitted Katsuhisa Fujii via kneebar in the finals to earn the crown.

Fujii earned a spot in the finals earlier in the evening with a second-round technical knockout of Masutatsu Yano.

Four other middleweights battled it out in Tokyo as well, as Eugene Jackson finished Keiichiro Yamamiya with a single left hook in the third round, and Joe Slick earned a first-round technical knockout win over Jason DeLucia, who retired due to a knee injury.

Knockout of the Night (unofficial): Rizzo vs. Kosaka

Fight of the Night (unofficial): Jackson vs. Yamamiya

UFC 24 *First Defense*

10 March 2000

Lake Charles Civic Center, Lake Charles, LA

Debuts: Shonie Carter, Brad Gumm, Scott Adams, Ian Freeman, David Velasquez, Bob Cook, Tiki Ghosn, Dave Menne, Lance Gibson, Jermaine Andre, Tedd Williams

Fighters			Division	Method	Time	Round
Main Card						
Tedd Williams	def.	Steve Judson	Heavyweight	Technical Knockout	3:23	1
Lance Gibson	def.	Jermaine Andre	Middleweight	Knockout	3:37	3
Dave Menne	def.	Fabiano Iha	Lightweight	Unanimous Decision	—	3
Bob Cook	def.	Tiki Ghosn	Lightweight	Submission - Rear Naked Choke	1:30	2
Jens Pulver	def.	David Velasquez	Lightweight	Technical Knockout	2:41	2
Preliminary Card						
Scott Adams	def.	Ian Freeman	Heavyweight	Submission - Heel Hook	3:09	1
Shonie Carter	def.	Brad Gumm	Lightweight	Unanimous Decision	—	2

It was a bizarre night at the Lake Charles Civic Center in Louisiana, as the Ultimate Fighting Championship lost its main event due to injury…not a week or two before the bout, or even days before, but *on* fight night, as UFC heavyweight champion Kevin Randleman slipped on several pipes while warming up backstage, fell to the concrete floor and hit his head, rendering him unconscious.

Randleman, who was scheduled to defend his crown against Brazil's Pedro Rizzo, was rushed to a local hospital, where he was diagnosed with a concussion.

With no main event, it was up to the rest of the 14 fighters on the card to step up their games, and with 11 of them making their UFC debuts, they were raring to go from the start.

Heavyweight newcomer Tedd Williams, a Bas Rutten protégé, proved to be too big for Steve Judson as he halted him in at 3:23 of the first round. The end came when Williams—who had taken some hard shots early broke open a slow-paced fight with a series of thudding head and body shots that produced a referee stoppage.

After dominating much of the fight at close range against the fence, Lance Gibson caught Jermain Andre napping in the third round of their middleweight bout and then put him to sleep with a single knee that sent Andre crashing to the canvas face first at 3:37 of the round.

Knockout of the Night (unofficial): Gibson vs. Andre

Rising star Jens Pulver continued his trek up the lightweight ladder, scoring a punishing technical knockout victory over a game David Velasquez. The Pat Miletich-trained Pulver used a series of unanswered ground strikes to finish matters at the 2:41 mark.

Fight of the Night (unofficial): Cook vs. Ghosn

Lightweight "Crazy" Bob Cook won a fast-paced battle of newcomers, submitting Tiki Ghosn in the second round.

On the attack from the opening bell, Cook looked for submissions while Ghosn scored with hard strikes while mixing in the occasional takedown. In the second, the bout strayed to the mat again, and when Ghosn gave up his back, Cook capitalized and choked out his foe via rear naked choke at the 1:30 mark.

Lightweight Dave Menne showed off a well-rounded attack in his bout with Brazilian jiu-jitsu ace Fabiano Iha, emerging with a three-round unanimous decision victory.

Iha tried to implement his submission game on Menne, but was unable to get his foe in trouble on the mat. Iha did mark up Menne's right eye, but the Midwestern veteran was undeterred, and as the bout progressed, he was able to inflict more and more punishment en route to a clear-cut victory.

In preliminary bouts, charismatic newcomer Shonie Carter began his UFC career with a unanimous decision win over Brad Gumm, and Scott Adams lived up to his nickname as the "King of Leglocks" as he submitted England's Ian Freeman with a heel hook at 3:09 of the opening round.

Submission of the Night (unofficial): Adams vs. Freeman

One Hit Wonders: Scott Adams, David Velasquez, Bob Cook, Jermaine Andre

Combined, Scott Adams and Bob Cook compiled a 13-1 pro mixed martial arts slate, but both fighters, who completed their careers at UFC 24, would eventually become known more for what they did outside the Octagon than in it. Adams, "The King of Leglocks", teamed up with Reed Harris to form the World Extreme Cagefighting (WEC) organization. "Crazy" Bob become one of the sport's leading managers and trainers, working with the stellar group of fighters that emerged from San Jose's American Kickboxing Academy.

UFC 25 *Ultimate Japan 3*

14
April
2000

Yoyogi National Gymnasium, Tokyo, Japan

Debuts: Satoshi Honma, Ikuhisa Minowa, Murilo Bustamante, Sanae Kikuta, Koji Oishi

Fighters			Division	Method	Time	Round
Main Card						
Tito Ortiz	def.	Wanderlei Silva	Middleweight	Unanimous Decision	—	5
Murilo Bustamante	def.	Yoji Anjo	Middleweight	Submission - Arm Triangle Choke	0:31	2
Sanae Kikuta	def.	Eugene Jackson	Middleweight	Submission - Armbar	4:39	1
Ron Waterman	def.	Satoshi Honma	Heavyweight	Unanimous Decision	—	3
Ikuhisa Minowa	def.	Joe Slick	Middleweight	Technical Knockout - Cuts	1:54	3
Laverne Clark	def.	Koji Oishi	Lightweight	Majority Decision	—	3

Fight of the Night (unofficial): Ortiz vs. Silva

After the stunning retirement of Frank Shamrock after UFC 22 in September of 1999, a vacancy was left atop the middleweight division. Top contenders Tito Ortiz and Wanderlei Silva stepped in to fill that void in the main event of UFC 25 in Tokyo, and when it was all over, "The Huntington Beach Bad Boy" was crowned champion via five-round unanimous decision.

"I worked very hard for this, to make this belt happen," said the 25-year-old Ortiz.

The two aggressive battlers circled each other warily to start the bout, with Silva's first offensive push getting met by an Ortiz takedown. Ortiz controlled matters from the top for the remainder of the round, landing short shots that didn't cause any significant damage but did score points.

Silva came out fast for the second frame, but a flurry from the Brazilian left him open for an Ortiz right hand that dropped him to the canvas. Silva cleared his head quickly, but soon he was on his back again, eating shots from Ortiz. The pattern continued for the remainder of the stanza, putting Ortiz up 2-0.

Looking winded, Silva needed to turn things around, but he apparently didn't have the energy to do so. Ortiz didn't push the pace either, with a failed takedown attempt the only significant action until until nearly two minutes in, when an exchange saw Silva finally rock his foe. Ortiz literally ran to clear his head, but after a few tight moments, he was able to get the bout back to the mat, where he again controlled the battle with positioning and ground strikes.

After a two-minute cat and mouse game, Ortiz took the bout back to the canvas, and it was clear that the key to victory for him was keeping Silva on his back. He did just that through the rest of the fight, with the Brazilian having no escape route from the smothering attack, making the unanimous decision for Ortiz a mere formality.

Highly touted Brazilian middleweight Murilo Bustamante was successful in his UFC debut, as he followed up a late first-round surge with a quick second-round takedown and submission of Yoji Anjo via arm triangle at the 31-second mark.

Submission of the Night (unofficial): Bustamante vs. Anjo

Promising UFC rookie Sanae Kikuta was impressive in his middleweight bout against hard-hitting Eugene Jackson, using a steady diet of ground strikes to set up an arm triangle and then an armbar, with the armbar forcing a tapout at 4:39 of the first round.

Heavyweights Ron Waterman and Satoshi Honma battled it out for 15 minutes, with Waterman, "The H2O Man", earning a three-round unanimous decision victory. Also going the distance were lightweights Laverne Clark and Koji Oishi, with Clark pulling out the majority decision victory.

Ikuhisa Minowa and Joe Slick engaged in a middleweight battle packed with solid ground work from both men and a number of guillotine attempts from Slick, but in the third round, a right kick to the head by Minowa cut Slick's forehead open, forcing a stoppage at the 1:54 mark. Octagonside commentator Mike Goldberg called it the second-best kick he had ever seen in the UFC, bested only by Pete Williams' head kick knockout of Mark Coleman at UFC 17.

Knockout of the Night (unofficial): Minowa vs. Slick

One Hit Wonders: Ikuhisa Minowa, Sanae Kikuta

With then-owners SEG finding the reality of keeping the UFC afloat an almost losing battle, the funds simply weren't there to keep solid international talent like Minowa and Kikuta around. Both would go on to impressive careers in their home country of Japan, Kikuta mainly in the Pancrase organization, and Minowa in Pancrase, PRIDE, Deep, and Dream.

UFC 26 *Ultimate Field of Dreams*

09
June
2000

Five Seasons Events Center, Cedar Rapids, IA

Debuts: Tyrone Roberts, Marcelo Aguiar, Joao Roque, Nate Schroeder, Adrian Serrano

Fighters			Division	Method	Time	Round
Main Card						
Kevin Randleman	def.	Pedro Rizzo	Heavyweight	Unanimous Decision	—	5
Pat Miletich	def.	John Alessio	Lightweight	Submission - Armbar	1:43	2
Tyrone Roberts	def.	David Dodd	Middleweight	Unanimous Decision	—	3
Amaury Bitetti	def.	Alex Andrade	Middleweight	Opponent Disqualified	0:43	2
Matt Hughes	def.	Marcelo Aguiar	Lightweight	Technical Knockout	4:34	1
Jens Pulver	def.	Joao Roque	Bantamweight	Unanimous Decision	—	3
Preliminary Card						
Ian Freeman	def.	Nate Schroeder	Heavyweight	Submission - Strikes	2:13	2
Shonie Carter	def.	Adrian Serrano	Lightweight	Unanimous Decision	—	2

The UFC has had its share of anticipated main events that turned into duds, but few hit rock bottom like the UFC 26 headliner between Kevin Randleman and Pedro Rizzo, a 25-minute war of nerves. The winner via unanimous decision was defending UFC heavyweight champion Randleman, but the losers were the ones watching the dreadful five-rounder at the Five Seasons Events Center in Cedar Rapids, Iowa.

"I understand the boos and I definitely deserve it," said Randleman. "But I can tell you this, I came in here to strike with a striker, not to come in here and wrestle him. I came in here with one plan, to stay on my feet, take him down when I could, and box with him. I think Pedro and I just respected each other too much. I apologize."

The bout was originally scheduled to take place at UFC 24, but a backstage fall by Randleman caused a concussion and a postponement of the title fight.

The first round set the tone for the rest of the bout, with Randleman scoring the takedown and controlling the fight on the mat, but being unable to put together any consistent offensive attack. For Rizzo's part, he waited and hoped to counter while standing, but the champion wouldn't give him that opportunity.

The fighters even got a talking-to from referee John McCarthy in round two to pick up the pace, but was to no avail save for a couple of good strikes from Rizzo late. Round three was hardly better, but this time was Randleman leaving the positive impression on the judges with a late surge.

Rounds four and five continued to bore the Cedar Rapids crowd, as neither fighter wanted to take the risks that would allow them to win the fight and the belt. When the 25 minutes of tedious "action" were done, Randleman had retained his title.

Local hero Pat Miletich saved the day for the fans in the night's other championship bout, as he retained his lightweight crown for the third time with a second-round submission of John Alessio.

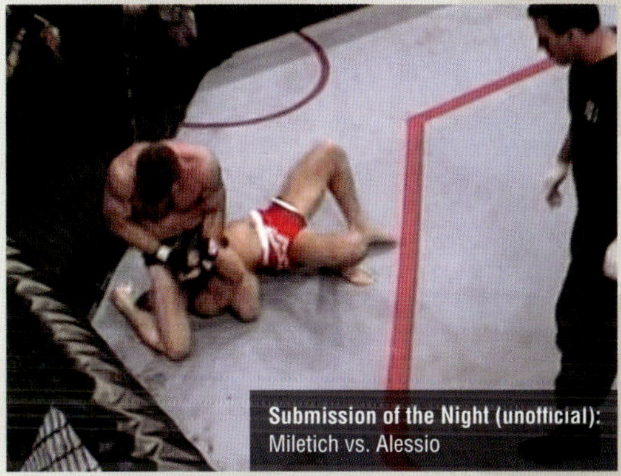

Submission of the Night (unofficial): Miletich vs. Alessio

The bout was fast-paced at the start, and Miletich used his standup to score the first takedown of the fight. Alessio sunk in a guillotine choke in response, but the champion fought loose and fired off some hard strikes from close range, allowing him to take the opening five minutes.

In the second, Miletich and Alessio locked up early, with Miletich using a slam to get the fight back to the mat. After a few moments, Miletich got into the full mount position and immediately grabbed Alessio's arm, forcing the tapout via armbar at 1:43 of the round.

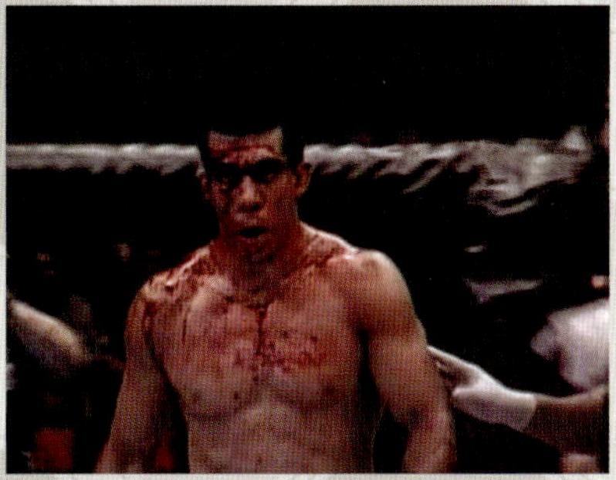

Miletich's gym mates, Matt Hughes and Jens Pulver, were victorious at home as well, with Hughes stopping Marcelo Aguiar via cuts in the first round and Pulver decisioning Joao Roque.

Middleweight bouts saw Tyrone Roberts decision David Dodd, and Amaury Bitetti win via disqualification over Alex Andrade after Andrade landed three illegal kicks.

UFC 27 *Ultimate Bad Boyz*

22
Sept.
2000

Lake Front Arena, New Orleans, LA

Debuts: Jeff Monson, Brad Gumm, CJ Fernandes

Fighters			Division	Method	Time	Round
Main Card						
Pedro Rizzo	def.	Dan Severn	Heavyweight	Submission - Strikes	1:33	1
Maurice Smith	def.	Bobby Hoffman	Heavyweight	Majority Decision	—	3
Jeremy Horn	def.	Eugene Jackson	Middleweight	Submission - Armbar	4:32	1
Fabiano Iha	def.	Laverne Clark	Lightweight	Submission - Armbar	1:10	1
Yuki Kondo	def.	Alexandre Dantas	Middleweight	Technical Knockout	2:28	3
Ian Freeman	def.	Tedd Williams	Heavyweight	Unanimous Decision	—	3
Preliminary Card						
Jeff Monson	def.	Tim Lajcik	Heavyweight	Unanimous Decision	—	2
Brad Gumm	def.	CJ Fernandes	Lightweight	Draw	—	2

"The Beast" was back for UFC 27 at the Lake Front Arena in New Orleans. But at 42, two-time UFC tournament champion Dan Severn just didn't have the firepower to hold off Pedro "The Rock" Rizzo, who rebounded from his dreadful decision loss to heavyweight champion Kevin Randleman three months earlier with a 93-second win.

"The old Pedro Rizzo is back," said Rizzo. "I come to knock everybody out, I want to get my rematch with Kevin because I think I deserve this match. Everybody knows what happened the last time."

Severn immediately looked for a takedown at the bell, but Rizzo simply tossed him to the canvas. The Brazilian appeared to be more aggressive, and even when he didn't land flush on Severn with a head kick, you could hear the impact of the skimming hit. Next came the leg kicks, and the first one to the inside dropped Severn. He rose immediately, but after a few seconds, another one to the same area crumbled Severn in pain, and he called off the bout.

The fight was Severn's first in the Octagon since UFC 12 in 1997.

Former UFC heavyweight champion Maurice Smith shook off the rust of a year layoff with a three-round majority decision win over Bobby Hoffman in the co-featured bout of the night.

In a long-awaited middleweight bout, Jeremy Horn showed off his well-rounded game as he nullified the attack of knockout artist Eugene Jackson, stayed patient, and then finished his foe with an armbar late in the first round.

After a 16-month wait, Fabiano Iha finally got his rematch with Laverne Clark. His UFC 20 bout with the Iowan was waved off due to cuts when he had a submission locked. Iha picked up where he left off as he finally finished his foe for real with an armbar 70 seconds into the first round.

Japanese middleweight contender Yuki Kondo made a successful UFC debut, stopping Alexandre Dantas via strikes at 2:28 of the third round. A knee followed by a ground strike ended the exhausted Dantas' night.

Submission of the Night (unofficial):
Iha vs. Clark

In the heavyweight main card opener, England's Ian Freeman decisioned Tedd Williams unanimously over three rounds.

Two UFC 27 preliminary bouts went the distance, with Jeff Monson decisioning Tim Lajcik in a heavyweight match, and lightweights Brad Gumm and CJ Fernandes battling to a draw.

Knockout of the Night (unofficial):
Kondo vs. Dantas

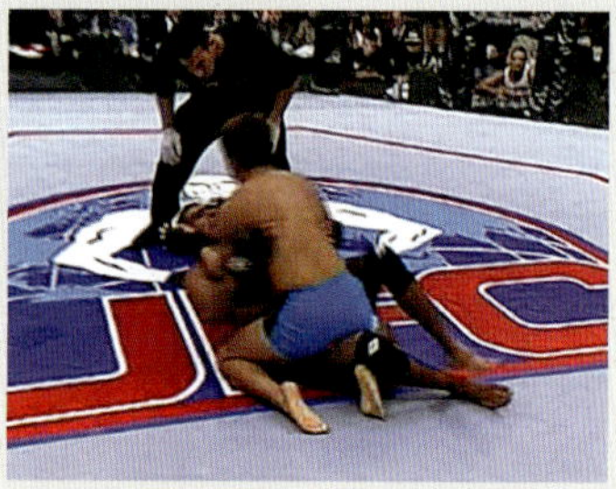

UFC 28 *High Stakes*

17 Nov. 2000

Mark G. Etess Arena, Atlantic City, NJ

Debuts: Renato Sobral, Gan McGee, Josh Barnett, Andrei Arlovski, Chris Lytle, Aaron Brink, Mark Hughes, Alex Stiebling, Ben Earwood

Fighters			Division	Method	Time	Round
Main Card						
Randy Couture	def.	Kevin Randleman	Heavyweight	Technical Knockout	4:13	3
Renato Sobral	def.	Maurice Smith	Heavyweight	Majority Decision	—	3
Josh Barnett	def.	Gan McGee	Super Heavyweight	Technical Knockout	4:34	2
Andrei Arlovski	def.	Aaron Brink	Heavyweight	Submission - Armbar	0:55	1
Jens Pulver	def.	John Lewis	Bantamweight	Knockout	0:15	1
Preliminary Card						
Mark Hughes	def.	Alex Stiebling	Middleweight	Unanimous Decision	—	2
Ben Earwood	def.	Chris Lytle	Lightweight	Unanimous Decision	—	2

UFC 28's event name, "High Stakes" said it all. SEG needed quality fights from quality fighters, and needed to cap it off with a main event worthy of a heavyweight championship if it wanted to attract Las Vegas for future shows. Well, the company and the crowd got what it needed, especially from heavyweight title combatants Randy Couture and Kevin Randleman.

For 14 minutes and 13 seconds, Couture and Randleman battled for Kevin's heavyweight title as if lives depended on the outcome. When it was all over, Couture walked away with the belt via third-round TKO, but both men left the arena with respect.

Fight of the Night (unofficial): Couture vs. Randleman

"This is not my time," said Randleman in a post-fight interview. "But I told you the only way I would be beaten is by a wrestler, and I got beat by one of the best wrestlers and best fighters in the world."

For Couture, it was a homecoming of sorts. He won the UFC heavyweight title in the ring, beating Maurice Smith at Ultimate Japan I in 1997. A contract dispute kept him out of the Octagon for almost three years, but what a way to return.

With Big John McCarthy's "Let's get it on" ringing in their ears, Randleman attacked Couture at the outset, eventually slamming him to the mat. The pro-Couture crowd worked itself into a frenzy when it looked like their man had ensnared Randleman in an arm bar, but with a show of strength from the Ohio native, he was able to escape.

In the second stanza, Randleman connected with a 1-2 combination that seemed to stun Couture. Both men locked up and Couture tried to score with some knee strikes. Randleman responded with more jarring blows to the head, some of which were blocked by Couture's gloves. Shortly after this flurry, Randleman took a knee to the head from the Washington native, and Couture was then able to take the champion to the floor. It looked like Randleman was stunned by the knee, and he possibly never recovered, because Couture dominated the action from that point on.

The "Ran-dy, Ran-dy" chants filled the Mark G. Etess Arena as action commenced in the third round. Knees by Couture put Randleman down again, and as a sustained flurry of blows ripped away at Randleman's defense, McCarthy halted the bout at the 4:13 mark.

In undercard action, 25-year-old Brazilian Renato "Babalu" Sobral made his UFC debut a successful one with a majority decision over former UFC heavyweight king Maurice Smith.

On paper it looked like it had the potential to be the fight of the night, but the battle between bantamweights Jens Pulver and John Lewis turned out to be a brutal mismatch, as Pulver starched Lewis with one left hand 15 seconds into the first round. "I let it go and it felt good," said Pulver.

In a battle of the big men, Josh Barnett survived an early onslaught by 6' 10" Gan McGee and scored a TKO at 4:34 of the second round.

Knockout of the Night (unofficial): Pulver vs. Lewis

Submission of the Night (unofficial): Arlovski vs. Brink

Andrei Arlovski defeated Aaron Brink via a tapout from an armbar at 55 seconds of the first round.

Ben Earwood defeated Chris Lytle via unanimous decision.

Mark Hughes defeated Alex Steibling via unanimous decision.

One Hit Wonders: Aaron Brink, Mark Hughes, Alex Stiebling, Ben Earwood

On a card where more than half of the competing fighters were making their Octagon debuts (including future standouts Sobral, Barnett, Arlovski, and Lytle), it was inevitable that some would fall by the wayside. Some, like Stiebling and Brink, went on to compete for several years in other organizations. Earwood, who beat Lytle, only fought twice more, retiring in 2001. Mark Hughes, the twin brother of Hall of Famer Matt, is still inseparable from his brother, but after a win over Leo Sylvest in 2003, he walked away from the game with a 6-2 record and no regrets.

UFC 29 *Defense of the Belts*

16 Dec. 2000

Differ Ariake Arena, Tokyo, Japan

Debuts: Dennis Hallman, Matt Lindland

Fighters			Division	Method	Time	Round
Main Card						
Tito Ortiz	def.	Yuki Kondo	Middleweight	Submission - Neck Crank	1:51	1
Pat Miletich	def.	Kenichi Yamamoto	Lightweight	Submission - Guillotine Choke	1:57	2
Matt Lindland	def.	Yoji Anjo	Middleweight	Technical Knockout	2:57	1
Fabiano Iha	def.	Daiju Takase	Lightweight	Technical Knockout	2:24	1
Evan Tanner	def.	Lance Gibson	Middleweight	Technical Knockout	4:48	1
Dennis Hallman	def.	Matt Hughes	Lightweight	Submission - Armbar	0:20	1
Chuck Liddell	def.	Jeff Monson	Middleweight	Unanimous Decision	—	3

December 16, 2000 marked the end of the first chapter in the history of the Ultimate Fighting Championship, as SEG put on the final event of their ownership of the company at the Differ Ariake Arena in Tokyo. Beginning with UFC 30, new owners Zuffa would take the sport into its next phase, but before that happened, there were still fights to be fought and titles to be defended. Both Tito Ortiz and Pat Miletich left Japan with their championship belts, as they submitted local contenders Yuki Kondo and Kenichi Yamamoto, respectively.

Fight of the Night (unofficial): Ortiz vs. Kondo

The main event saw "The Huntington Beach Bad Boy" retain his crown for the first time against Kondo, who was simply overpowered in their middleweight title bout. That's not to say Kondo didn't have his moments, as he rocked Ortiz with a kick and then dropped him with a knee in the opening minute. The champion immediately jumped back to his feet and scored the takedown, and then he began lowering the boom on Kondo with ferocious strikes from the top position. Kondo covered up as Ortiz fired away, yet amazingly, he made it back to his feet. Ortiz didn't let him stay upright long though, as he took Kondo back down and sunk in a neck crank that prompted a tap out at 1:51 of the first round.

Lightweight champion Pat Miletich also came in as champion and left the same way, as he made Kenichi Yamamoto tapout to a guillotine choke in the second round.

Yamamoto shot for a takedown at the bell, but Miletich sprawled out of danger and landed some knees to remind his foe that such a move wouldn't be advisable in the future. Returning to the standing position, Miletich turned the tables with a slam of the Japanese fighter, but quickly got back up again. When the bout did stray to the mat, Miletich controlled matters with his strikes and positioning, and the most impressive aspect of the bout was the champion's complete control of where the fight was going to take place.

At the end of the first round, Yamamoto look baffled as he went back to his corner, and in the second, Miletich added to his woes as he punished him standing and on the mat before sinking in a guillotine choke that produced a tap at the 1:57 mark. The successful title defense was Miletich's fourth.

After getting submitted in 17 seconds by Dennis Hallman back in October of 1998, Matt Hughes wanted some payback against the only man to beat him on the big stage of the UFC. It didn't happen though, as Hallman scored another quick finish, this time needing 20 seconds to rebound from two slams and catch Hughes in a fight-ending armbar.

Submission of the Night (unofficial): Hallman vs. Hughes

In a middleweight bout, Octagon newcomer Matt Lindland, a 2000 US Olympic Silver medalist in freestyle wrestling, moved to 4-0 in mixed martial arts with a first-round technical knockout of Yoji Anjo. Anjo surprised Lindland by trying to take him down, but "The Law" fought it off and ended matters at the 2:57 mark via strikes.

Brazilian jiu-jitsu ace Fabiano Iha showed off his punching power in lightweight action as he halted Daiju Takase with ground strikes in the first round.

Knockout of the Night (unofficial): Iha vs. Takase

Texas middleweight Evan Tanner scored a punishing first-round technical knockout of Lance Gibson, cutting his opponent's evening short with a barrage of ground strikes with two seconds left in the first round.

In lightweight action, Chris Lytle outpointed Ben Earwood via unanimous decision, and a middleweight bout saw Chuck Liddell score a unanimous decision victory as well, his coming over Jeff Monson.

UFC 30 *Battle on the Boardwalk*

23 Feb. 2001

Trump Taj Mahal, Atlantic City, NJ

Debuts: Caol Uno, Phil Johns, Elvis Sinosic, Mark Robinson, Phil Baroni, Curtis Stout, Sean Sherk

Fighters			Division	Method	Time	Round
Main Card						
Tito Ortiz	def.	Evan Tanner	Middleweight	Knockout	0:30	1
Jens Pulver	def.	Caol Uno	Bantamweight	Majority Decision	—	5
Fabiano Iha	def.	Phil Johns	Lightweight	Submission	1:38	1
Elvis Sinosic	def.	Jeremy Horn	Middleweight	Submission	2:59	1
Pedro Rizzo	def.	Josh Barnett	Heavyweight	Knockout	4:21	2
Bobby Hoffman	def.	Mark Robinson	Heavyweight	Knockout*	3:27	1
Preliminary Card						
Phil Baroni	def.	Curtis Stout	Middleweight	Unanimous Decision	—	2
Sean Sherk	def.	Tiki Ghosn	Lightweight	Submission - Injury	4:47	2

*Later overturned and ruled a No Contest when Hoffman failed a post-fight drug test.

On January 11, 2001, a company named Zuffa, manned by brothers Frank and Lorenzo Fertitta and their friend Dana White, purchased the struggling Ultimate Fighting Championship. Over the next ten years, they turned it into a sporting world juggernaut that has exceeded all early expectations. Every success story had to begin somewhere, and for Zuffa, the first test would be its first event, at the Trump Taj Mahal in Atlantic City, New Jersey.

Knockout of the Night (unofficial): Ortiz vs. Tanner

It was clear that night that for the new UFC to be successful, it needed a star. Huntington Beach, California's Tito Ortiz was that man, and like a main event fighter, the 205-pound champion knew how to close the show. In 30 seconds, Ortiz grabbed number one contender Evan Tanner in a bear hug, picked him up and slammed him to the mat, knocking him unconscious in the process. Follow-up punches to the prone Tanner were just window dressing before referee Big John McCarthy was able to push Ortiz off his opponent and end the bout.

In the co-feature, Jens Pulver won the UFC's first bantamweight title bout, taking a close majority decision over Japan's Caol Uno. "I'm just so excited, I can't believe it," said Pulver after the bout. Turning to his vanquished foe, Pulver said, "Uno, you are my idol. I respect you forever. If you ever want a rematch, I will give it to you." The fans at the Taj Mahal probably didn't like hearing that after booing throughout the five-round match. What the bout lacked in sustained action, it made up in strategy, as Pulver continually stalked, looking to land his power strikes, and Uno looked for openings to use his speed to lock up and submit "Lil' Evil".

In the end, Pulver's striking attacks and his utter disregard for Uno's power and strength proved to be the difference.

The Fight of the Night was staged between the big boys, heavyweights Josh Barnett and Pedro Rizzo. In 9:21 of some of the best striking attacks seen in a while in the UFC, the two combatants slugged it out on even terms until a vicious right hand by the Brazilian stunned Barnett. A follow-up right by Rizzo on his defenseless opponent left Barnett KO'd at the 4:21 mark of Round Two.

Fight of the Night (unofficial): Rizzo vs. Barnett

"To be honest, I really don't know what hit me," said Barnett, who lost for the first time in 25 mixed martial arts bouts. The Seattle resident, who remains one of the few to stand and trade with Rizzo for any length of time, would be heard from again.

Fabiano Iha made short work of Paul Johns, submitting him with an armbar in 1:47.

"The King of Rock and Rumble", Australia's Elvis Sinosic, made a huge splash in his UFC debut, submitting highly regarded Jeremy Horn with a triangle armbar at 2:59 of the first round.

Iowa's Bobby Hoffman was able to free himself from the clutches of 285-pound South African Mark Robinson long enough to land a brutal right elbow, ending the heavyweight match in 3:27.

Sean Sherk defeated Tiki Ghosn via verbal submission due to a dislocated shoulder at 4:47 of the second round.

Phil Baroni defeated Curtis Stout via unanimous decision.

One Hit Wonders: Phil Johns, Mark Robinson

When it came to fighting all comers on the Midwest circuit, Phil Johns was your man. A hard-nosed battler who faced Jens Pulver, Rumina Sato, Jeff Curran, Hermes Franca and Shonie Carter over his nine-year career, Johns may not have earned a return call to the UFC after UFC 30, but he could certainly fight.

THE OWNERS

UFC President and co-owner Dana White, perhaps the most influential figure in mixed martial arts history, wasn't a fan the first time he saw the sport back in 1993.

"I had seen the first two and then I stopped watching," said White. "I was a boxing guy. A bunch of us from the gym got together and rented it on Pay-Per-View and watched it. The stuff that (Royce) Gracie was doing you didn't understand and then I watched the second one and there wasn't really ground fighting, but laying and stalling on the ground."

Fast forward a few years.

White, who had moved from Boston back to Las Vegas, where he went to high school, had reconnected with an old classmate, Lorenzo Fertitta, who ran the Station Casinos along with his brother Frank Fertitta III. White was managing fighters and gyms in the area, and the three were at the Hard Rock when they ran into mixed martial artist and jiu-jitsu black belt John Lewis. One thing led to another and Lewis began instructing the trio in Brazilian jiu-jitsu. They were hooked and soon gravitated to MMA and the UFC.

The UFC was in trouble, on the verge of bankruptcy and extinction. White found out it was for sale and told Lorenzo Fertitta. Frank Fertitta came into the conversation and the decision was made. They were going to form a new company—Zuffa (an Italian word meaning scuffle)—and buy the promotion. Zuffa was born in January of 2001.

That was the easy part.

The hard part was taking a damaged brand and not only reviving it, but making it a sport, not a spectacle. With unified rules already in place, Zuffa began the task of running towards regulation and not away from it. The goal was to get the sport back on cable and get it sanctioned by athletic commissions around the world so that fights in England and Australia would be fought under the same rules as fights in New Jersey and Las Vegas.

It was a difficult task, but one the Zuffa trio was prepared to undertake. Slowly, the walls began coming down. The sport was sanctioned in the fight capital of the world, Nevada, and state after state followed. The media, once content to write the sport off as "human cockfighting," began to write about MMA as a sport, focusing on the lives and journeys of the fighters. The events, with matchmaker Joe Silva continuing to put on consistently compelling fights, got bigger and bigger.

The resurrection of the UFC hit a snag as Lorenzo Fertitta decided that the company was simply losing too much money to remain viable. One night he told White to look for a buyer. The next morning, he changed his mind and told his partner that he was willing to give it one more shot.

That shot had to hit its mark though, and in 2005, Zuffa's last-ditch effort was a reality show entitled *The Ultimate Fighter*. Remarkably, it worked, as the show was a ratings hit for Spike TV. But it wasn't until the live finale and the unforgettable war between Forrest Griffin and Stephan Bonnar that White believed his company had reached its tipping point.

UFC co-owners Lorenzo and Frank Fertitta with UFC President Dana White (middle)

Even today, White doesn't hesitate to say that "The biggest thing to ever happen to us was Forrest Griffin and Stephan Bonnar."

The UFC was alive and on its way to being well. It would have been the signal for most businessmen to take their foot off the gas. White and the Fertittas pushed the pedal to the metal, building a brand that is the juggernaut of the sport world.

White is the frontman, a tireless worker and a media favorite for his no-nonsense approach and uncanny ability to tell it like it is. Lorenzo and Frank Fertitta are content letting White take the lead while they work their magic behind the scenes. It is a synergistic relationship where one part can't work without the other two.

"If you look throughout history, anything that's started to fail, people start pointing fingers real quick," said White. "The Fertittas never did that. And when it flipped and everything started to get successful and you look at how much my life changed and how well-known I became, there was never any ego, never anything about money or who's getting press or who's doing this. We never fight about anything, and never did they say 'What are you doing? What are you saying? Why did you do this? Why did you do that?' They let me be me and run this thing."

Now sanctioned in 45 of the 48 states with athletic commissions in the United States, in 354 million homes nationwide and on television in over 145 countries, and home to shows over the last few years in England, Australia, Canada, Germany, Ireland, and Abu Dhabi, the UFC is not just a US phenomenon, but an international one.

"It's about building a sport, and our goal is to make this thing a sport everywhere," said White.

In 2008, to aid in the UFC's global expansion, Lorenzo Fertitta stepped down as Chairman of Station Casinos to work full-time with Zuffa. White calls it one of his personal highlights.

"The thing was getting so big and we had these goals, but I was one guy," he said. "I was stretched as thin as you could possibly stretch a human being. There was no way we were going to do what we needed to do with just me over here, so when the day came that Lorenzo actually left Station Casinos to come work for the UFC, it was a proud moment for me."

There would be more.

In April of 2011, the organization presented a show at Toronto's Rogers Centre that sold over 55,000 tickets, a North American record, and the UFC shows no signs of slowing down. What matters to White and the Fertittas is bringing the best fights and fighters to fans around the world while wrapping it in the best live sports experience around. That's something you can never put a price tag on.

"This company's so big and it's so different than it used to be when it started, and there's a lot of things that I've given up control on," he said. "But I will never give up control on the product itself and what happens that night in the arena and on TV. It's that experience that I really watch over."

UFC 31 *Locked & Loaded*

04 May 2001

Trump Taj Mahal, Atlantic City, NJ

Debuts: Matt Serra, Semmy Schilt, Ricardo Almeida, BJ Penn, Tony DeSouza, Steve Berger

Fighters			Division	Method	Time	Round
Main Card						
Randy Couture	def.	Pedro Rizzo	Heavyweight	Unanimous Decision	—	5
Carlos Newton	def.	Pat Miletich	Welterweight	Submission - Choke	2:50	3
Chuck Liddell	def.	Kevin Randleman	Light Heavyweight	Knockout	1:18	1
Shonie Carter	def.	Matt Serra	Welterweight	Knockout	4:51	3
Semmy Schilt	def.	Pete Williams	Heavyweight	Technical Knockout	1:28	2
Matt Lindland	def.	Ricardo Almeida	Light Heavyweight	Opponent Disqualified	4:21	3
Preliminary Card						
BJ Penn	def.	Joey Gilbert	Lightweight	Technical Knockout	4:57	1
Tony DeSouza	def.	Steve Berger	Welterweight	Unanimous Decision	—	3

Fight of the Night (unofficial): Couture vs. Rizzo

At UFC 31, Randy Couture and Pedro Rizzo waged a five-round war worthy of the heavyweight championship. In the end, Couture retained his title by a close but unanimous decision, yet there were no losers in Zuffa's second UFC show at the Trump Taj Mahal.

Couture took home a victory the old-fashioned way: he earned it. The 37-year-old champ, the man who was never supposed to win but who kept doing it, almost scored a spectacular first-round stoppage as he executed his ground and pound strategy to perfection early on. Rizzo, bloodied and caught under a barrage of punches, looked like he was done, and referee John McCarthy was inspecting the Brazilian very closely as he absorbed heaps of punishment.

The second round was a carbon copy of the first, but this time it was Rizzo doing the damage, pounding a winded Couture with lefts, rights and stiff leg kicks. Couture, now bleeding heavily from the nose, staggered with practically every blow, but Rizzo's reluctance to pounce on the champ proved to be his downfall. Couture barely survived the second round, and at that moment, a distance fight seemed highly unlikely.

In the third and fourth rounds, Couture stood up with Rizzo, and the challenger refused to press his advantage. A stoppage by McCarthy to allow the ring doctor to check Couture's nose gave the champion the second wind he needed, and as the pace slowed, he took the final two rounds and the fight.

In the co-main event, Carlos Newton and Pat Miletich waged the expected tactical battle, with Newton winning the war and the UFC welterweight title by choking out "The Croation Sensation" at 2:50 of the third round.

Submission of the Night (unofficial): Newton vs. Miletich

Chuck Liddell gave a rude welcome to Kevin Randleman in the light heavyweight debut of "The Monster", stopping him with a left hook a mere 1:18 into the first round. Randleman said before the bout that he wanted to keep the fight standing up. "The Iceman" obliged, but Randleman didn't keep his end of the bargain, getting dropped and stunned. McCarthy immediately stepped in and ended the contest.

Knockout of the Night (unofficial): Carter vs. Serra

In a night of great fights, Shonie Carter and Matt Serra fought one of the best, with Carter ending the bout suddenly with a spinning back fist at the 4:51 mark of the third and final round. Serra, dropped hard by the blow, left the ring under his own power after a thorough check by the ringside physicians.

At the time of the knockout, the winner of the bout was in doubt, as the match had a myriad of twists and turns, with each man having his moments.

The pride of Zuidlaren, Holland, Semmy Schilt, survived a rough first round to impressively stop the Lion's Den's Pete Williams at 1:28 of the second frame.

In somewhat of a surprise, favored Brazilian jiu-jitsu star Ricardo Almeida was defeated by 2000 Olympic Silver medalist Matt Lindland via disqualification. Almeida, warned twice for illegal head kicks, was sent packing by referee Mario Yamasaki at the 4:21 mark.

Rising star BJ "The Prodigy" Penn was impressive in his first UFC match, rolling over Joey Gilbert via first-round stoppage. Penn controlled the bout from the outset, and once he had Gilbert's back the fight was over. Penn rained unanswered blows on Gilbert until referee Mason White stopped the contest at the 4:57 mark.

Tony DeSouza defeated Steve Berger via unanimous decision.

One Hit Wonder: Joey Gilbert

Owner of a 2-3 pro record over the course of a career that lasted from 1998 to 2003, Gilbert's fighting legacy unfortunately has him pegged as a trivia question: who was the first pro opponent of future two-time UFC champion BJ Penn?

UFC 32 *Showdown In The Meadowlands*

29 June 2001

Continental Airlines Arena, East Rutherford, NJ

Debuts: Paul Rodriguez, Vladimir Matyushenko, Ricco Rodriguez, Din Thomas

Fighters			Division	Method	Time	Round
Main Card						
Tito Ortiz	def.	Elvis Sinosic	Light Heavyweight	Technical Knockout	3:32	1
BJ Penn	def.	Din Thomas	Lightweight	Technical Knockout	2:42	1
Josh Barnett	def.	Semmy Schilt	Heavyweight	Submission - Armbar	4:21	1
Pat Miletich	def.	Shonic Carter	Welterweight	Knockout	2:42	2
Caol Uno	def.	Fabiano Iha	Lightweight	Knockout	1:49	1
Preliminary Card						
Vladimir Matyushenko	def.	Yuki Kondo	Light Heavyweight	Unanimous Decision	—	3
Ricco Rodriguez	def.	Andrei Arlovski	Heavyweight	Technical Knockout	1:23	3
Tony DeSouza	def.	Paul Rodriguez	Lightweight	Submission - Choke	1:15	1

UFC light heavyweight boss Tito Ortiz successfully defended his title at UFC 32 with a relatively easy first-round stoppage of Aussie contender Elvis Sinosic.

Fight of the Night (unofficial): Rodriguez vs. Arlovski

The "King of Rock and Rumble" was swarmed from the outset, and though Sinosic fired back gamely, his kicks and punches had little effect on the champion.

Soon Ortiz had taken the fight to the ground, and while Elvis tried to keep his opponent close to him, the strikes by the "Huntington Beach Bad Boy" started to find their mark, and Sinosic's defense began to show holes.

Referee Big John McCarthy watched the action closely, but Sinosic's ring savvy allowed him to move and block enough to keep himself in the match. A stiff forearm to the head changed that though, as blood spurted from the forehead of the challenger. Ortiz picked up the pace with his strikes, and McCarthy had little choice but to rescue Sinosic from further punishment at the 3:32 mark of the opening round.

In the co-main event, Hawaiian wunderkind BJ Penn drilled highly regarded Din Thomas with a right knee to the chin, followed up with three hooks on his fallen opponent, and scored a first-round TKO, his second in as many UFC appearances.

Perceived by many to be a pick-em matchup, in the 2:42 the match lasted, the crowd was captivated by the speed and technique of Penn, and the striking power and ring smarts of the veteran Thomas. Though making his Octagon debut, Thomas was a well traveled fighter who held a victory over then-UFC lightweight champion Jens Pulver. In the end it was the versatility and surprising power of Penn that led "The Prodigy" to victory.

Josh Barnett looked like a new man in the Octagon thanks to a huge loss of weight, and also showed some new wrinkles in his game by submitting Semmy Schilt with an armbar late in the first round.

In a bout that should have been a co-feature, and probably would have been a main event anywhere else, Pat Miletich lived up to his promise of knockouts by stopping old nemesis Shonie Carter with a head kick in the second round.

Vladimir Matyushenko, or as he is affectionately known, the "Janitor", wasn't able to mop up Japanese contender Yuki Kondo, but he did do enough to gain a unanimous decision over him in a light heavyweight bout.

Knockout of the Night (unofficial): Miletich vs. Carter

In what looked on paper to be the fight of the night, Caol Uno stunned the New Jersey crowd with a relatively quick and easy win over Fabiano Iha via referee stoppage after only 1:49 of the first round had elapsed.

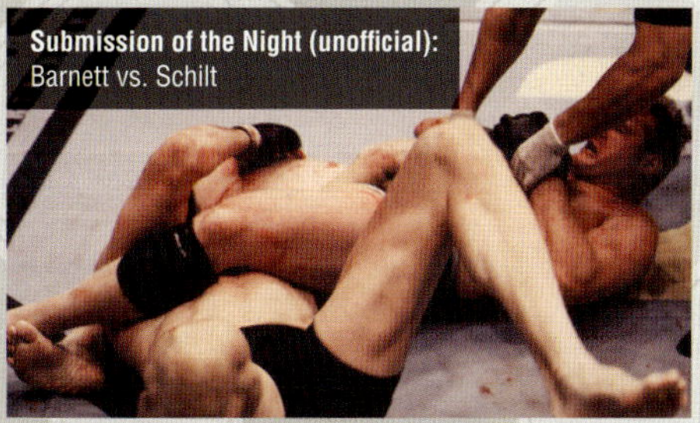

Submission of the Night (unofficial): Barnett vs. Schilt

Local hero Ricco Rodriguez (from Staten Island, NY), made his UFC debut a successful one, with an exciting third-round TKO victory over Andrei Arlovski. Both men had their moments throughout the bout, but it was Rodriguez who was able to wear down and finally catch up to Arlovski, who took an unanswered number of blows before being rescued by referee Mason White at 1:23 of the final round.

Tony DeSouza made it 2-for-2 in the Octagon with a quick (1:15) victory over well-regarded Paul Rodriguez, who got caught in a guillotine choke early, and was unable to escape.

One Hit Wonder: Paul Rodriguez

Paul Rodriguez' lone Octagon appearance was in a losing effort against Tony DeSouza, but there was no shame in his game. 10-8-2 over nine years as a pro, Rodriguez (who scored six wins by submission) never shied away from world-class competition, facing Dave Strasser, Dennis Hallman, Takanori Gomi, Tiki Ghosn, and Josh Neer.

UFC 33 *Victory in Vegas*

28 Sept. 2001

Mandalay Bay Events Center, Las Vegas, NV

Fighters			Division	Method	Time	Round
Main Card						
Tito Ortiz	def.	Vladimir Matyushenko	Light Heavyweight	Unanimous Decision	—	5
Jens Pulver	def.	Dennis Hallman	Lightweight	Unanimous Decision	—	5
Dave Menne	def.	Gil Castillo	Middleweight	Unanimous Decision	—	5
Chuck Liddell	def.	Murilo Bustamante	Light Heavyweight	Unanimous Decision	—	3
Matt Serra	def.	Yves Edwards	Welterweight	Majority Decision	—	3
Preliminary Card						
Jutaro Nakao	def.	Tony DeSouza	Welterweight	Knockout	0:15	2
Ricardo Almeida	def.	Eugene Jackson	Middleweight	Submission - Triangle Choke	4:06	1
Din Thomas	def.	Fabiano Iha	Lightweight	Unanimous Decision	—	3

There was good news and bad news when it came to UFC 33 on September 28, 2001. The good news was that at long last, the sport of mixed martial arts was sanctioned in the state of Nevada, allowing UFC events to be held in the universally accepted "Fight Capital of the World", Las Vegas. The UFC also made its way back to homes throughout the United States thanks to InDemand broadcasting fight cards on its Pay-Per-View system.

The bad news? Probably everything that came after the announcement that Vitor Belfort, the evening's headliner against UFC light heavyweight champ Tito Ortiz, had cut himself during training and was going to be forced out of the bout.

From there, despite the promise of three UFC championship bouts and an appearance from exciting knockout artist Chuck Liddell, it was all downhill, as the event didn't come close to meeting expectations.

In the main event, Ortiz went 25 minutes with replacement opponent Vladimir Matyushenko en route to a five-round unanimous decision win. Matyushenko, a world class wrestler from Belarus, didn't do anything in particular to threaten the reign of "The Huntington Beach Bad Boy", but he was tough enough to stick around for the entire fight…much to the chagrin of the Vegas crowd.

If the Ortiz-Matyushenko bout was disappointing, you could have excused it due to the late switch in opponents. There was no such soft-soaping the lightweight title fight between Jens Pulver and Dennis Hallman, a heated grudge match that didn't quite warm to above a slow boil. When it was over, it was another 25-minute war of nerves and another champion retaining his crown as Pulver won a five-round unanimous decision.

The third title fight was to crown the UFC's first 185-pound champion, and when the dust settled, there was more action in Dave Menne's win over gutsy Gil Castillo than in the other two title bouts, but it was another five-round bout that was fairly one-sided.

Even the soon-to-be legendary knockout artist Chuck "The Iceman" Liddell couldn't pull off one of his exciting wars or knockouts, as he worked his way to a methodical three-round decision win over Brazilian jiu-jitsu standout Murilo Bustamante.

In the final main card bout, exciting lightweight contenders Matt Serra and Yves Edwards engaged in a brisk, closely-contested three-rounder, with Serra emerging victorious via majority decision.

Brazilian jiu-jitsu ace Ricardo Almeida evened his UFC record to 1-1 in a middleweight bout as he submitted Eugene Jackson with a triangle choke at 4:06 of the opening round.

A horrific first round turned into an explosive second round for Japan's Jutaro Nakao, as he rebounded from a slow opening five minutes to knock out Tony DeSouza 15 seconds into round two.

Din Thomas and Fabiano Iha kicked off the UFC in Las Vegas era in style with an exciting three-round match won by Thomas via unanimous decision.

Fight of the Night (unofficial): Serra vs. Edwards

UFC 34 *High Voltage*

02 Nov. 2001

MGM Grand Garden Arena, Las Vegas, NV

Debuts: Homer Moore, Frank Mir, Roberto Traven

Fighters			Division	Method	Time	Round
Main Card						
Randy Couture	def.	Pedro Rizzo	Heavyweight	Technical Knockout	1:38	3
Ricco Rodriguez	def.	Pete Williams	Heavyweight	Technical Knockout	4:02	2
Matt Hughes	def.	Carlos Newton	Welterweight	Knockout	1:27	2
BJ Penn	def.	Caol Uno	Lightweight	Knockout	0:11	1
Josh Barnett	def.	Bobby Hoffman	Heavyweight	Submission - Strikes	4:25	2
Preliminary Card						
Evan Tanner	def.	Homer Moore	Light Heavyweight	Submission - Armbar	0:55	2
Matt Lindland	def.	Phil Baroni	Middlweight	Majority Decision	—	3
Frank Mir	def.	Roberto Traven	Heavyweight	Submission - Armbar	1:05	1

After a dismal debut in Las Vegas , the UFC bounced back with a UFC 34 card filled with knockouts, submissions, a little controversy, and the continued reign of the grand old man of mixed martial arts, Randy Couture.

Couture, 38, the UFC heavyweight champion, tightened his grip on the number-one spot in the world rankings. This dominant third-round technical knockout over a listless Pedro Rizzo in the main event was hardly reminiscent of the five-round war waged by the two six months earlier.

Coming out with leg kicks honed by training with former UFC king Maurice Smith, Couture led the action early in the first round. After trading knees in the clinch, Couture took Rizzo to the mat and proceeded to pound the Brazilian with anything at his disposal, be it punches, forearms or shoulders. Rizzo, either bored or confused, ended the round on his back and with a cut on the bridge of his nose for his trouble.

The second round provided more of the same, with Rizzo's lack of killer instinct painfully apparent. In the third, Couture ended things, dropping the challenger to the mat and raining down blows until referee John McCarthy rescued a bloody Rizzo from further punishment at the 1:38 mark.

Knockout of the Night (unofficial): Hughes vs. Newton

In the co-feature, Iowa's Matt Hughes scored a stunning upset to win the welterweight title, knocking out Carlos Newton in two rounds. The bout, dominated by Hughes, was not without a dose of controversy.

Hughes used his freakish strength to establish control from the outset. With slams, knees, and strikes, Hughes easily won the first round and was dominating the second when Newton was able to nab the Miletich team member in a triangle choke. The oohs and aahs could be heard throughout the MGM Grand when Hughes lifted Newton over his head and drove him into the fence.

The champion grabbed the top of the fence, but soon let go after being admonished by referee McCarthy. With Newton still over his head, and still sinking in the choke, Hughes took a step back and dropped his foe to the mat. Slamming his head on the canvas, Newton was out and McCarthy stopped the bout. Simple enough, but Hughes was dazed as well and needed to be told that he won the fight and the title. So who was out first? In Newton's post-fight interview, he stated that he believed he had choked Hughes out. But upon viewing different replay angles of the final slam, Hughes obviously had the presence of mind to take a step back, thus removing Newton from the cage and allowing him to fall. Regardless, the call stands.

It was supposed to be the fight of the night, and for pure excitement it was for the 11 seconds it lasted. Caol Uno and BJ Penn squared off for the right to face UFC lightweight champ Jens Pulver at UFC 35, and it was Penn who continued to be frighteningly effective in the Octagon.

Photography by: Susumu Nagao

Knockout of the Night (unofficial): Penn vs. Uno

Uno opened the bout with an attempted flying kick that captivated the crowd but did little to deter the focused Penn. Uno came at Penn again, only to be greeted with a barrage of punches. As Uno backpedaled with Penn in pursuit,"The Prodigy" landed a short right hand that sent his foe reeling into the fence. Penn pounced, landing right hand after right hand until a nearly unconscious Uno was rescued by referee Larry Landless at the 11-second mark.

Four of the UFC's top heavyweights were in action that night, and after impressive victories over Bobby Hoffman and Pete Williams, respectively, Josh Barnett and Ricco Rodriguez set Randy Couture in their sights.

Fight of the Night (unofficial): Lindland vs. Baroni

Middleweights Matt Lindland and Phil Baroni battled in a match worthy of the main card, with Lindland surviving some shaky moments and a point deduction for a foul to nab a three-round majority decision.

Evan Tanner returned to the Octagon for the first time since a brutal KO loss to Tito Ortiz with an easy two-round win over UFC rookie Homer Moore. After an uneventful first round between the two light heavyweights, Tanner caught Moore in an armbar in the second and won via tapout at the 55-second mark.

Submission of the Night (unofficial): Mir vs. Traven

Local Las Vegas heavyweight Frank Mir made his UFC debut a successful one, submitting Brazil's Roberto Traven with an armbar after 1:05 of the first round.

UFC 37 *High Impact*

10 May 2002

CenturyTel Center, Bossier City, LA

Debuts: Paul Creighton, Ivan Salaverry, Benji Radach, Robbie Lawler, Aaron Riley

Fighters			Division	Method	Time	Round
Main Card						
Murilo Bustamante	def.	Matt Lindland	Middleweight	Submission - Guillotine	1:26	3
Ricco Rodriguez	def.	Tsuyoshi Kohsaka	Heavyweight	Technical Knockout	3:26	2
BJ Penn	def.	Paul Creighton	Lightweight	Technical Knockout	3:22	2
Phil Baroni	def.	Amar Suloev	Middleweight	Technical Knockout	2:59	1
Caol Uno	def.	Yves Edwards	Lightweight	Unanimous Decision	—	3
Preliminary Card						
Ivan Salaverry	def.	Andrei Semenov	Middleweight	Technical Knockout	2:27	3
Benji Radach	def.	Steve Berger	Welterweight	Technical Knockout*	0:27	1
Robbie Lawler	def.	Aaron Riley	Welterweight	Unanimous Decision	—	3

*Result later changed to No Contest due to an incorrect referee stoppage.

Surviving an injured finger and a blown call by referee John McCarthy in the UFC 37 main event, Murilo Bustamante retained his middleweight title with a third-round submission win over Matt Lindland at the CenturyTel Center in Bossier City, Louisiana.

A guillotine choke forced Lindland to tap at 1:26 of the third, but it was a short right hand to the jaw that started "The Law" on the road to defeat. Bloodied and stunned, Lindland attempted to hold the champion off after being dropped to the canvas, but Bustamante was too much for the world-class wrestler to handle.

It almost wasn't a happy ending for the Brazilian. As a fast-paced first round was drawing to a close, Bustamante took Lindland down, and as the Oregon native tried to reverse, the champion caught the challenger in an armbar. Fully extending the arm, a tapout seemed to be seconds away. After seeing Lindland apparently tap, McCarthy broke up the two.

Submission of the Night (unofficial): Bustamante vs. Lindland

Bustamante fought off his disappointment in the second and effectively defended Lindland's knee attempts in the clinch. As the second progressed, Bustamante started to find his range with his punches, as well—a precursor of things to come.

Bustamante continued to press the action as the third round commenced, and once he got Lindland hurt, he refused to let him off the hook a second time.

Moving one step closer to a heavyweight title shot, the well-traveled Ricco Rodriguez continued to impress, stopping Tsuyoshi Kosaka via strikes at the 3:26 mark of round two.

Knockout of the Night (unofficial): Rodriguez vs. Kosaka

Entering the second phase of his MMA career, BJ Penn rebounded from the first loss of his career at the expense of Paul Creighton, stopping the New Yorker with punches at 3:22 of the second.

Long Island middleweight Phil Baroni withstood an illegal knee to the head early in round one to score a devastating first-round KO of Russia's Amar Suloev.

All action from the opening bell, both men were obviously looking to make good on the pre-fight war of words they engaged in. Suloev drew first blood with a flying knee, and a follow-up barrage stunned the New Yorker and put him to the canvas.

Suloev then ripped an illegal knee to Baroni's face that appeared to briefly KO him. As referee John McCarthy intervened, Baroni regained his senses and went at Suloev.

After a foul warning, Baroni refused McCarthy's offer of a minute's rest and went right back at the Russian. Suloev then attempted an armbar, and after escaping, Baroni got position on his foe. The end came seconds later as Baroni battered Suloev into submission. McCarthy wisely halted the bout at the 2:59 mark.

In the main card opener, Caol Uno got back on the winning track with a hard-earned unanimous decision over Texas' Yves Edwards in a lightweight contest. Scores were 29-28 twice and 30-29.

Fight of the Night (unofficial): Lawler vs. Riley

Robbie Lawler and Aaron Riley waged a main-card–worthy brawl in a welterweight preliminary bout, with both youngsters showing devastating power and iron chins throughout their three-round war. When it was over, Lawler had a unanimous decision victory. Official scores were 29-27 twice, and 29-28 for the newest representative of the Miletich team to make an Octagon appearance.

Almost KO'd in the first and submitted in the second, a bloodied Andrei Semenov finally succumbed to Ivan Salaverry, getting stopped via strikes at the 2:27 mark of the third and final round of yet another preliminary war, this one in the suddenly interesting middleweight division.

It was a quick hook by Mason White that changed the welterweight preliminary bout between Benji Radach and Steve Berger. After being dropped by a stiff right, Berger weathered a series of punches from Radach, and attempted a kneelock on his foe. White broke the hold and stopped the bout, awarding it to Radach at the 27-second mark of the first round, eliciting a series of boos from the CenturyTel Center crowd.

One Hit Wonder: Paul Creighton

UFC 37.5 *As Real As It Gets*

22 June 2002

Bellagio Hotel and Casino, Las Vegas, NV

Debuts: Joao Marcos Pierini, Rodrigo Ruas, Pete Spratt, Zach Light, Nick Serra

Fighters			Division	Method	Time	Round
Main Card						
Chuck Liddell	def.	Vitor Belfort	Light Heavyweight	Unanimous Decision	[illegible]	3
Benji Radach	def.	Nick Serra	Welterweight	Unanimous Decision	—	3
Pete Spratt	def.	Zach Light	Welterweight	Submission - Armbar	2:22	1
Robbie Lawler	def.	Steve Berger	Welterweight	Technical Knockout	0:27	2
Tony Fryklund	def.	Rodrigo Ruas	Middlweight	Technical Knockout	3:34	2
Yves Edwards	def.	Joao Marcos Pierini	Lightweight	Technical Knockout - Injury	1:19	1

Number-one UFC light heavyweight contender Chuck "The Iceman" Liddell left no doubt as to who the next challenger for Tito Ortiz' title should be, as he outpointed returning superstar Vitor Belfort over three rounds to win his ninth consecutive bout.

"I thought if I kept pressing him I could take the fight away from him," said Liddell.

Scores were 30-27 twice and 29-28. The fight was Belfort's first in the UFC since a first-round knockout of Wanderlei Silva in October of 1998.

Fight of the Night (unofficial): Liddell vs. Belfort

Liddell opened the bout with a head kick, but Belfort was able to block it. Surprisingly, Belfort's first doses of offense were two takedown attempts, both of which he nailed. Liddell fought well off his back though, landing some strikes before he used the fence to get back to his feet at the midway point. Still locked up, Liddell pinned Belfort to the fence and landed close-range strikes before breaking loose with a minute left. Belfort finished the round with another score, a hard leg kick.

After the close first round, Liddell went on the attack, stalking Belfort as the Brazilian looked to counter. A right hand jarred Belfort and prompted him to tie up. Liddell took the dominant position against the fence though, and he landed a series of knees before referee John McCarthy broke the two at the midway point. A spinning back kick by Liddell got the crowd roaring, and Belfort came back with one of his trademark flurries, even ending the round with a kick to the head in order to try and steal the round.

The 205-pounders traded leg kicks early in the third, and Liddell missed a spinning back fist as he mixed up his assault. The big shots were coming faster now, as Liddell and Belfort traded home run swings, but it was "The Iceman" who got the last word with a counter right hand in the midst of a furious exchange that sealed the decision for the Californian with less than two minutes left.

Prodigious knockout artist Robbie Lawler survived a spirited effort from seasoned competitor Steve Berger and delivered some thunder of his own in response, using a right hand to drop Berger and a follow up barrage to finish him on the ground at 27 seconds of round two.

Knockout of the Night (unofficial): Lawler vs. Berger

In welterweight action, Benji Radach outpointed New York's Nick Serra, taking a unanimous decision by scores of 30-27 twice, and 29-28.

Muay Thai ace Pete Spratt showed off his submission game in his bout with wrestler Zach Light, surviving a ground and pound assault to lock in an armbar and force a tapout at 2:22 of the first round.

Submission of the Night (unofficial): Spratt vs. Light

Veteran Tony Fryklund ruined the UFC debut of Marco Ruas' nephew Rodrigo, pounding away with ground strikes that bloodied the Brazilian and forced a stoppage at 3:34 of the second round.

The opening lightweight bout between highly-regarded Yves Edwards and Joao Marcos Pierini ended in abbreviated fashion when an injury forced a halt to the bout at 1:19 of the opening round. A right high kick from Edwards sent Pierini hard to the mat, but after the Brazilian rose, he wasn't able to continue due to a shoulder injury, rendering Edwards the technical knockout winner.

One Hit Wonders: Joao Marcos Pierini, Rodrigo Ruas, Zach Light, Nick Serra

The brother of former UFC welterweight champion Matt Serra, Nick Serra is a jiu-jitsu black belt under Renzo Gracie, and he won three of his final five MMA bouts before leaving the sport in 2008 to focus on teaching at the Serra jiu-jitsu academies in New York.

UFC 38 *Brawl at the Hall*

13 July 2002

Royal Albert Hall, London, England

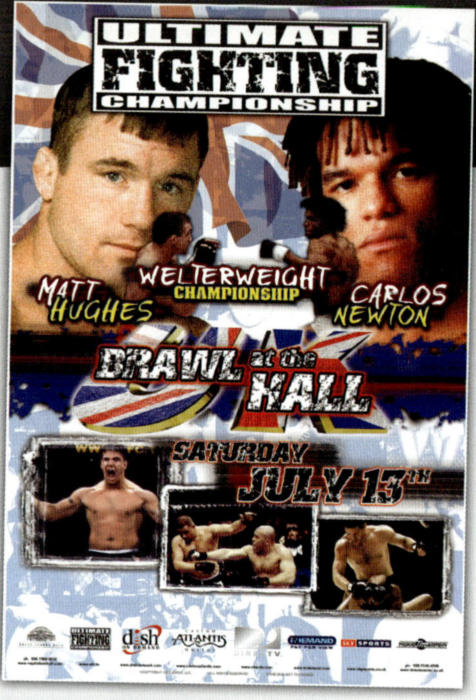

Debuts: Mark Weir, Genki Sudo, Leigh Remedios, James Zikic, Phillip Miller, Chris Haseman

Fighters			Division	Method	Time	Round
Main Card						
Matt Hughes	def.	Carlos Newton	Welterweight	Technical Knockout	3:37	4
Ian Freeman	def.	Frank Mir	Heavyweight	Technical Knockout	4:35	1
Mark Weir	def.	Eugene Jackson	Middlweight	Knockout	0:10	1
Genki Sudo	def.	Leigh Remedios	Lightweight	Submission - Rear Naked Choke	1:38	2
Phillip Miller	def.	James Zikic	Light Heavyweight	Unanimous Decision	—	3
Preliminary Card						
Renato Sobral	def.	Elvis Sinosic	Light Heavyweight	Unanimous Decision	—	3
Evan Tanner	def.	Chris Haseman	Light Heavyweight	Unanimous Decision	—	3

The first welterweight title bout between Matt Hughes and Carlos Newton ended in controversy. The new champion made sure there was none the next time around in the main event of UFC 38 as he defended his crown for the second time with a dominant fourth-round technical knockout of "The Ronin" in the UFC's first visit to England.

Hughes had knocked out Newton with a slam to win the 170-pound title at UFC 34 in 2001, but some speculated that Newton had first put Hughes to sleep with a triangle choke seconds before the end. There would be no doubts in the rematch.

After a slow beginning, it was Newton surprisingly shooting for the takedown, but Hughes was able to reverse the attempt and get on top. Newton almost locked up the champion's arm from the bottom, yet Hughes powered out and began working his strikes. Newton stayed busy and so did Hughes who was continually moving and using his shoulders, elbows and forearms to avoid a referee standup.

Hughes closed the distance quickly in round two, and the bout returned to the mat. Newton scrambled his way free and got back to his feet, but Hughes stayed close and put the challenger on his back again. From there, it was just a case of Hughes dominating on the mat and Newton trying in vain to escape. At the end of the round, Hughes began unleashing a ferocious series of elbows, cutting his foe in the process.

Newton had a brief window of opportunity when the third opened as Hughes missed a high kick, but seconds later, he was taken down. Newton gamely looked to turn things around with a submission, but the champion's offense and defense were on point. With under two minutes left, Hughes got the mount position and fired away with strikes, but there was no stoppage. Hughes even showed off some more aspects of his game as he went for an armbar, but Newton escaped and took Hughes' back. Time ran out on "The Ronin", though, killing his best comeback attempt.

Keeping it simple, Hughes took Newton down to start the fourth, and he patiently punished the challenger. With less than two minutes remaining, Newton got trapped, and after a series of unanswered blows, referee John McCarthy halted the bout at the 3:37 mark.

In the co-feature, unbeaten young gun Frank Mir got a rude welcome to England by local hero Ian Freeman, who scored an emotional first-round technical knockout win in a stunning upset.

The 23-year-old Mir, a submission specialist, traded with Freeman early, but then wisely went to the mat to look for the tapout. Freeman weathered the grappling attacks and began teeing off on his foe at close range when they stood. After the assault of knees, Mir got another takedown, this time looking to lock up the Brit's ankle. The 35-year-old veteran pounded his way loose. With the crowd roaring, Freeman continued to score, and with under a minute left, Mir lost his mouthpiece. McCarthy halted the bout to put the mouthpiece back in, but Mir could barely stand, forcing the stoppage with 25 seconds left in the round.

Fight of the Night (unofficial):
Freeman vs. Mir

Another battlin' Brit, Mark Weir, also sent his home country fans home happy as he knocked out veteran Eugene Jackson in just 10 seconds.

Knockout of the Night (unofficial):
Weir vs. Jackson

The two other British fighters on the main card weren't as fortunate though, as debuting Japanese star Genki Sudo submitted Leigh Remedios via rear naked choke at 1:38 of round two, and the United States' Phillip Miller scored a unanimous decision win over James Zikic.

Two of Australia's top MMA fighters also had a rough night, with former world title challenger Elvis Sinosic dropping a unanimous decision to Renato "Babalu" Sobral and late replacement Chris Haseman losing a three-round nod to Evan Tanner.

Submission of the Night (unofficial):
Sudo vs. Remedios

One Hit Wonders: Leigh Remedios, James Zikic, Chris Haseman

UFC 39 *The Warriors Return*

27 Sept. 2002

Mohegan Sun Arena, Uncasville, CT

Debuts: Wesley Correira, Tim Sylvia

Fighters			Division	Method	Time	Round
Main Card						
Ricco Rodriguez	def.	Randy Couture	Heavyweight	Submission - Strikes	3:04	5
Tim Sylvia	def.	Wesley Correira	Heavyweight	Technical Knockout	1:43	2
BJ Penn	def.	Matt Serra	Lightweight	Unanimous Decision	—	3
Caol Uno	def.	Din Thomas	Lightweight	Unanimous Decision	—	3
Gan McGee	def.	Pedro Rizzo	Heavyweight	Technical Knockout	5:00	1
Phil Baroni	def.	Dave Menne	Middleweight	Knockout	0:18	1
Preliminary Card						
Matt Lindland	def.	Ivan Salaverry	Middleweight	Unanimous Decision	—	3
Sean Sherk	def.	Benji Radach	Welterweight	Technical Knockout - Cuts	4:16	1

There was nothing "Suave" about Ricco Rodriguez' fifth-round win over Randy Couture at the Mohegan Sun Casino in Uncasville, Connecticut. In taking the UFC heavyweight title vacated by the suspension of Josh Barnett, Rodriguez showed guts, stamina, and a lot of heart.

Fight of the Night (unofficial): Rodriguez vs. Couture

After losing the first two rounds to the ageless 39-year-old Couture, a bloodied Rodriguez kept his composure and roared back into the fight, winning the next two stanzas and setting up a decisive fifth round with the former champion.

As the bout opened, Rodriguez surprisingly opted to keep the fight standing until Couture took Rodriguez down suddenly. Rodriguez was able to rise, but another effective takedown sat him down on the mat again as the round ended.

Couture controlled the second round even more convincingly, taking Rodriguez down early and keeping him there with an array of shoulders, punches, and forearms. With under a minute left, the fight rose to the standing position, but seconds later, Couture dropped Rodriguez again. Couture tried to finish the fight, but Rodriguez was able to weather the storm and survive the round.

In the third, Rodriguez finally mounted an offense and started landing some forearms and elbows, and he even scored a guillotine choke briefly as the round drew to a close.

Kicking off the fourth round with an impressive takedown, Rodriguez kept the momentum by pinning Couture against the fence and using his forearms and elbows to punish his foe. With 30 seconds left, Rodriguez got full mount and went for the former champion's arm, but Couture spun out and actually had the upper position as the round closed.

After eating a quick combination seconds into the final round, Rodriguez took Couture to the mat and pounded him until "The Natural" verbally submitted at the 3:04 mark of the fifth. It was the culmination of a dream for the new champion.

It wasn't the Fight of the Night as many expected, but BJ Penn still managed to earn his second shot at the UFC lightweight title with a razor-thin unanimous decision victory over Matt Serra. All three judges scored it 29-28 for Penn.

In the opening lightweight tournament bout, Caol Uno repeated his victory over Din Thomas, surviving some rocky first-round moments to nab a unanimous decision by scores of 29-27.

"We got a problem here," said ace cutman Leon Tabbs as Pedro Rizzo stumbled back to his corner after his first round with Gan McGee. He was right.

Drilled with a straight right hand seconds after landing one of his patented leg kicks, Rizzo staggered back to the fence, blood spurting from the bridge of his nose. The round ended, and so did Rizzo's immediate heavyweight title hopes as his trainer, Marco Ruas, disgustedly tossed a white towel to the canvas, signaling his charge's surrender.

It took Phil Baroni longer to thank his sponsors than to walk through former UFC champ Dave Menne in their middleweight bout. After 18 seconds of fury, Baroni had delivered a KO for the ages.

"I'm the best ever," he screamed, and while the "New York Bad Ass" was typically overstating his case, those who doubted the power of the Long Islander could be skeptical no longer.

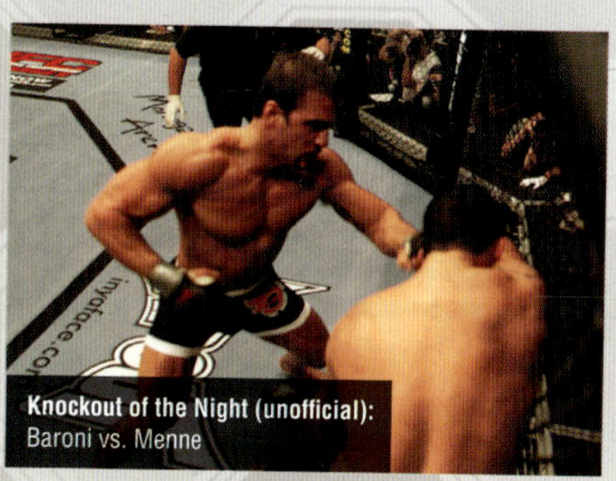
Knockout of the Night (unofficial): Baroni vs. Menne

After a few moments of mutual jabbing, Baroni landed flush with the first serious punch he threw, a right hand that staggered Menne, and for all intents and purposes, ended the fight.

A follow-up barrage by Baroni, that included eight flush head shots, brought in referee Larry Landless to halt the bout.

In heavyweight action, Tim Sylvia stopped Wesley Correira in the second round.

Matt Lindland decisioned Ivan Salaverry over three rounds, and Sean Sherk halted Benji Radach via cuts at 4:16 of the opening stanza.

UFC 40 *Vendetta*

22 Nov. 2002

MGM Grand Garden Arena, Las Vegas, NV

Debuts: Vladimir Matyushenko, Travis Wiuff

Fighters			Division	Method	Time	Round
Main Card						
Tito Ortiz	def.	Ken Shamrock	Light Heavyweight	Technical Knockout	5:00	3
Matt Hughes	def.	Gil Castillo	Welterweight	Technical Knockout - Cuts	5:00	1
Chuck Liddell	def.	Renato Sobral	Light Heavyweight	Knockout	2:55	1
Carlos Newton	def.	Pete Spratt	Welterweight	Submission - Kimura	1:41	1
Robbie Lawler	def.	Tiki Ghosn	Welterweight	Technical Knockout	1:29	1
Preliminary Card						
Andrei Arlovski	def.	Ian Freeman	Heavyweight	Technical Knockout	1:18	1
Vladimir Matyushenko	def.	Travis Wiuff	Heavyweight	Submission - Strikes	4:10	1
Phillip Miller	def.	Mark Weir	Middlweight	Submission - Rear Naked Choke	4:50	2

Fight of the Night (unofficial): Ortiz vs. Shamrock

Since the creation of the Ultimate Fighting Championship in 1993, there have been highly-anticipated fights and some bad blood grudge matches; but nothing matched the anticipation and fire behind the November 22 battle for the light heavyweight title between champion Tito Ortiz and challenger Ken Shamrock.

The high-intensity feud—years in the making—made UFC 40 the biggest event in UFC history up until that time, and if Ortiz wasn't a star before…his bout with the MMA pioneer and former pro wrestling star, his punishing three-round stoppage victory certainly did the trick.

After elaborate entrances from both men that ignited the packed house, the two combatants stared each other down from across the Octagon throughout Bruce Buffer's introductions and referee John McCarthy's instructions, antsy to hear the opening bell ring.

When it did, Ortiz came out with a quick right hand that missed, and Shamrock locked the champion up. Ortiz fought his way loose and nailed the challenger with a combination of punches and a knee. Shamrock fired off uppercuts from close range, but Ortiz kept throwing, with his opponent finally hitting the deck. Shamrock got up quickly and sent Ortiz to a knee with a right to the jaw and the two locked up after a furious first minute. In the second minute, Ortiz grabbed Shamrock in a clinch before scoring a takedown, and it was time for him to unleash his patented ground and pound attack. Unleash it he did, as he punished Shamrock for the remainder of the round, cutting him in the process, and making it evident that "The World's Most Dangerous Man" was going to have a rough night.

It was a night that would last another ten minutes, as Ortiz continued to dominate his 38-year-old foe, who simply had no answers for the prime champion either standing or on the mat. Finally, after a steady three-round pounding that left Shamrock's face almost unrecognizable, the corner had seen enough, and they halted the bout before the bell for the fourth stanza.

After the bout, the two apparently squashed their beef.

"I always respected Ken as a fighter, I always looked up to him," said Ortiz. "As a person we had our differences, and today we squared away our differences in the Octagon."

"Tito Ortiz is a true champion, he beat me fair and square, and he's the man," said Shamrock. "We settled our differences, and it's over and done with."

Or was it? Only time would tell.

In the co-feature, light heavyweight contender Chuck "The Iceman" Liddell put himself in line for a shot at his former training partner's title with a first-round knockout of Brazil's Renato "Babalu" Sobral.

Knockout of the Night (unofficial): Liddell vs. Sobral

Fresh from a win over Vitor Belfort, Liddell stalked Sobral confidently, and the Brazilian looked equally calm in the Octagon. After pushing aside his foe's first takedown attempt though, Liddell seemed to become even more intent on ending the bout early. That time would come soon enough, as he followed up some flush right hands with a surprise left kick to the head. Sobral fell hard to the canvas and as referee Larry Landless halted the bout at the 2:55 mark, Liddell yelled "I want my belt."

In the night's second championship bout, welterweight titleholder Matt Hughes continued to dominate the 170-pound weight class, this time owning Gil Castillo on the mat for five minutes before the bout was halted due to a cut suffered by the former middleweight title challenger. The win was Hughes' 11th in a row, and third in defense of his belt.

Submission of the Night (unofficial): Newton vs. Spratt

Former welterweight champion Carlos Newton was back in form in his first bout since losing his rematch to Hughes at UFC 38 as he submitted Pete Spratt via kimura at 1:41 of the first round.

The main card opener saw welterweight knockout artist "Ruthless" Robbie Lawler improve to 3-0 in the Octagon with a first-round technical knockout via strikes of Tiki Ghosn.

In preliminary action, Andrei Arlovski snapped a two-fight losing streak with a 78-second technical knockout of England's Ian Freeman; Vladimir Matyushenko submitted Travis Wiuff via strikes and Phillip Miller used a rear naked choke to produce a tapout from Mark Weir in round two.

UFC 41 *Onslaught*

28 Feb. 2003

Boardwalk Hall, Atlantic City, NJ

Debut: Rich Clementi

Fighters			Division	Method	Time	Round
Main Card						
Tim Sylvia	def.	Ricco Rodriguez	Heavyweight	Knockout	3:06	1
Frank Mir	def.	Tank Abbott	Heavyweight	Submission - Ankle Lock	0:46	1
BJ Penn	vs.	Caol Uno	Lightweight	Draw	—	5
Matt Lindland	def.	Phil Baroni	Middleweight	Unanimous Decision	—	3
Vladimir Matyushenko	def.	Pedro Rizzo	Heavyweight	Unanimous Decision	—	3
Preliminary Card						
Din Thomas	def.	Matt Serra	Lightweight	Split Decision	—	3
Gan McGee	def.	Alexandre Dantas	Heavyweight	Technical Knockout	4:49	1
Yves Edwards	def.	Rich Clementi	Lightweight	Submission - Rear Naked Choke	4:07	3

Barely champion for six months, heavily favored Ricco Rodriguez paid a dear price for trading punches with 6' 8" challenger Tim Sylvia, as a series of brutal right hands knocked the Staten Island native down and out at 3:06 of the first round in the UFC 41 main event before a packed (and shocked) house at the Boardwalk Hall.

Sylvia showed his ferocity once he got Rodriguez hurt with a stiff right hand shortly after the midway point of the first. It was almost a short night for Sylvia himself when, after some tentative punches thrown by both fighters, Rodriguez was able to secure an armbar two minutes into the contest.

Knockout of the Night (unofficial): Sylvia vs. Rodriguez

Sylvia's strength allowed him to escape, and Rodriguez continued to stand with the challenger, a decision that led to the unbeaten and unheralded Sylvia being declared champion.

In the co-feature, Tank Abbott learned first-hand how far the UFC had evolved since his last Octagon bout in 1998 when he was tapped out by jiu-jitsu ace Frank Mir in a mere 46 seconds.

"My submissions are devastating," said Mir. "When I'm on, they don't go that fast."

Mir was right on both counts, weathering a couple of Abbott haymakers to take the original UFC bad boy down to the mat and quickly securing not only an omoplata, but also an ankle lock. The ankle lock proved to be the finisher, as Abbott tried in vain to escape, but with no options left, he tapped.

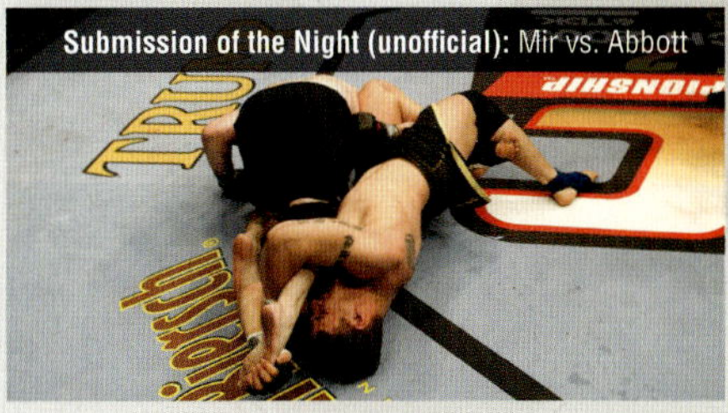

Submission of the Night (unofficial): Mir vs. Abbott

BJ Penn and Caol Uno showed the best of what the UFC lightweight division had to offer in their battle for the lightweight title, but at the end of five rounds of intriguing action, Jens Pulver's championship remained vacant after a draw was declared.

Both fighters came to win, with Penn looking to repeat his first-round blitz of Uno, and Uno looking to bring a UFC title home to Japan. In the end, it was Uno's valiant desire to avenge his loss and Penn's measured but spotty performance that produced the stalemate.

The draw was scored 48-47 Uno, 48-46 Penn, and 48-48.

Prior to their UFC 41 middleweight contest, the trash talk flew fast and furiously between Matt Lindland and Phil Baroni. In a twist rarely seen in the fight game, the match actually surpassed the hype, with Lindland pounding out a clear three-round decision over "The New York Bad Ass" in an early candidate for Fight of The Year.

Lindland opened the bout by driving Baroni to the fence and slamming him to the canvas, where he proceeded to pound him relentlessly.

The second round followed the same pattern, with Baroni absorbing copious amounts of punishment but refusing to give in to his nemesis, who had defeated him by decision in late-2001.

Fight of the Night (unofficial): Lindland vs. Baroni

Down on the scorecards, Baroni laid it all on the line in the final round. He landed a series of unanswered blows as the seconds ticked away, leaving him just short of what could have been an amazing comeback. All three judges scored it 29-28 for Lindland.

Perennial heavyweight contender Pedro Rizzo saw his hopes of a future title bout dashed even further as he suffered his second consecutive loss, this time via a three-round unanimous decision to Vladimir Matyushenko.

In a preliminary bout, top lightweight contenders Din Thomas and Matt Serra battled on fairly even terms for three rounds with Serra initially eking out an unpopular three-round split decision—a verdict which was turned over minutes later due to an announced miscalculation of the official scorecards. Shortly after the bout's conclusion, with both fighters back in the locker rooms, ring announcer Bruce Buffer re-announced the scores as 29-28 twice, and 28-30 for Thomas.

Heavyweight contender Gan McGee followed up his victory over Pedro Rizzo with another first-round stoppage, this one over Alexandre "Café" Dantas.

In the lightweight opener, Yves Edwards was impressive in scoring a third-round submission victory over Rich Clementi.

UFC 42 *Sudden Impact*

25 April 2003

American Airlines Arena, Miami, FL

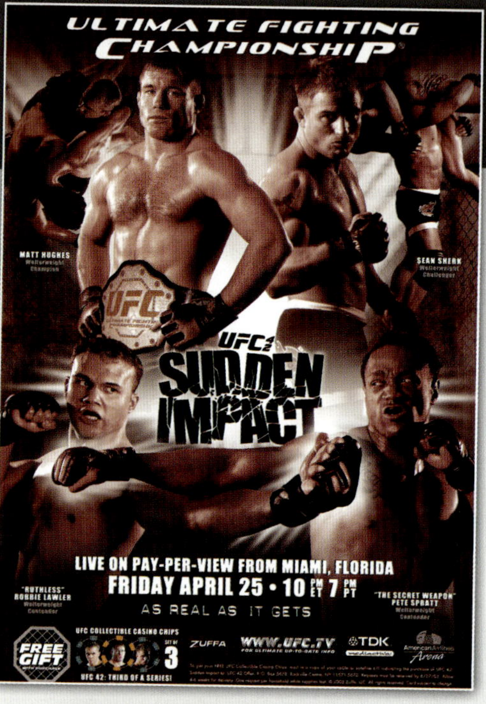

Debuts: Romie Aram, Sean Alvarez, Hermes Franca, Rich Crunkilton, David Loiseau, Rich Franklin

Fighters			Division	Method	Time	Round
Main Card						
Matt Hughes	def.	Sean Sherk	Welterweight	Unanimous Decision	—	5
Pete Spratt	def.	Robbie Lawler	Welterweight	Submission - Injury	2:28	2
Dave Strasser	def.	Romie Aram	Welterweight	Unanimous Decision	—	3
Wesley Correira	def.	Sean Alvarez	Heavyweight	Technical Knockout	1:46	2
Rich Franklin	def.	Evan Tanner	Light Heavyweight	Technical Knockout	2:40	1
Preliminary Card						
Duane Ludwig	def.	Genki Sudo	Lightweight	Unanimous Decision	—	3
Hermes Franca	def.	Rich Crunkilton	Lightweight	Unanimous Decision	—	3
David Loiseau	def.	Mark Weir	Middlweight	Knockout	3:52	1

Fight of the Night (unofficial): Hughes vs. Sherk

Unbeaten in 20 pro fights, powerhouse Minnesota wrestler Sean Sherk was expected to be the stiffest test for powerhouse Illinois wrestler Matt Hughes in the main event of UFC 43 at the American Airlines Arena in Miami. After 25 minutes, it was Hughes who still walked away with the UFC welterweight championship belt in his possession as he scored a five-round unanimous decision to retain the title for the fourth time.

Almost mirror images of each other, Hughes and Sherk squared off, with Hughes nailing his first takedown. The champion pushed Sherk to the fence and stayed busy with his strikes. Midway through the round, Sherk was bleeding over his right eye, but he was still able to spring to his feet. He wasn't upright long, as Hughes scored another takedown. Sherk threw strikes from the bottom position, but things weren't looking good for the Minnesotan as Hughes focused on the cut and finished up a dominant round.

The second round was a virtual repeat of the first, with Hughes remaining in control. Sherk needed to make a charge if he wanted to turn things around, and after being turned back on his first takedown attempt of the third stanza, he secured the second a minute in and quickly bulled Hughes to the fence. Sherk fired off strikes from the top, while Hughes almost locked up a kimura before "The Muscle Shark" powered free. Back on top, Sherk landed some shots, bloodying Hughes, but with a minute left referee John McCarthy restarted the action. That was fine with Sherk, who used an uppercut to set up another takedown.

As the championship rounds began, Sherk was back in the fight, but Hughes quickly diffused his opponent's early charge for a takedown and guillotine choke with a takedown, and he kept him there, punishing his foe for nearly the entire five-minute period.

Needing a finish to win, Sherk tried for a takedown to start round five, and after a long period against the fence, he finally got it. Sherk threw short punches at close range, but while points scoring, they weren't doing enough damage. With two minutes left, McCarthy stood the fight up, and Hughes refused to get taken down again. Instead, it was Hughes who ended up on top on the mat, and ultimately in the fight.

In the co-feature, rising welterweight star Robbie Lawler suffered the first loss of his pro career as he was forced to submit due to injury in the second round against Pete Spratt.

The finish came at 2:28 of the second round, when a dislocated hip ended Lawler's night.

Grappling ace Sean Alvarez had high hopes in his UFC debut, but they were dashed by Hawaiian brawler Wesley "Cabbage" Correira, who used an effective spawl and brawl strategy to wear his foe down and then finish him via technical knockout in round two.

Debutant Rich Franklin of Cincinnati was too strong for Evan Tanner in their light heavyweight bout, as he avoided a grappling match with the veteran and instead teed off with accurate strikes that eventually ended the bout via technical knockout at 2:40 of the first round.

In other action, Canadian newcomer David Loiseau put a stamp on his Octagon debut as he knocked out lanky British striker Mark Weir at 3:52 of the first round in a middleweight bout. Plus, Hermes Franca scored a close unanimous decision win over previously unbeaten Rich Crunkilton, and Duane Ludwig's bout with Genki Sudo was even closer, as "Bang" pounded out a three-round split decision win over the Japanese favorite. Also earning a judges' decision was welterweight Dave Strasser, who shut Romie Aram out over three rounds.

Knockout of the Night [unofficial] (Not Pictured): Loiseau vs. Weir

UFC 43 *Meltdown*

06 June 2003

Thomas and Mack Center, Las Vegas, NV

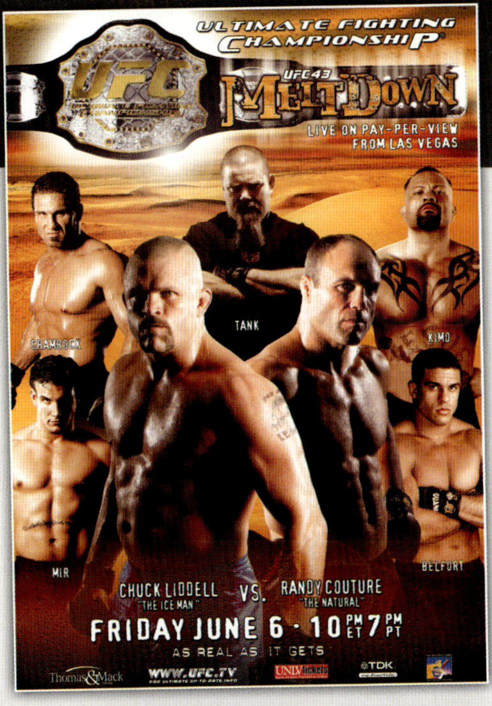

Debuts: Marvin Eastman, Wes Sims, Eddie Ruiz, Vernon White, Falaniko Vitale

Fighters			Division	Method	Time	Round
Main Card						
Randy Couture	def.	Chuck Liddell	Light Heavyweight	Technical Knockout	2:39	3
Kimo Leopoldo	def.	Tank Abbott	Heavyweight	Submission - Arm Triangle Choke	1:59	1
Yves Edwards	def.	Eddie Ruiz	Light Heavyweight	Unanimous Decision	—	3
Vitor Belfort	def.	Marvin Eastman	Light Heavyweight	Technical Knockout	1:07	1
Vernon White	vs.	Ian Freeman	Heavyweight	Draw	—	3
Frank Mir	def.	Wes Sims	Heavyweight	Opponent Disqualified	2:55	1
Preliminary Card						
Falaniko Vitale	def.	Matt Lindland	Middleweight	Technical Knockout	1:56	1
Pedro Rizzo	def.	Tra Telligman	Heavyweight	Technical Knockout	4:24	2

A couple weeks short of his 40th birthday—usually a death sentence for combat sports athletes—two-time UFC heavyweight champion Randy Couture had been written off by virtually everyone after losing back-to-back bouts against Josh Barnett and Ricco Rodriguez. A decision to drop to the light heavyweight division was seen as a last ditch effort to salvage his career, but Couture took the barbs with grace, even when he was made a significant underdog to number one 205-pound contender Chuck Liddell.

With Tito Ortiz' light heavyweight title in limbo, Couture stepped up and took the interim belt, stunning the mixed martial arts world with a third-round technical knockout of Liddell in the main event of UFC 43.

"I like being the underdog; it suits me well," said Couture, who became the first man in history to win UFC titles in two weight classes.

Fight of the Night (unofficial): Couture vs. Liddell

Couture avoided Liddell's thunder early, using some solid inside work to set up a slam in less than a minute. Liddell quickly rose, but Couture stayed attached to his foe, landing a knee before he let him go. Two minutes in, the two locked up again, but Liddell slugged his way loose. While standing, Couture showed no fear of Liddell's striking, and his high guard and quick strikes were serving him well. But just when Liddell settled in for a kickboxing match, Couture scored a takedown. Liddell rose with Couture on his back, and they ended the round in that position.

A solid right hand kicked off the second stanza for Couture, and he proceeded to close the distance for a brief lockup. After breaking, Couture's striking continued to catch Liddell off guard, and his 1-2s kept piling up the points. With 90 seconds left, Couture kicked Liddell's legs out from under him, putting "The Iceman" on the mat again. Liddell reversed position in the final 30 seconds, but he ran out of time to capitalize.

With two rounds in the books, things were beginning to heat up, but Liddell wasn't able to follow up his momentum from the end of the second frame, as Couture was giving better than he got in the standup, slowly draining the confidence from Liddell. Liddell kept firing back though, looking to land a haymaker, but after a thunderous takedown two minutes in, Couture got the mount position and finished things off with a furious barrage of ground strikes.

After his stirring win, Couture had a message for Ortiz, "Tito, if you want this belt, you're gonna have to come in here and take it."

In the co-feature, early UFC heroes Kimo Leopoldo and Tank Abbott met up in what was expected to be a brawl, but it was Kimo dominating on the mat and taking the drama out of the bout with an arm triangle choke that ended the bout via tapout at 1:59 of the opening round.

Submission of the Night (unofficial): Leopoldo vs. Abbott

Brazilian star Vitor Belfort earned his first UFC win since 1998, spoiling the debut of Marvin Eastman via technical knockout. Belfort's blistering hand speed was on display against "The Beastman", and after a tentative opening, he finished Eastman off with a barrage of ground strikes. It was a knee to the head that really spelled the end, as it opened Eastman's forehead and sent him to the canvas. From there, it was game over, with the official end coming at 1:07 of the first round.

Knockout of the Night (unofficial): Belfort vs. Eastman

Heavyweight vets Ian Freeman and Vernon White fought to a three-round draw, and lightweight star Yves Edwards scored a shutout three-round decision over Eddie Ruiz.

A wild heavyweight battle saw Frank Mir win via first-round disqualification over Hammer House newcomer Wes Sims when Sims stomped the head of Mir, who was on the canvas at the time.

In preliminary action, perennial heavyweight contender Pedro Rizzo kept his title hopes alive with a second-round technical knockout of Tra Telligman, and middleweight Falaniko Vitale got a bizarre technical knockout win when Matt Lindland knocked himself out executing a throw.

One Hit Wonder: Eddie Ruiz

UFC 44 *Undisputed*

26 Sept. 2003

Mandalay Bay Events Center, Las Vegas, NV

Debuts: Edwin Dewees, Karo Parisyan, Josh Thomson, Gerald Strebendt, Jeremy Jackson, Nick Diaz

Fighters			Division	Method	Time	Round
Main Card						
Randy Couture	def.	Tito Ortiz	Light Heavyweight	Unanimous Decision	—	5
Andrei Arlovski	def.	Vladimir Matyushenko	Heavyweight	Knockout	1:59	1
Tim Sylvia	def.	Gan McGee	Heavyweight	Technical Knockout	1:52	1
Jorge Rivera	def.	David Loiseau	Middleweight	Unanimous Decision	—	3
Rich Franklin	def.	Edwin Dewees	Light Heavyweight	Technical Knockout	3:35	1
Preliminary Card						
Karo Parisyan	def.	Dave Strasser	Welterweight	Submission - Kimura	3:52	1
Josh Thomson	def.	Gerald Strebendt	Lightweight	Knockout	2:45	1
Nick Diaz	def.	Jeremy Jackson	Welterweight	Submission - Armbar	2:02	3
Hermes Franca	def.	Caol Uno	Lightweight	Knockout	2:46	2

Just three months after his stirring win over Chuck Liddell for the interim UFC light heavyweight title, ageless Randy Couture was able to call himself an undisputed champion as he outpointed Tito Ortiz over five rounds in yet another time capsule fight for the 40-year-old superstar.

Fight of the Night (unofficial): Couture vs. Ortiz

Said Couture, "I guess I'm a late bloomer. Tito's been a great champion and I've been honored to fight him."

The loss was Ortiz' first since a 1999 defeat against Frank Shamrock. "The Huntington Beach Bad Boy" was back in the Octagon for the first time since defeating Shamrock's brother Ken at UFC 40 in November of 2002, but on this night, he had few answers for "The Natural", who dominated from start to finish as he won via scores of 50-44 twice and 50-45.

Using his wrestling both while locked up against the fence and on the mat, Couture turned the tables on the ground and pound master, punishing him throughout the five-rounder. The only serious trouble Ortiz was in came in the first stanza when Couture almost scored with a rear naked choke, but the 25-minute battering, which included a playful spanking of Ortiz in the closing seconds, left no doubt as to who the winner was when the final bell tolled. An emotionally distraught Ortiz was classy in defeat though, as he put the belt around the waist of the new champion before plotting his return to the top.

There was a battle of giants in the second title bout of the evening, but 6' 8" UFC heavyweight champion Tim Sylvia didn't leave it in the hands of the judges, as he stopped 6' 10" Gan McGee at 1:52 of the first round.

McGee seemed unbothered by the spectacle of the Octagon as he and Sylvia circled each other in the opening minute. In the second minute, Sylvia began stalking, and his high guard allowed him to deflect any incoming fire until a right hand drilled the challenger and sent him to the canvas. A follow-up barrage was a mere formality as referee John McCarthy intervened at the 1:54 mark.

Unfortunately, Sylvia's celebration was short-lived, as a positive post-fight drug test for steroids forced the champion to relinquish his belt. He admitted his guilt and was suspended by the Nevada State Athletic Commission.

Finding an opening to move into the title picture was a man long seen as one of the top young heavyweights in the game, Andrei Arlovski, who looked like he was beginning to put his full MMA game together as he stopped Vladimir Matyushenko in the first round to extend his winning streak to two fights. A right uppercut followed by a hammerfist on the mat ended the bout at the 1:59 mark.

Knockout of the Night (unofficial): Arlovski vs. Matyushenko

Middleweights kicked off the main card in Las Vegas, with Rich Franklin halting Edwin Dewees via strikes in the first round, and New Englander Jorge Rivera scoring an upset by pounding out an exciting three-round unanimous decision win over Canadian prospect David Loiseau.

Highly-touted judoka Karo Parisyan showed off an array of skills in his first Octagon bout before submitting Dave Strasser with a rare rolling kimura at 3:52 of the opening round.

Josh "The Punk" Thomson was impressive in his victory over debuting Gerald Strebendt, halting his foe with a series of ground strikes at 2:45 of the first round.

Welterweight up-and-comers Jeremy Jackson and Nick Diaz had split two fights on the local fight scene, and they settled their score in the Octagon, as the 20-year-old Diaz submitted his rival via armbar at 2:02 of the third round.

Submission of the Night (unofficial): Diaz vs. Jackson

Brazil's Hermes Franca made it 2-0 in the Octagon with a second-round knockout of former world title challenger Caol Uno. A right hand spelled doom for the Japanese star.

One Hit Wonder: Gerald Strebendt

UFC 45 *Revolution*

21 Nov. 2003

Mohegan Sun Arena, Uncasville, CT

Debuts: Frank Trigg, Chris Ligouri, Nick Agallar

Fighters			Division	Method	Time	Round
Main Card						
Matt Hughes	def.	Frank Trigg	Welterweight	Submission - Rear Naked Choke	3:54	1
Wesley Correira	def.	Tank Abbott	Heavyweight	Technical Knockout - Cuts	2:14	1
Evan Tanner	def.	Phil Baroni	Middleweight	Technical Knockout	4:42	1
Robbie Lawler	def.	Chris Lytle	Welterweight	Unanimous Decision	—	3
Matt Lindland	def.	Falaniko Vitale	Middleweight	Submission - Strikes	4:23	3
Preliminary Card						
Pedro Rizzo	def.	Ricco Rodriguez	Heavyweight	Unanimous Decision	—	3
Keith Rockel	def.	Chris Liguori	Middleweight	Submission - Guillotine Choke	3:29	1
Yves Edwards	def.	Nick Agallar	Lightweight	Technical Knockout	2:14	2

On November 21, 2003 at the Mohegan Sun Arena, UFC presented its tenth anniversary show, UFC 45 – Revolution, and used a mixture of old-school tributes and new talent to bridge the gap between past and present.

In the main event, welterweight champion Matt Hughes once again proved his superiority over the competition with a first-round submission win over a man expected to give him his sternest test—Frank Trigg.

Using wrestling skills honed on the collegiate level, Trigg gained the advantage early by taking Hughes down and working well on the ground against the Illinois native. Soon enough though, Hughes got his bearings and lifted Trigg to the sky before parading him across the ring and slamming him on his side.

Submission of the Night (unofficial): Hughes vs. Trigg

Trigg recovered quickly, and wrestled evenly with Hughes on the ground before a tactical misstep allowed the champion to get the challenger's back and sink in a fight-ending rear naked choke at the 3:54 mark.

In the "Revolution" co-feature, there was little finesse or skill shown in the heavyweight matchup between David "Tank" Abbott and Wesley "Cabbage" Correira, but there was plenty of action and blood, at least until a crimson gash on the forehead of Abbott forced a halt to the bout at 2:14 of the opening round.

Using his patented hand speed and power, Baroni stunned Tanner with a right hand seconds into the scheduled three-rounder, and follow-up bombs by the "New York Badass" had Tanner stumbling, cut, and in deep trouble. But after a brief break to have his cut inspected, Tanner used some effective knees in the clinch and finally took the Long Island native to the mat. As the seconds ticked away on the first round, Tanner gained a full mount position and rained elbows on his foe. Referee Larry Landless leaned in and repeatedly asked Baroni if he wanted the fight stopped. Baroni, thinking that the referee was asking if he was fit to continue, answered "yes." The bout was halted at 4:42 of the first, a controversial verdict that didn't sit well with Baroni.

Fight and Knockout of the Night (unofficial): Tanner vs. Baroni

Matt Lindland stayed in the hunt for the vacant 185-pound crown with a workmanlike third-round stoppage of Falaniko Vitale. The bout was a rematch of a June 2003 contest in which Lindland knocked himself out while throwing Vitale. "The Law" took no such chances this time, sticking to a steady but unspectacular ground and pound attack, which paid benefits late in the third as Vitale tapped with 37 seconds remaining in the match.

Welterweight bomber Robbie Lawler opened up the main card with a razor thin unanimous decision over tough Chris Lytle. All three scores were 29-28 for "Ruthless Robbie", who was making his first start since injuring his hip during a loss to Pete Spratt in April 2003.

Heavyweights Pedro Rizzo and Ricco Rodriguez showed little urgency in their matchup, with Rizzo winning a lackluster three-round decision over the former heavyweight champion.

Local middleweight Keith Rockel thrilled the fans who came down from nearby Massachusetts as he scored a first-round submission win over newcomer Chris Liguori.

In the first preliminary bout, lightweight contender Yves Edwards stayed busy with a second-round TKO of late sub Nick Agallar.

A pre-main event ceremony saw Royce Gracie and Ken Shamrock honored as the first inductees in the UFC Hall of Fame. Also in attendance to receive Viewer's Choice Awards were former UFC competitors Oleg Taktarov, Marco Ruas, Mark Coleman and Don Frye.

One Hit Wonders: Chris Ligouri, Nick Agallar

Both Ligouri and Agallar made early exits at UFC 45, prompting their releases from the organization, but neither stopped fighting. Agallar (who went 1-1 on the first two WEC cards) remains active today, and Ligouri, another active fighter who has been in with the likes of Jim Miller (twice), Matt Brown, and Marcus Aurelio, is a training partner of Frankie Edgar.

BROTHER ACTS

JUNIOR AND RAPHAEL ASSUNCAO

Natives of Recife, Brazil, Junior and Raphael Assuncao made their names in the mixed martial arts world while living in their adopted city of Atlanta, Georgia. Lightweight Junior—a black belt in jiu-jitsu and Capoeira—was the first to make it to the big show, and he went 1-2 in three UFC bouts in 2006-07. Younger brother Raphael, a featherweight, went 3-2 in five WEC outings, and he has since migrated to the UFC, where he hopes his brother will eventually join him.

NICK AND NATE DIAZ

Like most younger brothers, Nate Diaz wanted nothing more than to follow in his older sibling Nick's footsteps. That meant going to the gym.

"I started training when I was younger just because I didn't have much else to do, and that's what my brother did," said Nate. "I just went to the gym with him, he started fighting in the UFC, and I wanted to help him win fights so I did everything I could to help. I put on the gloves and sparred with him, and before I knew it I was getting a fight of my own."

Nick turned pro in 2001, and three years later, Nate was competing as well. Both garnered positive reputations for their hard-nosed demeanor, never-say-die attitude and skill both standing and on the ground. In 2007, Nate won *The Ultimate Fighter 5* and he's currently battling it out in multiple weight classes. Nick had an erratic UFC career from 2003 to 2006, but he has since become one of the top fighters in the world.

JEREMY HORN AND MATT ANDERSEN

The half-brother of Jeremy Horn, Matt Andersen lost his lone UFC bout to Rafael Carino in 1996, but he continued fighting on the Midwest circuit up until 2010. Horn remains an active fighter, with over 100 bouts to his name, including 13 in the UFC, where he fought Chuck Liddell for the light heavyweight championship in 2005.

MATT AND MARK HUGHES

Five minutes younger than his brother Matt, Mark Hughes held a wrestling victory over the future two-time welterweight champion when the two were in school. Even after compiling a 6-2 pro mixed martial arts record from 1999 to 2003, he decided that the fight game just wasn't for him. As for Matt, 45 pro wins, seven title defenses over two reigns and membership in the UFC Hall of Fame tell you just about all you need to know about his fighting ambitions.

JOE AND DAN LAUZON

Polar opposites outside of the Octagon, Joe and Dan Lauzon are aggressive clones inside it, making them two of the most exciting fighters in the game today. "He got the smarts, and I didn't really get them, so fighting's what I want to do for the rest of my life," laughed Dan shortly before he became the youngest fighter to ever compete in the UFC at 18 in 2006. "My parents always told me that fighting comes second, that you need a job, but I see it the other way—I see fighting coming first. When me and Joe train together and fight, we're almost the same person. We fight alike and train the same, but when it comes to working and doing jobs, we're the exact opposite. I hate work and he doesn't mind it. I'd rather just fight." Dan and Joe were the first brothers to fight on the same night in the UFC at UFC 108. Dan hasn't had much luck in the Octagon though, going 0-3. Joe, a former IT professional who appeared on *The Ultimate Fighter 5*, is a legit lightweight contender who currently owns a 6-3 UFC slate.

MINOTAURO RODRIGO AND ANTONIO ROGERIO NOGUEIRA

Brazilian twins Minotauro and Antonio Rogerio Nogueira comprise perhaps the greatest brother act in mixed martial arts history. Skilled groundfighters with knockout power while standing, both brothers first became stars in Japan's PRIDE organization, where Minotauro became the first heavyweight champion and Rogerio was a top light heavyweight standout. In recent years, the two entered the UFC Octagon, with Minotauro becoming an interim UFC champion and Rogerio seeking gold in the 205-pound weight class.

MATT AND NICK SERRA

Two of the top jiu-jitsu practitioners to ever hail from New York, Renzo Gracie black belts Matt and Nick Serra are masters on the mat and teachers of countless students in their Long Island academies. In the Octagon, younger brother Nick (4-3 overall) only competed once, losing a decision to Benji Radach at UFC 37.5 in 2002. On the other hand, Matt has been a UFC mainstay since 2001, with his unquestioned highlight being his 2007 knockout of Georges St-Pierre for the UFC welterweight title.

FRANK AND KEN SHAMROCK

Adopted by Bob Shamrock, Frank Juarez and Ken Kilpatrick may not have been blood brothers, but after becoming Frank and Ken Shamrock, they shared a competitive drive and the athletic ability to become mixed martial arts superstars. Ken competed in the first UFC event in 1993 and eventually earned a spot in the UFC Hall of Fame. Frank was the organization's first 205-pound champion, defending the crown four times before vacating the title in 1999.

JIM AND DAN MILLER

All you really need to know about the fighting Miller brothers of New Jersey comes in a statement from older brother Dan: "I know that if I put everything I have into it and I can't get up after that final bell, he will carry me out of the ring," he said. "It's good to know that he's there in my corner, and I know it's the same for him." In 2008, Dan and Jim both entered the Octagon for the first time after successful stints on the local circuit and each has found success at the elite level of the game, Dan winning five of nine bouts and Jim earning victories in nine of his 10 UFC outings.

UFC 46 *Super Natural*

31 Jan. 2004

Mandalay Bay Events Center, Las Vegas, NV

Debuts: Jeff Curran, Georges St-Pierre, Lee Murray, Renato Verissimo

Fighters			Division	Method	Time	Round
Main Card						
Vitor Belfort	def.	Randy Couture	Light Heavyweight	Technical Knockout - Cuts	0:49	1
BJ Penn	def.	Matt Hughes	Welterweight	Submission - Rear Naked Choke	4:39	1
Renato Verissimo	def.	Carlos Newton	Catchweight	Unanimous Decision	—	3
Frank Mir	def.	Wes Sims	Heavyweight	Knockout	4:21	2
Lee Murray	def.	Jorge Rivera	Middleweight	Submission - Triangle Choke	1:45	1
Preliminary Card						
Matt Serra	def.	Jeff Curran	Lightweight	Unanimous Decision	—	3
Josh Thomson	def.	Hermes Franca	Lightweight	Unanimous Decision	—	3
Georges St-Pierre	def.	Karo Parisyan	Welterweight	Unanimous Decision	—	3

Fresh off dominating wins over Chuck Liddell and Tito Ortiz, UFC light heavyweight champion Randy Couture had proven that at 40, "age ain't nothin' but a number." But against Brazil's Vitor Belfort, Couture was once again going to be facing a younger, more explosive opponent (albeit one he already held a 1997 victory over), making the UFC 46 main event a compelling one. Adding to the drama was the fact that Belfort's sister Priscila had disappeared weeks before the fight, leaving "The Phenom" in a mental state of either complete focus or complete disarray. Once the bout commenced, it was over almost as soon as it began.

After the two briefly sparred with each other, Belfort grazed Couture with a straight left. The two clinched against the fence, with Couture in obvious discomfort. Referee John McCarthy intervened, bringing in ringside physician Margaret Goodman to examine Couture's left eye, and she recommended that McCarthy call a halt to the bout at the 49-second mark, a stoppage that crowned Belfort the new champion. The culprit that ended the contest was a gashed lower left eyelid of Couture, a cut caused by a seam on Belfort's glove.

After a UFC career that saw him repeatedly touted as the sport's "Next Big Thing," Hawaii's BJ Penn was in an unusual position as he entered his welterweight championship match with Matt Hughes. Rising in weight from 155 pounds (where he failed in two title tries) to 170 to challenge a man considered to be one of the top pound-for-pound fighters in the world, Penn was seen by most to be committing athletic suicide against Hughes, who was making the sixth defense of his title.

Someone forgot to tell Penn, though, and in one of the sport's most memorable moments, he fulfilled all of his exceptional promise in a quick four minutes and 39 seconds.

Submission of the Night (unofficial): Penn vs. Hughes

From the opening bell, Penn dictated the action and even appeared to be bigger physically than the champion. Soon, Hughes found himself on the mat, and as the final minute of the first round got underway, it was a strike by Penn that turned the tide of the fight. Stunned by a blow that bloodied his nose, Hughes instinctively turned to the side, giving Penn his back. With breakneck speed, Penn took the most dominant position in the sport and immediately sunk in a rear naked choke. The tap by Hughes seconds later was a mere formality, and a new champion was crowned.

Another highly-touted young contender, Frank Mir, had been seemingly groomed for the heavyweight title since his UFC debut in 2001. On January 31, Mir fought a man who was last seen illegally stomping him in the head: Wes Sims.

In a disciplined performance, Mir erased any doubts surrounding his DQ win over Sims the previous June with a stunning second-round TKO of "The Project".

Knockout of the Night (unofficial): Mir vs. Sims

Great Britain's Lee Murray finally got to show his wares to U.S. fans with an impressive submission win over Jorge Rivera in a middleweight bout.

Hoping to place himself back in line to regain his welterweight title, Carlos Newton was surprisingly outclassed by UFC newcomer Renato Verissimo, who scored a lopsided unanimous decision over "The Ronin" in a three-rounder.

Fight of the Night (unofficial): St-Pierre vs. Parisyan

Canada's Georges St-Pierre, coming off a submission win over Pete Spratt, continued his hot streak in his UFC debut by scoring a unanimous three-round decision over fellow welterweight prospect Karo Parisyan.

In an undercard lightweight bout that had main card excitement written all over it, Josh "The Punk" Thomson eked out a unanimous decision over Hermes Franca.

In the UFC 46 opener, lightweight dervish Matt Serra evened his UFC slate at 3-3 with a shutout three-round decision over late replacement Jeff Curran.

One Hit Wonders: Jeff Curran, Lee Murray

The post–UFC 46 careers of Curran and Murray went in distinctly different directions. Curran proceeded to find a home in the featherweight and bantamweight divisions of the WEC, where he eventually challenged Urijah Faber for the WEC 145-pound crown. Murray, who got into the UFC after a highly publicized street fight in London with Tito Ortiz, fought just one more time, losing a decision to Anderson Silva. In 2010 he was convicted of masterminding a 2006 bank heist that saw him and his accomplices get away with 53 million pounds.

UFC 47 *It's On!*

02 April 2004

Mandalay Bay Events Center, Las Vegas, NV

Debuts: Mike Brown, Jonathan Wiezorek, Wade Shipp, Mike Kyle

Fighters			Division	Method	Time	Round
Main Card						
Chuck Liddell	def.	Tito Ortiz	Lightweight	Knockout	0:38	2
Chris Lytle	def.	Tiki Ghosn	Welterweight	Submission - Choke	1:55	2
Yves Edwards	def.	Hermes Franca	Lightweight	Split Decision	—	3
Andrei Arlovski	def.	Wesley Correira	Heavyweight	Technical Knockout	1:15	2
Nick Diaz	def.	Robbie Lawler	Welterweight	Knockout	1:31	2
Mike Kyle	def.	Wes Sims	Heavyweight	Knockout	4:59	1
Preliminary Card						
Genki Sudo	def.	Mike Brown	Lightweight	Submission - Triangle Choke	3:31	1
Jonathan Wiezorek	def.	Wade Shipp	Heavyweight	Technical Knockout	4:39	1

It was the grudge match to end all grudge matches, and a packed house at the Mandalay Bay Events Center saw Chuck Liddell and Tito Ortiz finally get it on in the main event of UFC 47.

After only five minutes and 38 seconds, it was "The Iceman" who was left standing, as he emphatically stopped the former light heavyweight champion in the second round. The action didn't go to the ground once during the match, with two Ortiz takedown attempts easily foiled by Liddell. Even though Liddell was in his element while standing, he was unable to penetrate Ortiz' tight defense for much of the opening round, as both men tentatively pawed at each other, not wanting to make a fatal mistake.

Fight of the Night (unofficial): Liddell vs. Ortiz

Late in the first, Liddell finally landed one of his patented bombs, exploding a right hand on Ortiz' jaw that staggered him. "The Iceman" followed with a kick to the head, and Ortiz' legs were rubbery at the bell, even as he jawed defiantly at Liddell.

Capitalizing on his good fortune, Liddell moved right in on Ortiz as the second round commenced, and once he landed a 1-2 combination to the chin of "The Huntington Beach Bad Boy", the end was just moments away.

Pinned to the cage by Liddell's furious barrages, Ortiz blocked most of the punches but then got drilled with a right to the jaw followed by a quick left that bloodied his face and put him down on the mat, forcing referee John McCarthy to halt the bout just 38 seconds into round two.

Scheduled to face Tim Sylvia for the vacant heavyweight crown, Andrei Arlovski instead took on Wesley "Cabbage" Correira in a non-title fight when it was revealed that Sylvia still had a trace amount of steroids left in his body from previous use (use that had gotten him stripped of the title in the first place), thus making him ineligible to compete.

Undeterred, Arlovski calmly re-established his credentials as he scored a one-sided stoppage over Correira, who was game but outgunned by the Belarusan. Arlovski drilled his foe with an assortment of punches, knees, and kicks throughout the 6:15 of action.

If anyone thought the welterweight bout between young guns Robbie Lawler and Nick Diaz would end in a knockout, they wouldn't expect that the man with his hand raised would be Diaz. But in a shocker, the Cesar Gracie jiu-jitsu ace disregarded his ground game completely, knocking out the knockout artist at 1:31 of the second round.

Knockout of the Night (unofficial): Diaz vs. Lawler

It had become commonplace for the bizarre to kick into high gear when 6' 10" heavyweight Wes Sims was in the Octagon, and his UFC 47 bout with newcomer Mike Kyle was no exception. Taking the bout on one day's notice, Sims had some early success on the mat with a couple of submission attempts, but soon Kyle's ground and pound weakened the Ohio native. After a standup by referee John McCarthy, Sims was spent. Initially turning his back on his foe, Sims turned around in enough time to be grabbed in a clinch, where Kyle landed some flush knees before landing a brutal right hand that sent "The Project" down and out at the 4:59 mark. Almost immediately, Sims was back on his feet—complaining of an alleged bite by Kyle, allegations the Californian dismissed as sour grapes.

Welterweight Chris Lytle followed up his spirited performance against Robbie Lawler at UFC 45 with an impressive two-round victory over Tiki Ghosn.

Submission of the Night (unofficial): Sudo vs. Brown

Eccentric lightweight contender Genki Sudo returned to the UFC for the first time since a decision loss to Duane Ludwig at UFC 42 and scored a submission victory over debuting Mike Brown.

In an evenly-matched lightweight bout, Yves Edwards eked out a three-round split decision over Hermes Franca.

In a battle of debuting heavyweights, Jonathan Wiezorek survived some shaky moments en route to a first-round stoppage win over Wade Shipp.

One Hit Wonders: Jonathan Wiezorek, Wade Shipp

UFC 48 *Payback*

19 June 2004

Mandalay Bay Events Center, Las Vegas, NV

Debuts: Ivan Menjivar, Trevor Prangley, Jay Hieron

Fighters			Division	Method	Time	Round
Main Card						
Frank Mir	def.	Tim Sylvia	Heavyweight	Submission	0:50	1
Ken Shamrock	def.	Kimo Leopoldo	Heavyweight	Technical Knockout	1:26	1
Frank Trigg	def.	Dennis Hallman	Welterweight	Technical Knockout	4:15	1
Matt Hughes	def.	Renato Verissimo	Welterweight	Unanimous Decision	—	3
Evan Tanner	def.	Phil Baroni	Middleweight	Unanimous Decision	—	3
Preliminary Card						
Matt Serra	def.	Ivan Menjivar	Lightweight	Unanimous Decision	—	3
Trevor Prangley	def.	Curtis Stout	Middleweight	Submission	1:05	2
Georges St-Pierre	def.	Jay Hieron	Welterweight	Technical Knockout	1:42	1

Submission of the Night (unofficial): Mir vs. Sylvia

It only took 50 seconds, but in that short span of time, heavyweights Frank Mir and Tim Sylvia put mixed martial arts into a blunt context that even the most disinterested observer could understand. When it was over, Mir—with a frightening armbar that caused not only referee Herb Dean to halt the bout, but Sylvia to make his way to the DL with two broken bones in his arm—had won the UFC heavyweight title. As for Sylvia, he showed the never-say-die mentality that forced him not to quit and even made him protest the stoppage when the fight was stopped.

That's mixed martial arts—where a split-second lapse can cause you to lose a fight, and where courage to take those risks can put you in a position to make decisions with no regard to your health.

With the heavyweight championship finally secure, UFC 48 was safe to be filed away in the record books as a success, complete with its requisite mix of upsets, KOs and decisions.

In the main event, UFC legend Ken Shamrock returned to the Octagon for the first time since his November 2002 loss to Tito Ortiz (and knee surgery) with a 1:26 stoppage of Kimo Leopoldo. The victory repeated Shamrock's 1996 victory over Leopoldo at UFC 8.

Fight of the Night (unofficial): Tanner vs. Baroni

In a highly-anticipated rematch that didn't produce nearly the amount of fireworks the first contest did, Evan Tanner used a disciplined attack to make it two for two against Phil Baroni in a middleweight bout. Tanner, who was awarded a 30-27 (twice), 29-28 unanimous decision, survived a late Baroni charge to win, much like he had held off an early attack by the New Yorker in their first bout. That match ended via a controversial stoppage in November 2003 that saw Baroni suspended for striking referee Larry Landless.

Matt Hughes showed no ill effects of his January loss to BJ Penn by taking a unanimous decision over talented Renato Verissimo in a fairly uneventful welterweight contest. Scores for Hughes were 30-27 (twice) and 29-28. It was Verissimo's first loss in six MMA bouts. Among his wins was a clearcut January decision over Carlos Newton.

Rounding out the main card was another rematch, with welterweight Frank Trigg making it a clean sweep for the first-time victors as he stopped Dennis Hallman at 4:15 of the opening round. Trigg defeated Hallman by TKO in their 2002 WFA bout.

Matt Serra scored his second consecutive win, decisioning debuting Canadian Ivan Menjivar over three rounds in lightweight action.

Menjivar's Canadian countryman, rising welterweight star Georges St-Pierre, made short work of late replacement Jay Hieron, stopping him at 1:42 of the first round.

Knockout of the Night (unofficial): St-Pierre vs. Hieron

South Africa's Trevor Prangley was impressive in his Octagon debut, submitting Curtis Stout with a neck crank in the first round.

UFC 49 *Unfinished Business*

21 Aug. 2004

MGM Grand Garden Arena, Las Vegas, NV

Debuts: Joe Doerksen, Joe Riggs, David Terrell, Justin Eilers, Ronald Jhun

Fighters			Division	Method	Time	Round
Main Card						
Randy Couture	def.	Vitor Belfort	Light Heavyweight	Technical Knockout - Doctor Stoppage	5:00	3
Joe Riggs	def.	Joe Doerksen	Middleweight	Submission - Strikes	3:39	2
Chuck Liddell	def.	Vernon White	Light Heavyweight	Knockout	4:05	1
David Terrell	def.	Matt Lindland	Middleweight	Knockout	0:24	1
Justin Eilers	def.	Mike Kyle	Heavyweight	Knockout	1:14	1
Preliminary Card						
Chris Lytle	def.	Ronald Jhun	Welterweight	Submission - Guillotine Choke	1:17	2
Karo Parisyan	def.	Nick Diaz	Welterweight	Split Decision	—	3
Yves Edwards	def.	Josh Thomson	Lightweight	Knockout	4:32	1

The entire light heavyweight division was biding their time, hoping that one day, any day, Randy Couture would start acting his age. That day was not August 21, 2004, when Couture, 41, regained the 205-pound title from Vitor Belfort with a three-round blowout of the Brazilian before a crowd of over 12,000 at the MGM Grand Garden Arena in Las Vegas.

It was the third bout between the two, with Couture's only setback being a quick January 2004 loss that occurred when a freak eye injury caused a controversial halt to the bout. This time, it wasn't even close. From the opening bell to the moment when the ringside physician decided a bloodied Belfort had taken enough punishment shortly before the start of the fourth round, the bout was all Couture as he put on a clinic in control and ground and pound.

Belfort's only attempts at offense were two armbar tries which went for naught. While "The Phenom" showed an incredible amount of heart to make it through three rounds of sustained punishment that saw his blood stain the Octagon mat and both fighters, he was simply outclassed by the top fighter of his generation. Liddell had succeeded in taking down his three greatest challenges at light heavyweight (Belfort, Chuck Liddell, Tito Ortiz) with relative ease.

In the UFC 49 co-feature, the aforementioned Chuck Liddell earned another shot at Couture with an exciting first-round stoppage of a game Vernon White, who continually battled back from concussive blows in that opening frame to give Liddell hell, only to be sent to defeat with a big right hand that ended matters conclusively at the 4:05 mark.

Fight of the Night (unofficial): Liddell vs. White

Two of the UFC's top 155-pounders showed why the lightweight division was still the place to go for fast-paced, high-quality action, as Yves Edwards and Josh Thomson battled it out for almost an entire five-minute round before Edwards pulled a right high kick out of a comic book frame and sent Thomson crashing to defeat at the 4:32 mark in one of the most spectacular knockouts anyone will see in combat sports. Unfortunately, this would be the last lightweight bout in the UFC until the division was reinstated at UFC 58 in 2006.

In another fast-paced battle between two of the UFC's young guns, Karo Parisyan scored a three-round split decision over Nick Diaz in a welterweight contest. Scores for Parisyan were 30-27, 29-28, and 28-29.

Knockout of the Night (unofficial): Terrell vs. Lindland

Debuting middleweight David Terrell made a huge splash on the UFC scene with a stunning 25-second knockout of number one 185-pounder Matt Lindland. Terrell, best known for his Cesar Gracie jiu-jitsu stylings, landed a huge right hand seconds into the bout and Lindland dropped hard to the mat, where Terrell pounced and followed up before Herb Dean stopped the bout.

Another UFC first-timer, Justin Eilers, showed that friendship ends once the bell rings as he whacked out childhood buddy Mike Kyle with a perfectly placed left hook to the jaw just 1:14 into their heavyweight clash.

Submission of the Night (unofficial): Lytle vs. Jhun

Heavy-handed Joe Riggs scored a second-round stoppage of fellow UFC newcomer Joe Doerksen in a middleweight contest.

Welterweight Chris Lytle continued to impress with a second-round submission win over veteran Ronald Jhun.

One Hit Wonder: Ronald Jhun

UFC 50 *The War of '04*

22 Oct. 2004

Boardwalk Hall, Atlantic City, NJ

Debuts: Travis Lutter, Patrick Cote

Fighters			Division	Method	Time	Round
Main Card						
Tito Ortiz	def.	Patrick Cote	Light Heavyweight	Unanimous Decision	—	3
Matt Hughes	def.	Georges St-Pierre	Welterweight	Submission - Armbar	4:59	1
Rich Franklin	def.	Jorge Rivera	Middleweight	Submission - Armbar	4:28	3
Frank Trigg	def.	Renato Verissimo	Welterweight	Technical Knockout	2:11	2
Evan Tanner	def.	Robbie Lawler	Middleweight	Submission - Triangle Choke	2:22	1
Preliminary Card						
Ivan Salaverry	def.	Tony Fryklund	Middleweight	Submission - Body Triangle	1:36	1
Travis Lutter	def.	Marvin Eastman	Light Heavyweight	Knockout	0:33	2

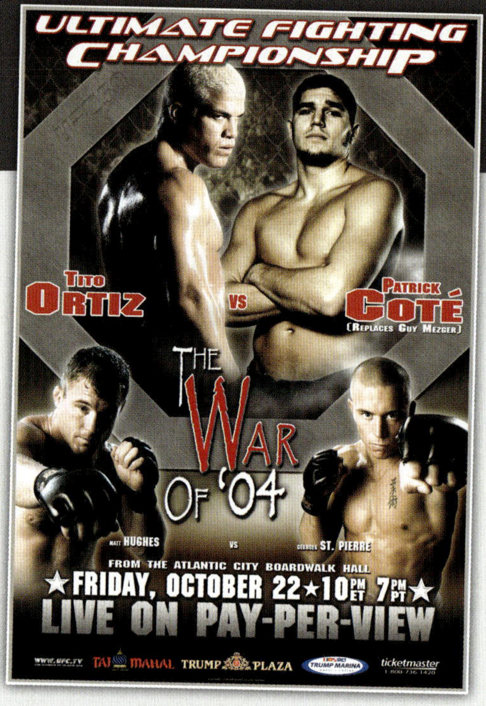

Former light heavyweight champion Tito Ortiz broke a two-fight losing streak in the main event of UFC 50 at Boardwalk Hall in Atlantic City, New Jersey, grounding and pounding out a lopsided unanimous decision over Quebec's Patrick Cote.

Scores were 30-27, and 30-26 twice for Ortiz, who was coming off defeats to current 205-pound champ Randy Couture and Chuck Liddell. Cote, who was making his UFC debut, was a late replacement for Guy Mezger, who suffered a training injury.

Appearing supremely relaxed, Cote came out with a quick right that Ortiz easily weathered. Another right seconds later was a different story though, as Ortiz went to a knee briefly. When Cote moved in for the kill, Ortiz put him on his back and the ground and pound attack that epitomized the bout began, continuing for much of the ensuing rounds.

In the co-feature, Matt Hughes regained the UFC welterweight crown vacated by BJ Penn by showing a new wrinkle in his arsenal, submitting game Georges St-Pierre with an armbar at 4:59 of the first round.

Submission of the Night (unofficial): Hughes vs. St-Pierre

After setting things up with a good jab, St-Pierre used an effective single leg takedown to put Hughes to the mat seconds into the fight. Both quickly stood, and it was Hughes who used his left hand to work his opponent to the fence. Of course, moments later Hughes lifted St-Pierre and dropped him to the mat. St-Pierre worked his way out of trouble and used a left kick to the midsection to stun the former champion.

With a little over a minute to go, Hughes was able to take St-Pierre down and he tried to work his ground and pound from the Canadian's guard. Suddenly though, with the round ticking away, Hughes swung into an armbar, and just when an upset seemed possible by the 23-year-old, the veteran had won the bout via tapout with a single second to go in the opening round.

Fight of the Night (unofficial): Trigg vs. Verissimo

Frank Trigg put himself back in line for a welterweight title shot against Hughes with an exciting second-round stoppage of Renato Verissimo. Clinching almost immediately, Trigg was able to force Verissimo to the fence while throwing knees. Once the two broke, "Charuto" landed a stiff right hand that jarred Trigg briefly, forcing a takedown. Verissimo attempted a couple of submissions on the ground, but Trigg was able to power his way out with strikes.

After a brief return to the feet, both went to the mat, and Verissimo sunk in a triangle choke. After a few dicey seconds, Trigg was able to break out, bringing a roar from the crowd.

Verissimo shot in to open the second, but a sprawl by Trigg nullified the takedown attempt. With both men trading blows, Verissimo got rocked, and Trigg pounded away, looking for the KO. Still groggy, Verissmimo got hit with an array of punches and forearms, and with no response coming from the jiu-jitsu ace, referee Herb Dean stepped in to halt the bout at 2:11 of round two.

In the main card opener, Evan Tanner gave Robbie Lawler a rude welcome to the middleweight division, submitting the former welterweight contender with a triangle choke in the first round.

Late replacement Travis Lutter made a stunning entrance into the UFC, knocking out Marvin Eastman with a single right hand 33 seconds into the second round of a scheduled three-round light heavyweight bout. Lutter, a jiu-jitsu black belt, showed that he had more than a little pop in his fists, dropping the Muay Thai kickboxer hard to the canvas after a fairly slow first round. The bout was stopped immediately when Eastman hit the mat.

Knockout of the Night (unofficial): Lutter vs. Eastman

In a battle of returning UFC middleweights, Ivan Salaverry submitted Tony Fryklund with a body triangle 96 seconds into the first round to throw his hat into the 185-pound title race.

Rising star Rich Franklin made his middleweight debut in the card's swing bout, gutting out a hard-fought submission victory over Jorge Rivera in an evenly-matched bout marked by impressive inside work by both men.

UFC 51 *Super Saturday*

05 Feb. 2005

Mandalay Bay Events Center, Las Vegas, NV

Debuts: Pete Sell, Paul Buentello, James Irvin, Gideon Ray, Drew Fickett

Fighters			Division	Method	Time	Round
Main Card						
Tito Ortiz	def.	Vitor Belfort	Light Heavyweight	Split Decision	—	3
Andrei Arlovski	def.	Tim Sylvia	Heavyweight	Submission - Achilles Lock	0:47	1
Evan Tanner	def.	David Terrell	Middleweight	Technical Knockout	4:35	1
Pete Sell	def.	Phil Baroni	Middleweight	Submission - Guillotine Choke	4:19	3
Paul Buentello	def.	Justin Eilers	Heavyweight	Knockout	3:34	1
Preliminary Card						
Mike Kyle	def.	James Irvin	Heavyweight	Knockout	1:55	1
David Loiseau	def.	Gideon Ray	Middleweight	Technical Knockout - Doctor Stoppage	5:00	1
Karo Parisyan	def.	Chris Lytle	Welterweight	Unanimous Decision	—	3
Nick Diaz	def.	Drew Fickett	Welterweight	Technical Knockout	4:40	1

At UFC 33 in 2001, light heavyweights Tito Ortiz and Vitor Belfort were supposed to be the headliners as the UFC finally returned to Pay-Per-View television. After injuries scrapped the bout, as well as a subsequent re-scheduling, it appeared that the dream fight would remain a dream. Then came UFC 51, and the two finally met, with Ortiz fighting his way back into the 205-pound title picture with an exciting three-round split decision victory.

Fight of the Night (unofficial): Ortiz vs. Belfort

Scores were 29-28, 29-28, and 28-29 for Ortiz, who won his second consecutive bout since losses to Randy Couture and Chuck Liddell.

This was a pitched battle from the outset, with neither superstar wanting to give in to the other, but in the end it was Ortiz' ground and pound attack and superior gas tank that nullified the rapid-fire striking of "The Phenom" and allowed "The Huntington Beach Bad Boy" to finish strong and emerge victorious.

In a battle of New York middleweights, debuting Pete "Drago" Sell put Phil Baroni's UFC career in question after handing the Long Islander his fourth consecutive loss via a come-from-behind guilltone choke submission. The end came at 4:19 of the third round in a bout Baroni appeared to be on his way to winning via decision.

Submission of the Night (unofficial): Arlovski vs. Sylvia

The long and frustrating wait for Belarusian bomber Andrei Arlovski was over, as he finally got his title shot and made the most of it, submitting former champ Tim Sylvia to earn the interim UFC heavyweight crown made available when champion Frank Mir was injured in a motorcycle accident in September of 2004.

Sylvia, who was sidelined himself when Mir broke his arm in their 2004 bout, looked comfortable in the opening moments of the bout until a clean right hand by Arlovski shockingly dropped the 6' 8" giant. After a frantic series of punches on his downed foe, Arlovski locked on a heel hook just as quickly and Sylvia had no option but to tap out, ending this championship bout in stunning fashion just 47 seconds into the bout.

Following a long dry period, the UFC finally got a middleweight champion after veteran Evan Tanner stopped David Terrell in the first round of a scheduled five-round title bout.

Terrell, in only his second UFC appearance, tried to repeat his early round KO of Matt Lindland with a whipping kick to the head seconds after the opening bell, but Tanner blocked the shot. Terrell was able to take Tanner down moments later, and even though the veteran quickly got to his feet, Terrell was firmly on the offensive as he chased Tanner around the Octagon.

Knockout of the Night (unofficial): Tanner vs. Terrell

Tanner kept his cool though, even after Terrell sunk in a guillotine choke and looked for the submission.

Gamely, he pounded his way out of the choke and with Terrell on the mat against the fence, Tanner opened fire with a series of punches and forearms.

With no response from Terrell, who appeared bewildered while on the defensive, referee Herb Dean had no choice but to stop the fight with a mere 25 seconds left in the first stanza.

San Jose heavyweight prospect Mike Kyle rebounded from a stoppage loss to Justin Eilers by dispatching of James Irvin in a single round.

Forget any groundwork in the Pay-Per-View opener between heavyweights Paul Buentello and Justin Eilers. Both of the big boys focused on the striking game from the outset, with each fighter having his moments of success in an evenly matched opening three minutes. But with less than two minutes to go, Buentello pounced, putting Eilers on rubbery legs with two lefts to the jaw before a right put him down and out at 3:34 of the first.

David Loiseau stopped late replacement Gideon Ray via cuts in a middleweight bout.

Welterweight Karo Parisyan defeated Chris Lytle via unanimous decision.

Drew Fickett got a rude welcome to the UFC when Nick Diaz stopped him at 4:40 of the first round of their welterweight contest.

The Ultimate Fighter 1 Finale

09 April 2005

Cox Pavilion, Las Vegas, NV

Debuts: Alex Karalexis, Josh Rafferty, Mike Swick, Alex Schoenauer, Nate Quarry, Lodune Sincaid, Josh Koscheck, Chris Sanford, Chris Leben, Jason Thacker, Sam Hoger, Bobby Southworth, Diego Sanchez, Kenny Florian, Forrest Griffin, Stephan Bonnar

Fighters			Division	Method	Time	Round
Main Card						
Rich Franklin	def.	Ken Shamrock	Light Heavyweight	Technical Knockout	2:42	1
Forrest Griffin	def.	Stephan Bonnar	Light Heavyweight	Unanimous Decision	—	3
Diego Sanchez	def.	Kenny Florian	Middleweight	Technical Knockout	2:46	1
Preliminary Card						
Sam Hoger	def.	Bobby Southworth	Light Heavyweight	Unanimous Decision	—	3
Chris Leben	def.	Jason Thacker	Middleweight	Technical Knockout	1:35	1
Josh Koscheck	def.	Chris Sanford	Middleweight	Knockout	4:21	1
Nate Quarry	def.	Lodune Sincaid	Middleweight	Technical Knockout	3:17	1
Mike Swick	def.	Alex Schoenauer	Middleweight	Knockout	0:20	1
Alex Karalexis	def.	Josh Rafferty	Welterweight	Technical Knockout	1:40	1

There was a life-changing UFC contract on the line at the Cox Pavilion in Las Vegas when Forrest Griffin fought Stephan Bonnar in the finale of *The Ultimate Fighter*'s first season, but they fought as if so much more was on the line. And there was, as their three-round war for the ages highlighted the UFC's first live event on basic cable television and introduced mixed martial arts to the masses.

Fight of the Night (unofficial): Griffin vs. Bonnar

When it was over, Griffin emerged with the razor-thin unanimous decision victory, but the fight was so amazing that both fighters were awarded UFC contracts. In fact, calling it amazing doesn't do it justice.

It took just seven seconds for the first blow to be thrown (a right by Griffin), and from there, it was game on. Griffin was the sharper of the two early as he scored well with combinations on the inside, but Bonnar didn't back down. With a little more than three minutes left, Bonnar delivered a couple of kicks and followed up with a series of punches that put Griffin on the defensive. Griffin quickly got back into the fray though, briefly rocking Bonnar with a punch as the round approached the midway point. As they grappled, the two tumbled to the mat, only to rise seconds later. There was no let-up to the action at all as the two threw shots at each other with abandon. With less than 20 seconds left, Griffin took Bonnar's back and then tried to secure an armbar, but the bell intervened.

The pace slowed down in round two—for about 40 seconds—until the two began slugging it out again. Bonnar looked to get the better of the exchange, and Griffin took the bout to the mat. Griffin emerged with a cut on his nose that brought a brief halt to the action, and when the fight resumed, so did the two light heavyweights. Bonnar tagged his foe with punches and appeared to have swung momentum in his favor. After a well-deserved breather against the fence, the two broke loose and began swinging for the fences again. In the closing minute, Bonnar put his foot on the gas and landed more good shots before the bell sent the two back to their corners.

Incredibly, the two found the energy to make it out for round three. After a minute, Griffin teed off with knees at close range and leg kicks from long range. Griffin's right hands were also finding their mark. With two minutes remaining, the two began their final charge, with each shot requiring incredible will at this late stage. Both were bloodied and battered, and with a minute left, the crowd rose to their feet in appreciation, and suitably, the fighters ended the bout the way it began, slugging it out.

In the night's main event, Rich "Ace" Franklin had a star-making turn in his light heavyweight bout against Ken Shamrock, stopping the UFC Hall of Famer in the first round.

Beginning the bout at a measured pace, Franklin shot out occasional strikes from long distance to get his range, and after winning the first exchange, he was able to capitalize when Shamrock slipped on the way inside and fell to the mat. In a scramble, Franklin worked for an omaplata, but the 41-year-old Shamrock pulled free and tried to lock up his opponent's leg. Franklin calmly worked himself loose and the two stood. After a brief lull, Franklin and Shamrock traded kicks, Franklin's landing and Shamrock's missing and causing another fall to the mat. This time, Franklin capitalized on his good fortune, and after an unanswered series of strikes, referee John McCarthy stopped the fight at the 2:42 mark.

In the night's other *Ultimate Fighter* final, this one in the middleweight division, Albuquerque's Diego Sanchez halted Boston's Kenny Florian in the first round to earn a UFC contract.

After a long feeling out process, Sanchez finally struck a minute into the bout, rushing Florian and pinning him to the fence. The fighters traded knees, with Florian getting the last word, allowing him to escape. Sanchez was undeterred though, and he rushed Florian again, this time getting the takedown. Sanchez began firing off strikes and then took the mount position. A bloodied Florian turned to escape, but there would not be one, as a continued series of punches brought Steve Mazzagatti to halt the bout 2:46 into the opening frame.

Sam Hoger scored the upset of the night when he decisioned veteran Bobby Southworth over three rounds.

Chris Leben needed only 95 seconds to halt Jason Thacker in his middleweight bout, but Mike Swick one-upped him with a 20-second finish of Alex Schoenauer.

Nate Quarry wasn't able to compete on *TUF1* due to injury, but he got his UFC career off right with a first-round TKO of Lodune Sincaid.

Knockout of the Night (unofficial): Koscheck vs. Sanford

Josh Koscheck also found the winner's circle with a knockout of Chris Sanford, and Alex Karalexis finished off Josh Rafferty with strikes 1:40 into their welterweight match.

One Hit Wonders: Josh Rafferty, Alex Schoenauer, Lodune Sincaid, Chris Sanford, Jason Thacker, Bobby Southworth

UFC 52 *Couture vs. Liddell 2*

16 April 2005

MGM Grand Garden Arena, Las Vegas, NV

Debuts: Jason Miller, John Marsh

Fighters			Division	Method	Time	Round
Main Card						
Chuck Liddell	def.	Randy Couture	Light Heavyweight	Knockout	2:06	1
Matt Hughes	def.	Frank Trigg	Welterweight	Submission - Rear Naked Choke	4:05	1
Renato Sobral	def.	Travis Wiuff	Light Heavyweight	Submission - Armbar	0:24	2
Matt Lindland	def.	Travis Lutter	Middleweight	Submission - Guillotine Choke	3:13	2
Georges St-Pierre	def.	Jason Miller	Welterweight	Unanimous Decision	—	3
Preliminary Card						
Ivan Salaverry	def.	Joe Riggs	Middleweight	Submission - Triangle Choke	2:42	1
Joe Doerksen	def.	Patrick Cote	Middleweight	Submission - Rear Naked Choke	2:35	3
Mike Van Arsdale	def.	John Marsh	Heavyweight	Unanimous Decision	—	3

It had been a long time coming for Chuck Liddell—seven years to be exact. After a series of disappointments and near-misses, "The Iceman" finally got his light heavyweight world championship after a stirring first-round knockout of Randy Couture in the main event of UFC 52. With the win, Liddell evened his record with Couture at 1-1 (Couture had stopped Liddell in three rounds in June of 2003).

After the customary touch of gloves, Liddell looked to counterpunch as Couture stalked. When Couture did get close, Liddell was able to use lateral movement to hit the champion and then move out of danger.

Knockout of the Night (unofficial): Liddell vs. Couture

With the crowd building to a frenzy, Couture landed a couple of shots before grabbing Liddell against the cage. After a brief skirmish, Liddell escaped and Couture backed out holding his right eye which had inadvertently been poked.

When action resumed, Couture immediately engaged, but was jarred by a short left hand. Couture kept moving forward and swinging, yet when Liddell stepped in with a right hand on the chin, Couture fell as if he had been shot. Liddell immediately jumped on his fallen foe, and after two more shots to the head, referee John McCarthy called a halt to the bout at 2:06 of the first round.

Fight and Submission of the Night (unofficial): Hughes vs. Trigg

UFC welterweight champ Matt Hughes made it two in a row over Frank Trigg in the evening's second title bout, sending "Twinkle Toes" to defeat via rear naked choke in a rematch that packed more drama into 4:05 than most do in five rounds.

After an opening staredown, the two combatants met at the center of the cage and traded punches until a lock-up. While against the cage, Trigg caught Hughes with a low knee that was not caught by referee Mario Yamasaki. As Hughes retreated and tried to regain his bearings, Trigg pounced and sent Hughes to the canvas with a left to the jaw. In serious trouble, Hughes caught a flurry of blows on the ground as Trigg worked his way into the mounted position.

Hughes tried to escape the bottom but wound up giving Trigg his back at the three-minute mark, and the challenger quickly capitalized with a rear naked choke. Hughes' face turned crimson, but amazingly he was able to escape and then follow up this good fortune by picking his foe up and carrying him across the cage before dropping him on his back with a trademark slam.

Now it was Hughes in control, and in the full mount he opened up on Trigg with both hands. With the packed house going wild, Trigg then turned and it was Hughes sinking in a rear naked choke, which produced a tapout at the 4:05 mark.

Renato "Babalu" Sobral made his return to the UFC for the first time in over two years a successful one, winning via second-round submission over Travis Wiuff.

Matt Lindland rebounded from his shocking first-round knockout loss to David Terrell at UFC 49, submitting Travis Lutter with a guillotine choke in the second round.

In the main card opener, rising welterweight star Georges St-Pierre pounded out a dominating three-round decision over Jason "Mayhem" Miller.

Comebacking veteran Mike Van Arsdale decisioned John Marsh over three rounds in a heavyweight bout.

Joe Doerksen submitted Canada's Patrick Cote via rear naked choke at 2:35 of the third and final round of their middleweight contest.

Ivan Salaverry defeated Joe Riggs via submission from a triangle choke at 2:42 of the first round in a middleweight matchup.

Adding to the importance of this historic event was the induction of Dan "The Beast" Severn into the UFC Hall of Fame.

One Hit Wonder: John Marsh

25 GREATEST KNOCKOUTS

UFC 77
ANDERSON SILVA VS. RICH FRANKLIN 2

It wasn't one blow that ended Anderson Silva's rematch with Rich Franklin, but the wide array of techniques displayed by the UFC middleweight champion that was a thing of beauty. The stunning barrage of blows left Franklin not only helpless, but with a look on his face wondering what the best pound for pound fighter in the world was going to unleash on him next.

UFC 52
CHUCK LIDDELL VS. RANDY COUTURE 2

For nearly two years, Chuck Liddell patiently waited for a shot at redemption for his upset 2003 loss against Randy Couture. In April of 2005, he got it, and with his trademark right hand, he exorcised his demons with a spectacular finish of "The Natural" to win the UFC light heavyweight championship

UFC 70
GABRIEL GONZAGA VS. MIRKO CRO COP

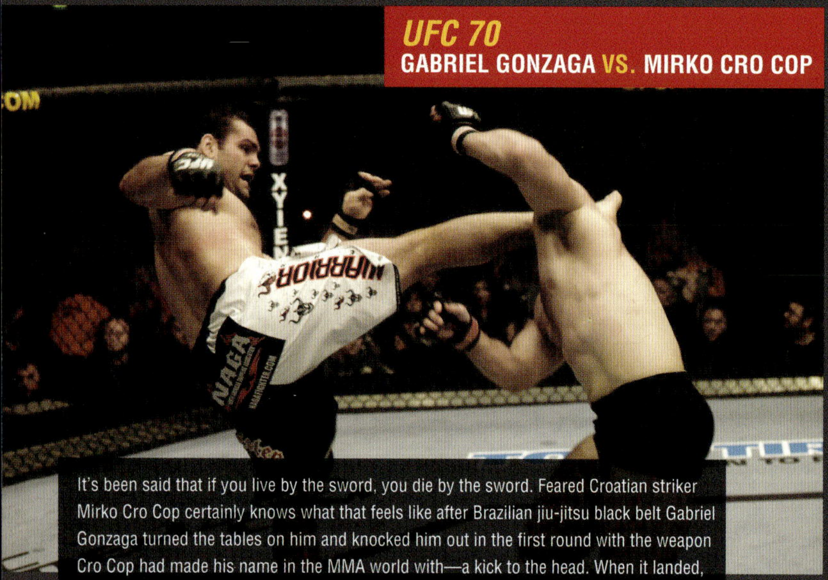

It's been said that if you live by the sword, you die by the sword. Feared Croatian striker Mirko Cro Cop certainly knows what that feels like after Brazilian jiu-jitsu black belt Gabriel Gonzaga turned the tables on him and knocked him out in the first round with the weapon Cro Cop had made his name in the MMA world with—a kick to the head. When it landed, Cro Cop fell like he was shot, grotesquely twisting his knee and ankle in the process. Not only was it shocking, but it was spectacular.

UFC 34
MATT HUGHES VS. CARLOS NEWTON 1

When UFC welterweight champion Carlos Newton sunk in a triangle choke on challenger Matt Hughes, it looked like it would just be a matter of time until Newton retained his title. But Hughes took matters into his own hands, lifted Newton over his head, and after some tense moments, he slammed his foe to the mat, winning the fight and knocking loose the 170-pound championship belt in the process.

TUF4 FINALE
SCOTT SMITH VS. PETE SELL

For pure aesthetic value, this unbelievable knockout wins every time. Smith and Sell became friends on the fourth season of *The Ultimate Fighter* reality show, but they fought like enemies in their bout as they traded power shots. In the second round, Sell looked like he had pulled ahead when he nailed his opponent with a body shot that doubled Smith over in pain as he backpedaled to the fence. Sell ran in recklessly to land the finisher, but Smith caught him with a perfect right hand to the jaw, and just like that, Smith had the TKO victory. It was straight out of a Hollywood script, and one of those endings you truly had to see to believe.

Photography by: Susumu Nagao

UFC 34
BJ PENN VS. CAOL UNO 1

After avoiding a wild flying knee from Caol Uno to start the 2001 bout, BJ Penn responded with a barrage of strikes which knocked the Japanese star out against the Octagon fence in just 11 seconds. How did Penn celebrate? By running from the cage and back to his locker room.

25 GREATEST KNOCKOUTS

UFC 77
ANDERSON SILVA VS. RICH FRANKLIN 2

It wasn't one blow that ended Anderson Silva's rematch with Rich Franklin, but the wide array of techniques displayed by the UFC middleweight champion that was a thing of beauty. The stunning barrage of blows left Franklin not only helpless, but with a look on his face wondering what the best pound for pound fighter in the world was going to unleash on him next.

UFC 52
CHUCK LIDDELL VS. RANDY COUTURE 2

For nearly two years, Chuck Liddell patiently waited for a shot at redemption for his upset 2003 loss against Randy Couture. In April of 2005, he got it, and with his trademark right hand, he exorcised his demons with a spectacular finish of "The Natural" to win the UFC light heavyweight championship

UFC 70
GABRIEL GONZAGA VS. MIRKO CRO COP

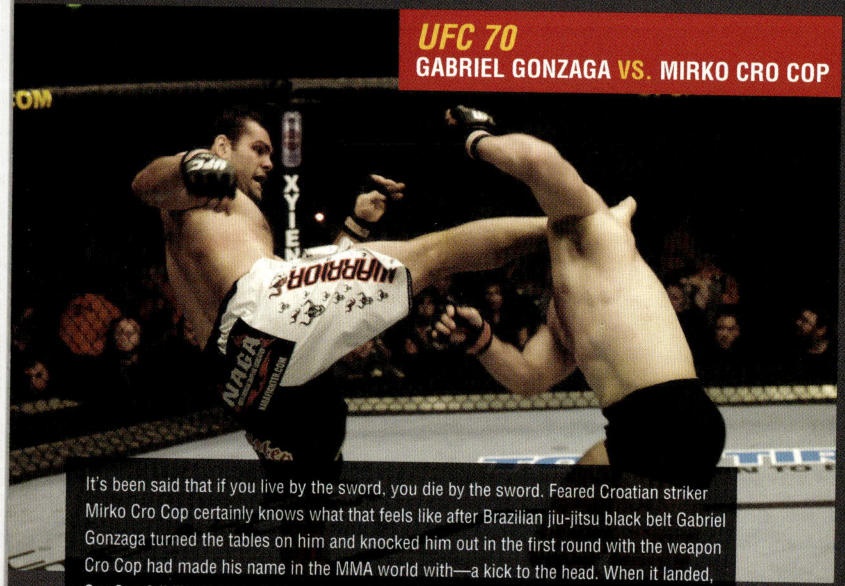

It's been said that if you live by the sword, you die by the sword. Feared Croatian striker Mirko Cro Cop certainly knows what that feels like after Brazilian jiu-jitsu black belt Gabriel Gonzaga turned the tables on him and knocked him out in the first round with the weapon Cro Cop had made his name in the MMA world with—a kick to the head. When it landed, Cro Cop fell like he was shot, grotesquely twisting his knee and ankle in the process. Not only was it shocking, but it was spectacular.

UFC 34
MATT HUGHES VS. CARLOS NEWTON 1

When UFC welterweight champion Carlos Newton sunk in a triangle choke on challenger Matt Hughes, it looked like it would just be a matter of time until Newton retained his title. But Hughes took matters into his own hands, lifted Newton over his head, and after some tense moments, he slammed his foe to the mat, winning the fight and knocking loose the 170-pound championship belt in the process.

TUF4 FINALE
SCOTT SMITH VS. PETE SELL

For pure aesthetic value, this unbelievable knockout wins every time. Smith and Sell became friends on the fourth season of *The Ultimate Fighter* reality show, but they fought like enemies in their bout as they traded power shots. In the second round, Sell looked like he had pulled ahead when he nailed his opponent with a body shot that doubled Smith over in pain as he backpedaled to the fence. Sell ran in recklessly to land the finisher, but Smith caught him with a perfect right hand to the jaw, and just like that, Smith had the TKO victory. It was straight out of a Hollywood script, and one of those endings you truly had to see to believe.

Photography by: Susumu Nagao

UFC 34
BJ PENN VS. CAOL UNO 1

After avoiding a wild flying knee from Caol Uno to start the 2001 bout, BJ Penn responded with a barrage of strikes which knocked the Japanese star out against the Octagon fence in just 11 seconds. How did Penn celebrate? By running from the cage and back to his locker room.

ULTIMATE BRAZIL
VITOR BELFORT VS. WANDERLEI SILVA

Though their spots in the MMA pecking order would eventually flip-flop, at the time of their Ultimate Brazil bout in 1998, the undisputed star was Vitor Belfort and Wanderlei Silva was just a raw up-and-comer. This prospect didn't get much time to settle in though, as Belfort blitzed "The Axe Murderer" with a blinding series of rights and lefts en route to a 44-second TKO win.

UFC 126
ANDERSON SILVA VS. VITOR BELFORT

Anderson Silva was more amped up than usual for his middleweight title defense against former training partner Vitor Belfort. He made sure "The Phenom" was aware of his intentions as he knocked him out with a front kick to the face that Silva's friend (and action film star) Steven Seagal claimed to have taught him.

UFC 17
PETE WILLIAMS VS. MARK COLEMAN

Exhausted after over 12 minutes of fighting, former UFC heavyweight champion Mark Coleman was just trying to survive against young contender Pete Williams in their 1998 bout. Williams gave Coleman the rest he craved midway through that 13th minute with a flush kick to the head that became one of the most enduring images of early UFC action.

UFC 8
GARY GOODRIDGE VS. PAUL HERRERA

It was perhaps the most brutal knockout in UFC history. After hearing that Paul Herrera had delivered some trash talk in his direction before their bout, Gary Goodridge responded by catching Herrera in a crucifix position moments into the fight. What followed was a crushing series of elbows that knocked Herrera out in just 13 seconds.

UFC 95
NATE MARQUARDT VS. WILSON GOUVEIA

Nate Marquardt probably could have coasted in the third round of his bout against Wilson Gouveia at UFC 95 and just grabbed a decision win, but in that final stanza it was as if something went off in his head. What followed was a dizzying array of fists, feet and knees that took Gouveia out at 3:10 of the round.

UFC 100
DAN HENDERSON VS. MICHAEL BISPING

Yes, Michael Bisping talked a lot leading up to his UFC 100 showdown with Dan Henderson. But the Brit's mouth had nothing to do with his demise at the hands of Hendo. Instead, once the former two-division PRIDE champion realized that Bisping wasn't hurting him and that he was pulling straight back AND circling into his power hand, the end was inevitable. And when Henderson's vaunted right hand crashed into Bisping's jaw in the second, it was lights out, with the final shot delivered to his downed opponent legal, but ultimately unnecessary.

UFC 69
MATT SERRA VS. GEORGES ST-PIERRE 1

As far as highlight reel knockouts go, there are better choices, but you can't help but give a nod to a knockout that belongs strictly for its historic and shock value. Matt Serra's upset of the seemingly unstoppable Georges St-Pierre definitely applies. A hard right hand that clipped a ducking St-Pierre took the champion's equilibrium, and as GSP tried to get his legs under him, Serra was calm, cool, collected and sending bombs down the pipe that were keeping the Canadian from getting back into the fight. Finally, a series of unanswered shots on the ground forced a halt to the bout, and the MMA world had a new champion in Matt "The Terror" Serra.

UFC 114
MIKE RUSSOW VS. TODD DUFFEE

Hot prospect Todd Duffee was on his way to another Octagon victory when he battered Mike Russow for two-plus rounds at UFC 114. But nothing's guaranteed in this game until the fight is over, and Duffee learned that the hard way, as Russow pulled out a right hand from nowhere in the final round that starched Duffee at the 2:35 mark, stunning all in attendance at the MGM Grand Garden Arena.

UFC 88
RASHAD EVANS VS. CHUCK LIDDELL

In the first round, Rashad Evans fought the perfect fight against Chuck Liddell, using movement and quick flurries to frustrate "The Iceman". So when Liddell came out recklessly and aggressively in the second stanza, Evans ended the perfect fight with the perfect punch—a right on the button that put the former light heavyweight king down and out.

UFC 54
JAMES IRVIN VS. TERRY MARTIN

To say the first five minutes of James Irvin's light heavyweight debut against Terry Martin were abysmal would be an understatement. But in the first nine seconds of round two, all was forgiven as "The Sandman" drilled Martin with a flying knee to the head that sent the Illinois native to sleep.

UFC 92
QUINTON JACKSON VS. WANDERLEI SILVA 3

As cathartic a knockout as you'll find in this game, Quinton Jackson finished off a rough 2008 campaign on a high note, not only with a victory, but with a victory over Wanderlei Silva, the man who knocked him out twice in PRIDE. The fact that he knocked out his heated rival with a single left hook made the win even sweeter.

UFC 6
TANK ABBOTT VS. JOHN MATUA

In the early days of the UFC, the knockouts came in a fast and furious fashion, and most were brutal reminders that this was a contact sport. But few were as emphatic as Tank Abbott's introduction to the world, an 18-second display of fury and right hands that left John Matua down on the canvas, arms and legs outstretched.

UFC 40
CHUCK LIDDELL VS. RENATO SOBRAL 1

Everyone was rightfully scared of Chuck Liddell's right hand, and game plans centered on how to avoid getting posterized by the most dangerous weapon in the UFC. Renato "Babalu" Sobral did an excellent job of not getting halted by Liddell's right, but instead, it was a left kick to the head that ended the Brazilian's night and put another notch in the belt of "The Iceman".

UFC 47
NICK DIAZ VS. ROBBIE LAWLER

With only one injury-induced loss and concrete blocks for fists, Robbie Lawler wasn't only expected to be a future UFC champ, but he was the one guy no one wanted to stand with. Well no one except brash groundfighter Nick Diaz, who beat Lawler at his own game and stunned the MMA world by knocking him out with a single right hand that sent Lawler face-first to the canvas.

UFC 49
YVES EDWARDS VS. JOSH THOMSON

It was the last lightweight fight in the UFC for nearly two years, but Yves Edwards made sure that fight fans remembered the 155-pounders. An attempted back fist by Josh Thomson was met by a flush right kick to the head by Edwards, and it was game over for "The Punk" and a spectacular knockout win for Edwards, the master and creator of "Thug Jitsu".

UFC 129
LYOTO MACHIDA VS. RANDY COUTURE

In pre-fight interviews, the legendary Randy Couture announced that after his UFC 129 bout against Lyoto Machida he would be retiring. Well, if Couture was having any second thoughts, Machida likely erased them with a flying front kick to the face in round two that looked like it came straight out of the ending of the first *Karate Kid* film.

UFN8
RASHAD EVANS VS. SEAN SALMON

In the lead-up to his bout with Sean Salmon, Rashad Evans started going by the moniker "Suga". Well, the former MSU Spartan showed a little spice in this fight, battling through a sluggish first round to put an emphatic end to Salmon's UFC debut in the second with a picture-perfect right kick to the head that put Salmon out on impact.

UFC 101
ANDERSON SILVA VS. FORREST GRIFFIN

If at one point in your life you can say that you witnessed greatness in person, you're lucky. Those fans in attendance at the Wachovia Center in Philadelphia for UFC 101 had that opportunity as middleweight champion Anderson Silva went back to the light heavyweight division and put on a clinic of precision striking, taking out former 205-pound titleholder Forrest Griffin at 3:23 of the first round. Call it over the top, but this performance was a potent mix of a Ted Williams swing, a John Coltrane solo and a Barry Sanders run out of the backfield.

UFC 129
JOHN MAKDESSI VS. KYLE WATSON

One of the most creative standup fighters in the UFC today, John "The Bull" Makdessi showed off a wide array of techniques in his bout against Kyle Watson. It was his picture-perfect spinning back fist that will live on in highlight films forever. Not just because it ended the bout in the third round, but due to the way Makdessi set it up with a fake that had Watson completely fooled before the final blow landed.

UFC 53 *Heavy Hitters*

04 June 2005

Boardwalk Hall, Atlantic City, NJ

Debuts: Charles McCarthy, Kevin Jordan, Bill Mahood

Fighters			Division	Method	Time	Round
Main Card						
Andrei Arlovski	def.	Justin Eilers	Heavyweight	Technical Knockout	4:10	1
Rich Franklin	def.	Evan Tanner	Middleweight	Technical Knockout	3:25	4
Karo Parisyan	def.	Matt Serra	Welterweight	Unanimous Decision	—	3
Forrest Griffin	def.	Bill Mahood	Light Heavyweight	Submission - Rear Naked Choke	2:18	1
Paul Buentello	def.	Kevin Jordan	Heavyweight	Submission - Guillotine Choke	4:00	1
Preliminary Card						
Nate Quarry	def.	Shonie Carter	Middleweight	Technical Knockout	2:37	1
David Loiseau	def.	Charles McCarthy	Middleweight	Technical Knockout	2:04	2
Nick Diaz	def.	Koji Oishi	Welterweight	Technical Knockout	1:24	1

Justin Eilers, who managed to secure a heavyweight title bout despite being knocked out in his last UFC bout against Paul Buentello, was easily dispatched by interim champ Andrei Arlovski at 4:10 of the first round of their UFC 53 championship bout at Atlantic City's Boardwalk Hall.

Working his leg kicks and heavy head shots from the outset, Arlovski was never in danger in the bout as Eilers simply backpedaled and hoped for the best. To his credit, Eilers was game, but overmatched against the Belarusian. Strangely enough, it was Eilers who doomed himself when he went to throw a right hand and blew out his right knee with just under a minute left, allowing Arlovski to jump on him and finish the fight with 50 seconds left in the opening round.

Fight of the Night (unofficial): Franklin vs. Tanner

The Franklin/Tanner fight was fast-paced from the start, with Tanner immediately taking the fight to the challenger. Both fighters traded heavy shots with some fans surprised by Tanner's willingness to keep the fight standing. Franklin jarred Tanner briefly with a high left kick, and Tanner quickly recovered, only to get rocked by an uppercut seconds later. Franklin's superior standup skills were evident, but Tanner kept moving forward, looking for an opening—an opening which came with 40 seconds left in the round as he dropped the challenger with a right hand to the jaw. Tanner got Franklin's back and briefly had an armbar, but Franklin cleared his head and was back in the fight by the bell. As Tanner went to his corner, he was bleeding from his ear, and things would only get worse as the fight progressed.

The pattern continued in the second and third rounds, with Franklin now mixing kicks and knees in with his accurate punches. Despite the fact that the fight was becoming one-sided, Tanner kept coming forward as he refused to give up his title without a fierce struggle. By the fourth round the outcome was no longer in doubt, and after a series of shots by Franklin with 1:35 to go in the round, referee Herb Dean halted the bout to allow the ringside physicians to check Tanner, and the fight was immediately stopped.

In a compelling welterweight matchup, Matt Serra started strong but faded late, dropping a three-round unanimous decision to judo ace Karo Parisyan. Seconds into the bout, Serra sent Parisyan face-first to the canvas with a stiff right hand to the head. Parisyan gamely held on as Serra opened up with both hands, and once his head cleared he started throwing back as Serra continued to land. But by the final minute of the first, Parisyan had taken control of the bout with some excellent grappling work, mixed in with a hearty ground and pound. The second and third rounds were Parisyan's, easily taking the final two frames en route to the decision win. Scores were 29-28, and 30-27 twice for Parisyan.

The light heavyweight winner of *The Ultimate Fighter* reality show, Forrest Griffin, made his highly anticipated UFC Pay-Per-View debut a successful one. Eschewing his usual hell-bent-for-leather style in favor of a more patient attack, Griffin took advantage of a missed Mahood kick to take control of the bout early on the ground. Griffin got his opponent's back, sinking in a rear naked choke and ending the fight impressively 2:18 into the opening frame.

In the Pay-Per-View opener, rising heavyweight contender Paul Buentello survived some rocky early moments against debuting Kevin Jordan en route to a first-round submission victory.

Submission of the Night (unofficial): Buentello vs. Jordan

Middleweight contender David "The Crow" Loiseau gave newcomer Charles McCarthy a harsh introduction to the UFC. McCarthy, a submission ace from Florida, briefly had Loiseau in trouble in the first round, but the Montreal native fought his way out. By the second round "The Crow" was back in control, hurting McCarthy with a back kick followed by a flying knee. A final flurry brought John McCarthy (no relation) in to stop the fight.

Knockout of the Night (unofficial): Loiseau vs. McCarthy

Nate Quarry, a member of *The Ultimate Fighter* cast, also made his UFC Pay-Per-View debut in an undercard bout, stopping veteran Shonie Carter in the first round of their middleweight bout.

In a welterweight preliminary bout, Nick Diaz had little difficulty with Yokohama, Japan's Koji Oishi, stopping the highly unorthodox fighter with a series of strikes at 1:24 of the first round.

One Hit Wonder: Bill Mahood

Despite his less-than-stellar performance against Forrest Griffin, Mahood was one of Canada's mixed martial arts pioneers, with nearly 20 wins (against the likes of Steve Steinbeiss, Chris Haseman and Jason MacDonald) over the course of more than a decade in the game.

Ultimate Fight Night 1

06 Aug. 2005

Cox Pavilion, Las Vegas, NV

Debuts: Nate Marquardt, Josh Neer

Fighters			Division	Method	Time	Round
Main Card						
Nate Marquardt	def.	Ivan Salaverry	Middleweight	Unanimous Decision	—	3
Chris Leben	def.	Patrick Cote	Middleweight	Split Decision	—	3
Stephan Bonnar	def.	Sam Hoger	Light Heavyweight	Unanimous Decision	—	3
Nate Quarry	def.	Pete Sell	Middleweight	Technical Knockout	0:42	1
Preliminary Card						
Josh Koscheck	def.	Pete Spratt	Welterweight	Submission - Rear Naked Choke	1:53	1
Mike Swick	def.	Gideon Ray	Middleweight	Technical Knockout	0:22	1
Kenny Florian	def.	Alex Karalexis	Welterweight	Technical Knockout	2:52	2
Drew Fickett	def.	Josh Neer	Welterweight	Submission - Rear Naked Choke	1:35	1

Just four months after the groundbreaking finale of *The Ultimate Fighter* reality show in April of 2005, eight members of the season one cast made their returns to the Octagon in an attempt to keep the momentum going as they look to take their game to the next level.

It was a bout between two veterans of the fight game that headlined the first Ultimate Fight Night event at the Cox Pavilion in Las Vegas, and it was former King of Pancrase Nate Marquardt scoring a victory in his Octagon debut as he outpointed Ivan Salaverry over three rounds.

The unanimous decision read 29-28 twice and 30-27 for "Nate The Great", who used his superior athleticism, speed and takedowns to win the 15-minute battle over Salaverry, who just couldn't figure his opponent out in time to turn the tables. What resulted was a bout that was far from action-packed, but as famed boxing trainer George Benton once said "Win today, look good tomorrow."

And that's what Marquardt did as he notched his first UFC victory in his first bout on US soil since 2003.

Yet while Marquardt's arrival immediately marked him as a contender for the middleweight title, such lofty titles were still some time away for the *Ultimate Fighter* alumni, who are now at the point in their careers when they wanted to make lasting impressions, and many of them did.

Fight of the Night (unofficial): Leben vs. Cote

In the co-feature, *TUF* middleweight Chris Leben kept Canada's Patrick Cote winless in three UFC outings as he won a razor-thin three-round split decision over "The Predator". A strong third-round finish by "The Crippler" made an impression on the judges, who awarded him the 30-27, 29-28, and 28-29 nod.

TUF1 finalist Stephan Bonnar, fresh from his classic with Forrest Griffin, got back in the win column against castmate Sam Hoger, who put up a stellar effort despite losing a shutout three-round decision to "The American Psycho".

Opening the main card was hard-hitting Nate Quarry, whose second Octagon win was shrouded in controversy. His 42-second knockout of Pete Sell was seen as the beneficiary of a quick hook by referee Cecil Peoples, and the angry Sell agreed but the call stood.

On the preliminary portion of the card, former national wrestling champion and *TUF1* alum Josh Koscheck moved to 4-0 as a pro with a first-round rear naked choke submission of veteran Pete Spratt. Also, Mike Swick was forced to go two seconds longer than he did when he knocked out Alex Schoenauer at the *TUF1* finale as he needed 22 seconds to finish off Gideon Ray with a blazing array of strikes.

Submission of the Night (unofficial): Koscheck vs. Spratt

Making his UFC welterweight debut after losing in the *TUF* finals to Diego Sanchez at middleweight, Kenny Florian was forced to finish off his castmate and fellow New Englander Alex Karalexis at 2:52 of the second round in a bout stopped due to an elbow-induced cut suffered by Karalexis.

Knockout of the Night (unofficial): Swick vs. Ray

Veteran Drew Fickett ended tough-as-nails rookie Josh Neer's night in the welterweight opener, submitting him via rear naked choke at 1:35 of the first round.

UFC 54 *Boiling Point*

20 Aug. 2005

MGM Grand Garden Arena, Las Vegas, NV

Debuts: Terry Martin, Brian Gassaway

Fighters			Division	Method	Time	Round
Main Card						
Chuck Liddell	def.	Jeremy Horn	Light Heavyweight	Technical Knockout	2:46	4
Tim Sylvia	def.	Tra Telligman	Heavyweight	Knockout	4:59	1
Randy Couture	def.	Mike Van Arsdale	Light Heavyweight	Submission - Anaconda Choke	0:52	3
Diego Sanchez	def.	Brian Gassaway	Welterweight	Submission - Strikes	1:56	2
Georges St-Pierre	def.	Frank Trigg	Welterweight	Submission - Rear Naked Choke	4:09	1
Preliminary Card						
Matt Lindland	def.	Joe Doerksen	Middleweight	Unanimous Decision	—	3
Trevor Prangley	def.	Travis Lutter	Middleweight	Unanimous Decision	—	3
James Irvin	def.	Terry Martin	Light Heavyweight	Knockout	0:09	2

UFC light heavyweight champion Chuck Liddell etched his name in the annals of mixed martial arts history on August 20, 2005. He not only avenged his first loss to Jeremy Horn via a fourth-round stoppage at the MGM Grand Garden Arena, but became the winningest fighter in the UFC history at the time. He notched his twelfth victory in the Octagon, surpassing Royce Gracie's mark of 11.

Fight of the Night (unofficial): Liddell vs. Horn

The two 205-pound standouts traded jabs and kicks early on, with Liddell holding a slight edge over the opening two minutes. Even Horn's high guard didn't help as Liddell dropped Horn with a stiff right hand straight down the middle. After a quick barrage on the ground by the Iceman, both fighters rose, and Horn still opted to trade with the champion despite being on wobbly legs.

Courageously, Horn survived the round and even jarred Liddell briefly in the second with a right hand of his own. In the third minute of the second round, Liddell's right hand dropped Horn a second time, and again, the challenger barely weathered the storm. Looking for some way to get back into the fight, Horn shot in for the takedown four times, but again Liddell was able to sprawl out of trouble.

Showing the scars of battle on his face, Horn came out gamely for the third round throwing leg kicks to try to loosen Liddell up. Horn kept the pressure on with his kicks in the fourth round as well, and Liddell got back on track with stiff jabs and 1-2s to the head. Later in the round, Horn was dropped for the third time by a right hand directly on the eye. As Horn rose, he told referee John McCarthy that he couldn't see, and the bout was halted at the 2:46 mark, giving Liddell his first successful light heavyweight title defense.

"He's a tough guy and he can take a lot of punishment," said Liddell. "I hit him hard quite a few times and he survived. He's a tough guy to stop."

In a light heavyweight bout, ageless Randy Couture made his first start in the Octagon since his knockout loss to Chuck Liddell, and was impressive in submitting Mike Van Arsdale via anaconda choke in the third round.

Submission of the Night (unofficial): Couture vs. Van Arsdale

Canadian welterweight contender Georges St-Pierre scored the most impressive victory of his young career, dominating two-time title challenger Frank Trigg from the outset en route to a first-round submission victory via rear naked choke.

The middleweight winner of the first season of *The Ultimate Fighter* reality show, Diego Sanchez, made his Pay-Per-View debut a successful one as he defeated veteran Brian Gassaway via a second-round tap out in a welterweight bout.

Former UFC heavyweight champion Tim Sylvia got back in the UFC win column after losses to Frank Mir and Andrei Arlovski with a decisive first-round knockout of veteran Tra Telligman.

Sylvia didn't have to worry about any submissions in this bout, as Telligman (who had competed in pro boxing) was unafraid of trading with the 6' 8" "Maine-iac" in the early going. But it was Sylvia who got the last word when he drilled Telligman with a kick to the head just before the bell, causing the bout to be halted immediately at 4:59 of the first round.

Middleweight contender Matt Lindland kept on track with a unanimous three-round decision over Joe Doerksen.

James Irvin electrified the crowd with a flying knee knockout of Terry Martin at nine seconds of the second round.

Trevor Prangley scored a clear-cut unanimous decision over Travis Lutter in a middleweight bout.

Knockout of the Night (unofficial): Irvin vs. Martin

One Hit Wonder: Brian Gassaway

A longtime training partner of Shonie Carter, Brian Gassaway already had compiled 38 pro fights by the time he stepped into the Octagon against Sanchez. Although he wasn't victorious in the UFC, he continued to fight against quality foes such as John Alessio, Jose Landi-Jons, Forrest Petz, and Mike Pyle, and he's still fighting today.

Ultimate Fight Night 2

03 Oct. 2005

Hard Rock Hotel and Casino, Las Vegas, NV

Debuts: Brandon Vera, Fabiano Scherner, Thiago Alves, Spencer Fisher, Brock Larson, Jon Fitch, Jonathan Goulet

Fighters			Division	Method	Time	Round
Main Card						
David Loiseau	def.	Evan Tanner	Middleweight	Technical Knockout	4:15	2
Chris Leben	def.	Edwin Dewees	Middleweight	Submission - Armbar	3:26	1
Brandon Vera	def.	Fabiano Scherner	Heavyweight	Technical Knockout	3:22	2
Drew Fickett	def.	Josh Koscheck	Welterweight	Submission - Rear Naked Choke	4:38	3
Preliminary Card						
Spencer Fisher	def.	Thiago Alves	Welterweight	Submission - Triangle Choke	4:43	2
Jon Fitch	def.	Brock Larson	Middleweight	Unanimous Decision	—	3
Jonathan Goulet	def.	Jay Hieron	Welterweight	Technical Knockout	1:05	3

Riding a four-fight winning streak and knowing that he was one more victory away from a world title shot, Canada's David "The Crow" Loiseau nonetheless tempted fate in his Ultimate Fight Night match with Evan Tanner, avoiding numerous submission attempts before halting the former middleweight champion via cuts in the second round.

The win set up Loiseau's challenge for Rich Franklin's middleweight belt.

Aggressively looking to bounce back from the loss of his title to Franklin four months earlier, Tanner found success crowding Loiseau and getting him to the mat, and surprisingly, the Montrealer gave up his back willingly as Tanner looked to lock in rear naked chokes. By the end of the round though, a failed Tanner armbar attempt left Loiseau the opening to rain down some hard ground strikes.

Fight of the Night (unofficial): Loiseau vs. Tanner

Undeterred, Tanner maintained the fast pace in round two, and he kept his eyes open for any submission attempts. But with a little bit more than two minutes left, Loiseau again found an opening for some ground strikes, and this time he made them count as he delivered a series of devastating elbows that cut Tanner. After a break for an inspection of the cut, the bout was allowed to continue, but Loiseau wasn't going to let his foe off the hook, and another barrage produced another stoppage, this one for good, as the bout was waved off due to the severity of Tanner's cuts at 4:15 of the round.

Unabashed middleweight brawler Chris Leben showed that he had a few tricks up his sleeve in the co-feature, as he remained unbeaten in the Octagon with a first-round submission of Edwin Dewees via armbar.

Undefeated heavyweight prospect Brandon Vera made his UFC debut with an impressive second-round TKO of Brazil's Fabiano Scherner. Even more notable than the knees that ended the bout at the 3:22 mark were Vera's comments after the bout, when he declared that he wanted to not only win the heavyweight title belt, but hold the light heavyweight belt at the same time.

Knockout of the Night (unofficial): Vera vs. Scherner

For much of Josh Koscheck's welterweight scrap with veteran Drew Fickett, the rising star had things his way. In fact, entering the final minute, all he needed to do was stay out of trouble and he would have walked away with a unanimous decision victory and his perfect MMA record intact. But he couldn't stay out of trouble, and with the seconds ticking away, Fickett put the first "1" in Koscheck's loss column as he locked in a rear naked choke that ended the fight with just 32 seconds remaining. And that's the beauty of mixed martial arts.

Submission of the Night (unofficial): Fickett vs. Koscheck

In preliminary matchups featuring five UFC newcomers, Canada's Jonathan Goulet nabbed a bloody TKO win over Jay Hieron, Jon Fitch outpointed Brock Larson unanimously in a battle of welterweight wrestling powerhouses, and Spencer Fisher spoiled Thiago Alves' 22nd birthday by submitting him in the second round via triangle choke.

UFC 55 *Fury*

07 Oct. 2005

Mohegan Sun Arena, Uncasville, CT

Debuts: Alessio Sakara, Ron Faircloth, Marcio Cruz, Keigo Kunihara, Chael Sonnen, Branden Lee Hinkle, Sean Gannon

Fighters			Division	Method	Time	Round
Main Card						
Andrei Arlovski	def.	Paul Buentello	Heavyweight	Knockout	0:15	1
Forrest Griffin	def.	Elvis Sinosic	Light Heavyweight	Technical Knockout	3:30	1
Renato Sobral	def.	Chael Sonnen	Light Heavyweight	Submission - Triangle Choke	1:20	2
Joe Riggs	def.	Chris Lytle	Welterweight	Technical Knockout - Cuts	2:00	2
Branden Lee Hinkle	def.	Sean Gannon	Heavyweight	Technical Knockout	4:14	1
Preliminary Card						
Jorge Rivera	def.	Dennis Hallman	Middleweight	Unanimous Decision	—	3
Marcio Cruz	def.	Keigo Kunihara	Heavyweight	Submission - Rear Naked Choke	1:02	2
Alessio Sakara	vs.	Ron Faircloth	Light Heavyweight	No Contest	0:10	2

UFC heavyweight champion Andrei Arlovski once again proved to be a step above his competition as he destroyed top contender Paul Buentello in a mere 15 seconds at the Mohegan Sun Arena in Uncasville, Connecticut.

Knockout of the Night (unofficial): Arlovski vs. Buentello

The main event of UFC 55: Fury was over almost as soon as it started. After a brief exchange, Arlovski drilled Buentello with a right hand on the jaw, and as Buentello fell face forward towards the canvas, referee Big John McCarthy immediately stepped in to halt the bout. The knockout and stoppage was so fast that it drew boos from the packed house—at least until replays showed the wisdom of McCarthy's quick actions.

In the UFC 55 co-feature, light heavyweight fan favorite Forrest Griffin stayed on the fast track to the top of the division with a first-round stoppage of former title challenger Elvis Sinosic. It was Griffin's second Octagon victory since winning the stirring finale of *The Ultimate Fighter* against Stephan Bonnar in April of 2005.

Fight of the Night (unofficial): Griffin vs. Sinosic

Both light heavies traded strikes early, with Sinosic doing surprisingly well on his feet. One minute in, a right by the Australian briefly rocked Griffin, and the battle was on in full force. With under two minutes left Griffin started to finally find his range, and though he was breathing heavily, he was getting closer and closer, and after a right uppercut followed by a left hook, Sinosic hit the mat hard. Griffin jumped in to finish the bout, but referee Mario Yamasaki saved him the trouble, erring on the side of caution and halting the bout at the 3:30 mark.

Brazil's Renato "Babalu" Sobral moved one step closer to a rematch with UFC 205-pound champion Chuck Liddell with a second-round submission victory over game UFC debutant Chael Sonnen in light heavyweight action.

Submission of the Night (unofficial): Sobral vs. Sonnen

The Pay-Per-View opener saw former super heavyweight Joe Riggs make his welterweight debut a successful one, as he handed Chris Lytle his first ever stoppage defeat via a cut-induced TKO at 2:00 of the second round.

In a heavyweight undercard bout, controversial underground fight participant Sean Gannon was game, but obviously not ready for prime time, as MMA veteran Branden Lee Hinkle sent the Boston cop crashing down to defeat in his UFC debut via a one-sided first-round beating.

Local New England hero Jorge Rivera gave Dennis Hallman a rude welcome to the middleweight division, scoring a convincing three-round unanimous decision win over the veteran, who was making his UFC debut in the 185-pound weight class. Scores were 30-27 across the board for Rivera.

Italian light heavyweight Alessio Sakara, a former pro boxer, showed his superior striking class in his UFC debut as he pounded Ron Faircloth throughout the opening round of their bout, but in round two, everything changed when Faircloth landed a kick to Sakara's groin, sending him to the canvas in pain and ending the fight as a no contest.

Marcio Cruz submitted Keigo Kunihara via rear naked choke in a heavyweight contest.

One Hit Wonders: Ron Faircloth, Sean Gannon

Ron Faircloth and Sean Gannon both made sizeable impressions in their lone UFC bouts, Faircloth because of his low blow that ended Alessio Sakara's night, and Gannon because of his unique backstory. Gannon, a Boston police officer, came to the attention of the world because of an underground video that showed him being the first person to defeat a young man nicknamed "Kimbo Slice". That attention got him noticed by the UFC, and a contract was signed. After his lone UFC loss, Gannon never fought again.

The Ultimate Fighter 2 Finale

05 Nov. 2005

Hard Rock Hotel and Casino, Las Vegas, NV

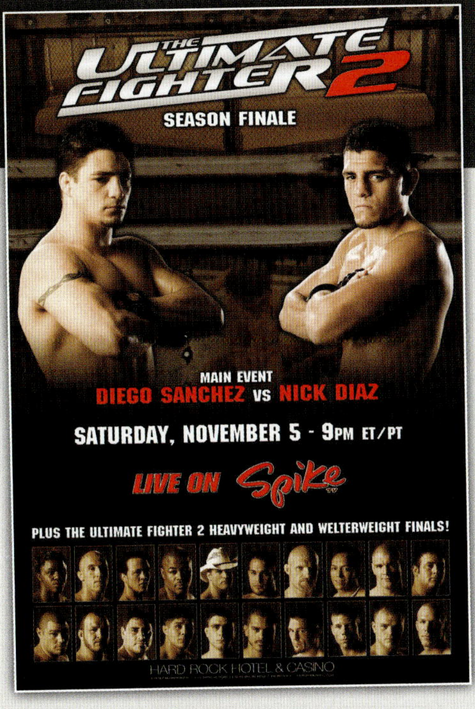

Debuts: Rashad Evans, Brad Imes, Joe Stevenson, Luke Cummo, Kit Cope, Josh Burkman, Sam Morgan, Melvin Guillard, Marcus Davis, Keith Jardine, Kerry Schall

Fighters			Division	Method	Time	Round
Main Card						
Diego Sanchez	def.	Nick Diaz	Welterweight	Unanimous Decision	—	3
Rashad Evans	def.	Brad Imes	Heavyweight	Split Decision	—	3
Joe Stevenson	def.	Luke Cummo	Welterweight	Unanimous Decision	—	3
Kenny Florian	def.	Kit Cope	Welterweight	Submission - Rear Naked Choke	0:37	2
Preliminary Card						
Josh Burkman	def.	Sammy Morgan	Welterweight	Knockout	0:21	1
Melvin Guillard	def.	Marcus Davis	Welterweight	Technical Knockout - Cuts	2:55	2
Keith Jardine	def.	Kerry Schall	Heavyweight	Technical Knockout	3:28	2

Rashad Evans and Joe Stevenson came into *The Ultimate Fighter 2* reality series from vastly different places in terms of expectations. At the end of the finale at the Hard Rock Hotel and Casino, the underdog and the favorite finally had something in common: They were ultimate fighters.

In the heavyweight finale, Evans outpointed Brad Imes via split decision in a classic slugfest, and Stevenson also won via points, unanimously outscoring Luke Cummo to earn this season's welterweight crown. Both Evans and Stevenson took home six-figure UFC contracts with their victories.

When the 5' 11", 224-pound Evans squared off against the 6' 7", 250-pound Imes, many expected the height and weight disparity between the two to be too high of a mountain to climb for the former Michigan State wrestler. Early on, things went according to form, with Evans' faster hands getting nullified by Imes' Thai clinch and knees.

Fight of the Night (unofficial): Evans vs. Imes

By late in the first round, Evans started finding a home for his left hooks, while just missing with a right hand finisher. It was an omen of things to come.

In the second, Imes again used his reach advantage to spear Evans from long range, and as fatigue started to become an issue for both men, the real fight began, with both athletes taking turns rocking each other with solid blows to the head. "He caught me with a couple of good shots, but I kept my feet moving, kept going, and I worked through it," said Evans.

The third round had the packed house on its feet, but Imes wasn't so lucky when Evans finally connected with the left-hook, right-hand combo, sending the Iowa resident crashing to the canvas. Evans pounced but was unable to finish.

"I thought I could have been more patient when I had him stunned," admitted Evans, who once standing again, left it all in the Octagon, as did Imes. So, needless to say, when the scores for Evans—29-28 (twice) and 28-29—were announced, the Lansing resident may have had his hand raised, but there were truly no losers between the two heavyweights.

Joe Stevenson entered his welterweight finale against Luke Cummo with a serious training injury that left his clavicle torn from his sternum. But he fought on…and he won.

"Joe pushed that out of his mind, went out there injured, and he did it," said Stevenson's coach Marc Laimon of the injury, which had occurred two weeks prior. Not only did Stevenson do it, but he did it in style, using his extensive ground game to pull ahead of Cummo in another bout that got the fans and fighters in attendance on their feet.

"That was Stephan Bonnar and Forrest Griffin, only on the ground," said UFC President Dana White, referring to the season one finale that captivated the mixed martial arts world.

In the card's main event, Diego Sanchez proved that he was a legitimate contender to the welterweight crown held by Matt Hughes as he scored a shutout three-round decision over heated rival Nick Diaz.

Submission of the Night (unofficial): Florian vs. Cope

Kenny Florian scored perhaps the most impressive victory of his mixed martial arts career, submitting Muay Thai champion Kit Cope with a rear naked choke at 37 seconds of the second round. It was actually the second submission of the night for Florian, who forced Cope to tap out to an armbar just as the horn ending the round sounded.

Knockout of the Night (unofficial): Burkman vs. Morgan

Welterweight Josh Burkman scored a frightening 21-second knockout of Sam Morgan, sending him to the canvas with a takedown that put the Minnesotan out almost immediately. A follow-up barrage then forced the stoppage, giving Burkman the win.

In another welterweight matchup, Melvin Guillard showed the explosive style that got him invited to *The Ultimate Fighter* series, thrashing a game Marcus Davis at 2:55 of the second round.

In the opener, Keith Jardine scored an impressive stoppage of Kerry Schall, using brutally effective leg kicks to send "The Meat Truck" to defeat in the second round.

One Hit Wonders: Kit Cope, Kerry Schall

UFC 56 *Full Force*

19 Nov. 2005

MGM Grand Garden Arena, Las Vegas, NV

Debuts: Nick Thompson, Keith Wisniewski, Ansar Chalangov, Jeff Newton, Gabriel Gonzaga

Fighters			Division	Method	Time	Round
Main Card						
Rich Franklin	def.	Nate Quarry	Middleweight	Knockout	2:32	1
Matt Hughes	def.	Joe Riggs	Catchweight	Submission - Kimura	3:28	1
Gabriel Gonzaga	def.	Kevin Jordan	Heavyweight	Knockout	4:37	3
Georges St-Pierre	def	Sean Sherk	Welterweight	Technical Knockout	2:51	2
Jeremy Horn	def	Trevor Prangley	Middleweight	Unanimous Decision	—	3
Preliminary Card						
Sam Hoger	def.	Jeff Newton	Light Heavyweight	Submission - Rear Naked Choke	2:00	2
Thiago Alves	def.	Ansar Chalangov	Welterweight	Technical Knockout	2:22	1
Nick Thompson	def.	Keith Wisniewski	Welterweight	Unanimous Decision	—	3

With extreme prejudice, UFC middleweight champion Rich Franklin and his welterweight counterpart Matt Hughes both dispatched of their opponents in the first round at the MGM Grand Garden Arena, effectively stating their case as two of mixed martial arts' best, pound for pound.

Fight of the Night (unofficial): Franklin vs. Quarry

In the UFC 56 main event, Franklin defended his title for the first time with a single-round knockout of Nate Quarry, and in the non-title co-feature, welterweight king Matt Hughes submitted Joe Riggs in the opening stanza.

Franklin-Quarry ended the night on a high note, as both fighters took the opportunity to test their substantial standup games.

After a respectful handshake at the center of the Octagon, Franklin and Quarry got down to business. Both jabbed and circled, with the first serious action coming when Quarry missed a high kick and fell to the mat. He quickly recovered and rose to his feet, opting to stand with the champ.

Bad move. Franklin stalked and picked his shots, hurting Quarry 1:30 in with a straight right to the jaw. Seconds later a right left hurt "Rock" even worse, breaking his nose as he fell to the canvas.

Knockout of the Night (unofficial): Franklin vs. Quarry

Quarry gamely rose and stood in the pocket, but he was on rubbery legs, and when Franklin stepped in with a beautiful straight left on the point of the chin, Quarry was knocked out before he hit the floor, prompting an immediate stoppage by referee John McCarthy at the 2:32 mark of the opening stanza.

Matt Hughes didn't need five rounds to beat Joe Riggs in the UFC 56 co-feature; he didn't even need three. It only took the UFC welterweight champion 3:28 to finish off Joe Riggs in their non-title bout, rendered as such after "Diesel" was unable to make weight for his first title challenge.

"That's my bread and butter," said Hughes of the kimura lock that forced Riggs to tap out.

Submission of the Night (unofficial): Hughes vs. Riggs

Rising star Georges St-Pierre continued his amazing run at 170 pounds, scoring a decisive second-round stoppage of former title challenger Sean Sherk in a highly-anticipated contest.

From the opening bell the fight was all St-Pierre, as the explosive Canadian controlled not only the standup game, as expected, but the ground action as well, avoiding Sherk's takedown attempts and scoring impressive takedowns of his own. Once "Rush" had Sherk on the ground, it was bombs away, with the end coming at 2:51 of the second round.

In the Pay-Per-View opener, Jeremy Horn dropped from light heavyweight to middleweight and had a tough battle in his 185-pound return, eking out an unpopular three-round unanimous decision over tough Trevor Prangley. All three judges scored it 29-28 for Horn.

The UFC 56 swing bout saw Gabriel Gonzaga score a final-minute TKO of Kevin Jordan in a heavyweight match that was repeatedly booed for lack of action.

"The Karate Kid" Jeff Newton showed that he had a bit of a ground game in his light heavyweight preliminary bout with Sam Hoger, but Hoger's superior skills on the mat shone through as he escaped some scary moments in the opening round to finish off Newton with a rear naked choke at 2:00 of round two.

Brazil's Thiago Alves evened his UFC record at 1-1 as he scored a first-round stoppage of Russia's Ansar Chalangov in a welterweight bout.

"It was the best win of my career," said Alves. "I knew it was going to be a hard fight, but I knew I was going to win."

In the welterweight opener, Nick Thompson pounded out a three-round unanimous decision over Keith Wisniewski. Scores were 30-27 across the board in a fight that was more competitive than the scores would indicate. In the end though, Thompson's faster hands and better ground work proved to be too much for the gutsy Wisniewski.

One Hit Wonders: Keith Wisniewski, Jeff Newton

Ultimate Fight Night 3

16
Jan.
2006

Hard Rock Hotel and Casino, Las Vegas, NV

Debuts: Assuerio Silva, Jason Von Flue

Fighters			Division	Method	Time	Round
Main Card						
Tim Sylvia	def.	Assuerio Silva	Heavyweight	Unanimous Decision	—	3
Stephan Bonnar	def.	James Irvin	Light Heavyweight	Submission	4:30	1
Chris Leben	def.	Jorge Rivera	Middleweight	Technical Knockout	1:44	1
Josh Burkman	def.	Drew Fickett	Welterweight	Submission - Guillotine Choke	1:07	1
Preliminary Card						
Josh Neer	def.	Melvin Guillard	Welterweight	Submission - Triangle Choke	4:20	1
Duane Ludwig	def.	Jonathan Goulet	Welterweight	Technical Knockout	0:11	1
Spencer Fisher	def.	Aaron Riley	Welterweight	Technical Knockout - Injury	5:00	1
Jason Von Flue	def.	Alex Karalexis	Welterweight	Submission	1:17	3

Tim Sylvia moved one step closer to a rematch with UFC heavyweight champion Andrei Arlovski. He won a three-round unanimous decision victory over Brazil's Assuerio Silva in the main event of Ultimate Fight Night at the Hard Rock Hotel.

"What a war," said Sylvia, who scored his third straight win since losing to Arlovski via decision in February of 2005. "That guy is tough."

Scores were 30-27 twice and 29-28 for Sylvia, who held off the onrushing Silva and controlled the action from a standing position while fighting a disciplined fight from bell to bell, with only some shaky moments in the second and third rounds keeping it from being a perfect evening for "The Maine-iac."

"I had him hurt a couple of times but I couldn't capitalize," said Sylvia.

Utilizing a wide variety of standup skills and improved kicking, and good work on the inside as well as long range, Sylvia kept Silva at bay in the first, as the Brazilian looked for one of two things—the takedown or a looping overhand right. In round two, Silva finally struck with the right hand, opening a small cut over Sylvia's left eye and jarring him briefly. Sylvia quickly recovered and outworked his foe for much of the round.

The third round saw Silva push the action, knowing that his only chance to get Sylvia in trouble was to get him to the mat. Sylvia avoided any serious difficulties, though, with some careful defense as well as a quick grab of the Octagon fence—an illegal move that drew a warning from referee John McCarthy—and rode out the victory to its conclusion.

"I've earned the right to get a title shot," said Sylvia. "I'm gonna train harder and get my belt back."

In the co-feature, light heavyweight Stephan Bonnar showed that he had a ground game to go with his striking skills as he submitted noted striker James Irvin at 4:30 of the first round.

Knockout of the Night (unofficial): Leben vs. Rivera

Welterweight prospect Josh Burkman left his "American-Who-Hit-U" fighting style in the dressing room and instead showed his versatility, submitting jiu-jitsu ace Drew Fickett in just over a minute.

Chris Leben, star of the first season of *The Ultimate Fighter* series, truly arrived on the world middleweight scene with an impressive first-round stoppage of seasoned vet Jorge Rivera.

Josh Neer survived one of the nastiest cut eyes ever in the fight game to submit Melvin Guillard at 4:20 of the first round of their welterweight bout.

Fight of the Night (unofficial): Neer vs. Guillard

"I was real worried," said Neer of his cut right eye, "but you keep going."

Absorbing a mix of offensive attacks from the explosive Guillard, Neer was cut by an elbow to the head but was still willing to go on. The ringside physician agreed, but it was probable that the fight was going to get halted between rounds if Neer didn't get something accomplished fast. He did, locking in a guillotine choke after Guillard strangely decided to take his foe to the mat. Guillard escaped, but a tapout followed soon after when Neer landed a triangle choke, and Neer evened his UFC record at 1-1 with a nice show of grace under pressure.

Big things were expected from Canadian welterweight standout Jonathan Goulet, but unfortunately "The Road Warrior" didn't get to display his wares for the packed house as a single right hand from Muay Thai standout Duane "Bang" Ludwig—the first punch of the fight—ended his night in just 11 seconds, what was then the fastest KO in UFC history.

Submission of the Night (unofficial): Von Flue vs. Karalexis

The predicted fight of the night between welterweights Spencer Fisher and Aaron Riley didn't exactly play out that way, but that was due more to a broken jaw suffered by Riley that forced a halt to the bout after the first round.

In the opener, Jason Von Flue made his UFC debut a successful one, submitting Alex Karalexis in the third and final round of their welterweight bout.

THE UFC CHAMPIONSHIP BELT

Some athletes fight for glory, some do it for the paycheck and still others do it just to quench their thirst for competition. But whatever reason they choose to fight for, when you've reached the pinnacle of your profession and have earned the right to be called champion of the world, it's nice to get a memento of that occasion that sets you apart from your peers. Nothing signifies being at the top of your game more than a world championship belt.

Photography by: Susumu Nagao

In the Ultimate Fighting Championship, the precious and coveted gold belt is the one accessory every fighter wants to own, but in the early days of the organization, tournament winners like Mark Kerr were awarded medals for their efforts.

It wasn't until UFC 5 that it was announced that the winner of the Superfight championship bout between Gracie and Ken Shamrock would receive a championship belt. But when the bout was ruled a draw, the belt stayed in its case. Tournament champions would also receive belts until UFC 12, when medals were reinstituted for most tourney winners.

At UFC 12 in 1997, Mark Coleman became the first UFC heavyweight champion, and from that event through to UFC 48, champions would receive a new title belt for each successful defense.

By the time Zuffa took over, the belts began a slow redesign phase to eventually resemble the championship belts worn today by the UFC's best of the best. It's been a long journey to get here, but whether you received a belt in 1997 or 2011, you can rest assured that you earned it and that it's something no one can ever take away.

UFC 57 *Liddell vs. Couture 3*

04 Feb. 2006

Mandalay Bay Events Center, Las Vegas, NV

Debuts: Gilbert Aldana, Mike Whitehead

Fighters			Division	Method	Time	Round
Main Card						
Chuck Liddell	def.	Randy Couture	Light Heavyweight	Knockout	1:28	2
Brandon Vera	def.	Justin Eilers	Heavyweight	Knockout	1:22	1
Marcio Cruz	def.	Frank Mir	Heavyweight	Technical Knockout	4:10	1
Renato Sobral	def	Mike Van Arsdale	Light Heavyweight	Submission – Rear Naked Choke	2:19	1
Joe Riggs	def	Nick Diaz	Welterweight	Unanimous Decision	—	3
Preliminary Card						
Alessio Sakara	def.	Elvis Sinosic	Light Heavyweight	Unanimous Decision	—	3
Paul Buentello	def.	Gilbert Aldana	Heavyweight bout	Technical Knockout	2:27	2
Jeff Monson	def.	Branden Lee Hinkle	Heavyweight bout	Submission – North-South Choke	4:35	1
Keith Jardine	def.	Mike Whitehead	Light Heavyweight	Unanimous Decision	—	3

At UFC 57, Chuck Liddell won the battle and the war. Before a sold-out Mandalay Bay Events Center, "The Iceman" retained his UFC light heavyweight crown with a second-round TKO of Randy Couture, giving him the final 2-1 edge in the trilogy between the light heavyweight greats. After the bout, Couture, 42, the only fighter in UFC history to win the heavyweight and light heavyweight titles, announced his retirement. He would return at UFC 68 a year later.

Fight of the Night (unofficial): Liddell vs. Couture

As for Liddell-Couture 3, the two future Hall of Famers circled each other warily early on, looking for openings as the crowd alternately cheered for their favorite fighter. Couture stalked behind a high guard, and his sporadic strikes seemed to take Liddell out of his rhythm. Liddell quickly recovered though, rocking Couture briefly with a right to the head. As Liddell moved in for the kill, Couture, his nose now bloodied, was able to recover and take the champion to the mat for the remainder of the round.

Knockout of the Night (unofficial): Liddell vs. Couture

Couture refused to deviate from his fight plan in the second round, as he followed Liddell around the Octagon while throwing in the occasional counter. Couture's luck ran out, and as he shot in with a left hand, Liddell landed the same short right hand that ended the pair's second fight, and Couture again crashed limply to the mat. Referee John McCarthy called a stop to the bout at 1:28 of the second stanza.

Former UFC heavyweight champion Frank Mir didn't get the welcome back he expected after a 20-month absence due to injury, getting stopped in the first round by Brazil's Marcio "Pe de Pano" Cruz in a stunning upset.

Mir immediately started throwing punches to start the fight, with Cruz looking for the takedown. By the one-minute mark, the two jiu-jitsu standouts were on the mat, with Cruz looking for a quick sub. It was the Brazilian's elbow that did the most damage though, as he opened a nasty cut over Mir's left eye that forced a look from the ringside physician. After the bout was allowed to continue, Cruz effectively worked the cut with both hands and his forearms. As Mir's face got covered in crimson, the crowd started cheering for the Las Vegan to come back, but it was not to be, as the constant punishment convinced referee Herb Dean to make the right decision and call the bout at the 4:10 mark.

Brazil's Renato "Babalu" Sobral cemented his position as the number-one challenger for the UFC light heavyweight belt as he submitted veteran Mike Van Arsdale in the first round of a scheduled three-round contest.

Joe Riggs showed off his impressive boxing skills in the Pay-Per-View opener, keeping himself in the welterweight title picture with a close unanimous decision over Nick Diaz in an entertaining three-round scrap. Scores for Arizona's Riggs were 29-28 twice and 30-27. Both he and Diaz were coming off defeats—Riggs to UFC welterweight champ Matt Hughes, Diaz to rising star Diego Sanchez.

A heavyweight swing bout between rising star Brandon Vera and Justin Eilers ended quickly and explosively, as "The Truth" dispatched of Eilers in 1:22 of round one.

In a light heavyweight bout, Elvis Sinosic put on a courageous performance against heavy-handed Alessio Sakara, but the Italian's superior striking and ground and pound were too much for him as he lost a lopsided unanimous decision. Scores for Sakara were 29-26 twice, and 29-25.

Heavyweights Paul Buentello and Gilbert Aldana kept the fans on their feet in their heavyweight bout, swinging for the fences with each shot until Buentello outlasted "El Peligroso", stopping him in the second round.

Submission of the Night (unofficial): Monson vs. Hinkle

Jeff Monson made a successful return to the Octagon in a heavyweight prelim bout, defeating Branden Lee Hinkle with a submission via North-South choke in the first round.

In the opener, Keith Jardine pounded out a three-round unanimous decision over Mike Whitehead. Scores were 29-28 across the board.

One Hit Wonder: Mike Whitehead

UFC 58 *USA vs. Canada*

04 Mar. 2006

Mandalay Bay Events Center, Las Vegas, NV

Debuts: Steve Vigneault, Mark Hominick, Rob MacDonald, Jason Lambert, Tom Murphy

Fighters			Division	Method	Time	Round
Main Card						
Rich Franklin	def.	David Loiseau	Middleweight	Unanimous Decision	—	5
Georges St-Pierre	def.	BJ Penn	Welterweight	Split Decision	—	3
Mike Swick	def.	Steve Vigneault	Middleweight	Submission - Guillotine Choke	2:09	1
Nate Marquardt	def.	Joe Doerksen	Middleweight	Unanimous Decision	—	3
Mark Hominick	def.	Yves Edwards	Lightweight	Submission - Triangle Armbar	1:52	2
Preliminary Card						
Sam Stout	def.	Spencer Fisher	Lightweight	Split Decision	—	3
Jason Lambert	def.	Rob MacDonald	Light Heavyweight	Submission - Kimura	1:54	1
Tom Murphy	def.	Icho Larenas	Heavyweight	Technical Knockout	1:59	3

Fight of the Night (unofficial): Franklin vs. Loiseau

UFC 58 was supposed to be Rich Franklin's toughest test yet, but after a five-round battering of courageous challenger David Loiseau at the Mandalay Bay Events Center, the UFC middleweight champion once again posted himself high above the rest of his division.

The unanimous five-round decision read 50-42 twice and 50-43 for Franklin, who defended his crown for the second time and did it with a broken left hand and broken foot suffered in the second round. He also had to rise from a third-round knockdown to turn back Canada's Loiseau.

Georges St-Pierre was the spitting image of a 9-to-5 businessman when he entered the UFC Octagon at 5:08pm local time to warm up in a suit, tie and no shoes. Once he returned to fight former UFC welterweight champion BJ Penn, he was all fighter, as he survived a bloody pounding in the first round to win the next two on two of the three judges' cards and earn a split decision in the highly-anticipated bout that lived up to the hype.

Scores were 29-28 twice and 28-29 for St-Pierre, who earned a rematch against current UFC welterweight king Matt Hughes with the win. Penn, who entered the bout wearing the championship belt he never lost in the Octagon, was disappointed with the verdict.

Fight of the Night (unofficial): St-Pierre vs. Penn

"I just feel that I probably did more damage," said Penn, making his first UFC appearance in two years after a contract dispute and lawsuit kept him out of the Octagon. "But he fought well."

Middleweight Mike Swick was forced past the 30-second mark for the first time in the UFC but he still didn't see round two, as he submitted Quebec's Steve Vigneault in the opening stanza of their swing bout.

In another middleweight battle, Wyoming native Nate Marquardt outlasted Manitoba's Joe Doerksen in a quality bout between two of the most seasoned veterans in the sport. All three judges scored the bout 30-27 in a bout that was a lot closer than the judges' scores would indicate.

Mark Hominick had plenty on his mind entering his UFC debut against one of MMA's pound-for-pound best, Yves Edwards. With his father's fight against cancer inspiring him, the Ontario lightweight upset the heavily favored Texan, submitting him in the second round of a scheduled three-rounder.

Submission of the Night (unofficial): Hominick vs. Edwards

In the first lightweight bout in the UFC since 2004, Sam Stout showed his "Hands of Stone" as he pounded out a close three-round split decision over Spencer Fisher in a bout that showed why the lightweight division had the most exciting fighters in mixed martial arts. Scores were 29-28 twice, and 28-29 for Stout, who was scheduled to fight Kenny Florian until a back injury forced Florian out and brought Fisher in on three days notice.

The wait to get to the UFC was a long one, but for Jason "The Punisher" Lambert it was worth it, as he submitted *The Ultimate Fighter*'s Rob MacDonald in less than two minutes in a light heavyweight bout.

In the heavyweight opener, Tom Murphy, a cast member of season two of *The Ultimate Fighter* reality show, got his first UFC victory with a dominating third-round stoppage of late replacement Icho Larenas, who took the fight on one day's notice after original opponent Christophe Midoux was forced out with a hernia.

One Hit Wonders: Steve Vigneault, Tom Murphy, Icho Larenas

Usually when a fighter is one and done in the UFC, he leaves with a loss. In the case of Tom Murphy, a Division III All-American wrestler and cast member on season two of *The Ultimate Fighter*, he left after a win, and a TKO victory at that. Following his success at UFC 58, Murphy took two years off from the game before coming back to win a single fight a year in 2008, 2009, and 2010.

Ultimate Fight Night 4

06 April 2006

Hard Rock Hotel and Casino, Las Vegas, NV

Debuts: Dan Christison, Luigi Fioravanti

Fighters			Division	Method	Time	Round
Main Card						
Stephan Bonnar	def.	Keith Jardine	Light Heavyweight	Unanimous Decision	—	3
Rashad Evans	def.	Sam Hoger	Light Heavyweight	Split Decision	—	3
Josh Neer	def.	Joe Stevenson	Welterweight	Unanimous Decision	—	3
Chris Leben	def.	Luigi Fioravanti	Middleweight	Unanimous Decision	—	3
Preliminary Card						
Luke Cummo	def.	Jason Von Flue	Welterweight	Unanimous Decision	—	3
Jon Fitch	def.	Josh Burkman	Welterweight	Submission - Rear Naked Choke	4:57	2
Dan Christison	def.	Brad Imes	Heavyweight	Submission - Armbar	3:37	3
Josh Koscheck	def.	Ansar Chalangov	Welterweight	Submission - Rear Naked Choke	3:29	1
Chael Sonnen	def.	Trevor Prangley	Middleweight	Unanimous Decision	—	3

In the main event of the Ultimate Fight Night card at the Hard Rock Hotel and Casino, light heavyweight Stephan Bonnar took home an unpopular three-round decision from season two alumnus Keith Jardine. The verdict was met with boos and jeers from the packed house.

Scores were 29-28 across the board for Chicago's Bonnar, who didn't see any cause for the negative reaction.

From the opening bell, both fighters worked their Muay Thai techniques efficiently, with Jardine holding a decided edge in the first round with crisper strikes and leg kicks that landed with audible thuds. Bonnar bounced back in the second, dropping his foe with a flush counterpunch and almost securing a rear naked choke before "The Dean of Mean" was able to escape. In round three, one of the better rounds of the year, both fighters left it all in the ring as each tried to land the homerun punch or kick. A solid left hook by Bonnar put Jardine down a second time, but he quickly recovered, and by the end of the round he was landing with punches and kicks on Bonnar, who was cut over both eyes when the bell sounded.

"I thought I earned the victory," said Jardine. "I guess the judges don't give too much credit to leg kicks."

TUF2 heavyweight winner Rashad Evans got a rude welcome to light heavyweight. Evans had all he could handle before winning a hard-fought split decision to a very game Sam Hoger.

Evans' *TUF2* counterpart at welterweight, Joe Stevenson, wasn't as fortunate when it came to the final result, as Josh Neer pulled off an upset three-round decision over the season two winner with a gritty display of striking, wrestling, and submission defense.

Fight of the Night (unofficial): Neer vs. Stevenson

"Sometimes you eat the bear," said Stevenson, "and sometimes the bear eats you."

The fast-paced three-rounder kept fight fans enthralled from start to finish, with Neer opening strong behind his strikes and Stevenson responding with myriad submission attempts. At one point in the first, Stevenson locked in a kneebar, and Neer fought off the pain and eventually escaped, to the amazement of many in attendance.

Though Stevenson failed on that attempt, he kept trying to tap Neer out throughout the fight. Iowa's Neer wouldn't play along though, and his ground and pound on the mat and crisper striking while standing was paying dividends on the judges' scorecards in rounds two and three. Soon, Stevenson's dyed blonde hair turned crimson due to cuts opened up by "The Dentist", and the fight appeared to be slipping away.

Stevenson didn't go down without a fight, as he rebounded from a strong Neer third round to flurry with both hands on the ground in the final minute, much to the delight of the crowd. It wasn't enough though, as Neer took the decision via scores of 29-28 on all three judges' cards.

In the main card opener, middleweight contender Chris Leben remained unbeaten in the UFC with a workmanlike three-round decision over Florida's previously unbeaten Luigi Fioravanti.

Long Island, New York's Luke Cummo worked his Muay Thai effectively throughout his three-round welterweight bout against Jason Von Flue and easily walked away with the shutout unanimous decision in a battle between *TUF2* alums.

Another battle between welterweight up-and-comers saw American Kickboxing Academy standout Jon Fitch put a momentary halt to the meteoric rise of Josh Burkman via a second-round submission.

There was little in the way of ground fighting when heavyweights Dan Christison and Brad Imes squared off, but no one in the Hard Rock complained as the two big men went for broke in a bloody and exciting war won by late replacement Christison via third-round submission.

Submission of the Night (unofficial): Koscheck vs. Chalangov

TUF1 alumnus Josh Koscheck made short work of Ansar Chalangov, winning via submission at 3:29 of the opening round.

In the opener, Chael Sonnen rebounded from his loss to Renato Sobral with a three-round unanimous decision win over AKA's Trevor Prangley in a middleweight bout.

UFC 59 *Reality Check*

15 April 2006

Arrowhead Pond, Anaheim, CA

Debuts: Justin Levens, Scott Smith, Derrick Noble

Fighters			Division	Method	Time	Round
Main Card						
Tim Sylvia	def.	Andrei Arlovski	Heavyweight	Technical Knockout	2:43	1
Tito Ortiz	def.	Forrest Griffin	Light Heavyweight	Split Decision	—	3
Sean Sherk	def.	Nick Diaz	Welterweight	Unanimous Decision	—	3
Evan Tanner	def.	Justin Levens	Middleweight	Submission - Triangle Choke	3:11	1
Jeff Monson	def.	Marcio Cruz	Heavyweight	Split Decision	—	3
Preliminary Card						
Karo Parisyan	def.	Nick Thompson	Welterweight	Submission - Strikes	4:44	1
David Terrell	def.	Scott Smith	Middleweight	Submission - Rear Naked Choke	3:08	1
Jason Lambert	def.	Terry Martin	Light Heavyweight	Technical Knockout	2:37	2
Thiago Alves	def.	Derrick Noble	Welterweight	Technical Knockout	2:54	1

In MMA, fortunes can change in a split second. Just ask Tim Sylvia and Andrei Arlovski. Within moments of rocking and dropping Sylvia with a big right hand, the champion soon found himself without a belt. Sylvia quickly rebounded and delivered a right to the jaw to Arlovski that allowed the Maine native to regain the championship belt he had sought for over two years.

Knockout of the Night (unofficial): Sylvia vs. Arlovski

The bout, which was held before a sold-out crowd of over 17,000 who witnessed the UFC's first show ever in California, was a rematch of a February 2005 bout won by Arlovski in the first round.

In the UFC 59 co-feature, the legend of Forrest Griffin grew. Despite dropping a split decision to former UFC light heavyweight champion Tito Ortiz, *The Ultimate Fighter 1* winner won over a partisan crowd and gained even more fans with a courageous performance and comeback that marked him as truly one of the best 205-pounders in the game.

It was Ortiz' night on the scorecards, though, as "The Huntington Beach Bad Boy" earned the close verdict via scores of 30-27, 28-29, and 29-27, as a huge first round and a few big moments in the final frame proved to be the difference.

Oddly enough, this instant classic was almost over in the first round. With the crowd erupting as John McCarthy waved the fighters into action, both fighters began trading, with Ortiz quickly securing a takedown and then opening up on Griffin, who had no answers for Ortiz' brutal ground and pound. Finally, with a little over a minute to go, Griffin escaped and opened up with both hands, briefly jarring Ortiz, who fired back and put his foe on the mat again as he pounded his way through the remainder of the round.

Fight of the Night: Ortiz vs. Griffin

Ortiz' jab was on target to begin round two, with Griffin's punches landing, but lacking pop. Later in the frame, Griffin stuffed some Ortiz takedown attempts and seemed to have regained his confidence as he tagged Ortiz with a series of roundhouse punches that may not have been hurting his foe, but they were scoring points, and suddenly it was a brand new fight entering the final round.

Looking to regain control, Ortiz tried the takedown twice more early in the third, only to be rebuffed each time. Finally, with under two minutes to go, Ortiz got his first takedown since the first round. This time it was Griffin doing much of the work from the bottom, though, and when the Georgian stood up and started trading with Ortiz it was a moment fight fans wouldn't forget.

Sean Sherk made his last fight at 170 pounds a winning one, as he outpointed Nick Diaz unanimously over three rounds in a bout that was much closer than the three scores of 30-27 would indicate.

Former UFC middleweight champion Evan Tanner bounced back impressively from consecutive losses to Rich Franklin and David Loiseau, submitting 185-pound prospect Justin Levens in the opening round.

Submission of the Night (unofficial): Tanner vs. Levens

Jeff Monson continued his rise up the heavyweight ranks with a split decision win over Marcio Cruz.

Karo Parisyan may have missed his first punch of the night, but he was rarely off the mark for the rest of the four minutes and forty-four seconds he pounded on Nick Thompson as he recorded a first-round submission due to strikes victory.

David Terrell made his return to the Octagon for the first time in over a year a successful one as he submitted Scott Smith with a rear naked choke in the first round of their middleweight bout.

Jason Lambert improved to 2-0 in the UFC with a second-round TKO win over Terry Martin.

In the welterweight opener, Thiago Alves erased the memory of a 2003 submission loss to Derrick Noble by stopping his foe with a barrage of strikes in the first round of a scheduled three.

One Hit Wonder: Derrick Noble

UFC 60 *Hughes vs. Gracie*

27 May 2006

STAPLES Center, Los Angeles, CA

Debuts: Rick Davis, Dean Lister, Matt Wiman

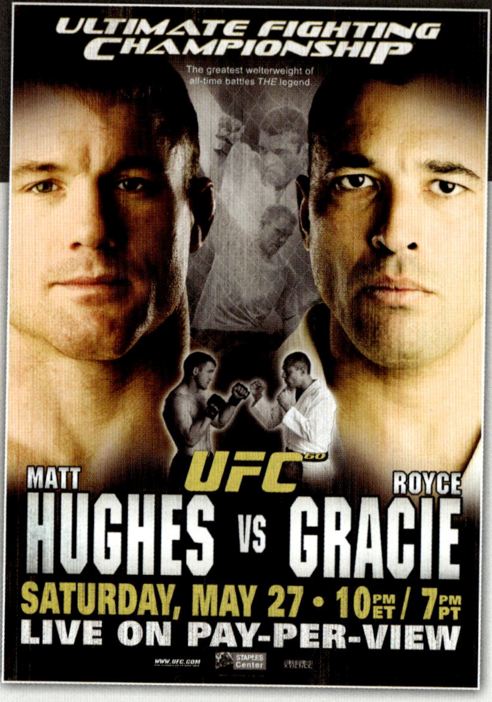

Fighters			Division	Method	Time	Round
Main Card						
Matt Hughes	def.	Royce Gracie	Catchweight	Technical Knockout	4:39	1
Diego Sanchez	def.	John Alessio	Welterweight	Unanimous Decision	—	3
Brandon Vera	def.	Assuerio Silva	Heavyweight	Submission - Guillotine Choke	2:39	1
Dean Lister	def.	Alessio Sakara	Light Heavyweight	Submission - Triangle Choke	2:20	1
Mike Swick	def.	Joe Riggs	Middleweight	Submission - Guillotine Choke	2:19	1
Preliminary Card						
Jeremy Horn	def.	Chael Sonnen	Middleweight	Submission - Armbar	1:13	2
Spencer Fisher	def.	Matt Wiman	Lightweight	Knockout	1:43	2
Gabriel Gonzaga	def.	Fabiano Scherner	Heavyweight	Technical Knockout	0:24	2
Melvin Guillard	def.	Rick Davis	Lightweight	Knockout	1:37	1

The talk before the UFC 60 main event between Matt Hughes and Royce Gracie was that the sport of mixed martial arts had passed the Brazilian legend by and that he couldn't compete with the new breed of mixed martial artist. Yet while Hughes was dominant in a first-round stoppage victory before a packed house at STAPLES Center, there is no doubting the toughness of Gracie, who not only made his return to the Octagon for the first time in over 10 years, but did it against the premier welterweight in the game.

The night truly belonged to Hughes, who may not have had his UFC welterweight crown on the line, but who fought as if it was his last bout as he dominated from start to finish against the jiu-jitsu ace from Rio de Janeiro.

Gracie opened the fight with a couple of range-finding kicks. Hughes answered with an overhand left that briefly jarred the Brazilian. Gracie quickly regained his bearings though and kept kicking at Hughes, who drove him into the fence. With 3:45 left in the round, the fight went to the mat, with the crowd erupting as Gracie looked for a submission. Hughes kept his cool though and worked his strikes from the top position, eventually locking up Gracie's left arm. After some tense moments, Gracie escaped, but soon Hughes got his back and opened up with elbows and strikes. Seconds later, after a series of unanswered blows to the head, referee John McCarthy had no choice but to halt the bout at 4:39 of the frame.

And then the boos turned to cheers for Hughes, and rightfully so.

World-class grappler Dean Lister made his long-awaited UFC debut a successful one as he stopped the run of hard-hitting Alessio Sakara with a first-round submission victory.

Diego Sanchez survived the toughest moments of his UFC career en route to an unpopular three-round unanimous decision over Canadian vet John Alessio, who fought a disciplined fight from start to finish but wasn't rewarded by the ringside judges, who saw it for the "Nightmare" by scores of 30-27, and 29-28 twice.

Maybe Brandon Vera was telling the truth all along. In a highly anticipated heavyweight bout, knockout artist Vera—who claimed to be more comfortable on the mat than standing—showed off his submission game in the UFC for the first time, forcing Brazil's Assuerio Silva to tap out in the first round of a scheduled three.

Rising middleweight contender Mike Swick once again lived up to his nickname of "Quick" as he submitted perennial contender Joe Riggs in the first round, running his unbeaten streak of first-round endings to four.

Submission of the Night (unofficial): Swick vs. Riggs

It may be safe to say that Jeremy Horn has Chael Sonnen's number as the veteran beat Sonnen for the third time in their middleweight bout, forcing a submission in the second round of their three-rounder.

Spencer "The King" Fisher continued his march up the lightweight ranks with a second-round knockout of Matt Wiman in an entertaining bout that saw the late replacement from Florida almost pull off the upset with a first-round guillotine choke. In the end though, Fisher's power and accuracy proved to be the difference.

Fight of the Night (unofficial): Fisher vs. Wiman

Heavyweight Gabriel Gonzaga improved to 2-0 in the UFC with a solid effort in stopping fellow Brazilian Fabiano Scherner in the second round.

In the opener, Melvin "The Young Assassin" Guillard made a successful drop to the 155-pound lightweight class, knocking out UFC debutant Rick Davis with a single right hand at 1:37 of the opening round.

Knockout of the Night (unofficial): Guillard vs. Davis

One Hit Wonder: Rick Davis

Schoolteacher Rick Davis raced out to a 3-0-1 record in his MMA career, though perhaps "raced" isn't the right word since those four fights were spread out from 2002 to 2004. In fact, when he took on Guillard at UFC 60, he hadn't fought in nearly two years, making the end result almost a foregone conclusion. Davis never fought again after UFC 60.

The Ultimate Fighter 3 Finale

24 June 2006

Hard Rock Hotel and Casino, Las Vegas, NV

Debuts: Michael Bisping, Josh Haynes, Kendall Grove, Ed Herman, Wilson Gouveia, Rory Singer, Ross Pointon, Kalib Starnes, Danny Abbadi, Solomon Hutcherson, Matt Hamill, Jesse Forbes, Wes Combs, Mike Nickels

Fighters			Division	Method	Time	Round
Main Card						
Kenny Florian	def.	Sam Stout	Lightweight	Submission - Rear Naked Choke	1:46	1
Michael Bisping	def.	Josh Haynes	Light Heavyweight	Technical Knockout	4:14	2
Kendall Grove	def.	Ed Herman	Middleweight	Unanimous Decision	—	3
Keith Jardine	def.	Wilson Gouveia	Light Heavyweight	Unanimous Decision	—	3
Preliminary Card						
Rory Singer	def.	Ross Pointon	Middleweight	Submission - Triangle Choke	0:44	1
Kalib Starnes	def.	Danny Abbadi	Middleweight	Submission - Rear Naked Choke	2:56	1
Luigi Fioravanti	def.	Solomon Hutcherson	Middleweight	Knockout	4:15	1
Matt Hamill	def.	Jesse Forbes	Light Heavyweight	Technical Knockout	4:47	1
Mike Nickels	def.	Wes Combs	Light Heavyweight	Submission - Rear Naked Choke	3:10	1

Despite the fact that there are only supposed to be two UFC contracts up for grabs in the finale of *The Ultimate Fighter* series, when you put on an epic battle like the one waged by middleweights Kendall Grove and Ed Herman, to paraphrase baseball great Ernie Banks, "Let's pay two."

Despite the largesse of the UFC awarding six-figure contracts to both combatants, there was a victor, and it was Grove. He eked out a 29-28 decision on all three judges' scorecards.

Fight of the Night (unofficial): Grove vs. Herman

It didn't look like it was going the distance in the early going, as Herman dropped Grove to the mat and opened up with strikes. Grove looked to secure an arm, but Herman used knees effectively to escape any trouble. With less than 90 seconds left in the round, Grove finally made it back to his feet, only to be dropped again by round's end.

Already down a round, Grove needed to make something happen, but it didn't look good when Herman again secured the takedown. This time though, Grove locked Herman's arm and looked to land a triangle seconds later. With the pro-Grove crowd roaring, Grove tightened the lock but Herman escaped, and this back and forth action epitomized the round and the fight.

It was more of the same in the final stanza, with the big scores of the round being Grove's triangles and a last-second rear naked choke, and Herman's own sub work on his foe's arm. By the time the final bell rang though, no one knew who had won, with strong arguments to be made for each fighter.

Knockout of the Night (unofficial): Bisping vs. Haynes

The other two finalists, light heavyweights Michael Bisping and Josh Haynes, had a tough act to follow in their bout, still there was enough compelling action to keep fight fans happy and also earn the pride of Manchester a UFC contract as he halted the courageous Haynes via strikes at 4:14 of the first round.

In the main event of the night, Kenny Florian, a season one *TUF* finalist who lost to Diego Sanchez in their bout in April of 2005, showed how far he had come in a little over a year, dismantling highly-touted prospect Sam Stout in just one minute and 46 seconds of the first round.

In a grueling light heavyweight bout, Keith Jardine rebounded from a horrific second round which saw him bloodied and bruised to win a unanimous three round decision over UFC debutant Wilson Gouveia.

Submission of the Night (unofficial): Singer vs. Pointon

TUF3 middleweights Rory Singer and Ross Pointon ended the preliminary action with a flourish, putting on a frantic 44-second brawl that saw Singer absorb Pointon's thunder and rebound to score a first-round submission win over "The Gladiator".

In perhaps the least surprising result of the night, Kalib Starnes took Danny Abbadi down to the mat and controlled the action of the meeting between *TUF3* middleweight alums until the end came via rear naked choke at 2:56 of the first stanza.

Late replacement Luigi Fioravanti survived some rocky moments in the early going against *TUF3*'s Solomon Hutcherson in their middleweight preliminary bout, but using his veteran guile, he kept his cool and lulled Hutcherson into a picture-perfect left hook that ended the bout at 4:15 of round one.

TUF3's Matt Hamill, who became the sentimental favorite of the show due to his wrestling as well as his determination to not let being deaf hold him back from a pro fighting career, made his big show debut a successful one as stopped fellow cast member Jesse Forbes at 4:47 of the opening round.

In the opener, Denver's Mike Nickels showed marked improvement over his stint on *The Ultimate Fighter* as he submitted highly touted Wes Combs in the first round of their light heavyweight bout.

One Hit Wonder: Solomon Hutcherson

Ultimate Fight Night 5

28 June 2006

Hard Rock Hotel and Casino, Las Vegas, NV

Debuts: Jorge Santiago, Kristian Rothaermel, Jorge Gurgel, Anderson Silva

Fighters			Division	Method	Time	Round
Main Card						
Anderson Silva	def.	Chris Leben	Middleweight	Knockout	0:49	1
Jonathan Goulet	def.	Luke Cummo	Welterweight	Majority Decision	—	3
Rashad Evans	def.	Stephan Bonnar	Light Heavyweight	Majority Decision	—	3
Mark Hominick	def.	Jorge Gurgel	Lightweight	Unanimous Decision	—	3
Preliminary Card						
Josh Koscheck	def.	Dave Menne	Welterweight	Unanimous Decision	—	3
Jason Lambert	def.	Branden Lee Hinkle	Light Heavyweight	Technical Knockout	5:00	1
Jon Fitch	def.	Thiago Alves	Welterweight	Technical Knockout	4:37	2
Rob MacDonald	def.	Kristian Rothaermel	Light Heavyweight	Submission - Armbar	4:01	1
Jorge Santiago	def.	Justin Levens	Middleweight	Knockout	2:13	1

UFC middleweight champion Rich Franklin received a new challenger to look out for, and his name was Anderson Silva.

The world-class Brazilian bomber, who was making his long-awaited UFC debut, walked through the usually durable Chris Leben in a mere 49 seconds, stunning the crowd at the Hard Rock Hotel and Casino and announcing his arrival with a flourish—a loud one.

Knockout of the Night (unofficial): Silva vs. Leben

Immediately establishing his striking dominance, Silva pumped a couple of jabs in Leben's face, and after a right hand by "The Crippler" grazed the Brazilian and opened a small cut over his eye, "The Spider" pounced with extreme prejudice, stunning Leben with a left kick and a three-punch combination that put him down and apparently out.

Leben regained his senses as he hit the mat. Instead of looking to clear his head with a takedown or some movement, he immediately tried to trade with Silva. After getting hit with a right uppercut, a thudding right knee put Leben down again, with the follow-up barrage bringing in referee John McCarthy to halt the bout. It was Leben's first loss in six UFC fights.

In the Ultimate Fight Night co-feature, Rashad Evans kept his unbeaten MMA record intact with a dominating three-round decision over fellow light heavyweight prospect Stephan Bonnar.

Two of Canada's finest won hard-fought bouts in the Octagon, with lightweight Mark Hominick and welterweight Jonathan Goulet each decisioning tough foes.

In the lightweight bout, Hominick outpointed Jorge Gurgel in a fast-paced three-rounder that saw the bout remain on the feet for the entire 15 minutes of action. Although the fans in attendance booed the 29-28 across-the-board verdict, Hominick's faster hands, takedown defense and accurate counters edged out Gurgel's aggressiveness and heavier shots.

Fight of the Night (unofficial): Goulet vs. Cummo

Goulet, looking to rebound from an 11-second knockout loss at the hands of Duane Ludwig in January, went the entire three rounds in outpointing Long Island's Luke Cummo.

Josh Koscheck notched the biggest win of his young career as he scored a solid if unspectacular unanimous decision over former UFC middleweight champ Dave Menne.

Long Beach, California's Jason Lambert improved to 3-0 in the UFC as he rebounded from a slow start to pound out Branden Lee Hinkle at the end of the first round in a light heavyweight bout.

Welterweight Jon Fitch may have moved from the realm of prospect to contender as he notched his third consecutive Octagon victory by stopping Brazil's Thiago Alves.

After some dicey early moments, when a kick and attempted guillotine choke by Alves put him on the defensive, Fitch roared back with an impressive array of ground-and-pound techniques as he controlled Alves for the remainder of the first round and much of the second.

Alves' last hope came late in the second stanza as he escaped Fitch's clutches and looked to take the offensive. Unfortunately, "Pitbull" was a little too eager, and an upkick from the prone Fitch put him on rubbery legs. Fitch pounced on his opponent and opened up with both hands, prompting a stoppage by referee Mario Yamasaki at the 4:37 mark.

Toronto's Rob MacDonald, an alumnus of *The Ultimate Fighter 2*, scored his first UFC victory with a first-round submission of season three's Kristian Rothaermel. The end came at 4:01 as "Maximus" locked in a picture-perfect armbar on his New Orleans foe.

Submission of the Night (unofficial): MacDonald vs. Rothaermel

American Top Team's Jorge Santiago opened up the evening in explosive fashion, knocking out California's Justin Levens with a single knee to the head at 2:13 of the first round in a middleweight contest.

One Hit Wonder: Kristian Rothaermel

UFC 61 *Bitter Rivals*

08 July 2006

Mandalay Bay Events Center, Las Vegas, NV

Debuts: Joe Jordan, Anthony Perosh, Cheick Kongo, Kurt Pellegrino

Fighters			Division	Method	Time	Round
Main Card						
Tim Sylvia	def.	Andrei Arlovski	Heavyweight	Unanimous Decision	—	5
Tito Ortiz	def.	Ken Shamrock	Light Heavyweight	Technical Knockout	1:18	1
Frank Mir	def.	Dan Christison	Heavyweight	Unanimous Decision	—	3
Joe Stevenson	def.	Yves Edwards	Lightweight	Technical Knockout - Cuts	5:00	2
Josh Burkman	def.	Josh Neer	Welterweight	Unanimous Decision	—	3
Preliminary Card						
Hermes Franca	def.	Joe Jordan	Catchweight	Submission - Triangle Choke	0:47	3
Jeff Monson	def.	Anthony Perosh	Heavyweight	Technical Knockout	2:43	1
Cheick Kongo	def.	Gilbert Aldana	Heavyweight	Technical Knockout - Cuts	4:13	1
Drew Fickett	def.	Kurt Pellegrino	Welterweight	Submission - Rear Naked Choke	1:20	3

The rubber match between Tim Sylvia and Andrei Arlovski didn't match the brief and explosive nature of their first two bouts, but Sylvia did enough to outlast "The Pit Bull" in their war of nerves at the Mandalay Bay Events Center. Scores were 48-47 twice and 49-46 for Ellsworth, Maine's Sylvia, who repeated his April 15, 2006 win over Arlovski.

The pace was measured early, with Arlovski working his leg kicks effectively and Sylvia looking for the big bomb. With a little under three minutes left, Sylvia's first heavy salvo rocked Arlovski briefly, but after a short clinch, "The Pit Bull" came firing back and fought with a relaxed ease as Sylvia appeared tense as he stalked the challenger.

The heavy punches kept coming in the second round, with Arlovski still scoring, but Sylvia answered by opening a cut on the left side of his foe's head. The tense drama continued to play out in round three, with Sylvia starting to show the scars of battle via a mouse under his right eye as Arlovski again landed the cleaner blows between sporadic bursts of activity from the champion.

The fourth round saw the crowd get restless, and Sylvia responded by picking up the pace and opening up cuts under Arlovski's right eye and on the side of his left eye, but the final round played out like the previous four, with both fighters having all too brief moments of scoring activity, and leaving the bout in the hands of the judges, much to the chagrin of the packed house.

In the UFC 61 co-featured bout, it was safe to say that the feud between Tito Ortiz and Ken Shamrock was far from over as Ortiz made it two in a row over his longtime rival, stopping the UFC Hall of Famer with a series of forearm strikes just 1:18 into the first round.

The bout was not without its share of controversy, as referee Herb Dean's stoppage drew loud boos from the capacity crowd and prompted the Las Vegas police to enter the Octagon to keep an irate Shamrock from getting at Ortiz. But despite the protests, there was little doubt that the stoppage was just, after Ortiz landed five consecutive forearms on the head of Shamrock, who was not defending himself.

Josh Burkman scored the biggest win of his UFC career, earning a hard fought three-round unanimous decision over Josh Neer in a welterweight bout. Scores were 29-28 twice, and 30-27.

Former UFC heavyweight champion Frank Mir won his first fight in over two years, eking out a three-round unanimous decision over Dan Christison.

All three judges scored the bout 29-28 for Mir, who was sidelined for 16 months due to a motorcycle accident in September of 2004. His first comeback fight, on February 4, 2006, had seen him get stopped by Brazil's Marcio Cruz.

Former welterweight Joe Stevenson made a successful jump to the 155-pound weight class with a bloody second-round stoppage of Yves Edwards, whose cut forehead prompted a halt to the bout after 10 minutes of spirited action.

Fight of the Night: Stevenson vs. Edwards

Submission of the Night: Franca vs. Jordan

Knockout of the Night: Monson vs. Perosh

Hermes Franca returned to the UFC for the first time since April 2, 2004, and did it in style, scoring an impressive third-round submission win over late replacement Joe Jordan.

Jeff Monson impressively stated his case for a heavyweight title shot as he halted Australia's Anthony Perosh in the first round.

French kickboxing star Cheick Kongo made his UFC debut a successful one as he used a series of knees and uppercuts to stop Phoenix's Gilbert Aldana via cuts in the first round.

The end came at 4:13, as a nasty gash over the right eye of Aldana prompted referee Yves Lavigne to halt the bout after consulting with the ringside physician.

Kurt Pellegrino lost his Octagon debut, as Drew Fickett submitted the New Jersey native in the lightweight opener of UFC 61.

One Hit Wonder: Joe Jordan

UFC Fight Night 6

17 Aug. 2006

Red Rock Resort Spa and Casino, Las Vegas, NV

Debuts: Pat Healy, Anthony Torres, Forrest Petz, Kristof Midoux, Jake O'Brien, Martin Kampmann, Crafton Wallace, Yuki Sasaki

Fighters			Division	Method	Time	Round
Main Card						
Diego Sanchez	def.	Karo Parisyan	Welterweight	Unanimous Decision	—	3
Chris Leben	def.	Jorge Santiago	Middleweight	Knockout	0:33	2
Dean Lister	def.	Yuki Sasaki	Middleweight	Unanimous Decision	—	3
Josh Koscheck	def.	Jonathan Goulet	Welterweight	Submission - Strikes	4:12	1
Preliminary Card						
Martin Kampmann	def.	Crafton Wallace	Middleweight	Submission - Rear Naked Choke	2:59	1
Joe Riggs	def.	Jason Von Flue	Welterweight	Submission - Triangle Choke	2:01	1
Jake O'Brien	def.	Kristof Midoux	Heavyweight	Technical Knockout	0:52	2
Forrest Petz	def.	Sam Morgan	Welterweight	Unanimous Decision	—	3
Anthony Torres	def.	Pat Healy	Welterweight	Submission - Rear Naked Choke	2:37	1

The critics were waiting in the wings, ready to pounce on Diego Sanchez as he looked for his eighteenth victory without a loss in the UFC Fight Night main event against Karo Parisyan. Sanchez' performance, which got him a unanimous decision victory in one of the best fights of 2006, left one lasting statement to those skeptics: Not tonight.

Fight of the Night (unofficial): Sanchez vs. Parisyan

Scores were 29-28 (twice) and 30-26 for Sanchez.

The welterweights immediately got down to business, with Sanchez landing a hard right uppercut before taking Parisyan down. "The Heat" was able to get back to his feet and score a takedown of his own, and the fast pace of the bout had the crowd roaring, especially when Parisyan struck with two judo throws that put Sanchez on the defensive.

The standup battle picked up where it left off in the first round, with Sanchez and Parisyan both taking good shots. One minute in, Parisyan picked Sanchez up and took him down, but Sanchez worked well enough from the bottom to stay out of serious trouble. With three minutes left, Sanchez rose and the welterweight contenders got back to trading punches. Sanchez finished stronger though with some late ground and pound.

Taking a well-deserved break for the first few seconds of the final round, both Sanchez and Parisyan soon resumed hostilities on the feet, with Sanchez landing the crisper punches. Parisyan got even though, taking Sanchez to the mat and working from the top. Sanchez got out of trouble quickly and tried to sink in a choke, but Parisyan escaped. Seconds later, things got even worse for "The Heat" as Sanchez got on top and started opening up with both hands. Parisyan showed the heart of a lion though, and with little under two minutes left he made it back to his feet. Sanchez scored with a series of uppercuts and a knee though (the knee knocking Parisyan's tooth out), and the fight appeared to be slipping away from "The Heat", something that was made a certainty as Sanchez pounded away until the final bell tolled.

Chris Leben rebounded from his stunning knockout defeat at the hands of Anderson Silva in June with a stunning KO of his own, as he took out Jorge Santiago early in the second round of a scheduled three-round middleweight bout.

Knockout of the Night (unofficial): Leben vs. Santiago

Dean Lister pulled out all the stops in his first middleweight start against Yuki Sasaki, but the UFC debutant from Tokyo refused to go away, gamely lasting the three-round distance but falling short on the scorecards to the California grappling master.

In the main card opener, Josh Koscheck continued on his way up the welterweight ladder with an exciting and dominating TKO win over Jonathan Goulet.

Middleweights Martin Kampmann and Crafton Wallace came to the UFC advertised as Muay Thai specialists, but after some early fireworks, the bout hit the mat and Kampmann's superior ground work proved to be the difference as he submitted Wallace with a rear naked choke at 2:59 of the first round.

Submission of the Night (unofficial): Riggs vs. Von Flue

Welterweight contender Joe Riggs bounced back from a middleweight loss to Mike Swick earlier this year with an impressive one-round blowout of Jason Von Flue.

Jake O'Brien, 21, made his UFC debut a successful one as he pounded out a second-round TKO win over Canada's Kristof Midoux.

Sammy Morgan barely avoided being on the short end of a third straight UFC knockout loss in a welterweight bout against newcomer Forrest Petz, but was clearly outpointed by the Cleveland native.

In a welterweight bout, Anthony Torres, a veteran of the second season of *The Ultimate Fighter* reality show, got the "W" in his first UFC bout, submitting fellow newcomer Pat Healy in the opening round.

One Hit Wonders: Pat Healy, Kristof Midoux, Crafton Wallace, Yuki Sasaki

UFC 62 *Liddell vs. Sobral*

26 Aug. 2006

Mandalay Bay Events Center, Las Vegas, NV

Debuts: Christian Wellisch, Jamie Varner, Eric Schafer, David Heath, Cory Walmsley, Yushin Okami, Alan Belcher

Fighters			Division	Method	Time	Round
Main Card						
Chuck Liddell	def.	Renato Sobral	Light Heavyweight	Technical Knockout	1:35	1
Forrest Griffin	def.	Stephan Bonnar	Light Heavyweight	Unanimous Decision	—	3
Nick Diaz	def.	Josh Neer	Welterweight	Submission - Kimura	1:42	3
Cheick Kongo	def.	Christian Wellisch	Heavyweight	Knockout	2:51	1
Hermes Franca	def.	Jamie Varner	Lightweight	Submission - Armbar	3:31	3
Preliminary Card						
Eric Schafer	def.	Rob MacDonald	Light Heavyweight	Submission - Arm Triangle Choke	2:26	1
Wilson Gouveia	def.	Wes Combs	Light Heavyweight	Submission - Rear Naked Choke	3:23	1
David Heath	def.	Cory Walmsley	Light Heavyweight	Submission - Rear Naked Choke	2:32	1
Yushin Okami	def.	Alan Belcher	Middleweight	Unanimous Decision	—	3

UFC light heavyweight champion Chuck Liddell was in fearsome form in the main event of UFC 62 at the Mandalay Bay Events Center, stopping Brazil's Renato "Babalu" Sobral for the second time in four years, this time pulling off the feat in just 95 seconds. Liddell had previously knocked out Sobral in 2:55 at UFC 40 in 2002.

Knockout of the Night: Liddell vs. Sobral

The early moments were tense, as both fighters looked for an opening, but once Sobral initiated the action with a series of strikes, Liddell landed an overhand right and followed up with a right uppercut, jarring Sobral and sending him to the canvas. It was just a matter of time after that, as Liddell opened up with a fierce barrage that Sobral was unable to recover from, forcing referee John McCarthy to halt the one-sided bout.

The rematch between Forrest Griffin and Stephan Bonnar wasn't as consistently frenetic as their first bout, but it was just as intense and just as close. Fortunately for Griffin, the result was the same as well, as he scored a three-round decision over Bonnar in their light heavyweight co-feature. Scores were 30-27 across the board for Griffin, in a bout that was much tighter than those numbers would indicate.

Needless to say, the action got started pretty quick between these two friendly rivals, though not exactly at the manic pace of their first fight. Griffin in particular showed a more methodical and patient attack, drawing blood from Bonnar's nose and scoring equally well with his punches and kicks.

Griffin continued his disciplined offensive in the second stanza, but Bonnar was able to open a cut under the Georgia native's right eye early on. The blood didn't deter Griffin, and he kept moving forward. In this round though, Bonnar attempted to stand his ground a little more, perhaps sensing that the judges would be scoring for fighter aggressiveness.

By the early stages of round three, Bonnar was cut over the left eye and on the bridge of the nose, Griffin added a cut in the corner of his right eye to his medical report, and with the result of the bout perhaps hanging in the balance and the punches were coming harder and faster from both fighters. The crowd loved it, roaring louder and louder as the seconds came down and technique gave way to an all-out brawl that completed a fitting second chapter to this epic series.

Nick Diaz got back in the win column in his welterweight bout with Josh Neer, showing a complete mixed martial arts game en route to a third-round submission victory.

Submission of the Night: Diaz vs. Neer

In heavyweight action, France's Cheick Kongo improved to 2-0 in the UFC as he stopped debuting Christian Wellisch with a single knee in the first round.

UFC rookie Jamie Varner came to fight in his Octagon debut, but veteran lightweight contender Hermes Franca proved to be too much for the 21-year-old, as the Brazilian came from behind to submit his foe in the third and final round.

Fight of the Night: Franca vs. Varner

Newcomer Eric Schafer was impressive in his Octagon debut, putting Rob MacDonald to sleep with an arm triangle at 2:26 of the first round in a light heavyweight bout.

American Top Team's Wilson Gouveia was in solid form, submitting Wes Combs via a rear naked choke in the first round.

Debuting light heavyweight Cory Walmsley claimed in a pre-fight interview that he would force newcomer David Heath to tap out, but instead it was Heath—believed to be primarily a striker—who scored the submission victory, landing a rear naked choke that forced a halt to the bout at 2:32 of the first round.

Japanese veteran Yushin Okami opened up the night's card by scoring his first UFC victory, a workmanlike three-round unanimous decision over fellow Octagon debutant Alan "The Talent" Belcher.

One Hit Wonder: Cory Walmsley

UFC 63 *Hughes vs. Penn*

23 Sept. 2006

Arrowhead Pond, Anaheim, CA

Debuts: Tyson Griffin, David Lee, Mario Neto, Eddie Sanchez, Roger Huerta, Jason Dent, Joe Lauzon, Gabe Ruediger

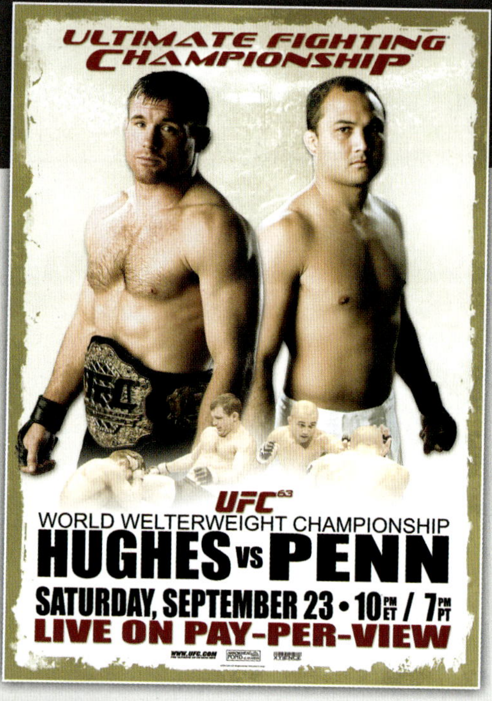

Fighters			Division	Method	Time	Round
Main Card						
Matt Hughes	def.	BJ Penn	Welterweight	Technical Knockout	3:53	3
Mike Swick	def.	David Loiseau	Middleweight	Unanimous Decision	—	3
Melvin Guillard	def.	Gabe Ruediger	Lightweight	Technical Knockout	1:01	2
Rashad Evans	def.	Jason Lambert	Light Heavyweight	Knockout	2:22	2
Joe Lauzon	def.	Jens Pulver	Lightweight	Knockout	0:47	1
Preliminary Card						
Roger Huerta	def.	Jason Dent	Lightweight	Unanimous Decision	—	3
Eddie Sanchez	def.	Mario Neto	Heavyweight	Knockout	0:17	2
Jorge Gurgel	def.	Danny Abbadi	Lightweight	Split Decision	—	3
Tyson Griffin	def.	David Lee	Lightweight	Submission - Rear Naked Choke	1:50	1

A champion's heart can never be underestimated. Just ask Matt Hughes, who survived blood, a poke in the eye, and crippling submission attempts from the last man to beat him, BJ Penn, to stop "The Prodigy" in the third round at the Arrowhead Pond and extend his reign as the UFC welterweight champion.

Fight of the Night: Hughes vs. Penn

Penn, who replaced injured number-one contender Georges St-Pierre in the UFC 63 main event, had submitted Hughes in their first bout in January of 2004, and after two rounds, it looked like he was on his way to a repeat, but Hughes wouldn't go away that easily.

"I knew I had lost the first two rounds," said Hughes. "That just meant I had three left."

Late in the second round, Penn almost finished the bout as he grabbed Hughes' back while the two grappled, bringing back memories of their first fight as the Hawaiian tried to lock up and submit his opponent. Yet Hughes survived the onslaught, barely, as the bell rang.

The crowd chanted for Hughes as the bout went to the mat again in round three, yet this time, the Illinois native imposed his will on Penn from the top position. Suddenly the challenger was taking flush shots to the face at an alarming rate and Penn was rendered defenseless, leaving McCarthy no choice but to stop the fight at 3:53 of the third round.

In the co-feature, it was 14 minutes of chess and one minute of war, but when it was over, Mike Swick moved one step closer to a shot at the UFC middleweight championship as he outpointed former world title challenger David Loiseau.

"It was a lot tougher than it looked," joked Swick, who took the first two frames before meeting some trouble in the final one, winning by scores of 29-28 across the board.

Lightweight Melvin Guillard survived some shaky moments at the end of the first round and roared back to improve to 3-2 in the UFC with a second-round TKO of local favorite Gabe Ruediger that was highlighted by a single body shot finish.

Rashad Evans moved from prospect to contender with the most impressive victory of his UFC career as he stopped Jason Lambert in the second round of their light heavyweight bout. Expected to be one of the most evenly matched bouts on the UFC 63 card, the fight turned out to be anything but.

Knockout of the Night: Lauzon vs. Pulver

Unheralded UFC newcomer Joe Lauzon stunned the mixed martial arts world in the main card opener, spoiling the return of former UFC lightweight champion Jens Pulver by stopping "Lil' Evil" in just 48 seconds.

It was Pulver's first fight in the UFC since his victory over BJ Penn in 2002.

UFC debutant Roger Huerta made his Octagon debut a successful one as he pounded out a three-round unanimous decision over Jason Dent in an exciting lightweight bout that was more competitive than the 30-27 judges' scores suggested.

Temecula, California's Eddie Sanchez made quite an impression in his UFC debut, knocking out well-regarded veteran Mario Neto in the second round of their heavyweight prelim bout.

Jorge Gurgel fought off a pre-fight knee injury to pound out a three-round unanimous decision over Danny Abbadi and earn his first UFC win in a lightweight battle pitting former cast members of *The Ultimate Fighter* reality show. Scores were 29-28 across the board for Gurgel.

Highly-touted lightweight newcomer Tyson Griffin got the card off to a rousing start as he submitted fellow debutant David Lee with a rear naked choke at 1:50 of the first round.

Submission of the Night: Griffin vs. Lee

Fight of the Night (Not Pictured): Huerta vs. Dent

One Hit Wonder: Mario Neto

Though unsuccessful in the Octagon, Mario "Sucata" Neto has had an impact on the UFC as the jiu-jitsu coach for England's Wolfslair team.

Ortiz vs. Shamrock 3: The Final Chapter

10 Oct. 2006

Seminole Hard Rock Hotel and Casino, Hollywood, FL

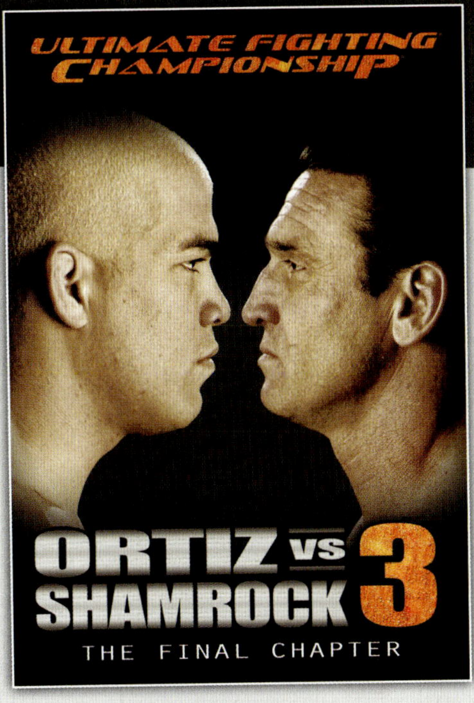

Debuts: Chris Price, Jason MacDonald, Seth Petruzelli, Dustin Hazelett

Fighters			Division	Method	Time	Round
Main Card						
Tito Ortiz	def.	Ken Shamrock	Light Heavyweight	Technical Knockout	2:24	1
Kendall Grove	def.	Chris Price	Middleweight	Submission - Strikes	3:59	1
Jason MacDonald	def.	Ed Herman	Middleweight	Submission - Triangle Choke	2:40	1
Matt Hamill	def.	Seth Petruzelli	Light Heavyweight	Unanimous Decision	—	3
Preliminary Card						
Nate Marquardt	def.	Crafton Wallace	Middleweight	Submission - Rear Naked Choke	1:14	2
Tony DeSouza	def.	Dustin Hazelett	Welterweight	Submission - Kimura	3:59	1
Rory Singer	def.	Josh Haynes	Middleweight	Unanimous Decision	—	3
Thiago Alves	def.	John Alessio	Welterweight	Unanimous Decision	—	3
Marcus Davis	def.	Forrest Petz	Welterweight	Submission - Guillotine Choke	4:58	1

Ken Shamrock got another minute and five seconds in his third bout with Tito Ortiz, but this time the controversy of their second bout in July 2006 was non-existent, as Ortiz once again proved his dominance against the UFC Hall of Famer by knocking him out at 2:24 of the first round at the Seminole Hard Rock Live Arena in what ultimately became the UFC swan song for "The World's Most Dangerous Man".

Knockout of the Night: Ortiz vs. Shamrock

"Congratulations to Tito Ortiz," said a gracious Shamrock. "I wish him and all the people in the UFC the best. Thanks for all the wonderful years."

Although Shamrock's career earned him a spot in the organization's Hall of Fame, the veteran of the first UFC back in 1993 was never a match for Ortiz, who defeated him via a third-round TKO in 2002, and repeated the feat in July in a bout rife with controversy due to a one-minute and 18-second stoppage that was deemed too quick by fans and some fight insiders.

Almost immediately, Ortiz drove Shamrock into the fence and tried to impose his will on the 42-year-old. Seconds later, Ortiz secured a takedown and started to open up with forearms in an almost carbon copy of their second bout. After Ortiz found some space to throw blows with both hands without any response, the result was the same, as well, and referee John McCarthy was forced to call a stop to the bout at 2:24. Although the bad blood between the two over the years was real, it was nice to see the two embrace in the Octagon after the bout and bury the hatchet in a great show of class from both fighters.

In the main undercard bout, Kendall Grove, middleweight winner of *The Ultimate Fighter* season three, kept the momentum going with a dominating first-round strike-induced submission of Chris "The Exorcist" Price.

The first fight of Ed Herman's new UFC contract was a disastrous one, as UFC newcomer Jason MacDonald submitted him with a triangle choke at 2:40 of the first round in their middleweight bout.

Submission of the Night: MacDonald vs. Herman

"If they brought me here as a steppingstone, that was a mistake, because I'm nobody's steppingstone," said MacDonald, a 25-fight veteran who was making his long-awaited debut in the Octagon. "It took me a long time to get here, but I'm here to stay."

The Ultimate Fighter 3's Matt Hamill kept his unbeaten record intact in the first fight of the main card as he grounded and pounded his way to a unanimous decision win over season two's Seth Petruzelli in a light heavyweight contest where a late rally by "The Silverback" wasn't enough to cope with the strength of the Ohio wrestler.

Fight of the Night: Hamill vs. Petruzelli

Middleweight contender Nate "The Great" Marquardt was in fine form against Crafton Wallace, submitting the Naples, Florida resident with a rear naked choke at 1:14 of the second round.

Tony DeSouza survived some rocky moments against 20-year-old Dustin Hazelett in his first UFC fight since 2001, but he eventually broke through the defenses of the youngster and submitted him in the first round of their welterweight bout.

Rory Singer and Josh Haynes may have been friends outside of the Octagon, but the two veterans of the third season of *The Ultimate Fighter* certainly fought like enemies in their three-round middleweight bout, in which Singer rose from the canvas in the second round to score a bloody three-round unanimous decision over his buddy.

Thiago Alves kept the fans in his adopted home state of Florida happy as he pounded out a three-round unanimous decision over John Alessio, who was still looking for his first UFC win after three tries.

In the welterweight opener, Marcus "The Irish Hand Grenade" Davis earned his first UFC victory by submitting Forrest Petz. Davis fought off a bad cut on his nose at the end of a frantic first round to right his ship with a fight-ending guillotine choke.

THE FIGHT HEARD 'ROUND THE WORLD

GRIFFIN vs. BONNAR

April 9, 2005. Light heavyweight hopefuls Forrest Griffin and Stephan Bonnar had survived six weeks in the fishbowl of reality television, and now they were one win away from glory, a UFC contract and a life-altering change to everything they had known previously.

Griffin and Bonnar fought as if their lives were at stake. In the final of *The Ultimate Fighter's* first season, the ensuing 15 minutes encapsulated the best of what this sport has to offer, and the best of these two fighters. If you didn't walk away from your television set a fan that night, check your pulse. About the only person disappointed with the three-round war was the winner.

"I only watched it once," admitted Griffin. "I guess I kinda had to. It was a hard, a lot of missed opportunities, and a lot of things where you know better. You know you can do this or do that, but you don't. But the bottom line is I felt like I fought a great first round. I felt like I came out and just started going at it."

GRIFFIN VS. BONNAR

Bonnar eagerly accepted Griffin's willingness to scrap, and the pattern and pace rarely changed throughout the bout. Griffin took the first round and Bonnar rebounded in the second, leaving his foe bloodied from a cut on the bridge of his nose.

"I don't know, man, you need to get popped; you need to get a little bit of something. It helps if you get backed into a corner."

—Stephan Bonnar

THE ULTIMATE FIGHTER

APRIL 9, 2005

***TUF1* Light Heavyweight Division**

Forrest Griffin

VS.

Stephan Bonnar

	TALE OF THE TAPE	
26	Age*	28
6' 3" (190cm)	Height	6' 4" (193cm)
205 lbs (93kg)	Weight	205 lbs (93kg)

*At the time of fight

Result: Griffin wins by Unanimous Decision

Backed into a corner by Bonnar's attack and exhausted by the furious pace of the first ten minutes, Griffin's chest visibly heaved for any air it could get. He continued to fight, and the third round became as memorable as the first two, with fans in attendance screaming and a Spike TV television audience growing with each punch and kick.

"I knew it was a good fight when the final bell rang and the crowd was going nuts and yelling for another round," said Bonnar. "Just looking into the crowd and at everyone's face, the energy level was so high, I said, 'it must have been a good one.'"

In the end, even though Griffin got the decision, both he and Bonnar received UFC contracts, and a sport got the jolt it needed. To this day, UFC President Dana White calls the bout the most important in UFC history.

"I felt like I came out and just started going at it."

—Forrest Griffin

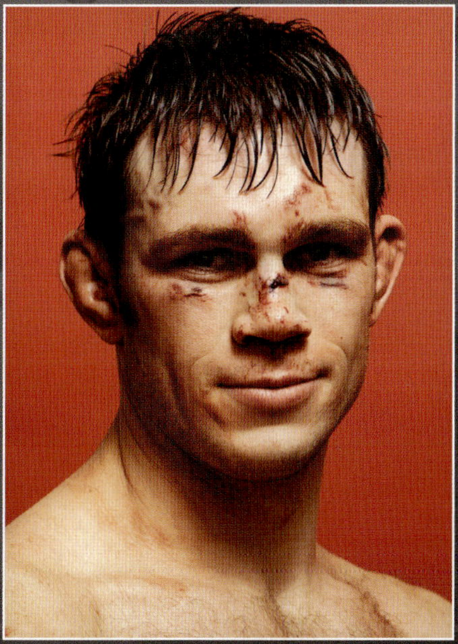

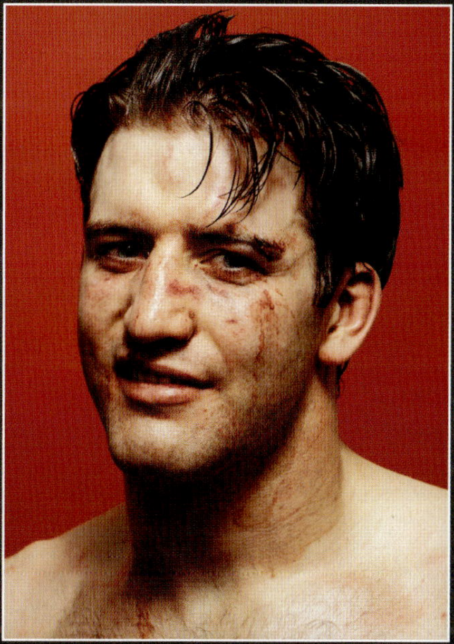

UFC 64 *Unstoppable*

14 Oct. 2006

Mandalay Bay Events Center, Las Vegas, NV

Debuts: Kuniyoshi Hironaka, Carmelo Marrero, Dan Lauzon, Justin James, Clay Guida, Junior Assuncao

Fighters			Division	Method	Time	Round
Main Card						
Anderson Silva	def.	Rich Franklin	Middleweight	Technical Knockout	2:59	1
Sean Sherk	def.	Kenny Florian	Lightweight	Unanimous Decision	—	5
Jon Fitch	def.	Kuniyoshi Hironaka	Welterweight	Unanimous Decision	—	3
Carmelo Marrero	def.	Cheick Kongo	Heavyweight	Split Decision	—	3
Spencer Fisher	def.	Dan Lauzon	Lightweight	Technical Knockout	4:38	1
Preliminary Card						
Yushin Okami	def.	Kalib Starnes	Middleweight	Technical Knockout	1:38	3
Clay Guida	def.	Justin James	Lightweight	Submission - Rear Naked Choke	4:42	2
Kurt Pellegrino	def.	Junior Assuncao	Lightweight	Submission - Rear Naked Choke	2:02	1

Leading up to the 185-pound title fight between Rich Franklin and Anderson Silva, many wondered if the Brazilian's 49-second blowout of Chris Leben in June of 2006 was a fluke. It wasn't, as Silva used a brutal Muay Thai clinch to dominate Franklin on the inside and stun the crowd in attendance for UFC 64 at the Mandalay Bay Events Center by scoring a first-round TKO over the Cincinnati native to win the UFC middleweight crown.

Knockout of the Night: Silva vs. Franklin

It was a war of nerves in the early going, but by the second minute of the first round, both fighters started opening up a bit more, with Silva securing a tight Thai clinch that produced a series of solid knees to the body and head, one of which jarred the champ briefly. Franklin waded right back into battle, but as he came in, Silva locked his hands around Franklin's neck again, and this time a huge right knee left Franklin stunned and open for a brutal follow-up that included two more kicks and a final left knee that sent Franklin to the canvas, where referee John McCarthy wisely halted the bout at the 2:59 mark.

In UFC 64's second title fight, it was a long time coming, but for the first time since 2002, the UFC had a lightweight champion. Sean Sherk grounded and pounded his way to a five-round unanimous decision victory over a courageous Kenny Florian, who had come a long way from his days on *The Ultimate Fighter* reality show, but was unable to stop the onslaught of the "Muscle Shark". Scores were 49-46 twice and 50-48 for Sherk.

Fight of the Night: Sherk vs. Florian

"I've been working for this moment my whole life," said Sherk, the first UFC lightweight champion since Jens Pulver abandoned the belt in 2002. "Nothing was gonna stop me."

Jon Fitch finally got his shot on television against Japan's Kuniyoshi Hironaka after three straight UFC wins, and he let the folks at home see what all the fuss was about as he pounded out a three-round unanimous decision in a highly anticipated welterweight bout.

Scores were 30-25 and 30-27 twice for Fitch.

UFC debutant Carmelo Marrero put a halt to the quick rise of France's Cheick Kongo, using his superior takedown ability to upset the heavyweight contender via a close split decision. Scores were 29-28 twice and 28-29 for Marrero.

Lightweight contender Spencer Fisher survived a spirited effort from 18-year-old Dan Lauzon and delivered a first-round stoppage of the New Englander, who was making his UFC debut in only his fifth pro fight.

Yushin Okami's second fight in the Octagon was his most impressive, as he was steady and consistent in stopping *The Ultimate Fighter 3*'s Kalib Starnes in the third and final round of their middleweight bout.

Ball of energy Clay Guida made his long-awaited UFC debut a successful one as he pounded his way through the defenses of Justin James and then sunk in a rear naked choke to defeat "The Pretty Boy" in the second round of their lightweight bout.

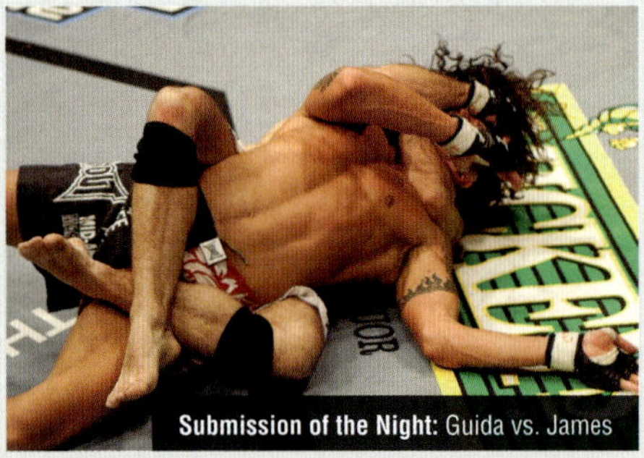
Submission of the Night: Guida vs. James

There was no questioning the dominance of New Jersey native Kurt Pellegrino, as he was in control from the start until he finished newcomer Junior Assuncao with a rear naked choke at 2:02 of the first round in the UFC 64 opener.

One Hit Wonder: Justin James

The Ultimate Fighter 4 Finale

11 Nov. 2006

Hard Rock Hotel and Casino, Las Vegas, NV

Debut: Thales Leites

Fighters			Division	Method	Time	Round
Main Card						
Matt Serra	def.	Chris Lytle	Welterweight	Split Decision		3
Travis Lutter	def.	Patrick Cote	Middleweight	Submission - Armbar	2:18	1
Din Thomas	def.	Rich Clementi	Lightweight	Submission - Rear Naked Choke	3:11	2
Jorge Rivera	def.	Edwin Dewees	Middleweight	Technical Knockout	2:38	1
Preliminary Card						
Pete Spratt	def.	Jeremy Jackson	Welterweight	Submission - Injury	1:11	2
Scott Smith	def.	Pete Sell	Middleweight	Knockout	3:25	2
Charles McCarthy	def.	Gideon Ray	Middleweight	Submission - Armbar	4:43	1
Martin Kampmann	def.	Thales Leites	Middleweight	Unanimous Decision	—	3

A second chance is a great thing—just ask Matt Serra and Travis Lutter, who bounced back into the UFC via Spike TV's *The Ultimate Fighter 4: The Comeback* series and then recorded victories against fellow veterans Chris Lytle and Patrick Cote, respectively, in the *TUF4* Finale at the Hard Rock Hotel and Casino to earn a host of prizes, and most importantly, a shot at their respective division's champion in 2007.

In the welterweight final, Matt Serra and Chris Lytle fought a war of attrition for three rounds that had judges and fans mixed in their opinions of the split verdict in Serra's favor.

Scores were 30-27 twice for Serra and 27-30 once for Lytle in a fight that was extremely difficult to score.

A slow first round picked up steam in the final two minutes as "Lights Out" took Serra down, but the Long Island jiu-jitsu ace fired back, trying to lock in a triangle choke that Lytle escaped from fairly easily.

Serra tried to push the pace a little bit more in the early stages of the second round as he pinned Lytle against the fence and landed with foot stomps in order to soften his foe up for the takedown. Lytle's defense was solid though, even though any offense was smothered by Serra.

Lytle initiated the striking in the third round, but Serra responded by firing off a spinning backfist. It didn't land, but it made Lytle hesitate enough that he fell victim to Serra's first solid takedown, a key factor in the New Yorker taking the last stanza.

In a pre-fight interview, Travis Lutter claimed that his *TUF4* middleweight final against Patrick Cote would play out as follows: "We'll circle, I'll take him down, and the fight's over."

Submission of the Night: Lutter vs. Cote

He was right, as he took just 42 seconds to put Cote on the mat, and he then went on to use his stellar Brazilian jiu-jitsu game to lock in an armbar and force Cote to submit at 2:18 of the opening round.

"I didn't expect it quite that fast," said Texas' Lutter, "but sometimes you get lucky."

There was no luck involved, and with the win, Lutter—in addition to the aforementioned prizes—earned a shot at UFC middleweight boss Anderson Silva in 2007.

Comebacking lightweight Din Thomas was impressive in his Octagon return, showing a sharp standup game before submitting Rich Clementi at 3:11 of the second round.

Jorge Rivera worked his standup gameplan to perfection against Edwin Dewees in the main card opener, swarming his *TUF4* castmate en route to a first-round TKO victory in their middleweight contest.

Pete "The Secret Weapon" Spratt got back in the UFC win column in his bout against fellow *TUF4* competitor Jeremy Jackson, gaining a second-round victory when Jackson tapped out due to a neck injury.

TUF4 middleweights Scott Smith and Pete Sell promised the fight of the night, and the two buddies certainly did their best to deliver on that promise, with an entertaining war that ended with what was unquestionably THE knockout of 2006.

Fight of the Night: Smith vs. Sell

After a first round that was punctuated by a laser-like left hand from Smith, a series of hellacious haymakers from Sell, and a couple of stoppages that saw both fighters stop, smile, and high five each other, the two combatants continued to throw leather in the second frame.

Sell trudged forward after Smith, fighting through a cut under his right eye, and finally hit paydirt with a brutal left to the body. Smith doubled over in pain and Sell moved in for the kill.

"I got drilled," said Smith. "I knew I only had one punch left in me."

That one punch, a right to the jaw of the onrushing Sell, dropped the New Yorker immediately and brought in referee John McCarthy to halt the bout at the 3:25 mark. As soon as the fight was stopped, Smith joined Sell in pain on the canvas. It was an unforgettable ending.

TUF4 middleweight Charles McCarthy got his first UFC win in the bank as he submitted fellow cast member Gideon Ray at 4:43 of the first round.

In a high-impact middleweight opener, Martin Kampmann moved to 2-0 in the Octagon with a punishing three-round unanimous decision win over UFC debutant Thales Leites.

UFC 65 *Bad Intentions*

18 Nov. 2006

ARCO Arena, Sacramento, CA

Debuts: Josh Schockman, Hector Ramirez, Antoni Hardonk, Sherman Pendergarst, Gleison Tibau, Dokonjonosuke Mishima, Drew McFedries

Fighters			Division	Method	Time	Round
Main Card						
Georges St-Pierre	def.	Matt Hughes	Welterweight	Technical Knockout	1:25	2
Tim Sylvia	def.	Jeff Monson	Heavyweight	Unanimous Decision	—	5
Brandon Vera	def.	Frank Mir	Heavyweight	Technical Knockout	1:09	1
Drew McFedries	def.	Alessio Sakara	Light Heavyweight	Technical Knockout	4:07	1
Joe Stevenson	def.	Dokonjonosuke Mishima	Light Heavyweight	Submission - Guillotine Choke	2:07	1
Preliminary Card						
Nick Diaz	def.	Gleison Tibau	Welterweight	Technical Knockout	2:27	2
Antoni Hardonk	def.	Sherman Pendergarst	Heavyweight	Technical Knockout	3:15	1
James Irvin	def.	Hector Ramirez	Light Heavyweight	Technical Knockout	2:36	2
Jake O'Brien	def.	Josh Schockman	Heavyweight	Unanimous Decision	—	3

Georges St-Pierre had never been shy in proclaiming Matt Hughes as his mixed martial arts idol, even citing it as a reason for his 2004 loss to the longtime champion. But at UFC 65, before a packed house at Arco Arena, St-Pierre showed no respect to his hero in their rematch, scoring a one-sided second-round TKO to win the UFC welterweight championship.

Knockout of the Night: St-Pierre vs. Hughes

St-Pierre pushed the pace early behind leg kicks and the occasional punch as Hughes took his time looking for an opening. At the one-minute mark of the round, it was St-Pierre picking the action up even more emphatically as he put Hughes on his heels with his impressive standup, which nonetheless brought a smile from the champion. Two low kicks from St-Pierre halted his momentum though as Hughes was forced to take a short break to recover. The Canadian kept his focus upon the restart and went right back to working his faster hands and feet on Hughes and tossing off the Illinois native's first half-hearted takedown attempt. With under 1:20 to go, St-Pierre opted to take the fight to the canvas and landed some strikes before standing and scoring with a knee. Hughes looked to get back into the scoring column by committing to a takedown, but St-Pierre brushed him off and finished with a right hand that dropped the champion just before the bell intervened.

Hughes began the second round with a smirk, but this was no laughing matter, as St-Pierre was not only winning the standup game, he was showing the physical strength to keep the champion at bay. With 3:45 left, St-Pierre hit paydirt, landing a high left kick that put Hughes on the mat again, this time, the bell wouldn't save the longtime champion, and with referee John McCarthy's stoppage at 1:25 of the second, a new king was crowned.

In the co-feature, Tim Sylvia retained his UFC heavyweight championship with a gritty five-round unanimous decision over Jeff Monson in a fight that was a lot closer than the 50-45 and 49-46 (twice) judges' verdicts.

There was no question who the victor was though, as the 6' 8" Sylvia's takedown defense and surprising submission attempts, coupled with harder striking, proved to be too much for the game Monson, who at 5' 9" was giving up almost a foot in height to the champion.

Brandon Vera left no doubt as to his viability as the leading contender for the UFC heavyweight championship as he only needed 69 seconds to blitz and stop former world champion Frank Mir.

Iowa's Drew McFedries promised to bring the heat against Alessio Sakara in his UFC debut and he delivered in punishing style, stopping his foe with ground strikes in the first round of their exciting light heavyweight contest.

Joe "Daddy" Stevenson made it 2-0 as a UFC lightweight, scoring a first-round submission win over Japanese standout Dokonjonosuke Mishima.

Submission of the Night: Stevenson vs. Mishima

Nick Diaz put together back-to-back UFC wins for the first time in over a year, impressively stopping Brazil's Gleison Tibau in the second round of a scheduled three-round welterweight contest.

Debuting UFC heavyweight Antoni Hardonk survived an early takedown from fellow debutant Sherman Pendergarst to roar back and knock out Tank with a left to the jaw and right kick to the upper thigh. The end came at 3:15 of the opening round.

Fight of the Night: Irvin vs. Ramirez

Light heavyweight James Irvin had the Sacramento fans in his corner entering his All-California bout with Hector Ramirez, and "The Sandman" delivered with an exciting second-round TKO of the tough Norwalk resident.

In the UFC 65 opener, unbeaten heavyweight Jake O'Brien notched his second Octagon victory with a less than compelling three-round decision over Josh Schockman. Scores were 30-27 across the board for "Irish" Jake, who issued Schockman his first mixed martial arts defeat.

One Hit Wonders: Josh Schockman, Sherman Pendergarst

UFC Fight Night 7

Sanchez vs. Riggs

13 Dec. 2006

MCAS Miramar, San Diego, CA

Debuts: Steve Byrnes, Logan Clark, Keita Nakamura, Victor Valimaki, Jeff Joslin

Fighters			Division	Method	Time	Round
Main Card						
Diego Sanchez	def.	Joe Riggs	Welterweight	Knockout	1:33	1
Josh Koscheck	def.	Jeff Joslin	Welterweight	Unanimous Decision	—	3
Karo Parisyan	def.	Drew Fickett	Welterweight	Unanimous Decision	—	3
Marcus Davis	def.	Shonie Carter	Welterweight	Unanimous Decision	—	3
Preliminary Card						
Alan Belcher	def.	Jorge Santiago	Middleweight	Knockout	2:45	3
Luigi Fioravanti	def.	Dave Menne	Welterweight	Technical Knockout	4:44	1
David Heath	def.	Victor Valimaki	Light Heavyweight	Split Decision	—	3
Brock Larson	def.	Keita Nakamura	Welterweight	Unanimous Decision	—	3
Logan Clark	def.	Steve Byrnes	Middleweight	Unanimous Decision	—	3

The fighter jets taking off with a thunderous roar at the Marine Corps Air Station Miramar had nothing on Diego Sanchez. The unbeaten welterweight contender impressively improved to 19-0 with a roar of his own in the form of a perfect right hand and right knee, which sent Joe Riggs down to a knockout defeat at 1:33 of the first round before 3,000 loud and appreciative United States Marines in the first live UFC event ever held on a military base.

The fight was mainly tactical in the opening moments, with Riggs looking good while stuffing a takedown and landing with a kick. But as Sanchez calmly stalked, he faked a left hook, came across with a right on the jaw and Riggs fell hard to the mat. Riggs quickly got his bearings, but as he shot forward, Sanchez ran in with a right knee that landed cleanly and put "Diesel" down a second time, this time for good, as a follow-up barrage was nothing but a formality before referee John McCarthy halted the contest.

"I said I'm just gonna be calm and let the techniques come into play," said Sanchez. "This is what happens."

In main card action, Josh Koscheck continued his rise up the welterweight ranks with a clear cut three-round unanimous decision over UFC debutant Jeff Joslin.

Welterweight contenders Karo Parisyan and Drew Fickett left it all in the Octagon during their three-round battle, but in the end, "The Heat" did enough to earn a unanimous decision over Fickett by three scores of 30-27.

Fight of the Night (unofficial): Parisyan vs. Fickett

Marcus Davis scored the biggest win of his mixed martial arts career in the Spike TV opener, winning a lopsided three-round decision over seasoned vet Shonie Carter in a welterweight bout.

Light heavyweight prospect David Heath remained unbeaten by pounding out a three-round split decision over Canadian newcomer Victor "The Matrix" Valimaki.

Biloxi, Mississippi's Alan Belcher evened his UFC record at 1-1 with a one-kick knockout of Jorge Santiago in middleweight preliminary action.

Knockout of the Night (unofficial): Belcher vs. Santiago

Retired U.S. Marine Luigi Fioravanti made a huge statement in his welterweight bout against Dave Menne, stopping the former middleweight champion in the first round.

Welterweight Brock Larson earned his first UFC victory in his second try as he scored a solid but unspectacular three-round unanimous decision over Keita Nakamura.

Another Marine Corps vet, "Sergeant" Steve Byrnes, got the night off to a rousing start, but the judges seemingly didn't agree, as they awarded a three-round unanimous decision to a game Logan Clark in a middleweight bout that marked the UFC debut for both fighters.

One Hit Wonders: Steve Byrnes, Logan Clark, Jeff Joslin

UFC 66 *Liddell vs. Ortiz 2*

30 Dec. 2006

MGM Grand Garden Arena, Las Vegas, NV

Fighters			Division	Method	Time	Round
Main Card						
Chuck Liddell	def.	Tito Ortiz	Light Heavyweight	Technical Knockout	3:57	3
Keith Jardine	def.	Forrest Griffin	Light Heavyweight	Technical Knockout	4:41	1
Jason MacDonald	def.	Chris Leben	Middleweight	Submission - Guillotine Choke	4:01	2
Andrei Arlovski	def.	Marcio Cruz	Heavyweight	Knockout	3:15	1
Michael Bisping	def.	Eric Schafer	Light Heavyweight	Technical Knockout	4:24	1
Preliminary Card						
Thiago Alves	def.	Tony DeSouza	Welterweight	Knockout	1:10	2
Gabriel Gonzaga	def.	Carmelo Marrero	Heavyweight	Submission - Armbar	3:22	1
Yushin Okami	def.	Rory Singer	Middleweight	Submission - Strikes	4:03	3
Christian Wellisch	def.	Anthony Perosh	Heavyweight	Unanimous Decision	—	3

Tito Ortiz came to fight at UFC 66 in 2006, and although he brought his "A" game, when you're facing the best light heavyweight on the planet, sometimes that's just not enough. Chuck Liddell defended his UFC crown for the fourth time with a third-round TKO of Ortiz before a sellout crowd of 14,607 at the MGM Grand Garden Arena in their long-awaited rematch.

Fight of the Night: Liddell vs. Ortiz

Even though Ortiz, a former UFC light heavyweight champion, showed courage and improved stand-up, it just wasn't enough to answer to the power of Liddell.

Ortiz opened the action aggressively, but Liddell calmly countered his offensive rushes, drawing a roar from the crowd as he cut Ortiz over the left eye and closed in for the kill. Moments later, it appeared that the end had arrived as Liddell put the challenger on the canvas with a left to the temple and pounded away furiously with both hands as referee Mario Yamasaki watched the action closely. Incredibly though, Ortiz survived the onslaught and made it to his feet, the crowd erupting as the bell rang.

There was more of the same in the second round, and while Ortiz finally got Liddell to the mat with a minute left, "The Iceman" easily made it back to his feet and out of danger to ride out the round.

In the third, Ortiz again showed no fear of the champion, but his ineffectiveness securing takedowns was proving to be his downfall, as Liddell took every opportunity to make the challenger pay for his misses. With under two minutes to go, Ortiz made his final mistake as he attempted to get into a firefight with Liddell and paid for it, as the champion sent his challenger to the canvas. A final barrage forced Yamasaki to halt the bout at 3:57 of the third stanza.

Knockout of the Night: Jardine vs. Griffin

In a light heavyweight bout, Keith Jardine loudly announced his arrival to the top ten, scoring a stirring first-round TKO of Forrest Griffin in a fight that lived up to its explosive billing. Griffin took an early edge in the bout behind his faster and more accurate strikes, but Jardine stayed in the pocket and gave as good as he got, eventually noticing that Griffin was putting his head down when the two would get into heated exchanges.

"I knew I'd catch him with the uppercut sooner or later," said Jardine, and he was right, as he landed a flush right uppercut and followed with a left cross that staggered Griffin. Jardine jumped in and fired off a furious barrage as both fighters hit the mat. The assault from "The Dean of Mean" on Griffin continued unabated, and referee John McCarthy had no choice but to stop the fight at the 4:41 mark.

Jason MacDonald made it back-to-back wins over members of *The Ultimate Fighter* cast as he submitted season one's Chris Leben in the second round of their middleweight bout.

Submission of the Night: MacDonald vs. Leben

"They can start calling me the *TUF* killer," joked MacDonald, who had defeated season three's Ed Herman two months earlier.

Former UFC heavyweight champion Andrei Arlovski returned to the Octagon and broke a two-fight losing streak with a first-round TKO of Brazil's Marcio "Pe de Pano" Cruz.

Unbeaten Michael Bisping, winner of the light heavyweight division of *The Ultimate Fighter* third season, fought off a game Eric Schafer en route to a first-round TKO victory in his first bout since June of 2006.

Thiago Alves ended 2006 on a victorious note as he knocked out veteran Tony DeSouza in the second round of a scheduled three-round welterweight contest.

Gabriel Gonzaga scored the most impressive win of his UFC career, dominating from the opening bell against previously unbeaten heavyweight Carmelo Marrero before submitting the Philadelphia native at 3:22 of the first round.

Yushin Okami improved to 3-0 in the Octagon with a third-round submission win (due to strikes) over Rory Singer in a middleweight bout.

In the opener, heavyweight prospect Christian Wellisch pounded out a hard-fought unanimous decision over Australia's Anthony Perosh.

UFC Fight Night 8

Evans vs. Salmon

25 Jan. 2007

Seminole Hard Rock Hotel and Casino, Hollywood, FL

Debuts: Chad Reiner, Heath Herring, Sean Salmon

Fighters			Division	Method	Time	Round
Main Card						
Rashad Evans	def.	Sean Salmon	Light Heavyweight	Knockout	1:06	2
Jake O'Brien	def.	Heath Herring	Heavyweight	Unanimous Decision	—	3
Hermes Franca	def.	Spencer Fisher	Lightweight	Technical Knockout	4:03	2
Preliminary Card						
Nate Marquardt	def.	Dean Lister	Middleweight	Unanimous Decision	—	3
Josh Burkman	def.	Chad Reiner	Welterweight	Unanimous Decision	—	3
Ed Herman	def.	Chris Price	Middleweight	Submission - Armbar	2:58	1
Din Thomas	def.	Clay Guida	Lightweight	Unanimous Decision	—	3
Rich Clementi	def.	Ross Pointon	Welterweight	Submission - Rear Naked Choke	4:52	2

With a perfectly timed kick to the head of Sean Salmon at the Seminole Hard Rock Live Arena, light heavyweight contender Rashad Evans may have permanently erased the notion that he is not a finisher, as he knocked out the former Ohio State wrestler in the second round to remain unbeaten and earn his second straight devastating knockout victory.

The end of the UFC Fight Night main event came at the 1:06 mark of round two.

Knockout of the Night: Evans vs. Salmon

The two former Division I wrestlers traded punches in the early going, with Evans holding the edge thanks to his faster hands. Two minutes in, Salmon was able to get Evans to the mat and he worked quickly to get into side control. Evans fought his way back up, only to get tagged by a left-right, and a few seconds later, Salmon got another takedown.

Early in the second, Evans got back in gear, hurting Salmon briefly with strikes to the head and a follow-up flurry. Smelling blood, Evans moved in carefully and threw a perfect right kick to the head. Salmon was out before he hit the mat.

International star Heath Herring got a rude welcome home in his UFC debut, as unbeaten 22-year-old Jake O'Brien stifled the offense of "The Texas Crazy Horse" for 15 minutes and took him down almost at will en route to a unanimous decision victory.

"I'm disappointed," said Herring, 28, who had previously fought in Japan for the PRIDE and K-1 organizations. "In my head, this fight wasn't supposed to go this way."

Fight of the Night: Franca vs. Fisher

Hermes Franca moved one step closer to a shot at UFC 155-pound champion Sean Sherk in the main card opener as he impressively halted Spencer Fisher in the second round of an exciting lightweight bout.

Fisher pushed the pace in the standup early as the purple-haired Franca took his time getting acclimated to the Octagon. A minute and a half in, Franca got the takedown and almost landed a submission on Fisher, but "The King" sprawled his way out of trouble and went back on the attack with punches and kicks. Franca was no slouch standing though, as he landed a couple of looping overhand rights on his opponent and then got another takedown with 1:30 left in the round. Franca then finished strong with strikes on the mat.

The fast pace continued in the second, with Fisher tightening up his striking and landing with more accuracy. An ill-advised kick on the grounded Franca almost got Fisher in trouble submission-wise, but he was able to escape, only to be put in a precarious position on the mat moments later as Franca worked an effective ground and pound on the Iowa resident. With 2:30 to go, referee Jorge Alonso stood the two fighters up and Fisher went back to sprawling the Brazilian around the Octagon. When Franca did stop, the two traded blows to the delight of the crowd, and with a little over a minute left, Franca stunned Fisher with a wide right hand. He followed with a knee and then poured it on his hurt opponent until Alonso had seen enough and wisely waved it off at the 4:03 mark.

Nate Marquardt made a strong case for a shot at UFC middleweight champion Anderson Silva with a shutout three-round decision win over Dean Lister.

Welterweight up-and-comer Josh Burkman returned from an injury-induced six-month layoff with a three-round unanimous decision over Octagon debutant Chad Reiner.

The Ultimate Fighter 3 finalist Ed Herman broke a two-fight losing streak by making short work of Chris Price, submitting "The Exorcist" in the first round of a scheduled three-round middleweight contest.

Submission of the Night: Herman vs. Price

Din Thomas' striking game and late takedown defense proved to be the difference in a hard-fought three-round war with game Clay Guida as he pounded out a close unanimous decision victory in their lightweight bout.

In the welterweight opener, Slidell, Louisiana's Rich Clementi showed a veteran's poise before taking Ross Pointon down and out at 4:52 of the second round via submission.

UFC 67 *All or Nothing*

03 Feb. 2007

Mandalay Bay Events Center, Las Vegas, NV

Debuts: Mirko Cro Cop, John Halverson, Quinton Jackson, Frankie Edgar, Lyoto Machida, Diego Saraiva

Fighters			Division	Method	Time	Round
Main Card						
Anderson Silva	def.	Travis Lutter	Middleweight	Submission - Elbows	2:11	2
Mirko Cro Cop	def.	Eddie Sanchez	Heavyweight	Technical Knockout	4:33	1
Quinton Jackson	def.	Marvin Eastman	Light Heavyweight	Knockout	3:49	2
Roger Huerta	def.	John Halverson	Lightweight	Technical Knockout	0:18	1
Patrick Cote	def.	Scott Smith	Middleweight	Unanimous Decision	—	3
Preliminary Card						
Terry Martin	def.	Jorge Rivera	Middleweight	Knockout	0:14	1
Frankie Edgar	def.	Tyson Griffin	Lightweight	Unanimous Decision	—	3
Lyoto Machida	def.	Sam Hoger	Light Heavyweight	Unanimous Decision	—	3
Dustin Hazelett	def.	Diego Saraiva	Lightweight	Unanimous Decision	—	3

Travis Lutter not only lost a chance at the UFC middleweight championship by coming in overweight for his UFC 67 main event bout, he also succeeded in making the champion, Anderson Silva, angry, resulting in a second-round submission win for "The Spider", who survived some rocky first-round moments to move to 3-0 in the Octagon.

Submission of the Night (unofficial): Silva vs. Lutter

Lutter stalked and looked for a takedown early on while Silva effortlessly moved away and out of danger. Trying for a flying knee moments later, Silva's attack was muffled by Lutter, who took the off-balance Brazilian down. Put to the mat for the first time in his UFC tenure, Silva fought off Lutter's attack and stood up, only to have the Texan grab his foot and put him down again. This time, Lutter was more aggressive offensively, but so was Silva, as he fought back from the bottom. Eventually, with one minute left, Lutter got to side control and then to the full mount. Lutter pounded away, but Silva weathered the storm and stood up, drawing a roar from the crowd.

Lutter opened the second with another takedown, but this time Silva responded with a kick to the head from the ground. Visibly hurt, Lutter fell into Silva's triangle choke attempt and the champion pounded away with both elbows until Lutter was forced to tap out at the 2:11 mark.

With the flags of his native Croatia waving in the crowd, heavyweight superstar Mirko Cro Cop made his long-awaited UFC debut and delivered in style for his legion of fans, stopping previously unbeaten Eddie Sanchez in the first round.

In the other highly anticipated Octagon debut of UFC 67, Quinton "Rampage" Jackson didn't announce his arrival to the UFC with one of his trademark slams, but he was on target with his punches, knocking out the first man to defeat him, Marvin Eastman, in the second round.

Roger "El Matador" Huerta played the bull in his lightweight swing bout against UFC newcomer John Halverson, halting "The Hurricane" in just 18 seconds.

Patrick Cote, who made it to *The Ultimate Fighter 4* final in November of 2006, but had never won a UFC match outside of the *TUF4* series, earned his first proper UFC victory in his fifth try, scoring a shutout three-round decision over Scott Smith in a middleweight bout.

Knockout of the Night: Martin vs. Rivera

Former light heavyweight Terry Martin made quite an impression in his middleweight debut, knocking out Jorge Rivera in a mere 14 seconds.

Unbeaten but unheralded lightweight Frankie Edgar handed highly-regarded Tyson Griffin his first loss in their preliminary bout, winning a hard-fought three-round unanimous decision.

Though fairly unknown in UFC circles, Edgar made it obvious that he came to win as he took the favored Griffin to the mat and survived a thunderous slam to rack up an impressive first round in the Octagon.

Griffin stunned Edgar on two occasions early in round two, with the New Jersey fighter opting for the takedown to get out of trouble. And while Griffin appeared to be controlling the action on the mat, just when Edgar seemed to be fading, he would come back, ending the round in the full mount position as he attempted to ground and pound his way to victory.

With the crowd firmly in his corner, Edgar again took a visibly winded Griffin down and also opened up with both hands while standing in an attempt to close the show in style. And though Griffin attempted to finish with a kneebar in the final seconds, as the round ticked away, it was Edgar pounding on Griffin's leg in time with the clock, drawing a roar with each shot.

Fight of the Night: Edgar vs. Griffin

Brazil's Lyoto Machida made a low-key UFC debut with a three-round unanimous decision win over Sam Hoger in a light heavyweight preliminary bout.

Lightweight prospect Dustin Hazelett opened the UFC 67 festivities in victorious fashion with a shutout three-round unanimous decision over late replacement Diego Saraiva.

UFC 68 *The Uprising*

03 March 2007

Nationwide Arena, Columbus, OH

Debuts: Rex Holman, Jason Gilliam

Fighters			Division	Method	Time	Round
Main Card						
Randy Couture	def.	Tim Sylvia	Heavyweight	Unanimous Decision	—	5
Rich Franklin	def.	Jason MacDonald	Middleweight	Technical Knockout	5:00	2
Matt Hughes	def.	Chris Lytle	Welterweight	Unanimous Decision	—	3
Martin Kampmann	def.	Drew McFedries	Middleweight	Submission - Arm Triangle	4:06	1
Jason Lambert	def.	Renato Sobral	Light Heavyweight	Knockout	3:36	2
Preliminary Card						
Matt Hamill	def.	Rex Holman	Lightweight	Technical Knockout	4:00	1
Jon Fitch	def.	Luigi Fioravanti	Welterweight	Submission	3:05	2
Gleison Tibau	def.	Jason Dent	Lightweight	Unanimous Decision	—	3
Jamie Varner	def.	Jason Gilliam	Lightweight	Submission - Rear Naked Choke	1:34	1

After losing two out of three fights to UFC light heavyweight champion Chuck Liddell and a tearful retirement in 2006, most believed that Randy Couture had run out of miracles. But before a packed house at the Nationwide Arena, the 43-year-old Hall of Famer shocked the world once again, dominating Tim Sylvia for five rounds, en route to a shutout five-round decision that earned Couture a third UFC heavyweight championship.

"Not bad for an old man," said Couture.

With the first right hand he threw to open the bout, Couture dropped the 6' 8", 263-pound champion and pounced on him, looking to end matters as the arena erupted. Soon, Couture had Sylvia's back, but the champion took his time calmly as he tried to escape the clutches of "The Natural". Couture continued to work for the finish throughout the rest of the round, though, as Sylvia arched backward in an effort to weigh down and tire the challenger until the bell rang.

Couture quickly closed the distance to open the second, and despite being tossed back by Sylvia on his first attempt, his next try was more successful as he drove "The Maine-iac" to the fence in an effort to get the takedown, which he got with 3:30 left. On the ground, Couture was active with both hands in order to not only score points but to keep his dominant position.

Sylvia pressed the action to begin round three, but Couture still amazed with his crisper standup and his impressive defense, complete with quick head movement and bobbing and weaving while he potshotted the 30-year-old champion.

Visibly winded between rounds, Couture had built enough of a lead that he could conceivably run out the clock for the next two rounds, but that just wasn't his style, so he kept pressing. For his part, Sylvia continued to try landing the equalizer, but it was not to be, and in the final 30 seconds, the crowd that had been behind him from the opening bell roared and stood in unison for the new king.

Ohio's own Rich Franklin showed no ill effects from his devastating first-round loss to Anderson Silva at UFC 64, as he broke down and eventually stopped tough contender Jason MacDonald in two rounds.

Former UFC welterweight champion Matt Hughes got back in the win column for the first time since losing his title to Georges St-Pierre at UFC 65 with a no-nonsense, three-round unanimous decision over Chris Lytle that saw the Hillsboro, Illinois native get back to his ground and pound basics.

Fight and Knockout of the Night:
Lambert vs. Sobral

Light heavyweight Jason Lambert scored the biggest win of his MMA career, stopping former UFC title challenger Renato "Babalu" Sobral in the second round of a back and forth 205-pound showdown.

In a middleweight swing bout, Martin Kampmann lost the stand-up battle to Drew McFedries, but he won the war, taking the bout to the mat and scoring a first-round submission to run his unbeaten UFC record to 3-0.

Fight and Submission of the Night:
Kampmann vs. McFedries

In a battle between Ohio wrestlers, Columbus' former Division I National Champion Rex Holman (Ohio State) may have shown the right stuff to throw off the attacks of Cincinnati's Division III National Champ Matt Hamill (Rochester Institute of Technology) had they been competing in a wrestling match. When it came to striking and a complete mixed martial arts game, "The Hammer" was leagues ahead of Holman as he pounded out an impressive first-round TKO win in a light heavyweight bout.

In welterweight action, highly-touted contender Jon Fitch delivered a second-round submission win over Luigi Fioravanti.

Gleison Tibau's first foray to the UFC lightweight division was a successful one as he out-pointed Jason Dent over three rounds in a fairly uneventful preliminary bout.

In the UFC 68 opener, Jamie Varner got it right his second time around in the Octagon, making short work of UFC newcomer Jason "The Gizzard" Gilliam with a rear naked choke submission at 1:34 of the first round.

One Hit Wonder: Rex Holman

UFC Fight Night 9

Stevenson vs. Guillard

05 April 2007

The Pearl at The Palms, Las Vegas, NV

Debuts: Thiago Tavares, Naoyuki Kotani, Roan Carneiro, Nate Mohr, Justin McCully

Fighters			Division	Method	Time	Round
Main Card						
Joe Stevenson	def.	Melvin Guillard	Lightweight	Submission - Guillotine Choke	0:27	1
Justin McCully	def.	Antoni Hardonk	Heavyweight	Unanimous Decision	—	3
Kenny Florian	def.	Dokonjonosuke Mishima	Lightweight	Submission - Rear Naked Choke	3:57	3
Preliminary Card						
Kuniyoshi Hironaka	def.	Forrest Petz	Welterweight	Unanimous Decision	—	3
Wilson Gouveia	def.	Seth Petruzelli	Light Heavyweight	Submission - Guillotine Choke	0:39	2
Drew Fickett	def.	Keita Nakamura	Welterweight	Unanimous Decision	—	3
Kurt Pellegrino	def.	Nate Mohr	Lightweight	Submission - Ankle Lock	2:58	1
Roan Carneiro	def.	Rich Clementi	Welterweight	Unanimous Decision	—	3
Thiago Tavares	def.	Naoyuki Kotani	Lightweight	Unanimous Decision	—	3

The bad blood was evident between lightweight contenders Joe Stevenson and Melvin Guillard leading up to their UFC Fight Night main event, but Stevenson was a cool customer once the bell rang, stunning all in attendance with a seemingly effortless 27-second submission win over "The Young Assassin".

Submission of the Night: Stevenson vs. Guillard

"I was nervous with his athletic ability and explosiveness and it could have gone just as fast the other way," said the gracious Stevenson.

Surprisingly it was Stevenson who landed the first telling blow on the fierce striker, briefly stunning Guillard with a left hand. It was the opening he needed as he got Guillard to the mat and quickly sunk in a guillotine choke, producing a stirring submission victory.

Justin McCully proved to be more than just Tito Ortiz' training partner in his heavyweight bout against Antoni Hardonk, pounding out a three-round decision win to gain his first UFC victory.

In the main card opener, lightweight contender Kenny Florian showed no ill effects from his title bout loss to Sean Sherk in October of 2006, notching the most impressive win of his MMA career with a third-round submission victory over Dokonjonosuke Mishima.

Fight of the Night: Florian vs. Mishima

After some brief standup from both men, the bout hit the mat late in the first minute of the opening round, with Mishima attempting to work his ground and pound on the Massachusetts native. Florian quickly worked his way out of trouble, getting into Mishima's guard at the midway point and opening up with both hands when the openings presented themselves. With a little over a minute left, the two stood, with Florian again pushing the pace and scoring with leg kicks while Mishima missed with a wild haymaker and a spinning back fist.

Florian's leg kicks continued to pay dividends early in the second, and Mishima was visibly bothered by them. A missed kick by the Japanese fighter brought the fight to the mat, and again, Florian controlled the action until he decided to rise and attack from a standing position. The fighters were only upright briefly though, as Florian put Mishima on his back and scored with a few blows before standing again. With under a minute left in the round, Florian's left kicks to the leg were caving Mishima in, but the 35-year-old veteran refused to give up.

The pace dipped early in the final round, but despite apparently having the fight secured, Florian kept the pressure on and it almost cost him as Mishima nearly landed a game-changing kneebar. It was Mishima's last stand, as Florian escaped and turned up the heat, sinking in a match-ending rear-naked choke with just 1:03 left in the bout.

Wilson Gouveia continued his trek up the light heavyweight ranks with a second-round submission win over Seth Petruzelli.

Drew Fickett survived an illegal downward elbow from Keita Nakamura in the second round of their welterweight bout to finish strong and win a unanimous decision over the gutsy Japan native in a highly entertaining scrap.

Kurt Pellegrino scored the first early ending of the UFC Fight Night card, fighting off game newcomer Nate Mohr before eventually securing an ankle lock that forced a tap out at the 2:58 mark.

Submission of the Night: Pellegrino vs. Mohr

Ohio's Forrest Petz had his moments against Kuniyoshi Hironaka, but the Japan native's ground attack was just too much as he pounded out a three-round decision win.

Brazilian 155-pounder Roan Carneiro made a successful UFC debut, unanimously outpointing veteran Rich Clementi via scores of 30-27 from all three Octagonside judges.

In the first bout of the evening, highly touted lightweight prospect Thiago Tavares upped his unbeaten record to 15-0 with a shutout three-round decision over Naoyuki Kotani.

UFC 69 *Shootout*

07 April 2007

Toyota Center, Houston, TX

Debut: Leonard Garcia

Fighters			Division	Method	Time	Round
Main Card						
Matt Serra	def.	Georges St-Pierre	Welterweight	Technical Knockout	3:25	1
Josh Koscheck	def.	Diego Sanchez	Welterweight	Unanimous Decision	—	3
Roger Huerta	def.	Leonard Garcia	Lightweight	Unanimous Decision	—	3
Yushin Okami	def.	Mike Swick	Middleweight	Unanimous Decision	—	3
Kendall Grove	def.	Alan Belcher	Middleweight	Submission – D'Arce Choke	4:37	2
Preliminary Card						
Heath Herring	def.	Brad Imes	Heavyweight	Unanimous Decision	—	3
Thales Leites	def.	Pete Sell	Middleweight	Unanimous Decision	—	3
Marcus Davis	def.	Pete Spratt	Welterweight	Submission - Ankle Lock	2:57	2
Luke Cummo	def.	Josh Haynes	Welterweight	Knockout	2:45	2

Odds mean nothing. The past means nothing. In mixed martial arts, what matters is what happens when the bell rings. When the bell rang at the Toyota Center for UFC 69, Matt Serra came to fight. When you do that, good things can happen, and they did for the Long Island native, who stunned the world with a first-round TKO win over Georges St-Pierre to win the UFC welterweight championship.

Serra had earned his title shot by winning season four of *The Ultimate Fighter* reality show. St-Pierre, in his first fight since taking the 170-pound title from Matt Hughes last November, was expected to roll over his challenger en route to bigger and better things.

Knockout of the Night: Serra vs. St-Pierre

It was not to be.

A smiling and relaxed Serra showed no fear of the champion as he met him in the middle of the Octagon to start the bout, but St-Pierre was sharp as he shot out kicks and the occasional quick flurry. The challenger responded with kicks of his own to the champion's legs, but St-Pierre appeared to be too fast for his foe, apparently just biding his time until he decided to pounce.

That's why they fight the fights, and just as soon as those words were written, Serra threw a looping right hand that grazed the back of St-Pierre's head, forcing him to lose his balance and stumble twice. It was all that the underrated Serra needed, as he swung for the fences and landed on the still-recovering champion, who got into deeper and deeper trouble with each shot the New Yorker landed.

Suddenly, St-Pierre was on the mat, and Serra followed him, never letting his hands stop moving until referee John McCarthy pulled him off at the 3:25 mark and declared him the new welterweight champion of the world.

"Tonight I got beat by a better fighter than myself," said a gracious St-Pierre. "He beat me fair and square. I'm very sad right now, but I will come back."

After the war of words between Josh Koscheck and Diego Sanchez, nothing less than an all-out shootout was expected between the two welterweight standouts. Unfortunately for Sanchez, the best shot he landed on Koscheck was the two-handed shove he delivered during Friday's weigh-in, as he was unable to mount any offense whatsoever during the real fight en route to a shutout decision loss in a bout that didn't deliver on the hype, but that did allow Koscheck to gain revenge on the man who beat him during the first season of *The Ultimate Fighter* while also handing the "Nightmare" his first professional defeat.

In stark contrast to Koscheck-Sanchez, Roger Huerta and Leonard Garcia put it all on the line in their lightweight swing bout, and though Huerta emerged with the decision win, there were no losers in one of the best 155-pound battles of recent years.

There was simply no feeling-out process between the two Texans, as they emerged in a fast and furious fashion as soon as they were waved out of their corners and barely let up for the next 15 minutes, drawing thunderous roars from the crowd throughout. Scores were 30-27 for Huerta.

Fight of the Night: Huerta vs. Garcia

The rise of Mike Swick up the middleweight ranks hit a snag, as he was clearly outpointed by Yushin Okami in a hotly contested three-rounder. Scores for Okami were 29-28 twice and 30-27.

TUF3 winner Kendall Grove continued to impress in his UFC campaign as he submitted fellow prospect Alan Belcher in the second round of a heated middle-weight battle.

Submission of the Night: Grove vs. Belcher

Longtime heavyweight contender Heath Herring rebounded from his debut UFC loss to Jake O'Brien with a three-round unanimous decision over Brad Imes.

Thales Leites dominated from start to finish against Pete Sell, winning their middleweight bout via unanimous three-round decision.

Welterweight Marcus Davis continued his progression as a mixed martial artist, impressively submitting Pete Spratt in the second round.

New Yorker Luke Cummo got the night off to a rousing start with a second-round stoppage of Josh Haynes in a welterweight bout.

UFC 70 *Nations Collide*

21 April 2007

M.E.N. Arena, Manchester, England

Debuts: Fabricio Werdum, Terry Etim, Matt Grice, Jess Liaudin, Dennis Siver, Paul Taylor, Edilberto Crocota

Fighters			Division	Method	Time	Round
Main Card						
Gabriel Gonzaga	def.	Mirko Cro Cop	Heavyweight	Knockout	4:51	1
Andrei Arlovski	def.	Fabricio Werdum	Heavyweight	Unanimous Decision	—	3
Michael Bisping	def.	Elvis Sinosic	Light Heavyweight	Technical Knockout	1:40	2
Lyoto Machida	def.	David Heath	Light Heavyweight	Unanimous Decision	—	3
Cheick Kongo	def.	Assuerio Silva	Heavyweight	Majority Decision	—	3
Preliminary Card						
Terry Etim	def.	Matt Grice	Lightweight	Submission - Guillotine Choke	4:45	1
Junior Assuncao	def.	David Lee	Lightweight	Submission - Rear Naked Choke	1:55	2
Alessio Sakara	def.	Victor Valimaki	Light Heavyweight	Technical Knockout	1:44	1
Jess Liaudin	def.	Dennis Siver	Welterweight	Submission - Armbar	1:19	1
Paul Taylor	def.	Edilberto Crocota	Welterweight	Technical Knockout	0:37	3

For years, Mirko Cro Cop had knocked opponents out in devastating fashion with fearsome kicks to the head. On April 21, 2007, before a packed house at the M.E.N. Arena, Gabriel Gonzaga gave the Croatian bomber a taste of his own medicine. At the UFC's first event in England since UFC 38, Gonzaga sent Cro Cop crashing to defeat with a single right kick to the head that earned him a shot at UFC heavyweight champion Randy Couture.

Knockout of the Night: Gonzaga vs. Cro Cop

Gonzaga came out of his corner determined to fight, and he immediately started tossing out rangefinding punches as he stood in the pocket with the feared striker. Cro Cop took his time while looking for an opening, but when he threw his first big kick to the body, Gonzaga was able to grab his opponent's leg and take him to the canvas. On the mat, Cro Cop tried to keep his cool in an attempt to force a standup, but Gonzaga would have none of it as he fired away with forearms to the head, one of which opened a cut on the Croatian's forehead. With 35 seconds left, apparently Cro Cop got a reprieve, but instead, he was sent crashing to the mat with a single right kick to the head at the 4:51 mark, throwing the arena into shock as the next challenger for the heavyweight crown was determined.

He who dared lost in the heavyweight bout between former UFC heavyweight champion Andrei Arlovski and Octagon newcomer Fabricio Werdum, as Arlovski won a unanimous decision in unspectacular fashion. The Brazilian jiu-jitsu black belt opted to stand and make a fight of it, but to no avail on the judges' scorecards. Scores were 30-27 twice and 29-28 for Arlovski.

The Great UK Hope, Michael Bisping, lived up to expectations in his light heavyweight bout against UFC gatekeeper Elvis Sinosic, bookending some rocky moments in the second round with a dominating performance that earned him a second-round TKO win.

As promised, Sinosic came out swinging, and Bisping eagerly obliged, firing back before throwing the Australian to the mat. Bisping followed his foe to the canvas and ferociously attacked with both hands, much to the delight of his roaring and chanting hometown fans, and within the next couple of minutes, "The Count" kept the pressure on, knocking Sinosic's mouthpiece out and opening up a cut on his forehead.

Fight of the Night: Bisping vs. Sinosic

Gamely, Sinosic came out for the second round, and he nearly hit paydirt, knocking Bisping down with a knee to the head and then almost securing a kimura lock. Just when it appeared Sinosic was on the verge of the upset, Bisping turned the tables, got in his opponent's guard and pounded away with both hands until referee Steve Mazzagatti halted the bout at the 1:40 mark.

Light heavyweight contender Lyoto Machida kept his unbeaten record intact by outpointing David Heath. The fans were less than thrilled with the bout, which was serenaded with boos for the majority of its 15 minutes due to a lack of action.

Heavyweight contender Cheick Kongo won a razor-thin majority decision over Sao Paulo, Brazil's Assuerio Silva.

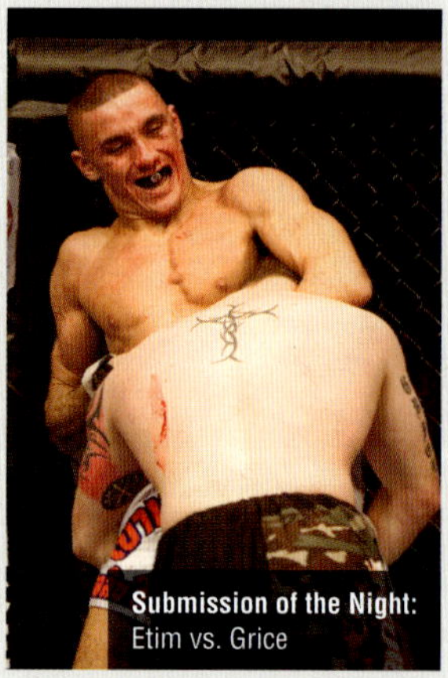
Submission of the Night: Etim vs. Grice

Liverpool lightweight Terry Etim upped his unbeaten record to 10-0 with a first-round submission victory over Matt Grice.

Brazil native Junior Assuncao earned his first UFC victory, submitting London's David Lee in the second round of their lightweight bout.

Italian light heavyweight Alessio Sakara broke a two-fight losing streak with an impressive first-round stoppage of Edmonton's Victor Valimaki.

It took 13 years for him to get there, but London-based Frenchman Jess Liaudin proved that he was no "Joker" as he made the most of his UFC debut by submitting Germany's Dennis Siver in just 1:19.

Walsall, England's "Relentless" Paul Taylor got the crowd into UFC 70 immediately with a third-round TKO of previously unbeaten Edilberto Crocota in their welterweight opener.

UFC 71 *Liddell vs. Jackson*

26 May 2007

MGM Grand Garden Arena, Las Vegas, NV

Debuts: Houston Alexander, Thiago Silva, Jeremy Stephens

Fighters			Division	Method	Time	Round
Main Card						
Quinton Jackson	def.	Chuck Liddell	Light Heavyweight	Knockout	1:53	1
Karo Parisyan	def.	Josh Burkman	Welterweight	Unanimous Decision	—	3
Terry Martin	def.	Ivan Salaverry	Middleweight	Technical Knockout	2:04	1
Houston Alexander	def.	Keith Jardine	Light Heavyweight	Knockout	0:48	1
Kalib Starnes	def.	Chris Leben	Middleweight	Unanimous Decision	—	3
Preliminary Card						
Thiago Silva	def.	James Irvin	Light Heavyweight	Technical Knockout - Injury	1:06	1
Alan Belcher	def.	Sean Salmon	Light Heavyweight	Submission Guillotine Choke	0:53	1
Din Thomas	def.	Jeremy Stephens	Lightweight	Submission - Armbar	2:44	2
Wilson Gouveia	def.	Carmelo Marrero	Light Heavyweight	Submission - Guillotine Choke	3:06	1

Chuck Liddell's right hand had exacted revenge for him on many occasions, leading him on a reign of terror at 205 pounds that saw him win seven fights in a row, by KO or TKO. At the MGM Grand Garden Arena on May 26, 2007, the streak came to an end at the hands of the last man to beat him, Quinton "Rampage" Jackson, who earned the UFC light heavyweight championship with a stunning first-round TKO.

Knockout of the Night: Jackson vs. Liddell

The tension was thick as camera flashes were seen throughout the arena. The action didn't match the atmosphere in the opening minute though, bringing a look of disdain and a wave in from Jackson to engage. Liddell obliged, but after Jackson absorbed a left hook from "The Iceman", he came back immediately with a right hook that dropped Liddell to the canvas hard. Rampage immediately pounced on the soon-to-be ex-champion, and after four unanswered blows, referee John McCarthy halted the bout at the 1:53 mark, and a new king was crowned at 205 pounds.

Welterweight contender Karo Parisyan moved one step closer to a title shot, outpointing fellow 170-pound standout Josh Burkman via unanimous decision.

Terry Martin made it 2-0 in the middleweight division with a first-round finish of returning UFC vet Ivan Salaverry.

UFC newcomer Houston Alexander made quite an impression in his debut, stunning 205-pound contender Keith Jardine via a devastating first-round knockout.

The bout was fought at a hellacious pace from the opening bell, with Jardine apparently hurting Alexander with a quick left hook that put the Nebraskan on the canvas briefly. Alexander quickly recovered though, and once the two clinched, he opened up with overhand rights that stunned the "Dean of Mean". Moments later, after a barrage of heavy shots, Jardine hit the canvas from a right uppercut. Another follow-up right uppercut put Jardine down face first, drawing the stoppage from referee Steve Mazzagatti, and just like that, the crowded light heavyweight division had a new face.

In an entertaining main card opener, Kalib Starnes and Chris Leben left it all the Octagon, but in the end, it was Starnes who took the close three-round decision in a battle between middleweight alumni from *The Ultimate Fighter* reality series.

Both fighters had their moments in the fast-paced opening round, Leben scoring with brief flurries and looping shots while Starnes landed the harder and crisper shots with counters straight down the middle to the head and body.

Fight of the Night: Starnes vs. Leben

Starnes upped the pressure in the second, stunning Leben with a straight right to the jaw and immediately following up with a hard takedown. Leben, true to form, would not go away quietly, and he finished the round strong.

Leben kept pursuing a backpedaling Starnes as the final round got underway, and a left to the body by Leben hurt his foe, allowing the fight to go to the mat. There, Leben worked his ground and pound effectively as the exhausted Starnes simply tried to survive. It appeared that Leben's previous work proved to be enough to earn him the nod. The judges disagreed though, giving the razor-thin decision to Starnes.

The expected standup war between Chute Boxe newcomer Thiago Silva and James "The Sandman" Irvin fizzled out early when a partial ACL tear caused Irvin to retire at 1:06 of the first round.

Alan Belcher came in on just two weeks' notice to replace the injured Eric Schafer against Sean Salmon, but stamina wasn't an issue for "The Talent" as he submitted Salmon just 53 seconds into the opening round.

Submission of the Night: Thomas vs. Stephens

Lightweight contender Din Thomas spoiled the Octagon debut of Jeremy Stephens, submitting the newcomer in the second round of a scheduled three.

Wilson Gouveia continued to show improvement in his game as he notched his third straight Octagon win by submitting Carmelo Marrero in the first round.

UFC Fight Night 10

Stout vs. Fisher

12 June 2007

Seminole Hard Rock Hotel and Casino, Hollywood, FL

Debuts: Luke Caudillo, Anthony Johnson, Jeff Cox, Tamdan McCrory, Jason Black, Jordan Radev

Fighters			Division	Method	Time	Round
Main Card						
Spencer Fisher	def.	Sam Stout	Lightweight	Unanimous Decision	—	3
Jon Fitch	def.	Roan Carneiro	Welterweight	Submission - Rear Naked Choke	1:07	2
Drew McFedries	def.	Jordan Radev	Middleweight	Knockout	0:33	1
Preliminary Card						
Thiago Tavares	def.	Jason Black	Lightweight	Submission - Triangle Choke	2:49	2
Forrest Petz	def.	Luigi Fioravanti	Welterweight	Unanimous Decision	—	3
Tamdan McCrory	def.	Pete Spratt	Welterweight	Submission - Triangle Choke	2:04	2
Gleison Tibau	def.	Jeff Cox	Lightweight	Submission - Arm Triangle Choke	1:52	1
Anthony Johnson	def.	Chad Reiner	Welterweight	Knockout	0:13	1
Nate Mohr	def.	Luke Caudillo	Lightweight	Unanimous Decision	—	3

They were lightweights on the scale only. When the bell rang at the Seminole Hard Rock Live Arena, and for the next 15 minutes of torrid give and take, Spencer Fisher and Sam Stout were heavyweights in heart, determination, and relentless action. When it was all said and done, Fisher had scored a unanimous three-round decision victory to even his series with Stout at one apiece.

Fight of the Night: Fisher vs. Stout

Scores for Fisher, which didn't reflect the closeness of the bout, were 30-27 across the board. Stout had scored a split decision win over Fisher at UFC 58 in March of 2006.

The leather was flying from the outset, and Fisher immediately made an impression with a series of flush shots to the face. And while Stout stood in the pocket and fired back, his looping punches weren't quick enough to land before Fisher's straight blows, which reddened the Ontario native's face and cut him in the side of his head. Stout wouldn't fold though, and he cut Fisher over the right eye and appeared to jar him briefly. In this classic round of ebb and flow, just when it appeared Stout had turned the corner and taken control, Fisher came firing back, putting the crowd on its feet when the bell ending the round finally intervened.

If anyone thought the fighters were going to take a breather in round two, they were wrong, as the non-stop action picked up right where it left off, with Fisher and Stout starting to add more kicks and knees to their arsenals of bad-intentioned punches to the head and body. Throughout the frame, it was dead even, with both taking turns leading the attack. Although Fisher's face continued to show the scars of battle from the onslaught of "Hands of Stone", "The King" continued to press and score enough to keep Stout honest and the contest too close to call.

With the fight possibly on the line, Fisher and Stout continued at an inhuman pace, taking turns drilling each other with shots that would have dropped lesser fighters. But as the round progressed, it was Fisher starting to take control, and his punches knocked his tiring foe back at various points in the round. Midway through the final stanza, a right hand dropped Stout to a knee briefly, but the 23-year-old battler came back firing despite the fact that his left eye was beginning to swell shut. The fight ticked down its final minute with the crowd standing and cheering, and both fighters gave whatever they had left. It was more than enough to stamp this one a classic.

Welterweight contender Jon Fitch was looking to impress in his main card debut, and he delivered, bouncing back from some shaky moments in the first round to switch gears and score a submission victory over Roan Carneiro.

Knockout of the Night: McFedries vs. Radev

In the main card opener, Drew McFedries made short work of former Bulgarian Olympic wrestling team member Jordan Radev, taking advantage of the UFC newcomer's porous defense with crisp right uppercuts down the middle. The final one put Radev on the mat, and another right hand knocked the Bulgarian out, but referee Jorge Alonso was a step slow stopping the bout, giving McFedries the KO win at the 33-second mark only after another couple of unnecessary shots landed.

Unbeaten Brazilian phenom Thiago Tavares spoiled Jason Black's long-awaited UFC debut, impressively submitting the Iowa veteran in the second round of their lightweight contest.

Submission of the Night: Tavares vs. Black

It wasn't World War III when welterweights Forrest Petz and Luigi Fioravanti locked horns, but Petz did enough effective work to win a three-round unanimous decision.

A star was born in the preliminary bout between Tamdan McCrory and Pete Spratt, as the 20-year-old New Yorker survived some rough moments and used a varied and energetic attack to submit Spratt in the second round of an action-packed welterweight contest.

Welterweight prospect Gleison Tibau made it two in a row in the Octagon, submitting newcomer Jeff Cox at 1:52 of the first round.

Late replacement Anthony "Rumble" Johnson warned Chad Reiner in a pre-fight interview: "Don't blink." Well, he was right, as two debilitating left hooks put Reiner down and out in just 13 seconds, heralding the birth of a new prospect in the packed 170-pound weight class.

In the lightweight opener, Nate Mohr was focused and followed his game plan perfectly as he scored an impressive three-round unanimous decision over UFC debutant Luke Caudillo.

UFC 72 *Victory*

16 June 2007

The Odyssey Arena, Belfast, Northern Ireland

Debuts: Colin Robinson, Steve Lynch, Jason Tan

Fighters			Division	Method	Time	Round
Main Card						
Rich Franklin	def.	Yushin Okami	Middleweight	Unanimous Decision	—	3
Forrest Griffin	def.	Hector Ramirez	Light Heavyweight	Unanimous Decision	—	3
Jason MacDonald	def.	Rory Singer	Middleweight	Technical Knockout	3:18	2
Tyson Griffin	def.	Clay Guida	Lightweight	Split Decision	—	3
Ed Herman	def.	Scott Smith	Middleweight	Submission - Rear Naked Choke	2:25	2
Preliminary Card						
Eddie Sanchez	def.	Colin Robinson	Heavyweight	Technical Knockout	0:32	2
Marcus Davis	def.	Jason Tan	Welterweight	Knockout	1:15	1
Dustin Hazelett	def.	Steve Lynch	Welterweight	Submission - Anaconda Choke	2:50	1

Former UFC middleweight champion Rich Franklin survived some dicey moments in the final round of his bout against Yushin Okami at the Odyssey Arena, but in the end, "Ace" had put in enough early work to earn a unanimous decision in the UFC 72 main event and another shot at the 185-pound title he lost in October of 2006.

Franklin-Okami headlined the UFC's first-ever trip to Ireland, and it was a rousing success, as 7,850 fans cheered throughout the eight-bout card and brought in an Odyssey Arena record gate of £603,600.

Most had come to see Franklin, who defeated Okami by scores of 29-28 on all three judges' scorecards.

Light heavyweight contender Forrest Griffin rebounded from a devastating first-round loss to Keith Jardine at UFC 66 by scoring a hard-fought but clear-cut three-round unanimous decision over Hector Ramirez.

"I'm Irish, I'm fighting in Ireland, I deserve a little luck," said Griffin, who didn't need any in upping his record to 14-4 via scores of 30-27 across the board.

Middleweight standout Jason MacDonald started slow but finished strong, stopping Rory Singer in the second round to improve to 20-8 and earn his third win over alumni from *The Ultimate Fighter* reality show.

In an action-packed lightweight bout that lived up to the hype, Tyson Griffin pounded out a close three-round split decision over Clay Guida.

Fight of the Night: Griffin vs. Guida

Scores were 29-28 twice and 28-29 for Griffin, a verdict that was booed by the fans in attendance who believed Guida had pulled out the win.

After a few tense early moments, the fight began in earnest in the second minute, with Griffin able to lock in a guillotine choke as the two fell to the mat. Guida eventually worked his way free and back to his feet, but Griffin kept the Illinois native locked up against the fence until deciding to let go and trade punches with under a minute left. Griffin's standup was crisp and varied, with Guida game, but a step behind.

Guida turned things around in round two, immediately rushing Griffin into the fence. The Californian wasn't rattled though, and his superior strength allowed him to free himself and continue with his standup attack, which was eagerly met and responded to by Guida. With under three minutes left, Griffin took Guida to the mat and got his back, but Guida escaped and went for Griffin's ankle. Griffin attempted to pound his way out, and eventually got loose, only to give up his back. With Guida on his back attempting a choke, Griffin stood, only to fall back down and break the hold while making it out of the round.

With the fight on the line, Griffin came out firing with punches, knees, and kicks in round three as Guida looked for the takedown. Eventually the fight went there, with both fighters looking to finish the bout, whether by submission or via strikes. Both had their moments, making the round difficult to judge. Guida's superior positioning and a late choke attempt seemed to be enough to sway the scores and give "The Carpenter" a victory, but it was not to be.

Middleweight prospect Ed Herman improved to 15-4 in the main card opener as he submitted Scott Smith in the second round of their 185-pound bout.

Submission of the Night: Herman vs. Smith

Welterweight Marcus Davis' hot streak continued as he stopped Jason Tan in the first round to nab his fourth UFC win in a row, and ninth overall.

"I just lived my dream," said Davis. "I got to fight in Ireland and I got a vicious KO."

Knockout of the Night: Davis vs. Tan

Heavyweights Eddie Sanchez and Colin Robinson went to war in their preliminary bout, but it was Sanchez who emerged victorious by way of a second-round TKO after some rough early moments.

Welterweight prospect Dustin Hazelett spoiled the homecoming for Steve Lynch in the opener, submitting the Antrim, UK product in the first round.

One Hit Wonder: Steve Lynch

The Ultimate Fighter 5 Finale

23 June 2007

The Pearl at The Palms, Las Vegas, NV

Debuts: Brian Geraghty, Allen Berube, Rob Emerson, Gray Maynard, Cole Miller, Andy Wang, Brandon Melendez, Doug Evans, Floyd Sword, Nate Diaz, Manny Gamburyan

Fighters			Division	Method	Time	Round
Main Card						
BJ Penn	def.	Jens Pulver	Lightweight	Submission - Rear Naked Choke	3:12	2
Nate Diaz	def.	Manny Gamburyan	Lightweight	Submission - Injury	0:20	2
Thales Leites	def.	Floyd Sword	Middleweight	Submission - Arm Triangle Choke	3:50	1
Roger Huerta	def.	Doug Evans	Lightweight	Technical Knockout	3:30	2
Preliminary Card						
Joe Lauzon	def.	Brandon Melendez	Lightweight	Submission - Triangle Choke	2:09	2
Cole Miller	def.	Andy Wang	Lightweight	Technical Knockout	1:10	1
Gray Maynard	def.	Rob Emerson	Lightweight	No Contest	0:39	2
Leonard Garcia	def.	Allen Berube	Lightweight	Submission - Rear Naked Choke	4:22	1
Matt Wiman	def.	Brian Geraghty	Lightweight	Technical Knockout	2:09	1

It took five years, but at the Pearl at the Palms Hotel, BJ Penn erased the most discouraging loss of his career in punishing style, submitting Jens Pulver in the second round to break a two-fight losing streak and begin the next phase of his career with a bruising exclamation point.

"The Prodigy" jarred Pulver with the first right hand he threw and then slammed him to the canvas. On the ground, Pulver's submission defense and heart kept him in the fight, but as Penn moved from submission to submission while adding in various punches and elbows, it appeared that it was just going to be a matter of time before the Hawaiian prevailed. Pulver refused to give in, fighting his way back to his feet and engaging in some heavy exchanges with Penn until the bell for the first round sounded.

In the second, though, Penn would not be denied, and despite Pulver's courageous effort, he was too much for "Lil' Evil" on this night, eventually getting his opponent's back and submitting him with a rear naked choke at 3:12 of the second round.

The Ultimate Fighter final was a bit of an anti-climax, especially considering the torrid wars fans usually expect from the final bouts of the series. But in season five's championship match, a dislocated shoulder suffered by Manny Gamburyan kept an interesting bout from truly heating up, and gave Nate Diaz the win and the six-figure UFC contract that goes to the winner of the Spike TV reality series.

What made the ending even more disappointing for Gamburyan was that he had won the first round with a relentless ground and pound attack and nullified the size and standup advantages enjoyed by Stockton, California's Diaz. Moments into the second round, Gamburyan shot in for another takedown and landed hard, dislocating his right shoulder and causing him to tap out from the excruciating pain. The end came 20 seconds into the round.

Rising lightweight star Roger Huerta got a scare in his bout against unbeaten UFC debutant Doug Evans, but "El Matador" eventually prevailed, pounding out a second-round TKO victory.

Middleweight up-and-comer Thales Leites put on a groundfighting clinic against Floyd Sword, eventually submitting the UFC newcomer in the first round.

Before season five of *The Ultimate Fighter* began, many tabbed Massachusetts' Joe Lauzon as a favorite to win it all. But while that plan didn't work out, Lauzon moved to 2-0 in his UFC career with a dominating submission win over castmate Brandon Melendez.

Submission of the Night: Lauzon vs. Melendez

TUF5's Cole Miller was impressive in his UFC debut, stopping Andy Wang at 1:10 of the first round.

Knockout of the Night: Miller vs. Wang

Gray Maynard saw an apparent victory get snatched away in his bout against *TUF5* teammate Rob Emerson, with the lightweight bout being ruled a no contest in the second round.

Maynard dominated the bout with his ground attack, and by the end of the first round, Emerson limped back to his corner with injured ribs. Looking to end things, Maynard jumped right in Emerson's face early in the second and picked him up for a thunderous slam.

Fight of the Night: Maynard vs. Emerson

Then things got cloudy, as Maynard put Emerson down hard on the canvas, prompting Emerson to tap out due to an aggravation of his rib injury. But after referee Steve Mazzagatti waved the bout off, apparently because of the tap, the verdict came back as a no contest, with the reasoning being that Maynard was knocked out by his own slam, rendering both fighters unable to continue.

Lightweight prospect Leonard Garcia improved to 14-2 with a first-round submission win over *TUF5*'s Allen Berube.

Matt Wiman evened his Octagon record at 1-1, blowing through his *TUF5* castmate Brian Geraghty at 2:09 of the first round. Referee Yves Lavigne stopped the bout after Wiman got in the mounted position and rained blows down on his foe.

One Hit Wonders: Floyd Sword, Brandon Melendez, Andy Wang, Brian Geraghty, Allen Berube

UFC 73 *Stacked*

07 July 2007

ARCO Arena, Sacramento, CA

Debuts: Alvin Robinson, Antonio Rodrigo "Minotauro" Nogueira, Mark Bocek

Fighters			Division	Method	Time	Round
Main Card						
Anderson Silva	def.	Nate Marquardt	Middleweight	Technical Knockout	4:50	1
Sean Sherk	def.	Hermes Franca	Lightweight	Unanimous Decision	—	5
Tito Ortiz	vs.	Rashad Evans	Light Heavyweight	Draw	—	3
Minotauro Nogueira	def.	Heath Herring	Heavyweight	Unanimous Decision	—	3
Kenny Florian	def.	Alvin Robinson	Lightweight	Technical Knockout	4:30	1
Preliminary Card						
Stephan Bonnar	def.	Mike Nickels	Light Heavyweight	Submission - Rear Naked Choke	2:14	1
Jorge Gurgel	def.	Diego Saraiva	Lightweight	Unanimous Decision	—	3
Chris Lytle	def.	Jason Gilliam	Welterweight	Submission - Inverted Triangle Choke	2:15	2
Frankie Edgar	def.	Mark Bocek	Lightweight	Technical Knockout	4:55	1

It was supposed to be one of Anderson Silva's toughest tests, but instead, his win over Nate Marquardt at ARCO Arena proved to be one of his greatest victories, as he defended his UFC middleweight crown for the first time with a first-round TKO in the UFC 73 main event.

Knockout of the Night: Silva vs. Marquardt

After briefly jarring Marquardt with a punch in the opening minute of the fight, Silva's attempt at an acrobatic follow-up kick earned him a trip to the canvas. While there, Silva worked effectively with strikes from the bottom, while Marquardt did his fair share of damage from the top. With 1:30 left, referee John McCarthy re-started the action despite the fact that both fighters were active on the ground, and Silva opened up, forcing Marquardt to look for the takedown. But just when it seemed that Marquardt had weathered the storm and would survive the round, Silva's brutal power erupted and he landed on the challenger with a series of right hands that forced McCarthy to halt the bout at 4:50 of the opening round.

A second-round foul cost Tito Ortiz dearly in his highly anticipated light heavyweight bout against rising star Rashad Evans, as a unanimous decision win instead turned into a three-round draw thanks to a point deducted from the former light heavyweight champion for holding the fence as Evans attempted to secure a takedown. Scores were 28-28 across the board.

UFC lightweight champion Sean Sherk stayed the course in his first title defense against Hermes Franca, grounding and pounding his way to a clear-cut five-round unanimous decision victory.

Former PRIDE heavyweight champion Antonio Rodrigo "Minotauro" Nogueira made his Octagon debut that night against a familiar face in Heath Herring, but "The Texas Crazy Horse" gave the Brazilian all he could handle before losing a close but unanimous three-round decision.

Scores were 29-28 for Minotauro, who also defeated Herring in 2001 and 2004, when the two were in the PRIDE organization.

Minotauro wasted no time getting acclimated to the Octagon, jarring Herring with a left to the head in the first round, and his crisper punch and knee attacks paid dividends as he put him on the defensive.

With under a minute to go though, Herring, bloodied and bruised, struck paydirt with a left kick to the face that put Minotauro flat on his back. Herring pounced on his dazed foe and appeared to be a punch or two from victory, but in an effort to make sure he wasn't submitted by the always dangerous Minotauro Nogueira, he let him up and scored with more flush shots before the bell intervened.

The pace was more measured in rounds two and three, and while Herring went down fighting, he had not done enough to break his losing streak against the Brazilian standout.

Although Lightweight contender Kenny Florian fought prior to the Silva-Marquardt main event, he performed as if he were the headliner as he fought off a game challenge from newcomer Alvin Robinson to stop the Denver fighter with ground strikes at 4:30 of the opening round.

The Ultimate Fighter 1 finalist Stephan Bonnar made a triumphant return to the Octagon in his first fight since a nine-month suspension, submitting Mike Nickels in the first round of their light heavyweight bout. Bonnar was suspended after his 2006 loss to Forrest Griffin after testing positive for the steroid boldenone.

Fight of the Night: Gurgel vs. Saraiva

Fortaleza can be proud of both Jorge Gurgel and Diego Saraiva, as the two Brazilian lightweights fought courageously for local bragging rights, with Gurgel emerging victorious via a three-round unanimous decision.

In a battle of Indiana welterweights, Indianapolis' Chris Lytle broke a two-fight losing streak in impressive fashion, grounding and pounding and then submitting late replacement Jason Gilliam of Muncie at 2:15 of the first round.

Submission of the Night: Lytle vs. Gilliam

In the lightweight opener, unbeaten Frankie Edgar continued to impress, following up his February win over Tyson Griffin with a first-round stoppage of Woodbridge, Ontario's Mark Bocek.

UFC 74 *Respect*

25 Aug. 2007

Mandalay Bay Events Center, Las Vegas, NV

Debuts: Marcus Aurelio, Ryan Jensen, Alberto Crane

Fighters			Division	Method	Time	Round
Main Card						
Randy Couture	def.	Gabriel Gonzaga	Heavyweight	Technical Knockout	1:37	3
Georges St-Pierre	def.	Josh Koscheck	Welterweight	Unanimous Decision	—	3
Roger Huerta	def.	Alberto Crane	Lightweight	Technical Knockout	1:50	3
Joe Stevenson	def.	Kurt Pellegrino	Lightweight	Unanimous Decision	—	3
Patrick Cote	def.	Kendall Grove	Middleweight	Knockout	4:45	1
Preliminary Card						
Renato Sobral	def.	David Heath	Light Heavyweight	Submission - Anaconda Choke	3:30	2
Frank Mir	def.	Antoni Hardonk	Heavyweight	Submission - Kimura	1:17	1
Thales Leites	def.	Ryan Jensen	Middleweight	Submission - Armbar	3:47	1
Clay Guida	def.	Marcus Aurelio	Lightweight	Split Decision	—	3

In the UFC 74 main event at the Mandalay Bay Events Center, the ageless Randy Couture did it again, successfully defending his UFC heavyweight title against a dangerous foe 16 years his junior, Gabriel Gonzaga, and he did it in spectacular fashion, stopping the Brazilian in the third round in yet another timeless performance for the 44-year-old known as "The Natural".

Fight of the Night: Couture vs. Gonzaga

With a quick 1-2 to open things up, Gonzaga announced his arrival in the match. A split second later, a left by Couture staggered Gonzaga to let him know that he wasn't ready to give up his belt just yet. After that quick burst of action, the two clinched against the fence, but after a short stalemate, both resumed throwing bombs until Couture grabbed hold of his challenger and slammed him to the mat. Gonzaga quickly rose and fired back at Couture, but he was also now nursing a bloody and possibly broken nose from an apparent clash of heads. Couture kept him pinned against the fence and fired away in brief spurts for the final two minutes of the round until a last-second surge by the Brazilian that almost saw him lock in a guillotine choke as the bell rang.

Following perhaps the worst five minutes of his UFC career, Gonzaga tried to turn things around early in the second with a high kick similar to the one that earned him his title shot when he knocked out Mirko Cro Cop. Couture caught the kick, though, and drove Gonzaga to the fence. Things then went from bad to worse for "Napao" as he was docked a point for grabbing the fence and then continued to get drilled by the champion with power shots as they clinched at close range.

Already down three points, Gonzaga looked to press the action in the third and he did score with a kick to the head that got Couture's attention. Apparently it only served to make the champion work harder, and after pushing Gonzaga to the fence, he took him down and proceeded to rain blows down on the challenger, who, overwhelmed, was unable to defend himself, prompting a stoppage from Herb Dean at 1:37 of the third frame.

Former UFC welterweight champion Georges St-Pierre showed no ill effects from his knockout loss to Matt Serra, impressively pounding out a three-round unanimous decision over Josh Koscheck in the UFC 74 co-feature that saw him regain a good dose of the luster diminished by the loss of his title four months earlier.

St-Pierre's resurgent fellow countryman, middleweight Patrick Cote, scored his second straight Octagon win in the UFC 74 main card opener, handing up-and-comer Kendall Grove his first UFC loss via first-round TKO.

Knockout of the Night: Cote vs. Grove

Rising lightweight star Roger Huerta made it 4-0 for 2007 as he fought off a spirited challenge from previously unbeaten Alberto Crane to score a third-round TKO victory.

Lightweight contender Joe Stevenson moved one step closer to a title shot with a hard-fought unanimous decision win over Kurt Pellegrino in a closely contested three-rounder.

Former light heavyweight title challenger Renato "Babalu" Sobral broke a two-fight losing streak in impressive fashion, grounding and pounding David Heath before submitting him in the second round of their UFC 74 preliminary bout at the Mandalay Bay Events Center, but his victory was marred by a classless display which saw the Brazilian keep a finishing hold locked on seconds after Heath tapped out and referee Steve Mazzagatti attempted to break the fighters to halt the bout.

Former UFC heavyweight champion Frank Mir showed that he still had some gas left in the tank as he easily submitted Antoni Hardonk at 1:17 of the first round.

Submission of the Night: Leites vs. Jensen

Thales Leites and Ryan Jensen gave the fans non-stop action in their middleweight bout, with some solid give-and-take eventually leading to a submission victory for Leites in the first round.

Lightweight dynamo Clay Guida fought a disciplined three-rounder against PRIDE Bushido veteran Marcus Aurelio, winning a split decision.

UFC 75 *Champion vs. Champion*

08 Sept. 2007

02 Arena, London, England

Debut: Tomasz Drwal

Fighters			Division	Method	Time	Round
Main Card						
Quinton Jackson	def.	Dan Henderson	Light Heavyweight	Unanimous Decision		5
Michael Bisping	def.	Matt Hamill	Light Heavyweight	Split Decision	—	3
Cheick Kongo	def.	Mirko Cro Cop	Heavyweight	Unanimous Decision	—	3
Marcus Davis	def.	Paul Taylor	Welterweight	Submission - Armbar	4:14	1
Houston Alexander	def.	Alessio Sakara	Light Heavyweight	Technical Knockout	1:01	1
Preliminary Card						
Gleison Tibau	def.	Terry Etim	Lightweight	Unanimous Decision	—	3
Thiago Silva	def.	Tomasz Drwal	Light Heavyweight	Technical Knockout	4:23	2
Dennis Siver	def.	Naoyuki Kotani	Lightweight	Knockout	2:04	2
Jess Liaudin	def.	Anthony Torres	Welterweight	Technical Knockout	4:10	1

Sometimes history can occur in seconds. In September 2007, it took 25 minutes as Quinton "Rampage" Jackson became the first man in MMA history to unify a major title, decisioning Dan Henderson over five rounds to defend his UFC light heavyweight championship and take home Henderson's PRIDE 205-pound belt in the process. Scores were 48-47 and 49-46 twice.

There was no feeling-out process in this one, as Jackson immediately tried swinging for the fences before pushing Henderson to the Octagon fence. Henderson responded well, reversing position and scoring with knees to the leg. With 3:30 to go in the round, Henderson worked free and went in for the takedown, putting Jackson on his back and then moving into side control. From there, Henderson again fired away with knees. The final 30 seconds of the opening frame saw Jackson rebound and land some strikes at close range, but Henderson had the last word with a knee to the head at the bell.

Henderson kept Jackson off balance in the beginning stages of round two, and he eventually made good on his feints with a solid takedown. After a stay on the mat, the two rose and battled it out on the fence before Jackson got his own takedown and opened up with point-scoring punches and forearms.

The action was tense early in the third, with both fighters finally letting go with punches at close range. Soon, the bout again went to the mat, with Jackson controlling things from the side for much of the round.

In round four, Jackson hurt Henderson with a left and followed his foe to the mat. Henderson reacted quickly, going for Jackson's arm. Within seconds, Jackson freed his arm and resumed his attack, and in a war of attrition like this one, every strike counts.

With the fight perilously close, Henderson and Jackson traded punches in the final round, with Rampage jarring Henderson and holding the edge. An ill-advised kick gave Henderson the opening he needed, though, and he took Jackson to the mat. On the ground, Henderson controlled matters, but Jackson worked his way up and then returned the favor, with the two firing away until the fight was over.

England's own Michael Bisping kept his unbeaten record intact in the main undercard bout of the UFC 75 card, eking out a close split decision over Matt Hamill in a light heavyweight contest that finally pitted the two unbeaten stars of *The Ultimate Fighter 3*.

Scores were 29-28 twice and 27-30 for Bisping.

What was expected to be Armageddon turned out to be more of a chess match, but in the end, Cheick Kongo was Garry Kasparov as he scored a three-round unanimous decision win over Mirko Cro Cop in a heavyweight upset that saw the former PRIDE star lose two fights in a row for the first time in his mixed martial arts career.

Knockout of the Night: Alexander vs. Sakara

Following his 48-second win over Keith Jardine at UFC 71, Houston Alexander was actually forced to fight 13 more seconds against Alessio Sakara, but he was just as devastating, as he stopped the Italian in one minute and one second in the main card opener.

Marcus Davis continued on his hot streak against Paul Taylor, but not before "The Irish Hand Grenade" was put through a gut check from his British foe, who gave a spirited effort before being submitted late in the opening round.

Fight and Submission of the Night: Davis vs. Taylor

Gleison Tibau notched his third straight UFC victory with a unanimous decision over previously unbeaten Terry Etim.

Using a steadily escalating rate of attack, Brazilian prospect Thiago Silva upped his unbeaten slate to 11-0 with a second-round stoppage of UFC debutant Tomasz Drwal.

After losing his UFC debut to Jess Liaudin, Dennis Siver made sure that lightning didn't strike twice in his second Octagon bout, as he fought off a tight triangle choke attempt in the first round to knock out Naoyuki Kotani in the second.

Jess Liaudin nabbed his second consecutive Octagon victory in the UFC 75 opener, a first-round TKO of Anthony Torres.

25 GREATEST FIGHTS

UFC 86
FORREST GRIFFIN VS. QUINTON JACKSON

This was everything you hope a championship fight is, and for five rounds, Forrest Griffin and Quinton Jackson fought as if more than just the UFC light heavyweight belt was on the line. Filled with knockdowns, tactical stalemates, bone-rattling power shots, submission attempts, and drama, this fight had it all. And though there were rumblings in certain sectors about the decision, this was a close fight that could have gone either way. Griffin didn't have to explain himself for winning, and Jackson shouldn't get down on himself for losing. Both men did the sport proud on this night.

UFN10
SPENCER FISHER VS. SAM STOUT 2

When the rematch between lightweight standouts Spencer Fisher and Sam Stout made their exciting first fight look like a boring, three-round waltz, you knew it was good. Think of Forrest Griffin-Stephan Bonnar 1 sped up and with even more flush shots landed. Both fighters left it all in the Octagon that June night in Florida, and while they had the bruises and cuts to show for it, they also had the type of battle that will be remembered long after Fisher's three-round decision win is forgotten.

UFC 79
CHUCK LIDDELL VS. WANDERLEI SILVA

Six years in the making, the showdown between the most dominant light heavyweights of this era—Chuck Liddell and Wanderlei Silva—was worth the wait. Punctuated by brutal close range exchanges, this was a fight that had patrons at the Mandalay Bay Events Center on their feet and people at home jumping off their couches. In the end, Liddell revived his career with a three-round win, and in defeat Silva remained one of the sport's true action heroes, a guy anyone would still pay to watch fight.

UFN6
DIEGO SANCHEZ VS. KARO PARISYAN

Elite 170-pounders Diego Sanchez and Karo Parisyan locked horns in a bout that you can show to skeptics to say "this is what mixed martial arts is all about." Sanchez' introduction came at Parisyan's expense via decision. "The Heat" should never hang his head for a performance that saw him land his patented judo throws on Sanchez. He continue to battle, even as the seemingly indefatigable Albuquerque native kept attacking for 15 torrid minutes. If you can't appreciate this fight for its technical and visceral brilliance, you're watching the wrong sport.

UFC 58
GEORGES ST-PIERRE VS. BJ PENN 1

The big question mark about Georges St-Pierre entering his fight against prodigal son BJ Penn was how would he react if he had to face adversity. The first time it happened against Matt Hughes, St-Pierre folded. Against Penn in a first round that saw him bloodied and battered, the Canadian bit down on his mouthpiece and went to war, winning the next two rounds to eke out a close decision and earn a rematch with Hughes. It was stirring stuff from GSP in a bout that was tense from start to finish, as two of the best 170-pounders in the world matched wits and fists for 15 minutes.

TUF6 FINALE
ROGER HUERTA VS. CLAY GUIDA

To be considered great, a fight has to have more than frantic action and back and forth momentum swings, though those attributes don't hurt. What a fight truly needs to enter the realm of the classics is drama, and the bout between Roger Huerta and Clay Guida lived up to that end of the bargain spectacularly. Down all three scorecards, Huerta needed a miracle. Amazingly, he stunned Guida with a knee before taking his back and locking in a victory-clenching rear naked choke. It was a fight that saw everybody in attendance rise in unison to salute the most memorable battle of 2007.

TUF1 FINALE
FORREST GRIFFIN VS. STEPHAN BONNAR 1

A pitched battle between two fighters who fought as if a six-figure UFC contract was on the line (and it was), Forrest Griffin and Stephan Bonnar gave fight fans a brawl to remember. Add in the fact that this standup war was being televised live to millions on Spike TV and the impact of this bout was even more profound. As far as the fight goes, it was bombs away from the opening bell, with both fighters growing progressively more tired as the rounds passed by but refusing to give ground. In the end the decision went to Griffin, but there were no losers here, especially with contracts being awarded to both fighters after the verdict was announced.

UFC 52
MATT HUGHES VS. FRANK TRIGG 2

Just a week after Forrest Griffin and Stephan Bonnar waged war and put the UFC on the mainstream map, veterans Matt Hughes and Frank Trigg showed mixed martial arts fans a little war of their own, this time at the highest levels of the game with the UFC welterweight crown on the line. As soon as the pre-fight staredown ended, these two 170-pound standouts got right down to business, with Trigg stunning Hughes with strikes (and an inadvertent low blow) early and locking in a rear-naked choke seconds later. The champion escaped and after slamming Trigg to the mat, he locked in a choke of his own, ending the frenetic instant classic at the 4:09 mark.

UFC 35
JENS PULVER VS. BJ PENN 1

To most observers, this fight should have been over before it started. No one gave reigning lightweight champ Jens Pulver a chance of beating "The Prodigy" BJ Penn in this one, yet after one of the grittiest performances in UFC history, "Lil' Evil" successfully defended his crown via a five-round decision. The loss crushed the heavily favored Hawaiian. "I didn't know what I was gonna do with my life or my career," Penn remembered. "Everything was in shambles. I didn't know what to think, I didn't know where to go. The only thing I was sure about was that it was a great learning experience."

UFC 31
RANDY COUTURE VS. PEDRO RIZZO 1

Heavy-handed Brazilian Pedro Rizzo was seen as the heir apparent to the heavyweight crown held by Randy Couture, and once again, "The Natural" was seen by many as the underdog. Once the bell rang though, it was Couture's will and heart that ruled the day as he pounded out a close but well-earned unanimous decision over "The Rock". Want to know how much heart he showed that night? Ask anyone who was at the post fight conference about Couture being barely able to walk to his seat on the podium after eating Rizzo's hellacious leg kicks for five rounds.

UFC 22
FRANK SHAMROCK VS. TITO ORTIZ

One of the most memorable fights from the early UFCs, and in the eyes of many the best of the pre-Zuffa era, Tito Ortiz and Frank Shamrock went to war for three rounds where it was safe to say that either man had a good chance of eventually pulling the fight out. By the fourth round though, Ortiz was losing steam and his conditioning betrayed him, as Shamrock pounced and stopped him, defending his title for the fourth time in his final UFC bout. Ortiz learned a valuable lesson that day. Never again would conditioning be an issue for "The Huntington Beach Bad Boy", who instead adopted a Spartan philosophy when it came to preparing for a fight.

UFC 102
MINOTAURO NOGUEIRA VS. RANDY COUTURE

At Octagonside that August night in Portland, some likened this fight to the 1975 "Thrilla in Manila" between Muhammad Ali and Joe Frazier. That opinion stands today, knowing that while Minotauro Nogueira and Randy Couture may have been in the final third of their storied careers, when you put two great fighters together, there's just something that turns the clock back and lets you get a look at what made them so special. This was 15 minutes of fighting that anyone who saw won't soon forget, and it was also a primer for the rest of those young bucks on how you represent the sport and yourself when the bell rings.

TUF3 FINALE
KENDALL GROVE VS. ED HERMAN

The fact the UFC awarded contracts to both Kendall Grove and Ed Herman (the first time that was done since Forrest Griffin and Stephan Bonnar waged war in the *TUF1* finale) should tell you right away how good this one was. Herman controlled the first round, Grove came back in the second, and both fighters fought hard for the contract in a third round that had more twists and turns than a rollercoaster. Both fighters seemed seconds away from victory or defeat depending on the moment. It was a memorable fight to say the least.

TUF6 FINALE
JON KOPPENHAVER VS. JARED ROLLINS

One of the first things an emotional Jon Koppenhaver said after stopping fellow *TUF6* castmate Jared Rollins was "J-Roc's my friend, I didn't want to have to fight him." Well, the two welterweights fought like bitter enemies in this knock-down, drag-out brawl that saw myriad twists and turns and plenty of blood before Koppenhaver rebounded from almost certain defeat in the third to stop Rollins with a series of strikes.

TUF9 FINALE
DIEGO SANCHEZ VS. CLAY GUIDA

If Diego Sanchez and Clay Guida stood in opposite corners and didn't engage for 14 minutes and 30 seconds, the first 30 seconds of their bout still would have earned them a spot here; that's how good the frenetic, toe-to-toe opening was. Luckily for us, they kept the pace high throughout the three-round battle, and this fight had something for everyone. If someone ever wonders why the lightweights are considered the most exciting division in the sport, show them this fight.

UFC 14
MAURICE SMITH VS. MARK COLEMAN

UFC heavyweight champion Mark Coleman was undefeated and deemed unbeatable when he met Maurice Smith (who was making his UFC debut) at UFC 14 in 1997. But it was the kickboxing ace who showed the world that a striker could be successful in MMA as he stunned "The Hammer" with stellar takedown defense and superior striking en route to decision win and the world title.

UFC 68
RANDY COUTURE VS. TIM SYLVIA

Turning back the clock after a one-year retirement and knockout losses in two of his previous three fights, Randy Couture cemented his legendary status by dominating 6' 8" Tim Sylvia for 25 minutes en route to taking the UFC heavyweight title for an unprecedented third time. What made this one even more special was that from the first right hand Couture landed (dropping Sylvia in the process), the packed house of 19,000 fans in Ohio stood, roared and didn't sit down for the rest of the five-round bout. It was a special night for Couture, but even more memorable for everyone who was watching it.

UFC 4
ROYCE GRACIE VS. DAN SEVERN

With dominating finishes of Anthony Macias and Marcus Bossett, world-class wrestler Dan "The Beast" Severn emerged on December 16, 2004's UFC 4—Revenge of The Warriors show as perhaps the only person capable of giving superstar Royce Gracie a fight. And what a fight he gave, battling hard for over 15 minutes until Gracie finally locked in the finishing triangle choke to win his third Ultimate Fighting Championship tournament title.

UFC 125
FRANKIE EDGAR VS. GRAY MAYNARD 2

Perennial underdog Frankie Edgar filled that role once again when he defended his lightweight crown for the second time against the only man to beat him, Gray Maynard. And in the first round, it looked like the end of Edgar's reign as he was knocked down multiple times by "The Bully". Yet amazingly, Edgar roared back and the two lightweights traded shifts of momentum until a fair draw verdict was rendered at the end of five fast-paced rounds.

UFC 117
ANDERSON SILVA VS. CHAEL SONNEN

The drama before this UFC 117 bout took place couldn't hold a candle to what happened on fight night, as Anderson Silva and Chael Sonnen engaged in a championship fight for the ages. Yes, Sonnen dominated the majority of the bout with his ground and pound attack, but each moment before he would take the previously-untouchable titleholder to the mat was filled with tension as Silva unleashed the strikes many believed would end the fight. But even though he got rocked on a few occasions, Sonnen was resolute in his attack, and as the seconds ticked by, he was getting closer and closer to one of the sport's great upsets and the realization of a dream. Then, like the truest of champions, Silva pulled off a fifth-round submission. Calling it a spectacular comeback simply doesn't do it justice.

UFC 31
SHONIE CARTER VS. MATT SERRA

On a night of great fights at UFC 31 in May of 2001, welterweights Shonie Carter and Matt Serra may have fought the best one, with Carter ending the bout suddenly with a spinning back fist at the 4:51 mark of the third and final round. At the time of the knockout, the outcome of the bout was in doubt, with each man having his moments both standing and on the mat.

UFC LIVE 3
DIEGO SANCHEZ VS. MARTIN KAMPMANN

Diego Sanchez' face betrayed him on this night in Louisville, but his heart kept beating strong against Martin Kampmann. Sanchez battled through numerous cuts and a rough first round to take the next two frames and the fight from "The Hitman", proving once again that in a torrid firefight, the one fighter you want on your side is the man formerly known as "Nightmare", but now going by the moniker "The Dream".

UFC 63
MATT HUGHES VS. BJ PENN 2

BJ Penn was at the top of his game for ten minutes against Matt Hughes in their September rematch, and the champion—who had lost his title the first time to the "Prodigy"—appeared to be on his way to a repeat defeat, even turning to prayer to help him out of a tight submission lock by Penn in the second round. But you can never underestimate the heart of a champion, and Hughes roared back to stop Penn in the third round and avenge his loss to the Hawaii native. "I knew I had lost the first two rounds; that just meant I had three left", said Hughes.

UFC 67
FRANKIE EDGAR VS. TYSON GRIFFIN

It was a spectacular way for Frankie Edgar to start his UFC career—handing highly regarded Tyson Griffin his first pro loss—but even more impressive than the give-and-take action from both men was how Edgar survived a kneebar late in the third round that would have crippled most fighters. "I hate to lose," said Edgar after the fight. "I put so much on the line in that fight, and then with 45 seconds left I get caught in that. But there was no way I could tap. It did pop a couple of times, but once it popped once, I said, 'Hey, the hell with it. I'd rather limp around for a while and get this 'W,' than take a loss.'"

UFC 116
CHRIS LEBEN VS. YOSHIHIRO AKIYAMA

On a stellar card that featured several Fight of the Night worthy bouts, Chris Leben and Yoshihiro Akiyama took that as a challenge, and they went on to put on not just the UFC 116 Fight of the Night, but one of the best to date. Featuring fierce toe-to-toe action, changes in momentum, and a shocking and exciting finish, this bout had it all. And in the process, Leben, fighting (and winning) for the second time in two weeks, completed his transformation from MMA's problem child to legit middleweight contender.

UFC Fight Night 11

Thomas vs. Florian

19 Sept. 2007

The Pearl at The Palms, Las Vegas, NV

Debut: Joe Veres

Fighters			Division	Method	Time	Round
Main Card						
Kenny Florian	def.	Din Thomas	Lightweight	Submission - Rear Naked Choke	4:31	1
Chris Leben	def.	Terry Martin	Middleweight	Knockout	3:56	3
Nate Diaz	def.	Junior Assuncao	Lightweight	Submission - Guillotine Choke	4:10	1
Nate Quarry	def.	Pete Sell	Middleweight	Knockout	0:44	3
Preliminary Card						
Dustin Hazelett	def.	Jonathan Goulet	Welterweight	Submission - Armbar	1:14	1
Thiago Alves	def.	Kuniyoshi Hironaka	Welterweight	Technical Knockout	4:04	2
Cole Miller	def.	Leonard Garcia	Lightweight	Unanimous Decision	—	3
Luke Cummo	def.	Edilberto Crocota	Welterweight	Technical Knockout	1:45	1
Gray Maynard	def.	Joe Veres	Lightweight	Knockout	0:09	1

Lightweight contender Kenny Florian threw down a bold gauntlet after his last fight when he declared, "I finish fights." At The Pearl at The Palms, Florian lived up to his mantra with a first-round submission win over fellow 155-pound standout Din Thomas in the UFC Fight Night main event.

Florian led off the scoring early with high kicks, straying low with a thud when he went for the midsection, forcing a brief stoppage of the action. When the action resumed with 3:30 left, Florian kept throwing kicks, but a miss allowed Thomas to get him on the mat briefly.

Once standing, Florian continued to press, and when Thomas shot in with 1:30 remaining in the round and missed face first, apparently hurting himself on the way in, the New Englander jumped on his foe and pounded away with his right hand repeatedly until he worked his way to Thomas' back. Once there, the end was a mere formality, and Florian sunk in a rear naked choke that produced a tap out at 4:31 of the opening round.

Knockout of the Night: Leben vs. Martin

Middleweight Chris Leben bounced back from a string that saw him lose three out of four fights, and he did so in spectacular fashion, shaking off two bombs from Terry Martin to land with a crushing shot of his own that ended matters in the third and final round.

The winner of season five of *The Ultimate Fighter*, lightweight rising star Nate Diaz, began his post-*TUF* career in impressive fashion, patiently battling it out with Junior Assuncao before lowering the boom and submitting his foe late in the first round.

The result of the middleweight rematch between comebacking Nate Quarry and Pete Sell was the same two years later, but the road to Quarry's knockout win was quite different. In their first bout in 2005, Sell was stopped in the first round by Quarry, a controversial stoppage that was deemed too quick by most fans and pundits. This time around, the Oregon native Quarry dug himself out of a hole on the scorecards to end the bout in the third and final round.

Eager to erase the memory of that first bout, Sell came out bombing, hurting Quarry with the first right hand he landed. But Quarry, fighting for the first time since back surgery took him out of commission following his loss to then-UFC middleweight champion Rich Franklin in November of 2005, came back with heavy shots of his own, and it continued this way for much of the first two rounds.

Yet while Quarry was game and got his licks in, Sell's left hook right cross combination continually hit the mark, and after Sell dropped "The Rock" in the second round, it looked like only a matter of time before "Drago" would finish the bout.

Fight and Knockout of the Night: Quarry vs. Sell

In round three, though, Quarry would survive another early onslaught of crisp punching by Sell, and he finally landed with a big right hand of his own that sent the New Yorker down to the canvas hard. Quarry hesitated momentarily, then jumped in with one more right to the head, and referee Mario Yamasaki had seen enough, halting the war 44 seconds into the final frame.

Edilberto Crocota mocked Luke Cummo and showboated constantly in the early stages of his UFC Fight Night undercard bout at The Pearl at The Palms, but it was the New Yorker who had the last laugh, as he drilled the Brazilian with three straight right hands to stop his foe and continue his climb up the welterweight ranks.

The Ultimate Fighter 5 saw Cole Miller make it 2-0 in the Octagon with an entertaining three-round unanimous win over always-tough Leonard Garcia.

Another *TUF5* alum, Gray Maynard, finally got his first UFC win, but he didn't stay around long to get it, landing his first left hook with a thud that dropped Octagon newcomer Joe Veres. Maynard pounced immediately and after a three-punch combination, referee Mario Yamasaki wisely stepped in, halting the lightweight bout after just nine seconds.

Thiago Alves returned to the Octagon for the first time in eight months and he picked up where he left off, stopping Japanese veteran Kuniyoshi Hironaka in the second round of their welterweight battle.

Submission of the Night: Hazelett vs. Goulet

Lightweight up-and-comer Dustin Hazelett opened up the UFC Fight Night show in style, using his solid ground game to submit Jonathan Goulet in the first round.

UFC 76 *Knockout*

22 Sept. 2007

Honda Center, Anaheim, CA

Debuts: Mauricio Rua, Kazuhiro Nakamura, Scott Junk

Fighters			Division	Method	Time	Round
Main Card						
Keith Jardine	def.	Chuck Liddell	Light Heavyweight	Split Decision	—	3
Forrest Griffin	def.	Mauricio Rua	Light Heavyweight	Submission - Rear Naked Choke	4:45	3
Jon Fitch	def.	Diego Sanchez	Welterweight	Split Decision	—	3
Lyoto Machida	def.	Kazuhiro Nakamura	Light Heavyweight	Unanimous Decision	—	3
Tyson Griffin	def.	Thiago Tavares	Lightweight	Unanimous Decision	—	3
Preliminary Card						
Rich Clementi	def.	Anthony Johnson	Catchweight	Submission - Rear Naked Choke	3:05	2
Jeremy Stephens	def.	Diego Saraiva	Lightweight	Unanimous Decision	—	3
Christian Wellisch	def.	Scott Junk	Heavyweight	Submission - Heel Hook	3:19	1
Matt Wiman	def.	Michihiro Omigawa	Lightweight	Unanimous Decision	—	3

Following a knockout loss earlier in the year, many expected Keith Jardine to be an easy mark for the return of another recent KO victim, former UFC light heavyweight champion Chuck Liddell. But in the UFC 76 main event at Honda Center, Jardine made it clear that there is no such thing as a sure thing in MMA, as he used an effective mix of kicks and punches and a second-round knockdown to win a split decision.

Scores were 29-28 twice and 28-29 for Jardine, who rebounded from his loss to Houston Alexander. Liddell was looking to come back from the loss of his title to Quinton "Rampage" Jackson on the same May card.

In the eyes of many, PRIDE veteran Mauricio "Shogun" Rua was one of the best light heavyweights in the world. In Rua's UFC debut, Forrest Griffin elevated his own status at the expense of the feared Brazilian, dominating him throughout their three-rounder and then finishing the bout with a submission at the 4:45 mark of the final round.

From the outset, Griffin showed no fear, landing with strikes and fighting off Rua's takedown attempts. With a little over a minute gone, Rua got his takedown and started to open up with forearms in Griffin's guard. Griffin fought his way back to his feet with a little under half the round gone, and after some trading of punches, he scored his own takedown, followed by some ground strikes. Soon the two combatants, both showing swelling on their faces, stood and traded again, with Rua getting Griffin to the mat with 30 seconds to go. By the end of the frame, Griffin had reversed position and was in control at the bell.

Again standing in the pocket with Rua, Griffin scored early with strikes in the second until Shogun got the takedown and bloodied his foe's forehead with ground strikes. Incensed at seeing his own blood, Griffin fought back harder, reversing position on Rua and landing with his own strikes on the mat before the two stood again. With under two minutes left in the round, the two traded punches, with Rua looking to be the more fatigued. Griffin, tired himself, nonetheless worked Rua over when the bout hit the mat again.

Rua opened his final round offense with a takedown, and Griffin tried to pull a fast one with a submission that was turned away. While on the ground, Rua fired away with the occasional elbow while Griffin fired back and continued to outwork his more celebrated opponent from all angles, eventually getting into a dominant position where he locked in a rear naked choke and finished off Rua with just 15 seconds left.

At the time of the stoppage, Griffin was leading 20-18 on all three scorecards.

Submission of the Night: F. Griffin vs. Rua

Jon Fitch scored the biggest win of his mixed martial arts career, nabbing a three-round split decision over Diego Sanchez in a bout that was as difficult to score as it was picking a pre-fight victor.

Scores for Fitch were 30-27, 29-28, and 28-29.

Light heavyweight contender Lyoto Machida improved to 11-0 with a shutout unanimous decision win over PRIDE veteran and UFC newcomer Kazuhiro Nakamura.

Fight of the Night: T. Griffin vs. Tavares

Rising stars Tyson Griffin and Thiago Tavares lived up to all expectations in their lightweight showdown, with Griffin putting another Fight of the Year candidate in his pocket as he outpointed Tavares over three torrid rounds.

Rich "No Love" Clementi handed Anthony Johnson his first professional loss, submitting him in the second round of a catchweight bout of 177 pounds.

Jeremy Stephens scored his first UFC win, earning a unanimous three-round decision over tough, but outgunned, Diego Saraiva.

Christian Wellisch got his second UFC win in a row, submitting late replacement Scott Junk in the first round of their heavyweight bout.

Lightweights Matt Wiman and Michihiro Omigawa opened the show with a bang, getting the crowd on its feet early as Wiman pounded out an exciting three-round unanimous decision.

One Hit Wonder: Scott Junk

UFC 77 *Hostile Territory*

20 Oct. 2007

U.S. Bank Arena, Cincinnati, OH

Debut: Demian Maia

Fighters			Division	Method	Time	Round
Main Card						
Anderson Silva	def.	Rich Franklin	Middleweight	Technical Knockout	1:07	2
Tim Sylvia	def.	Brandon Vera	Heavyweight	Unanimous Decision	—	3
Alvin Robinson	def.	Jorge Gurgel	Lightweight	Unanimous Decision	—	3
Stephan Bonnar	def.	Eric Schafer	Light Heavyweight	Technical Knockout	2:47	2
Alan Belcher	def.	Kalib Starnes	Middleweight	Technical Knockout - Cuts	1:39	2
Preliminary Card						
Yushin Okami	def.	Jason MacDonald	Middleweight	Unanimous Decision	—	3
Demian Maia	def.	Ryan Jensen	Middleweight	Submission - Rear Naked Choke	2:40	1
Josh Burkman	def.	Forrest Petz	Welterweight	Split Decision	—	3
Matt Grice	def.	Jason Black	Lightweight	Split Decision	—	3

If anyone doubted the validity of Anderson Silva's first win over Rich Franklin in 2006, they weren't doubting it any more. The UFC middleweight champion defended his crown for the second time with a second-round stoppage of Franklin. The fight was more competitive but equally dominant.

Franklin was busy early with leg kicks and quick jabs to the head. Silva didn't fire his first shot until 55 seconds had elapsed, and that was a knee to the body followed by an attempt at the same clinch that ended Franklin's title reign. This time though, Franklin fought the attempt off well, and after a brief scramble against the fence, the bout hit the mat. Silva would rise after a few moments, and Franklin got close and pushed Silva to the fence. After breaking, the two engaged, with a left kick to the face by Silva the most telling blow before Franklin was able to push his foe to the fence again. Once the two separated, Silva brought out his bag of tricks, which included spinning backfists and, of course, his devastating knees. It was a right hook to the head, though, that dropped Franklin at the bell, and forced his cornermen to assist him back to his stool.

Knockout of the Night: Silva vs. Franklin

With his legs back apparently back under him, Franklin aggressively took after Silva to begin round two, but when "Ace" got too close, the champion showed why he is the best fighter in the world, pound for pound, as he hurt Franklin with another right hand, then started sending a ferocious arsenal of knees the hometown hero's way again. Finally, Franklin collapsed under the assault, causing referee John McCarthy to call a stop to the bout at 1:07 of the round.

You can't teach size and you can't teach experience. Rising star Brandon Vera found that out the hard way at UFC 77, but he still acquitted himself well before falling short via a competitive three-round unanimous decision to former two-time UFC heavyweight champion Tim Sylvia.

Scores were 29-27, and 29-28 twice for Sylvia, who was victorious in his first start since losing his UFC heavyweight title to Randy Couture at UFC 68 and a subsequent back surgery.

Hometown favorite Jorge Gurgel saw his two-fight winning streak snapped in the lightweight swing bout as Alvin Robinson outworked him on the ground en route to a three-round unanimous decision win.

Stephan Bonnar followed up his UFC 73 win over Mike Nickels with a second-round TKO over Eric Schafer in their light heavyweight bout, giving "The American Psycho" his first two-fight winning streak since 2006.

In the main card opener, an exciting middleweight bout between prospects Alan Belcher and Kalib Starnes came to an abbreviated end when a nasty gash on the forehead of Starnes forced a halt to the contest in the second round.

Japan's Yushin "Thunder" Okami made his case for a shot at the middleweight crown in a preliminary bout, using a strong second and third-round surge to break open a close fight with Jason MacDonald and earn a unanimous decision victory.

Decorated grappling master Demian Maia improved to 7-0 in his UFC debut, submitting Ryan Jensen with a rear naked choke in the opening round of their middleweight matchup.

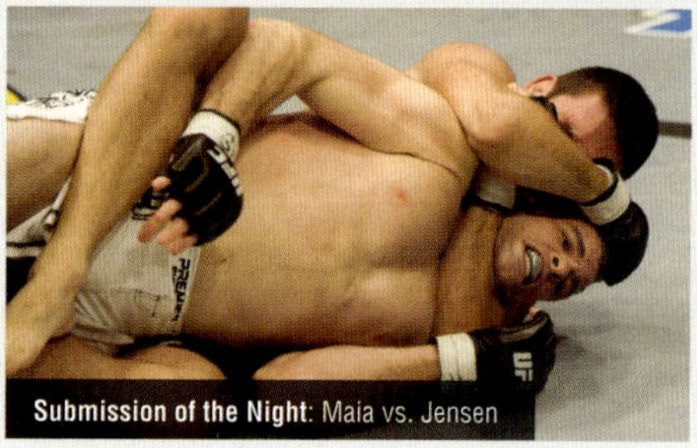

Submission of the Night: Maia vs. Jensen

A third-round knockdown may have been the deciding factor in the welterweight bout between Josh Burkman and Forrest Petz, with the single left hand allowing Burkman to escape with a three-round split decision victory.

For a few seconds, Matt Grice thought he would have to fight again for his first UFC victory after an exciting nip-and-tuck battle with Jason Black. But after a miscalculation of the scores was discovered in the UFC 77 opener, the Oklahoma lightweight was elated to find out he had earned a split decision victory in his second Octagon bout, and not a draw.

Fight of the Night: Grice vs. Black

UFC 78 *Validation*

17 Nov. 2007

Prudential Center, Newark, NJ

Debuts: Ryo Chonan, Jason Reinhardt, Akihiro Gono

Fighters			Division	Method	Time	Round
Main Card						
Rashad Evans	def.	Michael Bisping	Light Heavyweight	Split Decision	—	3
Thiago Silva	def.	Houston Alexander	Lightweight	Knockout	3:25	1
Karo Parisyan	def.	Ryo Chonan	Welterweight	Unanimous Decision	—	3
Ed Herman	def.	Joe Doerksen	Middleweight	Knockout	0:39	3
Frankie Edgar	def.	Spencer Fisher	Lightweight	Unanimous Decision	—	3
Preliminary Card						
Thiago Alves	def.	Chris Lytle	Welterweight	Technical Knockout - Cuts	5:00	2
Joe Lauzon	def.	Jason Reinhardt	Lightweight	Submission - Rear Naked Choke	1:14	1
Marcus Aurelio	def.	Luke Caudillo	Lightweight	Technical Knockout	4:29	1
Akihiro Gono	def.	Tamdan McCrory	Welterweight	Submission - Armbar	3:19	2

After his UFC 73 draw with Tito Ortiz, Rashad Evans' place in the talent-rich light heavyweight division was questioned. In the UFC 78 main event, he returned to his lofty spot in the 205-pound pecking order with a solid split decision win over Michael Bisping.

Scores were 29-28 twice and 28-29 for the unbeaten Evans, whose takedowns and quick right hands proved to be the deciding factor.

Evans kept Bisping off balance to begin the fight, eventually putting "The Count" on the canvas 30 seconds into the bout. Bisping battled back to his feet, but Evans quickly closed the gap with his faster hands and again pushed the fight to the fence as he looked for a takedown. After the two finally broke, Evans landed upstairs and Bisping responded with a kick, but Evans took advantage and put his foe on the mat and transitioned into side control. Evans, pushing the pace, scored with a couple of forearms before scoring yet another takedown just before the round ended.

Bisping came out fast to start the second, but Evans wasn't rattled. Instead, he scored with a right hand and then picked Bisping up for an Octagon-shaking slam. Bisping got his wits back almost instantly and after a short stalemate, referee Dan Miragliotta stood the fighters up. Bisping started to find his range briefly, only to again get nailed by Evans' 1-2s. But with under a minute to go, Bisping was unquestionably the busier and more effective of the two fighters.

With his strong second-round finish still in his mind, Bisping again pushed the pace in the final frame, but Evans drew first blood in the third with a takedown. Bisping turned the tables and reversed position with 3:30 left, but the two stood moments after and looked to make their fortunes on their feet. There, Evans was too fast and accurate with his strikes, and his right hands were almost inevitably followed by takedowns. Though Bisping gamely looked for a finishing haymaker in the final seconds, the rush was too little, too late.

Houston Alexander was everywhere in the weeks leading up to his bout against Thiago Silva, with newspapers and websites telling his story with a fervor, but when the two 205-pounders stepped into the Octagon, it was Silva who carved his own name into the headlines as he stopped the knockout artist in the first round.

Welterweight contender Karo Parisyan didn't thrill the fans in attendance with his bout against PRIDE vet Ryo Chonan, but he did do enough to get the victory as he scored a unanimous decision over the Japan native.

Knockout of the Night: Herman vs. Doerksen

In middleweight action, Ed Herman avenged a 2004 loss to Joe Doerksen, knocking out his foe in the third and final round.

Unbeaten Frankie Edgar thrilled the New Jersey crowd in the main card opener, scoring the biggest win of his young career by scoring a shutout three-round decision over Spencer Fisher in a bout that made up in dominance what it may have lacked in explosive action.

The welterweight war between Thiago Alves and Chris Lytle lived up to expectations for the first ten minutes, but two cuts suffered by Lytle prevented the final five minutes from being fought, allowing Alves to leave the Octagon with a second-round TKO victory on the UFC 78 undercard.

Joe Lauzon made quick work of UFC debutant Jason Reinhardt in their lightweight bout, submitting the previously unbeaten Illinois native at 1:14 of the first round.

Brazilian jiu-jitsu ace Marcus Aurelio notched his first UFC win in his second try, improving to 15-5 overall with a first-round TKO of Luke Caudillo.

In the welterweight opener, Akihiro Gono showed that while it's nice to be 21 years old, in MMA it's better to have experience in your pocket, as the PRIDE veteran shook off an early barrage from Tamdan McCrory to tap out the previously unbeaten youngster in the second round.

Fight of the Night: Alves vs. Lytle

Submission of the Night: Gono vs. McCrory

UFC 79 *Nemesis*

29 Dec. 2007

Mandalay Bay Events Center, Las Vegas, NV

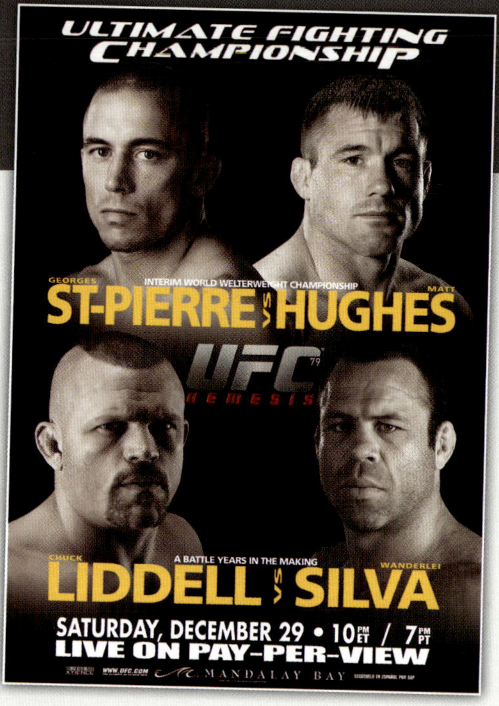

Debuts: Soa Palelei, Rameau Thierry Sokoudjou, Luiz Cane

Fighters			Division	Method	Time	Round
Main Card						
Georges St-Pierre	def.	Matt Hughes	Welterweight	Submission - Armbar	4:52	2
Chuck Liddell	def.	Wanderlei Silva	Light Heavyweight	Unanimous Decision	—	3
Eddie Sanchez	def.	Soa Palelei	Heavyweight	Technical Knockout	3:24	3
Lyoto Machida	def.	Rameau Thierry Sokoudjou	Light Heavyweight	Submission - Arm Triangle	4:20	2
Rich Clementi	def.	Melvin Guillard	Lightweight	Submission - Rear Naked Choke	4:40	1
Preliminary Card						
James Irvin	def.	Luiz Cane	Light Heavyweight	Opponent Disqualified	1:51	1
Manny Gamburyan	def.	Nate Mohr	Lightweight	Submission - Achilles Lock	1:31	1
Dean Lister	def.	Jordan Radev	Middleweight	Unanimous Decision	—	3
Roan Carneiro	def.	Tony DeSouza	Welterweight	Technical Knockout	3:30	2
Mark Bocek	def.	Doug Evans	Lightweight	Unanimous Decision	—	3

After a forgettable spring that saw him go through personal and professional turmoil which culminated in a knockout loss to Matt Serra at UFC 69, Georges St-Pierre rebounded spectacularly in the second half of 2007. He beat Josh Koscheck in August, then ended the year at the Mandalay Bay Events Center with a second-round submission win over Matt Hughes to take the interim UFC welterweight title and end their trilogy with a 2-1 edge.

"It's a good honor, but Matt Serra is the target," said St-Pierre of his interim title win. "Until I get my belt back, I'm not gonna consider myself a real champion."

"No excuses," said a gracious Hughes, who defeated St-Pierre in their first fight in 2004; St-Pierre returned the favor in November of 2006. "I came in 120 percent and really trained hard for this fight and had a great gameplan. Georges is the better fighter."

Submission of the Night: St-Pierre vs. Hughes

The crowd engaged more than the fighters in the opening 90 seconds, dueling with chants of "USA" and "GSP". But then the action picked up, with St-Pierre putting Hughes on his back. Hughes, in fairly unfamiliar territory, got pushed to the fence by the Montreal resident, who fired away with ground strikes on the two-time welterweight king. Hughes tried to stem the tide by holding St-Pierre close in order to force a standup, but a series of short slams diluted that plan quickly, and with seconds left St-Pierre appeared to be close to a finish before the bell rang.

St-Pierre's domination continued in the second round as he again took the wrestler down to the canvas. While there, St-Pierre's work rate was relentless as he fired away with strikes while looking to improve his position. Hughes, while game, was getting outhustled and outfought at every turn. And with under two minutes left, St-Pierre got his foe's back for a moment before the two stood. In the final minute Hughes tried for a slam but was instead tripped and thrown to the mat. The end followed, with St-Pierre sinking in an armbar that produced a verbal tap out at 4:52 of the round.

At UFC 79, fans received proof that there is a Santa Claus. And though he came six years and four days late, he finally showed up with a fight between the two most dominant light heavyweights in history, Chuck Liddell and Wanderlei Silva, and the ensuing three-round war lived up to all expectations, with Liddell emerging victorious via three-round unanimous decision.

Scores were 30-27 twice and 29-28 for the former UFC light heavyweight champion, who broke a two-fight losing streak with his win over the former PRIDE champion, who was trying to stop his own two-fight skid.

"It would have been a travesty if we wouldn't have fought because it's a great fight for the fans," said Liddell in the understatement of the year. "I knew it was a big fight for everybody, especially for me to get back on track."

"I gave my best," said Silva. "Win or lose, I like to give to my fans."

Both fighters did that and more.

Fight of the Night: Liddell vs. Silva

With flashbulbs lighting up the arena, both fighters circled each other warily early on, not wanting to be the first to make a fatal tactical error. Silva, after dropping his hands to taunt Liddell, engaged first, but none of his blows struck paydirt. Shortly thereafter, Liddell apparently hurt Silva, with Silva backing up to the fence either because his legs were rubbery or because he wanted to lure Liddell in. Whatever the reason, it worked, and the two threw bombs at each other, with Silva getting the worst of it as he emerged with a mouse under his left eye. Silva soon got his licks in and the crowd erupted, growing even louder as Liddell and Silva both scored with power shots that would have crumbled lesser men. After some more furious exchanges, the bell rang, ending one of the most exciting rounds of the year.

The action in round two heated up immediately, with Silva winging bombs at Liddell, whose straighter punches were leaving their mark on the Brazilian's face. Not surprisingly though, Silva kept trudging forward, eager to engage and loving the battle. A minute and a half in, Silva started to land more on Liddell, but "The Iceman" was accurate with his return fire. A slip to the canvas by Liddell put fans on their feet, but the Californian rose quickly, only to eat some power shots, one of which put him down for real, seconds later. With under two minutes to go, Liddell and Silva clinched near the fence, and Silva, now bleeding from over his right eye, took the worst of it. Silva wouldn't surrender though, and the ensuing exchanges to the bell were nothing short of spectacular.

"I hit him with a lot of big shots and he kept coming," said Liddell.

Looking to close the show, Liddell, cut under his left eye, shot in and took Silva down to start the final round, but the two quickly rose back to their feet. The pace dipped for about 20 seconds after that before the haymakers started flying again. Liddell scored with a flush right that Silva shook off, and Silva responded with a shot off the top of the head that Liddell walked through. Surprisingly, a spinning backfist by Liddell jarred Silva, and a follow-up barrage got "The Axe Murderer" in serious trouble against the fence. Just when referee Herb Dean moved in to watch the action closely for a possible stoppage, Silva started firing back with both hands. At this point, with under two minutes left, it appeared that Liddell was winning this war, yet nothing stopped Silva's forward march, and he gamely followed the tired Liddell in search of the equalizer. Though it never came, there was no question that the years of waiting for the fight were worth it, regardless of who won and who lost.

Maybe it was the aggressive style of UFC newcomer Rameau Thierry Sokoudjou brought to the Octagon that brought out the best in light heavyweight contender Lyoto "The Dragon" Machida, but whatever it was, that's what fans got, as the Brazilian scored the biggest and most impressive win of his UFC career by submitting the highly-touted Cameroon native in the second round.

There was no resolution to the bad blood between lightweights Rich Clementi and Melvin Guillard, even after Clementi submitted his bitter rival late in the first round of the Louisiana grudge match.

Heavyweight hopeful Eddie Sanchez continued his rise up the ranks with a second-round TKO of UFC newcomer Soa Palelei.

Knockout of the Night:
Sanchez vs. Palelei

Lightweight up-and-comer Manny Gamburyan wasted no time getting back in the saddle after his disappointing injury-induced loss to Nate Diaz in *The Ultimate Fighter 5* finale, showing no ill effects from his shoulder surgery en route to a first-round submission win over Nate Mohr.

James Irvin got his first UFC win since November of 2006 the hard way when he was drilled by a knee to the head from Octagon newcomer Luiz "Banha" Cane while down on the mat, causing the Brazilian to be disqualified at 1:51 of the first round.

It was far from compelling stuff, but middleweight Dean Lister scored a three-round unanimous decision over Jordan Radev.

Roan Carneiro improved to 2-1 in the UFC with a second-round TKO win over Tony DeSouza.

Mark Bocek scored his first UFC victory in his second attempt, outpointing Doug Evans.

One Hit Wonder: Soa Palelei

PRIDE

Launched in 1997, the PRIDE Fighting Championships quickly became the gold standard for mixed martial arts in Japan, and over the years, the organization was the only serious competition for the United States-based UFC in terms of winning over the loyalties of fight fans.

Home to such superstars such as Wanderlei Silva, Kazushi Sakuraba, Antonio Rodrigo "Minotauro" Nogueira, Mauricio "Shogun" Rua, Fedor Emelianenko, Takanori Gomi, Mirko Cro Cop and Quinton "Rampage" Jackson, PRIDE fights matched spectacle with sport to create a phenomenon in the Land of the Rising Sun.

In the early days, the promotion relied on the star power of fighters like Rickson and Renzo Gracie and former UFC stars Kimo Leopoldo, Dan Severn, Gary Goodridge and Oleg Taktarov to sell their product in Asia. But as the shows progressed, new stars emerged.

The first great star to make his name in PRIDE was the homegrown Kazushi Sakuraba, who scored victories over UFC vets Carlos Newton and Vitor Belfort before earning the nickname "The Gracie Hunter" for his wins against Royler, Royce, Renzo and Ryan. His 90-minute epic with Royce Gracie in the opening round of the 2000 PRIDE Openweight Grand Prix is consistently mentioned as one of the greatest fights of all-time, and his wars with Jackson and Silva are also key parts of his legacy.

In that 2000 Grand Prix, it was old pro Mark Coleman who scored four emotional victories to win the title and resurrect a career that had gone sour in the United States. The win by "The Hammer" opened the door for more vets to make their way to Japan. At the same time, a new breed of fighter was emerging, and soon it was Minotauro Nogueira, Silva, Ricardo Arona, Murilo Bustamante and Shogun and "Ninja" Rua who were dominating the circuit.

In the heavyweight ranks, the resilient Minotauro became the first PRIDE heavyweight champion. He would hold the belt until Russian powerhouse Fedor Emelianenko seized the throne in 2003.

Some of the organization's best fights were taking place at 205 pounds though, as a heated rivalry erupted between Wanderlei Silva and Rampage Jackson. They would fight twice in PRIDE, with Silva winning both. Even UFC star Chuck Liddell got into the act, as he was sent to Japan three times to fight in PRIDE bouts.

In 2003, the PRIDE Bushido series was launched, and with it came star-making turns by Shogun Rua, Takanori Gomi and even former UFC lightweight champ Jens Pulver.

With all this action going on, fight fans quickly grasped on to anything and everything involving PRIDE. Since the rules varied from UFC matches, it gave aficionados a different look than what they were used to. First, PRIDE matches took place in a ring as opposed to the Octagon. The rounds system was also different, head stomps and soccer kicks were legal, and there was a yellow card system where the referee could penalize a fighter for a lack of action, causing the fighter to lose 10 percent of his purse.

Despite their significant run of success, and even two events in the United States in 2006-07, the company was eventually sold in March of 2007. Luckily, it fell into good hands in the form of UFC majority owners Lorenzo and Frank Fertitta, two fans who vowed that the legacy of PRIDE would not be forgotten.

Soon the likes of Minotauro, Cro Cop, Silva, Gomi, Rua and Jackson made their way into the UFC Octagon. Fans finally got to see the dream fights they had been waiting years for. But PRIDE is not gone; in fact it's still alive through the Spike TV series *The Best of PRIDE Fighting Championships*, where fans old and new can relive the greatest MMA fights ever seen in the ring.

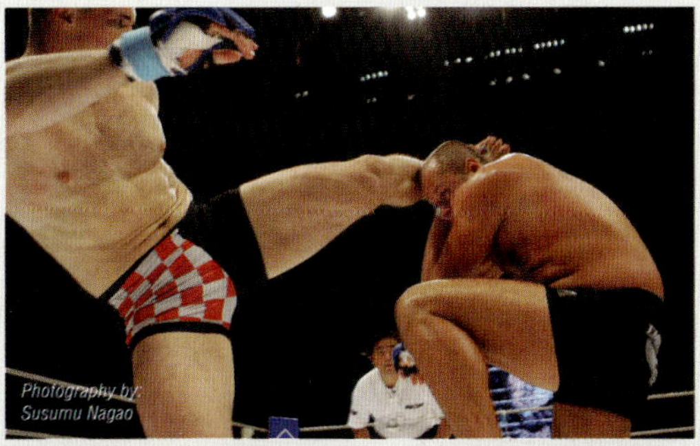

Photography by Susumu Nagao

PRIDE CHAMPIONSHIP ROSTER

HEAVYWEIGHT

 Antonio Rodrigo Nogueira

 Fedor Emelianenko

MIDDLEWEIGHT

(205 POUNDS – EQUIVALENT TO UFC LIGHT HEAVYWEIGHT)

 Wanderlei Silva

 Dan Henderson

WELTERWEIGHT

(183 POUNDS – ROUGHLY EQUIVALENT TO UFC MIDDLEWEIGHT)

 Dan Henderson

LIGHTWEIGHT

(161 POUNDS – ROUGHLY EQUIVALENT TO UFC LIGHTWEIGHT)

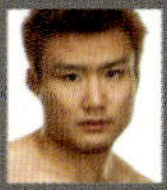 Takanori Gomi

GRAND PRIX CHAMPIONS

 Mark Coleman

 Mauricio "Shogun" Rua

 Mirko Cro Cop

 Wanderlei Silva

 Dan Henderson

 Kazuo Misaki

 Fedor Emelianenko

 Takanori Gomi

UFC CHAMPIONS WHO HAVE FOUGHT IN PRIDE

 Josh Barnett

 Chuck Liddell

 Kevin Randleman

 Vitor Belfort

 Carlos Newton

 Ricco Rodriguez

 Murilo Bustamante

 Antonio Rodrigo Nogueira

 Anderson Silva

 Mark Coleman

 Jens Pulver

 Maurice Smith

 Quinton Jackson

The Ultimate Fighter 6 Finale

Team Hughes vs. Team Serra

08 Dec. 2007

The Pearl at The Palms, Las Vegas, NV

Debuts: Troy Mandaloniz, Richie Hightower, Roman Mitichyan, Dorian Price, Paul Georgieff, Matt Arroyo, John Kolosci, Ben Saunders, Dan Barrera, George Sotiropoulos, Billy Miles, Jared Rollins, Jon Koppenhaver, Mac Danzig, Tommy Speer

Fighters			Division	Method	Time	Round
Main Card						
Roger Huerta	def.	Clay Guida	Lightweight	Submission - Rear Naked Choke	0:51	3
Mac Danzig	def.	Tommy Speer	Welterweight	Submission - Rear Naked Choke	2:01	1
Jon Koppenhaver	def.	Jared Rollins	Welterweight	Technical Knockout	1:59	3
George Sotiropoulos	def.	Billy Miles	Welterweight	Submission - Rear Naked Choke	1:36	1
Ben Saunders	def.	Dan Barrera	Welterweight	Unanimous Decision	—	3
Preliminary Card						
Matt Arroyo	def.	John Kolosci	Welterweight	Submission - Armbar	4:42	1
Jonathan Goulet	def.	Paul Georgieff	Welterweight	Submission	4:42	1
Roman Mitichyan	def.	Dorian Price	Welterweight	Submission - Ankle Lock	0:23	1
Troy Mandaloniz	def.	Richie Hightower	Welterweight	Technical Knockout	4:20	1

Roger Huerta didn't think defeating Clay Guida was going to be easy, but he didn't expect it to be this hard either. But after losing the first ten minutes of their fight, Huerta won the next 51 seconds, and those were the ones that counted, as "El Matador" scored a third-round submission victory.

Fight of the Night: Huerta vs. Guida

Guida got off to a good start on the mat, putting Huerta on his back and working his strikes while trying to improve position. Before the bell tolled, both fighters took turns trading the dominant position, displaying the type of action fight fans expected going into the bout.

There was more of the same in the second. Yet late in the round, it was clear that Guida's punches were doing more and more damage, this time dropping the Minnesotan and almost putting him out in the final 30 seconds, but by the end of the round, Huerta was fighting back and ready for the final five minutes.

With the fight on the line, Huerta walked right at Guida. Guida met him with the same hard punches that he had thrown and landed in the early rounds, but this time Huerta walked through them and let loose with his own bombs. And after landing a couple of big shots, Guida was visibly dazed. Huerta moved in for the kill as Guida desperately tried to get a takedown and weather the storm. Huerta wouldn't be denied though, and as the bout hit the mat, he sunk in a rear naked choke that ended the bout via tap out at 51 seconds of the final round.

Entering the final round, Huerta trailed 20-18 twice, and 20-17 on the judges' scorecards.

The Ultimate Fighter 6 welterweight finale between Mac Danzig and Tommy Speer was dubbed as a battle of technique (Danzig) versus strength (Speer)

Technique won, with Danzig controlling the action from the opening bell to the finish two minutes and one second later. With a rear naked choke submission win, the California veteran's long journey to the Octagon was finally complete as he earned the UFC contract he had sought for years.

Fight and Knockout of the Night: Koppenhaver vs. Rollins

In an action-packed, back-and-forth battle that caused the Palms crowd to erupt on a number of occasions, Jon Koppenhaver survived some rocky moments to pull out a stirring third-round stoppage victory over fellow Californian Jared Rollins.

George Sotiropoulos made a successful transition from the *TUF6* house to the Octagon, submitting Billy Miles in the first round of their welterweight bout.

Ben Saunders and Dan Barrera put on arguably the best fight of the sixth season of *The Ultimate Fighter*, with Saunders rising from the canvas to score a decision win. Their rematch didn't live up to the standard set by the first one, but the end result was the same, with Saunders earning a clear-cut three-round verdict over Barrera in the main card opener.

Ultimate Fighter teammates Troy Mandaloniz and Richie Hightower didn't fight like buddies in preliminary action, going toe-to-toe for much of the opening round until the heavy-handed Mandaloniz finished Hightower late in the first frame of their welterweight bout.

Matt Arroyo earned his first UFC win with a jiu-jitsu clinic against *TUF6* teammate John Kolosci, submitting his foe with an armbar in the first round.

Submission of the Night: Arroyo vs. Kolosci

Roman Mitichyan didn't get to show what he could do on *The Ultimate Fighter* due to injury, but he made quite an impression in his first UFC fight by taking Dorian Price to the mat almost immediately and sinking in an ankle lock which forced Price to tap out in just 23 seconds.

Jonathan Goulet proved that there is no substitute for experience, putting Paul Georgieff of *TUF6* to sleep with a rear naked choke in the first round.

One Hit Wonders: Richie Hightower, Dorian Price, Paul Georgieff, John Kolosci, Dan Barrera, Billy Miles, Jared Rollins

UFC 80 *Rapid Fire*

19 Jan. 2008

Metro Radio Arena, Newcastle Upon Tyne, England

Debuts: James Lee, Per Eklund, Paul Kelly

Fighters			Division	Method	Time	Round
Main Card						
BJ Penn	def.	Joe Stevenson	Lightweight	Submission - Rear Naked Choke	4:02	2
Fabricio Werdum	def.	Gabriel Gonzaga	Heavyweight	Technical Knockout	4:34	2
Marcus Davis	def.	Jess Liaudin	Welterweight	Knockout	1:04	1
Wilson Gouveia	def.	Jason Lambert	Light Heavyweight	Knockout	0:37	2
Jorge Rivera	def.	Kendall Grove	Middleweight	Technical Knockout	1:20	1
Preliminary Card						
Antoni Hardonk	def.	Colin Robinson	Heavyweight	Technical Knockout	0:17	1
Paul Kelly	def.	Paul Taylor	Welterweight	Unanimous Decision	—	3
Alessio Sakara	def.	James Lee	Light Heavyweight	Technical Knockout	1:30	1
Sam Stout	def.	Per Eklund	Lightweight	Unanimous Decision	—	3

It took BJ Penn more than 11 rounds—59 minutes and two seconds to be exact. Finally, in his third try, BJ Penn made history, submitting Joe Stevenson in the second round to become the UFC lightweight champion and join Randy Couture as the only two men in UFC history to win titles in two different weight classes.

Penn had fallen short in two previous 155-pound title tries, losing to Jens Pulver in 2002 and drawing with Caol Uno In 2003. He held the UFC welterweight title briefly in 2004, submitting Matt Hughes to win the belt.

Submission of the Night: Penn vs. Stevenson

It was a fight that almost ended as soon as it began, as Penn rocked and dropped Stevenson with a right hand that finished his opening barrage of the bout. He immediately looked for an opening on the mat to finish, but Stevenson's 40 fights of experience kicked in and he got his way out of danger. Penn never stopped working, though, and his subsequent ground and pound attack scored points and opened up a nasty cut on his opponent's forehead with a right elbow moments before the bell rang to end the round.

With blood streaming down his forehead, Stevenson came out with a sense of urgency to begin the second, closing the gap quickly and attempting to land with big shots when inside. The heavy-handed Penn kept his cool, countering Stevenson well and trying to keep him at the end of his punches. After a short break two minutes in for the Octagonside physician to check on Stevenson's cut, the action resumed and Penn tried to make sure the outcome wouldn't be decided by anyone but him. After jarring Stevenson and following him to the mat, he got in the full mount position and began to rain blows on the Californian, who showed the heart of a lion in continuing to battle against the odds. The fight would end shortly thereafter, as Stevenson gave up his back and Penn sunk in a rear naked choke, producing the tapout and the victory at 4:02 of the second round.

The Metro Radio Arena in England was a long way from Manaus, Brazil, but when heavyweights Fabricio Werdum and Gabriel Gonzaga met for the second time, the result was the same as it was in 2003, as Werdum stopped the former heavyweight title challenger in the second round.

"I fought Gonzaga before, so I know he is a very tough guy," said Werdum, who stopped Gonzaga in three rounds in their first fight in Brazil, when both had under five fights to their credit.

Marcus Davis didn't engage in the Fight of the Night that many expected, but he did make a strong case for Knockout of the Night honors (an award that eventually went to Wilson Gouveia) as he blasted out Jess Liaudin in a little over a minute to run his MMA winning streak to 11 fights.

Middleweight veteran Jorge Rivera revived his career at 35 years old, stunning and stopping *The Ultimate Fighter* winner Kendall Grove in just 80 seconds.

Wilson Gouveia rebounded from a rough first round against fellow light heavyweight contender Jason Lambert to score an emphatic knockout over "The Punisher" in the second stanza that earned UFC 80 Knockout of the Night honors.

Knockout of the Night: Gouveia vs. Lambert

Liverpool's Paul Kelly and Walsall's Paul Taylor did the British Isles proud in their welterweight battle that night, battling it out for three closely contested rounds, with Octagon debutant Kelly emerging victorious via a unanimous decision on the UFC 80 undercard at the Metro Radio Arena.

Fight of the Night: Kelly vs. Taylor

Heavyweight prospect Antoni Hardonk made short work of Northern Ireland's Colin Robinson, improving to 6-4 with a 17-second stoppage.

Italy's Alessio Sakara got back in the win column in his final bout as light heavyweight, scoring a first-round TKO of Detroit's James Lee.

In the opener, up-and-coming lightweight Sam Stout put together a disciplined gameplan and adhered to it for three rounds, winning a unanimous decision over Per Eklund.

One Hit Wonder: James Lee

UFC Fight Night 12

Swick vs. Burkman

23 Jan. 2008

The Pearl at The Palms, Las Vegas, NV

Debuts: Justin Buchholz, Corey Hill

Fighters			Division	Method	Time	Round
Main Card						
Mike Swick	def.	Josh Burkman	Welterweight	Majority Decision	—	3
Patrick Cote	def.	Drew McFedries	Middleweight	Technical Knockout	1:44	1
Thiago Tavares	def.	Michihiro Omigawa	Lightweight	Unanimous Decision	—	3
Nate Diaz	def.	Alvin Robinson	Lightweight	Submission - Triangle Choke	3:39	1
Preliminary Card						
Kurt Pellegrino	def.	Alberto Crane	Lightweight	Technical Knockout	1:55	2
Gray Maynard	def.	Dennis Siver	Lightweight	Unanimous Decision	—	3
Jeremy Stephens	def.	Cole Miller	Lightweight	Technical Knockout	4:44	2
Corey Hill	def.	Joe Veres	Lightweight	Technical Knockout	0:37	2
Matt Wiman	def.	Justin Buchholz	Lightweight	Submission - Rear Naked Choke	2:56	1

Former middleweight contender Mike Swick may have heard boos for the first time in his UFC career, but he was able to secure a victory in his welterweight debut, scoring a razor-thin three-round majority decision over Josh Burkman at The Palms.

Scores were 29-28 twice and 29-29, a decision that was not popular with the fans in attendance.

After four consecutive losses in the Octagon from 2004 to 2006, Patrick Cote's future in the UFC was anything but secure. But the Quebec fighter kept his nose to the grindstone, won twice in the organization in 2007, and at The Palms he ran his winning streak to three with an impressive first-round stoppage of hard-hitting Drew McFedries.

Knockout of the Night:
Cote vs. McFedries

Predictably, there was no feeling-out process between the two middleweight bangers, with each fighter landing heavy shots—both punches and kicks—in the early going. Cote was the more aggressive of the two, though, and after he absorbed a power shot from McFedries and jarred his foe with a return right to the head, it was the opening he needed. Cote opened with both hands, and McFedries could only cover up as he backed into the fence and down to the canvas. After a series of unanswered blows from "The Predator", referee Herb Dean had no choice but to halt the bout at 1:44 of the round.

Thiago Tavares bounced back from his first pro loss to Tyson Griffin, outpointing Japan's Michihiro Omigawa unanimously over three rounds in a lightweight contest.

Lightweights Nate Diaz and Alvin Robinson kicked off main card action with an energetic and skillful display of groundfighting, and Diaz eventually emerging with a first-round submission win.

Submission of the Night:
Diaz vs. Robinson

Lightweight contender Kurt Pellegrino went back home to Jupiter, Florida with a hole in his mouth after a first-round kick from Alberto Crane sent his teeth through his lip, but he also went home with a victory, as he rebounded from a rough start to stop Crane in the second round of their UFC Fight Night preliminary bout.

Crane's left kick opened the bout with a thud, bloodying Pellegrino and sending him to the canvas. The jiu-jitsu master immediately looked for a fight-ending submission, but Pellegrino cleared his head and fought his way free. The two would stand for much of the remaining part of the round, with Pellegrino's crisper and more accurate shots bruising Crane before the bell.

Fight of the Night:
Pellegrino vs. Crane

In the second, Crane immediately looked to take the fight down to the mat, where he could work his ground magic, but Pellegrino's return striking was setting the pace and keeping Crane off balance. Eventually, a big right hand from Pellegrino landed flush on the now-bloodied Crane, forcing the Californian to turn his back. Pellegrino landed a couple more unanswered shots, and referee Herb Dean stepped in, halting the fight at the 1:55 mark of round two.

Gray Maynard expected to be coasting to an easy victory in the first round of his lightweight bout with Dennis Siver, but the Germany-based Russian rebounded in the second round and showed a great deal of heart and determination throughout the fight, eventually falling short via a three-round unanimous decision.

In a battle of two 155-pound young guns, 21-year-old Jeremy Stephens emerged victorious against 23-year-old Cole Miller, stopping him in the second round of their scheduled three-rounder.

UFC Fight Night 12 saw Corey Hill finally making his long-awaited UFC debut and he lived up to expectations, stopping Joe Veres in the second round of their lightweight bout.

Matt Wiman held off a spirited early charge from UFC newcomer Justin Buchholz in the opener, submitting the Alaska native at 2:56 of the first round.

UFC 81 *Breaking Point*

02 Feb. 2008

Mandalay Bay Events Center, Las Vegas, NV

Debuts: Brock Lesnar, Rob Yundt, Kyle Bradley, Tim Boetsch

Fighters			Division	Method	Time	Round
Main Card						
Minotauro Nogueira	def.	Tim Sylvia	Heavyweight	Submission - Guillotine Choke	1:28	3
Frank Mir	def.	Brock Lesnar	Heavyweight	Submission - Kneebar	1:30	1
Nate Marquardt	def.	Jeremy Horn	Middleweight	Submission - Guillotine Choke	1:37	2
Ricardo Almeida	def.	Rob Yundt	Middleweight	Submission - Guillotine Choke	1:08	1
Tyson Griffin	def.	Gleison Tibau	Lightweight	Unanimous Decision	—	3
Preliminary Card						
Chris Lytle	def.	Kyle Bradley	Welterweight	Technical Knockout	0:33	1
Marvin Eastman	def.	Terry Martin	Middleweight	Unanimous Decision	—	3
Tim Boetsch	def.	David Heath	Light Heavyweight	Technical Knockout	4:52	1
Rob Emerson	def.	Keita Nakamura	Lightweight	Split Decision	—	3

For a little over a minute, highly-touted newcomer Brock Lesnar looked like he was going to have his way with former UFC heavyweight champion Frank Mir in his Octagon debut. At this level of the game, it only takes one mistake to end up on the losing end of the equation, and Mir proved it, submitting Lesnar 90 seconds into the opening round.

Submission of the Night: Mir vs. Lesnar

Within seconds of the opening bell, Lesnar had dumped Mir on the canvas and started reigning down blows. An inadvertent shot to the back of the head by Lesnar forced a stoppage of the action and a deduction of a point by referee Steve Mazzagatti, though, and gave Mir a chance to clear his head.

While he would be put on the mat a second time, now by a right hand from Lesnar, this time Mir would weather the storm while fighting to sink in an armbar, and as Lesnar looked to finish, Mir grabbed his leg and sunk in the fight-ending kneebar.

After surviving a horrific childhood accident in which he was run over by a truck, it's hard to count Antonio Rodrigo "Minotauro" Nogueira out of anything, let alone a fight. So after he took a pounding from Tim Sylvia for ten minutes of their bout, he finally found the opening he needed in round three and submitted Sylvia to win the interim UFC heavyweight championship. In doing so, he became the first man in history to hold the UFC and PRIDE heavyweight championship belts.

Sylvia was sharp in the first round, and with under three minutes left, he scored with a left hook before shooting a right hand over the top that dropped the Brazilian. Minotauro survived the ensuing onslaught, but once the fight rose again, his legs had lost some spring and he was showing the scars of battle on his face.

Minotauro looked to secure a takedown in the second, but Sylvia fought off the attempt and picked at his foe with strikes from long range that scored with frightening regularity. He continued to battle, as is his custom, but Sylvia's takedown defense was stellar, and it left Minotauro with few options other than standing and trading with the much larger man.

Up two rounds, Sylvia kept to the game plan in round three, drilling Minotauro with right-hand leads and counters. Minotauro finally got his takedown, and after sweeping Sylvia, he sunk in a guillotine choke and forced the tap out at the 1:28 mark.

Fight of the Night: Minotauro vs. Sylvia

Middleweight contender Nate Marquardt said he learned a valuable lesson in his losing effort against UFC champion Anderson Silva the previous July, one about letting his hands go and fighting to win and not just to avoid losing. Well, he proved it at the Mandalay Bay Events Center, scoring perhaps his most exciting UFC victory to date by submitting veteran Jeremy Horn in the second round.

Middleweight Ricardo Almeida made a triumphant return to mixed martial arts and the UFC, winning his first MMA fight since 2004 by submitting late replacement Rob Yundt in just 68 seconds.

Lightweight contender Tyson Griffin showed poise and discipline in pounding out a three-round unanimous decision over Gleison Tibau.

Veteran UFC welterweight Chris Lytle wasn't interested in eking out decisions or putting on exciting fights that went the distance anymore. He came to finish, plain and simple, and "Lights Out" lived up to his new attitude, blasting out Octagon newcomer Kyle Bradley in just 33 seconds.

Knockout of the Night: Lytle vs. Bradley

Short notice was no problem for light heavyweight Tim Boetsch, as he made a successful UFC debut by stopping David Heath in the first round.

It took almost five years, but middleweight veteran Marvin Eastman finally got in the win column in the UFC as he scored a three-round unanimous decision over Terry Martin.

In the opener, *The Ultimate Fighter 5*'s Rob Emerson nabbed his first UFC win, outpointing Japan's Keita Nakamura via split decision in a lightweight bout.

UFC 82 *Pride of a Champion*

01
March
2008

Nationwide Arena, Columbus, OH

Debuts: Chris Wilson, David Bielkheden

Fighters			Division	Method	Time	Round
Main Card						
Anderson Silva	def.	Dan Henderson	Middleweight	Submission - Rear Naked Choke	4:52	2
Heath Herring	def.	Cheick Kongo	Heavyweight	Split Decision	—	3
Yushin Okami	def.	Evan Tanner	Middleweight	Knockout	3:00	2
Chris Leben	def.	Alessio Sakara	Middleweight	Knockout	3:16	1
Jon Fitch	def.	Chris Wilson	Welterweight	Unanimous Decision	—	3
Preliminary Card						
Andrei Arlovski	def.	Jake O'Brien	Heavyweight	Technical Knockout	4:17	2
Josh Koscheck	def.	Dustin Hazelett	Welterweight	Technical Knockout	1:24	2
Diego Sanchez	def.	David Bielkheden	Welterweight	Technical Knockout	4:43	1
Luigi Fioravanti	def.	Luke Cummo	Welterweight	Unanimous Decision	—	3
Jorge Gurgel	def.	John Halverson	Lightweight	Unanimous Decision	—	3

UFC middleweight champion Anderson Silva lost the first round to PRIDE 183-pound titleholder Dan Henderson in their UFC 82 title unification bout. In round two, Silva turned up the heat and finished Henderson with a rear naked choke to make it game over and another victory for the most dominant fighter in the sport.

Fight of the Night: Silva vs. Henderson

The opening seconds were tense as Henderson moved forward behind probing kicks to the leg. Silva fired back with a leg kick of his own 70 seconds into the bout, but a brief follow-up exchange produced no fireworks. As the bout approached the three-minute mark, Silva was trying to work his kicks, but it was Henderson who broke the ice scoring-wise with a takedown. Silva did his best to keep Henderson tied up as the Californian fired off a series of hammerfists at close range, and with under 30 seconds left Henderson briefly got into side control before ending up in Silva's guard by round's end.

Silva came out with more urgency in the second round, firing off kicks that Henderson was able to brush off with little difficulty. Henderson fired back with some haymakers, but while Silva waved his foe on, the close exchanges allowed Henderson to grab hold of "The Spider" and tie him up against the fence. Once the two separated, Henderson landed with a couple of hard strikes, but Silva responded with a right knee to the head that appeared to jar "Hendo". Henderson looked for the takedown, but Silva jumped into the top position and tried to land a finisher. As the round entered its final two minutes, Henderson's head was clear, but Silva was actively working, and with under a minute to go, the UFC champion got his foe's back and sunk in a rear naked choke. Henderson valiantly tried to fight it off and make it to the end of the round, but at the 4:52 mark he was forced to tap out.

Submission of the Night: Silva vs. Henderson

Standout 170-pound Josh Koscheck bounced back from his August 2007 loss to Georges St-Pierre in impressive fashion, stopping up-and-comer Dustin Hazelett in the second round.

Welterweight contender Diego "Nightmare" Sanchez broke a two-fight losing streak in style, forcing Octagon newcomer David Bielkheden to tap out due to strikes late in the first round of a scheduled three-rounder.

After a slow start, former UFC heavyweight champion Andrei Arlovski kicked his game into gear in the second round, stopping previously unbeaten Jake O'Brien to score his third straight victory and first stoppage since he knocked out Marcio Cruz at UFC 66 in December of 2006.

Florida's Luigi Fioravanti upped his record to 13-3 in his welterweight bout with Luke Cummo, snapping the two-fight winning streak of "The Silent Assassin" with a unanimous decision win while putting his own two-fight UFC losing streak to rest.

After a disappointing loss in his home state of Ohio at UFC 77, Cincinnati's Jorge Gurgel got it right the second time around, earning a three-round unanimous decision win over John Halverson.

Following a debut year in the UFC that saw him struggle to a 1-2 record in 2007, Heath Herring got 2008 off to a much better start, using some heavy shots standing and on the ground to earn a close three-round split decision win over Cheick Kongo.

Yushin Okami paved the way for a rematch against middleweight champion Anderson Silva with an emphatic second-round stoppage of comebacking former 185-pound champion Evan Tanner.

It had been eight UFC fights and eight wins for welterweight contender Jon Fitch, and though his victory over Octagon newcomer Chris Wilson saw the San Jose resident survive some hard strikes and a late triangle choke attempt, his unanimous decision win put him firmly in line for a world title shot.

Many expected the bout between middleweights Chris Leben and Alessio Sakara to be an all-out slugfest, and it lived up to expectations, with Leben's better chin and heavy hands proving to be the difference as he stopped "Legionarius" in the first round.

Knockout of the Night: Leben vs. Sakara

UFC Fight Night 13

Florian vs. Lauzon

02 April 2008

Broomfield Event Center, Broomfield, CO

Debuts: Samy Schiavo, Ryan Roberts

Fighters			Division	Method	Time	Round
Main Card						
Kenny Florian	def.	Joe Lauzon	Lightweight	Technical Knockout	3:28	2
Gray Maynard	def.	Frankie Edgar	Lightweight	Unanimous Decision	—	3
Thiago Alves	def.	Karo Parisyan	Welterweight	Technical Knockout	0:34	2
Matt Hamill	def.	Tim Boetsch	Light Heavyweight	Technical Knockout	1:25	2
Nate Diaz	def.	Kurt Pellegrino	Lightweight	Submission - Triangle Choke	3:06	2
James Irvin	def.	Houston Alexander	Light Heavyweight	Knockout	0:08	1
Preliminary Card						
Josh Neer	def.	Din Thomas	Lightweight	Unanimous Decision	—	3
Marcus Aurelio	def.	Ryan Roberts	Lightweight	Submission - Armbar	0:16	1
Manny Gamburyan	def.	Jeff Cox	Lightweight	Submission - Guillotine Choke	1:41	1
Clay Guida	def.	Samy Schiavo	Lightweight	Technical Knockout	4:15	1
George Sotiropoulos	def.	Roman Mitichyan	Welterweight	Technical Knockout	2:24	2
Anthony Johnson	def.	Tommy Speer	Welterweight	Knockout	0:51	1

In all sports, local rivalries tend to bring out the best in competitors. That was the case when New England standouts Kenny Florian and Joe Lauzon battled tooth and nail in their fast-paced UFC Fight Night main event until Florian broke the fight open in the second round, stopping Lauzon with a series of strikes at the 3:28 mark.

Fight of the Night: Florian vs. Lauzon

Lauzon had the crowd in his corner from the opening bell, but it was Florian who drew first blood with a series of elbows to the head when the two New Englanders hit the mat. The barrage caused a stoppage of the action and drew a warning from referee Herb Dean to Florian for using strikes that strayed to the back of the head. When the action resumed, Lauzon regained the lead, only to see Florian turn the tables and finish strong with some more ground strikes.

Florian pressed the action while standing early in the second, and as the first minute wound down, he got a takedown and moved into the mount position, where he fired away with his right hand and left elbow. Lauzon escaped the mount, drawing a roar from the crowd, but Florian fought back into the dominant position, firing strikes all the while. Eventually, the series of unanswered blows was too much, and Dean was forced to halt the bout.

Knockout of the Night: Irvin vs. Alexander

The UFC Fight Night bout between light heavyweight James Irvin and Houston Alexander promised explosive action, and it delivered for the eight seconds it lasted, with Irvin halting Alexander to nab the biggest win of his UFC career and join Don Frye as owner of the record for the fastest knockout in organization history (a mark later broken by Todd Duffee).

Brazil's Thiago Alves put a serious dent in the title aspirations of Karo Parisyan, halting the Armenian contender in the second round of a pivotal welterweight bout.

The Ultimate Fighter 5 winner Nate Diaz was impressive in the UFC when he was the hammer. On April 2, 2008, fight fans found out what he can do when he's the nail as he roared back from a horrible first round to submit Kurt Pellegrino in the second frame of a crowd-pleasing lightweight bout that was epitomized not only by a display of skill from the 22-year-old, but heart and determination as well.

Submission of the Night: Diaz vs. Pellegrino

Matt Hamill's return to the Octagon was a successful one, as he continued to show new dimensions to his game in stopping Tim Boetsch in the second round of their light heavyweight contest.

Unbeaten Gray Maynard pinned the first pro loss on fellow lightweight prospect Frankie Edgar, using his size, strength, and wrestling to earn a hard-fought unanimous decision victory.

Lightweight contender Clay Guida promised wins and finishes in 2008, and he lived up to his word in his first bout of the year, stopping French newcomer Samy Schiavo in the first round.

Josh Neer made a successful return to the UFC as a lightweight, pounding out a three-round unanimous decision victory over Din Thomas.

Marcus Aurelio was decisive and devastating in his opening round win over late replacement Ryan Roberts in a lightweight bout, taking just 16 seconds to up his record to 16-5.

Manvel "The Anvil" Gamburyan showed off his submission skills in the Octagon once again, following up his December 2007 win over Nate Mohr with a first-round victory over Cleveland's Jeff Cox in a lightweight contest.

The Ultimate Fighter 6's George Sotiropoulos nabbed his second straight UFC win, stopping tough fellow castmate Roman Mitichyan in the second round of their welterweight bout.

Budding welterweight star Anthony Johnson improved to 5-1 in the opener with an emphatic first-round knockout win over *The Ultimate Fighter 6* finalist Tommy Speer.

One Hit Wonder: Ryan Roberts

UFC 83 *Serra vs. St-Pierre 2*

19 April 2008

Bell Centre, Montreal, Quebec, Canada

Debuts: Jason Day, Cain Velasquez, Brad Morris

Fighters			Division	Method	Time	Round
Main Card						
Georges St-Pierre	def.	Matt Serra	Welterweight	Technical Knockout	4:45	2
Rich Franklin	def.	Travis Lutter	Middleweight	Technical Knockout	3:01	2
Michael Bisping	def.	Charles McCarthy	Middleweight	Technical Knockout	5:00	1
Nate Quarry	def.	Kalib Starnes	Middleweight	Unanimous Decision	—	3
Mac Danzig	def.	Mark Bocek	Lightweight	Submission - Rear Naked Choke	3:48	3
Preliminary Card						
Jason Day	def.	Alan Belcher	Middleweight	Technical Knockout	3:58	1
Demian Maia	def.	Ed Herman	Middleweight	Submission - Triangle Choke	2:27	2
Jason MacDonald	def.	Joe Doerksen	Middleweight	Technical Knockout	0:56	2
Rich Clementi	def.	Sam Stout	Lightweight	Split Decision	—	3
Cain Velasquez	def.	Brad Morris	Heavyweight	Technical Knockout	2:10	1
Jonathan Goulet	def.	Kuniyoshi Hironaka	Welterweight	Technical Knockout	2:07	2

It was loud at the Bell Centre on April 19, 2008—chair-shaking, eardrum-breaking, can't-hear-ring-announcer-Bruce-Buffer loud. Just when you thought the decibels couldn't go higher, they did, as hometown hero Georges St-Pierre regained his UFC welterweight crown from Matt Serra via a second-round TKO, putting a fitting cap on UFC 83, the organization's first-ever show in Canada.

Five seconds into the bout, St-Pierre secured a takedown, trying to ensure that there would be no repeat of April 7, 2007, the night Serra took his title via a first-round knockout. St-Pierre worked his punches and forearms while muscling the New Yorker to keep him down, and the Canadian kept firing away, wrapping up a dominant opening round.

The second round didn't start much better for Serra, as he found himself on his back again. For his part, St-Pierre kept moving and kept throwing punches, and even when the two stood, St-Pierre was throwing everything in his arsenal at Serra to keep him off balance, which led to another takedown with under three minutes left. The 33-year-old Serra, as expected, would not surrender to his younger foe, but for everything he tried, St-Pierre had an answer, and with under 30 seconds left, the Montrealer opened up and let all the frustration of the last year out in the form of vicious knees to the body. Again, Serra wouldn't quit under the onslaught, but referee Yves Lavigne intervened, stopping the bout at the 4:45 mark and crowning St-Pierre champion once again.

Based on the reception he got from the packed house at the Bell Centre, one would have thought that Rich Franklin was Canadian. But the former UFC middleweight champion from Cincinnati justified those cheers in emphatic fashion, posting his most impressive win in over two years by stopping Travis Lutter in the second round of their UFC 83 co-main event.

After a heated war of words with Charles McCarthy, Michael Bisping made his final statement in the Octagon, stopping the *Ultimate Fighter 4* alum at the end of the first round, notching a successful middleweight debut in the process.

The Ultimate Fighter 6 winner Mac Danzig began his post-reality-show UFC career in style as he submitted Toronto's Mark Bocek in the third and final round of their lightweight bout.

Nate Quarry tried to make a fight out of it against Surrey, British Columbia's Kalib Starnes, but it was to no avail, as what promised to be an exciting middleweight bout turned into a track meet. Starnes ran from Quarry the entire fight. Quarry cruised to a unanimous decision victory that was easy for him, but dreadful for the fans.

Knockout of the Night: MacDonald vs. Doerksen

Edmonton, Alberta's Jason MacDonald made it two in a row over Joe Doerksen in their middleweight bout, surviving some dicey moments in the opening round to stop his foe in round two. The two first fought in October of 2005, with MacDonald winning via a fourth-round submission.

Lethbridge, Alberta's Jason "Dooms" Day showed no signs of the first-time UFC jitters in his middleweight bout against Alan Belcher, impressively stopping his foe in the first round.

Submission of the Night: Maia vs. Herman

Brazilian middleweight Demian Maia made the jump from prospect to contender as he submitted a game Ed Herman with a triangle choke in the second round of an intriguing ground battle.

Streaking lightweight veteran Rich Clementi spoiled the Canadian homecoming of London, Ontario's Sam Stout, pounding out a hard-earned three-round split decision to run his unbeaten streak to five fights.

The pre-fight talk about Cain Velasquez labeled him as the heavyweight division's next big thing. The former Arizona State wrestling standout did nothing to dismiss that notion in his UFC debut, as he improved to 3-0 as a pro with a first-round TKO win over Brad Morris.

Fight of the Night: Goulet vs. Hironaka

Welterweights Jonathan Goulet and Kuniyoshi Hironaka got the UFC era in Canada off to a rousing start, putting on an exciting bout with plenty of twists and turns before Victoriaville, Quebec's Goulet ended matters via strikes in the second round.

UFC 84 *Ill Will*

24 May 2008

MGM Grand Garden Arena, Las Vegas, NV

Debuts: Goran Reljic, Antonio Mendes, Rousimar Palhares, Yoshiyuki Yoshida, Dong Hyun Kim, Shane Carwin

Fighters			Division	Method	Time	Round
Main Card						
BJ Penn	def.	Sean Sherk	Lightweight	Technical Knockout	5:00	3
Wanderlei Silva	def.	Keith Jardine	Light Heavyweight	Knockout	0:36	1
Goran Reljic	def.	Wilson Gouveia	Light Heavyweight	Technical Knockout	3:15	2
Lyoto Machida	def.	Tito Ortiz	Light Heavyweight	Unanimous Decision	—	3
Thiago Silva	def.	Antonio Mendes	Light Heavyweight	Submission - Strikes	2:24	1
Preliminary Card						
Rousimar Palhares	def.	Ivan Salaverry	Middleweight	Submission - Armbar	2:36	1
Rameau Thierry Sokoudjou	def.	Kazuhiro Nakamura	Light Heavyweight	Technical Knockout	5:00	1
Rich Clementi	def.	Terry Etim	Light Heavyweight	Unanimous Decision	—	3
Yoshiyuki Yoshida	def.	Jon Koppenhaver	Welterweight	Submission - Anaconda Choke	0:56	1
Dong Hyun Kim	def.	Jason Tan	Welterweight	Technical Knockout	0:25	3
Shane Carwin	def.	Christian Wellisch	Heavyweight	Knockout	0:44	1

After shutting down former champ Sean Sherk via third-round TKO in the UFC 84 main event at the MGM Grand Garden Arena, UFC lightweight champion BJ Penn was content that there were no more questions—either about his cardio or his claim to the title.

It was Sherk's first bout since July 2007, after which he was suspended by the California State Athletic Commission for a positive test for nandrolone. Sherk vehemently protested the result, but he was subsequently stripped of his belt. His game performance in defeat earned him a significant measure of redemption, though that was little consolation to the Minnesotan.

Sherk's punches were crisp in the early going, but Penn's jabs started to find their mark more as the round progressed, reddening the challenger's face and bruising him under his right eye.

Penn's reach was becoming more and more of an issue in round two, even though Sherk still aggressively pursued his foe and was able to score well when he got in close. But at long range, it was all Penn, who was able to control the pace behind his jab.

Cut under both eyes, Sherk strode out in determined fashion for round three, but his attempts to jab with Penn were unsuccessful. With under two minutes left, Sherk tried leg kicks to soften up Penn and met with some success, though not enough to put together a sustained assault that could turn the fight around. Just when it seemed like Sherk had survived another round, Penn attacked with a fury in the seconds remaining, catching Sherk with a left knee to the head as he came off the fence. Sherk dropped to the mat and Penn followed with flush strikes. The bell sounded but Sherk was deemed unable to continue by referee Mario Yamasaki, ending the bout in emphatic fashion.

With his trademark ferocity on full display, former PRIDE legend Wanderlei Silva broke a three-fight losing streak and won his first UFC fight since 1999, stopping highly regarded light heavyweight contender Keith Jardine in just 36 seconds.

Knockout of the Night: Silva vs. Jardine

It was an emotional night for former UFC light heavyweight champion Tito Ortiz in the final fight of his current contract with the organization, but it was equally so for unbeaten Lyoto Machida, who scored the biggest win of his career with an almost technically flawless three-round decision.

Fight of the Night: Reljic vs. Gouveia

UFC newcomer Goran Reljic made plenty of fans in his Octagon debut, halting Wilson Gouveia in the second round of an entertaining light heavyweight clash.

Unbeaten light heavyweight contender Thiago Silva made it to 13 the hard way, rising from an early knockdown to force newcomer Antonio "Samuray" Mendes to tap out due to strikes in the first round.

Submission of the Night: Palhares vs. Salaverry

Brazilian Top Team's Rousimar Palhares showed some slick jiu-jitsu in his Octagon debut, making it look easy as he submitted longtime UFC standout Ivan Salaverry with an armbar in the first round.

Rameau Thierry Sokoudjou earned his first UFC victory in impressive style, stopping Japanese vet Kazuhiro Nakamura at the end of the first round.

Rich Clementi survived a rough first round against British up-and-comer Terry Etim, but the ground game and savvy of veteran "No Love" proved too much as he pounded out a three-round unanimous decision victory, his sixth in a row.

One of two fourth-degree judo black belts on the show, Yoshiyuki Yoshida made short work of *The Ultimate Fighter 6*'s Jon Koppenhaver, submitting his foe with an anaconda choke in under a minute.

Dong Hyun Kim made a huge impact—literally—in his first UFC fight, slamming and stopping England's Jason Tan in the third round of their welterweight bout.

Highly-touted heavyweight prospect Shane Carwin delivered in his Octagon debut, stopping Christian Wellisch in the first round of the UFC 84 opener.

25 GREATEST SUBMISSIONS

UFC 1
ROYCE GRACIE VS. KEN SHAMROCK 1

When Royce Gracie submitted Art Jimmerson in the first UFC tournament in 1993, observers were confused. When the skinny gi-wearing Brazilian did the same thing to the imposing Ken Shamrock, this time by rear-naked choke in just under a minute, a sport was born. This is where it all began.

Photography by: Susumu Nagao

UFC 48
FRANK MIR VS. TIM SYLVIA

Remember the way a prime Mike Tyson approached his fights when he was the heavyweight boxing champion? Well, Frank Mir attacked submissions the way Tyson sought knockouts: He wanted to take an arm or leg home, and he almost got his wish against Tim Sylvia when he broke his opponent's arm with an armbar to earn the UFC heavyweight crown in 2004.

UFC 52
MATT HUGHES VS. FRANK TRIGG 2

After taking an inadvertent low blow and almost getting choked out by Frank Trigg, Matt Hughes not only broke free from the hold, but he picked Trigg up, carried him across the Octagon, and slammed him before sinking-in a fight-ending rear naked choke. This wasn't just one of the greatest submissions ever; it was one of the best fights in UFC history.

UFC 4
ROYCE GRACIE VS. DAN SEVERN

After winning two of the first three UFC tournaments, Royce Gracie was the undisputed king of MMA. But after two big wins at UFC 4, Dan Severn was a serious threat to the crown, and he looked to be putting the finishing touches on his *coup d'etat* before Gracie pulled off a triangle choke that turned the tables after nearly 16 minutes of combat.

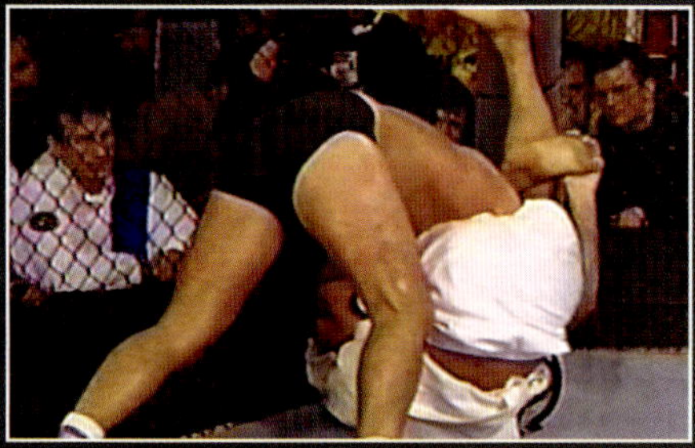

UFC 81
FRANK MIR VS. BROCK LESNAR

For a little over a minute, UFC newcomer Brock Lesnar was well on his way to one of the most impressive debuts of all-time. Yet against a crafty vet like Frank Mir, all it took was one slip-up, and that's just what happened to the overaggressive Lesnar, as he got caught in a kneebar that resurrected Mir's career in emphatic fashion.

UFC 117
ANDERSON SILVA VS. CHAEL SONNEN

Great champions aren't defined by their dominance, but by how they react to adversity. Anderson Silva took nearly five rounds worth of punishment from trash-talking Chael Sonnen, but just when it appeared that the UFC middleweight champion's title was slipping away, he pulled off a final-round submission of Sonnen that forever etched his name in the record books as one of the sport's best ever.

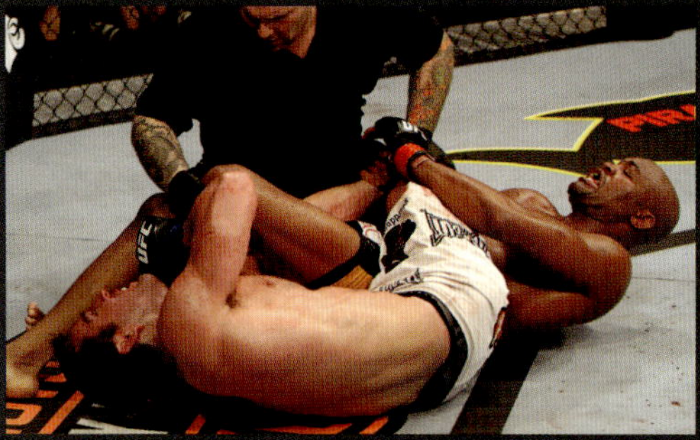

UFC 46
BJ PENN VS. MATT HUGHES 1

Riding a 13-fight winning streak that included six victories in UFC title fights, welterweight champion Matt Hughes was understandably being referred to as invincible. But former lightweight BJ Penn wasn't called "The Prodigy" for nothing, and the confident Hawaiian shocked the world with a rear naked choke submission of Hughes at UFC 46.

UFC 50
MATT HUGHES VS. GEORGES ST-PIERRE 1

Nine months after losing his welterweight title to BJ Penn, Matt Hughes got the opportunity to wear gold around his waist once again when he took on Canadian phenom Georges St-Pierre for the vacant belt. And though GSP soon became the future of the division, on this night, Hughes was the present as he sunk in an armbar that made St-Pierre tap with just one second left in the first round.

UFC 73
CHRIS LYTLE VS. JASON GILLIAM

At this level, if you have stellar technique and can get a well-trained opponent to make enough of a mistake that you can capitalize and submit him, it's safe to say that you're a pretty good fighter. Lock your opponent up in two submission holds at once? That's what Chris Lytle did in his win over Jason Gilliam, catching his foe in a triangle and an armlock to get the tapout.

UFC 44
KARO PARISYAN VS. DAVE STRASSER

Shocking those who didn't believe judo had a place in mixed martial arts, Karo "The Heat" Parisyan blasted those critics as he gave a clinic against veteran Dave Strasser at UFC 44 before finishing matters less than four minutes into the first round with a rare rolling kimura.

TUF7 FINALE
DUSTIN HAZELETT VS. JOSH BURKMAN

Just 22 years old at the time, Dustin Hazelett quickly earned a reputation as one of the UFC's most impressive ground fighters, thanks to accomplishments like his win over the always-tough Josh Burkman, a fight that was ended by what Joe Rogan described as "the sweetest armbar I have ever seen in mixed martial arts."

UFC 37
MURILO BUSTAMANTE VS. MATT LINDLAND

We should probably give Murilo Bustamante two spots on this list, considering he submitted Matt Lindland twice in the same bout. And while Bustamante's armbar finish was disallowed because Lindland claimed he didn't tap, in the third round the middleweight champ did finally end things with a guillotine choke.

UFC 95
DEMIAN MAIA VS. CHAEL SONNEN

It's hard to not be impressed with Brazilian jiu-jitsu black belt Demian Maia. And it's not just his technique, it's the fact that every time he steps into the Octagon, his opponents know what he's going to do—and most of the time they still can't stop it. In this fight, it was a beautiful takedown right into a triangle choke that spelled doom for Chael Sonnen and gave Maia another submission win.

UFC 82
ANDERSON SILVA VS. DAN HENDERSON

He's scored highlight reel-worthy knockouts, is a jiu-jitsu black belt, and is universally recognized as THE state-of-the-art mixed martial artist. So how does Anderson Silva top that? Rebound from a shaky first round against Dan Henderson to win by submission in the second stanza of a historic UFC/PRIDE unification bout.

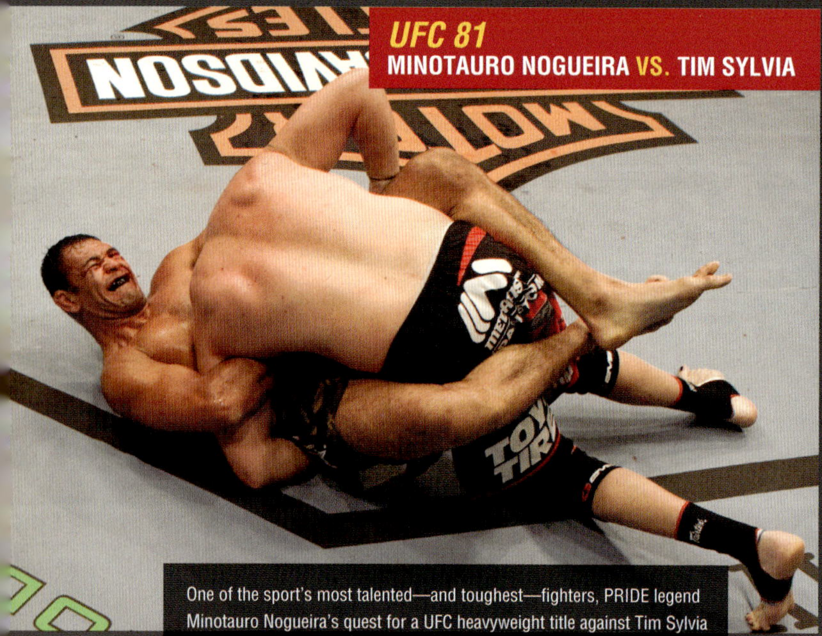

UFC 81
MINOTAURO NOGUEIRA VS. TIM SYLVIA

One of the sport's most talented—and toughest—fighters, PRIDE legend Minotauro Nogueira's quest for a UFC heavyweight title against Tim Sylvia wasn't going too well early on. But as Minotauro explained his eventual win by guillotine choke, "I played his game for almost three rounds. He played my game for two minutes and I won the fight."

UFC 76
FORREST GRIFFIN VS. MAURICIO "SHOGUN" RUA

Sometimes the best submissions aren't ones that are memorable for spectacular technique or the "wow" factor, but rather ones that live on for what they meant at that particular moment in time. When Forrest Griffin closed the show on the heavily-favored PRIDE import Shogun Rua with a rear naked choke in the final minute, it was an exclamation mark on a result no one saw coming, especially Rua, a Brazilian jiu-jitsu black belt.

UFC 3
ROYCE GRACIE VS. KIMO LEOPOLDO

Royce Gracie is rightfully revered for his technical acumen and impact on the sport of mixed martial arts, but what sometimes gets lost is that he is also one of the toughest and most determined fighters ever. That won't be disputed by Leopoldo, whose shocking beatdown of Gracie turned into a defeat in seconds thanks to a tight armbar.

UFC 108
COLE MILLER VS. DAN LAUZON

Talented lightweight prospect Cole Miller always seems to pull off a highlight reel submission, but he may have even topped himself at UFC 108 with an inverted reverse triangle/kimura combination that you certainly don't see too often. Unfortunately for his opponent—in this case, Dan Lauzon—what happens next is inevitably a tapout.

UFN13
NATE DIAZ VS. KURT PELLEGRINO

A lot of fighters are great at being the hammer; not so many can come back after being the nail. But after a rough first round, Nate Diaz proved he can talk tough and walk tough as he roared back and caught Kurt Pellegrino in a fight-ending triangle choke in the second while thrusting his fists in the air in triumph.

UFC 51
ANDREI ARLOVSKI VS. TIM SYLVIA 2

Andrei "The Pit Bull" Arlovski showed just how well-rounded a fighter he had become in this 2005 battle for the interim UFC heavyweight title, not only knocking 6-foot-8 Tim Sylvia to the mat, but then landing the ankle lock that forced "The Maine-iac" to tap out less than a minute into the bout.

UFN23
CHAN SUNG JUNG VS. LEONARD GARCIA

In the rematch with Garcia, the "Korean Zombie" pulled off—for the first time in the UFC—an amazing twister submission. With it Jung earned his first submission of the night bonus and avenged the earlier controversial defeat. In his post-fight interview, Jung credited Eddie Bravo and internet videos.

UFC 31
CARLOS NEWTON VS. PAT MILETICH

Reminiscent of those old schoolyard fights, complete with side headlocks, respected veteran Pat Miletich got the bully treatment from Carlos Newton at UFC 31 in 2001. He was forced to submit to the Canadian's bulldog choke in the third round, relinquishing his 170-pound crown to "The Ronin" in the process.

UFC 19
JEREMY HORN VS. CHUCK LIDDELL 1

Before he was celebrated as "The Iceman", Chuck Liddell was just another prospect working his way up the ranks. When he was paired with 30-fight vet Jeremy Horn, the future champion was taught a thing or two as Horn used his experience and technique to put Liddell to sleep with an arm triangle choke.

TUF6 FINALE
ROGER HUERTA VS. CLAY GUIDA

Down on all three scorecards entering the final round, Roger Huerta turned the tables on Clay Guida in an amazing show of heart as well as skill, hurting his foe first with a knee and then finishing him off with an improbable rear naked choke that made the fans at The Palms in Las Vegas erupt.

UFN2
DREW FICKETT VS. JOSH KOSCHECK

More impressive for the actual lead-up to the finish than the technique itself, veteran Drew Fickett was far behind on the scorecards when he landed a kick that stunned *The Ultimate Fighter 1* prospect Josh Koscheck. Fickett immediately pounced, sinking in the rear naked choke that secured this miracle final-minute victory.

UFC 85 *Bedlam*

07 June 2008

O2 Arena, London, England

Debut: Kevin Burns

Fighters			Division	Method	Time	Round
Main Card						
Thiago Alves	def.	Matt Hughes	Catchweight	Technical Knockout	1:02	2
Michael Bisping	def.	Jason Day	Middleweight	Technical Knockout	3:42	1
Mike Swick	def.	Marcus Davis	Welterweight	Unanimous Decision	—	3
Thales Leites	def.	Nate Marquardt	Middleweight	Split Decision	—	3
Fabricio Werdum	def.	Brandon Vera	Heavyweight	Technical Knockout	4:40	1
Preliminary Card						
Martin Kampmann	def.	Jorge Rivera	Middleweight	Submission - Guillotine Choke	2:44	1
Matt Wiman	def.	Thiago Tavares	Lightweight	Knockout	1:57	2
Kevin Burns	def.	Roan Carneiro	Welterweight	Submission - Triangle Choke	3:53	2
Luiz Cane	def.	Jason Lambert	Light Heavyweight	Technical Knockout	2:07	1
Paul Taylor	def.	Jess Liaudin	Welterweight	Split Decision	—	3
Antoni Hardonk	def.	Eddie Sanchez	Heavyweight	Knockout	4:15	2

Entering his UFC 85 main event against Matt Hughes, Thiago Alves' right ankle was sprained and heavily taped, but apparently his left knee was just fine as he used it to score a stunning second-round TKO over the former two-time UFC welterweight champion in front of 15,327 fans at The O2 Arena.

The gameplans were clear in this one: Hughes wanted it on the mat, Alves wanted to keep it standing, and Hughes immediately looked for the takedown. He was rebuffed the first time, and the second time saw him pull guard to get Alves down. While there, Alves was able to draw blood from Hughes' nose and get back to his feet. By the midway point of the round, Hughes had Alves down again; this time, he was controlling matters from the top. By the end of the round, though, Alves had turned the tables, landing with some ground strikes until the bell sounded.

Knockout of the Night: Alves vs. Hughes

Hughes' first takedown attempt of the second round was greeted by a knee to the head, and the blood began flowing again as Hughes went to his back. Alves scored with a couple of ground strikes and the fight resumed on foot. Hughes tried to get Alves back down but couldn't, and as they stood apart, Alves shot in himself—this time it was with a flying left knee that caught Hughes flush. Hughes fell to the canvas, with Alves' follow-up forcing a stoppage from referee Herb Dean at 1:02 of the round.

In front of his home country fans, Manchester middleweight Michael Bisping justified all the attention he received in the lead-up to the UFC 85 co-main event, scoring a dominating first-round TKO over Jason Day.

It wasn't the all-out war most people expected, but Mike Swick stuck to his gameplan and executed it, outpointing Marcus Davis in their welterweight bout and snapping the 11-fight win streak of "The Irish Hand Grenade" in the process.

The middleweight matchup between Thales Leites and Nate Marquardt was bumped to the pay-per-view portion of the show, and the fans viewing at home were the true winners, as both fighters battled it out tooth and nail for 15 minutes, with Leites emerging victorious via split decision in a bout that would have gone Marquardt's way if not for two point deductions for fouls.

Controversy also reigned in Fabricio Werdum's first-round TKO of Brandon Vera. The quick stoppage overshadowed what was another strong performance by the Brazilian heavyweight, who was coming off a big TKO win over Gabriel Gonzaga at UFC 80.

Middleweight contender Martin "The Hitman" Kampmann returned to the Octagon for the first time since March of 2007. He picked up where he left off before his knee surgery, submitting Jorge Rivera in the first round of UFC 85 preliminary action.

Even though lightweight up-and-comer Matt Wiman was getting married the week after his UFC 85 bout, it would have been hard for the *Ultimate Fighter* alum to top the feeling of his knockout victory over Thiago Tavares—without question the most important and impressive win of his career thus far.

Fight of the Night: Wiman vs. Tavares

Submission of the Night: Burns vs. Carneiro

Octagon newcomer Kevin "The Fire" Burns showed no sign of UFC jitters as he came in on short notice for injured Ryo Chonan and made the most of his opportunity, submitting Roan Carneiro in the second round of their welterweight bout.

Brazilian light heavyweight Luiz Cane got his first UFC victory in style, impressively stopping Jason "The Punisher" Lambert in the first round of their scheduled three-rounder.

Walsall's Paul Taylor broke a two-fight losing streak over an old foe, winning a three-round split decision over Jess Liaudin in their welterweight match, repeating his 2003 win over "The Joker".

Heavyweight up-and-comer Antoni Hardonk survived two knockdowns and an aggressive assault from late replacement Eddie Sanchez to score a second-round TKO victory in the entertaining UFC 85 opener.

The Ultimate Fighter 7 Finale

Team Rampage vs. Team Forrest

21 June 2008

The Pearl at The Palms, Las Vegas, NV

Debuts: Rob Kimmons, Matt Brown, Matthew Riddle, Dante Rivera, Amir Sadollah, CB Dollaway

Fighters			Division	Method	Time	Round
Main Card						
Kendall Grove	def.	Evan Tanner	Middleweight	Split Decision	—	3
Amir Sadollah	def.	CB Dollaway	Middleweight	Submission - Armbar	3:02	1
Diego Sanchez	def.	Luigi Fioravanti	Welterweight	Technical Knockout	4:07	3
Spencer Fisher	def.	Jeremy Stephens	Lightweight	Unanimous Decision	—	3
Matthew Riddle	def.	Dante Rivera	Middleweight	Unanimous Decision	—	3
Preliminary Card						
Dustin Hazelett	def.	Josh Burkman	Welterweight	Submission - Armbar	4:46	2
Drew McFedries	def.	Marvin Eastman	Middleweight	Technical Knockout	1:08	1
Matt Brown	def.	Matt Arroyo	Welterweight	Technical Knockout	3:40	2
Dean Lister	def.	Jeremy Horn	Middleweight	Submission - Guillotine Choke	3:52	1
Rob Kimmons	def.	Rob Yundt	Middleweight	Submission - Guillotine Choke	3:58	1

In theory and in practice, reality television shows are at their best when the underdog rises from nowhere to win it all. On June 21, 2008, Amir Sadollah completed his improbable run through *The Ultimate Fighter: Team Rampage vs. Team Forrest*, submitting CB Dollaway a second time to win the competition and a UFC contract.

A fighter with no professional bouts when he joined the Spike TV reality show, Sadollah gained a legion of fans and a ton of respect as he defeated Steve Byrnes, Gerald Harris, Matt Brown, and Dollaway to earn a shot in the final. And though Dollaway seemed to be in control just before the bout ended, Sadollah's "never say die" attitude prevailed once again.

Dollaway opened the bout strong with a hard leg kick but was answered by Sadollah's own kicks to the belly. As the bout approached its second minute, Dollaway scored a takedown and worked his ground and pound game. Within a minute, Dollaway was in side control, but only briefly as he found himself back in Sadollah's guard and landed ground strikes again. Sadollah, as was his custom throughout the show, pulled victory from the jaws of defeat, locking in an armbar. Dollaway tried to slam his way out but was unable to, and he tapped out at 3:02 of the opening round.

After back-to-back losses to Patrick Cote and Jorge Rivera, Kendall Grove's future in the UFC's 185-pound division may have been riding on the result of his bout against Evan Tanner. Subsequently, the Hawaii native put on perhaps his most disciplined performance as he decisioned the former UFC middleweight champion in the main event of *The Ultimate Fighter 7 Finale.*

Welterweight contender Diego Sanchez was sharp and focused in his bout against Luigi Fioravanti, stopping the American Top Team product in the third round of an exciting bout that was fought predominantly on the feet.

Lightweight contender Spencer "The King" Fisher rebounded from his loss to Frankie Edgar, pounding out a three-round unanimous decision over Jeremy Stephens.

Nothing like making your pro debut in front of a national television audience, but if anyone could handle it, it was probably precocious 22-year-old Matthew Riddle, who made it 1-0 in the pro ranks with a three-round unanimous decision win over *TUF* castmate Dante Rivera in the main card opener.

Knockout of the Night: McFedries vs. Eastman

Middleweight Drew McFedries roared out of his corner at the start of his preliminary bout against Marvin Eastman Saturday night and he didn't stop throwing until he had ended his opponent's night, just 68 seconds into their bout.

After a somewhat erratic start to his UFC stint, welterweight Dustin Hazelett put it all together as he scored the biggest win of his career over Josh Burkman. The end came via submission at 4:46 of the second round.

Fight of the Night: Hazelett vs. Burkman

Submission of the Night: Hazelett vs. Burkman

Burkman was aggressive throughout the first round as he tried to inflict punishment on Hazelett from his ground and pound attack. This aggression cost "The People's Warrior" as Hazelett tried submission after submission in an attempt to finish Burkman off.

The pace dipped in the second round, as Burkman scored with a takedown and some hard strikes that kept Hazelett off balance. Just when it looked as if the bout was going to go to a third round, Hazelett found his opening and locked in an armbar that forced Burkman to tap out with 14 seconds left in the stanza.

Grappling wizard Dean Lister evened the score with Jeremy Horn in their middleweight bout, avenging a 2003 decision loss to the Utah resident via a first-round submission victory.

It was a different day but the same result in the welterweight bout between Matt Brown and Matt Arroyo, as Brown stopped Arroyo in the second round, mimicking his November 2006 win over the *Ultimate Fighter 6* competitor.

Late replacement Rob Kimmons made the most of his opportunity against Rob Yundt in the middleweight opener, submitting the Alaska native to win his UFC debut and improve to 21-3.

One Hit Wonder: Dante Rivera

UFC 86 *Jackson vs. Griffin*

05 July 2008

Mandalay Bay Events Center, Las Vegas, NV

Fighters			Division	Method	Time	Round
Main Card						
Forrest Griffin	def.	Quinton Jackson	Light Heavyweight	Unanimous Decision	—	5
Patrick Cote	def.	Ricardo Almeida	Middleweight	Split Decision	—	3
Joe Stevenson	def.	Gleison Tibau	Lightweight	Submission - Guillotine Choke	2:57	2
Josh Koscheck	def.	Chris Lytle	Welterweight	Unanimous Decision	—	3
Tyson Griffin	def.	Marcus Aurelio	Lightweight	Unanimous Decision	—	3
Preliminary Card						
Gabriel Gonzaga	def.	Justin McCully	Heavyweight	Submission - Americana	1:57	1
Justin Buchholz	def.	Corey Hill	Lightweight	Submission - Rear Naked Choke	3:57	2
Melvin Guillard	def.	Dennis Siver	Lightweight	Knockout	0:36	1
Cole Miller	def.	Jorge Gurgel	Lightweight	Submission - Triangle Choke	4:48	3

In the days leading up to the UFC light heavyweight championship bout between Forrest Griffin and Quinton "Rampage" Jackson, fans and pundits almost unanimously agreed that, on paper, the champion, Jackson, should win. Yet those comments were always followed by the word 'but' and some way of describing how one could never count Griffin out.

At the sold-out Mandalay Bay Events Center, Griffin took all the 'buts' out of the equation, overturning the odds and pounding out a thrilling unanimous five-round decision win over Jackson to take the 205-pound world championship and etch his name in the history books.

"This is the greatest night of my life," said Griffin, the first winner of *The Ultimate Fighter* reality show and now the second *TUF* winner to earn a world title, following former welterweight boss Matt Serra.

Scores were 48-46 twice and 49-46 for Griffin.

Griffin took the fight to the champion immediately, working behind his jab and some quick kicks to the head and legs. When the two would exchange at close range, Jackson was in his element and he was able to land with more consistency, and with under three minutes left he was able to jar Griffin briefly with a left hook. The challenger recovered quickly and flurried back, but a right uppercut by Jackson with a little over a minute left dropped Griffin.

Griffin opened the second with more leg kicks, this time buckling Jackson's left leg. As the champion staggered backward, Griffin moved in, clinching and landing knees at close range before trying to sink in a guillotine. Jackson escaped that trouble but wound up in more as the bout subsequently moved to the mat, with Griffin working for submissions and grounding and pounding Jackson steadily for the remainder of the round.

"You've got to make him fight you," trainer Juanito Ibarra told Jackson between rounds two and three as the champion's left knee was iced, and Rampage showed his heart as he entered the fray again for round three. Griffin, not getting overly aggressive, pecked away from long range as Jackson concentrated on avoiding more leg kicks and on catching the challenger with haymakers as he came into range. As the round entered its final two minutes, Jackson appeared to be back in business as he scored with body shots and hard counters to the head when Griffin tried to open up.

As the fight entered the championship rounds, Jackson's urgency was evident as he stalked Griffin and landed with heavy shots to the head. Griffin responded with a takedown, with Jackson ending up in his challenger's guard. With 3:40 left, Griffin locked in a triangle choke, and the response from Jackson was what you would expect: a slam that broke the hold and allowed Jackson to resume his ground and pound attack. The two fighters rose with two minutes remaining, and Jackson again jarred Griffin with shots to the side of the head. But predictably, the round ended with a toe-to-toe exchange.

Fight of the Night: F. Griffin vs. Jackson

Tyson Griffin continued to improve as he moved closer to a lightweight title shot with a clear-cut unanimous decision win over Marcus Aurelio in the main card opener.

Gabriel Gonzaga impressively broke a two-fight losing streak, submitting his foe Justin McCully less than two minutes into their bout.

Griffin opened the final round with more leg kicks, hoping to repeat his second-round success, and 90 seconds in, he added pinpoint strikes to the head. That woke Jackson back up as he landed flush shots to the head and body, but Griffin took everything in stride and kept moving forward, jarring the champion with his own return fire. The final minute saw the packed house rise in appreciation for the effort of both men, and neither stopped swinging until the final bell ended, putting an exclamation point on an unforgettable night.

After an 0-4 start to his UFC career, Patrick Cote continued his improbable comeback, scoring a razor-thin split decision win over Ricardo Almeida in a contest that was more tactical than explosive.

Seven-year-old Joe Stevenson, Jr. saw his father fight live for the first time that night, and he certainly went home with a smile on his face as "Joe Daddy" survived some rough patches to submit Gleison Tibau with a guillotine choke in the second round of their lightweight matchup.

In recent history, cuts had been the Achilles' heel of Chris "Lights Out" Lytle, and at UFC 86 they cost him again, as Josh Koscheck's ground and pound attack opened up two cuts that helped Kos cruise to a unanimous three-round decision win.

Jorge Gurgel was apparently on his way to his most impressive UFC victory against up-and-comer Cole Miller in their lightweight bout, but with 40 seconds left in the bout, Miller locked in a triangle choke, and 28 ticks of the clock later, Gurgel was forced to tap out, giving "Magrinho" his biggest win to date at the 4:48 mark of the final round.

Submission of the Night: Miller vs. Gurgel

A focused Melvin Guillard has always been a dangerous prospect for the rest of the 155-pound division. That was never more evident than in his bout against Dennis Siver, a 36-second blitz that saw Guillard notch his 40th pro win and get back on track after consecutive UFC losses to Rich Clementi and Joe Stevenson.

Knockout of the Night: Guillard vs. Siver

Despite a rocky first round, Justin Buchholz showed that in MMA, capitalizing on one mistake can erase any negatives as he submitted Corey Hill with a rear naked choke in the second round.

UFC Fight Night 14

Silva vs. Irvin

19 July 2008

The Pearl at The Palms, Las Vegas, NV

Debuts: Brad Blackburn, James Giboo, Rory Markham, Brodie Farber, Dale Hartt, Shannon Gugerty, Nate Loughran, Johnny Rees, Tim Credeur, Cale Yarbrough, Jesse Taylor, Reese Andy

Fighters			Division	Method	Time	Round
Main Card						
Anderson Silva	def.	James Irvin	Light Heavyweight	Knockout	1:01	1
Brandon Vera	def.	Reese Andy	Light Heavyweight	Unanimous Decision	—	3
Frankie Edgar	def.	Hermes Franca	Lightweight	Unanimous Decision	—	3
Cain Velasquez	def.	Jake O'Brien	Heavyweight	Knockout	2:02	1
Kevin Burns	def.	Anthony Johnson	Welterweight	Technical Knockout	3:35	3
CB Dollaway	def.	Jesse Taylor	Middleweight	Submission - Peruvian Necktie	3:58	1
Preliminary Card						
Tim Credeur	def.	Cale Yarbrough	Middleweight	Technical Knockout	1:54	1
Nate Loughran	def.	Johnny Rees	Middleweight	Submission - Triangle Choke	4:21	1
Shannon Gugerty	def.	Dale Hartt	Lightweight	Submission - Rear Naked Choke	3:33	1
Rory Markham	def.	Brodie Farber	Welterweight	Knockout	1:37	1
Brad Blackburn	def.	James Giboo	Welterweight	Technical Knockout	2:29	2

UFC middleweight champion Anderson Silva didn't see his pound-for-pound crown tarnished at all in his UFC light heavyweight debut against James Irvin. Instead, his 61-second knockout win showed that if anything, he's getting better and more fearsome with each outing.

After the ritual touch of gloves, both fighters traded kicks to start the festivities. A few tense moments later, Irvin fired a right kick to the side, which Silva caught. "The Spider" proceeded to fire a right hand straight down the pipe at Irvin that landed flush and put him on his back. Silva pounced with a series of shots, but just when "The Sandman" appeared to be weathering the storm, a final right hand knocked him out at the 1:01 mark.

It was yet another clip for Silva's highlight reel, but as for a permanent stay at light heavyweight, the pride of Curitiba still preferred to take care of business at 185 pounds unless bigger fights present themselves.

There was good news and bad news for Brandon "The Truth" Vera in his light heavyweight debut. The good was that he got the unanimous decision victory over Reese Andy. The bad: he didn't get the definitive finish he wanted after a tougher-than-expected weight cut from heavyweight.

Lightweight contender Frankie Edgar impressively rebounded from his loss to Gray Maynard, pounding out a shutout three-round decision over Hermes Franca. Scores were 30-27 across the board for Edgar.

Fight of the Night: Edgar vs. Franca

The fighters went to the mat early, with Edgar doing work from the top as he pounded away on Franca. With 2:30 left, Franca sprung into action with an armbar that appeared to be locked in. Edgar showed the benefit of his recent training with Ricardo Almeida and was able to escape, and when the two stood, he held his own, striking with the heavy-handed Brazilian prior to scoring another takedown before the end of the frame.

Franca came out for round two with a big knot between his eyes and plenty of urgency. Despite this, Edgar refused to back down, and after some crisp exchanges, he scored the takedown and resumed the ground and pound attack that worked so well for him in the opening stanza.

Trying to turn the tide, Franca tried with all he had to take Edgar out, but even when he landed, the New Jersey native took each shot without flinching, except for a right knee that appeared to rock him momentarily.

Heavyweight prospect Cain Velasquez probably gained even more believers as he pounded out fellow up-and-comer Jake O'Brien in just two minutes and two seconds.

A competitive welterweight bout between up-and-comers Kevin Burns and Anthony Johnson ended in controversial fashion when an inadvertent poke in the eye by Burns led to an unpopular third-round TKO victory for the Iowan.

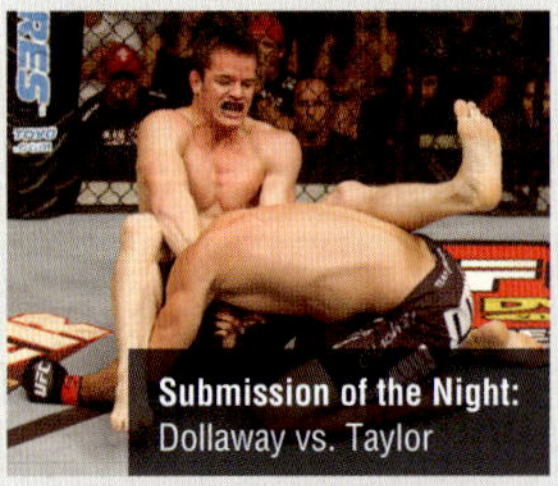
Submission of the Night: Dollaway vs. Taylor

Ultimate Fighter cast member CB Dollaway dismantled fellow *TUF* fighter Jesse Taylor, whom he submitted with a Peruvian Necktie in the first round of their middleweight contest.

The Ultimate Fighter 7 contender Tim Credeur showed off his ever-improving striking, knocking out his foe in under two minutes.

Knockout of the Night: Markham vs. Farber

Veteran knockout artist Rory Markham lived up to his reputation in his first UFC bout, spectacularly taking out Brodie Farber with a kick to the head in just 97 seconds of their UFC Fight Night preliminary bout.

Nate Loughran may not have looked like he won his middleweight debut, but despite a cut and a nasty welt on his face, he emerged victorious, submitting "The Hater Hurter" in one round.

Brad Blackburn was certainly "Bad" news for James Giboo, stopping the Iowan with pinpoint strikes in the second round of their welterweight clash.

California's Shannon Gugerty did his mentor Dean Lister proud in the opener, submitting Maine's Dale Hartt in the first round of their lightweight bout.

One Hit Wonders: James Giboo, Jesse Taylor

UFC 87 *Seek And Destroy*

09 Aug. 2008

Target Center, Minneapolis, MN

Debuts: Dan Evensen, Jon Jones, Andre Gusmao, Steve Bruno, Ryan Thomas

Fighters			Division	Method	Time	Round
Main Card						
Georges St-Pierre	def.	Jon Fitch	Welterweight	Unanimous Decision		5
Brock Lesnar	def.	Heath Herring	Heavyweight	Unanimous Decision	—	3
Kenny Florian	def.	Roger Huerta	Lightweight	Unanimous Decision	—	3
Rob Emerson	def.	Manny Gamburyan	Lightweight	Knockout	0:12	1
Demian Maia	def.	Jason MacDonald	Middleweight	Submission - Rear Naked Choke	2:44	3
Preliminary Card						
Tamdan McCrory	def.	Luke Cummo	Welterweight	Unanimous Decision	—	3
Cheick Kongo	def.	Dan Evensen	Heavyweight	Technical Knockout	4:55	1
Jon Jones	def.	Andre Gusmao	Light Heavyweight	Unanimous Decision	—	3
Chris Wilson	def.	Steve Bruno	Welterweight	Unanimous Decision	—	3
Ben Saunders	def.	Ryan Thomas	Welterweight	Submission - Armbar	2:28	2

It's an old fight game adage that it's harder to defend a title than win one. In the main event of UFC 87 at Target Center, UFC welterweight champion Georges St-Pierre got things right in his second reign as champion, defending his crown for the first time with a shutout five-round decision win over number one contender Jon Fitch. Scores were 50-43 and 50-44 twice.

Fight of the Night: St-Pierre vs. Fitch

The bout hit the mat immediately, with St-Pierre in Fitch's guard, but the challenger did good work from the bottom, even though he ate his share of thudding strikes. When Fitch was able to get back to his feet, the champion dropped him almost immediately with a right hand and followed up with a ferocious series of strikes that bruised Fitch's face. With less than 1:30 left in the round, Fitch gamely rose again, but with his legs rubbery, St-Pierre opened fire on the feet and the ground, keeping the Indiana native in serious trouble.

Fitch looked to stand with St-Pierre in round two, but the Canadian's speed, accuracy and footwork bloodied the challenger, and also allowed him to scoot out of danger before any of Fitch's wild strikes hit home.

If there was any renewed confidence from Fitch, it was probably removed seconds into the third round when he got his mouthpiece knocked out by a St-Pierre right hand, and the Canadian continued to pile up the points.

As the championship rounds began, Fitch drew blood from over St-Pierre's left eye, but the Montreal native was undaunted and remained in the pocket, pecking away at Fitch and denying takedown attempts.

Fitch opened the fifth and final round with a couple of solid shots, looking to rescue the fight for himself, but St-Pierre answered with a thudding back fist and a takedown, impressively refusing to sit on his lead as he pounded his way to victory.

After losing to Frank Mir in his Octagon debut at UFC 81, many wondered whether former pro wrestling superstar Brock Lesnar was more hype than substance. After a shutout three-round decision win over perennial heavyweight contender Heath Herring in the UFC 87 co-feature, there was no question that Lesnar may very well be the division's next big thing.

Roger Huerta showed that he could compete with the best at 155 pounds in his highly anticipated showdown with Kenny Florian, but it was Florian who proved that he was ready for another shot at the lightweight crown as he scored a shutout three-round decision win over the hometown hero, claiming his fifth straight bout in the process.

Submission of the Night: Maia vs. MacDonald

In an exciting display of groundfighting between two of the middleweight division's top submission artists, unbeaten Demian Maia outlasted Jason MacDonald, submitting his opponent with a rear naked choke in the third round of a torrid battle.

Knockout of the Night: Emerson vs. Gamburyan

The action was fast and furious in the lightweight match between *The Ultimate Fighter 5* vets Rob Emerson and Manny Gamburyan—at least for the 12 seconds it lasted before a right hand standing and a left hand on the mat spelled the end for Gamburyan.

Heavyweight contender Cheick Kongo got back in the win column in his first bout since his decision loss to Heath Herring in March, wasting no time in stopping Dan Evensen in a single round.

Welterweight up-and-comer Tamdan McCrory returned to the UFC after a nine-month layoff and showed little evidence of Octagon rust as he pounded out a clear-cut three-round unanimous decision win over fellow New Yorker Luke Cummo.

Endicott, New York's Jon Jones, the UFC's youngest fighter at 21 years old, made an impressive debut in the Octagon with a three-round unanimous decision win over Brazil native Andre Gusmao.

Team Quest's Chris Wilson nabbed his first UFC victory, scoring a dominant three-round unanimous decision over Steve Bruno.

In the opener, welterweight prospect Ben Saunders upped his unbeaten record to 6-0-2 with a second-round submission win over Octagon newcomer Ryan Thomas.

UFC 88 *Breakthrough*

06 Sept. 2008

Philips Arena, Atlanta, GA

Debut: Michael Patt

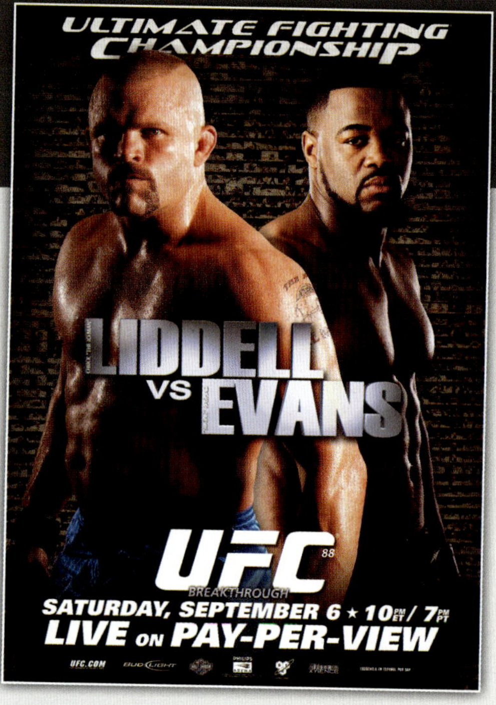

Fighters			Division	Method	Time	Round
Main Card						
Rashad Evans	def.	Chuck Liddell	Light Heavyweight	Knockout	1:51	2
Rich Franklin	def.	Matt Hamill	Light Heavyweight	Technical Knockout	0:39	3
Dan Henderson	def.	Rousimar Palhares	Middleweight	Unanimous Decision	—	3
Nate Marquardt	def.	Martin Kampmann	Middleweight	Technical Knockout	1:28	1
Dong Hyun Kim	def.	Matt Brown	Welterweight	Split Decision	—	3
Preliminary Card						
Kurt Pellegrino	def.	Thiago Tavares	Lightweight	Unanimous Decision	—	3
Ryo Chonan	def.	Roan Carneiro	Welterweight	Split Decision	—	3
Tim Boetsch	def.	Michael Patt	Light Heavyweight	Technical Knockout	2:03	1
Jason MacDonald	def.	Jason Lambert	Middleweight	Submission - Rear Naked Choke	1:21	2

Rashad Evans fought the perfect fight in the UFC 88 main event against former light heavyweight champion Chuck Liddell, and at 1:51 of the second round, he finished the perfect fight with the perfect punch, stunning a packed house at Philips Arena with a one-hit knockout of "The Iceman".

"You've got to go straight for the horns," said Evans. "You can't fight him going for take-downs all night. That's the way you get knocked out. I wanted to beat him at his own game."

Evans appeared loose before the opening bell, undaunted by the task ahead of him, and once the fight began, he used movement and angles to make Liddell use his legs. "The Iceman" simply stalked, waiting for the opportunity to unleash his right hand. With a little over three minutes left, he grazed Evans, knocking him off balance briefly. The crowd roared and Evans danced away, showing that he was unhurt. What really proved his readiness, though, was a hard kick to Liddell's leg. As the round entered its final two minutes, the crowd started to get restless at the lack of sustained action, and Liddell seemed to be getting impatient as well, as he picked up his forward march in pursuit of his elusive foe. Evans stayed out of trouble, however, and it was Liddell walking back to his corner at the end of the round with a cut under his right eye.

Knockout of the Night: Evans vs. Liddell

Liddell continued to stalk as round two began. This time, when he closed in, Evans would fire back in flurries that weren't doing damage but were keeping his foe honest. Moments later, Liddell, with his fist cocked and looking to be unworried by incoming fire, shot off a right uppercut from long range at the same time Evans blasted a right hand. Evans landed first, and Liddell, knocked unconscious instantly, fell hard to the canvas, where he remained for a few tense moments until he was able to make it up and out of the Octagon under his own power.

Former UFC middleweight champion Rich Franklin made a seamless return to the light heavyweight division, outgunning a game Matt Hamill with a steady striking attack in the UFC 88 co-main event.

It was Franklin's first fight at 205 pounds since his first-round TKO of Ken Shamrock in April of 2005. Middleweight contender and former 205- and 183-pound PRIDE champion Dan Henderson got back in the win column, breaking a two-fight losing streak by defeating Rousimar Palhares via a three-round unanimous decision that gave Henderson his first UFC win since 1998.

Perennial middleweight contender Nate Marquardt made an impressive statement in his bout with Martin Kampmann, stopping "The Hitman" via strikes in just 88 seconds, handing the Denmark native his first UFC loss.

Ultimate Fighter alumnus Matt Brown may have made more fans in defeat than victory, as his gutsy effort against Dong Hyun Kim won over the Atlanta fans that booed his three-round split decision loss to the still-unbeaten South Korea native.

Fight of the Night: Pellegrino vs. Tavares

If the early moments of the lightweight battle between Kurt Pellegrino and Thiago Tavares were any indication, Tavares had no right getting out of the opening round. But the game Brazilian hung on, survived, and became one-half of one of the most entertaining 155-pound battles of the year, with Pellegrino impressively pounding out a three-round unanimous decision in UFC 88 preliminary action.

Submission of the Night: MacDonald vs. Lambert

Light heavyweight Tim Boetsch got back in the win column after his April loss to Matt Hamill, blasting out newcomer Michael Patt in the first round.

Jason MacDonald gave Jason Lambert a rude welcome to the middleweight division, surviving some dicey moments before submitting the former light heavy-weight in the second round.

Ryo Chonan made it two in a row over Roan Carneiro in the opener, grabbing a close split decision victory over the local product in a welterweight bout. Scores were 29-28, 29-28, and 28-29 for Chonan, who had defeated Carneiro via cuts in a 2005 bout in Japan.

UFC Fight Night 15

Diaz vs. Neer

17 Sept. 2008

Omaha Civic Auditorium, Omaha, NE

Debuts: Dan Miller, Mike Massenzio, Jason Brilz, Joe Vedepo

Fighters			Division	Method	Time	Round
Main Card						
Nate Diaz	def.	Josh Neer	Lightweight	Split Decision	—	3
Clay Guida	def.	Mac Danzig	Lightweight	Unanimous Decision	—	3
Alan Belcher	def.	Ed Herman	Middleweight	Unanimous Decision	—	3
Eric Schafer	def.	Houston Alexander	Light Heavyweight	Submission - Arm Triangle Choke	4:53	1
Preliminary Card						
Alessio Sakara	def.	Joe Vedepo	Middleweight	Knockout	1:27	1
Wilson Gouveia	def.	Ryan Jensen	Middleweight	Submission - Armbar	2:04	2
Joe Lauzon	def.	Kyle Bradley	Lightweight	Technical Knockout	1:34	2
Jason Brilz	def.	Brad Morris	Light Heavyweight	Technical Knockout	2:54	2
Mike Massenzio	def.	Drew McFedries	Middleweight	Submission - Kimura	1:28	1
Dan Miller	def.	Rob Kimmons	Middleweight	Submission - Rear Naked Choke	1:27	1

Two of mixed martial arts' purest fighters locked up in the main event of UFC Fight Night at the Omaha Civic Auditorium, and lightweight up-and-comers Nate Diaz and Josh Neer didn't disappoint, with Diaz eking out a three-round split decision in an entertaining bout that let the world know that at 155 pounds, the future was in good hands.

Fight of the Night: Diaz vs. Neer

Scores were 29-28 twice, and 28-29 for Diaz, whose brother Nick had submitted Neer at UFC 62 in August of 2006. With the win, Diaz improved to 10-2; Neer fell to 24-7-1.

Popular local light heavyweight Houston Alexander promised a new level of aggression in his homecoming bout against Eric Schafer, but while "The Assassin" certainly did his part in pushing the pace, it was the non-stop ground attack of Schafer that ruled the day as he submitted Alexander in their furiously paced bout.

With the arena filling to the chants of "Houston, Houston," Alexander immediately responded with a series of vicious knees that put Schafer on the mat. As the hometown hero pounced, Schafer tried to grab a leg for a submission, but Alexander escaped and rose to his feet. At close range, the two locked up and traded knees, with Schafer getting a takedown midway through the round. Schafer got into side control and looked to be close to a finish, but Alexander escaped, and seconds later he averted another submission, this time a guillotine choke. Schafer was relentless in keeping a dominant position, and he fired off a series of heavy strikes from the mount position. The crowd tried to get their man back into the fight with deafening cheers, but Schafer wasn't about to let him off the hook, and after he sunk in an arm triangle, Alexander was forced to tap out at the 4:53 mark of the opening round.

Lightweight contender Clay Guida was relentless and effective in his bout against Mac Danzig, using a smothering attack to score a three-round unanimous decision win over the *Ultimate Fighter 6* winner.

In a competitive middleweight bout, Alan Belcher bounced back from an April loss to Jason Day, using his superior striking to nab a three-round unanimous decision over Ed Herman. Scores were 29-28 across the board and for Belcher. The verdict was originally announced as split, but a scoring discrepancy was corrected after the announcement was made.

The Garden State of New Jersey was well represented at the Omaha Civic Auditorium, with UFC debutants Mike Massenzio and Dan Miller both scoring big first-round submission wins in UFC Fight Night action.

Paterson's Massenzio made an immediate impact in his Octagon debut, scoring a first-round submission win over vet Drew McFedries in their middleweight contest.

Knockout of the Night: Sakara vs. Vedepo

Submission of the Night: Gouveia vs. Jensen

Debuting lightweight Miller was impressive in his initial Octagon appearance as well, making it two for two for New Jersey by submitting Rob Kimmons in the first round of the night's opening prelim bout.

Known primarily for his boxing, middleweight Alessio Sakara showed that his kicks are pretty deadly too, as he knocked out UFC newcomer Joe Vedepo in just 87 seconds.

Surviving a spirited effort from Omaha native Ryan Jensen, Wilson Gouveia made his UFC middleweight debut a successful one with a second-round submission win.

Rising lightweight star Joe Lauzon bounced back from his April loss to Kenny Florian in impressive fashion, halting Kyle Bradley in the second round to improve to 16-4.

Omaha's own Jason Brilz made the local fans happy in his UFC debut against Brad Morris, dominating from the opening bell until the fight was stopped in the second frame of their light heavyweight match.

UFC 89 *Bisping vs. Leben*

18 Oct. 2008

National Indoor Arena, Birmingham, England

Debuts: Neil Wain, Dan Hardy, Jim Miller, David Baron

Fighters			Division	Method	Time	Round
Main Card						
Michael Bisping	def.	Chris Leben	Middleweight	Unanimous Decision	—	3
Keith Jardine	def.	Brandon Vera	Light Heavyweight	Split Decision	—	3
Luiz Cane	def.	Rameau Thierry Sokoudjou	Light Heavyweight	Technical Knockout	4:15	2
Chris Lytle	def.	Paul Taylor	Welterweight	Unanimous Decision	—	3
Marcus Davis	def.	Paul Kelly	Welterweight	Submission - Guillotine Choke	2:16	2
Preliminary Card						
Shane Carwin	def.	Neil Wain	Heavyweight	Technical Knockout	1:31	1
Dan Hardy	def.	Akihiro Gono	Welterweight	Split Decision	—	3
Terry Etim	def.	Sam Stout	Lightweight	Unanimous Decision	—	3
David Bielkheden	def.	Jess Liaudin	Lightweight	Unanimous Decision	—	3
Jim Miller	def.	David Baron	Lightweight	Submission - Rear Naked Choke	3:19	3
Per Eklund	def.	Samy Schiavo	Lightweight	Submission - Rear Naked Choke	1:47	3

The UK can rest easy. At a packed National Indoor Arena in Birmingham, England, national hero Michael Bisping passed his sternest test in the middleweight division, scoring a unanimous three-round decision over Chris Leben in the UFC 89 main event. Scores were 30-27 twice and 29-28 for Bisping, a former light heavyweight.

With the crowd roaring, Leben calmly stalked Bisping, landing with a series of kicks to the body and midsection. Bisping took his time getting into the offensive column, eventually scoring with some quick counters as he used all of the Octagon real estate to stay out of harm's way. Leben wasn't rattled as he kept trying to push the pace, but as the round progressed, he was starting to eat more and more flush counter shots, leaving his nose bloodied as he went back to the corner.

Bisping continued to keep Leben at bay in the second round, picking and pecking at "The Crippler" and cutting him under the eye as he came in. With under three minutes left, an accidental low kick interrupted the action, but when the fight resumed, the pattern already established remained unchanged, as Leben wasn't quick enough to avoid Bisping's counters or to cut off the Manchester resident's lateral movement. Leben's desperate measure of dropping his hands paid dividends in the closing moments of the round though, as he was able to score with a couple of haymakers before the bell rang.

Leben opened the second with a hard left hand, looking to turn the tide, but any momentum was lost when there was a stoppage in the action as Bisping complained of something in his eye. After the brief break, the cat-and-mouse game continued, and Bisping, unmarked, kept to his disciplined fight plan. With under two minutes left, Leben surprised his foe with a takedown, but when he started to throw ground strikes, it gave Bisping the opening he needed to get back to his feet and return to the business of keeping Leben at bay with long-range strikes, which he did until the final bell sounded.

In his first bout since a first-round loss to Wanderlei Silva at UFC 84, light heavyweight contender Keith Jardine got a much needed career boost as he scored a three-round split decision win over Brandon Vera. Scores were 29-28 twice and 28-29 for Jardine. The loss was Vera's first at light heavyweight, and third in his last four bouts overall.

Knockout of the Night: Cane vs. Sokoudjou

Light heavyweight up-and-comer Luiz "Banha" Cane made a major statement in his third UFC bout, halting highly-regarded Rameau Thierry Sokoudjou in the second round.

Paul Taylor earned his third Fight of the Night award in five UFC outings, but unfortunately he wasn't able to get his third Octagon win, as he was outscored by veteran Chris Lytle in a hard-fought three-round welterweight battle.

Fight of the Night: Lytle vs. Taylor

Welterweight contender Marcus Davis was in fine form in his first bout since losing to Mike Swick in June, submitting previously unbeaten Paul Kelly with a guillotine choke in the second round.

Rising heavyweight star Shane Carwin spoiled the night of England's Neil Wain, needing only 91 seconds to stop him via strikes.

Highly-touted newcomer Dan Hardy got his first UFC win, eking out a split decision over Japanese veteran Akihiro Gono.

Submission of the Night: Miller vs. Baron

Also earning decision wins were Terry Etim, who defeated Sam Stout, and David Bielkheden, who outpointed Jess Liaudin.

Two submission wins opened the card, as Jim Miller finished David Baron with a rear naked choke in the third round, and Per Eklund did the same thing to Samy Schiavo, also in the final frame.

Following the event, main event middleweight Leben tested positive for the banned substance Stanozolol and was fined and suspended for nine months.

One Hit Wonders: Neil Wain, David Baron

UFC 90 *Silva vs. Cote*

25 Oct. 2008

Allstate Arena, Rosemont, IL

Debuts: Junior dos Santos, Matt Horwich

Fighters			Division	Method	Time	Round
Main Card						
Anderson Silva	def.	Patrick Cote	Middleweight	Technical Knockout - Injury	0:39	3
Thiago Alves	def.	Josh Koscheck	Welterweight	Unanimous Decision	—	3
Gray Maynard	def.	Rich Clementi	Lightweight	Unanimous Decision	—	3
Junior dos Santos	def.	Fabricio Werdum	Heavyweight	Knockout	1:20	1
Sean Sherk	def.	Tyson Griffin	Lightweight	Unanimous Decision	—	3
Preliminary Card						
Thales Leites	def.	Drew McFedries	Middleweight	Submission - Rear Naked Choke	1:18	1
Spencer Fisher	def.	Shannon Gugerty	Lightweight	Submission - Triangle Choke	3:56	3
Dan Miller	def.	Matt Horwich	Middleweight	Unanimous Decision	—	3
Hermes Franca	def.	Marcus Aurelio	Lightweight	Unanimous Decision	—	3
Pete Sell	def.	Josh Burkman	Welterweight	Unanimous Decision	—	3

As expected, Anderson Silva successfully defended his UFC middleweight title against heavy underdog Patrick Cote in the UFC 90 main event at Allstate Arena. What no one saw coming was the ending, as a competitive fight ended prematurely when Cote blew out his knee in the third round, awarding the bout to Silva via TKO.

The win was Silva's eighth in the UFC against no losses, and his fourth successful title defense. Contrary to what oddsmakers believed prior to the match, Cote was no easy mark for the pound-for-pound king.

Cote calmly stalked in the early going, moving his head side to side to avoid getting hit with a quick KO punch or kick. With under two minutes left, the crowd and Cote started getting restless, and the Canadian attacked wildly. Silva avoided serious trouble and fired back with a knee to the chin that Cote took well.

Silva struck early in round two, first with a jarring left to the head. Moments later the two briefly locked up against the fence, but after breaking, Silva kept the pressure on, eventually forcing Cote to the canvas. While there, Cote stayed busy with strikes from the bottom, and the two stood up seconds later. Silva was seemingly toying with the challenger, but Cote was all business as he shot for two takedowns, both of which were rebuffed.

Both fighters closed the distance quickly to start round three, but just as suddenly, as Cote planted his foot to move in on the champion, he buckled his right knee and fell to the canvas in pain. After making an attempt to rise, he fell again, and referee Herb Dean had no choice but to stop the fight at the 39-second mark.

Thiago "Pitbull" Alves made a strong case for being next in line for a shot at the welterweight crown with a methodical yet exciting three-round unanimous decision win over gutsy fellow contender Josh Koscheck in the UFC 90 co-feature.

Gray Maynard continued his trip up the 155-pound ranks with a shutout three-round decision win over Rich Clementi, breaking the six-fight winning streak of "No Love".

Knockout of the Night: dos Santos vs. Werdum

In the flash of a single right uppercut from UFC debutant Junior dos Santos, heavyweight contender Fabricio Werdum saw a title shot in the near future disappear, as he was knocked out just 80 seconds into the first round.

Fight of the Night: Sherk vs. Griffin

Lightweight contenders Sean Sherk and Tyson Griffin fought at a torrid pace in the UFC main card opener, and after 15 minutes of war, it was Sherk, the former lightweight champion, emerging victorious via a close but unanimous decision.

The UFC 90 prelim bout between middleweights Thales Leites and Drew McFedries was destined to end in one of two ways—Leites by submission or McFedries by knockout. It was Leites who survived an early bombing run by McFedries to submit the Iowan in 78 seconds.

Submission of the Night: Fisher vs. Gugerty

Going into the lightweight clash between Spencer Fisher and Shannon Gugerty, conventional wisdom held that were someone to score a submission win, it would be the Dean Lister-trained Gugerty. In an exciting turn of events, it was Fisher pulling off a triangle choke submission win late in the third round.

New Jersey middleweight Dan Miller showed heart and stellar submission defense in his three-round decision win over Matt Horwich, surviving a series of dicey situations in the second frame to grab his second UFC victory in as many months.

Hermes Franca entered the Octagon for his grudge match with Marcus Aurelio by bumping his former teacher, but for the next three rounds it was Franca who put on a Muay Thai clinic as he fired off continuous volleys of leg kicks en route to a three-round unanimous decision win.

In a must-win bout for both welterweights, Pete Sell recovered from a slow start to win a close three-round unanimous decision over Josh Burkman in the UFC 90 opener.

UFC 91 *Couture vs. Lesnar*

15 Nov. 2008

MGM Grand Garden Arena, Las Vegas, NV

Debuts: Josh Hendricks, Rafael dos Anjos

Fighters			Division	Method	Time	Round
Main Card						
Brock Lesnar	def.	Randy Couture	Heavyweight	Technical Knockout	3:07	2
Kenny Florian	def.	Joe Stevenson	Lightweight	Submission - Rear Naked Choke	4:03	1
Dustin Hazelett	def.	Tamdan McCrory	Welterweight	Submission - Armbar	3:59	1
Gabriel Gonzaga	def.	Josh Hendricks	Heavyweight	Technical Knockout	1:01	1
Demian Maia	def.	Nate Quarry	Middleweight	Submission - Rear Naked Choke	2:13	1
Preliminary Card						
Aaron Riley	def.	Jorge Gurgel	Lightweight	Unanimous Decision	—	3
Jeremy Stephens	def.	Rafael dos Anjos	Lightweight	Knockout	0:39	3
Mark Bocek	def.	Alvin Robinson	Lightweight	Submission - Rear Naked Choke	3:16	3
Matt Brown	def.	Ryan Thomas	Welterweight	Submission - Armbar	0:57	2

The first man in UFC history to win the heavyweight championship in his fourth fight was Randy Couture. In the UFC 91 main event, Couture was forced to make room in the history books for the second man to achieve the monumental feat, Brock Lesnar, who stopped Couture in the second round to take the belt.

Couture—a five-time UFC champion and a member of the organization's Hall of Fame—had made a career of overcoming the odds, and although he had his moments in the scheduled five-rounder, in the end, the power and size of the 6-3½, 265-pounder was too much for the 220-pound Couture to overcome, especially at 45. Couture, fighting for the first time since August of 2007, didn't blame ring rust or age for the loss. Instead, all praise went to the new king.

"Those were some big hamhocks coming at me," laughed Couture after the fight. "He's a big guy and he caught me with a big shot."

With the crowd chanting "Randy! Randy!" the bell rang for what was dubbed "the biggest fight in UFC history." Couture scored with a quick right hand and Lesnar attempted a couple of knees before tying the champion up against the fence, trying to wear Couture down with his 265 pounds. After a brief stalemate, the two separated and circled before Lesnar shot in for a takedown. Couture fought it off, but wound up pinned against the fence briefly before Lesnar finally finished the takedown and put Couture on his back. As soon as he was down, Couture reversed position and the crowd erupted. Lesnar quickly regained control, though, and again tried to use his size to exhaust Couture. With under a minute left, Couture made his move and got back to his feet. The two traded knees and Couture looked for the takedown, but the bell intervened.

The second began with Couture landing a couple of quick punches, which were answered by a right from Lesnar that briefly wobbled the champion. The two reconvened at the fence, and both fighters landed with hard shots as they separated. The ensuing exchange saw Lesnar get cut over the right eye, but as Couture moved in, the fighters locked up at the fence again. After they broke, a right hand behind the ear dropped Couture, and Lesnar immediately pounced, landing a series of hammerfists to the head that forced referee Mario Yamasaki to halt the bout at 3:07 of the second round.

If there were any doubts as to the identity of the number one contender to the lightweight crown, Kenny Florian removed them as he submitted Joe Stevenson in the first round.

Submission of the Night: Hazelett vs. McCrory

Dustin Hazelett showed off his brand new Brazilian jiu-jitsu black belt in style, scoring an entertaining first-round submission win over Tamdan McCrory in a battle of welterweight up-and-comers.

Heavyweight contender Gabriel Gonzaga wasted no time in his bout with Octagon newcomer Josh Hendricks, stopping him via strikes in just 61 seconds.

Unbeaten middleweight contender Demian Maia continued to impress in the main card opener, as he took Nate Quarry down and then took him out, winning via submission in the opening round.

The third time was the charm for veteran Aaron Riley, as he finally got his first UFC win in three tries with a razor-thin unanimous decision victory over Jorge Gurgel in an exciting lightweight bout.

Up-and-comer Jeremy Stephens survived some slick submission work by newcomer Rafael dos Anjos to knock the Brazilian out with a blistering uppercut in the third and final round of their lightweight scrap.

Knockout of the Night: Stephens vs. dos Anjos

Lightweight Mark Bocek scored the most impressive win of his UFC career, submitting a game Alvin Robinson in the third round.

The Ultimate Fighter 7's Matt Brown continued to show improvement in his game, submitting Ryan Thomas in the second round of their welterweight bout.

Fight of the Night: Riley vs. Gurgel

One Hit Wonder: Josh Hendricks

UFC Fight for the Troops 1 (Fight Night 16)

10 Dec. 2008

Crown Coliseum, Fayetteville, NC

Debuts: Brandon Wolff, Steve Cantwell, Razak Al-Hassan

Fighters			Division	Method	Time	Round
Main Card						
Josh Koscheck	def.	Yoshiyuki Yoshida	Welterweight	Knockout	2:15	1
Mike Swick	def.	Jonathan Goulet	Welterweight	Knockout	0:33	1
Steve Cantwell	def.	Razak Al-Hassan	Light Heavyweight	Submission - Armbar	4:04	1
Tim Credeur	def.	Nate Loughran	Middleweight	Technical Knockout	5:00	2
Jim Miller	def.	Matt Wiman	Lightweight	Unanimous Decision	—	3
Preliminary Card						
Luigi Fioravanti	def.	Brodie Farber	Catchweight	Unanimous Decision	—	3
Steve Bruno	def.	Johnny Rees	Welterweight	Submission - Rear Naked Choke	3:44	2
Ben Saunders	def.	Brandon Wolff	Welterweight	Technical Knockout	1:49	1
Dale Hartt	def.	Corey Hill	Lightweight	Technical Knockout - Injury	0:20	2
Justin McCully	def.	Eddie Sanchez	Heavyweight	Unanimous Decision	—	3

It used to be that you would always see welterweight contender Josh Koscheck's looping right hand coming. With each passing fight, Koscheck shortened and honed the punch, and in front of a Crown Coliseum filled with U.S. military men and women, he showed the fruits of his labors as he knocked out Yoshiyuki Yoshida in the first round of the main event of the UFC Fight for the Troops card, held to benefit the Intrepid Fallen Heroes Fund.

Knockout of the Night: Koscheck vs. Yoshida

"What an honor to fight in front of all you guys," said Koscheck, addressing the troops after his third win of 2008.

Both fighters started the bout cautiously, with Yoshida scoring with sporadic kicks. In the second minute, Koscheck started opening up with his trademark right hand and he landed a couple just as range-finders. Once he got his distance, though, the rights came with more damaging intentions, and after one solid shot froze Yoshida, a second one sent him down and out, with referee Mario Yamasaki's halting of the contest at the 2:15 mark merely a formality.

After two lackluster wins at welterweight, Mike Swick was looking to make a statement in his third bout at 170 pounds Wednesday night. He did, scoring a devastating 33-second stoppage of Jonathan Goulet in the co-featured bout on the UFC Fight for the Troops card.

Steve Cantwell, the last man to hold the WEC light heavyweight title, made a smooth transition into life in the UFC, impressively submitting fellow debutant Razak Al-Hassan in the first round of an exciting and competitive 205-pound contest.

Submission of the Night: Cantwell vs. Al-Hassan

Brazilian jiu-jitsu black belt Tim Credeur continued to show improvement in his striking game as he halted previously unbeaten Nate Loughran after two rounds of their middleweight match.

Fight of the Night: Miller vs. Wiman

Lightweight prospect Jim Miller made the best of his last-minute replacement gig against Matt Wiman, drilling out a three-round unanimous decision win that broke the Texan's four-fight winning streak.

Welterweight prospect Ben Saunders scored the most impressive win of his UFC career, taking out Octagon newcomer Brandon Wolff with a ferocious assault that prompted a halt to the UFC Fight for the Troops preliminary bout in just 109 seconds.

In a bout fought at a catchweight of 173 pounds when neither fighter made the welterweight limit, former U.S. Marine Luigi Fioravanti pounded out a three-round unanimous decision over a resilient Brodie Farber.

Former U.S. Naval Air Crewman and Rescue Swimmer Steve Bruno picked the perfect occasion for his first UFC win, submitting Johnny Rees in the second round of their welterweight bout.

A lightweight bout between Dale Hartt and Corey Hill ended in unfortunate and sudden fashion in the second round when Hill broke his right leg as his kick was blocked, rendering Hartt the victor by TKO.

"Me and Corey cut weight together and Corey is an awesome dude," said Hartt of the injury suffered by his foe. "I wanted to beat him, but I would never want something like that to happen."

Justin McCully bounced back from his loss to Gabriel Gonzaga in style with a hard-fought three-round unanimous decision win over Eddie Sanchez in the heavyweight opener.

UFC / MILITARY

With the UFC being home to many veterans of the United States Armed Forces, there is little question that supporting the men and women serving overseas and at home is an important cause for not only the fighters, but for UFC President Dana White, co-owners Lorenzo and Frank Fertitta and the rest of the organization.

That includes numerous visits to military bases and hospitals, both here in the United States and as far away as Afghanistan, Iraq and Germany. A veteran of the US Army, Hall of Famer Randy Couture recalls one such trip to Iraq in 2007.

"Most of the guys couldn't believe that they were actually meeting Rich (Franklin) and I in person," said Couture. "They had seen us on TV. They show the UFC over there quite frequently on the Armed Forces network, and I don't know how many guys told us that all they do to pass the time when they have down time is watch the DVDs. They work 12-hour shifts and they're stuck on these little FOB's (Forward Operation Bases) where there's a gym and there's food, but outside of that, there's not a whole lot else to do."

Each day's activities on these bases vary, but staples of each visit would be Q&A and autograph sessions, as well as meet-and-greets with the soldiers.

"They recognized that we're willing to put our butts on a plane and take time out to fly over there and meet them where they're working, see what they do, listen to what they have to say, and put forth that effort, outside of the typical celebrity that's either speaking out against the war or says they support the troops, but wouldn't get on a plane and go to a warzone," said Couture. "And the comment was made to us on several occasions that 'We can't believe you guys actually came over here. Thank you so much, you made my year.' Most of those guys are over there for 12-month deployments away from their families and their children. So I had the feeling that they were very excited that we went over and it gave them something to talk about and something to think about other than the day to day grind."

For those who are lucky enough to get into the packed on-base clinics, it's a highlight they won't soon forget. The clinics weren't just held for entertainment purposes though, as the Combatives Program is a key part of the Army's training program.

"The reason I initially contacted the Ultimate Fighting Championship was that it seemed to be the perfect type of tour that would cater to the troops," said Sgt. Bart A. Murphy of the United States Army. "The U.S. military utilizes combatives in training, so I thought it would be appropriate for the troops to visit with some of the UFC icons that they look up to."

The UFC doesn't limit their support of the troops to just visits though. In December of 2006, the organization took its UFC Fight Night event to the military base at the MCAS Miramar in San Diego, and with the exception of a few seats auctioned off to civilians for charity, the crowd was made up of United States Marines stationed there.

In 2008 and 2011, the UFC teamed up with the Intrepid Fallen Heroes Fund and Spike TV to deliver two Fight for the Troops events that raised millions to provide assistance to military personnel critically injured in the performance of their duties.

That's a cause that hits close to home for the UFC's most decorated veteran, United States Marine Corps Captain Brian Stann, who was awarded the Silver Star for valor in battle during his time in Iraq. Stann now works with his own foundation, Hire Heroes USA, to aid and support his fellow armed forces members.

"It's awesome to travel around the country and work with wounded warriors and transitioning warriors and talk about their experiences and try to help them to succeed later in life", said Stann. "It really is therapeutic for me and it probably helps me more than it does help these veterans. It's a huge part of my life right now that will never go away."

Just like the UFC's support of the heroes of the military will never go away.

UFC 92 *The Ultimate 2008*

27 Dec. 2008

MGM Grand Garden Arena, Las Vegas, NV

Debuts: Mostapha Al-Turk, Mike Wessel, Pat Barry

Fighters			Division	Method	Time	Round
Main Card						
Rashad Evans	def.	Forrest Griffin	Light Heavyweight	Technical Knockout	2:46	3
Frank Mir	def.	Minotauro Nogueira	Heavyweight	Technical Knockout	1:54	2
Quinton Jackson	def.	Wanderlei Silva	Light Heavyweight	Knockout	3:21	1
CB Dollaway	def.	Mike Massenzio	Middleweight	Technical Knockout	3:01	1
Cheick Kongo	def.	Mostapha Al-Turk	Heavyweight	Technical Knockout	4:37	1
Preliminary Card						
Yushin Okami	def.	Dean Lister	Middleweight	Unanimous Decision	—	3
Antoni Hardonk	def.	Mike Wessel	Heavyweight	Technical Knockout	2:09	2
Matt Hamill	def.	Reese Andy	Light Heavyweight	Technical Knockout	2:19	2
Brad Blackburn	def.	Ryo Chonan	Welterweight	Unanimous Decision	—	3
Pat Barry	def.	Dan Evensen	Heavyweight	Technical Knockout	2:36	1

For two rounds in the UFC 92 main event at the MGM Grand Garden Arena, it looked like Forrest Griffin's height and reach advantage was going to be too much for Rashad Evans to deal with. When you haven't lost in your previous 18 pro fights, you find a way to win, and that's what Evans did, roaring back in the third round to stop Griffin and win the UFC light heavyweight championship.

"It was a great fight," said Evans. "It took me a while to get warmed up, but I got there. I didn't want to go in there with one mindset because sometimes when you do that, you get messed up."

After ten minutes of sporadic success, Evans—winner of *The Ultimate Fighter 2*—attacked. Less than three minutes later, he was a world champion.

Fight of the Night: Evans vs. Griffin

Both fighters got their ranges in the opening minute, with Evans opening up minute number two with a haymaker that likely would have ended the fight had it landed. But it didn't, and the two combatants continued to circle each other at close range, adding tension to each exchange, as both fighters had their moments of success. Griffin especially found a home for his low kicks, and though Evans was the faster puncher of the two, he appeared to be having difficulty getting inside on his taller opponent.

Griffin continued to stalk in round two, briefly jarring Evans and pinning him against the fence. The flurry got the crowd chanting "For-rest, For-rest!" but it also re-focused Evans, who now made a concerted effort to close the distance on Griffin. Each step closer caused Evans to pay a price, though, whether with kicks low or punches high. When Evans did score, with a crisp 1-2 or a thudding body kick, it drew a roar. It was Griffin ending the round with the hardest shot, a right to the head at the bell.

In round three, Evans finally found his opening as he grabbed one of Griffin's kicks and sent the champion to the canvas with a flurry of punches. Evans tried to finish matters on the ground, but Griffin weathered the storm and quickly recovered. Evans remained in control on the ground, periodically erupting with hard strikes to the head. Griffin appeared to take the shots well until one ferocious barrage that began with a right hand stunned Griffin and put him out, with referee Steve Mazzagatti halting the contest at 2:46 of round three.

Frank Mir completed an amazing career comeback at UFC 92 by dominating and stopping Minotauro Nogueira in the second round to regain a portion of the UFC heavyweight title he never lost in the Octagon.

"I faced such demons after my wreck," said an emotional Mir, who came back from a devastating motorcycle accident in 2004 that broke his leg in two places and forced him to the sidelines for almost two years, getting his title stripped in the process. "To come back from that, I'm proof you can do things. I didn't even think I could beat Minotauro."

He did, and in addition to winning the interim UFC heavyweight title, he became the first fighter to finish Minotauro, the former PRIDE heavyweight champion and a future Hall of Famer.

Mir was busy with his kicks to start the fight, and he tossed in a jarring right uppercut for good measure, eventually taking the fight to the mat. After some ground strikes, Mir even chose to let the fight go back to the feet, so confident was he in his striking. Once standing, Mir continued to score effectively, eventually dropping Minotauro with a straight left with under two minutes left. Again, Mir followed up briefly before stepping back and standing the fight up again. By the closing moments of the round, Mir was loose and looking like he was having fun as he put Minotauro down just as the round ended.

Needing to get back in the fight, Minotauro came out aggressively in the second, only to continue getting tagged by Mir. Less than two minutes into the round, Mir lowered the boom with two left hooks to the jaw that put the Brazilian legend on the mat again. A follow-up barrage was a mere formality, as referee Herb Dean rescued Minotauro from further punishment at 1:54 of round two.

After a tumultuous 2008 that saw Quinton Jackson lose his light heavyweight title, change his managerial and training teams, and deal with out-of-the-Octagon issues, Rampage finished off the year by knocking out his old nemesis Wanderlei Silva in the first round of their UFC 92 bout.

It was Jackson's first win in three tries against Silva, who defeated the Memphis native in PRIDE bouts in 2003 and 2004. Opting to fight without the customary touch of gloves, these fierce rivals engaged almost immediately, with Jackson stalking and Silva looking to counter. A minute in, the crowd started chanting for Silva, followed shortly after by a chant for Rampage, and both men circled, neither wanting to make a fight-ending mistake. That mistake would come with under two minutes left, as Silva came in wide with a left hook and ate one in return, sending the Brazilian down to the canvas. A follow-up from Jackson was mere window dressing as referee Yves Lavigne intervened at the 3:21 mark.

Knockout of the Night: Jackson vs. Silva

Middleweight hopeful CB Dollaway made it 2-0 against Mike Massenzio as he halted his former college wrestling opponent in the first round. Dollaway had first defeated Massenzio in the junior college wrestling nationals in 2003.

Heavyweight contender Cheick Kongo moved a step further up the ranks, progressively picking up speed before emphatically stopping Octagon newcomer Mostapha Al-Turk in the first round.

Heavyweight prospect Antoni Hardonk got a spirited effort out of late replacement Mike Wessel in their UFC 92 preliminary bout, but in the end, the experience and stamina of Hardonk won out as he TKO'd Wessel in the second round.

Former kickboxing standout Pat Barry promised a spectacular showing in his UFC debut, and he delivered, moving to 4-0 with a first-round stoppage of Dan Evensen in their heavyweight bout.

Middleweight contender Yushin Okami continued his steady, if unspectacular rise up the 185-pound ranks with an uneventful three-round unanimous decision win over Dean Lister.

Light heavyweight prospect Matt Hamill bounced back from his UFC 88 loss to Rich Franklin, halting Reese Andy in the second round.

Brad Blackburn survived a furious late rally from Ryo Chonan to take a close three-round unanimous decision.

One Hit Wonder: Mike Wessel

The Ultimate Fighter 8 Finale

Team Nogueira vs. Team Mir

13 Dec. 2008

The Pearl at The Palms, Las Vegas, NV

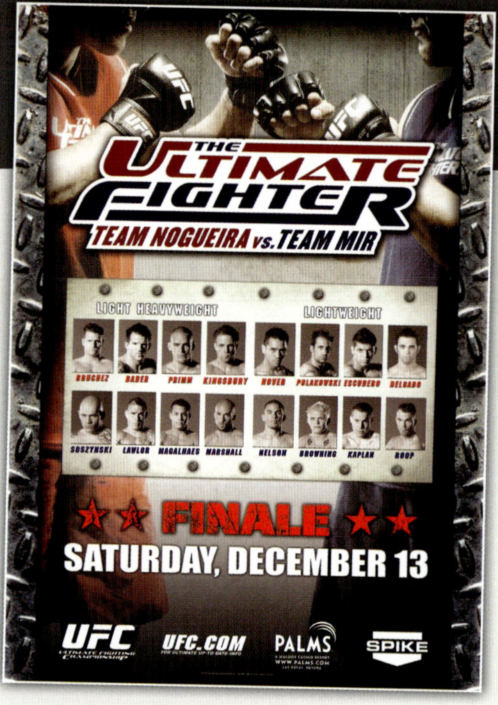

Debuts: Rolando Delgado, John Polakowski, Shane Nelson, George Roop, Kyle Kingsbury, Tom Lawlor, Eliot Marshall, Jules Bruchez, Krzysztof Soszynski, Shane Primm, Junie Browning, Dave Kaplan, Ryan Bader, Vinicius Magalhaes, Phillipe Nover, Efrain Escudero

Fighters			Division	Method	Time	Round
Main Card						
Efrain Escudero	def.	Phillipe Nover	Lightweight	Unanimous Decision	—	3
Ryan Bader	def.	Vinicius Magalhaes	Light Heavyweight	Knockout	2:18	1
Anthony Johnson	def.	Kevin Burns	Welterweight	Knockout	0:28	3
Wilson Gouveia	def.	Jason MacDonald	Catchweight	Submission - Strikes	2:18	1
Junie Browning	def.	Dave Kaplan	Lightweight	Submission - Armbar	1:32	2
Preliminary Card						
Krzysztof Soszynski	def.	Shane Primm	Light Heavyweight	Submission - Kimura	3:27	2
Eliot Marshall	def.	Jules Bruchez	Light Heavyweight	Submission - Rear Naked Choke	1:27	1
Tom Lawlor	def.	Kyle Kingsbury	Light Heavyweight	Unanimous Decision	—	3
Shane Nelson	def.	George Roop	Lightweight	Split Decision	—	3
Rolando Delgado	def.	John Polakowski	Lightweight	Submission - Guillotine Choke	2:18	2

Interim UFC heavyweight champion Minotauro Nogueira saw his fighters sweep honors at *The Ultimate Fighter: Team Nogueira vs. Team Mir Finale*, as lightweight Efrain Escudero and light heavyweight Ryan Bader both kept their perfect records intact at the expense of Phillipe Nover and Vinicius Magalhaes, respectively.

Both Escudero and Bader earned six-figure UFC contracts with their victories, which came after six weeks on Spike TV's *The Ultimate Fighter*.

It was a battle between friends and teammates in the *TUF8* lightweight final, with Escudero pounding out a disciplined three-round unanimous decision over Brooklyn's Nover. Scores were 29-28 across the board for Escudero.

Team Nogueira's 205-pound representative, "Darth" Bader, didn't even need to use his All-American wrestling skills against Team Mir's Brazilian jiu-jitsu ace, Magalhaes. Instead, the Reno native's standup attack was sufficient to stop Magalhaes in the first round and become *The Ultimate Fighter 8* light heavyweight winner.

The opening moments were tense, as both fighters pecked at each other and looked for fight-ending openings. Bader's strikes were harder though, and they quickly reddened Magalhaes' face. Around a minute later, Bader finished things, rocking and dropping Magalhaes with a right hand. As the Brazilian fell awkwardly, Bader pounced with a ferocious follow-up assault that forced a halt to the proceedings by referee Herb Dean at 2:18 of the opening stanza.

The second bout between welterweight up-and-comers Anthony Johnson and Kevin Burns ended in the third round just like the first one, but this time there was no controversy, as "Rumble" won a closely contested bout with an emphatic one-kick knockout of Burns.

Knockout of the Night: Johnson vs. Burns

Burns' third-round win over Johnson in July 2008 was bathed in controversy after an inadvertent poke in the eye ended the bout as a TKO for Burns instead of a disqualification victory for Johnson. This fight would hold no such debates.

Wilson Gouveia didn't make weight for his bout against Jason MacDonald, but he did come to fight, stopping the Canadian standout in the first round of their catchweight contest.

Fight of the Night: Browning vs. Kaplan

Controversial Team Mir member Junie Browning made a lot of noise during his stint on *The Ultimate Fighter*. In his first post-show UFC fight, the lightweight from Lexington, Kentucky showed that he could fight, too, as he submitted his teammate David Kaplan in the second round.

Submission of the Night: Soszynski vs. Primm

Team Mir light heavyweight Krzysztof Soszynski earned his first UFC victory with a second-round submission win over Team Nogueira's Shane Primm.

Eliot Marshall gave Jules Bruchez a rude welcome to the pro ranks, dominating his foe en route to an 87-second submission victory in their light heavyweight bout.

In light heavyweight action, Team Mir's Tom Lawlor pounded out a three-round unanimous decision win over Team Nogueira's Kyle Kingsbury.

It was a competitive lightweight battle between Team Mir teammates Shane Nelson and George Roop, but in the end, Nelson outlasted Roop via a three-round split decision.

Roli Delgado's ground game proved to be the difference in the lightweight opener, as "The Crazy Cuban" submitted his Team Nogueira teammate John Polakowski in the second round.

One Hit Wonders: John Polakowski, Jules Bruchez, Shane Primm

UFC 93 *Franklin vs. Henderson*

17 Jan. 2009

The O2 Dublin, Dublin, Ireland

Debuts: Denis Kang, Thomas Egan, John Hathaway, Alexandre Barros, Ivan Serati

Fighters			Division	Method	Time	Round
Main Card						
Dan Henderson	def.	Rich Franklin	Light Heavyweight	Split Decision	—	3
Mauricio Rua	def.	Mark Coleman	Light Heavyweight	Technical Knockout	4:36	3
Rousimar Palhares	def.	Jeremy Horn	Middleweight	Unanimous Decision	—	3
Alan Belcher	def.	Denis Kang	Middleweight	Submission - Guillotine Choke	4:30	2
Marcus Davis	def.	Chris Lytle	Welterweight	Split Decision	—	3
Preliminary Card						
John Hathaway	def.	Thomas Egan	Welterweight	Technical Knockout	4:36	1
Martin Kampmann	def.	Alexandre Barros	Welterweight	Technical Knockout	3:07	2
Eric Schafer	def.	Antonio Mendes	Light Heavyweight	Technical Knockout	3:35	1
Tomasz Drwal	def.	Ivan Serati	Light Heavyweight	Knockout	2:02	1
Dennis Siver	def.	Nate Mohr	Light Heavyweight	Technical Knockout	3:47	3

Before a packed house of 9,369 fans, Dan Henderson outlasted Rich Franklin via split decision in the main event of UFC 93, answering the recurring question of who would win between the two longtime MMA superstars. Scores were 29-28 twice for Henderson, with the third judge scoring it 30-27 for Franklin.

After a tactical opening, Henderson landed the first major blow of the fight with his patented right hand. But as Henderson rushed in to capitalize, he slipped. Midway through the round, Franklin got back to his feet, and "Ace" started to get his own offense into gear with hard kicks to the midsection and leg

Henderson aggressively chased after his foe at times in the second round, but Franklin's patient countering nullified the rushes. In the second half of the round, Henderson finally sought refuge back on the mat, where he could work his ground and pound.

Franklin began the final round with more urgency, but his aggression also allowed him to get taken down by Henderson, who pounded away again. Neither fighter wanted to give up an inch of Octagon real estate, making the fight compelling to watch. When Franklin rose to his feet, he again went on the offensive, much to the delight of the crowd. An inadvertent poke in the eye by Henderson sent Franklin to the mat and brought a stop to the action with under 40 seconds left, but after the break, Franklin got right back in the pocket, looking to finish. Henderson did the same with his lethal right hand, but neither man would get his wish, sending the bout to the scorecards.

After a loss to Forrest Griffin in 2007 and two knee surgeries, light heavyweight contender Mauricio "Shogun" Rua needed a win in a bad way, and he got it in the UFC 93 co-main event, stopping Mark Coleman in the third round of their rematch. The lasting image of the bout may not be Rua evening the score with his rival, but of the courageous Coleman leaving it all in the Octagon in his return to the organization where he made his name in the sport from 1996 to 1999.

Rousimar Palhares and Jeremy Horn showed off some solid groundwork in their bout, but Palhares proved himself to be the better fighter on that night as he scored a shutout three-round decision win.

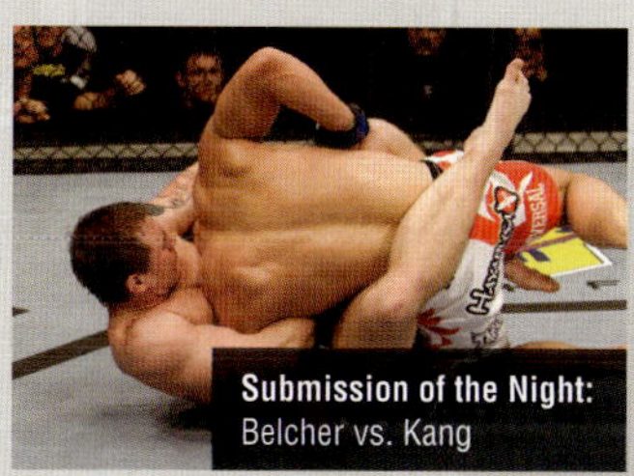
Submission of the Night: Belcher vs. Kang

Everything went wrong for Alan Belcher in his bout against international star Denis Kang except the final 24 seconds, and that's all that mattered, as he spoiled Kang's UFC debut with a second-round submission victory.

Fight of the Night: Davis vs. Lytle

Marcus Davis and Chris Lytle promised fireworks in their UFC 93 main card opener and they delivered beyond the shadow of a doubt, battling it out for 15 minutes before Davis emerged victorious via a three-round split decision.

With fans in The O2 Dublin Arena screaming themselves hoarse, it sounded like a main event before the UFC 93 preliminary bout between Dublin's own Tom Egan and England's John Hathaway, but in the end, the more experienced Hathaway had to disappoint Irish fans as he stopped the local hero in the first round of their bout.

Former middleweight contender Martin Kampmann did well in his welterweight debut, stopping Brazil's Alexandre Barros in the second round.

Eric Schafer made it four wins in a row, following up his victory over Houston Alexander with a first-round TKO of Antonio Mendes in a light heavyweight contest.

Poland's Tomasz Drwal enjoyed a successful return to the Octagon after an absence of over a year due to injury, knocking out newcomer Ivan Serati in the first round.

Dennis Siver kicked off the evening's festivities in style, ending his entertaining lightweight bout with Nate Mohr via third-round TKO.

Knockout of the Night: Siver vs. Mohr

Fight of the Night (Not Pictured): Rua vs. Coleman

One Hit Wonders: Thomas Egan, Alexandre Barros, Ivan Serati

UFC 94 *St-Pierre vs. Penn 2*

31 Jan. 2009

MGM Grand Garden Arena, Las Vegas, NV

Debuts: John Howard, Dan Cramer

Fighters			Division	Method	Time	Round
Main Card						
Georges St-Pierre	def.	BJ Penn	Welterweight	Technical Knockout	—	4
Lyoto Machida	def.	Thiago Silva	Light Heavyweight	Knockout	4:59	1
Jon Jones	def.	Stephan Bonnar	Light Heavyweight	Unanimous Decision	—	3
Karo Parisyan	def.	Dong Hyun Kim	Welterweight	Split Decision*	—	3
Clay Guida	def.	Nate Diaz	Lightweight	Split Decision	—	3
Preliminary Card						
Jon Fitch	def.	Akihiro Gono	Welterweight	Unanimous Decision	—	3
Thiago Tavares	def.	Manny Gamburyan	Lightweight	Unanimous Decision	—	3
John Howard	def.	Chris Wilson	Welterweight	Split Decision	—	3
Jake O'Brien	def.	Christian Wellisch	Light Heavyweight	Split Decision	—	3
Dan Cramer	def.	Matt Arroyo	Welterweight	Split Decision	—	3

*Result was changed to a no contest after Parisyan tested positive for banned painkillers.

It was the biggest fight of Georges St-Pierre's career, and against BJ Penn, the UFC welterweight champion delivered a master class, shutting down the lightweight champion completely before forcing a stoppage at the end of the fourth round in the UFC 94 main event.

It was a sweet victory for St-Pierre, who had scored a split decision win over Penn in their first fight in 2006. This one wasn't nearly as close.

The two champions locked up at the bell, with St-Pierre bulling his smaller foe into the fence while throwing the occasional short-range strike. Throughout the round, St-Pierre looked for a takedown but couldn't get it, and while the champion couldn't take Penn down, his crisp strikes and busy workrate gave him an early edge.

The second opened with some exchanges, but the crowd booed as St-Pierre pushed Penn to the fence and sought another takedown. This time St-Pierre got it, and the two commenced their first battle on the mat. St-Pierre's ground strikes were effective, and he quickly worked into side control, putting Penn in trouble as he fired away with punches.

St-Pierre raced out of his corner to start the third and his strikes sent blood spurting from Penn's nose. Moments later, St-Pierre took Penn down and looked to continue the ground assault he instituted in the previous round. He succeeded, pounding away as Penn tried to find an opening for a submission from his back. With two minutes left, after eating a series of shots to the face, Penn rose and looked for his own takedown as he pinned St-Pierre to the fence. GSP reversed the position, though, and got yet another takedown, this one the most emphatic of the fight thus far.

The left jab was St-Pierre's primary weapon in the beginning of round four, and after landing a few of those, he took Penn to the mat and landed in side control, where the punches started to rain down again. Pinned to the canvas, Penn was unable to get out of the way of St-Pierre's blows, and the end seemed to be near for the lightweight champion.

Knockout of the Night: Machida vs. Silva

There wouldn't be a fifth round for Penn, who was wisely kept in his corner by Octagonside physician William Berliner.

Criticized for his unorthodox countering style, Lyoto Machida silenced the critics in the co-main event of UFC 94, walking through Thiago Silva en route to a first-round knockout win.

Jon Jones proved that he was for real in UFC 94 action as the unbeaten 21-year-old stunned returning light heavyweight star Stephan Bonnar with a varied and aggressive attack that earned him a three-round unanimous decision win.

Welterweight contender Karo Parisyan returned to the Octagon for the first time since April of 2008 and handed Dong Hyun Kim his first pro loss via a closely contested but less than compelling three-round split decision. Afterwards, the result was ruled a no contest as Parisyan tested positive for painkillers.

In the main card opener, Clay Guida halted the Octagon unbeaten streak of Nate Diaz, drilling out a workmanlike three-round split decision.

Fight of the Night: Guida vs. Diaz

Japan's Akihiro Gono may have won the battle of the Octagon entrances in UFC 94 preliminary action, but once the bell rang, it was all Jon Fitch, as the no-nonsense welterweight contender pounded out a three-round unanimous decision victory.

Thiago Tavares broke a two-fight losing streak while issuing Manny Gamburyan his second straight loss, winning a three-round unanimous decision in their lightweight bout.

Fight of the Night: Howard vs. Wilson

UFC newcomer John "Doomsday" Howard became the latest New Englander to make his mark in the Octagon as he won an impressive three-round split decision over veteran Chris Wilson.

Former heavyweight prospect Jake O'Brien made his 205-pound debut a successful one, scoring a three-round split decision over another heavyweight turned light heavy, Christian Wellisch.

The Ultimate Fighter 7's Dan Cramer didn't get any breaks by making his professional MMA debut in the UFC, but after three hard-fought rounds, he eked out a split decision win over season six cast member Matt Arroyo.

UFC Fight Night 17

Lauzon vs. Stephens

07 Feb. 2009

USF Sun Dome, Tampa, FL

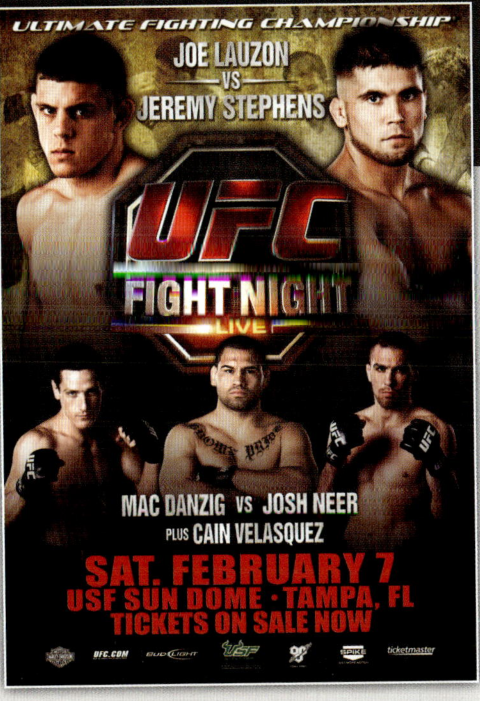

Debuts: Denis Stojnic, Jake Rosholt, Matt Veach, Derek Downey, Nick Catone

Fighters			Division	Method	Time	Round
Main Card						
Joe Lauzon	def.	Jeremy Stephens	Lightweight	Submission - Armbar	4:42	2
Cain Velasquez	def.	Denis Stojnic	Heavyweight	Technical Knockout	2:34	2
Josh Neer	def.	Mac Danzig	Lightweight	Submission - Triangle Choke	3:36	2
Anthony Johnson	def.	Luigi Fioravanti	Welterweight	Technical Knockout	4:39	1
Preliminary Card						
Kurt Pellegrino	def.	Rob Emerson	Lightweight	Submission - Rear Naked Choke	3:14	2
Dan Miller	def.	Jake Rosholt	Middleweight	Submission - Guillotine Choke	1:03	1
Matt Veach	def.	Matt Grice	Lightweight	Technical Knockout	4:34	1
Gleison Tibau	def.	Rich Clementi	Lightweight	Submission - Guillotine Choke	4:35	1
Nick Catone	def.	Derek Downey	Middleweight	Submission - Keylock	1:15	2
Matthew Riddle	def.	Steve Bruno	Welterweight	Unanimous Decision	—	3

The first time Joe Lauzon was in a UFC main event, against Kenny Florian in April of 2008, he admitted that he got a bit unnerved by his headlining status. But at the USF Sun Dome in Tampa, Florida, there were no such nerves as "J-Lau" used a varied attack before submitting Jeremy Stephens in the second round of the UFC Fight Night main event.

Submission of the Night: Lauzon vs. Stephens

Lauzon wasted no time taking the bout to the mat, and even though Stephens made it back to his feet rather quickly, Lauzon kept his foe locked up, and he fired away from close range before dropping to the mat for a leg lock attempt. Stephens got out of it quickly but was sent right back to the canvas moments later. This time, Lauzon worked his ground and pound attack, and with two minutes left, he moved into the mount position before trying for an armbar. Again, Stephens escaped, and he pushed Lauzon into the fence, where he could fire off his own ground strikes as the clock ticked down. The two stood in the final 30 seconds, with Stephens finishing the round off with a hard slam.

Stephens, who was a late replacement for the injured Hermes Franca, opened the second throwing bombs, but Lauzon was able to fight his way inside, and with a fireman's carry takedown, he put the fight back in his realm on the mat. Lauzon quickly moved to side control, and midway through the round, he got full mount before taking Stephens' back. At the three-minute mark, Stephens broke loose and got into Lauzon's guard. While there, he bulled Lauzon into the fence and opened a cut on the New Englander's forehead. Lauzon kept battling, though, and as he got into the mount position again, he went hard for the finish and got it, submitting Stephens with an armbar at 4:42 of the second round.

"I knew we were getting close to the end of the round so I was trying and trying, and I got the stoppage," said Lauzon.

Fight of the Night: Neer vs. Danzig

Lightweight Josh Neer scored the biggest win of his UFC career at the USF Sun Dome, impressively disregarding a badly cut eye to submit Mac Danzig in the second round of their UFC Fight Night bout.

Unbeaten heavyweight Cain Velasquez was in control from the opening bell against Octagon newcomer Denis Stojnic, showing off his standup attack before finishing the bout on the mat in the second round.

Knockout of the Night: Velasquez vs. Stojnic

In the main card opener, Anthony Johnson continued to build his rep as the most explosive striker at 170 pounds as he stopped Luigi Fioravanti in the first round.

After a breakout year in 2008, lightweight contender Kurt Pellegrino got 2009 off to a good start with a second-round submission win over Rob Emerson in UFC Fight Night prelim action.

It was a rollercoaster ride, but by the time it was over, unbeaten Matt Veach survived some rocky moments to stop Matt Grice in an exciting lightweight bout.

Dan Miller made it 3-0 in the Octagon in less than five months, issuing UFC debutant Jake Rosholt his first pro loss via first-round submission.

Gleison Tibau broke a two-fight losing streak in impressive fashion as he issued Rich Clementi a first-round submission defeat in their lightweight contest.

After two fights with Amir Sadollah were scrapped, New Jersey middleweight Nick Catone finally got the chance to step into the Octagon and he made the most of it, submitting Derek Downey in the second round.

In welterweight action, *The Ultimate Fighter 7* contender Matt Riddle upped his pro record to 2-0 with a three-round unanimous decision over Steve Bruno.

One Hit Wonder: Derek Downey

UFC 95 *Sanchez vs. Stevenson*

21 Feb. 2009

The O2, London, England

Debuts: Paulo Thiago, Brian Cobb, Stefan Struve, Evan Dunham, Mike Ciesnolevicz, Neil Grove

Fighters			Division	Method	Time	Round
Main Card						
Diego Sanchez	def.	Joe Stevenson	Lightweight	Unanimous Decision	—	3
Dan Hardy	def.	Rory Markham	Welterweight	Knockout	1:09	1
Nate Marquardt	def.	Wilson Gouveia	Middleweight	Technical Knockout	3:10	3
Demian Maia	def.	Chael Sonnen	Middleweight	Submission - Triangle Choke	2:37	1
Paulo Thiago	def.	Josh Koscheck	Welterweight	Knockout	3:29	1
Preliminary Card						
Terry Etim	def.	Brian Cobb	Lightweight	Technical Knockout	0:10	2
Junior dos Santos	def.	Stefan Struve	Heavyweight	Technical Knockout	0:54	1
Evan Dunham	def.	Per Eklund	Lightweight	Knockout	2:14	1
Mike Ciesnolevicz	def.	Neil Grove	Heavyweight	Submission - Heel Hook	1:03	1
Paul Kelly	def.	Troy Mandaloniz	Welterweight	Unanimous Decision	—	3

Former welterweight contender Diego Sanchez made an immediate statement in his debut at 155 pounds, scoring a hard-fought three-round unanimous decision victory over Joe Stevenson in the main event of UFC 95.

Fight of the Night: Sanchez vs. Stevenson

Entering the Octagon to the strains of Queen's "We Will Rock You", Sanchez' intensity was evident. Stevenson was less demonstrative, but his focus was clear once the bell rang as he pursued Sanchez and worked in straight counters as Sanchez flurried in spurts. As the midway point of the round approached, Sanchez picked up the pace and began to land with more frequency and power, even rocking his foe with an uppercut.

Sanchez opened the second with a hard right hand to the head, followed by a knee and a takedown that immediately put Stevenson on the defensive. The two got right back up to their feet and resumed the battle, locking up against the fence, and as Stevenson locked in a guillotine choke, Sanchez slammed his foe and broke loose. A frantic ground scramble ensued, and when the two rose, the crowd cheered appreciatively. The round progressed with Stevenson closing the striking gap a bit due to his aggression, but by the end of the frame Sanchez was back in control.

Both fighters met in the center of the Octagon at the start of the third and exchanged punches, with Sanchez perhaps getting the worst of it as he shook his hand after landing a right to the head, possibly injuring it. In ensuing exchanges, Stevenson seemed to be enjoying the action, as he took after Sanchez with a blood-stained grin and exhorted the crowd to keep cheering after he stuffed a Sanchez takedown attempt. Sanchez finally started to show signs of wearying as the bout entered its final two minutes, but as Stevenson began to land, Sanchez found a second wind and scored well with some punches and a kick to the head, which bloodied Stevenson's left eye just before a frenetic final flurry by both men got the crowd roaring.

The chatter before the UFC 95 bout between welterweights Dan Hardy and Rory Markham dictated that when it came to punching power, Markham was the man to watch out for. Nottingham's Hardy took issue with such talk, and he responded with his fists as he knocked Markham out in 69 seconds.

Submission of the Night: Maia vs. Sonnen

Knockout of the Night: Thiago vs. Koscheck

Middleweight contender Nate Marquardt continued to state his case for a rematch with 185-pound champion Anderson Silva as he impressively halted Wilson Gouveia in the third round.

Brazilian jiu-jitsu phenom Demian Maia further moved up the middleweight ladder with a first-round submission win over Chael Sonnen, his fifth tapout victory in five tries in the UFC.

UFC debutant Paulo Thiago scored the first major upset of 2009, knocking out welterweight contender Josh Koscheck in the first round of their main card opener.

Heavyweight up-and-comer Junior dos Santos made it two for two when it came to big knockout victories in the UFC, following up his win over Fabricio Werdum at UFC 90 with a 54-second destruction of Octagon newcomer Stefan Struve.

Terry Etim put together his most impressive UFC performance to date as he used a ferocious Muay Thai attack to halt Brian Cobb in the second round.

Evan Dunham made the most of his opportunity to step in for injured David Baron in UFC 95 on short notice, knocking out Swedish veteran Per Eklund in the first round of their lightweight bout.

Longtime MMA veteran Mike Ciesnolevicz finally got his shot to compete in the UFC Octagon, and even though he jumped up to heavyweight to do it, he was able to emerge victorious as he made short work of Essex' Neil Grove via 63-second submission.

Paul Kelly got the local fans up and roaring immediately as he pounded out a three-round unanimous decision over Troy Mandaloniz in the rousing welterweight opener.

One Hit Wonders: Brian Cobb, Neil Grove

UFC 96 *Jackson vs. Jardine*

07 March 2009

Nationwide Arena, Columbus, OH

Debuts: Mark Munoz, Ryan Madigan

Fighters			Division	Method	Time	Round
Main Card						
Quinton Jackson	def.	Keith Jardine	Light Heavyweight	Unanimous Decision	—	3
Shane Carwin	def.	Gabriel Gonzaga	Heavyweight	Knockout	1:09	1
Matt Brown	def.	Pete Sell	Welterweight	Technical Knockout	1:32	1
Matt Hamill	def.	Mark Munoz	Light Heavyweight	Knockout	3:53	1
Gray Maynard	def.	Jim Miller	Lightweight	Unanimous Decision	—	3
Preliminary Card						
Tamdan McCrory	def.	Ryan Madigan	Welterweight	Submission - Punches	3:35	1
Kendall Grove	def.	Jason Day	Middleweight	Technical Knockout	1:32	1
Jason Brilz	def.	Tim Boetsch	Light Heavyweight	Unanimous Decision	—	3
Brandon Vera	def.	Michael Patt	Light Heavyweight	Technical Knockout	1:27	2
Shane Nelson	def.	Aaron Riley	Lightweight	Technical Knockout	0:44	1

Former UFC light heavyweight champion Quinton "Rampage" Jackson didn't get an easy road to his 30th pro win, but after a hard-fought three-round unanimous decision win over Keith Jardine in the UFC 96 main event, he not only got the victory, he cleared the way for a title shot.

It took a while for the fight to heat up, but as the bout approached the four-minute mark, Jackson was starting to find his range as he caught the unorthodox Jardine on a couple of occasions.

Jardine led off the action in the second round, but his wild shots weren't landing with any consistency. Jackson continued to stalk quietly, looking for his chance to counter, and with 3:05 left, his opportunity came as he dropped Jardine with a hard left hook. Rampage immediately pounced, looking to finish off his foe, but Jardine made it to his feet and survived the onslaught, only to see Jackson finish strong with another barrage before the bell.

Fight of the Night: Jackson vs. Jardine

Jackson and Jardine met in the center of the Octagon for the final round and immediately started throwing strikes at each other. After the initial burst of action, the two circled, looking to potshot each other. The crowd alternated chants for each fighter, and with 3:45 remaining, Jackson took Jardine to the mat. "The Dean of Mean" rose quickly, and after they tangled along the fence, the standup battle resumed. As the round went into its final 2:30, Jardine became the busier of the two, but Jackson still got his shots in, and in the final minute he started tagging the tiring Jardine with power shots. After some dicey moments, Jardine got back into the fray, but a final knockdown scored by Jackson's left hook sealed the deal for the Memphis native. Scores were 29-28 twice and 30-27 for Jackson.

It only took 69 seconds for unbeaten Shane Carwin to graduate from prospect to contender, and he did it with a show-stopping right hand that knocked out former heavyweight title challenger Gabriel Gonzaga.

Welterweight Matt Brown continued to impress, halting Pete Sell in the first round with a furious blitz that took Sell by surprise and never allowed him to get into the fight.

Matt Hamill didn't want any part of wrestling with former Division I National Champion Mark Munoz in their light heavyweight bout, and for good reason, because "The Hammer" had a secret weapon to unleash: a kick to the head that knocked Munoz out in spectacular fashion in the first round.

Knockout of the Night: Hamill vs. Munoz

Lightweight Gray Maynard scored one of the most impressive wins of his career in the main card opener, using a striking-based attack and rock-solid defense to pound out a three-round unanimous decision win over Jim Miller.

Light heavyweight Brandon "The Truth" Vera put together his best performance (and first stoppage) since he beat Frank Mir in 2006, halting Michael Patt in the second round with a brutal assault of leg kicks in their UFC 96 prelim bout.

Tamdan McCrory bounced back from a November loss to Dustin Hazelett, handing newcomer Ryan Madigan his first pro loss via a first-round TKO.

Out of action since his win over Evan Tanner the previous June, Kendall Grove took little time to add another win to his record as he stopped Jason Day in the first round of their middleweight bout.

In 205-pound action, Jason Brilz improved to 17-1-1 with a three-round unanimous decision victory over Tim Boetsch.

In the opener, veteran Aaron Riley was on the wrong end of a horrendous call by referee Rick Fike, causing him to lose his lightweight bout to Shane Nelson via a first-round TKO. "It was definitely an early stoppage," said Riley. "Everybody saw me take a whole lot worse than that. I had all my faculties about me then, and I still do."

One Hit Wonder: Ryan Madigan

ODD FACTS

7 Seconds
Fastest KO in UFC History
Todd Duffee over Tim Hague

618 Pounds
Heaviest UFC Fighter Ever
Emmanuel Yarborough

36 Minutes
Longest UFC Fight
Royce Gracie vs. Ken Shamrock II

10 Most UFC Knockouts
Chuck Liddell

7
Number of Brazilian fighters to win a UFC title
Anderson Silva, Vitor Belfort, Mauricio Rua, Murilo Bustamante, Jose Aldo, Minotauro Nogueira, Lyoto Machida

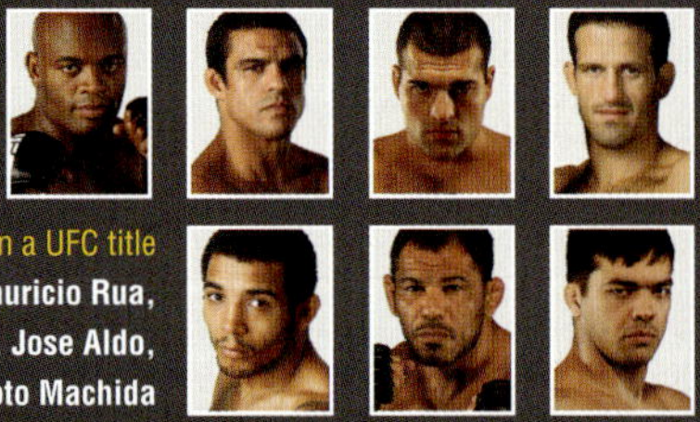

11 Most UFC Submissions
Royce Gracie

3
Number of *The Ultimate Fighter* season winners to win a UFC title
Forrest Griffin, Matt Serra, Rashad Evans

5
Number of UFC champions faced by Stephan Bonnar
Lyoto Machida, Forrest Griffin, Rashad Evans, Jon Jones, Mark Coleman

9 Seconds
Fastest Submission in UFC History
Oleg Taktarov over Anthony Macias

9-0
Georges St-Pierre's record in fights that go the distance

5
Number of UFC world titles won by
Randy Couture

8
Number of post-fight bonus awards won by
Anderson Silva and Chris Lytle

45
Age of the Oldest UFC titleholder
Randy Couture

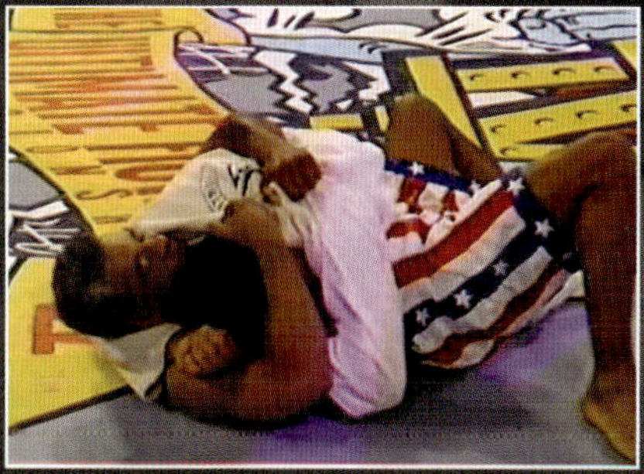

51
Age of the Oldest UFC Fighter
Ron Van Clief

38 Feet
Exterior size in diameter of the **UFC Octagon**

23 Years old
Age of the youngest titleholder in UFC history
Jon Jones

1
Number of fights ended by the twister submission
Chan Sung Jung over Leonard Garcia

55,724
Number of people in attendance for
UFC 129 in Toronto

84.5 Inches
Jones' reach, the longest in UFC history

7
Number of fighters to have won all three post-fight awards: KO, Sub, and Fight of the Night
Anderson Silva, Dennis Siver, Josh Koscheck, Chris Lytle, Paulo Thiago, Marcus Davis, Wilson Gouveia

UFC Fight Night 18

Condit vs. Kampmann

01 April 2009

Sommet Center, Nashville, TN

Debuts: Carlos Condit, Jesse Sanders, Nissen Osterneck, Tim McKenzie, Aaron Simpson

Fighters			Division	Method	Time	Round
Main Card						
Martin Kampmann	def.	Carlos Condit	Welterweight	Split Decision	—	3
Ryan Bader	def.	Carmelo Marrero	Light Heavyweight	Unanimous Decision	—	3
Tyson Griffin	def.	Rafael dos Anjos	Lightweight	Unanimous Decision	—	3
Cole Miller	def.	Junie Browning	Lightweight	Submission - Guillotine Choke	1:58	1
Preliminary Card						
Gleison Tibau	def.	Jeremy Stephens	Catchweight	Unanimous Decision	—	3
Ricardo Almeida	def.	Matt Horwich	Middleweight	Unanimous Decision	—	3
Brock Larson	def.	Jesse Sanders	Welterweight	Submission - Rear Naked Choke	2:01	1
Tim Credeur	def.	Nick Catone	Middleweight	Submission - Guillotine Choke	3:45	2
Jorge Rivera	def.	Nissen Osterneck	Middleweight	Split Decision	—	3
Rob Kimmons	def.	Joe Vedepo	Middleweight	Submission - Guillotine Choke	1:54	1
Aaron Simpson	def.	Tim McKenzie	Middleweight	Technical Knockout	1:40	1

Former WEC welterweight champion Carlos Condit didn't get any gimmes in his first UFC bout at the Sommet Center, and even though he proved he belonged with the best 170-pounders in the world, the night belonged to his opponent, Martin Kampmann "The Hitman" used a series of submission attempts to take a razor-thin split decision in a fast-paced battle between two of the division's rising stars. Scores were 29-28, 29-28, and 28-29 for Kampmann, who seemed close to finishing Condit with a guillotine choke at the end of the first round.

The evenly-matched nature of the bout was evident almost immediately as the two locked horns in the middle of the Octagon. Kampmann broke the stalemate with a takedown and a subsequent guillotine choke attempt. After a few tense moments, Condit broke loose and got back to his feet, but it was a brief respite, as both men went back to the canvas in order to work from there. The two got back to their feet and began to trade, with Condit holding the edge behind sweeping kicks and strikes. By the end of the round, it was Kampmann again locking in the guillotine choke, with only the bell intervening.

Trading kicks to open the second, the pace remained high, and Kampmann looked to continue his ground success as he took Condit to the mat. With the round approaching the midway point, Condit fought his way back to his feet and landed some hard strikes before pinning Kampmann against the fence. Kampmann fired back and drove Condit across the Octagon before sinking in his third guillotine choke. Condit, refusing to go away that easily, escaped and tried a rear naked choke on Kampmann as the crowd erupted in appreciation for both fighters' efforts.

The fighters picked up where they left off in the third, with Kampmann scoring a takedown and firing off punches while Condit punched back from the bottom and looked for submissions.

"It was deep—I thought I had him, but Carlos is a really tough man," said Kampmann. "That was a war."

Known primarily for their ground games, lightweights Tyson Griffin and Rafael dos Anjos instead showed off their striking prowess, and the result was an entertaining three-round scrap that saw Griffin survive some dicey moments before emerging victorious via unanimous decision.

Fight of the Night: Griffin vs. dos Anjos

In pre-fight banter, Cole Miller promised a dominant win over *The Ultimate Fighter 8* contender Junie Browning, and once the bell rang, the Georgia native delivered, submitting his foe in the first round of their lightweight bout.

The Ultimate Fighter 8 winner Ryan Bader kept his unbeaten record intact as he used his wrestling attack to cruise to a shutout three-round win over Carmelo Marrero.

"Crazy" Tim Credeur made it three in a row since his stint on *The Ultimate Fighter*, handing middleweight prospect Nick Catone his first pro defeat via an impressive second-round submission in UFC Fight Night preliminary action at the Sommet Center.

It was an emotional victory for middleweight veteran Jorge Rivera, who, fighting for the first time since the tragic death of his 17-year-old daughter Janessa in August 2008, pounded out a split decision win over Nissen Osterneck.

In a bout fought at a catchweight after both fighters weighed in over the lightweight limit, Gleison Tibau (156.5) scored a three-round unanimous decision win over Jeremy Stephens (158).

Middleweight contender Ricardo Almeida improved to 10-3 with a shutout three-round decision over Matt Horwich.

Former WEC welterweight title challenger Brock Larson made his first UFC fight since December of 2006 a successful one as he dominated Octagon newcomer Jesse Sanders before submitting him at 2:01 of the opening round.

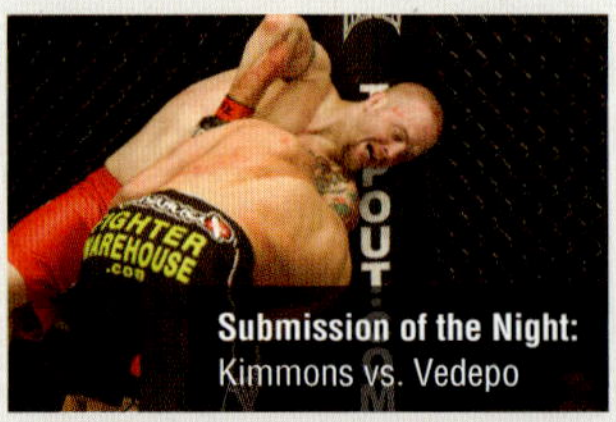
Submission of the Night: Kimmons vs. Vedepo

Middleweight Rob Kimmons impressively notched his second UFC win, submitting Joe Vedepo in the first round.

Knockout of the Night: Simpson vs. McKenzie

In the first bout of the evening, middleweight Aaron Simpson made short work of Tim McKenzie, stopping him in the first round of a clash between former WEC standouts.

One Hit Wonders: Jesse Sanders, Nissen Osterneck, Tim McKenzie

UFC 97 *Redemption*

18 April 2009

Bell Centre, Montreal, Quebec, Canada

Debuts: Brian Stann, Xavier Foupa-Pokam, TJ Grant

Fighters			Division	Method	Time	Round
Main Card						
Anderson Silva	def.	Thales Leites	Middleweight	Unanimous Decision	—	5
Mauricio Rua	def.	Chuck Liddell	Light Heavyweight	Technical Knockout	4:28	1
Sam Stout	def.	Matt Wiman	Lightweight	Unanimous Decision	—	3
Krzysztof Soszynski	def.	Brian Stann	Light Heavyweight	Submission - Kimura	3:53	1
Cheick Kongo	def.	Antoni Hardonk	Heavyweight	Technical Knockout	2:29	2
Luiz Cane	def.	Steve Cantwell	Light Heavyweight	Unanimous Decision	—	3
Preliminary Card						
Denis Kang	def.	Xavier Foupa-Pokam	Middleweight	Unanimous Decision	—	3
Nate Quarry	def.	Jason MacDonald	Middleweight	Technical Knockout	2:27	1
Ed Herman	def.	David Loiseau	Middleweight	Unanimous Decision	—	3
Mark Bocek	def.	David Bielkheden	Lightweight	Submission - Rear Naked Choke	4:57	1
TJ Grant	def.	Ryo Chonan	Welterweight	Split Decision	—	3
Eliot Marshall	def.	Vinicius Magalhaes	Light Heavyweight	Unanimous Decision	—	3

In his first five-rounder, UFC middleweight champion Anderson Silva earned the UFC record for most consecutive wins and tied the mark for most consecutive title defenses with his unanimous decision win over Thales Leites, but the lackluster 25-minute bout earned more boos than cheers from the sold-out crowd at the Bell Centre for its sometimes bizarre lack of action.

"It's unfortunate that things sometimes turn out that way, but when you're not in here, it's hard to tell what's going on sometimes," said Silva. "Sorry."

With a confident sneer and a dose of Slayer leading him into the Octagon, 39-year-old UFC superstar Chuck Liddell had all the pieces in place for a triumphant return after a knockout loss to Rashad Evans at UFC 88. Four minutes and 28 seconds later, it was his opponent, Mauricio "Shogun" Rua, who broke back into the ranks of the winning as he knocked Liddell out and resurrected his own ailing career.

Knockout of the Night: Rua vs. Liddell

With flashbulbs lighting up the Bell Centre, Liddell and Rua circled, poking each other with kicks to find their range. Twice in the opening minute, Liddell fired off his lethal right hand, but Rua's defense was solid. In a subsequent exchange, Rua left with a cut high on his forehead, but it did not deter the Brazilian from trading with the former UFC Light Heavyweight boss. At the midway point of the round, Rua took Liddell to the mat and looked for a submission, but Liddell broke loose, got back to his feet, and looked to reset his offense. When Liddell would attack, Rua would counter effectively, and suddenly with less than a minute remaining, a left hook to the head dropped Liddell hard to the canvas. Liddell, stunned, tried to clear his head, but Rua wouldn't let him, and a series of right hands brought in Mario Yamasaki to stop the fight at the 4:28 mark of the round.

London, Ontario's Sam Stout showed an improved all-around game and thrilled his home country fans with a close three-round unanimous decision win over Matt Wiman in a fast-paced and entertaining lightweight scrap.

The Ultimate Fighter 8's Krzysztof Soszynski scored his most impressive UFC win to date as he submitted Brian Stann in the first round.

Fight of the Night: Stout vs. Wiman

Cheick Kongo moved further up the heavyweight ranks in his battle with fellow striker Antoni Hardonk, using an effective ground and pound attack to halt his foe in the second round.

Submission of the Night: Soszynski vs. Stann

Light heavyweight up-and-comers Luiz Cane and Steve Cantwell opened up the main card with a bruising three-round battle that saw Brazil's Cane emerge victorious via a three-round unanimous decision.

Nova Scotia product TJ Grant made a statement in his first trip to the Octagon, winning a three-round split decision over Ryo Chonan in an entertaining welter-weight contest.

In middleweight action, Denis Kang scored his first UFC victory, outpointing newcomer Xavier Foupa-Pokam over three rounds.

Nate Quarry stopped Jason MacDonald in the first round with a series of ground strikes.

It was a disappointing return for David Loiseau, who was soundly beaten over three rounds by Ed Herman, who went home with a comfortable three-round unanimous decision victory.

Mark Bocek scored an impressive first-round win over David Bielkheden in a clash of light-weight grapplers, using a single-minded attack to secure the fight-ending submission.

What was expected to be a battle between two of the best young groundfighters in the light heavyweight division instead turned into a 15-minute kickboxing match, with Eliot Marshall doing enough to score a three-round unanimous decision win over his *TUF* teammate Vinny Magalhaes.

UFC 98 *Evans vs. Machida*

23 May 2009

MGM Grand Garden Arena, Las Vegas, NV

Debuts: Mike Pyle, Tim Hague

Fighters			Division	Method	Time	Round
Main Card						
Lyoto Machida	def.	Rashad Evans	Light Heavyweight	Knockout	3:57	2
Matt Hughes	def.	Matt Serra	Welterweight	Unanimous Decision	—	3
Drew McFedries	def.	Xavier Foupa-Pokam	Middleweight	Technical Knockout	0:37	1
Chael Sonnen	def.	Dan Miller	Middleweight	Unanimous Decision	—	3
Frankie Edgar	def.	Sean Sherk	Lightweight	Unanimous Decision	—	3
Preliminary Card						
Brock Larson	def.	Mike Pyle	Welterweight	Submission - Arm Triangle Choke	3:06	1
Tim Hague	def.	Pat Barry	Heavyweight	Submission - Guillotine Choke	1:42	1
Kyle Bradley	def.	Phillipe Nover	Lightweight	Technical Knockout	1:03	1
Krzysztof Soszynski	def.	Andre Gusmao	Light Heavyweight	Knockout	3:17	1
Yoshiyuki Yoshida	def.	Brandon Wolff	Welterweight	Submission - Guillotine Choke	2:24	1
George Roop	def.	Dave Kaplan	Lightweight	Split Decision	—	3

"Karate's back," shouted Lyoto Machida, and it was hard to argue with him once the words "UFC light heavyweight champion" preceded his name following a spectacular second-round knockout of Rashad Evans in the main event of UFC 98.

As expected, the two 205-pound stalwarts searched for openings from a distance as the bout started, feinting to see the reaction coming back from each other. With 90 seconds gone, the two got within striking range, and with two minutes gone, it was Machida who landed the first strike, a kick to the head that knocked Evans off balance. The champion fired back a flurry but missed, and the two calmly went back to their tactical chess match. As the round entered its final stages, Machida's kicks were finding a home, and with under a minute left, one landed, and a follow-up left hand dropped Evans. Machida moved in for the finish, but Evans quickly recovered, got back to his feet, and made it to the bell.

The first offense of the second round came from Machida's feet again, but the Brazilian was rebuffed on his takedown attempt. Moments later, Machida landed a hard punch, but Evans responded with a flurry that put the challenger on the defensive for the first time in the fight. Though they were blocked, Evans started throwing back his kicks in the second half of the stanza. With 1:30 left, Machida hurt Evans with a straight left to the head and dropped him. Evans got up and courageously fired back, trying to get back into the fight, but Machida's pinpoint accuracy was too much for the New York native to handle, and after a ferocious overhand right followed by a left hook, Evans was sent to the canvas for good, prompting referee Mario Yamasaki to halt the bout at the 3:57 mark.

Knockout of the Night: Machida vs. Evans

After a closely-contested 15-minute battle in the co-main event of UFC 98, fierce rivals and former welter-weight champions Matt Hughes and Matt Serra finally settled their differ-ences in the Octagon, with Hughes emerging victorious via razor-thin unanimous decision. Scores were 29-28 across the board for Hughes.

Fight of the Night: Hughes vs. Serra

No one expected the middleweight fight between Drew McFedries and Xavier Foupa-Pokam to last long, and the fans certainly weren't disappointed, as McFedries blitzed Foupa-Pokam and stopped him in a single round.

Veteran middleweight Chael Sonnen issued Dan Miller the first loss of his UFC career as he pounded out a three-round unanimous decision victory.

Matt Hughes. Georges St-Pierre. BJ Penn. Now add the name Frankie Edgar to the short and prestigious list of people to beat former UFC lightweight champ Sean Sherk. Edgar did so impressively by winning a shutout three-round unanimous decision in the main card opener.

Former K-1 kickboxer Pat Barry struck hard and fast in his UFC 98 heavyweight bout against Tim Hague, but the debuting "Thrashing Machine" got the last word in, submitting Barry at 1:42 of the first round.

Welterweight Brock Larson continued his UFC resurgence, making it two in a row in 2009 by submitting late replacement Mike Pyle in the first round.

Submission of the Night: Larson vs. Pyle

Kyle Bradley finally got his first UFC win in three tries, scoring an unpopular first-round stoppage of *The Ultimate Fighter 8* finalist Phillipe Nover.

Krzysztof Soszynski made it three straight in the UFC since his stint on the eighth season of *The Ultimate Fighter*, knocking out Andre Gusmao in the first round.

Japanese welterweight Yoshiyuki "Zenko" Yoshida made a successful return to the Octagon, submitting Brandon Wolff in the first round.

The Ultimate Fighter 8 alumni George Roop and Dave Kaplan battled it out for three closely contested rounds, with Roop pulling out the split decision win.

UFC 99 *The Comeback*

13 June 2009

Lanxess Arena, Cologne, Germany

Debuts: Peter Sobotta, Rick Story

Fighters			Division	Method	Time	Round
Main Card						
Rich Franklin	def.	Wanderlei Silva	Catchweight	Unanimous Decision	—	3
Cain Velasquez	def.	Cheick Kongo	Heavyweight	Unanimous Decision	—	3
Mirko Cro Cop	def.	Mostapha Al-Turk	Heavyweight	Technical Knockout	3:06	1
Mike Swick	def.	Ben Saunders	Welterweight	Technical Knockout	3:47	2
Spencer Fisher	def.	Caol Uno	Lightweight	Unanimous Decision	—	3
Dan Hardy	def.	Marcus Davis	Welterweight	Split Decision	—	3
Preliminary Card						
Terry Etim	def.	Justin Buchholz	Lightweight	Submission - D'Arce choke	2:38	2
Dennis Siver	def.	Dale Hartt	Lightweight	Submission - Rear Naked Choke	3:23	1
Paul Taylor	def.	Peter Sobotta	Welterweight	Unanimous Decision	—	3
Paul Kelly	def.	Rolando Delgado	Lightweight	Unanimous Decision	—	3
Stefan Struve	def.	Denis Stojnic	Heavyweight	Submission - Rear Naked Choke	2:37	2
John Hathaway	def.	Rick Story	Welterweight	Unanimous Decision	—	3

It's said that fighting is a young man's sport. Sometimes that's true, but veterans Rich Franklin and Wanderlei Silva proved that they still had some tricks to show the kids, as they engaged in an entertaining three-round battle that saw Franklin emerge victorious via unanimous decision in the UFC 99 main event.

After a touch of gloves to start the action, Franklin and Silva circled, each waiting for the right moment to engage. Ninety seconds in, sporadic bursts of action started appearing, building a tension that would remain throughout the bout.

Fight of the Night: Franklin vs. Silva

Franklin tried his luck with kicks early in round two, and when he added in punches to the head, he put Silva off balance as he tried to counter. As the round entered its third minute, Silva began to get a look in his eye like he was about to ignite a match on the war, but Franklin's effective movement and accurate shots kept "The Axe Murderer" at bay. With 1:15 left, Silva landed an overhand right, his best punch of the fight to that point, and moments later, he landed another, staggering Franklin.

The exchanges were coming more and more frequently in the third round, with the crowd starting to get behind Franklin for his efforts in the Octagon. And soon the packed house erupted as Silva paused from his attack to raise his hands for more cheers. He didn't need to ask, though, as the tension mounted in the final two minutes. Buoyed by the roars, Silva attacked Franklin and landed with some hard shots. Franklin kept his composure, scoring the takedown, but as the two rose and Franklin got his foe's back, Silva fired off a series of elbows until the bout ended, drawing a deserved standing ovation from the 12,854 in attendance.

Heavyweight Cain Velasquez still had the "0" at the end of his record after his three-round unanimous decision win over Cheick Kongo at the Lanxess Arena. What the end result didn't show is the heart both fighters showed in engaging in a memorable 15-minute war that saw Velasquez graduate to contender status while Kongo solidified his spot in the heavyweight pecking order.

An eye poke began what most believed was an inevitable conclusion in the return of Mirko Cro Cop, as he stopped Mostapha Al-Turk in the first round, showing that—foul excluded—he still had the power in his strikes.

Mike "Quick" Swick put together perhaps his most impressive win at 170 pounds, calmly controlling his bout against previously unbeaten Ben Saunders until taking "Killa B" out with pinpoint strikes in the second round.

Knockout of the Night: Swick vs. Saunders

Lightweight contender Spencer Fisher made it three in a row as he drilled out a three-round unanimous decision over two-time title challenger Caol Uno, who was making his first UFC start since 2003.

The trash talk was fast, furious, and personal between welterweights Dan Hardy and Marcus Davis in the weeks leading up to their bout that night, but it was Nottingham's Hardy who was able to take home bragging rights after a razor-thin split decision victory.

Mannheim's Dennis Siver made the fans at the Lanxess Arena happy, impressively submitting Dale Hartt in the first round of their lightweight bout.

Submission of the Night: Etim vs. Buchholz

Terry Etim continued to show new facets of his game, rising from a first-round knockdown to roar back in the second and submit Justin Buchholz in a clash of lightweight prospects.

Welterweight Paul Taylor spoiled the UFC debut of Germany's Peter Sobotta, outpointing the home country favorite via unanimous decision.

Paul Kelly made his lightweight debut a successful one, rebounding from a slow start to outpoint Roli Delgado unanimously over three rounds.

21-year-old Stefan Struve survived a nasty cut on his forehead in the first round and roared back in the second, submitting Denis Stojnic in an entertaining heavyweight bout.

John Hathaway remained unbeaten with a hard-fought three-round unanimous decision win over UFC debutant Rick Story.

UFC 100

11 July 2009

Mandalay Bay Events Center, Las Vegas, NV

Debut: Yoshihiro Akiyama

Fighters			Division	Method	Time	Round
Main Card						
Brock Lesnar	def.	Frank Mir	Heavyweight	TKO	1:48	2
Georges St-Pierre	def.	Thiago Alves	Welterweight	Unanimous Decision	—	5
Dan Henderson	def.	Michael Bisping	Middleweight	Knockout	3:20	2
Jon Fitch	def.	Paulo Thiago	Welterweight	Unanimous Decision	—	3
Yoshihiro Akiyama	def.	Alan Belcher	Middleweight	Split Decision	—	3
Preliminary Card						
Mark Coleman	def.	Stephan Bonnar	Light Heavyweight	Unanimous Decision	—	3
Jon Jones	def.	Jake O'Brien	Light Heavyweight	Submission - Guillotine Choke	2:43	2
Jim Miller	def.	Mac Danzig	Lightweight	Unanimous Decision	—	3
Dong Hyun Kim	def.	TJ Grant	Welterweight	Unanimous Decision	—	3
Tom Lawlor	def.	CB Dollaway	Middleweight	Submission - Guillotine Choke	0:55	1
Shannon Gugerty	def.	Matt Grice	Lightweight	Submission - Guillotine Choke	2:36	1

Brock Lesnar may not have made many fans in the Mandalay Bay Events Center that Saturday night by stopping local hero Frank Mir in the second round of their long-awaited UFC 100 rematch, but if there was one thing made clear, it's that beating the UFC heavyweight champion was going to be a tall order for anyone in the division.

Forty seconds in, the two engaged, with Lesnar taking Mir to the mat. Lesnar stayed close and kept his cool, making sure he didn't get overaggressive like he did in their first fight, which would allow Mir to take advantage and attempt a submission. The crowd didn't care for Lesnar's patient approach, but it was scored for the champion as he used his bulk to tire Mir while mixing in short but effective punches to the head and body. By the time the bell sounded, Mir's face showed the scars of battle.

Lesnar dumped Mir on the mat early in round two, but the champion let him right back up. That almost looked to be a mistake as Mir scored with some good shots and almost caught Lesnar's neck before they toppled to the canvas with the Minnesotan on top. Despite the chants of the crowd to stand up the fighters, Lesnar was consistently working, and after another series of huge ground strikes, Mir was left with nowhere to go, forcing referee Herb Dean to halt the bout at the 1:48 mark.

Welterweight champion Georges St-Pierre made it look easy in the UFC 100 co-feature. But it was far from that, as his five-round unanimous decision win over number one contender Thiago Alves was categorized not only by a gritty challenger who refused to go away without a fight, but a third-round groin injury that forced the Canadian superstar to dig deep in order to finish off the championship rounds.

With the crowd chanting "GSP," Alves looked to silence them with kicks to the champion's legs. St-Pierre responded with a takedown, and each time Alves tried to rise, the Montreal native had an answer. By the time two minutes had passed, St-Pierre appeared to be closing in on a submission from the back, but Alves took the opportunity to get back to his feet, and he again began attacking his opponent's legs. With 90 seconds remaining, Alves stuffed St-Pierre's next takedown attempt, but when he landed a few strikes and got over-aggressive, "Rush" put Alves on his back again. By the end of the round, the Brazilian scrambled back to his feet but went back to his corner with a cut over his right eye.

Judging by the early second-round action, St-Pierre was just getting warmed up in the first, as he pulled off a slick superman punch/low kick combo before scoring another takedown. While on the mat, St-Pierre controlled matters with not only strikes, but his always-impressive athleticism. With under a minute left, the bloodied Alves took advantage of a lull to get back to his feet, but he was unable to make anything happen before the bell rang.

Alves, still resilient, kept marching forward, but as soon as he moved in to land more than one punch, St-Pierre would drop him with another takedown. And late in the round, he put Alves down with a right hand but ran out of time before he could finish "The Pitbull".

The fourth round began like the others, with St-Pierre getting his takedown and keeping Alves from mounting any offense. With two minutes gone, Alves finally turned the tables and got into St-Pierre's guard, where he fired away with punches until the two rose with under two minutes left. Despite this being his first time into the fourth round, Alves didn't look fatigued, although getting dropped by a right hand in the final 30 seconds didn't help matters.

With only five minutes to turn things around, Alves' intensity was evident as he came out for the final round, but St-Pierre was not about to let his foot off the gas, and he took the bout back to where he had dominated from the start: the mat. Alves battled his way up quickly this time around, and he marched forward, oblivious to pain and fatigue. What he couldn't stop were St-Pierre's takedowns, and that ultimately proved to be his undoing.

Michael Bisping had the right stick-and-move plan heading into his middleweight bout with Dan Henderson, but when dealing with the former two-division PRIDE champion, it only takes one wrong move and one right hand to end matters. That's exactly what happened as Henderson knocked out "The Count" in the second round of the long-awaited showdown between the coaches of *The Ultimate Fighter 9*.

Knockout of the Night: Henderson vs. Bisping

Welterweight contender Jon Fitch continued his climb back toward a title shot, handing Paulo Thiago his first pro loss via unanimous decision.

Japanese star Yoshihiro Akiyama made a smooth transition to the UFC, scoring an exciting split decision win over Alan Belcher in his Octagon debut. Scores in the punishing three-rounder were 30-27, 29-28, and 28-29 for Akiyama.

Belcher's advantage in size was evident from the start, but Akiyama didn't shy away from exchanges as he traded kicks with his foe. Unfortunately, a low kick by Belcher forced a halt to the action. Once the fight resumed, both got right back to business, this time trading punches that reddened both men's faces. With 2:15 left, Belcher dropped Akiyama with a punch to the jaw, but the Japan native quickly rose to his feet and resumed his pursuit of Belcher, landing some flush shots in the process. Belcher responded with punches of his own before bulling his opponent into the fence. After the two broke, Akiyama landed with a right hand that dropped Belcher, but before he could capitalize, the bell rang.

Fight of the Night: Akiyama vs. Belcher

After trading kicks at the start of the second round, Akiyama immediately closed the distance and took Belcher down. Belcher scrambled to get loose, but Akiyama was just as busy as he moved into side control. With under four minutes left, Akiyama got into Belcher's guard and fired away with strikes. Eventually, Belcher got back to his feet, and despite fatigue setting in, he was still able to pick up points with sporadic punches upstairs and kicks downstairs.

With the fight still close, Akiyama and Belcher stood at close range and looked for the home run that would finish things. This resulted in brief bursts of action that saw each man getting his shots in, but with not enough oomph to take the other out of there. With 1:30 left, Akiyama—his left eye swollen nearly shut—put Belcher down a second time, and even though the Biloxi product rose quickly, Akiyama scored a late takedown and secured the victory.

It took 12 years, but Mark "The Hammer" Coleman finally got back in the UFC win column, grounding and pounding out a three-round unanimous decision over Stephan Bonnar, delighting the fans who hoped the 44-year-old Hall of Famer would be able to turn back the clock one more time.

With lightweights Jim Miller and Mac Danzig both coming off losses (and Danzig coming off two straight defeats), the stakes were understandably high in their three-rounder and they fought like it, with Miller emerging victorious by way of an exciting unanimous decision.

In submitting Jake O'Brien in the second round, rising light heavyweight star Jonny "Bones" Jones upped his pro record to 9-0 with a disciplined attack followed by his trademark flash, once again impressing his growing legion of fans with the maturation of his MMA game.

Korean star Dong Hyun Kim remained unbeaten in welterweight action, improving to 12-0-1, 1 NC with a workmanlike three-round decision win over TJ Grant.

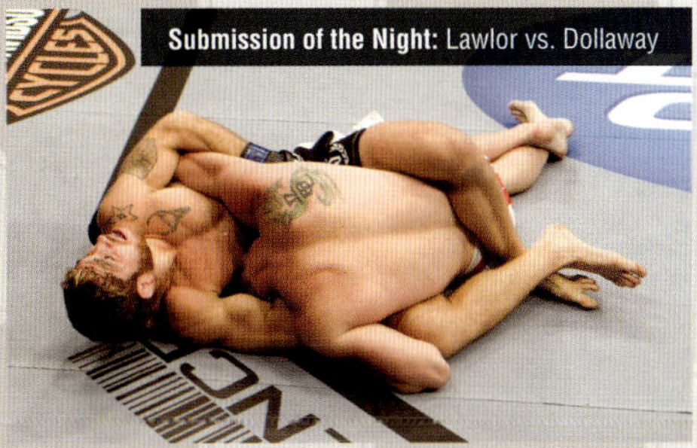

Submission of the Night: Lawlor vs. Dollaway

After an entertaining walk to the Octagon that included *Ultimate Fighter* alum Seth Petruzelli on a leash as the song "Who Let the Dogs Out" played, Tom Lawlor delivered when the bell rang, as well, submitting CB Dollaway in less than a minute.

Shannon Gugerty kicked off the evening's festivities with a first-round submission win over Matt Grice.

The Ultimate Fighter 9 Finale

United States vs. United Kingdom

20 June 2009

The Pearl at The Palms, Las Vegas, NV

Debuts: DaMarques Johnson, James Wilks, Andre Winner, Ross Pearson, Edgar Garcia, Frank Lester, Nick Osipczak, Cameron Dollar

Fighters			Division	Method	Time	Round
Main Card						
Diego Sanchez	def.	Clay Guida	Lightweight	Split Decision	—	3
James Wilks	def.	DaMarques Johnson	Lightweight	Submission - Rear Naked Choke	4:52	1
Ross Pearson	def.	Andre Winner	Lightweight	Unanimous Decision	—	3
Chris Lytle	def.	Kevin Burns	Welterweight	Unanimous Decision	—	3
Joe Stevenson	def.	Nate Diaz	Lightweight	Unanimous Decision	—	3
Preliminary Card						
Melvin Guillard	def.	Gleison Tibau	Lightweight	Split Decision	—	3
Brad Blackburn	def.	Edgar Garcia	Welterweight	Split Decision	—	3
Tomasz Drwal	def.	Mike Ciesnolevicz	Catchweight	Technical Knockout	4:48	1
Nick Osipczak	def.	Frank Lester	Welterweight	Submission - Rear Naked Choke	3:40	1
Jason Dent	def.	Cameron Dollar	Lightweight	Submission - Anaconda Choke	4:46	1

On paper, it should have been a war to remember. And in reality, it delivered, as Diego Sanchez and Clay Guida put on a Fight of the Year candidate at The Palms. When it was all over, someone had to take home the victory, and it was Sanchez pounding out the split decision win. Scores were 29-28, 29-27, and 28-29 for Sanchez.

The walk-ins alone were more intense than some fights, with Guida and Sanchez both getting themselves and the fans amped up for the opening bell. From the start, the two went toe-to-toe exchanging a furious barrage of punches that got the crowd on its feet. It was Sanchez, though, who took the early lead with more accurate blows and the occasional knee to the head. With a minute gone, the bloodied Guida cleared his head and took Sanchez to the mat, firing off elbows in an effort to extract his own form of revenge. Sanchez, not used to being in this predicament, stayed cool nonetheless, and got back to his feet, landing a hard kick that dropped Guida. "The Carpenter" rose and swung back aggressively, but Sanchez' harder shots were doing all the damage, and a takedown with under a minute left punctuated the round for the "Nightmare".

Fight of the Night: Sanchez vs. Guida

"The guy has a tremendous chin," said Sanchez of his courageous foe. "He is an animal."

Guida got the takedown early in round two, and he fired off with any limb he had free. Sanchez did the same from the bottom position, but it was clear that Guida was having more luck on the mat than when he was standing, and the fans chanting his name only pushed him further. Sanchez was not about to let Guida get the round that easily though, and he reeled off a series of elbows from his back that bloodied Guida on his forehead.

The opening minute of the final round was a tense one, and when the two started to flurry at each other, it was Sanchez again being the crisper puncher. That's not to say Guida wasn't getting his licks in, and he certainly landed enough shots to get Sanchez' respect. With two minutes left, Guida shot for a takedown, but Sanchez eluded it and went for the fight-ending choke. Guida escaped, but Sanchez went to finish him via kimura, only to see "The Carpenter" escape and land a ground strike seconds before the final bell sounded.

In the welterweight final of *TUF9*, James Wilks blitzed DaMarques Johnson at the opening bell and didn't stop attacking until he had submitted his foe and earned recognition as season nine's 170-pound *Ultimate Fighter*.

The Ultimate Fighter lightweight final was fought toe-to-toe for 15 minutes, and when it was over, it was Ross Pearson who emerged victorious over his UK teammate Andre Winner to earn the unanimous decision win and the season nine title at 155 pounds.

Chris Lytle and Kevin Burns left it all in the Octagon in their three-round welterweight bout, and after 15 spirited minutes of back-and-forth action, it was Lytle emerging victorious via a close unanimous decision.

In the main card opener, former world lightweight title challenger Joe Stevenson broke a two-fight losing streak by going back to his groundfighting roots and drilling out an exciting three-round unanimous decision win over Nate Diaz.

Submission of the Night: Dent vs. Dollar

Up-and-comer Melvin Guillard showed the maturation of his fight game in his bout with Gleison Tibau at The Palms, allowing him to improve his pro record to 41-8-3.

Brad Blackburn took home his third straight UFC win in welterweight action, earning an unpopular three-round split decision over previously unbeaten Edgar Garcia.

Knockout of the Night: Drwal vs. Ciesnolevicz

Polish up-and-comer Tomasz Drwal scored his second straight first-round win, halting Iowa's Mike Ciesnolevicz in the first round of their light heavyweight bout.

Team UK welterweight Nick Osipczak made short work of Frank Lester, submitting the Team USA fighter in the first round.

Jason Dent from *TUF9* got his first UFC win in the lightweight opener, coming back from a rocky start to submit Cameron Dollar in the first round.

Fight of the Night (Not Pictured): Stevenson vs. Diaz, Lytle vs. Burns

One Hit Wonders: Frank Lester, Cameron Dollar

UFC 101 *Declaration*

08
Aug.
2009

Wachovia Center, Philadelphia, PA

Debuts: Johny Hendricks, Danillo Villefort, Jesse Lennox

Fighters			Division	Method	Time	Round
Main Card						
BJ Penn	def.	Kenny Florian	Lightweight	Submission - Rear Naked Choke	3:45	4
Anderson Silva	def.	Forrest Griffin	Light Heavyweight	Knockout	3:23	1
Aaron Riley	def.	Shane Nelson	Lightweight	Unanimous Decision	—	3
Johny Hendricks	def.	Amir Sadollah	Welterweight	Technical Knockout	0:29	1
Ricardo Almeida	def.	Kendall Grove	Middleweight	Unanimous Decision	—	3
Kurt Pellegrino	def.	Josh Neer	Lightweight	Unanimous Decision	—	3
Preliminary Card						
John Howard	def.	Tamdan McCrory	Welterweight	Split Decision	—	3
Alessio Sakara	def.	Thales Leites	Middleweight	Split Decision	—	3
Matthew Riddle	def.	Dan Cramer	Welterweight	Unanimous Decision	—	3
George Sotiropoulos	def.	George Roop	Lightweight	Submission - Kimura	1:59	2
Jesse Lennox	def.	Danillo Villefort	Welterweight	Technical Knockout - Cut	3:37	3

Written off by many after his failed quest for the welterweight title against Georges St-Pierre in January, BJ Penn returned to the lightweight division and showed why he was still the best 155-pounder in the world as he submitted number one contender Kenny Florian in the fourth round of their UFC 101 main event bout.

Submission of the Night: Penn vs. Florian

In the fourth round, Penn broke open a competitive fight by ripping off a flurry and then taking the challenger to the canvas. While there, Penn went on the attack, getting into the mount and then taking Florian's back as he fired off kicks and strikes. The kicks did the trick, as Florian left his neck exposed for the split second Penn needed to sink in a rear naked choke. Florian fought valiantly to break free, but it was to no avail, with the tap out coming at 3:45 of the fourth round.

UFC middleweight champion Anderson Silva heard the boos, and he knew what the fans thought of his previous two bouts against Patrick Cote and Thales Leites. So what did the best fighter in the world do in the UFC 101 co-feature at the Wachovia Center that Saturday night? He put on one of the most spectacular striking displays ever seen in the Octagon, knocking out former UFC light heavyweight champion Forrest Griffin in less than four minutes of the first round. When it was over, all he heard were cheers.

As advertised, Griffin came right at Silva, and the crowd was behind him immediately, chanting "Let's go, Forrest." The former light heavyweight champ threw out some range-finding kicks and jabs but was unable to land on Silva, who caught Griffin's first serious kick and tried to finish things with a right hand, but was unable to. Moments later, Silva got into the fray and dropped Griffin with a right hand. Griffin quickly recovered, but Silva was warmed up and ready to go. As Griffin rose, Silva stood in the pocket, ducked and dodged everything Griffin threw at him, and dropped his opponent again with a left hand. Griffin, game to the end, stood again, but as he came in, Silva threw a right hand while moving backward and caught Griffin flush. The Las Vegan dropped to his back, but as Silva moved in, Griffin decided he had had enough, and the bout was waved off by referee Kevin Mulhall at 3:23 of the opening round.

Fight and Knockout of the Night: Silva vs. Griffin

The fans may not have liked it, believing Amir Sadollah got the short end of a quick hook, but Johny Hendricks certainly was impressive before the finish, as he halted *The Ultimate Fighter 7* winner in just 29 seconds.

Hamilton, New Jersey resident Ricardo Almeida was steady throughout his middleweight bout with Kendall Grove, shutting out "Da Spyder" over three rounds.

Kurt Pellegrino stuck to what he did best in the main card opener, using his wrestling to drill out a disciplined three-round decision win over Josh Neer.

After a controversial stoppage loss the first time around, Aaron Riley got even against Shane Nelson, winning a shutout three-round decision over the game Hawaiian.

In a closely contested battle of welterweight prospects, John Howard scored a three-round split decision win over Tamdan McCrory.

In an uninspiring middleweight bout, Alessio Sakara took a three-round split decision win over former title challenger Thales Leites.

Allentown's Matthew Riddle gave Pennsylvania fans something to cheer about as he pounded out a three-round unanimous decision win over Dan Cramer.

The Ultimate Fighter alum George Sotiropoulos returned to the Octagon for the first time in over a year and did so in impressive fashion, submitting another *TUF* veteran, George Roop, in the second round.

The opener between WEC vets Jesse Lennox and Danillo Villefort ended in bizarre fashion as Villefort looked for a time out after being cut, prompting a stoppage in the third round of what had been an exciting welterweight scrap.

One Hit Wonder: Danillo Villefort

OCTAGON GIRLS

ARIANNY CELESTE

Arianny Celeste became a UFC Octagon Girl in typical fashion— through a modeling casting call—but ever since she made her debut in 2006, life has been anything but typical for the Las Vegas native, who saw her first live mixed martial arts fight that night. Since then, this striking Latina has become a fixture at UFC events and a fan favorite who has also appeared on the covers of *Playboy* and *Maxim* magazines.

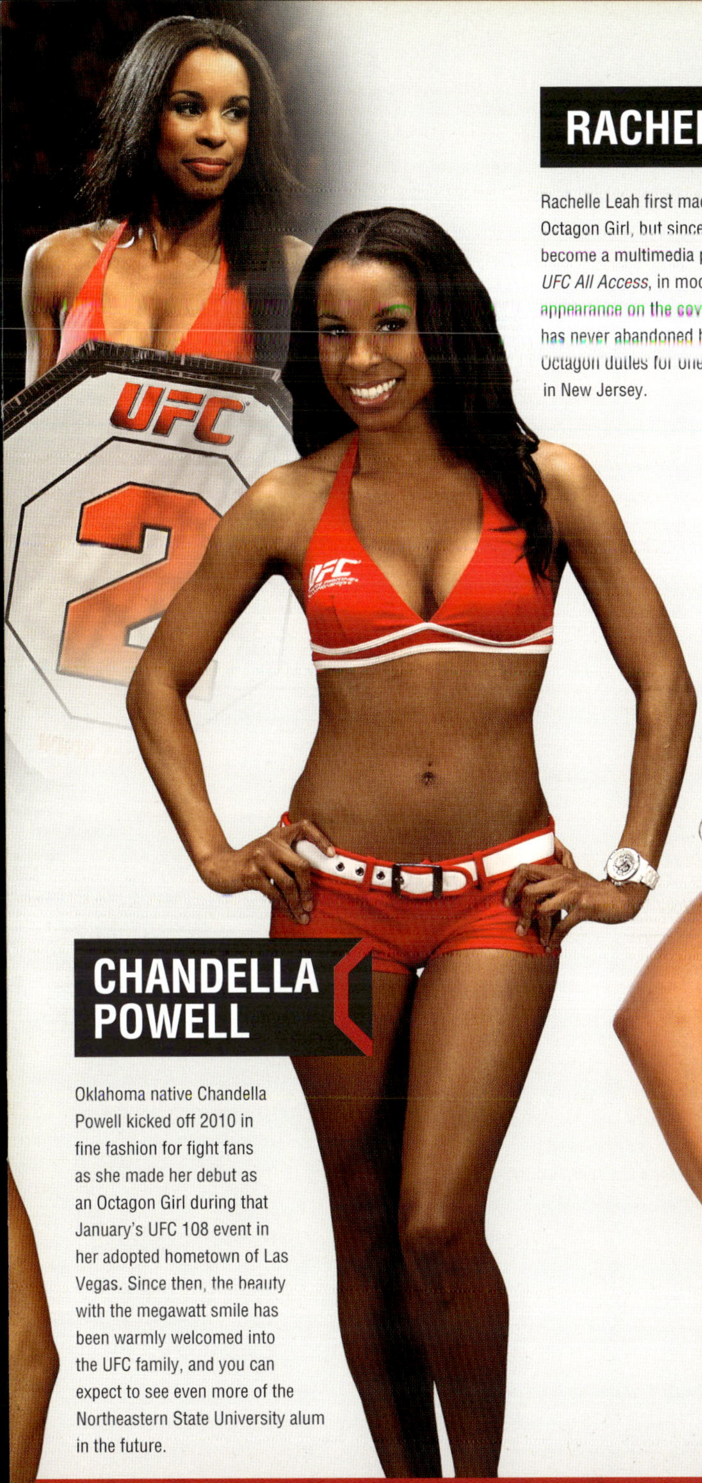

RACHELLE LEAH

Rachelle Leah first made her name in the UFC as an Octagon Girl, but since then, the Bay Area-born beauty has become a multimedia powerhouse as the host of Spike TV's *UFC All Access*, in modeling and acting gigs and with an appearance on the cover of *Playboy* magazine. But Rachelle has never abandoned her first love, so she resumed her Octagon duties for one night only at 2010's UFC 111 event in New Jersey.

CHANDELLA POWELL

Oklahoma native Chandella Powell kicked off 2010 in fine fashion for fight fans as she made her debut as an Octagon Girl during that January's UFC 108 event in her adopted hometown of Las Vegas. Since then, the beauty with the megawatt smile has been warmly welcomed into the UFC family, and you can expect to see even more of the Northeastern State University alum in the future.

BRITTNEY PALMER

Las Vegas' Brittney Palmer first came to mixed martial arts after a stint as a boxing ring card girl, and once she got her first dose of WEC action, she was hooked. "There's really no comparison," said Palmer. "When you're watching MMA, it's just so much better." Now gracing the UFC Octagon, nothing makes the brunette bombshell happier than working a big room, like she does every night the UFC takes its show on the road.

PREVIOUS OCTAGON GIRLS

- Edith Labelle
- Holly Madison
- Amber Nichole
- Ali Sonoma
- Logan Stanton
- Natasha Wicks

UFC 102 *Couture vs. Nogueira*

29 Aug. 2009

Rose Garden, Portland, OR

Debuts: Chris Tuchscherer, Mike Russow, Todd Duffee

Fighters			Division	Method	Time	Round
Main Card						
Minotauro Nogueira	def.	Randy Couture	Heavyweight	Unanimous Decision	—	3
Thiago Silva	def.	Keith Jardine	Light Heavyweight	Knockout	1:35	1
Jake Rosholt	def.	Chris Leben	Middleweight	Submission - Arm Triangle Choke	1:30	3
Nate Marquardt	def.	Demian Maia	Middleweight	Knockout	0:21	1
Brandon Vera	def.	Krzysztof Soszynski	Light Heavyweight	Unanimous Decision	—	3
Preliminary Card						
Gabriel Gonzaga	def.	Chris Tuchscherer	Heavyweight	Technical Knockout	2:27	1
Mike Russow	def.	Justin McCully	Heavyweight	Unanimous Decision	—	3
Aaron Simpson	def.	Ed Herman	Middleweight	Technical Knockout - Injury	0:17	2
Todd Duffee	def.	Tim Hague	Heavyweight	Knockout	0:07	1
Mark Munoz	def.	Nick Catone	Middleweight	Split Decision	—	3
Evan Dunham	def.	Marcus Aurelio	Lightweight	Split Decision	—	3

It wasn't in Manila, but mixed martial arts had its "Thrilla" as veteran heavyweight legends Minotauro Nogueira and Randy Couture turned back the clock. Like Muhammad Ali and Joe Frazier did in 1975, the bout reminded fight fans just what greatness is in a three-round war won by Minotauro in the main event of UFC 102.

Fight of the Night: Minotauro vs. Couture

Minotauro outpointed Couture by scores of 30-27 (twice) and 29-28 in a fight that was much more competitive and drama-filled than the 30-27 numbers would indicate.

The bout began with a spirited standup exchange, and the pace remained high, with Couture beating Minotauro to the punch. Minotauro remained patient, however, and soon hit paydirt, dropping Couture with a hard right hand. Minotauro almost finished things with a choke, but Couture fought his way free and the two rose and exchanged punches as the crowd rose to its feet.

Minotauro hurt Couture again early in the second round, but he slipped as he tried to pull guard for the submission. Couture took advantage by following Minotauro to the mat and firing away with his trademark ground and pound attack, as the crowd roared with each shot landed by the hometown favorite. Just when things looked bad for Minotauro, he reversed and got into the mount position.

Going on the attack immediately to start round three, Minotauro dropped Couture hard with a right hand, and the follow-up barrage looked to be the one to finish off "The Natural", but Couture, showing the resilience that has always been Minotauro's trademark, survived the assault and looked to pull off the miracle comeback. With a cut now over his right eye, Couture was running out of time, and Minotauro wanted to shorten that time even more as he got Couture's back and looked for a choke. The crowd erupted, trying to will their man to victory, but a win was not in the cards that night.

If Thiago Silva was gun-shy in his first fight since losing for the first time against Lyoto Machida at UFC 94, he certainly didn't show it in the co-main event, as he blasted Keith Jardine into defeat in just 95 seconds.

After a series of spectacular submission victories, the only question that remained about middleweight contender Demian Maia was how he would react when caught by a flush shot from a world-class foe. Nate Marquardt asked that question early with a big right hand, and at the 21-second mark of the first round, he had scored the biggest victory of his UFC career, handing Maia his first pro loss.

Knockout of the Night: Marquardt vs. Maia

Jake Rosholt got his first UFC victory in a big way, submitting Portland veteran Chris Leben in the third round of a hard-fought middleweight bout.

Submission of the Night: Rosholt vs. Leben

Brandon Vera scored his second straight victory at 205 pounds, unanimously outpointing Krzysztof Soszynski over three rounds.

Aaron Simpson continued to impress, as he spoiled the homecoming of Ed Herman via second-round TKO in UFC 102 preliminary action.

Heavyweight Gabriel Gonzaga ruined the UFC debut of Brock Lesnar training partner Chris Tuchscherer, stopping "The Crowbar" less than three minutes into the first round.

Chicago police officer Mike Russow laid down the law in his UFC debut, winning a three-round unanimous decision over Justin McCully.

It didn't take long for highly touted heavyweight prospect Todd Duffee to make an impact in his UFC debut as he scored with a straight left to the jaw of Tim Hague and followed up with a ferocious ground assault, forcing Mario Yamasaki to halt the fight just seven seconds into the first round, giving Duffee the fastest knockout in UFC history.

In an exciting three-round war, Mark Munoz scored a razor-thin split decision win over Nick Catone in his middleweight debut.

Unbeaten Evan Dunham got the evening off to a good start for the local boys, pounding out a three-round split decision over Marcus Aurelio in an entertaining lightweight bout.

UFC Fight Night 19

Diaz vs. Guillard

16 Sept. 2009

Cox Convention Center, Oklahoma City, OK

Debuts: Jake Ellenberger, Jay Silva, Mike Pierce, Steve Steinbeiss

Fighters			Division	Method	Time	Round
Main Card						
Nate Diaz	def.	Melvin Guillard	Lightweight	Submission - Guillotine Choke	2:13	2
Gray Maynard	def.	Roger Huerta	Lightweight	Split Decision	—	3
Carlos Condit	def.	Jake Ellenberger	Welterweight	Split Decision	—	3
Nate Quarry	def.	Tim Credeur	Middleweight	Unanimous Decision	—	3
Preliminary Card						
Brian Stann	def.	Steve Cantwell	Light Heavyweight	Unanimous Decision	—	3
Mike Pyle	def.	Chris Wilson	Welterweight	Submission - Guillotine Choke	2:15	3
CB Dollaway	def.	Jay Silva	Middleweight	Unanimous Decision	—	3
Jeremy Stephens	def.	Justin Buchholz	Lightweight	Technical Knockout - Cut	3:23	1
Mike Pierce	def.	Brock Larson	Welterweight	Unanimous Decision	—	3
Ryan Jensen	def.	Steve Steinbeiss	Middleweight	Submission - Guillotine Choke	3:56	1

Lightweight prospect Nate Diaz wanted someone to fight him, someone to go to war with. He got a willing participant in Melvin Guillard, and after Diaz was dropped and cut in the first round, he could have rethought that request. Not this Stockton, California native, who roared back in round two to turn things around with a submission win that punctuated a memorable UFC Fight Night card.

Submission of the Night: Diaz vs. Guillard

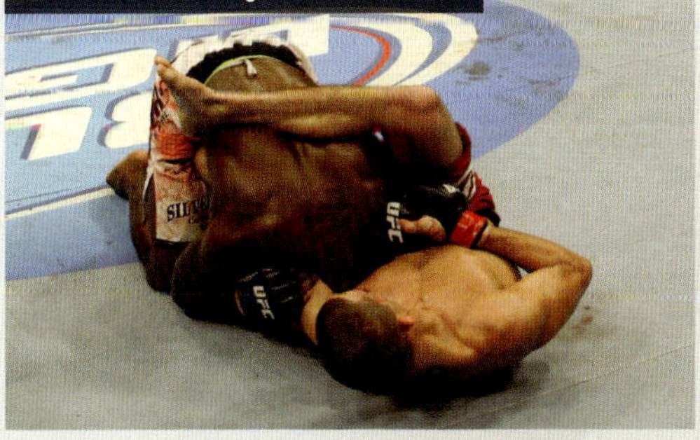

The action almost started before the opening bell as the two combatants got in each other's faces, and Guillard wasted no time introducing himself more formally after the bell rang, dropping Diaz with the first right hand he landed. Diaz quickly cleared his head and got back to his feet. With a minute gone he shot for a takedown and got it. Guillard immediately got up and returned the favor with a throw of Diaz to the mat before standing and resuming the standup battle.

Diaz, cocky as ever, mugged for the crowd before round two, but Guillard kept his cool, drilling his foe with a thudding kick to the body. Diaz kept the pressure on, trying to make something happen standing and on the ground, but it was Guillard who was still landing the harder shots. After getting caught with a jab and playing possum as if he were hurt, Guillard rushed Diaz and got caught in a guillotine. Seconds later, Guillard tapped out at the 2:13 mark, giving Diaz one of the biggest wins of his career.

In what was Roger Huerta's last UFC fight, "El Matador" may not have won, but he certainly went down fighting in a closely contested bout with Gray Maynard. Yet when the scores were tallied, it was the unbeaten Maynard who emerged victorious, using his takedowns, more accurate punching, and a third-round kimura attempt to earn a three-round split decision victory in the lightweight matchup.

Rising welterweight star Carlos Condit saw stars for much of the first round against Octagon debutant Jake Ellenberger, but the Albuquerque native weathered the early storm and got stronger as the fight progressed, eventually eking out a hard-fought and entertaining split decision win over Ellenberger.

Fight of the Night: Quarry vs. Credeur

Among diehard fight fans, the Nate Quarry/Tim Credeur match was widely recognized as the one bout on the UFC Fight Night card that was likely to steal the show. Well, it did. Both Quarry and Credeur lived up to expectations with a memorable middleweight war, and in the end, it was Quarry emerging with the victory via a close unanimous decision.

Middleweight prospect CB Dollaway got back in the win column following his UFC 100 loss to Tom Lawlor. "The Doberman" was pushed to the brink while earning a unanimous three-round decision over newcomer Jay Silva, who certainly made a name for himself with a spirited effort and some bone-rattling strikes in their UFC Fight Night preliminary bout.

It was Greg Jackson 101 in the rubber match between former WEC Light Heavyweight champions Brian Stann and Steve Cantwell, as Stann used a disciplined stick-and-move fight plan and stuck to it for 15 minutes en route to a three-round unanimous decision win over Cantwell. Scores were 30-27 twice and 29-28 for Stann. The two traded TKO wins in the WEC in 2007 and 2008.

Mike Pyle earned the victory over Chris Wilson in a battle of veteran welterweights, submitting his foe via guillotine choke in the third round.

Lightweights Jeremy Stephens and Justin Buchholz looked like they were on their way to a memorable war when a cut suffered by Buchholz forced a halt to the action, earning Stephens a TKO win in a bout that certainly gave the fans their money's worth for the 3:23 it lasted.

Knockout of the Night: Stephens vs. Buchholz

UFC newcomer Mike Pierce made the most of his Octagon debut, scoring a steady but unspectacular unanimous decision win over veteran welterweight contender Brock Larson.

Ryan Jensen got his first UFC victory in four tries in the opener, but a bad call by referee Gary Ritter put a damper on the middleweight veteran's first-round win over Octagon newcomer Steve Steinbeiss.

UFC 103 *Franklin vs. Belfort*

19 Sept. 2009

American Airlines Center, Dallas, TX

Debuts: Paul Daley, Steve Lopez, Rafaello Oliveira, Nik Lentz, Brian Foster, Igor Pokrajac

Fighters			Division	Method	Time	Round
Main Card						
Vitor Belfort	def.	Rich Franklin	Catchweight	Knockout	3:02	1
Junior dos Santos	def.	Mirko Cro Cop	Heavyweight	Submission - Injury	2:00	3
Paul Daley	def.	Martin Kampmann	Welterweight	Technical Knockout	2:31	1
Josh Koscheck	def.	Frank Trigg	Welterweight	Technical Knockout	1:25	1
Tyson Griffin	def.	Hermes Franca	Catchweight	Knockout	3:26	2
Preliminary Card						
Efrain Escudero	def.	Cole Miller	Lightweight	Technical Knockout	3:36	1
Tomasz Drwal	def.	Drew McFedries	Middleweight	Submission - Rear Naked Choke	1:03	2
Jim Miller	def.	Steve Lopez	Lightweight	Technical Knockout - Injury	0:48	2
Nik Lentz	def.	Rafaello Oliveira	Lightweight	Unanimous Decision	—	3
Rick Story	def.	Brian Foster	Welterweight	Submission - Arm Triangle Choke	1:09	2
Eliot Marshall	def.	Jason Brilz	Light Heavyweight	Split Decision	—	3
Vladimir Matyushenko	def.	Igor Pokrajac	Light Heavyweight	Unanimous Decision	—	3
Rafael dos Anjos	def.	Rob Emerson	Lightweight	Unanimous Decision	—	3

In his first UFC bout since 2005, former light heavyweight champion Vitor Belfort showed a glimpse of the speed and finishing power that made him one of the most beloved fighters in mixed martial arts as he knocked out Rich Franklin in the first round of the UFC 103 main event. It was Belfort's first knockout win in the UFC since he halted Marvin Eastman at UFC 43 in 2003.

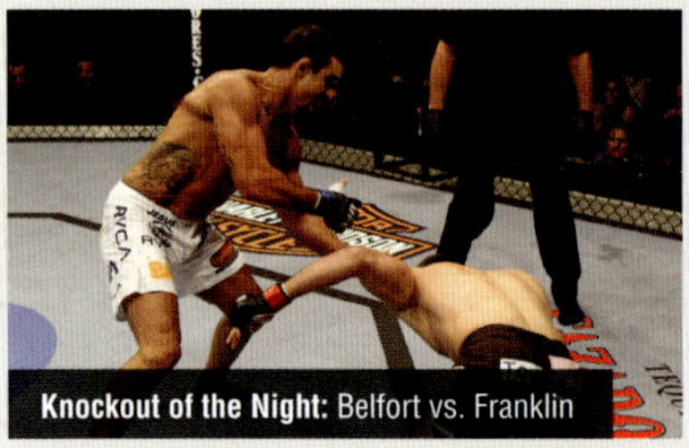

Knockout of the Night: Belfort vs. Franklin

"I miss this vibe, and I'm here for a reason," said Belfort. "I trained so hard and I've been away from my family for three months."

The training showed, as his timing was on when the opening presented itself against the former middleweight champion. Initially, the two southpaws circled each other at close range, with both Franklin and Belfort throwing out the occasional range-finding punch or kick. After a tense few minutes, the two exchanged blows, with Belfort landing a left to the top of the head that took Franklin's legs out from under him. Belfort, showing the quickness that first got him dubbed "The Phenom" as a 19-year-old in the UFC, pounced and scored with a left to the jaw that rocked Franklin, with referee Yves Lavigne intervening to stop the fight at 3:02 of the opening round.

"Once you get clipped, everything kinda goes blank," said Franklin of the final sequence.

Rising star Junior dos Santos had already displayed the ability to blast opponents out with ease. At UFC 103, he showed that he could stick to his gameplan, punish, and then finish a foe late, as he forced Mirko Cro Cop to verbally submit in the third round of their pivotal heavyweight bout.

The last time Martin Kampmann was one win away from a UFC title shot, he got injured before a middleweight fight with Rich Franklin. At UFC 103, after Mike Swick was injured, Nottingham, England's Paul Daley stepped in and went on to upset Kampmann via a first-round stoppage in welterweight action.

Considering the wrestling acumen of both Josh Koscheck and Frank Trigg, it was expected that the deciding factor in their welterweight fight would be the standup. And it was, with Koscheck's lethal right hand paving the way for an emphatic first-round TKO that spoiled Trigg's first UFC bout since 2005.

Lightweight contender Tyson Griffin scored the biggest win of his career in the opener, stopping Hermes Franca in the second round and earning his first UFC finish since his Octagon debut against David Lee in 2006.

It took more than nine months for *Ultimate Fighter* winner Efrain Escudero to get his first UFC win, but it was certainly worth it for "Hecho en Mexico" as he thrilled fans at American Airlines Center with a first-round stoppage of Cole Miller.

Tomasz Drwal made his middleweight debut a successful one, winning his third fight in a row by submitting Drew McFedries in the second round.

The UFC debut of Indiana lightweight Steve Lopez ended in abbreviated fashion, as a dislocated shoulder ended his bout against Jim Miller and awarded Miller the second-round TKO victory.

UFC newcomers Nik Lentz and Rafaello Oliveira both came to fight in their entertaining lightweight scrap, but it was El Paso native Lentz who took home the victory via unanimous decision.

Lightweight prospects Rick Story and Brian Foster let it rip for 6:09 seconds in their bout: it was Story who pulled off the victory via second-round submission.

Light heavyweight prospect Eliot Marshall rode an effective takedown defense and some long-distance striking to an uneventful split decision win over Jason Brilz, who was aggressive but largely ineffective throughout the bout.

Fight and Submission of the Night: Story vs. Foster

Former UFC light heavyweight title challenger Vladimir Matyushenko made a triumphant return to the Octagon at the expense of Mirko Cro Cop protégé Igor Pokrajac, who was outpointed unanimously by "The Janitor" over three rounds.

Brazil's Rafael dos Anjos earned the first UFC victory of his career, pounding out a unanimous decision over Rob Emerson.

UFC 104 *Machida vs. Shogun*

24 Oct. 2009

STAPLES Center, Los Angeles, CA

Debuts: Ben Rothwell, Chase Gormley

Fighters			Division	Method	Time	Round
Main Card						
Lyoto Machida	def.	Mauricio Rua	Light Heavyweight	Unanimous Decision	—	5
Cain Velasquez	def.	Ben Rothwell	Heavyweight	Technical Knockout	0:58	2
Gleison Tibau	def.	Josh Neer	Catchweight	Unanimous Decision	—	3
Joe Stevenson	def.	Spencer Fisher	Lightweight	Submission - Strikes	4:02	2
Anthony Johnson	def.	Yoshiyuki Yoshida	Catchweight	Technical Knockout	0:41	1
Preliminary Card						
Ryan Bader	def.	Eric Schafer	Light Heavyweight	Unanimous Decision	—	3
Pat Barry	def.	Antoni Hardonk	Heavyweight	Technical Knockout	2:30	2
Chael Sonnen	def.	Yushin Okami	Middleweight	Unanimous Decision	—	3
Jorge Rivera	def.	Rob Kimmons	Middleweight	Technical Knockout	1:53	3
Kyle Kingsbury	def.	Razak Al-Hassan	Light Heavyweight	Split Decision	—	3
Stefan Struve	def.	Chase Gormley	Heavyweight	Submission - Triangle Choke	4:04	1

At UFC 104, Lyoto Machida was shown to be human. He also remained the UFC light heavyweight champion after a grueling five-round unanimous decision win over Mauricio Rua in a bout that may have shown more about the challenger than about the champion, as Shogun finally showed UFC fans the form that saw him terrorizing 205-pounders in Japan's PRIDE organization.

Rua closed the distance quickly to open the bout, only to be greeted by a series of knees from the champion. Rua continued to press, scoring with long-range kicks before grabbing hold of Machida and walking him into the fence, where he scored with knees at close range before Machida broke free, albeit with a red welt on his stomach.

The kicks kept coming from Rua in round two, as he had more success against Machida than any UFC opponent to date. Machida was still getting his shots in, though, with a 1-2 knocking Rua backward briefly. With 3:20 left, Rua looked to take Machida down but was turned away, and now Shogun was showing redness around his belly from Machida's shots.

Exchanges between Machida and Rua began to take on more urgency in round three, with Shogun able to take Machida's shots and still fire back making it a difficult bout for either fighter to break wide open. As the two battled, Rua's thudding kicks were starting to land with more and more frequency. It may have been what Machida needed, as he kicked into gear with a furious flurry that seemed to startle Rua—at least until Shogun started firing back, much to the delight of the crowd.

Round four was tense, with the pace suiting the more methodical Machida, who landed hard kicks to keep Rua at bay.

Rua came out for the final round intent on bringing a world title back to Curitiba, and he pressed the action, even bloodying Machida's lip during an exchange.

Scores were 48-47 across the board for Machida. The decision was greeted with boos from the Los Angeles crowd, but in a bout as tough to score as this one, it was hard to find fault with the final verdict.

With a one-sided second-round thumping of highly regarded Ben Rothwell, it was clear that Cain Velasquez wasn't just the future of the heavyweight division; he was ready to be its present.

Joe Stevenson continued his recent resurgence, making it two wins in a row as he pounded out a second-round submission win due to strikes over Spencer Fisher.

Gleison Tibau was efficient and effective throughout his three-round catchweight battle with Josh Neer, doing enough to earn a unanimous decision win over "The Dentist".

Chatter before the opener between Anthony Johnson and Yoshiyuki Yoshida was that "Rumble" was going to be too big and strong for Yoshida. Well, after Johnson missed weight by six pounds, he was even bigger than his foe, and it led to a first-round blowout victory.

Fight and Knockout of the Night: Barry vs. Hardonk

Former training partners Pat Barry and Antoni Hardonk assured a standup war in their UFC 104 heavyweight clash and they delivered on their promise, duking it out for seven minutes and 30 seconds until Barry emerged victorious via an exciting second-round TKO.

The Ultimate Fighter 8 winner Ryan Bader showed no ill effects from an April injury, as he returned to the Octagon with a hard-fought three-round unanimous decision win over "Red" Schafer.

Middleweight contender Chael Sonnen pulled off the biggest win of his second stint in the UFC, dominating Yushin Okami for three rounds en route to a shutout decision victory.

Jorge Rivera continued to turn back the clock at 37 as he notched his second straight UFC win with an impressive third-round stoppage of Rob Kimmons.

Submission of the Night: Struve vs. Gormley

The Ultimate Fighter 8's Kyle Kingsbury earned his first Octagon win in light heavyweight action as he scored a close split decision victory over Iowa's Razak Al-Hassan.

Stefan Struve handed Octagon debutant Chase Gormley his first pro loss, submitting the Los Angeles resident in the first round.

UFC 105 *Couture vs. Vera*

14 Nov. 2009

M.E.N Arena, Manchester, England

Debuts: Alexander Gustafsson, Jared Hamman

Fighters			Division	Method	Time	Round
Main Card						
Randy Couture	def.	Brandon Vera	Light Heavyweight	Unanimous Decision	—	3
Dan Hardy	def.	Mike Swick	Welterweight	Unanimous Decision	—	3
Michael Bisping	def.	Denis Kang	Middleweight	Technical Knockout	4:24	2
Matt Brown	def.	James Wilks	Welterweight	Technical Knockout	2:26	3
Ross Pearson	def.	Aaron Riley	Lightweight	Technical Knockout - Doctor Stoppage	4:34	2
Preliminary Card						
John Hathaway	def.	Paul Taylor	Welterweight	Unanimous Decision	—	3
Terry Etim	def.	Shannon Gugerty	Lightweight	Submission - Guillotine Choke	1:24	2
Nick Osipczak	def.	Matthew Riddle	Welterweight	Technical Knockout	3:53	3
Dennis Siver	def.	Paul Kelly	Lightweight	Technical Knockout	2:53	2
Alexander Gustafsson	def.	Jared Hamman	Light Heavyweight	Knockout	0:41	1
Andre Winner	def.	Rolando Delgado	Lightweight	Knockout	3:22	1

It was another win for the seemingly ageless Randy Couture at the M.E.N Arena as he took a close three-round unanimous decision over Brandon Vera in the somewhat anti-climactic main event of UFC 105. Scores were 29-28 across the board for "The Natural" who was making his first start at 205 pounds since a loss to Chuck Liddell in 2006.

Vera tried to blitz Couture as soon as the bell rang, landing with a kick before Couture tied him up and pushed him into the fence, an effective strategy throughout the bout for him.

The UFC Hall of Famer got back to business in round two, mauling Vera along the fence in search of a takedown. To his credit, Vera was showing strong wrestling defense in keeping the bout upright, which didn't help the action level of the fight and was beginning to draw boos from the crowd. Vera responded by landing with two kicks, and then he followed up with a close range knee to the body that dropped Couture. Vera pounced on his foe, but Couture cleared his head quickly and looked to stall the action enough for a standup. He got his wish, scoring some much-needed points before the bell.

Couture marched forward to begin the final round, and he landed with some solid close range punches, drawing a smile from Vera, who nonetheless found himself with his back up against the fence yet again. With 2:16 left, Vera started to get his range with his kicks, but only briefly, as Couture was able to get inside again. Vera turned the tables this time, as he pushed Couture into the fence, and with 45 seconds left, he got the takedown and moved into a dominant top position. Couture broke free before any damage could be done, and as the seconds ticked away, the two exchanged blows until the fight ended.

"The Outlaw" was the hero at the M.E.N Arena, as Nottingham's Dan Hardy silenced some critics and also established himself as a legitimate challenger for the welterweight crown with a three-round unanimous decision win over Mike Swick in the UFC 105 co-main event.

To say Michael Bisping's back was against the wall after his UFC 100 loss to Dan Henderson would be a huge understatement. Bisping responded to the pressure in spectacular fashion in his hometown, as he stopped world-class contender Denis Kang in the second round to get back in the win column and re-establish himself in the 185-pound pecking order.

Fight of the Night: Bisping vs. Kang

Welterweight up-and-comer Matt Brown scored his third straight Octagon victory, pounding out a third-round TKO over game Leicester native James Wilks, who was competing for the first time since winning the welterweight division of season nine of *The Ultimate Fighter*.

Sunderland's Ross Pearson made a huge statement in his first bout since winning the lightweight division of *The Ultimate Fighter 9*, dominating veteran Aaron Riley before finishing him off via cuts in the second round.

In the main prelim bout, unbeaten welterweight prospect John Hathaway was in frightening form in his bout with countryman Paul Taylor, dominating the veteran for three rounds en route to a shutout unanimous decision victory.

Submission of the Night: Etim vs. Gugerty

Rising lightweight star Terry Etim continued to shine, submitting Shannon Gugerty in the first round to thrill the fans who came in from Liverpool to cheer him on.

The Ultimate Fighter 9's Nick Osipczak put another one in Team UK's win column as he handed Matthew Riddle his first pro loss via a third round TKO.

Knockout of the Night: Siver vs. Kelly

Germany's Dennis Siver scored his fourth straight win, third in the UFC, using a spinning back kick to doom Liverpool's Paul Kelly in the second round of their lightweight bout.

Unbeaten light heavyweight Alexander Gustafsson improved to 9-0 with an impressive 41-second stoppage of California's Jared Hamman in a battle of Octagon debutants.

TUF9 finalist Andre Winner kicked the night off on the right note for the hometown crowd, as the Leicester lightweight scored a first-round knockout of Arkansas' Roli Delgado.

UFC 106 *Ortiz vs. Griffin 2*

21 Nov. 2009

Mandalay Bay Events Center, Las Vegas, NV

Debuts: Jacob Volkmann, Antonio Rogerio Nogueira, Fabricio Camoes

Fighters			Division	Method	Time	Round
Main Card						
Forrest Griffin	def.	Tito Ortiz	Light Heavyweight	Split Decision	—	3
Josh Koscheck	def.	Anthony Johnson	Welterweight	Submission - Rear Naked Choke	4:47	2
Paulo Thiago	def.	Jacob Volkmann	Welterweight	Unanimous Decision	—	3
Antonio Rogerio Nogueira	def.	Luiz Cane	Light Heavyweight	Knockout	1:56	1
Amir Sadollah	def.	Phil Baroni	Welterweight	Unanimous Decision	—	3
Preliminary Card						
Ben Saunders	def.	Marcus Davis	Welterweight	Knockout	3:24	1
Kendall Grove	def.	Jake Rosholt	Middleweight	Submission - Triangle Choke	3:59	1
Brian Foster	def.	Brock Larson	Welterweight	Technical Knockout	3:25	2
Caol Uno	vs.	Fabricio Camoes	Lightweight	Majority Draw	—	3
George Sotiropoulos	def.	Jason Dent	Lightweight	Submission - Armbar	4:36	2

After Forrest Griffin and Tito Ortiz' two fights together, one thing was crystal clear: very little separates the two former light heavyweight champions. Their rematch at the Mandalay Bay Events Center was the latest example, as Griffin avenged his split decision loss to Ortiz in 2006 with a split decision win of his own over "The Huntington Beach Bad Boy". Scores were 30-27, 29-28, and 28-29 for Griffin.

Ortiz opened the bout with some wide strikes that showed the effects of being out of action since May of 2008. As the round progressed, Ortiz started to find his range, and once he did, he shot in for—and got—a takedown. While there, Ortiz fired away, but Griffin took his time and got back to his feet before he took too much damage. The two then locked up against the fence, with Griffin able to push off and get out of trouble. The combatants proceeded to trade punches, with Griffin starting to land with more frequency, and the Las Vegan also eluded Ortiz' next takedown attempt with ease before finishing the round strong with strikes.

Ortiz and Griffin began round two with haymakers that missed the mark, but Ortiz was on with his next offensive move as he put Griffin on his back with a quick takedown. Griffin did a good job of keeping Ortiz close, and as the two neared the fence, Griffin was able to get to his feet. While standing, Griffin was starting to get sharper, even knocking Ortiz' mouthpiece out with a kick, and Ortiz was beginning to look winded. Suddenly Ortiz sprang into action with a lightning-quick takedown, and he began to find room for his punches and elbows. In the final 30 seconds, Griffin got back into action, reversing position as he ended the round with a ground and pound assault of his own.

Griffin came out fast in round three, scoring with punches and a kick to the head as the crowd chanted his name. Ortiz fired back sporadically but did little damage while Griffin got stronger as the fight progressed, sealing his victory.

Fight and Submission of the Night:
Koscheck vs. Johnson

With the combined knockout power of welterweight contenders Josh Koscheck and Anthony Johnson, many expected their UFC 106 co-main event to end in quick and explosive fashion. But it was Koscheck, a former NCAA National Champion, going back to his roots to take Johnson down and submit him in the second round.

Antonio Rogerio Nogueira, the twin brother of heavyweight superstar Minotauro Nogueira, made his long-awaited UFC debut a successful one as he scored a spectacular first-round stoppage of countryman Luiz Cane.

Knockout of the Night:
Nogueira vs. Cane

Welterweight up-and-comer Paulo Thiago notched his second UFC win of the year, pounding out a hard-fought three-round unanimous decision over newcomer Jacob Volkmann.

The Ultimate Fighter 7 winner Amir Sadollah scored his first post-*TUF* win in the opening main card bout, weathering an early assault from Octagon returnee Phil Baroni to take a clear-cut three-round unanimous decision.

Before his clash with Marcus Davis, welterweight prospect Ben Saunders said that he hoped to become the first fighter to knock "The Irish Hand Grenade" out. His wish came true, as he used his deadly knees to halt the veteran contender in the first round.

Season three winner Kendall Grove made sure he didn't join Chris Leben as *Ultimate Fighter* alumni to fall to middleweight prospect Jake Rosholt, submitting the former college wrestling standout in the first round.

Illinois welterweight Brian Foster nabbed his first UFC win in his second try, impressively stopping veteran Brock Larson in the second round.

In lightweight action, a second-round point deduction from debuting Brazilian Fabricio "Morango" Camoes proved to be the deciding factor as he battled to a three-round majority draw with Japanese veteran Caol Uno.

Lightweight up-and-comer George Sotiropoulos opened up the UFC 106 card with his fourth straight Octagon victory, submitting Jason Dent in a battle of *The Ultimate Fighter* alumni.

The Ultimate Fighter 10 Finale

05 Dec. 2009

The Pearl at The Palms, Las Vegas, NV

Debuts: Joe Brammer, Rodney Wallace, Jon Madsen, Justin Wren, Darrill Schoonover, James McSweeney, Marcus Jones, Matt Mitrione, Kimbo Slice, Brendan Schaub, Roy Nelson

Fighters			Division	Method	Time	Round
Main Card						
Roy Nelson	def.	Brendan Schaub	Heavyweight	Knockout	3:45	1
Matt Hamill	def.	Jon Jones	Light Heavyweight	Opponent Disqualified	4:14	1
Kimbo Slice	def.	Houston Alexander	Catchweight	Unanimous Decision	—	3
Frankie Edgar	def.	Matt Veach	Lightweight	Submission - Rear Naked Choke	2:22	2
Matt Mitrione	def.	Marcus Jones	Heavyweight	Knockout	0:10	2
Preliminary Card						
James McSweeney	def.	Darrill Schoonover	Heavyweight	Technical Knockout	3:20	3
Jon Madsen	def.	Justin Wren	Heavyweight	Split Decision	—	3
Brian Stann	def.	Rodney Wallace	Light Heavyweight	Unanimous Decision	—	3
John Howard	def.	Dennis Hallman	Welterweight	Knockout	4:55	3
Mark Bocek	def.	Joe Brammer	Lightweight	Submission	3:36	1

Roy Nelson came into the Octagon at The Pearl at The Palms to the strains of Weird Al Yankovic's *I'm Fat*, but behind his physique and self-effacing humor lies a real fighter, and "Big Country" proved it with a devastating first-round knockout of previously unbeaten Brendan Schaub that earned Nelson *The Ultimate Fighter 10* title.

Knockout of the Night: Nelson vs. Schaub

Schaub's striking was working beautifully in the opening stages of the fight as he drove Nelson back against the fence. Nelson shook off the shots, got off a wide hook and then was able to get Schaub to the canvas, where he quickly took his trademark side control position. Surprisingly, Schaub found his way free and resumed his striking attack, but the Colorado fighter's defense was porous, and that was a sign of things to come, as Nelson took Schaub's punches and kept moving forward, eventually landing with a flush right hand to the temple that sent Schaub down hard to the canvas. A follow-up shot finished things off, with referee Herb Dean calling the bout off at the 3:45 mark.

For much of his fight against Matt Hamill, it looked like rising light heavyweight star Jon Jones was sailing to a tenth consecutive victory without a loss, but it was not to be, as an illegal elbow from Jones prompted a first-round disqualification from referee Steve Mazzagatti.

"They say that after you lose, you become a better, stronger person," said Jones. "Everything happens for a reason."

Jones and Hamill kept it standing early, with Jones holding the edge thanks to some quick kicks and punches, as well as solid takedown defense when Hamill decided to shoot in. By the third minute, Hamill was reddened on the face and body, and Jones was getting into a rhythm. Next came a takedown by Jones, who moved into mount and began firing away with a dizzying array of strikes. Hamill hung tough under the assault, but Jones was relentless with punches, forearms and elbows. One of the strikes was an illegal downward elbow, drawing a stoppage and a point deduction from referee Steve Mazzagatti. Yet when Hamill was unable to continue, Mazzagatti disqualified Jones at the 4:14 mark.

It wasn't the expected Armageddon, but after three rounds, the long-awaited UFC debut of Kimbo Slice ended in a unanimous decision win over Houston Alexander for the former streetfighting legend.

Lightweight contender Frankie Edgar got his first finish in over two years, as he withstood a strong effort from Matt Veach to submit the Illinois native in the second round.

Fight of the Night: Edgar vs. Veach

TUF10 heavyweights (and NFL vets) Matt Mitrione and Marcus Jones squared off in the main card opener, and after surviving some tight spots in the first round, Mitrione finished matters off in the second with two big right hands.

In comic books, Doomsday was the only character to defeat Superman. At The Pearl at The Palms, welterweight prospect John "Doomsday" Howard repeated that victory, roaring back from two rounds down to stop returning veteran Dennis "Superman" Hallman with just five seconds left in the third and final round of their preliminary bout on *The Ultimate Fighter: Heavyweights Finale* card.

James McSweeney earned his first UFC victory, halting *TUF10* teammate Darrill Schoonover in the third round of their heavyweight bout.

Submission of the Night: Bocek vs. Brammer

In the night's first clash of *TUF10* heavyweights, Jon Madsen scored a three-round split decision over Justin Wren.

Light heavyweight Brian Stann handed Octagon newcomer Rodney Wallace his first pro loss, pounding out a workmanlike three-round unanimous decision victory.

In the opener, lightweight up-and-comer Mark Bocek spoiled the UFC debut of Joe Brammer, submitting the Iowan in the first round.

One Hit Wonders: Justin Wren, Darrill Schoonover, Marcus Jones

UFC 107 *Penn vs. Sanchez*

12 Dec. 2009

FedEx Forum, Memphis, TN

Debuts: Ricardo Funch, Lucio Linhares

Fighters			Division	Method	Time	Round
Main Card						
BJ Penn	def.	Diego Sanchez	Lightweight	Technical Knockout - Cut	2:37	5
Frank Mir	def.	Cheick Kongo	Heavyweight	Submission - Guillotine	1:12	1
Jon Fitch	def.	Mike Pierce	Welterweight	Unanimous Decision	—	3
Kenny Florian	def.	Clay Guida	Lightweight	Submission - Rear Naked Choke	2:19	2
Stefan Struve	def.	Paul Buentello	Heavyweight	Majority Decision	—	3
Preliminary Card						
Alan Belcher	def.	Wilson Gouveia	Catchweight	Technical Knockout	3:03	1
Matt Wiman	def.	Shane Nelson	Lightweight	Unanimous Decision	—	3
Johny Hendricks	def.	Ricardo Funch	Welterweight	Unanimous Decision	—	3
Rousimar Palhares	def.	Lucio Linhares	Middleweight	Submission - Heel Hook	3:21	2
DaMarques Johnson	def.	Edgar Garcia	Welterweight	Submission Triangle Choke	4:03	1
TJ Grant	def.	Kevin Burns	Welterweight	Technical Knockout	4:57	1

If you listened to some observers, BJ Penn had no cardio, no dedication, and no business being on top of the 155-pound weight class. Well, Penn must be doing something right, because at UFC 107, the pride of Hilo, Hawaii established himself as the greatest lightweight champion in UFC history with a fifth-round stoppage of Diego Sanchez that saw him frustrate, punish, and dominate a talented challenger en route to his record third successful title defense in the main event of UFC 107.

Penn struck first and fast with a thudding right hand that put Sanchez on the canvas. Penn's follow-up attack was furious, but somehow Sanchez survived and managed to get to his feet. This early assault set the tone for the rest of the fight.

Sanchez made every effort to get Penn to the canvas in rounds two and three, but was unsuccessful. By now, Sanchez was bleeding from the mouth and ear, and although he kept trying to get the fight to the mat, it was becoming a losing battle, especially as Penn was doing his best to punish Sanchez at close range during every failed takedown attempt.

At the start of round four, Penn and Sanchez raced to the center of the Octagon and traded blows briefly, with no serious damage being done by either fighter. Sanchez, with a look of determination on his face, was not about to give in, but Penn's striking accuracy and takedown defense was making it impossible for the challenger to get any sort of offense together.

The final round began with a familiar pattern of Sanchez trying, and failing, to get Penn to the mat in order to mount an attack. Finally, the look on Sanchez' face began to show frustration, and then a kick to the head by Penn opened up a nasty gash on the challenger's forehead. With blood covering his face, referee Herb Dean brought in the Octagonside physician, who recommended that the bout be halted. Dean agreed, stopping the fight at the 2:37 mark.

Former UFC heavyweight champion Frank Mir bounced back from his UFC 100 loss to Brock Lesnar and kept his dreams of a rubber match with the champ alive with a spectacular first-round submission win over Cheick Kongo.

Fight of the Night: Belcher vs. Gouveia

In one of the most highly-anticipated UFC 107 bouts, two of the top lightweights in the game battled it out, and when it was over, Kenny Florian bounced back from his title fight loss against BJ Penn four months earlier with an impressive second-round submission of Clay Guida.

Submission of the Night: Johnson vs. Garcia

Washington's Mike Pierce gave welterweight contender Jon Fitch all he could handle in their three-rounder before Fitch emerged victorious with a hard-fought three-round unanimous decision win.

In a heavyweight bout, 6' 11" prospect Stefan "Skyscraper" Struve spoiled the UFC return of former world title challenger Paul Buentello by scoring an entertaining three-round majority decision win.

Alan Belcher left no one disappointed in UFC 107 action Saturday, as he halted Wilson Gouveia in the first round of a slugfest contested at a catchweight of 195 pounds.

In lightweight action, Matt Wiman broke a two-fight losing streak with a shutout three-round decision over Shane Nelson.

In a clash of welterweight unbeatens, Johny Hendricks pounded out a lopsided three-round unanimous decision over UFC debutant Ricardo Funch.

Middleweight Rousimar Palhares made his first start since a leg fracture earlier in the year a successful one as he submitted Octagon newcomer Lucio Linhares in the second round.

There was a little bit of everything for fight fans when DaMarques Johnson took on Edgar Garcia in a back and forth welterweight battle, but when the dust settled, it was Johnson who emerged victorious via first-round submission.

Knockout of the Night: Grant vs. Burns

Canada's TJ Grant made a statement in his welterweight match against Kevin Burns, rebounding from an early knockdown to finish his foe with seconds remaining in an exciting opening round.

25 GREATEST UPSETS

UFC 1
ROYCE GRACIE VS. KEN SHAMROCK 1

All you needed to do was look at Royce Gracie and Ken Shamrock side by side to wonder "how in the world is this skinny kid from Brazil going to beat this monster?" Throw in the fact that Shamrock knew the "mysterious" submission game employed by Gracie as well, and the odds in Shamrock's favor shot even higher. However, on this night, Gracie was not to be denied as he put a new sport on the map with a brilliant three fight / three win performance that was epitomized by the victory in the middle over Shamrock.

UFC 76
FORREST GRIFFIN VS. MAURICIO RUA

No one thought Forrest Griffin was going to lie down and take a beating from high-profile PRIDE import Mauricio Rua when they met in Anaheim in 2007. Griffin was going to show up, be competitive, swing for the fences and eventually get put away by Shogun—at least that's what the Hollywood script called for. Griffin didn't get the memo though, and he not only beat Rua, he dominated him, putting the icing on the cake with a submission in the final minute to cap the upset victory.

UFC 46
BJ PENN VS. MATT HUGHES 1

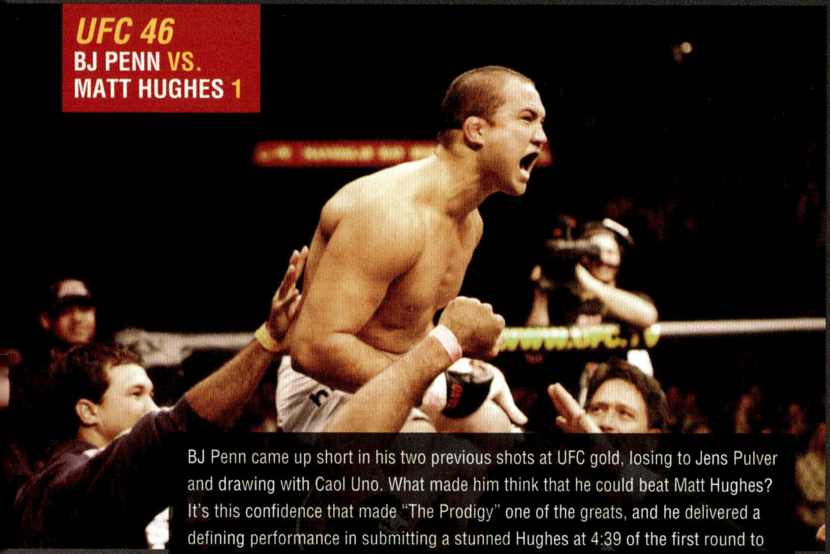

BJ Penn came up short in his two previous shots at UFC gold, losing to Jens Pulver and drawing with Caol Uno. What made him think that he could beat Matt Hughes? It's this confidence that made "The Prodigy" one of the greats, and he delivered a defining performance in submitting a stunned Hughes at 4:39 of the first round to win the UFC 170-pound title.

UFC 112
FRANKIE EDGAR VS. BJ PENN 1

Few outside of his native New Jersey gave Frankie Edgar a shot at defeating BJ Penn for the UFC lightweight title in their April 2010 bout. With crisp striking and effective movement, as well as a couple points-scoring takedowns, Edgar stunned fans at Abu Dhabi with a unanimous decision win. And if that wasn't enough, Edgar repeated the feat in more dominant fashion four months later at UFC 118, proving that the first win was no fluke.

UFC 63
JOE LAUZON VS. JENS PULVER

After more than four years away, Jens Pulver's return to the UFC in 2006 was supposed to be a celebration. And it was—for opponent Joe Lauzon, who knocked "Lil' Evil" out in less than a minute, momentarily derailing the former lightweight champion's comeback. As for Lauzon, he was back at work on Monday morning as an IT professional.

UFC 43
RANDY COUTURE VS. CHUCK LIDDELL 1

After taking back-to-back losses at heavyweight to the much bigger Ricco Rodriguez and Josh Barnett, Randy Couture's drop to the 205 pound weight class was seen as a move of desperation to save a career on the downswing. Facing the feared Chuck Liddell in his first light heavyweight bout was just going to hasten Couture's demise. But the one person not counting Couture out was the man himself, and he not only beat Liddell, he stopped him in the third round and began the second act of one of the fight game's most amazing careers.

UFC 70
GABRIEL GONZAGA VS. MIRKO CRO COP

Sure, Gabriel Gonzaga was an underdog against the feared Croatian striker, but there were more than a few people who figured the Brazilian jiu-jitsu black belt had the right stuff to beat Cro Cop—on the ground. Beating Cro Cop with a single kick to the head? Those are the kinds of odds that wouldn't even show up in Vegas. But Gonzaga pulled it off, earning himself a shot at the heavyweight title and a permanent spot in UFC highlight reels.

UFC 69
MATT SERRA VS. GEORGES ST-PIERRE 1

2007 was the year of the upset, but when it came to a fighter who was given virtually no chance to take down a champion expected to reign atop his division for as long as he chose to, Matt Serra's stoppage of Georges St-Pierre was not only the biggest upset of that year, but of all-time. And the Renzo Gracie jiu-jitsu black belt did it with his fists, not his ground game, as he clipped GSP early and kept punching until referee John McCarthy halted the bout and raised the hand of the new welterweight champion.

UFC 15
RANDY COUTURE VS. VITOR BELFORT 1

As you can tell with a quick glance of this list, Randy Couture made a career out of beating the oddsmakers, and it all began with his October 1997 thrashing of then-unbeaten Vitor Belfort. At the time, the question wasn't who would eventually beat "The Phenom", but if he would ever lose. Couture took all of eight minutes and 17 seconds to answer both questions as he pounded out a TKO victory.

UFC 90
JUNIOR DOS SANTOS VS. FABRICIO WERDUM

If you didn't know who Junior dos Santos was before October 25, 2008, you were not alone. But if you still didn't know who this Brazilian bomber was after his 81-second demolition of Fabricio Werdum at UFC 90, where were you? In a little over a minute, dos Santos smashed his way into the rankings with a ferocious KO of the consensus top-five Werdum, and suddenly, this young man had plenty of fans around the MMA world waiting to see what he was going to do next.

UFC 71
HOUSTON ALEXANDER VS. KEITH JARDINE

Practically no one knew who Houston Alexander was when he stepped into the Octagon against Keith Jardine at UFC 71. The basics: he was a radio DJ on the side and a father of six. But everyone knew who he was after his 48-second blitz of the highly-regarded "Dean of Mean", who was bludgeoned into defeat with a high-impact assault that electrified the packed house at the MGM Grand in Las Vegas.

UFC 105
DAN HARDY VS. MIKE SWICK

Nottingham's Dan Hardy could talk a great game—that there was no doubt. He could punch a little too, and he had quickly soared to a 3-0 UFC record by the time of his 2009 showdown with veteran Mike Swick. But Swick had been through the wars, and he was in better form than ever at 170 pounds. So what happened? Hardy put on a career-defining performance in dismantling Swick over three rounds to score the upset win and earn himself a shot at the UFC welterweight crown.

UFC 68
RANDY COUTURE VS. TIM SYLVIA

Sure, it was Randy Couture, but after the former heavyweight and light heavyweight champion's year long layoff (and knockout losses in two of his previous three fights), finding someone who was picking "The Natural" to beat the 6' 8" Sylvia was near impossible. Couture pulled off yet another miracle in winning a shutout five-round decision, delighting a packed house at the Nationwide Arena in Columbus, Ohio, in the process.

UFC 3
KEITH HACKNEY VS. EMMANUEL YARBOROUGH

In the early days of the UFC, it was hard to get a read on some of the competitors in this brand-new fighting venue, so you usually judged fighters by their appearances. When 200-pound Keith Hackney faced off against 600-pound Emmanuel Yarborough, you feared for Hackney's safety. Well, at least you did until the fight started and Hackney dropped his opponent with the first strike he landed. From there, it was all Hackney as he halted Yarborough in less than two minutes.

UFC 14
MAURICE SMITH VS. MARK COLEMAN

Just as jiu-jitsu ruled the early days of the Octagon, wrestling had taken over in 1996, and as 1997 dawned, the man on the top of the heap was "The Godfather of Ground and Pound", Mark Coleman. But kickboxing star Maurice Smith was about to turn the MMA world on its ear, and at UFC 14, he stunned observers with a style that was soon to be known as "Sprawl and Brawl", as he tossed off Coleman's takedown attempts and pounded out a decision win that earned him the UFC heavyweight title and handed "The Hammer" his first ever loss.

UFC 4
ROYCE GRACIE VS. DAN SEVERN

With 10 wins and no losses in the UFC, Royce Gracie was the undisputed king of the early Octagon. But the man many believed to have his number was a former college wrestling star known as "The Beast", Dan Severn. And as Severn romped over his first two opponents in the 1994 tournament, and then battered Gracie through the first 15 minutes of their final bout, it was no surprise to anyone. But then Gracie pulled off a triangle choke at the 15:49 mark, the crowd roared, and a legend's legacy was cemented for all-time.

UFC 57
MARCIO CRUZ VS. FRANK MIR

Less than two years removed from a serious motorcycle accident that took his UFC heavyweight title and almost his life, Frank Mir returned to the Octagon in February of 2006 to face jiu-jitsu specialist Marcio Cruz at UFC 57. But this wasn't the same Mir who was on top of the world a couple years earlier, and Cruz proved it by bloodying and stopping the former champion in the first round. It wouldn't be until 2007 that the "real" Mir once again made his presence known.

UFC 95
PAULO THIAGO VS. JOSH KOSCHECK

At the time of this 2009 bout, it was assumed that the unbeaten but unknown Paulo Thiago would be taken care of fairly easily by highly-regarded contender Josh Koscheck. The Brazilian had his supporters, but it would be safe to guess that not even Thiago's biggest fans expected their man to score with a right uppercut followed by a clean-up left hand to win by first-round knockout. This one stunned everyone, especially Koscheck.

UFC 17
PETE WILLIAMS VS. MARK COLEMAN

Despite his loss to Maurice Smith 10 months earlier, Mark Coleman was still "The Hammer" and still a feared man in the Octagon. Originally scheduled to face fellow wrestler Randy Couture, Coleman was instead matched with young prospect Pete Williams, and the Lion's Den product made an immediate name for himself with a highlight-reel head kick knockout of an exhausted Coleman at the 12:38 mark of their 1998 bout.

UFN8
JAKE O'BRIEN VS. HEATH HERRING

No, it wasn't the most compelling fight you'll ever see. In terms of having a gameplan, sticking to it, and executing it flawlessly, Jake O'Brien was spectacular in defusing the attack of PRIDE and K-1 star Heath Herring. Herring came to the Octagon with plenty of fanfare, but wwas instead soundly outpointed by O'Brien, a veteran of only 10 pro fights.

UFC 92
FRANK MIR VS. MINOTAURO NOGUEIRA

Going into this 2008 battle of *The Ultimate Fighter 8* coaches, conventional wisdom said that Minotauro, one of the sport's all-time greatest heavyweights, was just too good everywhere for Mir. So when Mir started lighting up Minotauro on the feet almost as soon as the bell rang, warning signs started flashing and with the former UFC heavyweight champ growing more confident with each knockdown of the Brazilian, he did what no fighter had ever done to the former PRIDE champ—he finished him in the second round to win the interim UFC heavyweight belt.

UFC 35
JENS PULVER VS. BJ PENN 1

Despite his status as UFC lightweight champion and a veteran competitor of the sport, Jens Pulver was a prohibitive underdog when he took on "The Prodigy" BJ Penn, at UFC 35 in 2002. And for two rounds, the oddsmakers were right, as Penn dominated and almost submitted the champion at the end of round two. But for the next three rounds, "Lil' Evil" emerged, pounding out a five-round majority decision that was the time capsule moment in the career of the UFC's popular (and first) lightweight champion.

UFC 38
IAN FREEMAN VS. FRANK MIR

In 2002, Frank Mir was the UFC's Golden Boy in waiting, a charismatic young heavyweight with off-the-charts talent. Ian Freeman, competing in front of his countrymen in the UFC's first visit to England, was a grizzled veteran fighting with a heavy heart due to the illness of his father. Inspired, Freeman shocked Mir and the world with an emotional first-round TKO win. But the celebration was tempered by the news that Freeman's father had passed away shortly before the bout, with "The Machine" not being told until after the fight concluded.

UFC 76
KEITH JARDINE VS. CHUCK LIDDELL

Before UFC 71, Chuck Liddell was the most dominant light heavyweight in the world, while Keith Jardine was coming off a stoppage of Forrest Griffin and seemed close to a title shot. Even after Liddell lost to Quinton Jackson, he was still expected to make short work of Jardine. What a difference a night makes. With a disciplined game plan and some hellacious kicks, Jardine put Liddell's career on ice for the moment with a three-round split decision win.

UFC 47
NICK DIAZ VS. ROBBIE LAWLER

A no-nonsense knockout artist, "Ruthless" Robbie Lawler was turning into the UFC's version of Mike Tyson and the fans loved him for it. Even an injury-induced loss to Pete Spratt didn't quiet the buzz around Lawler, but jiu-jitsu ace Nick Diaz certainly did the trick with his stunning one-punch finish of Lawler. But Diaz was no Buster Douglas, as he went on to a successful career of his own in the ensuing years.

UFC 108 *Evans vs. Silva*

02 Jan. 2010

MGM Grand Garden Arena, Las Vegas, NV

Debuts: Gilbert Yvel, John Gunderson

Fighters			Division	Method	Time	Round
Main Card						
Rashad Evans	def.	Thiago Silva	Light Heavyweight	Unanimous Decision	—	3
Paul Daley	def.	Dustin Hazelett	Catchweight	Knockout	2:24	1
Sam Stout	def.	Joe Lauzon	Lightweight	Unanimous Decision	—	3
Jim Miller	def.	Duane Ludwig	Lightweight	Submission - Armbar	2:31	1
Junior dos Santos	def.	Gilbert Yvel	Heavyweight	Technical Knockout	2:07	1
Preliminary Card						
Martin Kampmann	def.	Jacob Volkmann	Welterweight	Submission - Guillotine Choke	4:03	1
Cole Miller	def.	Dan Lauzon	Lightweight	Submission - Modified Kimura	3:05	1
Mark Munoz	def.	Ryan Jensen	Middleweight	Submission - Strikes	2:30	1
Jake Ellenberger	def.	Mike Pyle	Welterweight	Technical Knockout	0:22	2
Rafaello Oliveira	def.	John Gunderson	Lightweight	Unanimous Decision	—	3

For much of their UFC 108 main event, Rashad Evans dominated Thiago Silva behind effective wrestling and Octagon control. For a few moments in the final round, Silva had victory within reach thanks to his right hand, only to let it slip away behind some ill-advised showboating that allowed Evans to recover, get to the end of the bout, and earn the three-round unanimous decision win.

Scores were 29-28 across the board for Evans, who won his first bout since losing his UFC light heavyweight crown to Lyoto Machida by going back to his wrestling roots.

Evans tore after Silva at the bell, closing the distance quickly and tying his foe up. Within 40 seconds, Evans had slammed Silva to the mat and he moved into full mount. Silva fought his way loose, though, and got back to his feet. Evans stayed close with his foe against the fence, eventually breaking off in order to trade with Silva before scoring with another takedown. Again, Silva rose to his feet, but he was unable to get his rhythm while standing. With under a minute to go, Evans flurried against the fence and followed up with a takedown, solidifying the round for himself.

Evans fought the second round like he did the first, and with the same results. Silva was a little more active while pinned against the fence, but whenever he would get too loose, Evans would dump him on the canvas.

Little changed in round three, with Evans again managing matters with his takedowns and Octagon control. With under three minutes left, Silva started playing to the crowd and showboating in an effort to get Evans to stand and trade with him, but the former champion wouldn't bite. Silva bit back hard, rocking Evans badly with a right to the head and following up with more strikes as Evans staggered and tried to regain his composure. Unfortunately for the Brazilian, his continued showboating gave Evans the time he needed to get his bearings back, and he was able to pin Silva against the fence in the final minute and keep him there until the bell sounded.

Knockout of the Night: Daley vs. Hazelett

It was two UFC fights and two devastating knockout wins for Nottingham, England's Paul "Semtex" Daley, who struck hard and fast against Dustin Hazelett in the UFC 108 co-main event, taking out the jiu-jitsu ace in the first round.

Fight of the Night: J.Lauzon vs. Stout

Ontario lightweight Sam Stout turned in the most impressive performance of his UFC career, surviving some dicey early moments to decisively decision fellow up-and-comer Joe Lauzon over three rounds.

Jim Miller had three opponents for his UFC 108 fight, thanks to injuries to Tyson Griffin and Sean Sherk, but when it counted, Miller took care of the man who stepped into the Octagon with him, impressively dropping, then submitting, returning veteran Duane Ludwig in the first round of their lightweight bout.

In the main card opener, heavyweight contender Junior dos Santos continued to impress as he halted a former PRIDE fighter for the third time in four UFC fights, this time taking out Gilbert Yvel with a furious first-round barrage.

Submission of the Night: C.Miller vs. D.Lauzon

Lightweight up-and-comer Cole Miller came out on a mission to rebound from his loss to Efrain Escudero and he succeeded in style, rising from an early knockdown to submit fellow prospect Dan Lauzon in the first round of their UFC 108 preliminary bout.

Welterweight contender Martin "The Hitman" Kampmann got back in the win column following his TKO loss to Paul Daley at UFC 103, submitting Jacob Volkmann in the first round of an action-packed scrap.

Mark Munoz made it two straight in the middleweight division as he used his ground and pound attack to stop Ryan Jensen in the first round.

In welterweight action, Jake Ellenberger kicked off the New Year with his first UFC win as he impressively halted veteran Mike Pyle in the second round.

The first bout of the night saw Rafaello Oliveira pound out a methodical three-round unanimous decision win over Octagon newcomer John Gunderson.

UFC Fight Night 20

Maynard vs. Diaz

11 Jan. 2010

Patriot Center, Fairfax, VA

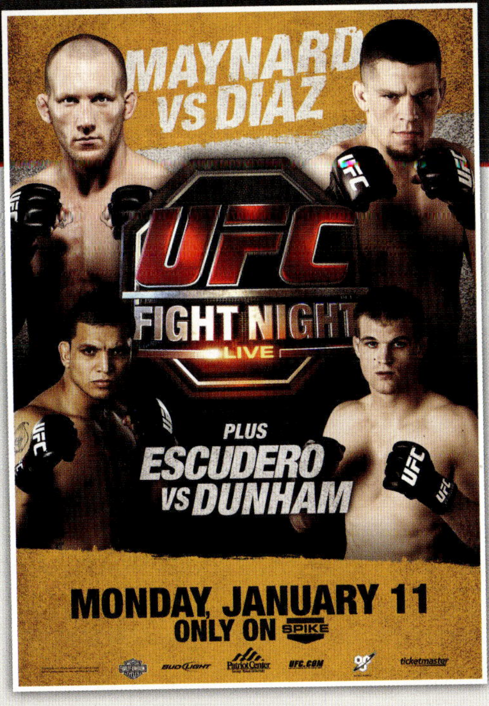

Debuts: Mike Guymon, Rory MacDonald, John Salter, Gerald Harris

Fighters			Division	Method	Time	Round
Main Card						
Gray Maynard	def.	Nate Diaz	Lightweight	Split Decision	—	3
Evan Dunham	def.	Efrain Escudero	Lightweight	Submission - Armbar	1:59	3
Aaron Simpson	def.	Tom Lawlor	Middleweight	Split Decision	—	3
Amir Sadollah	def.	Brad Blackburn	Welterweight	Unanimous Decision	—	3
Preliminary Card						
Chris Leben	def.	Jay Silva	Middleweight	Unanimous Decision	—	3
Rick Story	def.	Jesse Lennox	Welterweight	Split Decision	—	3
Thiago Tavares	vs.	Nik Lentz	Lightweight	Draw	—	3
Rory MacDonald	def.	Mike Guymon	Welterweight	Submission - Armbar	4:27	1
Rafael dos Anjos	def.	Kyle Bradley	Lightweight	Unanimous Decision	—	3
Gerald Harris	def.	John Salter	Middleweight	Technical Knockout	3:24	3
Nick Catone	def.	Jesse Forbes	Middleweight	Split Decision	—	3

It probably wasn't the way lightweight contender Gray Maynard pictured it, but before a sold-out crowd at the Patriot Center, he got the "W" he wanted more than any other, as he was awarded a close three-round split decision victory over Nate Diaz in the UFC Fight Night main event, a win that avenged his defeat to Diaz on *The Ultimate Fighter 5*.

Diaz stalked Maynard calmly to open the bout, and Maynard responded with the occasional wild haymaker. The shorter Maynard was having trouble getting his range, but Diaz wasn't piling up the points either as the round entered its final two minutes. With the round up for grabs, the two upped the pace in the last 120 seconds.

Both Diaz and Maynard got a little busier in round two, with Maynard landing the best punch of the fight thus far—90 seconds in—when he nailed Diaz with a thudding right hand. Diaz was unmoved by the shot and went back to his unorthodox southpaw attack, but a knee by Maynard dropped the Californian briefly and another right hand knocked him off balance moments later. Neither blow appeared to hurt Diaz, but they definitely made an impression on the judges. Diaz went back to showboating in the final minute, and Maynard joined in for a moment, but nothing resulted from their show of bravado, and the crowd let them hear it.

Diaz was the more active fighter in round three, and while Maynard trudged forward, he was not scoring enough to keep Diaz from apparently piling up the points in this pivotal round. Even in the clinch, Diaz was showing no signs of wear, but Maynard did finish strong, apparently doing enough to secure the victory on the judges' scorecards.

Submission of the Night: Dunham vs. Escudero

Scores for Maynard were 30-27, 29-28 and 28-29.

Unbeaten but unheralded Evan Dunham scored the biggest win of his young UFC career, moving to 3-0 in the organization with a come-from-behind third-round submission victory over *The Ultimate Fighter 8* winner Efrain Escudero, who suffered his first pro defeat in the UFC Fight Night co-feature.

Fight of the Night: Simpson vs. Lawlor

Middleweight Aaron Simpson kept his perfect record intact the hard way, surviving a full-on first-round striking assault from Tom Lawlor to battle back and earn a razor-thin three-round split decision victory.

Richmond's Amir Sadollah delivered for his hometown fans, showing off an impressive array of striking skills both standing and on the ground heading for a three-round unanimous decision win over veteran "Bad" Brad Blackburn in the welterweight main card opener.

Following two straight Octagon losses, middleweight Chris Leben desperately needed a win in his UFC Fight Night bout against Jay Silva. And he got it, bringing his ground and pound game out of mothballs to drill out a clear-cut three-round victory.

Vancouver, Washington's Rick Story made it two in a row in the UFC's welterweight division as he scored a three-round split decision win over Jesse Lennox.

Nik Lentz had insult added to injury in his lightweight bout with Thiago Tavares, as two low blows and a bruised face were added to an unpopular three-round majority draw that would have been a victory for Tavares if not for a third-round point deduction from the Brazilian.

The UFC welterweight division may have found another star North of the Border, as 20-year-old Rory MacDonald showed off an impressive ground game in his Octagon debut, submitting veteran (and fellow UFC newcomer) Mike Guymon in the first round.

Lightweight up-and-comer Rafael dos Anjos continued to impress in prelim action, as he pounded out a shutout three-round decision win over game Louisiana native Kyle Bradley.

Gerald Harris made his long-awaited UFC debut, stopping previously unbeaten John Salter in the third round of a middleweight bout.

Knockout of the Night: Harris vs. Salter

Middleweight prospect Nick Catone broke a two-fight losing streak in the opener, eking out a close split decision win over *The Ultimate Fighter 3* alum Jesse Forbes.

UFC 109 *Relentless*

06
Feb.
2010

Mandalay Bay Events Center, Las Vegas, NV

Debuts: Ronys Torres, Phil Davis, Joey Beltran, Rolles Gracie

Fighters			Division	Method	Time	Round
Main Card						
Randy Couture	def.	Mark Coleman	Light Heavyweight	Submission - Rear Naked Choke	1:09	2
Chael Sonnen	def.	Nate Marquardt	Middleweight	Unanimous Decision	—	3
Paulo Thiago	def.	Mike Swick	Welterweight	Submission – D'Arce choke	1:54	2
Demian Maia	def.	Dan Miller	Middleweight	Unanimous Decision	—	3
Matt Serra	def.	Frank Trigg	Welterweight	Knockout	2:23	1
Preliminary Card						
Mac Danzig	def.	Justin Buchholz	Lightweight	Unanimous Decision	—	3
Melvin Guillard	def.	Ronys Torres	Lightweight	Unanimous Decision	—	3
Rob Emerson	def.	Phillipe Nover	Lightweight	Unanimous Decision	—	3
Phil Davis	def.	Brian Stann	Light Heavyweight	Unanimous Decision	—	3
Chris Tuchscherer	def.	Tim Hague	Heavyweight	Majority Decision	—	3
Joey Beltran	def.	Rolles Gracie	Heavyweight	Technical Knockout	1:31	2

It was a bout nearly 12 years in the making, and for Randy Couture, it was certainly worth the wait, as he was on point against Mark Coleman from the opening bell until he submitted his fellow Hall of Famer in the second round.

"I'm having a blast," said Couture, who was scheduled to face Coleman in 1998 before an injury scrapped their UFC 17 bout. "I feel like I'm improving each time."

Both fighters landed their jabs effectively in the opening stages of the bout, with Couture adding a right hand to the mix. Coleman wasn't shying away from exchanges, though, and he was able to land some hard shots on the inside. With a little over three minutes left, Couture rocked Coleman with punches upstairs and his follow-up knees were just as effective before he bulled "The Hammer" into the fence.

Couture's more accurate strikes again paid off early in the second, as he rocked Coleman and then took him down to the mat. Couture proceeded to deliver some ground and pound to the master of the technique before sinking in a rear naked choke. Coleman attempted to hang on, but to no avail, as he went to sleep, forcing referee Steve Mazzagatti to halt the bout at 1:09 of the round.

Fight of the Night: Sonnen vs. Marquardt

Chael Sonnen is the worst kind of fighter to be in the Octagon with. Not because he will knock you out in 30 seconds or submit you in the same amount of time: it's because he will punish you and make you miserable for 15 minutes, and that's precisely what he did to Nate Marquardt in the UFC 109 co-main event, pounding out a unanimous decision victory that earned him a shot at the middleweight crown.

The first round may have not been something to write home about, but in round two of the welterweight battle between Paulo Thiago and Mike Swick, Thiago was dazzling, dropping Swick with a left hook before submitting him seconds later to further his climb up the 170-pound ranks.

Submission of the Night: Thiago vs. Swick

Brazil's Demian Maia bounced back from his 2009 knockout loss to Nate Marquardt with a workmanlike three-round unanimous decision win over Dan Miller.

Former UFC welterweight champion Matt Serra's first birthday gift to his daughter came a week early, as he drilled out a devastating first-round knockout victory over Frank Trigg, which ensured that "The Terror" would be unscathed for little Angelina's party.

Knockout of the Night: Serra vs. Trigg

When the heat was on, Mac Danzig delivered, as *The Ultimate Fighter 6* winner broke a three-fight losing streak with an impressive unanimous decision win over Justin Buchholz.

Melvin Guillard's debut with the Greg Jackson camp was a successful one, as "The Young Assassin" scored a close, but unanimous, decision win over debuting Brazilian Ronys Torres.

Veteran lightweight Rob Emerson kept *The Ultimate Fighter 8* finalist Phillipe Nover winless in the Octagon as he scored a steady but unspectacular unanimous decision victory.

Former NCAA Division I National champion wrestler Phil Davis didn't look like a UFC debutant with only four previous fights to his name as he made quite an impression with a dominant three-round unanimous decision win over Brian Stann.

North Dakota's Chris Tuchscherer nabbed his first UFC win in heavyweight action, surviving a late surge from Tim Hague to take a three-round majority decision.

Unheralded and unknown, Joey Beltran entered the Octagon after only a week's notice to replace Mostapha Al-Turk against highly-touted Rolles Gracie, but by the time the bout ended, fight fans found out who the California power hitter was, as he stopped Gracie in the second round to spoil the debut of the first Gracie to compete in the UFC since Hall of Famer Royce.

One Hit Wonder: Rolles Gracie

Rolles Gracie couldn't match the success of his cousin, as he gassed out after a strong start and was stopped in the second round. He was released from the UFC after the fight.

UFC 110 *Nogueira vs. Velasquez*

20 Feb. 2010

Acer Arena, Sydney, Australia

Debut: James Te Huna

Fighters			Division	Method	Time	Round
Main Card						
Cain Velasquez	def.	Minotauro Nogueira	Heavyweight	Knockout	2:20	1
Wanderlei Silva	def.	Michael Bisping	Middleweight	Unanimous Decision	—	3
George Sotiropoulos	def.	Joe Stevenson	Lightweight	Unanimous Decision	—	3
Ryan Bader	def.	Keith Jardine	Light Heavyweight	Knockout	2:10	3
Mirko Cro Cop	def.	Anthony Perosh	Heavyweight	Technical Knockout - Doctor Stoppage	5:00	2
Preliminary Card						
Krzysztof Soszynski	def.	Stephan Bonnar	Light Heavyweight	Technical Knockout - Cut	1:04	3
Chris Lytle	def.	Brian Foster	Welterweight	Submission - Kneebar	1:41	1
CB Dollaway	def.	Goran Reljic	Middleweight	Unanimous Decision	—	3
James Te Huna	def.	Igor Pokrajac	Light Heavyweight	Technical Knockout	3:26	3

If there were any doubts that Cain Velasquez was the real deal, the unbeaten phenom answered them emphatically in the UFC's first event in Australia as he scored a spectacular first-round knockout of future Hall of Famer Antonio Rodrigo "Minotauro" Nogueira in the UFC 110 main event at Acer Arena.

Knockout of the Night: Velasquez vs. Minotauro

Velasquez was sharp from the start, and after getting into a nice rhythm, he landed with a thudding left-right-left combination to the head that dropped Minotauro hard to the mat. A ferocious barrage of ground strikes followed and forced referee Herb Dean to halt the bout at the 2:20 mark.

With losses in three of his last four fights, PRIDE legend Wanderlei Silva felt the pressure heading into his UFC 110 co-main event against Michael Bisping, but with flashes of his ferocious brilliance late in rounds two and three, he was able to eke out a close, but unanimous, decision over "The Count" at Acer Arena.

Scores were 29-28 across the board for Silva.

Bisping walked right at Silva to start the bout, and after some tentative standup, he surprised "The Axe Murderer" at the one-minute mark with a takedown. Silva got right back to his feet and began his own stalking of "The Count". Bisping again scored with a takedown midway through the round but was unable to keep his foe on the mat.

Bisping continued to stand in the pocket with Silva in round two, eventually getting a takedown with under two minutes left. Once standing, Silva was still throwing sporadic bombs, but he wasn't landing enough to put Bisping down or to hurt him. Strangely enough, the end almost came in the final seconds when Silva responded to a Bisping takedown attempt with a tight guillotine choke that was interrupted only by the bell.

Silva opened up the final round with leg kicks, adding in the occasional punch upstairs. Bisping was standing in front of Silva, but not being active enough. With the crowd chanting his name, Silva moved forward, looking to land a big right hand, and just as the bout was ready to conclude, he finally hit paydirt with the right, dropping Bisping. A final left did even more damage, but then the bell intervened, sending the bout to the judges.

If George Sotiropoulos was awed by the idea of being the leading man for Australia in the first UFC event "Down Under", he didn't show it once the bell rang, as he scored the most impressive victory of his career, a shutout three-round decision win over longtime lightweight contender Joe Stevenson.

Fight of the Night: Sotiropoulos vs. Stevenson

For 12 minutes, unbeaten Ryan Bader had a tough time figuring out the riddle of perennial light heavyweight contender Keith Jardine, but in the next 10 seconds, the former Arizona State standout found the opening he needed and he made the most of it, stopping "The Dean of Mean" in the third round.

Sydney's own Anthony Perosh showed the heart of a lion when he agreed to fight on the UFC 110 card on just days notice, but veteran heavyweight contender Mirko Cro Cop was too much for him, stopping him in two rounds.

Submission of the Night: Lytle vs. Foster

Known for his striking prowess, welterweight vet Chris "Lights Out" Lytle went to Plan B at UFC 110, submitting Brian Foster with a first-round kneebar.

A clash of heads ended the entertaining light heavyweight bout between Krzysztof Soszynski and Stephan Bonnar early, with the final verdict being a third-round TKO win for Soszynski after a cut on Bonnar's forehead was judged to be too severe for him to continue.

Former *Ultimate Fighter* finalist CB Dollaway continued to show the progression of his fight game as he spoiled Goran Reljic's middleweight debut and his perfect record, scoring a unanimous decision victory.

The opener felt more like a main event, and rightfully so, as Australia based New Zealander James Te Huna gave the local fans what they wanted as he halted Igor Pokrajac in the third round of their light heavyweight bout.

UFC Live On Versus 1

Vera vs. Jones

21 March 2010

1STBANK Center, Broomfield, CO

Debuts: Darren Elkins, Daniel Roberts, Julio Paulino

Fighters			Division	Method	Time	Round
Main Card						
Jon Jones	def.	Brandon Vera	Light Heavyweight	Technical Knockout	3:19	1
Junior dos Santos	def.	Gabriel Gonzaga	Heavyweight	Knockout	3:53	1
Cheick Kongo	def.	Paul Buentello	Heavyweight	Submission - Strikes	1:16	3
Alessio Sakara	def.	James Irvin	Middleweight	Technical Knockout	3:01	1
Preliminary Card						
Clay Guida	def.	Shannon Gugerty	Lightweight	Submission - Arm Triangle Choke	3:40	2
Vladimir Matyushenko	def.	Eliot Marshall	Light Heavyweight	Split Decision	—	3
Darren Elkins	def.	Duane Ludwig	Lightweight	Technical Knockout - Injury	0:44	1
John Howard	def.	Daniel Roberts	Welterweight	Knockout	2:01	1
Brendan Schaub	def.	Chase Gormley	Heavyweight	Technical Knockout	0:47	1
Mike Pierce	def.	Julio Paulino	Welterweight	Unanimous Decision	—	3
Jason Brilz	def.	Eric Schafer	Light Heavyweight	Unanimous Decision	—	3

There is no question. Jon Jones is the real deal. For evidence, look no further than the New Yorker's first-round TKO of perennial contender Brandon Vera, which not only lifted his record to 10-1, but lifted him into the upper echelon of the 205-pound weight class in the first UFC Live event at 1STBANK Center.

Knockout of the Night: Jones vs. Vera

"I try not to pay attention to it (the hype), but I'm aware that it's there," said the 22-year-old Jones. "I just want to try to live up to my potential."

Right now, that potential seems limitless.

The fighters immediately engaged in the middle of the Octagon, with Jones drawing first blood with a takedown of Vera. Vera fought his way back up, but moments later Jones took him back to the canvas. While there, Vera fired off strikes from the bottom position as Jones tried to land the one big shot from the top. In the midst of the action, Vera drilled Jones with an illegal upkick to the head, drawing a point deduction from referee Herb Dean.

When the action resumed on the mat, Jones again worked his strikes while Vera kept his eyes open for a possible submission. Yet just when it looked like the action was going to stall, Jones fired off a flush left elbow to the jaw. Vera winced and turned his head to the side, and Jones pounced, firing off strike after strike, and with Vera not answering back, Dean halted the bout at 3:19 of the opening round.

Brazilian bomber Junior dos Santos added another high-profile name to his resume as he knocked out former world title challenger Gabriel Gonzaga in the first round of their UFC Live co-main event.

Knockout of the Night: dos Santos vs. Gonzaga

In a battle of heavyweight strikers, France's Cheick Kongo threw a wrench into the works, using a ground and pound strategy to take Paul Buentello out of his element and score a third-round victory over "The Headhunter".

Italy's Alessio Sakara spoiled James Irvin's middleweight debut in the main card opener, showing off his boxing skills in scoring a first-round TKO over "The Sandman".

After a rough 2009 campaign that saw him lose two of three bouts, lightweight contender Clay Guida returned to form on the inaugural UFC Live card with an impressive second-round submission win over Shannon Gugerty.

Submission of the Night: Guida vs. Gugerty

Welterweight prospect John "Doomsday" Howard made it four in a row in the UFC with a devastating first-round knockout of UFC debutant Daniel "Ninja" Roberts.

The Ultimate Fighter 10 finalist Brendan Schaub didn't want to disappoint his home state fans in his contest against Chase Gormley, and he certainly lived up to all expectations, as he blitzed his foe and stopped him in under a minute, much to the delight of the Colorado faithful.

Hometown favorite Eliot Marshall saw his three-fight UFC winning streak snapped in light heavyweight action, as veteran Vladimir Matyushenko scored a three-round split decision victory.

A freak ankle injury during a takedown forced a premature halt to the lightweight bout between Duane Ludwig and Darren Elkins, awarding Elkins the fight via first-round TKO.

Up-and-comer Mike Pierce sailed to victory in his welterweight bout with Julio Paulino, spoiling the Alaskan's Octagon debut via a shutout three-round unanimous decision.

In the light heavyweight opener, Nebraska's Jason Brilz got back in the win column after his September 2009 loss to Eliot Marshall, pounding out a hard-fought three-round unanimous decision win over Eric "Red" Schafer.

Knockout of the Night (Not Pictured): Howard vs. Roberts

UFC 111 *St-Pierre vs. Hardy*

27 March 2010

Prudential Center, Newark, NJ

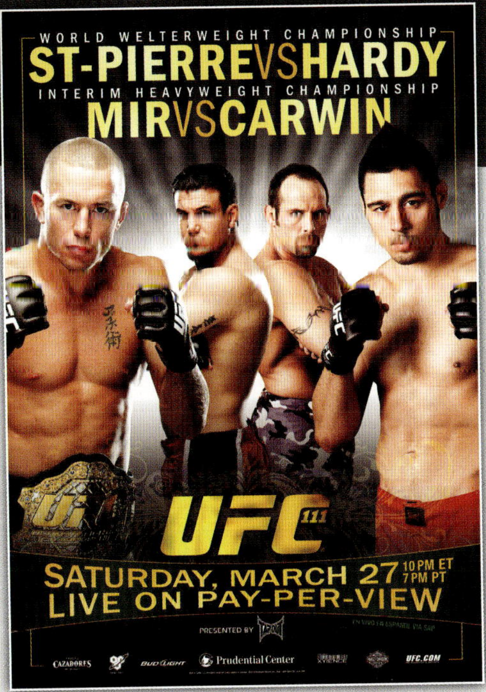

Debut: Greg Soto

Fighters			Division	Method	Time	Round
Main Card						
Georges St-Pierre	def.	Dan Hardy	Welterweight	Unanimous Decision	—	5
Shane Carwin	def.	Frank Mir	Heavyweight	Knockout	3:48	1
Kurt Pellegrino	def.	Fabricio Camoes	Lightweight	Submission - Rear Naked Choke	4:20	2
Jon Fitch	def.	Ben Saunders	Welterweight	Unanimous Decision	—	3
Jim Miller	def.	Mark Bocek	Lightweight	Unanimous Decision	—	3
Preliminary Card						
Nate Diaz	def.	Rory Markham	Catchweight	Technical Knockout	2:47	1
Ricardo Almeida	def.	Matt Brown	Welterweight	Submission - Rear Naked Choke	3:30	2
Rousimar Palhares	def.	Tomasz Drwal	Middleweight	Submission - Heel Hook	0:45	1
Jared Hamman	def.	Rodney Wallace	Light Heavyweight	Unanimous Decision	—	3
Matthew Riddle	def.	Greg Soto	Welterweight	Opponent Disqualified	1:30	3

After a gutsy effort by Dan Hardy, England may still belong to him, but Georges St-Pierre had the rest of the world wrapped up as he defended his UFC welterweight championship for the fourth time with a shutout five-round decision win.

St-Pierre was all business, taking the Nottingham native to the canvas moments into the bout. St-Pierre quickly moved to side control, then took Hardy's back as he tried to escape. Hardy was able to elude trouble on the mat, but as he escaped and got to his feet, St-Pierre made it a brief respite as he took "The Outlaw" back down. With 1:30 left, St-Pierre got into the mount position before again taking Hardy's back. A late armbar attempt by the champion appeared to spell the end, but the challenger gamely got free.

After his first-round dominance, St-Pierre went back to what was already working in round two, taking Hardy down one minute into the second stanza and keeping him on the mat for much of the round.

St-Pierre grounded Hardy again in round three, this time posturing up to add some more muscle to his strikes. Hardy, not surprisingly, remained game—even trying to grab the Canadian's arm for a submission attempt—but his odds of pulling off the upset victory were dwindling with each punch. With 90 seconds left, St-Pierre started working for the finish, but he was unable to break his foe.

Barely breathing heavy, St-Pierre ran through the championship rounds with more takedowns and ground work. Hardy's attempts to get back to his feet were rebuffed, but he wouldn't give in, even after a tight kimura attempt by St-Pierre that should have ended matters. It was a small battle won for Hardy, who, though lasting the distance, was simply unable to deal with the ground attack of St-Pierre.

Scores were 50-43, 50-44 and 50-45.

Knockout of the Night: Carwin vs. Mir

At UFC 111, Shane Carwin was extended past the two-minute, 11-second mark for the first time in his career, but there was no fade, no sudden implosion, only more of the same from the Colorado giant as he earned the interim UFC heavyweight championship with a first-round knockout of Frank Mir.

"It's a lifetime of work right here…I'm speechless," said Carwin. The victory now set up a bout with current heavyweight boss Brock Lesnar, whose bout with diverticulitis forced the creation of the interim title.

Submission of the Night: Pellegrino vs. Camoes

Jersey shore standout Kurt Pellegrino continued his rise up the lightweight ranks as he rebounded from some dicey moments in the first round to submit Brazil's Fabricio Camoes in the second.

When Thiago Alves was forced to withdraw from his welterweight bout against Jon Fitch, his American Top Team teammate Ben Saunders eagerly requested the bout. He may be rethinking that gutsy call after being on the short end of a dominant three-round decision win by Fitch.

Whippany, New Jersey lightweight Jim Miller was victorious in the main card opener as he pulled off a three-round unanimous decision win over always tough Mark Bocek.

When Rory Markham tipped the scales at 177 pounds for his welterweight bout with Nate Diaz, who was making his debut in the division, it was assumed that the former lightweight was going to have some difficulty dealing with the strength and power of the veteran knockout artist. But it was Diaz laying the hurt down on Markham as he scored a first-round TKO win.

Ricardo Almeida's welterweight debut was a successful one, as the former middleweight contender thrilled the fans in his adopted home of New Jersey with a second-round submission of Matt Brown.

Brazilian middleweight Rousimar Palhares scored a huge win in his preliminary bout, impressively submitting Tomasz Drwal with a heel hook in less than a minute.

Light heavyweight prospect Jared Hamman earned his first UFC victory, scoring a unanimous decision over Rodney Wallace in a furiously paced three-rounder.

In the opener, Matthew Riddle got the victory over Point Pleasant, New Jersey's Greg Soto via third-round disqualification after Soto landed an illegal upkick.

Fight of the Night: Hamman vs. Wallace

10 BIZARRE MOMENTS

GERARD GORDEAU GIVES TEILA TULI SOME FREE DENTAL WORK

It was the world's first exposure to the Ultimate Fighting Championship in November of 1993, and what an impression it was, as Gerard Gordeau sent Teila Tuli's tooth flying from his mouth with a kick (while Tuli was down, no less) that let everyone know that this wasn't some gimmick—this event was for real.

KEVIN RANDLEMAN TAKES ON PIPES...AND LOSES

Former Ohio State wrestling star Kevin Randleman was the UFC heavyweight champion and big things were expected from "The Monster". But first he would have to get past Pedro "The Rock" Rizzo in his first title defense at UFC 24. Unfortunately, Randleman had another issue to deal with before he even made it to the Octagon when he slipped on some pipes backstage and hit his head on the concrete floor, knocking him unconscious and making him the first fighter in history to get knocked out BEFORE his fight.

THE "JUST BLEED" GUY

Shirtless, with a drink in his hand, and painted with "UFC" on his forehead and "just bleed" on his chest, the "just bleed" guy probably hit all the bases when it came to the stereotypical early UFC fan. Luckily, we all got to see him immortalized when he was put on camera during the introduction of the Mark Kerr vs. Greg Stott bout at UFC 15 in Bay St. Louis, Mississippi. Mention him to any longtime fan, and they'll remember him, with current UFC middleweight Tom Lawlor even paying homage to him during the weigh-in for his UFC 100 bout against CB Dollaway.

JEFF MONSON CHANNELS JOHN LENNON BEFORE TITLE FIGHT

The walkout song: not only does it get the crowd pumped up and ready for the fight, but it can motivate a fighter. On November 18, 2006, Jeff Monson, always one to follow the beat of his own drummer, used John Lennon's *Imagine* to lead him into the Octagon before he challenged Tim Sylvia for the UFC heavyweight title.

KEITH HACKNEY SLAYS THE GIANT

When 5' 11", 200-pound Keith Hackney was matched up against 6' 8", 600-pound Emmanuel Yarborough at UFC 3 in 1994, one of three things probably popped into everyone's head: 1) Someone didn't like Keith Hackney, 2) The matchmaker certainly had a sense of humor or 3) How would Hackney avoid getting destroyed by this mountain of a man? But then the bell rang and Hackney dropped Yarborough with the first right hand he landed. A seemingly endless array of punches followed, with Hackney eventually winning at the 1:59 mark. David 1, Goliath 0.

PETE SELL SNATCHES DEFEAT FROM THE JAWS OF VICTORY

There was never such a swing in emotions as when Pete Sell fought Scott Smith in 2006. It was the second round of what had been an action-packed standup battle, and the two buddies continued to throw caution to the wind, much to the delight of the crowd. While it looked like Smith was pulling into the lead, Sell fired back with a shot to the body that hurt Smith and sent him reeling backward. The end was probably a punch or two away, and Sell knew it. But in his haste to finish, he got careless, and Smith—who admitted he had only one punch left in him—swung for the fences and scored the improbable KO win.

THE BUFFER 360

UFC 100 was the biggest event in UFC history, and in the weeks leading up to the bout, many wondered whether Octagon announcer Bruce Buffer would up the ante on his 180° technique of introducing the fighters to do what was going to be dubbed the Buffer 360. During his introduction of heavyweight champion Brock Lesnar, it happened, and the Buffer 360 became the talk of MMA message boards around the internet.

BJ PENN HAS LEFT THE BUILDING

How do you top an 11-second knockout over a world-class contender like Caol Uno? If you're BJ Penn, you finish the job and immediately run out of the Octagon and back to your locker room without interviews, congratulatory handshakes or poses for the camera. This was Penn getting caught up in the emotion of the moment and it firmly established him as one of the UFC's legendary free spirits.

Photography by: Susumu Nagao

BUSTAMANTE GETS TWO TAPS FOR THE PRICE OF ONE

Renowned ground fighter Murilo Bustamante has the jiu-jitsu skills to force anyone to tap out. But when he defended his UFC middleweight title against Matt Lindland at UFC 37 in May of 2002, he had to do it twice in one fight. Early in the bout, he caught Lindland in an armbar, and after an apparent tap, he released the hold. Lindland protested and referee John McCarthy decided to restart the action, but Bustamante was able to pull off the submission again, this time via guillotine choke in the third round.

WHO WAS KNOCKED OUT FIRST?

In the record books, it will be noted as the night a new era began, but back when Matt Hughes defeated Carlos Newton at UFC 34 in 2001 for the 170-pound title, it was one of the more controversial endings to a fight. Some believed Hughes was choked unconscious by a triangle choke when he slammed Newton to the mat for a finishing KO. Looking at it again, it appears that Hughes was still awake because he had the presence of mind to step back before lowering the boom, but he was certainly on his way to la-la land before he pulled off the miracle finish.

UFC Fight Night 21

Florian vs. Gomi

31 March 2010

Bojangles Coliseum, Charlotte, NC

Debuts: Takanori Gomi, Mario Miranda, Charlie Brenneman, Jason High

Fighters			Division	Method	Time	Round
Main Card						
Kenny Florian	def.	Takanori Gomi	Lightweight	Submission - Rear Naked Choke	2:52	3
Roy Nelson	def.	Stefan Struve	Heavyweight	Technical Knockout	0:39	1
Jorge Rivera	def.	Nate Quarry	Middleweight	Technical Knockout	0:29	2
Ross Pearson	def.	Dennis Siver	Lightweight	Unanimous Decision	—	3
Preliminary Card						
Andre Winner	def.	Rafaello Oliveira	Lightweight	Unanimous Decision	—	3
Jacob Volkmann	def.	Ronys Torres	Lightweight	Split Decision	—	3
Nik Lentz	def.	Rob Emerson	Lightweight	Unanimous Decision	—	3
Gleison Tibau	def.	Caol Uno	Lightweight	Technical Knockout	4:13	1
Yushin Okami	def.	Lucio Linhares	Middleweight	Technical Knockout - Doctor Stoppage	2:47	2
Gerald Harris	def.	Mario Miranda	Middleweight	Technical Knockout	4:49	1
Charlie Brenneman	def.	Jason High	Welterweight	Unanimous Decision	—	3

For two rounds Kenny Florian looked like a southpaw Larry Holmes as he peppered former PRIDE star Takanori Gomi with jab after jab. In the third, the lightweight contender took the fight to the mat and finished it there, spoiling Gomi's long-awaited UFC debut via submission.

Submission of the Night: Florian vs. Gomi

The two southpaws circled each other warily as the fight opened, with early strikes from both men coming up short. In the second minute, Florian began landing his punches and getting Gomi's attention, and the New Englander's tight defense deflected any return fire. As the round progressed, Florian's jabs began landing with increasing frequency, and the sporadic kick thrown in was scoring as well, capping off a dominant first five minutes.

Florian continued to pepper Gomi with jabs in the second round, with the Japanese star's lack of head movement making him an easy target. For his part, Gomi tried opening up more frequently in an effort to force Florian into a firefight, but his successes were few and far between, and his frustration was evident as he missed with a wide haymaker in the final minute.

With two rounds apparently in the bank, Florian looked for a takedown to start the final frame, yet was stopped in his tracks by Gomi. A minute in, Gomi landed with a solid combination, but was met with a successful takedown moments later for his trouble. Soon, Florian got the mount, and when Gomi gave up his back, Florian sunk in a rear naked choke that produced a tap out at the 2:52 mark of the third round.

The Ultimate Fighter 10 winner Roy Nelson quickly cut down Stefan "Skyscraper" Struve in the first round of their heavyweight bout.

Knockout of the Night: Nelson vs. Struve

After a power outage in the arena stalled the opening of the bout, Nelson and Struve went right to work when the lights came back on, with Nelson aggressively closing the distance. Once in range, Nelson struck, dropping his foe with a right hand. Struve was unable to recover, with a follow-up barrage of strikes bringing in referee Dan Miragliotta to halt the bout at the 39-second mark.

Veteran middleweight Jorge Rivera scored his third straight UFC victory in devastating fashion, stopping Nate Quarry in the second round with a blistering striking attack.

Fight of the Night: Pearson vs. Siver

The Ultimate Fighter 9 winner Ross Pearson continued to impress as he pounded out an exciting three-round unanimous decision win over always-tough Dennis Siver.

Japanese middleweight contender Yushin Okami put together one of his most impressive UFC performances to date at the Bojangles Coliseum as he halted Lucio Linhares in the second round after a clinic of precision striking.

British lightweight Andre Winner made it two in a row, following his knockout victory over Rolando Delgado with a three-round unanimous decision win over Rafaello Oliveira.

Jacob Volkmann scored his first UFC win in his lightweight debut, earning a three-round split decision over Brazil's Ronys Torres.

Nik Lentz got stronger as his fight with Rob Emerson went on, and he eventually pounded out a three-round unanimous decision victory to move to 2-0-1 in the UFC.

Brazilian jiu-jitsu black belt Gleison Tibau promised a knockout in his lightweight bout against Caol Uno and he delivered, finishing off the Japanese star late in the first round.

Gerald Harris made it two knockouts in two UFC tries, as he halted previously unbeaten debutant Mario Miranda in the first round of a back and forth middleweight scrap.

In a clash of debuting welterweights, Charlie Brenneman got his first Octagon victory, outpointing Jason High unanimously over three rounds.

One Hit Wonder: Jason High

UFC 112 *Invincible*

10 April 2010

Yas Island, Abu Dhabi, United Arab Emirates

Debut: Renzo Gracie

Fighters			Division	Method	Time	Round
Main Card						
Anderson Silva	def.	Demian Maia	Middleweight	Unanimous Decision	—	5
Frankie Edgar	def.	BJ Penn	Lightweight	Unanimous Decision	—	5
Matt Hughes	def.	Renzo Gracie	Welterweight	Technical Knockout	4:40	3
Rafael dos Anjos	def.	Terry Etim	Lightweight	Submission - Armbar	4:30	2
Mark Munoz	def.	Kendall Grove	Middleweight	Technical Knockout	2:50	2
Preliminary Card						
Phil Davis	def.	Alexander Gustafsson	Light Heavyweight	Submission - Anaconda Choke	4:55	1
Rick Story	def.	Nick Osipczak	Lightweight	Split Decision	—	3
DaMarques Johnson	def.	Brad Blackburn	Welterweight	Technical Knockout	2:08	3
Paul Kelly	def.	Matt Veach	Lightweight	Submission - Guillotine Choke	3.41	2
Jon Madsen	def.	Mostapha Al-Turk	Heavyweight	Unanimous Decision	—	3

UFC middleweight champion Anderson Silva's return to the Octagon after an eight-month absence wasn't as explosive as his previous battle with Forrest Griffin.

Not even close.

Although he retained his belt with a five-round unanimous decision victory over Demian Maia in the UFC 112 main event at Yas Island in Abu Dhabi, it was a bout filled with more stalemates than submissions, and more posing than punching, forcing Silva to apologize more than celebrate after the final bell sounded.

"Demain actually surprised me with some of his punches," said Silva. "I apologize to everybody; I don't know what got into me. I wasn't as humble as I should have been. It was just the ring rust and a little bit of everything. I can guarantee that next time it won't happen." Scores for Silva were 50-45 twice and 49-46.

There was plenty of drama in the co-main event though, as heavy underdog Frankie Edgar used a solid standup attack to score a five-round unanimous decision victory over BJ Penn to win the UFC lightweight championship. Scores were 50-45, 48-47, and 49-46 for Edgar.

Edgar made a concerted effort to stick and move in the bout, and though Penn remained patient, soon the points started adding up against him as the fight got into the later rounds. Through it all, Edgar seemed unbothered by the magnitude of the occasion, and he stuck to his game plan from rounds one through five as he shocked the MMA world with the biggest upset seen in quite some time.

Soon to be Hall of Famer Matt Hughes put a victory over another Gracie on his resume, spoiling the debut of Renzo Gracie via a third-round TKO. "I was pretty happy," said Hughes, who defeated Gracie's cousin Royce in 2006. "Renzo was throwing looping punches, so I tried to stay in close and keep things simple."

Submission of the Night: Dos Anjos vs. Etim

Brazil's Rafael dos Anjos continued to impress in lightweight action, submitting British prospect Terry Etim in the second round to score his third straight UFC win.

Fight of the Night: Munoz vs. Grove

Middleweight prospect Mark Munoz pulled off the biggest win of his young career, roaring back from a horrid first round to stop Kendall Grove via a ferocious second-round ground and pound attack.

"I was (hurt), but you have to have the will to survive in the cage," said Munoz. "You need that if you want to be a champion."

Preliminary action kicked off with a war of attrition between heavyweights Jon Madsen and Mostapha Al-Turk, with the unbeaten Madsen lasting out a 29-28 decision.

Thankfully, things picked up from there, as Paul Kelly submitted Matt Veach via guillotine choke at 3:41 of the second round, and DaMarques Johnson delivered the Knockout of the Night, finishing Brad Blackburn at 2:08 of the third stanza in welterweight action.

Knockout of the Night: Johnson vs. Blackburn

Also in the 170-pound division, Rick Story pulled out a close split decision win over Nick Osipczak by scores of 29-28 twice, and 28-29, and in a light heavyweight bout, "Mr. Wonderful" Phil Davis remained unbeaten with a anaconda choke submission of Alexander Gustafsson that came at 4:55 of the opening round.

UFC 113 *Machida vs. Shogun 2*

08
May
2010

Bell Centre, Montreal, Quebec, Canada

Fighters			Division	Method	Time	Round
Main Card						
Mauricio Rua	def.	Lyoto Machida	Light Heavyweight	Knockout	3:34	1
Josh Koscheck	def.	Paul Daley	Welterweight	Unanimous Decision	—	3
Jeremy Stephens	def.	Sam Stout	Lightweight	Split Decision	—	3
Matt Mitrione	def.	Kimbo Slice	Heavyweight	Technical Knockout	4:24	2
Alan Belcher	def.	Patrick Cote	Middleweight	Submission - Rear Naked Choke	3:25	2
Preliminary Card						
Joe Doerksen	def.	Tom Lawlor	Middleweight	Submission - Rear Naked Choke	2:10	2
Marcus Davis	def.	Jonathan Goulet	Welterweight	Technical Knockout	1:23	2
Johny Hendricks	def.	TJ Grant	Welterweight	Majority Decision	—	3
Joey Beltran	def.	Tim Hague	Heavyweight	Unanimous Decision	—	3
Mike Guymon	def.	Yoshiyuki Yoshida	Welterweight	Unanimous Decision	—	3
John Salter	def.	Jason MacDonald	Middleweight	Technical Knockout - Injury	2:42	1

Mauricio "Shogun" Rua was once written off as a serious contender after he lost his UFC debut to Forrest Griffin in 2007. At UFC 113, Rua became the UFC light heavyweight champion of the world after a stunning first-round knockout of previously unbeaten Lyoto Machida.

The bout was a rematch of a UFC 104 bout that saw Machida win a disputed five-round unanimous decision over Rua. This time, he left no doubts or questions.

Rua opened the fight with a kick to the legs and one of his patented flurries. Machida fired back with a punch upstairs that got Rua's attention, but the Curitiba, Brazil native was clearly intent on pushing the action and keeping Machida on the defensive. Machida bravely stood in the pocket with his dangerous foe, but after missing a left hand, Rua clipped the champion with a right hand that dropped him to the mat. It was then that one of the game's great finishers showed his stuff once again as he went immediately into the mount position and fired off a crushing series of punches that forced referee Yves Lavigne to stop the fight at the 3:34 mark.

Knockout of the Night: Rua vs. Machida

Josh Koscheck incensed Montreal fans at the Bell Centre, not only by predicting that the Pittsburgh Penguins would defeat the beloved Canadiens in their Stanley Cup playoff series, but by scoring a shutout three-round unanimous decision over Paul Daley in the co-main event of UFC 113. It was a bout that will win no votes for Fight of the Year, but that did earn Koscheck a shot at Georges St-Pierre's welterweight title and a coaching spot against GSP on *The Ultimate Fighter 12.*

Unfortunately, the bout was marred by a post-fight sequence that saw Daley take a swing at Koscheck after the fight ended, prompting referee Dan Miragliotta to intervene and UFC President Dana White to release Daley from the UFC due to the cheap shot.

"I'm probably the most lenient guy in sports and this is probably one of the most lenient organizations, and we're all human, we all make mistakes, things happen…but there's no excuse for that," said White at the post-fight press conference. "These guys are professional athletes, and you don't ever hit a guy blatantly after the bell like that, whether you're frustrated or not."

Fight of the Night: Stephens vs. Stout

Jeremy Stephens and Sam Stout left it all in the Octagon during their three-round lightweight war, with Stephens' heavier hands proving to be the difference as he pounded out a three-round split decision victory.

It was one of the most highly anticipated bouts on the UFC 113 card, and heavyweights Matt Mitrione and Kimbo Slice certainly entertained the Bell Centre faithful, with Mitrione outlasting Slice and showing off a varied array of skills before halting his *Ultimate Fighter 10* castmate in the second round.

Rising middleweight star Alan Belcher scored the most impressive victory of his UFC career, submitting former middleweight title challenger Patrick Cote in the second round.

Submission of the Night: Belcher vs. Cote

Middleweight prospect Tom Lawlor had the better Octagon entrance, but Manitoba veteran Joe Doerksen had the better exit, as he roared back from a shaky first round to submit *The Ultimate Fighter 8* alum in the second stanza.

Welterweight veteran Marcus Davis halted his two-fight losing streak in style, stopping Jonathan Goulet in the second round.

Unbeaten Johny Hendricks kept that perfect record intact with a hard-fought three-round majority decision win over Nova Scotia's TJ Grant in a fast-paced battle between two of the welterweight division's top prospects.

Joey Beltran made it two in a row in the Octagon, following up his win over Rolles Gracie earlier in 2010 with an entertaining three-round unanimous decision win over Edmonton's Tim Hague.

It was an emotional win for longtime MMA veteran Mike "Joker" Guymon, who scored his first UFC victory with a workmanlike three-round unanimous decision win over Yoshiyuki Yoshida.

The return of Jason MacDonald to the UFC came to an abrupt and unfortunate conclusion, as a knee injury rendered the Edmonton middleweight unable to continue in the first round.

UFC 114 *Rampage vs. Evans*

29 May 2010

MGM Grand Garden Arena, Las Vegas, NV

Debuts: Waylon Lowe, Cyrille Diabate

Fighters			Division	Method	Time	Round
Main Card						
Rashad Evans	def.	Quinton Jackson	Light Heavyweight	Unanimous Decision	—	3
Michael Bisping	def.	Dan Miller	Middleweight	Unanimous Decision	—	3
Mike Russow	def.	Todd Duffee	Heavyweight	Knockout	2:35	3
Antonio Rogerio Nogueira	def.	Jason Brilz	Light Heavyweight	Split Decision	—	3
John Hathaway	def.	Diego Sanchez	Welterweight	Unanimous Decision	—	3
Preliminary Card						
Dong Hyun Kim	def.	Amir Sadollah	Welterweight	Unanimous Decision	—	3
Efrain Escudero	def.	Dan Lauzon	Lightweight	Unanimous Decision	—	3
Melvin Guillard	def.	Waylon Lowe	Lightweight	Knockout	3:28	1
Cyrille Diabate	def.	Luiz Cane	Light Heavyweight	Technical Knockout	2:13	1
Aaron Riley	def.	Joe Brammer	Lightweight	Unanimous Decision	—	3
Ryan Jensen	def.	Jesse Forbes	Middleweight	Submission - Guillotine Choke	1:06	1

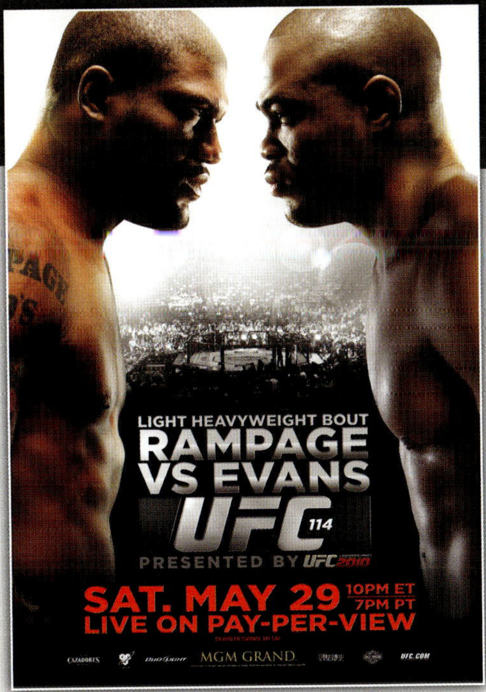

At times, the long-awaited grudge match between former light heavyweight champions "Suga" Rashad Evans and Quinton "Rampage" Jackson looked like the calm after the storm of trash talk and bad blood. An action-packed third round and a solidly executed gameplan from Evans will remain in the minds of fight fans as he pounded out a three-round unanimous decision win over his rival.

Scores were 30-27 twice and 29-28 for Evans.

Jackson, whose rivalry with Evans escalated when the two were coaches on the tenth season of *The Ultimate Fighter* reality show, raced across the Octagon at the bell to get in Evans' face, but it was Evans who got the first shot in, a lightning fast right hand that rocked Jackson and sent him sprawling into the cage. Jackson weathered the ensuing storm but wasn't able to get his offense in gear in the opening stanza.

There was more of the same in the second, as Evans smothered Jackson at every turn. In the third, Rampage came out determined to make something happen as he stalked his foe. With a minute gone, Jackson finally got his shot and took advantage of it, rocking and dropping Evans with a right hand.

A series of ground strikes followed and the end appeared to be near, but Evans was able to shake the cobwebs loose and make it back to his feet with 2:40 remaining. With under two minutes to go, Evans got a takedown and began raining punches down on Jackson, who was pinned against the fence. Jackson, game to the end, made it back to his feet, only to be taken down again by the rejuvenated Evans.

Michael Bisping was sharp, disciplined, and in fine form in his bout with Dan Miller, as he used a pinpoint striking attack to score a three-round unanimous decision victory over the New Jersey native.

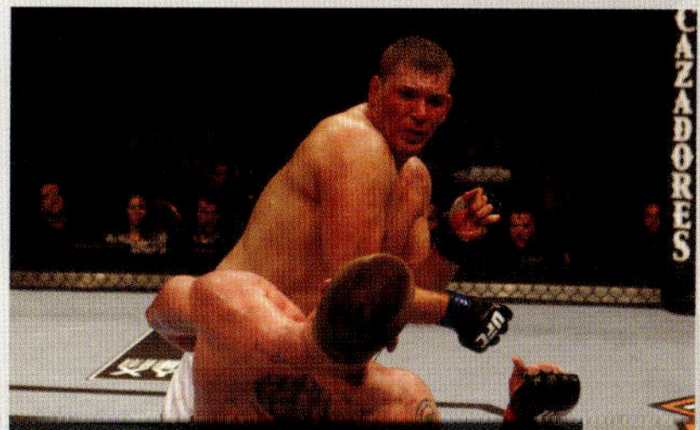

Knockout of the Night: Russow vs. Duffee

For 12 minutes and 30 seconds, highly-touted Todd Duffee was sailing to his second UFC win in as many tries. In what turned out to be the final five seconds of the bout, Mike Russow turned the tables and turned Duffee's lights out with a stirring third round knockout victory.

When Jason Brilz was brought in as a late replacement for the injured Forrest Griffin to face Antonio Rogerio Nogueira, many thought the Omaha product was a lamb being led to slaughter. Undeterred, Brilz thought he was going to win, and the 6.5-to-1 underdog almost did, putting together a career-best performance before falling short on the scorecards via an unpopular three-round split decision that was booed by the packed house.

Fight of the Night: Nogueira vs. Brilz

John Hathaway may not be the flashiest or most brash fighter to emerge from the United Kingdom, but the British prospect may eventually turn out to be the best, if his form in shutting out perennial contender Diego Sanchez is any indication.

Dong Hyun Kim kept it conservative in his welterweight bout against Amir Sadollah, but his smothering ground attack was enough to allow him to pound out a three-round unanimous decision win over the former *Ultimate Fighter* winner.

Efrain Escudero brought a disciplined gameplan into the Octagon against former training partner Dan Lauzon and he executed it perfectly to claim a three-round unanimous decision victory.

Submission of the Night: Jensen vs. Forbes

Melvin Guillard continued his ride up the 155-pound ladder, winning his fifth bout in his last six tries with a first-round knockout of Octagon newcomer Waylon Lowe.

Cyrille Diabate made a successful entry into the UFC as he rebounded from an early knockdown to stop Brazil's Luiz Cane via strikes later in the opening round.

Aaron Riley got back in the win column in his first bout since a loss to Ross Pearson at UFC 105 with a methodical three-round unanimous decision victory over Joe Brammer.

It was one of the wildest 30-second turnarounds seen in a long time as Ryan Jensen bounced back from an almost certain defeat to submit Jesse Forbes in the first round of the middleweight opener.

UFC 115 *Liddell vs. Franklin*

12 June 2010

General Motors Place, Vancouver, British Columbia, Canada

Debut: Claude Patrick

Fighters			Division	Method	Time	Round
Main Card						
Rich Franklin	def.	Chuck Liddell	Light Heavyweight	Knockout	4:55	1
Mirko Cro Cop	def.	Pat Barry	Heavyweight	Submission - Rear Naked Choke	4:30	3
Martin Kampmann	def.	Paulo Thiago	Welterweight	Unanimous Decision	—	3
Ben Rothwell	def.	Gilbert Yvel	Heavyweight	Unanimous Decision	—	3
Carlos Condit	def.	Rory MacDonald	Welterweight	Technical Knockout	4:53	3
Preliminary Card						
Evan Dunham	def.	Tyson Griffin	Lightweight	Split Decision	—	3
Matt Wiman	def.	Mac Danzig	Lightweight	Submission - Guillotine Choke	1:45	1
Mario Miranda	def.	David Loiseau	Middleweight	Technical Knockout	4:07	2
James Wilks	def.	Peter Sobotta	Welterweight	Unanimous Decision	—	3
Claude Patrick	def.	Ricardo Funch	Welterweight	Submission - Guillotine Choke	1:48	2
Mike Pyle	def.	Jesse Lennox	Welterweight	Submission - Triangle Choke	4:44	3

With a broken left arm but an unyielding will to win, Rich Franklin scored perhaps his most important victory since he took the middleweight title in 2005, as he knocked out returning Hall of Famer Chuck "The Iceman" Liddell in devastating fashion in the first round of their UFC 115 main event.

Knockout of the Night: Franklin vs. Liddell

"I broke my hand before and didn't quit," said Franklin with a smile after the bout. The injury occurred earlier in the first round due to a Liddell kick, but Franklin not only soldiered on, he knocked out one of the sport's most feared strikers in a bittersweet victory for fans of Liddell, who saw the 40-year-old light heavyweight legend lose his third straight fight by knockout.

Franklin's gameplan was clear at the outset: quick left hands down the middle with leg kicks to keep Liddell from setting his feet to throw his lethal right hand. Liddell adjusted well to this strategy, using his own kicks more than we've seen recently, and when the two did exchange, Liddell still had some speed on the fastball. Just before the midway point, Liddell was able to get the fight to the mat, another wrinkle in his game that had been missing, but as the two rose, Liddell emerged with a cut between his eyes.

Encouraged, Franklin began to let his hands go a little more, but with 1:10 left, Liddell hit paydirt with the right hand, staggering Franklin briefly. The Ohio native recovered quickly and came firing back, and as Liddell looked to engage, he walked into a flush right hand that dropped him to the mat. Liddell's head hit the mat hard, and referee Herb Dean halted the bout at the 4:55 mark, giving Franklin new life in the light heavyweight title picture.

Submission of the Night: Cro Cop vs. Barry

Anyone who proclaimed that the UFC 115 co-main event between world-class strikers Mirko Cro Cop and Pat Barry was going to go nearly three rounds would have been called crazy. Anyone who predicted it would end by submission would have been committed. That's just what happened as Cro Cop rose from two first-round knockdowns to submit Barry in the final round of a memorable heavyweight scrap.

It may not have been the most explosive performance of Martin Kampmann's career, but it was certainly one of the welterweight contender's most dominating and impressive ones as he outpointed Paulo Thiago unanimously over three rounds.

It wasn't pretty, especially in the second half of the fight, but Ben Rothwell got his first UFC win as he scored a three-round unanimous decision over Gilbert Yvel.

Fight of the Night: Condit vs. MacDonald

Kelowna, British Columbia's Rory MacDonald may have suffered his first pro loss in the main card opener, but his display of toughness against veteran Carlos Condit will certainly be remembered by fight fans as much as Condit's impressive finish in a third round that broke open an exciting welterweight battle.

The wins keep getting bigger and bigger for rising lightweight star Evan Dunham, who kept his perfect record intact with a three-round split decision win over highly regarded contender Tyson Griffin in UFC 115 prelim action.

What was promising to be an interesting lightweight scrap between Matt Wiman and Mac Danzig instead ended prematurely after referee Yves Lavigne mistakenly thought Danzig had been rendered unconscious by a Wiman guillotine choke and halted the bout in the first round.

It was a disappointing Octagon return for Montreal's David Loiseau, as "The Crow" was stopped in the second round of a one-sided fight by Brazil's "Super" Mario Miranda.

The Ultimate Fighter 9 winner James Wilks nabbed his first post-*TUF* victory in welterweight action, outpointing Peter Sobotta unanimously over three rounds.

Toronto's Claude Patrick made his long-awaited Octagon debut, and the welterweight delivered for his home country fans, submitting Brazil's Ricardo Funch in the second round.

Veteran Mike Pyle lived up to his nickname "Quicksand", luring Jesse Lennox in and then trapping him in a triangle choke that produced a submission victory with less than 30 seconds left in the third round.

The Ultimate Fighter 11 Finale

Team Liddell vs. Team Ortiz

19 June 2010

The Pearl at The Palms, Las Vegas, NV

Debuts: Court McGee, Kris McCray, Jamie Yager, Rich Attonito, Mark Holst, Brad Tavares, Seth Baczynski, Kyle Noke, Josh Bryant, James Hammortree, Chris Camozzi, Travis Browne

Fighters			Division	Method	Time	Round
Main Card						
Court McGee	def.	Kris McCray	Middleweight	Submission - Rear Naked Choke	3:41	2
Matt Hamill	def.	Keith Jardine	Light Heavyweight	Majority Decision	—	3
Chris Leben	def.	Aaron Simpson	Middleweight	Technical Knockout	4:17	2
Dennis Siver	def.	Spencer Fisher	Light Heavyweight	Unanimous Decision	—	3
Rich Attonito	def.	Jamie Yager	Middleweight	Technical Knockout	4:25	2
Preliminary Card						
John Gunderson	def.	Mark Holst	Light Heavyweight	Unanimous Decision	—	3
Brad Tavares	def.	Seth Baczynski	Middleweight	Unanimous Decision	—	3
Kyle Noke	def.	Josh Bryant	Middleweight	Technical Knockout	3:12	2
Chris Camozzi	def.	James Hammortree	Middleweight	Unanimous Decision	—	3
Travis Browne	def.	James McSweeney	Heavyweight	Technical Knockout	4:32	1

The journey of Court McGee from drug addict to *The Ultimate Fighter* reality show was well-documented. At The Pearl at The Palms on June 19, his inspiring tale had a fitting finish, as he submitted Kris "Savage" McCray to win the season 11 title and a UFC contract.

Submission of the Night: McGee vs. McCray

After some standup to begin the bout, McGee took control as soon as the fight hit the mat, landing with ground strikes until McCray was able to get back on his feet and fire off punches. McGee immediately closed the gap, taking his foe right back to the mat. The resilient McCray worked himself upright, and resumed swinging away, but his defense was porous and McGee countered him well until the bell.

McCray did some good body work as the fighters locked up to start round two, but McGee's takedowns were proving to be a tough hurdle for "Savage" to overcome. On the mat, McGee looked for a choke from the mount position, and when that didn't work, he took his foe's back, but McCray used that opening to get back on his feet. That moment standing was short lived, as McGee scored another takedown. "The Crusher" proceeded to take McCray's back again, and this time he closed the show, sinking in a rear naked choke that produced a tap out at the 3:41 mark of the second round.

Fight of the Night: Hamill vs. Jardine

Following disappointing performances in their previous fights, both Keith Jardine and Matt Hamill needed to pull off something big in their light heavyweight bout, and they did, engaging in a memorable three-rounder won by Hamill via majority decision.

There's no substitute for experience, and *Ultimate Fighter 1* alum Chris Leben proved it in his bout against Aaron Simpson as he handed the middleweight prospect his first pro loss via second-round TKO.

Knockout of the Night:
Leben vs. Simpson

Germany's Dennis Siver scored the biggest win of his UFC career, surviving a bad cut over his left eye to pound out a close but unanimous decision over veteran contender Spencer Fisher in a hard-fought lightweight contest.

It took *TUF11* middleweight Rich Attonito a little while to warm up in the main card opener, but once he did, he was tough to stop as he halted castmate Jamie Yager with ground strikes in the second round.

Kyle Noke may not have won *The Ultimate Fighter 11*, but on the finale card he showed why he was seen as an early favorite on the show, scoring an impressive second-round TKO of semifinalist Josh Bryant.

Their first bout on *The Ultimate Fighter 11* was one of the most memorable of the season, and the second time around, Brad Tavares put an exclamation point on his second win over Seth Baczynski, scoring a three-round unanimous decision win.

Las Vegas lightweight John Gunderson spoiled the UFC debut of Ottawa's Mark Holst, winning a clear-cut three-round unanimous decision.

TUF11 middleweights Chris Camozzi and James Hammortree put on a crowd-pleasing three-rounder, with Camozzi emerging victorious via unanimous decision.

In a heavyweight bout, Octagon rookie Travis "Hapa" Browne kept his unbeaten record intact with a first-round stoppage of veteran James McSweeney.

One Hit Wonders: Jamie Yager, Seth Baczynski, Josh Bryant, James Hammortree

UFC 116 *Lesnar vs. Carwin*

03 July 2010

MGM Grand Garden Arena, Las Vegas, NV

Debuts: Ricardo Romero, Dave Branch, Karlos Vemola

Fighters			Division	Method	Time	Round
Main Card						
Brock Lesnar	def.	Shane Carwin	Heavyweight	Submission - Arm Triangle Choke	2:19	2
Chris Leben	def.	Yoshihiro Akiyama	Middleweight	Submission - Triangle Choke	4:40	3
Chris Lytle	def.	Matt Brown	Welterweight	Submission - Triangle/Armbar	2:02	2
Stephan Bonnar	def.	Krzysztof Soszynski	Light Heavyweight	Technical Knockout	3:08	2
George Sotiropoulos	def.	Kurt Pellegrino	Lightweight	Unanimous Decision	—	3
Preliminary Card						
Brendan Schaub	def.	Chris Tuchscherer	Heavyweight	Technical Knockout	1:07	1
Ricardo Romero	def.	Seth Petruzelli	Light Heavyweight	Submission - Armbar	3:05	2
Kendall Grove	def.	Goran Reljic	Middleweight	Split Decision	—	3
Gerald Harris	def.	Dave Branch	Middleweight	Knockout	2:35	3
Daniel Roberts	def.	Forrest Petz	Welterweight	Split Decision	—	3
Jon Madsen	def.	Karlos Vemola	Heavyweight	Unanimous Decision	—	3

For a few minutes in the first round of the UFC 116 main event, it looked like the heavy hands of Shane Carwin were going to forcibly remove the UFC heavyweight title from the grasp of Brock Lesnar. With an amazing show of heart and resilience, and a chin of steel, Lesnar survived the first round and then closed the show in the second with a submission victory that kept the belt around the waist of the premier heavyweight in the game today.

Submission of the Night: Lesnar vs. Carwin

"This isn't about me tonight," said Lesnar, who was forced to the sidelines for nearly a year due to a bout with diverticulitis. "This is about my family, my doctors, all my training partners and staff. I am blessed by God. I stand before you a humble champion, but I'm still the toughest SOB around."

At the bell, Carwin and Lesnar circled each other warily, Lesnar shooting out a couple jabs that fell short. As the champion moved closer, Carwin scored with a short right hand and Lesnar shot for a takedown that was turned away. In an ensuing exchange, Carwin rocked Lesnar with an uppercut and sent him sprawling across the Octagon. Carwin threw a series of unanswered blows but wasn't able to finish Lesnar off. Lesnar briefly cleared his head and tried to score with a knee, but Carwin got his foe to the mat and again began teeing off. Lesnar, his face now bloodied from a cut over his left eye, amazingly didn't give in to the increasing assault, doing just enough to keep referee Josh Rosenthal from stopping the fight. With less than two minutes left, Lesnar finally made his move and got back to his feet.

Lesnar smiled as the second round began and he touched gloves with Carwin at the bell. This time Lesnar made the move to get off first, and after a right hand didn't do the trick, a takedown moments later did. Now in control on the mat, Lesnar locked in an arm triangle with a little over three minutes left. Although Carwin gallantly tried to break loose, he was eventually forced to tap at the 2:19 mark.

Fight of the Night: Leben vs. Akiyama

It was the conclusion to one of the most amazing stretches in UFC history, and middleweight Chris Leben pulled it off, winning his second fight in two weeks by taking an action-packed war against Japanese contender Yoshihiro Akiyama via third-round submission.

Leben, *The Ultimate Fighter 1* alumnus who replaced the injured Wanderlei Silva in the UFC 116 bout, was coming off a knockout victory over Aaron Simpson on June 19, 2010.

After catching Leben's opening kick and putting him on the deck, Akiyama was able to land with the first blows of the fight, but Leben quickly rose and went back on the attack. Though he engaged, he got thrown to the mat for his trouble. While in the bottom position, Leben looked to trap Akiyama's arm on two occasions, but the Asian star broke loose and tried to return the favor. With 1:30 left, Leben pulled off an escape of his own, yet Akiyama kept the pressure on as he tried to lock in an arm triangle. Again, Leben got free, this time getting to his feet as well. It was Akiyama with the last word, though, as he scored with a throw just before the bell.

The fighters traded strikes early in round two, Akiyama landing with a spinning back fist and Leben scoring with his trademark left hand. Within moments, the two began slugging each other with flush shots, and Leben was taking the worst of it. Akiyama sensed this and followed up with a takedown on the now fatigued and bloodied Leben. With under a minute to go, the two again traded with reckless abandon. This time it was Leben forcing Akiyama to hold on until the bell.

With the crowd roaring, the two respectfully touched gloves to begin the third round and decided to continue where they left off. Leben held an early edge, but Akiyama was able to catch a kick and land a punch to get the fight back to where he wanted it—on the mat. Leben was busy from the bottom, again looking for his opponent's arm, but Akiyama wasn't having it, and he shook loose. Then the slugging continued, only this time it was as the two jostled on the canvas. Finally, Akiyama got sloppy and left his arm dangling in front of Leben for too long, and the Oregon native made the most of it, locking in an arm triangle that produced a tap out at the 4:40 mark.

After three straight losses, including a defeat against the man facing him at UFC 116, Krzysztof Soszynski, light heavyweight Stephan Bonnar needed a win in the worst way, but he didn't just get the victory against "The Polish Experiment"; he and his opponent engaged in an instant classic that saw the Las Vegan emerge victorious via a second-round TKO.

There was no feeling-out process in this one, with both fighters picking up where they left off earlier in the year. Bonnar was able to land the first big punch of the fight, but it was Soszynski who almost pulled off an armbar moments later as they grappled on the canvas. In the ensuing scramble, Bonnar got back to his feet and the two traded blows, with Soszynski holding a slight edge. Bonnar bounced back, punctuating his next flurry with a hard knee to the head, but it was "The American Psycho" emerging with a cut under his right eye. The blood didn't deter Bonnar, and the two just kept throwing, with both men trading turns in momentum and earning a well-deserved roar from the crowd at the bell.

Fight of the Night: Bonnar vs. Soszynski

Now cut over the left eye as well, Bonnar walked right back into the fray in round two, only to be greeted by a flurry of shots from Soszynski. Bonnar quickly got his bearings back and fired off an array of punches of his own, and after a brief pause, he landed with a knee, more punches and even a kick before taking Soszynski down at the two-minute mark. After a brief stay on the mat, the two rose, but Bonnar kept the pressure on, dropping Soszynski with a right knee to the head. Soszynski tried to weather the storm, but Bonnar wouldn't let him off the hook, and after a series of unanswered blows, referee Mario Yamasaki halted the bout at the 3:00 mark.

Veteran Chris Lytle made it two in a row over Matt Brown in welterweight action, repeating his 2007 submission win with another victory due to tap out over "The Immortal".

It was another fight, another win, and another statement for lightweight contender George Sotiropoulos, who followed up his UFC 110 victory over Joe Stevenson with an equally impressive three-round unanimous decision over Kurt Pellegrino in the main card opener.

All that training with Shane Carwin must have rubbed off on heavyweight prospect Brendan Schaub, as the former *Ultimate Fighter* competitor made it two quick knockouts in a row on the UFC 116 undercard, halting Chris Tuchscherer in just 67 seconds.

New Jersey's latest hot prospect, Ricardo Romero, walked through fire to get his first UFC win, shaking off hard shots and submission attempts from Seth Petruzelli to submit the returning Octagon vet in the second round of an exciting light heavyweight scrap.

Kendall Grove pulled one out of the well yet again, bouncing back from a UFC 112 loss to Mark Munoz with a three-round split decision victory over Goran Reljic in a back-and-forth middleweight battle.

"It was a big win," said Grove. "I'm like a cockroach. I'm hard to get rid of."

Knockout of the Night: Harris vs. Branch

Middleweight Gerald "Hurricane" Harris made it 3-0 in the UFC in 2010 with his third straight knockout—this time taking out previously unbeaten newcomer David Branch with a thunderous, highlight-reel slam in the third round.

Welterweight prospect Daniel "Ninja" Roberts used his takedowns and ground game to earn his first UFC victory as he scored a three-round split decision over returning vet Forrest Petz.

Heavyweight Jon Madsen spoiled the UFC debut and the perfect record of London's Karlos Vemola, but he didn't win any new fans with his methodical three-round unanimous decision win.

UFC 117 *Silva vs. Sonnen*

07 Aug. 2010

Oracle Arena, Oakland, CA

Debuts: Todd Brown, Christian Morecraft

Fighters			Division	Method	Time	Round
Main Card						
Anderson Silva	def.	Chael Sonnen	Middleweight	Submission - Triangle Choke	3:10	5
Jon Fitch	def.	Thiago Alves	Catchweight	Unanimous Decision	—	3
Clay Guida	def.	Rafael dos Anjos	Lightweight	Submission - Injury	1:51	3
Matt Hughes	def.	Ricardo Almeida	Welterweight	Submission - Choke	3:15	1
Junior dos Santos	def.	Roy Nelson	Heavyweight	Unanimous Decision	—	3
Preliminary Card						
Rick Story	def.	Dustin Hazelett	Welterweight	Technical Knockout	1:15	2
Phil Davis	def.	Rodney Wallace	Light Heavyweight	Unanimous Decision	—	3
Johny Hendricks	def.	Charlie Brenneman	Welterweight	Technical Knockout	0:40	2
Tim Boetsch	def.	Todd Brown	Light Heavyweight	Unanimous Decision	—	3
Stefan Struve	def.	Christian Morecraft	Heavyweight	Knockout	0:21	2
Dennis Hallman	def.	Ben Saunders	Welterweight	Unanimous Decision	—	3

Chael Sonnen promised he would give UFC middleweight champion Anderson Silva a fight in their UFC 117 main event and he lived up to his word as he dominated the first four rounds of their bout. In the fifth, it was Silva pulling off an incredible triangle choke that allowed him to retain his title and get the last word on the challenger.

"I knew that I was losing the first four rounds," said Silva, who made the seventh successful defense of his title. "Chael put on a helluva fight tonight."

"It was a tough fight, he's a tough guy—I came in second," said Sonnen, whose pre-fight trash talk reached epic proportions and also made this one of the most highly anticipated bouts of the year.

And it lived up to its billing.

Steel-faced, Sonnen seemed to be in a rush to make it into the Octagon for the biggest fight of his career. Silva, on the other hand, was as cool as ever, bowing to the crowd as he made his walk into battle. Sonnen impatiently paced, pointing at and calling for Silva as he waited.

He would have his chance soon enough, as referee Josh Rosenthal called both men to the center of the Octagon. Sonnen immediately closed the gap on Silva but was unable to get him to the mat. He didn't need to, as a left hand rocked Silva briefly, forcing the champion to get the fight to the mat as he looked to clear his head. After a few seconds, the two rose, and Sonnen continued to land with strikes until taking Silva down hard and pinning him against the fence. There, Sonnen unleashed ground strikes on Silva, who was in the most trouble of his UFC career. By the midway point, it looked like Silva had cleared his head, even though Sonnen kept landing punches while looking for a choke. After spinning out of trouble briefly, Silva fell back into danger, courtesy of the challenger's fists, and the crowd erupted. Finally, the bell rang, giving Silva a much-needed break from the assault.

Silva came out fast for round two, intent on getting his respect from Sonnen. But after losing his balance, Silva was put on his back, and Sonnen fired away again, even resorting to boxing Silva's ears and slamming him as the champion tried to hang on and force a restart. With none forthcoming, Silva tried to land some elbows from the bottom as Sonnen peppered him, but the shots were having no effect on the Oregon native. Instead, Sonnen seemed to get stronger as the round progressed, with Silva having no answers for him. With under a minute to go, Silva finally made his move, almost locking up Sonnen's arm, but it was not to be, and the bell soon intervened.

Fight of the Night: Silva vs. Sonnen

A big right hand from Silva opened up round three as Sonnen rushed him, and he followed up seconds later with a spinning back kick. None seemed to affect Sonnen, who took Silva back to the mat. A series of knees to the thigh and punches to the head followed, with Silva making no attempt to escape. With 1:30 gone, the champion was able to escape, but he still wound up in the bottom position as the crowd chanted the challenger's name. Sonnen kept his followers happy with more ground strikes, wrapping up another one-sided round in his favor.

Silva finally got the fight where he wanted it in round four, rocking Sonnen with a series of bad-intentioned strikes before getting the challenger on his back. But his furious assault may have gassed him out, as Sonnen cleared his head and reversed position on "The Spider".

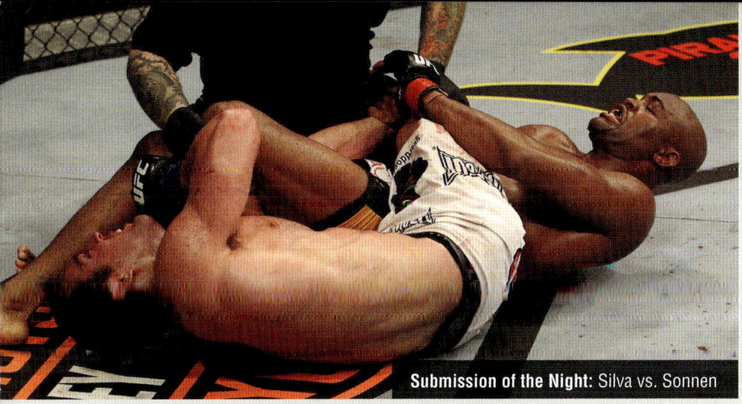

Submission of the Night: Silva vs. Sonnen

While on his back, Silva tried to hold on to force a restart, but Sonnen's continued activity made that an impossibility, as he landed with whatever strikes he had at his disposal. Silva gamely fought back from the bottom, opening a nasty cut over Sonnen's left eye, but as the bell rang, he would only have five minutes to save his crown.

A short left hand knocked Silva off balance and down early in the final stanza, and Sonnen immediately pounced on him and continued the attack that had won him the first four rounds. Again, Silva tried to potshot from the bottom, but it was clear that he was going to need a miracle to win the belt. With a little more than two minutes to go, he got it, as he sunk in a triangle choke. Sonnen tried to resist, but he eventually tapped at the 3:10 mark. Though Sonnen protested the tap, replays showed otherwise, and the belt remained in the hands of the pride of Curitiba.

Jon Fitch was in solid form once again as he delivered a shutout three-round unanimous decision win in his long-awaited rematch with Brazilian powerhouse Thiago "Pitbull" Alves.

In his first bout since being inducted into the UFC Hall of Fame in May 2010, Matt Hughes notched his third straight win in spectacular fashion, submitting Ricardo Almeida in the first round with a choke Hughes simply described as "an old wrestling move."

Submission of the Night: Hughes vs. Almeida

It was inevitable that heavyweight contender Junior dos Santos would eventually run into the man he couldn't finish in the UFC. At UFC 117, Roy Nelson was that man, and the result was a grueling three-round battle that may have been one-sided on the scorecards, yet was anything but in reality, as dos Santos drilled out an impressive three-round unanimous decision over the courageous Nelson.

Clay Guida scored his second consecutive victory, forcing Rafael dos Anjos to submit in the third round due to an injured jaw.

Rick "The Horror" Story's third consecutive UFC win was his most impressive by far, as he blitzed Dustin Hazelett from the opening bell to the time the referee halted the one-sided welterweight contest in the second round.

Light heavyweight prospect Phil Davis made it three in a row in the UFC, scoring a shutout three-round decision win over Rodney Wallace.

It was power vs. speed in the welterweight contest between Johny Hendricks and Charlie Brenneman, and power won, as Hendricks halted his foe in the second round of a fast-paced scrap.

Tim Boetsch made his return to the Octagon a successful one as he pounded out a three-round unanimous decision win over UFC debutant Todd Brown.

A battered and bloodied Stefan Struve roared back from a rough first stanza against newcomer Christian Morecraft to stop the previously unbeaten New Englander in the second round of an exciting battle of heavyweight prospects.

Knockout of the Night: Struve vs. Morecraft

It was a nearly ten-year wait, but Dennis "Superman" Hallman got back in the UFC win column with a three-round unanimous decision victory over Ben Saunders.

UFC Live On Versus 2

Jones vs. Matyushenko

01 Aug. 2010

San Diego Sports Arena, San Diego, CA

Debut: Charles Oliveira

Fighters			Division	Method	Time	Round
Main Card						
Jon Jones	def.	Vladimir Matyushenko	Light Heavyweight	Technical Knockout	1:52	1
Yushin Okami	def.	Mark Munoz	Middleweight	Split Decision	—	3
Jake Ellenberger	def.	John Howard	Welterweight	Technical Knockout - Doctor Stoppage	2:21	3
Takanori Gomi	def.	Tyson Griffin	Lightweight	Knockout	1:04	1
Preliminary Card						
Jacob Volkmann	def.	Paul Kelly	Lightweight	Unanimous Decision	—	3
Matthew Riddle	def.	DaMarques Johnson	Catchweight	Technical Knockout	4:29	2
Igor Pokrajac	def.	James Irvin	Light Heavyweight	Submission - Rear Naked Choke	2:29	1
Brian Stann	def.	Mike Massenzio	Middleweight	Submission - Triangle Choke	3:10	3
Charles Oliveira	def.	Darren Elkins	Lightweight	Submission - Armbar	0:41	1
Rob Kimmons	def.	Steve Steinbeiss	Middleweight	Unanimous Decision	—	3

It was quick, it was dominant, and it was something the light heavyweight division would have to get used to, as 205-pound phenom Jon Jones passed another test with breakneck speed, halting veteran Vladimir Matyushenko in less than two minutes.

"I trained the hardest I could possibly train and I knew it was going to be my toughest fight," said Jones, who certainly didn't make it look like his toughest fight, as he controlled the bout from start to finish against the rugged Belarus native, whose only previous losses were to Tito Ortiz, Antonio Rogerio Nogueira, Andrei Arlovski and Vernon White.

Loose and relaxed, Jones—who was coming off a first-round TKO of Brandon Vera in March 2010—came at Matyushenko slowly yet with a determined stride. A kick to the leg and a spinning back kick opened up the scoring for "Bones", and he quickly followed up with a takedown. Within a few moments, Jones had pinned Matyushenko down and then came a series of ferocious forearms that forced referee Herb Dean to call a halt to the bout at the 1:52 mark.

In the co-main event, 185-pound contender Yushin Okami held off the charge of local favorite Mark Munoz to earn a three-round split decision win.

Just when he was written off, Japanese superstar Takanori Gomi resurrected his career with a single right hand in the main card opener, knocking out Tyson Griffin in the first round.

Knockout of the Night: Gomi vs. Griffin

Welterweight up-and-comer Jake Ellenberger ate some hard shots from John Howard in their eagerly anticipated bout, but with unstoppable takedowns and an effective ground attack that nearly swelled his opponent's eye shut, he was able to score a third-round TKO over the Boston native.

In pre-fight interviews, Brian Stann said he wasn't worried about going to the mat against Mike Massenzio. In their middleweight bout—Stann's first at 185 pounds—he proved it as he scored the first submission win of his career via triangle choke in the third round.

Massenzio was effective with his takedowns and a guillotine choke in the opening round, but Stann's improved ground game was evident as he fought his way out of trouble, landing some hard strikes that reddened his foe's face.

The second frame was almost a mirror image of the first one, complete with takedowns and a choke attempt from Massenzio and a ground and pound assault from Stann.

Fight of the Night: Stann vs. Massenzio

Early in the third, Stann rocked Massenzio briefly, and while he got taken down in the midst of his follow-up, when the two stood he was able to hurt the New Jersey native again. This time, his attempt to finish was foiled when he missed a kick to the head and slipped to the mat, and Massenzio took the opportunity to clear his head before getting back to his feet. Another Massenzio takedown followed, but this time Stann was waiting for him as he sunk in a fight-ending triangle choke at the 3:10 mark.

Minnesota's Jacob Volkmann made it two in a row in the Octagon, scoring a three-round unanimous decision over the UK's Paul Kelly in lightweight action.

Welterweight prospect Matthew Riddle put together the best performance of his UFC career, halting veteran DaMarques Johnson in the second round of a battle between *The Ultimate Fighter* alumni.

Submission of the Night: Oliveira vs. Elkins

Light heavyweight Igor Pokrajac secured his first UFC win in three tries, and he did it in impressive fashion as he used his standup attack to set up a slam and an eventual submission win over James Irvin in less than three minutes of the first round.

Unbeaten Brazilian Charles "Do Bronx" Oliveira wasted no time getting acquainted with the UFC Octagon in his organizational debut, submitting Darren Elkins in less than a minute in lightweight action.

In the middleweight opener, veteran Rob Kimmons bounced back from a rough first round to score a close, but unanimous, decision win over Steve Steinbeiss.

UFC 118 *Edgar vs. Penn 2*

28 Aug. 2010

TD Garden, Boston, MA

Debuts: James Toney, Amilcar Alves

Fighters			Division	Method	Time	Round
Main Card						
Frankie Edgar	def.	BJ Penn	Lightweight	Unanimous Decision	—	5
Randy Couture	def.	James Toney	Heavyweight	Submission - Arm Triangle Choke	3:19	1
Demian Maia	def.	Mario Miranda	Middleweight	Unanimous Decision	—	3
Gray Maynard	def.	Kenny Florian	Lightweight	Unanimous Decision	—	3
Nate Diaz	def.	Marcus Davis	Welterweight	Submission - Guillotine Choke	4:02	3
Preliminary Card						
Joe Lauzon	def.	Gabe Ruediger	Lightweight	Submission - Armbar	2:01	1
Nik Lentz	def.	Andre Winner	Lightweight	Unanimous Decision	—	3
Dan Miller	def.	John Salter	Middleweight	Submission - Anaconda Choke	1:53	2
Greg Soto	def.	Nick Osipczak	Welterweight	Unanimous Decision	—	3
Mike Pierce	def.	Amilcar Alves	Welterweight	Submission - Armbar	3:11	3

In what was almost a continuation of their first bout, UFC lightweight champion Frankie Edgar shut out the man he beat for the belt at UFC 112, BJ Penn, via unanimous decision in the UFC 118 main event, silencing any naysayers who called the first win a fluke.

Edgar took the bout via three scores of 50-45.

The action got underway immediately, with the two trading punches and Edgar following up with a takedown of the former champ. Back standing, Edgar settled in, getting into the rhythm of striking and movement that won him the belt in the first place. This time, though, he was throwing more wrestling into the mix, as he put Penn on the mat a second time.

Better adjusting to Edgar's speed and head movement, Penn's strikes began landing with more frequency early in round two, but the champion was undeterred as he stuck to his gameplan while continuing to mix up his strikes.

Penn came out of his corner with more urgency in round three, and while he had some success early on, by the third minute of the frame, it was Edgar back in control, as the crowd chanted his name.

Early in round four, Penn switched gears and took Edgar to the canvas, garnering a roar from the crowd. Edgar grabbed Penn and tried to keep him close but then suddenly broke free in a lull and got back to his feet. Looking to get even scoring-wise, Edgar became the standup aggressor, even kicking Penn's legs out and sending him to the mat.

Penn shot for—and got—the takedown again to start round five, and even when Edgar scrambled up, Penn was relentless in getting him back to the mat. Edgar was just as active, and his perpetual motion kept Penn from putting together a late rally.

It was the first UFC bout between a world-class boxer and an equally proficient mixed martial artist, and the UFC 118 co-main event went as most expected. Randy Couture impressively sent three-division world champ James "Lights Out" Toney to defeat via submission in the first round.

Unbeaten contender Gray Maynard earned a shot at the UFC lightweight crown as he scored a solid, but fairly uneventful, three-round unanimous decision win over Brookline, Massachusetts' Kenny Florian.

It wasn't from a lack of effort, but middleweight contender Demian Maia was unable to submit tough up-and-comer Mario Miranda, and was forced to settle for a three-round unanimous decision win in his first bout since his five-round championship loss to Anderson Silva at UFC 112.

Fight of the Night: Diaz vs. Davis

Nate Diaz was in top form in the main card opener, dominating the standup against former pro boxer and welterweight veteran Marcus Davis before finishing matters via submission in the third round.

Submission of the Night: Lauzon vs. Ruediger

There were no hometown jitters for Bridgewater's Joe Lauzon, who thrilled his local fans with a one-sided submission victory over his *Ultimate Fighter 5* teammate Gabe Ruediger, who saw his Octagon return spoiled by a first-round armbar.

Nik Lentz remained unbeaten in the Octagon, scoring an uneventful three-round unanimous decision win over Andre Winner in a lightweight bout.

In middleweight action, Dan Miller broke his three-fight losing streak with a second-round submission win over Alabama's John Salter.

Lightweight prospect Greg Soto looked like a different fighter than the one who debuted in the Octagon back at UFC 111, as he survived a nasty cut over his left eye to pound out a three-round unanimous decision win over Nick Osipczak.

Mike Pierce made sure that the Octagon debut of Amilcar Alves ended with a loss, submitting the Brazil native in the third round.

One Hit Wonder: James Toney

A future boxing Hall of Famer, multi-division world champion Toney talked himself into a fight at UFC 118 despite having no previous MMA training. He deserves credit for taking the plunge, but it was clear from the outset that this one wasn't going to end well for him.

UFC Fight Night 22

Marquardt vs. Palhares

15
Sept.
2010

Frank Erwin Center, Austin, TX

Debuts: Rafael Natal, TJ Waldburger, David Mitchell

Fighters			Division	Method	Time	Round
Main Card						
Nate Marquardt	def.	Rousimar Palhares	Middleweight	Technical Knockout	3:28	1
Charles Oliveira	def.	Efrain Escudero	Catchweight	Submission - Rear Naked Choke	2:25	3
Jim Miller	def.	Gleison Tibau	Lightweight	Unanimous Decision	—	3
Cole Miller	def.	Ross Pearson	Lightweight	Submission - Rear Naked Choke	1:49	2
Preliminary Card						
Yves Edwards	def.	John Gunderson	Lightweight	Unanimous Decision	—	3
Kyle Kingsbury	def.	Jared Hamman	Light Heavyweight	Unanimous Decision	—	3
Dave Branch	def.	Tomasz Drwal	Middleweight	Unanimous Decision	—	3
Rich Attonito	def.	Rafael Natal	Middleweight	Unanimous Decision	—	3
TJ Waldburger	def.	David Mitchell	Welterweight	Unanimous Decision	—	3
Brian Foster	def.	Forrest Petz	Welterweight	Technical Knockout	1:07	1

Middleweight contender Nate Marquardt got back in the win column in his first bout since losing to Chael Sonnen at UFC 109, stopping grappling ace Rousimar Palhares in the first round at the Frank Erwin Center to put himself back on the road to a 185-pound title shot.

Palhares looked nervous moments before his first UFC main event, and Marquardt wasn't about to let him get settled, using his movement and angles as the bout opened to keep his foe from getting his bearings for a takedown. It wasn't the most scintillating start, and the fans let the fighters know it, but with the stakes high, one false move would be all it took to end the bout.

Midway through the round, Palhares was able to secure a takedown, yet after trying to lock up Marquardt's leg and failing to do so, Palhares looked to referee Herb Dean to say his opponent's legs were greased. In the midst of this sequence, Marquardt landed a right hand down the pipe, hurting the Rio de Janeiro product. A follow-up barrage of punches finished matters seconds later, with Dean calling the fight at 3:28 of the opening round.

Submission of the Night: Oliveira vs. Escudero

After the bout, Dean and members of the Texas commission checked Marquardt's legs and found them free of any illegal substances.

After winning his first UFC fight in August 2010 in just 41 seconds, 20-year-old lightweight phenom Charles Oliveira took a little longer the second time around, but it was the same result, as he impressively submitted Efrain Escudero in the third round of the UFC Fight Night co-main event.

Lightweight contender Jim Miller made it five wins in a row, using a solid standup attack to drill out a three-round unanimous decision victory over Gleison Tibau.

Rising lightweight star Cole Miller made an emphatic statement to his 155-pound peers in the main card opener, shaking off a slow start to submit fellow up-and-comer Ross Pearson in the second round.

Submission of the Night: C.Miller vs. Pearson

If you want an example of leaving it all in the Octagon, look no further than the light heavyweight bout between Kyle Kingsbury and Jared Hamman at the Frank Erwin Center, as both fighters went for broke in a punishing 15-minute battle won by Kingsbury via unanimous decision.

Fight of the Night: Kingsbury vs. Hamman

Veteran Yves Edwards returned to the Octagon for the first time since 2006 and in front of his hometown fans in Austin, he delivered a strong performance as he won a three-round unanimous decision over John Gunderson.

The action wasn't particularly compelling, but New York middleweight David Branch got his first UFC win, outpointing Poland's Tomasz Drwal over three rounds.

The Ultimate Fighter 11 saw Rich Attonito make it two in a row in the Octagon as he spoiled the UFC debut of Rafael Natal with a workmanlike three-round unanimous decision win.

UFC newcomers TJ Waldburger and David Mitchell put on an exciting three-round groundfighting clinic in their welterweight bout, but when it was over, it was Waldburger who issued Mitchell his first pro loss via unanimous decision.

Welterweight Brian Foster got the night off to a quick start—literally—stopping Forrest Petz in just 67 seconds.

Knockout of the Night: Foster vs. Petz

UFC 119 *Mir vs. Cro Cop*

25 Sept. 2010

Conseco Fieldhouse, Indianapolis, IN

Debuts: Pat Audinwood, Mark Hunt, Sean McCorkle

Fighters			Division	Method	Time	Round
Main Card						
Frank Mir	def.	Mirko Cro Cop	Heavyweight	Knockout	4:02	3
Ryan Bader	def.	Antonio Rogerio Nogueira	Light Heavyweight	Unanimous Decision	—	3
Chris Lytle	def.	Matt Serra	Welterweight	Unanimous Decision	—	3
Sean Sherk	def.	Evan Dunham	Lightweight	Split Decision	—	3
Melvin Guillard	def.	Jeremy Stephens	Lightweight	Split Decision	—	3
Preliminary Card						
CB Dollaway	def.	Joe Doerksen	Middleweight	Submission - Guillotine Choke	2:47	1
Matt Mitrione	def.	Joey Beltran	Heavyweight	Unanimous Decision	—	3
Thiago Tavares	def.	Pat Audinwood	Lightweight	Submission - Guillotine Choke	3:47	1
Waylon Lowe	def.	Steve Lopez	Lightweight	Split Decision	—	3
TJ Grant	def.	Julio Paulino	Welterweight	Unanimous Decision	—	3
Sean McCorkle	def.	Mark Hunt	Heavyweight	Submission - Armbar	1:03	1

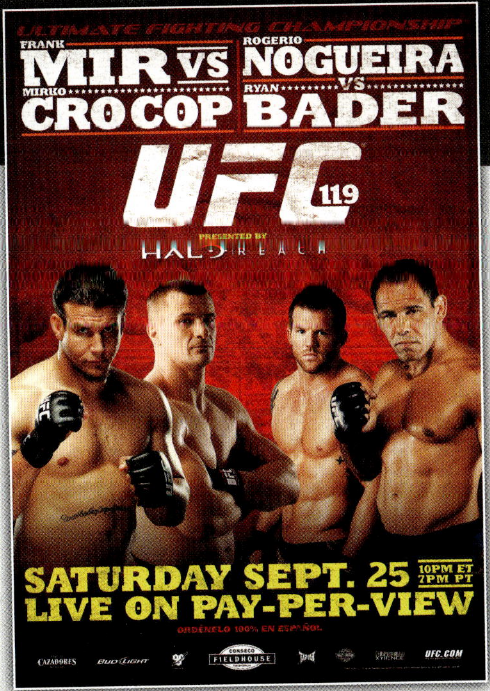

For nearly 14 minutes, it wasn't pretty. But Frank Mir ended the UFC's first show in Indianapolis with a bang, knocking out Mirko Cro Cop in the final minute of the third round in the UFC 119 main event at the Conseco Fieldhouse.

After a dismal first two rounds, Cro Cop got into the position of aggressor to begin the final round, but Mir's bouncing movement threw him off his own rhythm. With two minutes gone, he was able to land a hard shot to the side of the head, but Mir didn't budge, opting instead to pin his foe against the fence, which brought another re-start from referee Herb Dean with under two minutes left. Now Cro Cop showed more urgency to finish, but in the process, he left himself open for a counter left knee that sent him hard to the canvas. A follow-up barrage ended matters moments later, with Dean calling a stop to the bout at the 4:02 mark.

Unbeaten rising star Ryan Bader followed up his UFC 110 win over Keith Jardine with another big victory in the UFC 119 co-main event, outpointing longtime light heavyweight contender Antonio Rogerio Nogueira over three rounds.

In a punishing welterweight battle, good buddies Chris Lytle and Matt Serra erased the memory of their dismal 2006 bout, going toe-to-toe for three rounds, with Lytle emerging victorious by a three-round unanimous decision.

Evan Dunham may have suffered his first pro loss via split decision in an exciting 15-minute battle against former UFC champion Sean Sherk, but his stock only rose in defeat. He fought through a nasty cut over his right eye to almost finish the former UFC lightweight champion several times before the final bell rang.

The judges' unpopular verdict read 29-28 twice and 28-29 for Sherk.

"I knew I had the first round—the second round was close, the third round was close," said Sherk. "I felt it could have gone either way."

Fight of the Night: Sherk vs. Dunham

Most in attendance booed the decision, letting it be known which way they wanted it to go, but what wasn't in question was the high-level display of mixed martial arts and heart both 155-pounders showed over three fast-paced rounds.

Fight of the Night: Mitrione vs. Beltran

Lightweight Melvin Guillard won his third in a row and sixth of his last seven, patiently picking apart Jeremy Stephens en route to a three-round split decision victory.

Heavyweights Matt Mitrione and Joey Beltran delivered on their promise for a standup war in UFC 119 prelim action, and after three hard-fought and entertaining rounds, it was Mitrione who kept his unbeaten record intact via close but unanimous decision.

Middleweight prospect CB Dollaway pulled off one of his most impressive UFC wins, as he submitted Joe Doerksen via guillotine choke in the first round.

Thiago Tavares was in top-notch form in his first Octagon bout since January of 2010, submitting previously unbeaten newcomer Pat Audinwood in the first round.

Submission of the Night: Dollaway vs. Doerksen

Indiana native Steve Lopez was unsuccessful in his second bid for a UFC victory, losing a three-round split decision to Waylon Lowe.

Canadian prospect TJ Grant shut out Julio Paulino in welterweight action, earning a three-round unanimous decision victory.

With a raucous crowd in his corner, Indianapolis' own Sean McCorkle delivered in his UFC debut, submitting former K-1 and PRIDE star Mark Hunt in just 63 seconds.

UFC 120 *Bisping vs. Akiyama*

16 Oct. 2010

The O2 Arena, London, England

Debuts: Fabio Maldonado, Curt Warburton, Paul Sass, Vinicius Queiroz, Rob Broughton

Fighters			Division	Method	Time	Round
Main Card						
Michael Bisping	def.	Yoshihiro Akiyama	Middleweight	Unanimous Decision	—	3
Carlos Condit	def.	Dan Hardy	Welterweight	Knockout	4:27	1
Mike Pyle	def.	John Hathaway	Welterweight	Unanimous Decision	—	3
Cheick Kongo	vs.	Travis Browne	Heavyweight	Draw	—	3
Claude Patrick	def.	James Wilks	Welterweight	Unanimous Decision	—	3
Preliminary Card						
Alexander Gustafsson	def.	Cyrille Diabate	Light Heavyweight	Submission - Rear Naked Choke	2:41	2
Rob Broughton	def.	Vinicius Queiroz	Heavyweight	Submission - Rear Naked Choke	1:43	3
Paul Sass	def.	Mark Holst	Lightweight	Submission - Triangle Choke	4:45	1
Spencer Fisher	def.	Curt Warburton	Lightweight	Unanimous Decision	—	3
Fabio Maldonado	def.	James McSweeney	Light Heavyweight	Technical Knockout	0:48	3

"The Count" is back. In his first fight on home soil since defeating Denis Kang in November of 2009, British superstar Michael Bisping extended his winning streak to two with a Fight of the Night battle with Yoshihiro Akiyama.

The three scores for the Manchester middleweight's unanimous decision victory read 30-27 in a bout that was a lot more competitive than that margin would indicate. It was Akiyama's second UFC loss in three tries, but each contest earned Fight of the Night honors.

Fight of the Night: Bispina vs. Akiyama

The exciting Japanese fighter actually had his best moment in the early stages of the fight, as he clipped Bisping with a right hand that rocked him momentarily. Bisping, using effective Octagon generalship, moved quickly to clear his head, and now fully engaged, he began tagging the heavy-handed Akiyama with quick and accurate strikes.

Bisping threw more takedowns into the mix in round two, continually keeping Akiyama from getting a read on him. Well aware that he was down on the scorecards, Akiyama turned up the heat in the final frame, throwing caution to the wind as he swung at the Brit in the hopes of scoring a come from behind knockout. Bisping, not afraid of the exchanges, gave better than he got, again using straight and fast strikes to wrap up the third round and the fight.

In the co-feature, British favorite Dan "The Outlaw" Hardy learned the hard way that you don't hook with a hooker, as a trade of simultaneous left hooks with Carlos Condit in the final minute of the opening round left Hardy starting up at the lights, the victim of a knockout at the 4:27 mark.

Knockout of the Night: Condit vs. Hardy

The bad news continued for the Brits in another featured bout on the UFC 120 card, as rising welterweight star John Hathaway suffered the first loss of his pro career when he was decisioned over three rounds by grizzled veteran Mike Pyle, who controlled the bout from start to finish, en route to the 30-27 shutout win.

Repeated fouls by French heavyweight contender Cheick Kongo cost him in his less than scintillating bout against unbeaten Travis Browne, as a third-round point deduction for grabbing his opponent's shorts led to a 28-28 unanimous draw verdict.

Another tedious three-rounder, this time in the welterweight division, saw Canada's Claude Patrick remain unbeaten in the Octagon with a three-round decision win over Leicester native and former *Ultimate Fighter* winner James Wilks. Scores were 30-27 on all cards.

The preliminary card provided a lot more consistently compelling action, as well as a little more good news for the British faithful.

Waving the flag successfully were heavyweight Rob Broughton and lightweight Paul Sass, both of whom scored submission victories. Broughton finished Brazil's Vinicius Queiroz in the third round with a rear naked choke, and Sass used a triangle choke to end the night of Canada's Mark Holst.

Submission of the Night: Sass vs. Holst

Promising light heavyweight Alexander "The Mauler" Gustafsson made a statement in his bout with veteran kickboxer Cyrille Diabate, submitting "The Snake" via rear naked choke at 2:41 of the second round.

The only distance fight of the prelim portion of the card was turned in by Spencer Fisher, who pulled out a hard-fought three-round decision win over UK newcomer Curt Warburton.

The opening bout of the night was in the light heavyweight division, as Brazil's Fabio Maldonado halted England's James McSweeney at 0:48 of the third round.

One Hit Wonder: Vinicius Queiroz

At 6' 7", 243 lbs, with all five of his previous wins coming by knockout, Vinicius Queiroz had plenty of hype around him as entered his UFC debut, but after a late loss to Rob Broughton and a subsequent failed drug test for the banned performance enhancer Stanozolol, the Brazilian giant's UFC career was over as fast as it started when he was released in November of 2010.

UFC 121 *Lesnar vs. Velasquez*

23 Oct. 2010

Honda Center, Anaheim, CA

Debuts: Dongi Yang, Jake Shields

Fighters			Division	Method	Time	Round
Main Card						
Cain Velasquez	def.	Brock Lesnar	Heavyweight	Technical Knockout	4:12	1
Jake Shields	def.	Martin Kampmann	Welterweight	Split Decision	—	3
Diego Sanchez	def.	Paulo Thiago	Welterweight	Unanimous Decision	—	3
Matt Hamill	def.	Tito Ortiz	Light Heavyweight	Unanimous Decision	—	3
Brendan Schaub	def.	Gabriel Gonzaga	Heavyweight	Unanimous Decision	—	3
Preliminary Card						
Court McGee	def.	Ryan Jensen	Middleweight	Submission - Arm Triangle Choke	1:21	3
Tom Lawlor	def.	Patrick Cote	Middleweight	Unanimous Decision	—	3
Daniel Roberts	def.	Mike Guymon	Welterweight	Submission - Anaconda Choke	1:13	1
Sam Stout	def.	Paul Taylor	Lightweight	Split Decision	—	3
Chris Camozzi	def.	Dongi Yang	Middleweight	Split Decision	—	3
Jon Madsen	def.	Gilbert Yvel	Heavyweight	Technical Knockout	1:48	1

Too small, they said. But Cain Velasquez had other plans in the UFC 121 main event, and despite giving up more than 20 pounds to Brock Lesnar, he held off an initial charge from the 6' 3", 265-pounder to take the Minnesotan down, and then finish him off in the first round to win the UFC heavyweight championship.

"I expected nothing less," said a gracious Lesnar. "He's a great fighter. What can I say? He was better than me tonight."

Lesnar attacked with a takedown attempt immediately, but Velasquez met it with a flurry of punches. Lesnar eagerly fired back and even shot off a flying knee, and the crowd erupted. With less than 30 seconds of frantic action gone, Lesnar got his takedown, but Velasquez shot up quickly. Lesnar immediately bulled his foe into the fence and got another takedown, but Velasquez got up almost immediately and bloodied Lesnar's face with more shots. At the 2:53 mark, Velasquez scored with a takedown of his own, and amazingly the crowd got even louder. Lesnar made it back to his feet, but his balance was off and Velasquez took advantage with more accurate blows that sent Lesnar scrambling face-first to the mat. The champion weathered the initial storm, but after getting up again, Velasquez made sure he was not to be denied, as he dropped Lesnar again. This time, the humble kid from San Jose finished what he had started years ago on a wrestling mat, and after a barrage of strikes, referee Herb Dean halted the bout and Cain Velasquez began a new reign atop the heavyweight division.

Knockout of the Night: Velasquez vs. Lesnar

With the win, Velasquez, the first fighter of Mexican descent to win a major heavyweight title in combat sports, remained undefeated.

The highly anticipated UFC debut of Jake Shields was a victorious one, but his three-round split decision win over Martin Kampmann wasn't exactly the showcase many expected, as a mix of fatigue and Kampmann's defense kept the longtime welterweight and middleweight star from making the statement he wanted to.

Fight of the Night: Sanchez vs. Thiago

Many wondered whether Diego Sanchez' move back to 170 pounds was a wise one. In one of his best performances to date, the former lightweight title challenger silenced any doubters with an action-packed three-round unanimous decision win over Paulo Thiago.

It was teacher versus student, but the student, Matt Hamill, took the drama out of the showdown, using a steady ground and pound attack and effective standup striking to earn a three-round unanimous decision victory.

Rising heavyweight star Brendan Schaub added a sizeable notch to his belt in the main card opener as he defeated longtime contender Gabriel Gonzaga via three-round unanimous decision.

It didn't look good early on for Court McGee, but "The Crusher" roared back from a slow start to impressively finish off veteran middleweight Ryan Jensen in UFC 121 prelim action.

Middleweight prospect Tom Lawlor put in a workman-like effort over his three-rounder with Patrick Cote, winning a shutout unanimous decision over the former middleweight title challenger.

Daniel Roberts' Octagon evolution continued as he submitted veteran Mike Guymon just 73 seconds into the first round for his second straight UFC win.

Submission of the Night: Roberts vs. Guymon

Sam Stout and Paul Taylor delivered plenty of bad-intentioned punches and kicks over the course of an exciting three-rounder won by Canada's Stout via split decision.

The Ultimate Fighter 11 alum Chris Camozzi spoiled the UFC debut and perfect record of South Korea's Dongi Yang, pounding out a three-round split decision win in a compelling middleweight bout.

Heavyweight prospect Jon Madsen delivered the most impressive performance of his UFC career thus far, moving to 4-0 in the Octagon with a first-round TKO of veteran Gilbert Yvel.

WEC

The names are synonymous with mixed martial arts excellence: Jose Aldo, Urijah Faber, Ben Henderson, Anthony Pettis, Dominick Cruz, Jens Pulver, Chris Leben, Brian Stann, Carlos Condit, Nate Diaz, Brandon Vera, Mike Brown and Miguel Angel Torres. What do they all have in common? At one time or another they all graced the cage of the World Extreme Cagefighting organization, a breeding ground for not only consistently exciting fights, but for the best lighter-weight fighters in the world.

Founded in 2001 by Scott Adams and Reed Harris, the WEC was revered by hardcore fans for producing many instant classics. But for years, the organization was also MMA's best kept secret, like that great band you used to see at a local club that you knew would hit it big as soon as they got the right record deal.

Under the ownership of Zuffa, the WEC suddenly secured a national television deal with the VERSUS network, made Las Vegas its home base, and focused its energies on not only MMA's established weight classes, but the featherweight and bantamweight divisions that rarely got exposure in the United States.

The impact was immediate, aided in great part by the organization's featherweight champion Urijah Faber, a talented and charismatic fighter whose appeal cut across all demographics and brought in fans by the truckload, especially in the hometown of "The California Kid", Sacramento. Luckily, Faber was on board to do whatever was necessary to show the world just how exciting the lighter weight fighters were.

"People are gonna fall in love with our weight classes," said Faber during a media stop in New York before his 2007 bout against Chance Farrar. "You're gonna find that it's faster, it's more explosive and it's extremely entertaining."

Faber had plenty of help in his quest, as some of the early stars of the Zuffa-owned WEC were current household names like Brian Stann and Miguel Angel Torres, exciting battlers willing to put it all on the line once the bell rang.

But the WEC was just getting started, and as a new breed of dynamic fighters started to filter into the organization like Jose Aldo, Dominick Cruz, Ben Henderson, and Anthony Pettis, the fights featuring these standouts were routinely finding their way on to end-of-year "Best Of" lists.

Classics like Leonard Garcia-Chan Sung Jung, Miguel Angel Torres-Takeya Mizugaki, Urijah Faber-Jens Pulver 1, Ben Henderson-Donald Cerrone 1, and Anthony Pettis-Ben Henderson captivated fans and made any WEC event a must-see for the true fight fan.

In October of 2010, Zuffa announced that the UFC would be adding the featherweight and bantamweight divisions and merging the remainder of the WEC fighters into the world's premier MMA organization. While the WEC is no more, the excitement the organization brought to fight fans won't ever be forgotten.

"As the UFC continues to evolve and grow globally, we want to be able to give fans title fights in every weight division," said White. "This is a big day for the sport and the athletes who will have the opportunity to fight on the biggest stage in the world."

WEC CHAMPIONSHIP ROSTER

SUPER HEAVYWEIGHT
- Ron Waterman

HEAVYWEIGHT
- James Irvin
- Brian Olsen

LIGHT HEAVYWEIGHT
- Frank Shamrock
- Doug Marshall
- Jason Lambert
- Brian Stann
- Scott Smith
- Steve Cantwell
- Lodune Sincaid

MIDDLEWEIGHT
- Chris Leben
- Paulo Filho
- Joe Riggs

WELTERWEIGHT
- Nick Diaz
- Mike Pyle
- Shonie Carter
- Carlos Condit
- Karo Parisyan

LIGHTWEIGHT
- Gilbert Melendez
- Jamie Varner
- Gabe Ruediger
- Ben Henderson
- Hermes Franca
- Anthony Pettis
- Rob McCullough

FEATHERWEIGHT
- Cole Escovedo
- Mike Brown
- Urijah Faber
- Jose Aldo

BANTAMWEIGHT
- Eddie Wineland
- Brian Bowles
- Chase Beebe
- Dominick Cruz
- Miguel Angel Torres

NOTABLE WEC ALUMNI

Jose Aldo
John Alessio
Olaf Alonso
Raphael Assuncao
Antonio Banuelos
Renan Barao
Chase Beebe
Joseph Benavidez
Brian Bowles
Jonathan Brookins
Mike Brown
Steve Cantwell
Chris Cariaso
Shonie Carter
Shane Carwin
Gil Castillo
Danny Castillo
Donald Cerrone
Dan Christison
Carlos Condit
Kit Cope
Wesley Correira
Rich Crunkilton
Dominick Cruz
Jeff Curran
Mac Danzig
LC Davis
Nick Diaz
Nate Diaz
Joe Doerksen
Danny Downes
Yves Edwards
Cole Escovedo
Urijah Faber
Wagnney Fabiano
Paulo Filho
Hermes Franca
Manny Gamburyan
Leonard Garcia
Pablo Garza
Tiki Ghosn
Josh Grispi
Clay Guida
Ben Henderson
Johny Hendricks
Jay Hieron
Mark Hominick
Jeremy Horn
Chris Horodecki
Matt Horwich
Brad Imes
James Irvin
Yves Jabouin
Demetrious Johnson
Scott Jorgensen
Chan Sung Jung
Alex Karalexis
Tim Kennedy
Rob Kimmons
Erik Koch
Mike Kyle
Jason Lambert
Brock Larson
Chris Leben
Chris Lytle
Doug Marshall
Terry Martin
Rob McCullough
Gilbert Melendez
Chad Mendes
Ivan Menjivar
Micah Miller
Jason Miller
Takeya Mizugaki
Mark Munoz
Anthony Njokuani
Diego Nunes
Jake O'Brien
Nick Pace
Damacio Page
Bart Palaszewski
Karo Parisyan
Kurt Pellegrino
Anthony Pettis
Nam Phan
Brad Pickett
Carlo Prater
Jens Pulver
Mike Pyle
Joe Riggs
Andre Roberts
Ricco Rodriguez
Shane Roller
George Roop
Gabe Ruediger
Mackens Semerzier
Dan Severn
Kamal Shalorus
Frank Shamrock
Aaron Simpson
Wes Sims
Scott Smith
Rameau Thierry Sokoudjou
Chael Sonnen
Brian Stann
Cub Swanson
Mike Swick
Miguel Angel Torres
Charlie Valencia
Jamie Varner
Javier Vazquez
Ron Waterman
Mark Weir
Vernon White
Eddie Wineland
Rani Yahya
Tiequan Zhang

UFC 122 *Marquardt vs. Okami*

13 Nov. 2010

König Pilsener Arena, Oberhausen, Germany

Debuts: Alexandre Ferreira, Pascal Krauss, Mark Scanlon, Carlos Eduardo Rocha

Fighters			Division	Method	Time	Round
Main Card						
Yushin Okami	def.	Nate Marquardt	Middleweight	Unanimous Decision	—	3
Dennis Siver	def.	Andre Winner	Lightweight	Submission - Rear Naked Choke	3:37	1
Amir Sadollah	def.	Peter Sobotta	Welterweight	Unanimous Decision	—	3
Krzysztof Soszynski	def.	Goran Reljic	Light Heavyweight	Unanimous Decision	—	3
Duane Ludwig	def.	Nick Osipczak	Welterweight	Split Decision	—	3
Preliminary Card						
Vladimir Matyushenko	def.	Alexandre Ferreira	Light Heavyweight	Technical Knockout	2:20	1
Pascal Krauss	def.	Mark Scanlon	Welterweight	Unanimous Decision	—	3
Kyle Noke	def.	Rob Kimmons	Middleweight	Submission - Rear Naked Choke	1:33	2
Karlos Vemola	def.	Seth Petruzelli	Light Heavyweight	Technical Knockout	3:46	1
Carlos Eduardo Rocha	def.	Kris McCray	Welterweight	Submission - Kneebar	2:36	1

Having spent more than four years building his resume in the UFC, Japan's Yushin Okami earned a shot at the world middleweight championship after a close three-round unanimous decision victory over perennial contender Nate Marquardt in the UFC 122 main event.

Okami shot first, looking for an early takedown, but Marquardt fought it off with a brief guillotine choke attempt before working his way into his opponent's guard. Okami's defense was airtight, and a second, even briefer, guillotine attempt allowed the Kanagawa native to get into the top position. From there, it was a stalemate and the two scrambled to their feet. Marquardt landed with a quick right as Okami shot in, but "Thunder" was unmoved by the shot and he proceeded to pin Marquardt against the fence before taking him down just before the bell.

Marquardt easily threw aside Okami's first takedown effort of the second round, but his retaliatory single leg attempt came up empty, as well. The two middleweight contenders then locked up against the fence, with Marquardt reversing Okami's leg trip attempt and winding up on top. After Marquardt was able to land with some strikes, Okami scrambled to his feet and looked for his own takedown. It didn't come, and the two separated, unable to make anything significant happen before the end of the stanza.

Early in the final round, Okami's punches opened a cut under Marquardt's right eye, and buoyed by his success, he began to chase the Wyoming native. For his part, Marquardt, who was beginning to look fatigued, tried to counter Okami's advances, but as the round progressed, Okami showed even more confidence in his striking while the crowd chanted his name. With under two minutes left, Marquardt began to pick up his pace, landing a few strikes before taking Okami to the mat. Okami got back to his feet quickly and resumed his stalking of Marquardt, who landed a hard counter right before the two locked up against the fence and traded knees until the end of the bout.

Submission of the Night: Siver vs. Winner

Dennis Siver and Andre Winner brought fireworks to the König Pilsener Arena in their UFC 122 lightweight battle, but it was Mannheim's Siver who had dynamite in his gloves as he dropped Winner and then submitted him in a one-round scrap that ignited the crowd and moved him further up the 155-pound ladder.

Amir Sadollah got back on the winning track after his UFC 114 loss to Dong Hyun Kim, earning a clear-cut three-round unanimous decision victory over Germany's Peter Sobotta.

Krzysztof Soszynski continued his development in the UFC's light heavyweight class, pounding out a shutout three-round decision win over Goran Reljic, who was making his first start in the division since May of 2008.

Veteran striker Duane "Bang" Ludwig rebounded from a March 2010 ankle injury with a close three-round split decision win over *Ultimate Fighter* alumnus Nick Osipczak.

Fight of the Night: Krauss vs. Scanlon

In an exciting battle of unbeaten welterweight prospects on the UFC 122 undercard, Freiburg, Germany's own Pascal Krauss kept his "0" intact with a hard-fought three-round unanimous decision win over Mark Scanlon.

Veteran light heavyweight Vladimir Matyushenko spoiled the UFC debut of Alexandre "Cacareco" Ferreira, halting the Chute Boxe team member in the first round.

The Ultimate Fighter 11 alum Kyle Noke earned his second impressive UFC victory in a row, submitting tough vet Rob Kimmons in round two of their middleweight bout.

Knockout of the Night: Vemola vs. Petruzelli

Czech Republic native Karlos Vemola delivered the goods in his 205-pound debut, halting Seth Petruzelli in the first round to earn his first Octagon victory.

Hamburg-based Brazilian Carlos Eduardo Rocha got the crowd into matters immediately, submitting *The Ultimate Fighter 11* finalist Kris McCray in the first round of welterweight action.

UFC 123 *Rampage vs. Machida*

20 Nov. 2010

The Palace of Auburn Hills, Auburn Hills, MI

Debuts: Maiquel Falcao, Mike Lullo, Edson Barboza, TJ O'Brien

Fighters			Division	Method	Time	Round
Main Card						
Quinton Jackson	def.	Lyoto Machida	Light Heavyweight	Split Decision	—	3
BJ Penn	def.	Matt Hughes	Welterweight	Knockout	0:21	1
Maiquel Falcao	def.	Gerald Harris	Middleweight	Unanimous Decision	—	3
Phil Davis	def.	Tim Boetsch	Light Heavyweight	Submission - Modified Kimura	2:55	2
George Sotiropoulos	def.	Joe Lauzon	Lightweight	Submission - Kimura	2:43	2
Preliminary Card						
Brian Foster	def.	Matt Brown	Welterweight	Submission - Guillotine Choke	2:11	2
Mark Munoz	def.	Aaron Simpson	Middleweight	Unanimous Decision	—	3
Dennis Hallman	def.	Karo Parisyan	Welterweight	Technical Knockout	1:47	1
Edson Barboza	def.	Mike Lullo	Lightweight	Technical Knockout	0:26	3
Paul Kelly	def.	TJ O'Brien	Lightweight	Technical Knockout	3:18	2
Nik Lentz	def.	Tyson Griffin	Lightweight	Split Decision	—	3

Quinton Jackson brought out the PRIDE theme song, his old aggression, some wild haymakers, and nearly a trademark slam to the UFC 123 main event, and while it wasn't vintage Rampage, his willingness to push the pace throughout the first two rounds and to hold off a late charge from Lyoto Machida allowed him to earn a three-round split decision in the battle of former UFC light heavyweight champions.

Scores were 29-28 twice and 28-29 for Jackson.

Jackson came out of his corner aggressively, trying to corner Machida. "The Dragon" wasn't buying it, and he used his movement and some well-placed kicks to the inside of Jackson's legs to slow him down.

There was no change to the strategy for Jackson in round two, but this time he was able to pin Machida to the Octagon fence. With three minutes left, Jackson scored the first takedown of the fight, but there was precious little scoring from either man.

Machida's defense left Jackson in the cold to open the third, and the fans began booing. But with under four minutes left, Machida opened up his own arsenal, rocking Jackson with a series of shots. Jackson cleared his head quickly and fired back with both hands, finally giving the fans what they had been waiting to see. And it was enough for Jackson to eke out the win.

Knockout of the Night: Penn vs. Hughes

Twenty-one seconds. That and the idea of fighting an old rival was all it took for BJ Penn to get his mojo back, and he did just that, knocking out Matt Hughes in their rubber match to break a two-fight losing skid and send the crowd at The Palace of Auburn Hills into a frenzy during the UFC 123 co-main event.

"Matt you're my idol—you will always be my idol," said Penn, who ran out of the Octagon after the bout, recalling the time he did the same thing after halting Caol Uno in 11 seconds in 2001. When he returned, it was as a triumphant hero in his first welterweight bout since 2009. The win also brought him back to prominence after he lost his lightweight title and back-to-back bouts to Frankie Edgar.

With a burst of intense exchanges bookended by nearly two rounds of a tedious chess match, Brazilian middleweight Maiquel Falcao scored his first UFC win, ending Gerald Harris' three-fight Octagon winning streak via unanimous decision.

Submission of the Night: Davis vs. Boetsch

Unbeaten light heavyweight prospect Phil "Mr. Wonderful" Davis delivered perhaps his most impressive UFC performance to date, dominating always-tough Tim Boetsch before submitting him in the second round.

Lightweight George Sotiropoulos finished 2010 with a bang, ending a 3-0 run for the year with an impressive second-round submission win over Joe Lauzon in a bout named Fight of the Night.

Anyone wondering whether the UFC 123 prelim bout between Brian Foster and Matt Brown would end up on the mat would have thought it possible only if one of the two welterweight bangers got knocked out. Foster flipped the script on "The Immortal", moving seamlessly from striking to submission mode to force Brown to tap out in the second round.

Fight of the Night: Sotiropoulos vs. Lauzon

Longtime college wrestling buddies Mark Munoz and Aaron Simpson certainly didn't fight like friends in their middleweight bout, trading vicious punches and equally impressive ground techniques over an entertaining 15-minute battle won by Munoz via a close, but unanimous, decision.

Veteran Dennis Hallman continued his resurgence, stopping returning contender Karo Parisyan in the first round of their welterweight bout.

Unbeaten Brazilian newcomer Edson Barboza's Muay Thai attack delivered as advertised in his lightweight prelim bout against late replacement Mike Lullo, as a devastating series of kicks to the leg ended matters in the third round.

Liverpool's Paul Kelly got back in the win column in style, stopping Octagon debutant TJ O'Brien in the second round of an action packed lightweight battle.

Minnesota's Nik Lentz remained unbeaten in the Octagon, scoring an unpopular three-round split decision over Tyson Griffin in the lightweight opener.

The Ultimate Fighter 12 Finale

Team GSP vs. Team Koscheck

04 Dec. 2010

The Pearl at The Palms, Las Vegas, NV

Debuts: Jonathan Brookins, Michael Johnson, Nam Phan, Cody McKenzie, Aaron Wilkinson, Tyler Toner, Ian Loveland, Sako Chivitchian, Kyle Watson, Will Campuzano, Nick Pace, Fredson Paixao, Pablo Garza

Fighters			Division	Method	Time	Round
Main Card						
Jonathan Brookins	def.	Michael Johnson	Lightweight	Unanimous Decision	—	3
Stephan Bonnar	def.	Igor Pokrajac	Light Heavyweight	Unanimous Decision	—	3
Demian Maia	def.	Kendall Grove	Middleweight	Unanimous Decision	—	3
Rick Story	def.	Johny Hendricks	Welterweight	Unanimous Decision	—	3
Leonard Garcia	def.	Nam Phan	Featherweight	Split Decision	—	3
Preliminary Card						
Cody McKenzie	def.	Aaron Wilkinson	Lightweight	Submission - Guillotine Choke	2:03	1
Ian Loveland	def.	Tyler Toner	Featherweight	Unanimous Decision	—	3
Kyle Watson	def.	Sako Chivitchian	Lightweight	Unanimous Decision	—	3
Nick Pace	def.	Will Campuzano	Catchweight	Submission - Choke	4:32	3
Pablo Garza	def.	Fredson Paixao	Featherweight	Knockout	0:51	1
Dave Branch	def.	Rich Attonito	Middleweight	Unanimous Decision	—	3

After his three-round unanimous decision win over Michael Johnson, Jonathan Brookins earned *The Ultimate Fighter 12* title, but what will be most remembered about the match is Brookins' ultimate comeback from a rocky first round to pull off the stirring victory over the next two frames.

Scores were 29-28 twice and 29-27 for Brookins, who, like Johnson, represented Georges St-Pierre's Team GSP on the Spike TV reality series.

Trading strikes to open the bout, Johnson was the crisper puncher of the two lightweights, prompting Brookins to look for a takedown. Johnson's defense was solid, though, and he refused the trip to the canvas. With a little over three minutes remaining, a left to the head rocked Brookins and put him on the mat. Brookins weathered the storm, but after rising, Johnson delivered the hurt again with another left. With two minutes to go, a right uppercut jarred the Floridian, but the game Brookins was able to hold on and clear his head. By this time, Johnson was starting to impose his will on his opponent, not just turning away take-down attempts but pushing them off with ease, capping off a big first round.

Looking to turn the tide, Brookins made an almost desperate takedown attempt early in round one, and while it wasn't pretty, he got it, following up with a series of ground strikes as he battled his way back into the fight.

With five minutes left, there would be no saving it for next time with these two 155-pounders, and after Johnson briefly rocked Brookins with a shot to the face, Brookins took Johnson back to the mat, where he had so much success in the previous round. After working to break Johnson's defense, Brookins found himself in the mount position, but Johnson escaped, got back to his feet, and looked to fire off some fight-ending strikes. Brookins responded with another takedown and more ground strikes, and this late flurry of activity sealed the final round for the Orlando product.

Fight of the Night: Garcia vs. Phan

Stephan Bonnar continued his 2010 resurgence, following up his UFC 116 knockout of Krzysztof Soszynski with a clear-cut three-round unanimous decision win over Croatia's Igor Pokrajac.

In middleweight action, Demian Maia drilled out a close but unanimous three-round decision win over Kendall Grove.

Welterweight up-and-comer Rick Story made it five wins in a row, capturing a hard-fought three-round unanimous decision over previously unbeaten Johny Hendricks.

The Ultimate Fighter 12's Nam Phan got a tough assignment in his UFC debut against Leonard Garcia. It appeared to most observers that the Team Koscheck member had done enough to earn his first Octagon victory, but the judges didn't agree, awarding an unpopular three-round split decision to Garcia.

Submission of the Night: McKenzie vs. Wilkinson

Everyone knew it was coming, but Aaron Wilkinson still couldn't stop Cody McKenzie's guillotine in the first round of their lightweight bout.

Late replacement Ian Loveland made the most of his opportunity in featherweight action, parlaying two knockdowns into a unanimous decision victory over Tyler Toner.

Veteran Illinois lightweight Kyle Watson issued Sako Chivitchian his first pro defeat via unanimous decision in a meeting of *TUF12* alumni.

The first bantamweight bout in UFC history saw Nick Pace finish strong and submit Will Campuzano in the third round.

Fargo, North Dakota's Pablo Garza gave UFC fans an explosive introduction to the featherweight division, scoring a single knee first-round knockout of veteran Fredson Paixao in the first 145-pound fight in UFC history.

Brooklyn's David Branch won his second in a row in the opener, outpointing Rich Attonito in a clash of middleweight prospects.

Knockout of the Night: Garza vs. Paixao

One Hit Wonders: Aaron Wilkinson, Tyler Toner, Sako Chivitchian, Fredson Paixao

UFC 124 *St-Pierre vs. Koscheck 2*

11 Dec. 2010

Bell Centre, Montreal, Quebec, Canada

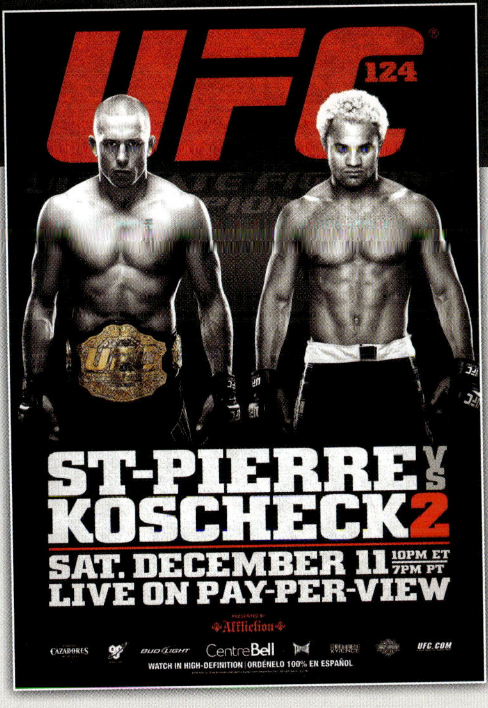

Debuts: Jesse Bongfeldt, Sean Pierson, John Makdessi

Fighter			Division	Method	Time	Round
Main Card						
Georges St-Pierre	def.	Josh Koscheck	Welterweight	Unanimous Decision	—	5
Stefan Struve	def.	Sean McCorkle	Heavyweight	Technical Knockout	3:55	1
Jim Miller	def.	Charles Oliveira	Lightweight	Submission - Kneebar	1:59	1
Mac Danzig	def.	Joe Stevenson	Lightweight	Knockout	1:54	1
Thiago Alves	def.	John Howard	Welterweight	Unanimous Decision	—	3
Preliminary Card						
Dan Miller	def.	Joe Doerksen	Middleweight	Split Decision	—	3
Mark Bocek	def.	Dustin Hazelett	Lightweight	Submission - Triangle Choke	2:33	1
Jesse Bongfeldt	vs.	Rafael Natal	Middleweight	Majority Draw	—	3
Sean Pierson	def.	Matthew Riddle	Welterweight	Unanimous Decision	—	3
Ricardo Almeida	def.	TJ Grant	Welterweight	Unanimous Decision	—	3
John Makdessi	def.	Pat Audinwood	Lightweight	Unanimous Decision	—	3

The last man to take a round from UFC welterweight champion Georges St-Pierre in a prize fight was Josh Koscheck, back in August of 2007. More than three years later, before 23,000-plus fans at the Bell Centre, Montreal's own St-Pierre made sure that wasn't going to be the case the second time around, as he repeated his victory over the number one contender, this time by way of a shutout five-round unanimous decision.

Fight of the Night: St-Pierre vs. Koscheck

Scores were 50-45 across the board for St-Pierre, who defended his title for the fifth consecutive time.

St-Pierre was eager to get down to business, and he did just that, taking Koscheck down within 20 seconds of the opening bell. Koscheck got back up but seemed content to let St-Pierre lead, looking for a chance to counter. St-Pierre had no problem with leading as he peppered Koscheck with jabs to the face, occasionally following up with a right hand or kick.

As Koscheck walked back to his corner after round one, a swelling under his right eye was evident, and as the fight progressed, it only got worse. A confident St-Pierre walked out of his corner and again began to deliver quick lefts and rights. Koscheck seemed to be in a trance at the end of St-Pierre's punches, unable to get his offense in gear.

Both fighters put a little more heat on their strikes to begin round three, but the pace dipped. Between rounds three and four, the Octagonside physician took a long look at Koscheck's nearly closed eye, then allowed the fight to continue. St-Pierre went at his foe at the bell, punctuating another round won with a thudding slam.

St-Pierre began leading with his left hook as the final round began, and Koscheck wasn't even seeing them coming. The challenger gamely looked for a takedown twice, only to come up short both times. What followed was more of the same from St-Pierre as he pecked and poked at Koscheck and was safely out of reach when any return fire came.

It wouldn't be a Stefan Struve fight without some adversity, but as is the young heavyweight's custom, that adversity is usually followed by triumph, and such was the case once again at UFC 124 as Struve survived an early kimura attempt to come back and stop Sean McCorkle in the first round.

Lightweight contender Jim Miller made no secret of his desire to move to the next level after five consecutive UFC wins. Well, he made an example of unbeaten phenom Charles Oliveira, handing the 21-year-old his first pro loss via first-round submission to make it six in a row.

Knockout of the Night: Danzig vs. Stevenson

After losing four of his previous five fights, lightweight Mac Danzig's career got a much needed boost as he scored a one-punch first-round knockout of Joe Stevenson in a clash of former *Ultimate Fighter* winners.

Welterweight contender Thiago Alves broke a two-fight losing streak in impressive style, using a precision Muay Thai attack to drill out a three-round unanimous decision win over John Howard.

Submission of the Night: Bocek vs. Hazelett

Mark Bocek took the drama out of his anticipated UFC 124 bout with fellow jiu-jitsu black belt Dustin Hazelett early and emphatically, impressively submitting his foe with a triangle choke in the first round.

In middleweight action, Dan Miller squeezed out a close three-round split decision win over Joe Doerksen.

A big last round from Jesse Bongfeldt allowed the debuting Ontario middleweight to eke out a three-round majority draw against Rafael Natal.

It was a debut years in the making, but veteran Ontario welterweight Sean Pierson made the most of it, winning an exciting three-round scrap with Matt Riddle via unanimous decision.

Ricardo Almeida bounced back from his UFC 117 loss to Matt Hughes with a three-round unanimous decision win over Nova Scotia's TJ Grant in welterweight action.

Debuting Montrealer John Makdessi set the tone for the hometown crowd immediately as he scored a shutout three-round unanimous decision over Pat Audinwood in the lightweight opener.

UFC 125 *Resolution*

01 Jan. 2011

MGM Grand Garden Arena, Las Vegas, NV

Debuts: Josh Grispi, Dustin Poirier, Diego Nunes, Antonio McKee

Fighters			Division	Method	Time	Round
Main Card						
Frankie Edgar	vs.	Gray Maynard	Lightweight	Draw	—	5
Brian Stann	def.	Chris Leben	Middleweight	Technical Knockout	3:37	1
Thiago Silva	vs.	Brandon Vera	Light Heavyweight	No Contest*	—	3
Dong Hyun Kim	def.	Nate Diaz	Welterweight	Unanimous Decision	—	3
Clay Guida	def.	Takanori Gomi	Lightweight	Submission	4:27	2
Preliminary Card						
Jeremy Stephens	def.	Marcus Davis	Lightweight	Knockout	2:33	3
Dustin Poirier	def.	Josh Grispi	Featherweight	Unanimous Decision	—	3
Brad Tavares	def.	Phil Baroni	Middleweight	Technical Knockout	4:20	1
Diego Nunes	def.	Mike Brown	Featherweight	Split Decision	—	3
Daniel Roberts	def.	Greg Soto	Welterweight	Submission - Kimura	3:45	1
Jacob Volkmann	def.	Antonio McKee	Lightweight	Split Decision	—	3

*Result was changed to a no contest after Silva tested positive for banned substances.

By all rights, Frankie Edgar never should have made it out of the first round of his UFC 125 main event against Gray Maynard. After surviving multiple knockdowns in the opening frame, the UFC lightweight champion roared back to retain his belt with a five-round draw in an exciting bout that kicked off the 2011 fight year in style.

Fight of the Night: Edgar vs. Maynard

Maynard announced his arrival to the championship level a little more than a minute in with a left hook that hurt and dropped the champion. Edgar got up, only to be sent back down by a right uppercut. Maynard pounced, but amazingly Edgar weathered the assault, and by the end of the round, he was firing back.

Edgar opened the second round with his legs back under him as he moved around the Octagon and poked at the challenger with quick flurries. With less than 90 seconds left and the crowd chanting his name, Edgar responded with a quick flurry that opened a cut under Maynard's left eye, and he followed up with a thunderous slam that ignited the crowd.

The champion again used his stick and move strategy to perfection in round three while also keeping Maynard from putting him on his back. Maynard kept stalking, and with less than 90 seconds left, he began to get closer with his power shots before landing a takedown in the final minute.

Edgar went on the offensive with a takedown and guillotine choke attempt to begin the fourth round, and while Maynard got up and escaped, the champion called on his wrestling for another takedown seconds later.

With five minutes to go, each shot carried the weight of the outcome on it, and each of these gutsy lightweights had their moments in the first half of the frame. In the second half, it was clear that the bout would be settled on the feet, and both were bloodied as they went toe-to-toe until the final bell. Scores were 48-46 Maynard, 48-46 Edgar and 47-47.

In the co-main event, middleweight up-and-comer Brian Stann asked for Chris Leben, a bold move to say the least, given the experience level of "The Crippler". However, the U.S. Marine Corps veteran delivered when it counted, as he scored a stirring first-round TKO win.

Light heavyweight contender Thiago Silva returned from a year-long layoff with a clear-cut three-round unanimous decision victory over slumping former contender Brandon Vera. In April, the fight was ruled a no contest as Silva failed the pre-fight drug test.

Korean welterweight Dong Hyun Kim remained unbeaten, holding off a late charge from Nate Diaz to win a close and hard-fought three-round unanimous decision.

Submission of the Night: Guida vs. Gomi

Lightweight contender Clay Guida got the big name scalp he was looking for in the main card opener, submitting former PRIDE champion Takanori Gomi with a guillotine choke in the second round.

Jeremy Stephens spoiled the lightweight debut of Marcus Davis, scoring a chilling third-round knockout of the former welterweight contender in UFC 125 preliminary action.

Knockout of the Night: Stephens vs. Davis

Josh Grispi could have been fighting for a world title at UFC 125. Instead, he ran into a buzzsaw named Dustin Poirier, who delivered a championship-level performance in winning a shutout three-round decision.

The Ultimate Fighter 11's Brad Tavares continued to impress in middleweight action as he stopped veteran Phil Baroni in the first round.

Brazil's Diego Nunes scored the biggest win of his pro career, defeating former WEC featherweight champion Mike Brown via split decision in an exciting three-rounder.

Daniel "Ninja" Roberts continued his rise up the welterweight ranks, smoothly submitting fellow prospect Greg Soto with a kimura in the first round.

It was a typical Antonio McKee fight, with the veteran standout going the distance for the 22nd time in his career, but this time he wasn't able to pull off the victory, as he dropped an uneventful three-round split decision to Jacob Volkmann in the lightweight opener.

One Hit Wonder: Antonio McKee

UFC Fight for the Troops 2 (Fight Night 23)

22 Jan. 2011

Fort Hood, Killeen, TX

Debuts: Rani Yahya, Willamy Freire, Chris Cariaso

Fighters			Division	Method	Time	Round
Main Card						
Melvin Guillard	def.	Evan Dunham	Lightweight	Technical Knockout	2:58	1
Matt Mitrione	def.	Tim Hague	Heavyweight	Technical Knockout	2:59	1
Mark Hominick	def.	George Roop	Featherweight	Technical Knockout	1:28	1
Pat Barry	def.	Joey Beltran	Heavyweight	Unanimous Decision	—	3
Matt Wiman	def.	Cole Miller	Lightweight	Unanimous Decision	—	3
Preliminary Card						
Yves Edwards	def.	Cody McKenzie	Lightweight	Submission – Rear Naked Choke	4:33	2
DaMarques Johnson	def.	Mike Guymon	Welterweight	Submission– Body Triangle	3:22	1
Rani Yahya	def.	Mike Brown	Featherweight	Unanimous Decision	—	3
Waylon Lowe	def.	Willamy Freire	Lightweight	Unanimous Decision	—	3
Charlie Brenneman	def.	Amilcar Alves	Welterweight	Unanimous Decision	—	3
Chris Cariaso	def.	Will Campuzano	Bantamweight	Unanimous Decision	—	3

"Young Assassin", indeed. Longtime lightweight talent Melvin Guillard delivered a defining performance in the main event of the UFC Fight for the Troops 2 card, stopping highly regarded Evan Dunham with a blistering mix of speed and power that announced his arrival as a major player at 155 pounds.

After the ritual touch of gloves, Dunham kicked off the action with a kick, but it was Guillard who landed a big right hand that got the Oregonian's attention. Dunham immediately shot for a takedown, and eventually got it. Guillard fought his way back to his feet and tagged Dunham with a series of punches, reddening his face. Calm in the pocket, Guillard danced around and shot in with dynamite when the opening presented itself. That opening came midway through the round as another right hand stunned Dunham and dropped him. Dunham looked for the takedown but it was nowhere to be found. Instead, Guillard drilled his foe with a left knee to the head that staggered him once again. Dunham started to fall to the canvas and Guillard wouldn't let him off the hook, prompting referee Mario Yamasaki to halt the bout at 2:58 of the opening round.

Knockout of the Night: Guillard vs. Dunham

Looking more confident than ever, rising heavyweight star Matt Mitrione scored his fourth pro win without a loss, knocking out Tim Hague in the first round of the Fight for the Troops 2 co-main event.

Mark Hominick guaranteed himself a title shot at UFC featherweight champion Jose Aldo, stopping former teammate George Roop in emphatic fashion in the first round.

Hominick didn't look like "The Machine"; in this fight; it was more like "The Terminator" as he walked Roop down with a determined look that made it clear he meant business. After tagging his foe with practically everything he threw, he dropped Roop with a left hook. Another left followed while Roop sat on the seat of his pants, and while he kicked at Hominick to break loose, referee Don Turnage halted the bout at the 1:28 mark. Roop protested the stoppage, but as he rose, he staggered on wobbly legs, making it clear that Turnage made the right call.

Heavyweight prospect Pat Barry got off to a slow start against Joey Beltran, but his trademark kicks started paying dividends as the bout progressed, allowing him to pound out a three-round unanimous decision win.

Fight of the Night: Edwards vs. McKenzie

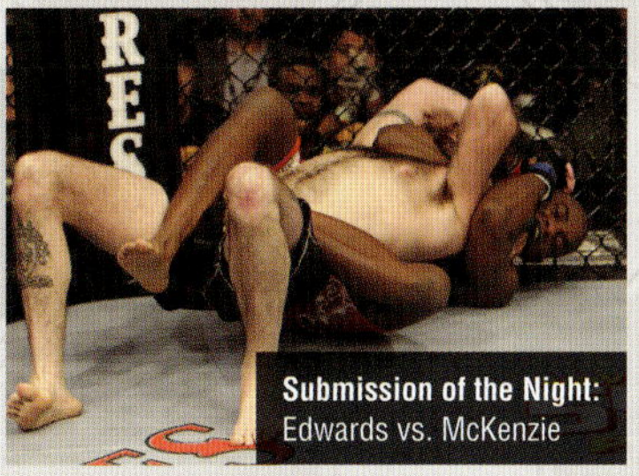
Submission of the Night: Edwards vs. McKenzie

Following a rough 2010 plagued by injuries, lightweight Matt Wiman got 2011 off to a stellar start with an impressive three-round unanimous decision win over his *Ultimate Fighter 5* castmate Cole Miller.

Veteran contender Yves Edwards showed that there is plenty of gas left in his tank, as he submitted young gun Cody McKenzie in the second round, handing the *Ultimate Fighter 12* alum his first pro loss in Fight for the Troops 2 prelim action.

Welterweight prospect DaMarques Johnson rebounded from his loss to Matt Riddle last August, scoring a first-round verbal submission win over Mike Guymon.

"My back popped bad; I can't even sit down," said Guymon, who retired after the bout. "I'm just so happy, it's been such a long road—it's so hard to explain. It's so many years fighting, I'm so happy to be done. I just accomplished everything I wanted to with fighting."

Returning to the featherweight division for his UFC debut, Brazil's Rani Yahya outlasted former WEC champ Mike Brown, winning a three-round unanimous decision.

Waylon Lowe made it two in a row in lightweight action, spoiling the debut of highly touted Willamy Freire via unanimous decision.

Welterweight prospect Charlie Brenneman left no doubts in his bout against Amilcar Alves, dominating on the mat from start to finish en route to a shutout three-round unanimous decision win.

Bantamweight Chris Cariaso made his UFC debut a successful one, scoring a close three-round unanimous decision win over Will Campuzano.

One Hit Wonder: Willamy Freire

UFC 126 *Silva vs. Belfort*

05 Feb. 2011

Mandalay Bay Events Center, Las Vegas, NV

Debuts: Miguel Angel Torres, Antonio Banuelos, Donald Cerrone, Chad Mendes, Norifumi "Kid" Yamamoto, Demetrious Johnson, Kenny Robertson

Fighters			Division	Method	Time	Round
Main Card						
Anderson Silva	def.	Vitor Belfort	Middleweight	Knockout	3:25	1
Forrest Griffin	def.	Rich Franklin	Light Heavyweight	Unanimous Decision	—	3
Jon Jones	def.	Ryan Bader	Light Heavyweight	Submission - Guillotine Choke	4:20	2
Jake Ellenberger	def.	Carlos Eduardo Rocha	Welterweight	Split Decision	—	3
Miguel Angel Torres	def.	Antonio Banuelos	Bantamweight	Unanimous Decision	—	3
Preliminary Card						
Donald Cerrone	def.	Paul Kelly	Lightweight	Submission - Rear Naked Choke	3:48	2
Chad Mendes	def.	Michihiro Omigawa	Featherweight	Unanimous Decision	—	3
Demetrious Johnson	def.	Norifumi "Kid" Yamamoto	Bantamweight	Unanimous Decision	—	3
Paul Taylor	def.	Gabe Ruediger	Lightweight	Knockout	1:42	2
Kyle Kingsbury	def.	Ricardo Romero	Light Heavyweight	Technical Knockout	0:21	1
Mike Pierce	def.	Kenny Robertson	Welterweight	Technical Knockout	0:29	2

Vitor Belfort was widely considered to be the most dangerous threat to Anderson Silva's middleweight title reign. So Silva did what one is supposed to do to such threats: he eliminated him immediately, knocking out Belfort in the first round to retain his crown for the eighth time in the UFC 126 main event at the Mandalay Bay Events Center. In the process, Silva broke a tie with Matt Hughes for most successful title defenses in UFC history.

Knockout of the Night: Silva vs. Belfort

"That's just one of the tricks I was working on," said Silva, who, for all intents and purposes, ended the bout with a spectacular front kick to the chin.

The chants of "Vitor, Vitor!" came from the rafters as soon as referee Mario Yamasaki called the two fighters to battle. But there would be no initial fireworks, as the two cautiously circled each other for the first 90 seconds until Belfort landed a range-finding leg kick. At the midway point, with still no meaningful action, Silva began showboating, with Belfort finally firing off a 1-2. Moments later, Belfort caught a Silva kick and the two tumbled to the mat. They rose quickly, and Silva, significantly warmed up, eluded a Belfort haymaker and came back with a blistering left front kick to the chin that dropped "The Phenom". Quickly moving in, Silva landed a 1-2 on his prone foe, and that was enough for Yamasaki to call a halt to the bout at the 3:25 mark.

"He caught me with a great kick," said Belfort. "Anderson Silva is a great fighter."

After more than a year away, Forrest Griffin had doubts about his ability to perform in the UFC 126 co-main event against Rich Franklin, but Griffin got through three fast-paced rounds the way he always does—by working—and the result was a close but unanimous decision win.

Right after Jon Jones scored the biggest win of his career by submitting previously unbeaten Ryan Bader with a guillotine choke in the second round of their UFC 126 bout, he told color commentator Joe Rogan, "I feel like it's my time."

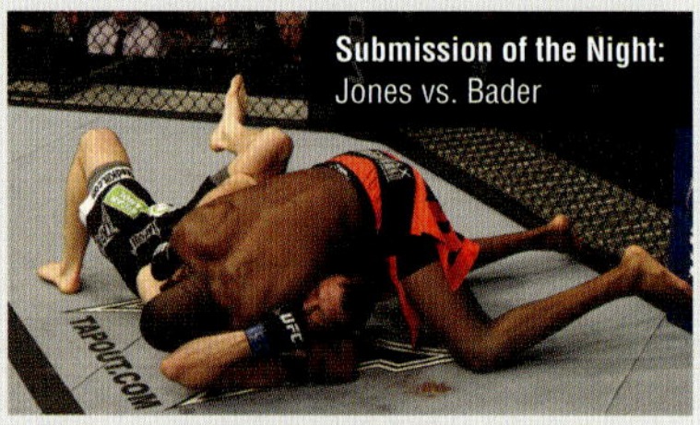

Submission of the Night: Jones vs. Bader

He had no idea how prophetic those words would be, as UFC President Dana White offered him a shot at Mauricio "Shogun" Rua's light heavyweight title at UFC 128 after it was revealed that Rua's original opponent, Rashad Evans, was forced out of the bout due to a knee injury.

Needless to say, Jones accepted. "I feel great," he said. "I'm going for a world title, baby."

Jake Ellenberger pinned the first pro loss on Carlos Eduardo Rocha's record, winning a close three-round split decision over the Brazilian.

Former WEC bantamweight champion Miguel Angel Torres was successful in his UFC debut as he scored a shutout three-round unanimous decision win over Antonio Banuelos.

In lightweight action, former WEC title challenger Donald "Cowboy" Cerrone weathered a gutsy effort from England's Paul Kelly and scored a second-round submission win.

Fight of the Night: Cerrone vs. Kelly

Unbeaten featherweight contender Chad Mendes put an impressive notch in his belt, scoring a workmanlike three-round unanimous decision win over returning Japanese standout Michihiro Omigawa.

Washington State's bantamweight Demetrious Johnson showed no sign of nerves in his UFC debut, defeating highly touted Japanese star Norifumi "Kid" Yamamoto via unanimous decision.

British banger Paul Taylor scored one of his most impressive Octagon wins in lightweight action, knocking out Gabe Ruediger with a single head kick in the second round.

The Ultimate Fighter 8 alumnus Kyle Kingsbury delivered one of the most impressive displays of knee strikes seen in some time, using them to set up a 21-second stoppage of Ricardo Romero.

Welterweight up-and-comer Mike Pierce turned in double duty in the opener, spoiling Kenny Robertson's UFC debut and his perfect MMA record via second-round stoppage.

One Hit Wonders: Kenny Robertson, Antonio Banuelos

UFC 127 *Penn vs. Fitch*

26 Feb. 2011

Acer Arena, Sydney, Australia

Debuts: Brian Ebersole, Nick Ring, Riki Fukuda, Tom Blackledge, Tiequan Zhang, Maciej Jewtuszko

Fighters			Division	Method	Time	Round
Main Card						
BJ Penn	vs.	Jon Fitch	Welterweight	Majority Draw	—	3
Michael Bisping	def.	Jorge Rivera	Middleweight	Technical Knockout	1:54	2
Dennis Siver	def.	George Sotiropoulos	Lightweight	Unanimous Decision	—	3
Brian Ebersole	def.	Chris Lytle	Welterweight	Unanimous Decision	—	3
Kyle Noke	def.	Chris Camozzi	Middleweight	Submission - Rear Naked Choke	1:35	1
Preliminary Card						
Ross Pearson	def.	Spencer Fisher	Lightweight	Unanimous Decision	—	3
Alexander Gustafsson	def.	James Te Huna	Light Heavyweight	Submission - Rear Naked Choke	4:27	1
Nick Ring	def.	Riki Fukuda	Middleweight	Unanimous Decision	—	3
Anthony Perosh	def.	Tom Blackledge	Light Heavyweight	Submission - Rear Naked Choke	2:45	1
Tiequan Zhang	def.	Jason Reinhardt	Featherweight	Submission	0:48	1
Mark Hunt	def.	Chris Tuchscherer	Heavyweight	Knockout	1:41	2
Curt Warburton	def.	Maciej Jewtuszko	Lightweight	Unanimous Decision	—	3

Perennial welterweight contender Jon Fitch finished up his UFC 127 main event against former two division champion BJ Penn with as dominant a round as you can have without a knockout or submission, but it was not enough to take the nod, as the three judges rendered a draw verdict.

Scores were 29-28 Fitch, and 28-28 twice.

Penn shot for a takedown immediately, and when it came up short, he bulled Fitch into the fence. Penn held off Fitch's takedown attempts and got the match to the mat, quickly taking his foe's back. After some tense moments, Fitch escaped and got back to his feet.

Fitch and Penn traded wild strikes to begin the second, with Fitch using the opportunity to take his foe to the mat. Penn battled back to his feet, but Fitch stayed attached to him against the fence. With two minutes left, the fighters broke, with Penn shooting in quickly and getting a takedown. Again he took Fitch's back, but the Indiana native was able to turn and get in Penn's guard, allowing him the opportunity to land his strikes and finish the round strong.

Opening with an overhand right and a takedown, Fitch started the third on the offensive and he didn't stay away from his foe for long, firing away with both hands as he bulled Penn to the fence, with the former two division champion having no escape route. This scenario finished up the bout, with Fitch dominating the final five minutes.

Middleweight contender Michael Bisping had the last word in his trash-talking battle with Jorge Rivera, ending the co-main event with his fists via TKO in the second round.

Bisping was sharp in the first round, but in an early scramble, he landed an illegal left knee on the downed Rivera, drawing a point deduction from referee Marc Goddard and a halt to the action as the Octagonside physicians checked the New Englander out. Rivera made it back to his feet and insisted that he could continue, and the action resumed.

Rivera rocked Bisping with his first right hand of the second round, but "The Count" recovered quickly and went on the offensive to get even. With 90 seconds gone, he scored with a right hand of his own and a follow-up barrage hurt Rivera. Another right hand put the veteran on the canvas and seconds later Goddard stepped in to halt the bout at the 1:54 mark of round two.

Germany's Dennis Siver made it three in a row and seven of his last eight, upsetting fellow lightweight contender George Sotiropoulos via unanimous decision.

Fight of the Night:
Ebersole vs. Lytle

Indiana native and Australia resident Brian Ebersole finally got his UFC shot after more than 60 fights, and he made the most of it, upsetting Chris Lytle via three-round decision in an action-packed welterweight scrap. Scores were 30-27, and 29-28 twice in the UFC 127 Fight of the Night.

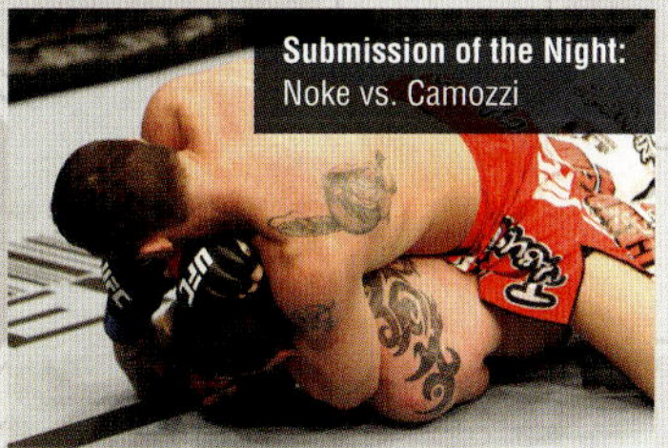
Submission of the Night:
Noke vs. Camozzi

Dubbo, New South Wales native Kyle Noke continued to impress in the Octagon as he scored his third consecutive UFC win by submitting fellow *Ultimate Fighter 11* castmate Chris Camozzi in the first round of the main card opener.

The Ultimate Fighter 9 winner Ross Pearson scored one of the biggest wins of his young career, pounding out a three-round unanimous decision over veteran contender Spencer Fisher.

Sweden's Alex Gustafsson submitted Aussie standout James Te Huna via rear naked choke in the first round of their light heavyweight matchup. Also delivering submission wins were Tiequan Zhang and hometown hero Anthony Perosh, who finished off Jason Reinhardt and Tom Blackledge, respectively.

Knockout of the Night:
Hunt vs. Tuchscherer

In middleweight action, *The Ultimate Fighter 11*'s Nick Ring was awarded an unpopular unanimous decision win over fellow debutant Riki Fukuda.

Former PRIDE standout Mark Hunt thrilled fans in his adopted home country by scoring a Knockout of the Night victory over Chris Tuchscherer in the second round of their heavyweight match.

Lightweight Curt Warburton got the evening's festivities started with a unanimous decision win over Maciej Jewtuszko.

UFC Live On Versus 3

Sanchez vs. Kampmann

03 March 2011

KFC YUM! Center, Louisville, KY

Debuts: Chris Weidman, Brian Bowles, Damacio Page, Danny Castillo, Shane Roller, Reuben Duran, Takeya Mizugaki

Fighters			Division	Method	Time	Round
Main Card						
Diego Sanchez	def.	Martin Kampmann	Welterweight	Unanimous Decision	—	3
Mark Munoz	def.	CB Dollaway	Middleweight	Knockout	0:54	1
Chris Weidman	def.	Alessio Sakara	Middleweight	Unanimous Decision	—	3
Brian Bowles	def.	Damacio Page	Bantamweight	Submission - Guillotine Choke	3:30	1
Preliminary Card						
Cyrille Diabate	def.	Steve Cantwell	Light Heavyweight	Unanimous Decision	—	3
Danny Castillo	def.	Joe Stevenson	Lightweight	Unanimous Decision	—	3
Shane Roller	def.	Thiago Tavares	Lightweight	Knockout	1:28	2
Takeya Mizugaki	def.	Reuben Duran	Bantamweight	Split Decision	—	3
Dongi Yang	def.	Rob Kimmons	Middleweight	Technical Knockout	4:47	2
Rousimar Palhares	def.	Dave Branch	Middleweight	Submission - Kneebar	1:44	2
Igor Pokrajac	def.	Todd Brown	Light Heavyweight	Technical Knockout	5:00	1

He calls himself "The Dream" now, but the fighter formerly known as "Nightmare" showed that he didn't lose the ability to dig deep and deliver a jaw-dropping performance, as Diego Sanchez did just that in a punishing three-round war with Martin Kampmann that saw the Albuquerque native and former *Ultimate Fighter* winner take a razor-thin unanimous decision victory.

Fight of the Night: Sanchez vs. Kampmann

Scores were 29-28 across the board for Sanchez.

After trading quick flurries of standup strikes, Sanchez looked for a takedown in the second minute of the fight, only to be turned away at the door by Kampmann, who proceeded to nail his foe with a knee and a quick right to the head that produced a flash knockdown.

Still determined to get the fight to the mat, Sanchez chased Kampmann in the early stages of round two, but he was still coming up short. On the other hand, Kampmann's pinpoint accurate strikes had now opened a cut under Sanchez' right eye. Sanchez kept pressing, and soon Kampmann was bleeding from a cut around his right eye, and Sanchez opened up with both hands as he got Kampmann against the fence.

Sanchez started to get even closer with his hooks in the final round, and he jarred his opponent with thudding shots. The takedowns still weren't getting done, but Kampmann wasn't matching Sanchez' success rate standing anymore. With a little more than two minutes remaining, Sanchez finally got his takedown, but Kampmann quickly got back to his feet. Sanchez wasn't going to be denied, though, and in the final minute, despite a new cut under his left eye, he fired away with reckless abandon until the bell.

What was expected to be a pitched 15-minute battle instead turned into a defining win for middleweight contender Mark Munoz, who lived up to his nickname "The Filipino Wrecking Machine" by finishing off CB Dollaway by TKO in just 54 seconds.

A star may have been born in the middleweight division as Long Island's Chris Weidman lived up to all the pre-fight hype about his UFC debut and scored a dominant three-round unanimous decision over Alessio Sakara. And he did it on just two weeks notice, replacing Rafael Natal against "Legionarius".

Former WEC bantamweight champion Brian Bowles made a triumphant return after a year-long layoff due to injury, submitting Damacio Page for the second time in two tries via guillotine choke in the UFC debut for both men. Ironically, the end came at the 3:30 mark, the same time Bowles finished him in with a guillotine choke the first time they fought in August of 2008.

Submission of the Night: Bowles vs. Page

After a number of stops and starts, former WEC light heavyweight champion Steve Cantwell finally returned to the Octagon, but he may have wanted to stay on the sidelines, considering the one-sided thrashing he took at the hands of Cyrille "The Snake" Diabate, who defeated the Las Vegan with a shutout three-round decision.

Former WEC standout Danny Castillo was on top of his game in his bout against Joe Stevenson, as he scored a hard-fought three-round unanimous decision win to notch his first UFC victory.

Knockout of the Night: Roller vs. Tavares

WEC veteran Shane Roller made a successful UFC debut in lightweight action, knocking out Thiago Tavares in the second round.

Japan's Takeya Mizugaki got a handful from late replacement Reuben Duran, but the bantamweight contender was able to hold off the newcomer for a close split decision win.

South Korean Dongi Yang was impressive in his second UFC outing, halting veteran middleweight Rob Kimmons in the second round.

Brooklyn's middleweight Dave Branch held off leg lock master Rousimar Palhares for one round, but in the second, the Brazilian won via submission for his fourth victory in his last five bouts.

Igor Pokrajac's superior striking was on display in the light heavyweight opener as he used a combination of kicks, knees and punches to stop Indiana's Todd Brown at the end of the first round.

UFC 128 *Shogun vs. Jones*

19 March 2011

Prudential Center, Newark, NJ

Debuts: Raphael Assuncao, Erik Koch, Costa Philippou, Joseph Benavidez, Anthony Njokuani, Kamal Shalorus, Urijah Faber, Eddie Wineland

Fighters			Division	Method	Time	Round
Main Card						
Jon Jones	def.	Mauricio Rua	Light Heavyweight	Technical Knockout	2:37	3
Urijah Faber	def.	Eddie Wineland	Bantamweight	Unanimous Decision	—	3
Jim Miller	def.	Kamal Shalorus	Lightweight	Technical Knockout	2:15	3
Nate Marquardt	def.	Dan Miller	Middleweight	Unanimous Decision	—	3
Brendan Schaub	def.	Mirko Cro Cop	Heavyweight	Technical Knockout	3:44	3
Preliminary Card						
Luiz Cane	def.	Eliot Marshall	Light Heavyweight	Knockout	2:15	1
Edson Barboza	def.	Anthony Njokuani	Lightweight	Unanimous Decision	—	3
Mike Pyle	def.	Ricardo Almeida	Welterweight	Unanimous Decision	—	3
Gleison Tibau	def.	Kurt Pellegrino	Lightweight	Split Decision	—	3
Joseph Benavidez	def.	Ian Loveland	Bantamweight	Unanimous Decision	—	3
Nick Catone	def.	Costa Philippou	Catchweight	Unanimous Decision	—	3
Erik Koch	def.	Raphael Assuncao	Featherweight	Knockout	2:32	1

Champion. At 23 years old, Jon Jones put that title next to his name after a dominating third-round stoppage of Mauricio "Shogun" Rua that justified all the pre-fight hype and may one day have fight fans asking "where were you when 'Bones' Jones won his world light heavyweight championship?"

Winning the title wasn't even all he did, as Jones—in the history books as the UFC's youngest world champion ever, replacing Josh Barnett—foiled an attempted robbery earlier on fight day.

Jones tried to end things immediately with a flying knee, and though it didn't land flush, the blow did rattle Rua, who got taken down moments later and kept there for much of the round.

Rua was still unable to get his offense in gear in round two, with Jones continuing to dominate both standing and on the mat.

Entering round three, Jones' face was unmarked, while Rua's showed the effects of the previous ten minutes, and soon, the challenger unleashed his full arsenal on the battered champion one crushing shot at a time. Rua courageously staggered to his feet, but all that was left was a finishing series of shots from Jones that dropped Rua and brought in referee Herb Dean to end the bout at 2:37 of the third round.

Two former WEC champions met in the UFC Octagon for the first time in the co-main event of UFC 128, and it was Urijah Faber beginning a new chapter in his storied career as he bounced back from some rough moments in the first round to defeat Eddie Wineland via unanimous decision in a bantamweight bout.

Knockout of the Night: Schaub vs. Cro Cop

After winning his seventh consecutive UFC bout, this time halting previously unbeaten Kamal Shalorus in the third round, Jim Miller certainly made it clear that he was ready for a lightweight title shot.

Middleweight contender Nate Marquardt put on his hard hat and went to work against Dan Miller, drilling out a shutout decision win over his New Jersey foe in a grueling three-rounder.

Brendan Schaub got a gut check and a highlight reel memory the day after his 28th birthday, as he battled through adversity, blood, and a second-round point deduction to knock out Mirko Cro Cop in the third round of the heavyweight main card opener.

Light heavyweight knockout artist Luiz "Banha" Cane got back on track after a two fight losing streak, stopping returning Eliot Marshall in the first round of their UFC 128 preliminary bout.

Fight of the Night: Barboza vs. Njokuani

Unbeaten Edson Barboza kept his perfect record intact with a close and exciting unanimous decision victory over Anthony Njokuani that earned both men Fight of the Night honors.

Welterweight vet Mike Pyle didn't show the spectacular form he displayed in his UFC 120 win over John Hathaway in October 2010, but he did enough on the judges' scorecards to take a three-round unanimous decision win over Ricardo Almeida.

Brazil's Gleison Tibau spoiled the homecoming of Point Pleasant's Kurt Pellegrino, scoring a close split decision victory over "Batman" in a lightweight bout.

Sporting a new nickname and a new fight venue, former WEC bantamweight contender Joseph Benavidez made a smooth transition to the Octagon with a hard-fought three-round unanimous decision win over scrappy Ian Loveland.

Late replacement Costa Philippou was game throughout his catchweight bout against Nick Catone, but the Brick, New Jersey native was too much for him on the mat as he pounded out a three-round unanimous decision win.

Former WEC featherweight Erik "New Breed" Koch introduced himself to UFC fans with a bang, knocking out veteran Raphael Assuncao in the first round to land himself a $70,000 Knockout of the Night bonus.

Knockout of the Night: Koch vs. Assuncao

UFC Fight Night 24

Nogueira vs. Davis

26 March 2011

KeyArena, Seattle, WA

Debuts: Michael McDonald, Edwin Figueroa, Alex Caceres, Mackens Semerzier, Chan Sung Jung

Fighters			Division	Method	Time	Round
Main Card						
Phil Davis	def.	Antonio Rogerio Nogueira	Light Heavyweight	Unanimous Decision	—	3
Anthony Johnson	def.	Dan Hardy	Welterweight	Unanimous Decision	—	3
Amir Sadollah	def.	DaMarques Johnson	Welterweight	Submission - Strikes	3:27	2
Chan Sung Jung	def.	Leonard Garcia	Featherweight	Submission - Twister	4:59	2
Preliminary Card						
Mike Russow	def.	Jonathan Madsen	Heavyweight	Technical Knockout - Injury	—	2
Mackens Semerzier	def.	Alex Caceres	Featherweight	Submission - Rear Naked Choke	3:18	1
John Hathaway	def.	Kris McCray	Welterweight	Split Decision	—	3
Michael McDonald	def.	Edwin Figueroa	Bantamweight	Unanimous Decision	—	3
Christian Morecraft	def.	Sean McCorkle	Heavyweight	Submission - Guillotine Choke	4:10	2
Johny Hendricks	def.	TJ Waldburger	Welterweight	Technical Knockout	1:35	1
Aaron Simpson	def.	Mario Miranda	Middleweight	Unanimous Decision	—	3
Nik Lentz	def.	Waylon Lowe	Light Heavyweight	Submission - Guillotine Choke	2:24	3

It wasn't the coronation many expected, but in the UFC Fight Night main event at KeyArena on March 26, fight fans got to see the continuing education of rising star Phil Davis as he won a three-round unanimous decision over veteran contender Antonio Rogerio Nogueira.

Davis began the fight with range-finding kicks. Nogueira stalked calmly, but wasn't getting off with his punches. The Brazilian's takedown defense was solid, though, and by the end of the round, Nogueira even began finding his range with his strikes.

The exchanges came with more drama in round two, with Davis firing off kicks and Nogueira trying to time those shots with counterpunches. Again, Nogueira was able to fight off Davis' takedown attempts, and as the round approached its midway point, he scored with his own kick to the head. With two minutes left, Davis was able to take Nogueira to the mat, and even though the veteran scrambled up to his feet, Davis kept him locked up, and in the final minute he put Nogueira down again and finished the round with a barrage of strikes.

Going on the attack to begin the final round, Davis threw kicks and a knee at Nogueira before taking him down to the mat. Nogueira fought his way up briefly, but Davis had found his takedown rhythm now, and he again took the top position on the ground. Midway through the round, Nogueira got to his feet and began pursuing Davis aggressively. That led to another takedown, and the mat was where he kept his foe for the remainder of the bout.

Anthony Johnson used the Georges St-Pierre blueprint to defeat Dan Hardy in their highly anticipated welterweight bout, and while it wasn't the most scintillating bout, the three-round unanimous decision win was a disciplined and effective return to action for "Rumble", who was making his first start since a loss to Josh Koscheck in November of 2009.

Amir Sadollah survived a spirited effort from late replacement DaMarques Johnson, stopping his opponent in the second round of a fast-paced welterweight bout.

It wasn't the "Fight of the Decade" like their first WEC bout was, but Chan Sung Jung made a good case for earning Submission of the Year consideration after he finished Leonard Garcia in the second round with the first twister in the history of the UFC.

Submission of the Night: Jung vs. Garcia

Fight of the Night: McDonald vs. Figueroa

Twenty-year-old bantamweight phenom Michael McDonald got a battle out of late replacement Edwin Figueroa en route to a unanimous decision victory that saw the stock of both 135-pounders rise in their UFC Fight Night prelim bout.

WEC veteran Mackens Semerzier spoiled the UFC debut of former *Ultimate Fighter 12* competitor Alex Caceres, submitting the precocious Miami native in the first round of their featherweight bout.

Heavyweight Mike Russow made it 3-0 in his UFC career as he stopped previously unbeaten Jon Madsen due to injury after two rounds.

England's John Hathaway dug deep to pound out a hard-fought split decision win over Kris McCray in a welterweight bout.

Christian Morecraft earned his first UFC win in heavyweight action, staying in control from the opening bell before finishing Sean McCorkle via submission in round two.

Welterweight prospect Johny Hendricks bounced back from the lone loss of his career against Rick Story last December, stopping Texas' TJ Waldburger just 95 seconds into the first round.

Knockout of the Night: Hendricks vs. Waldburger

Former Arizona State standout Aaron Simpson ran a wrestling clinic on local favorite Mario Miranda, dominating from start to finish en route to a three-round unanimous decision win that broke a two-fight losing skid.

Lightweight Nik Lentz kept his unbeaten UFC record intact the hard way in the opener, scoring a come-from-behind third-round submission win over Waylon Lowe to improve to 5-0-1 in the Octagon.

UFC 129 *St-Pierre vs. Shields*

30 April 2011

Rogers Centre, Toronto, Ontario, Canada

Debuts: Charlie Valencia, Ben Henderson, Jose Aldo

Fighters			Division	Method	Time	Round
Main Card						
Georges St-Pierre	def.	Jake Shields	Welterweight	Unanimous Decision	—	5
Jose Aldo	def.	Mark Hominick	Featherweight	Unanimous Decision	—	5
Lyoto Machida	def.	Randy Couture	Light Heavyweight	Knockout	1:05	2
Vladimir Matyushenko	def.	Jason Brilz	Light Heavyweight	Knockout	0:20	1
Ben Henderson	def.	Mark Bocek	Lightweight	Unanimous Decision	—	3
Preliminary Card						
Rory MacDonald	def.	Nate Diaz	Welterweight	Unanimous Decision	—	3
Jake Ellenberger	def.	Sean Pierson	Welterweight	Knockout	2:42	1
Claude Patrick	def.	Daniel Roberts	Welterweight	Unanimous Decision	—	3
Ivan Menjivar	def.	Charlie Valencia	Bantamweight	Technical Knockout	1:30	1
Jason MacDonald	def.	Ryan Jensen	Middleweight	Submission - Triangle Choke	1:37	1
John Makdessi	def.	Kyle Watson	Lightweight	Knockout	1:27	3
Pablo Garza	def.	Yves Jabouin	Featherweight	Submission - Flying Triangle Choke	4:31	1

By the time welterweight champion Georges St-Pierre finished his UFC 129 main event bout with Jake Shields before a record UFC crowd of over 55,000 fans at Rogers Centre, he looked like he had been in a fight. And two of the three judges agreed, as St-Pierre retained his title by two razor-thin scores of 48-47 and one more comfortable margin of 50-45.

Entering the bout, St-Pierre had won 30 consecutive rounds. Tonight that streak was broken, but he retained his undisputed title for the sixth time by keeping Shields from getting the bout to the mat to work his stellar jiu-jitsu game.

It looked like a typical dominant performance for UFC featherweight champion Jose Aldo early in the UFC 129 co-main event, but Ontario's own Mark Hominick refused to go away, fighting off a series of facial bumps, bruises and cuts to finish strong in the fifth round and leave his own courageous effort as the lasting image of the 145-pound title fight, which was ultimately won clearly and unanimously by Aldo. Scores were 48-45, 48-46, and 49-46 for Aldo.

Fight of the Night:
Aldo vs. Hominick

Karate is back again. Though if you ask former UFC light heavyweight champion Lyoto Machida, he'll tell you it never left, and to prove it, he sent UFC legend Randy Couture into retirement with a spectacular jumping front kick in UFC 129 main card action.

After slow first round, Machida seemed intent on ending the bout in round two, and soon enough, he did, taking a leap in the air, and while faking his left, landed flush with a right front kick. Couture fell flat on his back, and as Machida moved in for the finish on his hurt opponent, referee Yves Lavigne intervened, stopping the bout at the 1:05 mark.

Knockout of the Night:
Machida vs. Couture

Couture retired with a 19-11 record, five UFC titles in two divisions, status as a UFC Hall of Famer, and the eternal gratitude of all who watched him fight over the last 14 years, more than 55,000 of which stood and gave him an ovation after this final bout.

It was clean-up time for "The Janitor" in light heavyweight action as Vladimir Matyushenko took only 20 seconds to knock out Jason Brilz.

Former WEC lightweight champion Ben Henderson didn't deliver his usual Fight of the Night performance, but he was effective in his UFC debut, shutting out Mark Bocek over three rounds.

Some fighters are never the same after a crushing loss. Others get better. The latter scenario was fitting for Canada's Rory MacDonald, as he rebounded from last June's loss to Carlos Condit with a shutout three-round decision win over Nate Diaz.

Short notice was no problem for Jake Ellenberger in welterweight action, as he knocked out Toronto's Sean Pierson in the first round.

Toronto's own Claude Patrick thrilled his home province fan in welterweight action, eking out a grueling three-round unanimous decision win over Daniel Roberts.

Bantamweight veteran Ivan Menjivar returned to the Octagon for the first time since UFC 48 in 2004, and he made the most of it, ending Charlie Valencia's night with a vicious elbow in less than two minutes.

Longtime middleweight standout Jason MacDonald's comeback to the UFC after three consecutive Octagon losses and a series of injuries finally hit an upturn, as he submitted Ryan Jensen in the first round for his first UFC win since he defeated Jason Lambert in 2008.

He was more matador than "Bull" for much of his lightweight bout against *The Ultimate Fighter 12*'s Kyle Watson, but in the third round, John Makdessi exploded, finishing matters in emphatic fashion with a spinning backfist.

Featherweight up and comer Pablo Garza may have upset the local fans in the opener, but "The Scarecrow" made an impression on everyone in attendance with a first-round submission victory over Yves Jabouin of Montreal that featured a rare flying triangle.

Submission of the Night:
Garza vs. Jabouin

THE INTERNATIONAL SCENE

It's easy to look at the explosion of mixed martial arts—and the Ultimate Fighting Championship in particular—over the last several years and forget that there was a time not so long ago when the sport was in dire straits and possibly on the verge of being extinct.

The UFC, the major brand in the sport, was in deep trouble, and though the Zuffa ownership team of Lorenzo Fertitta, Frank Fertitta and Dana White had fought and won battles along the way—such as getting the sport back on easily accessible Pay-Per-View—it came at a heavy price, somewhere around $44 million, and the end seemed near.

"It was brutal," said White, UFC President. "We were waiting any day for the plug to be pulled. We felt like we were getting momentum and getting traction, but it wasn't enough to dig us out of the hole that we were in and it didn't look like there was any light at the end of the tunnel. When was this gonna turn? Then, boom, *The Ultimate Fighter*."

The fighting reality show, financed by Zuffa, took off when it aired on Spike TV in 2005, and the series finale, pitting Forrest Griffin against Stephan Bonnar, was the first UFC fight ever aired live on basic cable. Since then, the company has been a juggernaut, dominating an industry that is gaining more supporters every day.

Yet while perceptions about the sport of MMA have changed as casual fans and mainstream media have come aboard, what hasn't changed is Zuffa's single-minded pursuit of excellence, epitomized by the hard-charging White, whose hellacious pace isn't rivaled by the head of any major sport. The main goal? International expansion, a quest that began in earnest at UFC 70 in 2007, when the UFC returned to England for the first time in nearly five years. Key to this return was that it wasn't a one-shot deal; the UFC opened an office in the UK, and other offices would follow in Canada and China, showing the organization's commitment to these regions.

White's global journeys continued unabated. The company pursued its rapid expansion into Europe, Canada and beyond. Lorenzo Fertitta, White's best friend, high school classmate, and business partner, decided that he was going to work full-time with the UFC, an announcement made official in 2008.

For Fertitta, the sport's incredible trajectory prompted his decision to devote all his time to the UFC.

"We've seen this explosive growth of the UFC, and particularly the opportunity we now have internationally, so we felt like it was time for me to come aboard and help the team grow and expand," said Fertitta. "I've always been a believer that this was going to be the biggest sport on the planet," he said. "That's what our goal is and that's where we're taking it."

Over the next four years, the UFC would host events in England, Ireland, Australia, Germany, the United Arab Emirates and Canada. Each event was an unqualified success, with UFC 129 in April of 2011 cementing itself as the biggest night in UFC history with over 55,000 fans in attendance at Rogers Centre in Toronto, Ontario, Canada.

But that's just the beginning, as the UFC has cut television deals throughout the world to bring the fights and fighters of the Octagon into homes that were never within reach before. Even more exotic locales will be seeing UFC action live in the coming years. It's a long way from the dark ages of mixed martial arts, and Fertitta only sees bright days ahead.

"The plans are all coming into place," said Fertitta. "We're going to be moving the show around the world, and we're creating the UFC global footprint."

UFC 130 *Rampage vs. Hamill*

28 May 2011

MGM Grand Garden Arena, Las Vegas, NV

Debuts: Renan Barao, Cole Escovedo

Fighters			Division	Method	Time	Round
Main Card						
Quinton Jackson	def.	Matt Hamill	Light Heavyweight	Unanimous Decision	—	3
Frank Mir	def.	Roy Nelson	Heavyweight	Unanimous Decision	—	3
Travis Browne	def.	Stefan Struve	Heavyweight	Knockout	4:11	1
Rick Story	def.	Thiago Alves	Welterweight	Unanimous Decision	—	3
Brian Stann	def.	Jorge Santiago	Middleweight	Technical Knockout	4:29	2
Preliminary Card						
Demetrious Johnson	def.	Miguel Angel Torres	Bantamweight	Unanimous Decision	—	3
Tim Boetsch	def.	Kendall Grove	Middleweight	Unanimous Decision	—	3
Gleison Tibau	def.	Rafaello Oliveira	Lightweight	Submission - Rear Nake Choke	3:28	2
Michael McDonald	def.	Chris Cariaso	Bantamweight	Split Decision	—	3
Renan Barao	def.	Cole Escovedo	Bantamweight	Unanimous Decision	—	3

It wasn't the action-packed war that he wanted to deliver, but former UFC light heavyweight champion Quinton "Rampage" Jackson was dominant in the UFC 130 main event at the MGM Grand Garden Arena Saturday night as he pounded out a three-round unanimous decision victory over Matt Hamill.

Matt Hamill's tough, I tried to knock him out," said Jackson, who claimed to have entered the bout with a fractured hand. "I did what I had to do, I scraped out the win." Scores were 30-27 across the board for Jackson.

Hamill fired off kicks to the head and legs before shooting for his first takedown, but Jackson pushed him off and fired a flurry in return. Hamill showed no trepidation about standing in the pocket with his hard-hitting foe, which was made easier because Jackson wasn't being particularly busy outside of a quick uppercut that just missed the mark but still jarred Hamill. Hamill's leg kicks kept him on the scoreboard, but whenever he got too aggressive, Jackson would fire off a few shots to keep the Ohio native honest. With 90 seconds left, Jackson began to increase his punch output, and he began adding knees to his arsenal to avoid takedowns. With 30 seconds left, Hamill's legs looked to be unsteady, and Jackson sensed it, finishing the round strong and bloodying his opponent's mouth.

Hamill wasn't the only one showing the scars of battle, as Jackson was treated between rounds for a cut over his right eye. As the second frame began, Jackson stayed busy with his strikes while still not allowing Hamill to take the bout to the mat. In fact, he made it a point to punish his foe every time a takedown came up empty. But as Hamill eased off the gas pedal, so did Jackson, leading to a series of boos from the crowd. With under a minute remaining in the round, Jackson appeared to rock Hamill momentarily, and again he left his foe with plenty to think about between rounds.

A superman punch began the final round for Hamill, but barely produced an eye blink from Jackson, who again peppered his opponent and then rejected a takedown attempt with a knee to the body. The pace slowed again, as Jackson looked to counter and Hamill's offense stalled. As the three minute mark approached, Jackson picked up his work rate briefly, and Hamill gamely fired back, but then the action dipped and brought the boo birds out again. With 20 seconds left, Jackson made a last ditch effort to finish, but it was not to be, and the crowd wasn't happy about it.

Knockout of the Night: Browne vs. Struve

Two-time heavyweight champion Frank Mir kept his hopes alive for another title shot in the UFC 130 co-main event at the MGM Grand Garden Arena, showing off a varied array of skills that allowed him to dominate and defeat fellow Las Vegan Roy Nelson via three-round unanimous decision.

Unbeaten banger Travis Browne kept his "0" intact with a spectacular first-round knockout of highly-touted Stefan Struve in a clash of heavyweight prospects.

Welterweight up and comer Rick Story moved further up the ranks in his bout with Thiago Alves, as he outworked and survived some hard incoming fire from the former world title challenger to win a close, but unanimous, decision.

Fight of the Night: Stann vs. Santiago

On Memorial Day weekend, the most important holiday break on his calendar, United States Marine Corps veteran Brian Stann left his armed forces comrades happy as he dominated returning middleweight contender Jorge Santiago before ending the bout via TKO late in the second round.

Rising bantamweight star Demetrious Johnson scored the biggest win of his pro career in UFC 130 prelim action, outpointing former WEC champion Miguel Angel Torres over three rounds.

Tim Boetsch made a successful jump to the middleweight division, just having too much muscle and wrestling for Kendall Grove, who was outpointed unanimously by "The Barbarian" over three rounds.

Submission of the Night: Tibau vs. Oliveira

Lightweight strongman Gleison Tibau made it two in a row with a second-round submission victory over returning Rafaello Oliveira, who was a late replacement for the injured Bart Palaszewski.

Bantamweight phenom Michael McDonald kept his UFC hot streak going, impressively scoring a three-round split decision over fellow Californian Chris Cariaso.

Brazil's Renan Barao won a battle of debuting bantamweights over Cole Escovedo, earning a three-round unanimous decision.

ANNOUNCERS

BRUCE BUFFER

Bruce Buffer knew he had found his calling in life. The only dilemma was finding a way to convince SEG, then-owners of the Ultimate Fighting Championship, that he was the man to be "The Voice of The Octagon".

The Oklahoma native had already established himself in the business world as the manager of renowned boxing ring announcer Michael Buffer, but as a martial artist himself, Bruce felt an immediate affinity towards the sport of mixed martial arts.

Despite filling in on undercards and making one-off appearances, the full-time gig eluded him until an appearance on the hit NBC sitcom *Friends* with UFC fighter Tank Abbott and referee John McCarthy gave him the leverage he needed to negotiate his way into a full-time job beginning with UFC 13 in May of 1997.

Since then, Buffer has become synonymous with the UFC, with his catchphrase "It's time" and signature move "The Buffer 180" setting him far apart from his peers in the announcing business. He's also survived the dark ages of the UFC, with the turning point coming when Forrest Griffin and Stephan Bonnar put on an epic battle in the finale of *The Ultimate Fighter* in 2005.

"The tide started to turn when Dana (White) and the Fertitta brothers rolled the dice on *The Ultimate Fighter*. We not only made Spike TV, but Spike TV made us," said Buffer. "As a result, that's when I noticed that we started to really capture the hearts and minds of the 18 to 34 year olds. It started to bring in millions of new fans, but at the same time, the nucleus of fans that we had all along that had watched us since they were 12, they grew up, and they come up to me now at 25 or older and say 'I grew up watching you.' It's just a matter of timing."

Now, there are action figures, video games, trading cards, a poker room named after him at the Luxor hotel in Las Vegas, over 38,000 followers on Twitter, and a weekly radio show, but if you ask him about the best part of his success, he narrows it down to the time spent in the Octagon with two fighters waiting to do battle.

"I block out the audience to a degree," he said. "I feed off their energy but I'm not looking at them. To me, it's the fighters and me and that's it."

OTHER ANNOUNCERS

- **Michael Buffer** – The man known for the immortal phrase "Let's Get Ready to Rumble", Michael took a break from his work in boxing for a couple turns in the UFC before his brother Bruce eventually took over as "The Voice of The Octagon".
- **Manny Garcia** – Worked the Ultimate Ultimate 2 and UFC 12 in 1996-97
- **Rich Goins** – A cult favorite among fight fans to this day, the "G-Man" was the most recognizable man in the middle of the Octagon in the early days of the UFC.
- **Ron Jeremy** – No, not the adult film star. This Ron Jeremy worked the Octagon as the announcer for UFC 5.
- **Senshiro Matsuyama** – Worked UFC 23 and 29 in Japan.

LEADERBOARDS *(stats provided by FightMetric*)*

MOST UFC BOUTS

Rank	Fighter	# of Bouts
1	Matt Hughes	24
2	Randy Couture	23
3	Chuck Liddell	23
4	Tito Ortiz	23
5	BJ Penn	20
6	Chris Lytle	19
7	Josh Koscheck	18
8	Rich Franklin	18
9	Tank Abbott	18
10	Georges St-Pierre	17
11	Frank Mir	17
12	Evan Tanner	17
13	Chris Leben	17

SHORTEST AVERAGE FIGHT TIME

(minimum 5 UFC fights)

Rank	Fighter	Time
1	Drew McFedries	2:20
2	James Irvin	2:53
3	Shane Carwin	2:54
4	Frank Trigg	3:55
5	Houston Alexander	4:13
6	Yoshiyuki Yoshida	4:15
7	Frank Mir	4:29
8	Ken Shamrock	4:34
9	Ryan Jensen	4:38
10	Manvel Gamburyan	4:45

MOST UFC WINS

Rank	Fighter	# of Wins
1	Matt Hughes	18
2	Randy Couture	16
3	Chuck Liddell	16
4	Georges St-Pierre	15
5	Tito Ortiz	14
6	Anderson Silva	13
7	Jon Fitch	13
8	Josh Koscheck	13
9	Rich Franklin	13
10	Diego Sanchez	12
11	Frank Mir	12
12	BJ Penn	12

SIGNIFICANT STRIKES LANDED

Rank	Fighter	# of Strikes
1	Georges St-Pierre	892
2	BJ Penn	746
3	Rich Franklin	722
4	Forrest Griffin	708
5	Randy Couture	703
6	Chris Lytle	691
7	Michael Bisping	644
8	Sam Stout	607
9	Tim Sylvia	585
10	Frank Edgar	572

MOST CONSECUTIVE WINS

Rank	Fighter	# of Wins
1	Anderson Silva	13
2	Royce Gracie	11
3	Georges St-Pierre	8
4	Jon Fitch	8
5	Lyoto Machida	8
6	Gray Maynard	8
7	Chuck Liddell	7 (twice)
8	Randy Couture	7
9	Jim Miller	7
10	Thiago Alves	7
11	Rich Franklin	7
12	Pat Miletich	7
13	Cain Velasquez	7
14	George Sotiropoulos	7

LONGEST AVERAGE FIGHT TIME

(minimum 5 UFC fights)

Rank	Fighter	Time
1	Frankie Edgar	16:14
2	Sean Sherk	15:35
3	Heath Herring	15:00
4	Jorge Gurgel	14:58
5	Dan Henderson	14:38
6	Nik Lentz	14:34
7	Dong Hyun Kim	14:14
8	Jens Pulver	14:03
9	Jon Fitch	13:55
10	BJ Penn	13:42

KNOCKDOWNS LANDED

Rank	Fighter	# of Knockdowns
1	Chuck Liddell	14
2	Anderson Silva	13
3	Rich Franklin	10
4	Thiago Alves	9
5	Melvin Guillard	9
6	Lyoto Machida	9
7	Andrei Arlovski	8
8	Quinton Jackson	8
9	Nate Marquardt	8
10	Jorge Rivera	8
11	Georges St-Pierre	8

BEST SIGNIFICANT STRIKE ACCURACY

(minimum 5 UFC fights and 350 significant strike attempts)

Rank	Fighter	Percentage
1	Anderson Silva	68.3%
2	Cheick Kongo	61.3%
3	Cain Velasquez	60.9%
4	Lyoto Machida	60.1%
5	Evan Tanner	59.0%
6	Randy Couture	58.7%
7	Georges St-Pierre	56.2%
8	Matt Hughes	55.2%
9	Caol Uno	54.6%
10	Brandon Vera	54.3%

SIGNIFICANT STRIKE DEFENSE

(minimum 5 UFC fights and 350 significant strike attempts by opponents)

Rank	Fighter	Percentage
1	Ryan Bader	76.1%
2	Ross Pearson	74.9%
3	Yushin Okami	74.2%
4	Frankie Edgar	73.8%
5	Georges St-Pierre	73.6%
6	Rafael dos Anjos	72.8%
7	Jim Miller	72.6%
8	Eliot Marshall	72.1%
9	Michael Bisping	71.2%
10	Luigi Fioravanti	70.7%
11	George Sotiropoulos	70.7%

STRIKES ABSORBED PER MINUTE

(minimum 5 UFC fights)

Rank	Fighter	Strikes
1	Phil Davis	0.38
2	Pete Spratt	0.89
3	Georges St-Pierre	0.99
4	Ivan Salaverry	1.01
5	Chael Sonnen	1.02
6	Ricardo Almeida	1.05
7	Vladimir Matyushenko	1.09
8	Cain Velasquez	1.10
9	Ricco Rodriguez	1.10
10	Lyoto Machida	1.12

TOTAL STRIKES LANDED

Rank	Fighter	# of Strikes
1	Jon Fitch	1973
2	Georges St-Pierre	1924
3	BJ Penn	1516
4	Chris Leben	1477
5	Chris Lytle	1399
6	Randy Couture	1332
7	Sean Sherk	1274
8	Tito Ortiz	1185
9	Nick Diaz	1082
10	Chael Sonnen	1028

TAKEDOWN ACCURACY

(minimum 5 UFC fights and 20 takedown attempts)

Rank	Fighter	Percentage
1	Georges St-Pierre	77.7%
2	Nate Marquardt	72.9%
3	Jon Jones	72.0%
4	John Howard	71.4%
5	Jonathan Goulet	70.0%
6	Cheick Kongo	68.8%
7	Cain Velasquez	68.2%
8	Renato Sobral	66.7%
9	CB Dollaway	66.7%
10	Rich Franklin	65.0%

BEST TAKEDOWN DEFENSE

(minimum 5 UFC fights and 20 takedown attempts by opponents)

Rank	Fighter	Percentage
1	Andrei Arlovski	89.5%
2	Georges St-Pierre	86.4%
3	Lyoto Machida	83.8%
4	Chuck Liddell	83.6%
5	Yushin Okami	83.3%
6	Dong Hyun Kim	80.8%
7	Martin Kampmann	80.7%
8	Dan Henderson	80.0%
9	Gray Maynard	80.0%
10	Ben Saunders	80.0%

STRIKES LANDED PER MINUTE

(minimum 5 UFC fights)

Rank	Fighters	Strikes
1	Junior dos Santos	7.12
2	Cain Velasquez	7.11
3	Shane Carwin	6.48
4	Luiz Cane	5.37
5	Amir Sadollah	5.25
6	Drew McFedries	5.13
7	Nate Quarry	4.96
8	Brad Blackburn	4.49
9	Forrest Griffin	4.49
10	Michael Bisping	4.41

MOST CAREER TAKEDOWNS

Rank	Fighter	# of Takedowns
1	Georges St-Pierre	66
2	Gleison Tibau	54
3	Karo Parisyan	53
4	Jon Fitch	52
5	Sean Sherk	50
6	Randy Couture	46
7	Rashad Evans	44
8	Clay Guida	41
9	Matt Hughes	40
10	Frankie Edgar	35

** Started in 2007, FightMetric® is the world's only comprehensive mixed martial arts statistics and analysis system. FightMetric is the official statistics provider of the UFC®.*

UFC CHAMPIONSHIP HISTORY

HEAVYWEIGHT TITLE *(206 to 265 pounds)*

1

Mark Coleman – defeats Dan Severn at UFC 12 (7 Feb. 1997) to become the first UFC heavyweight champion.

2

Maurice Smith – defeats Mark Coleman at UFC 14 (27 July 1997). Smith defends the title once, against Tank Abbott.

3

Randy Couture – defeats Maurice Smith at Ultimate Japan (21 Dec. 1997). Couture loses his title after a contract dispute.

4

Bas Rutten – defeats Kevin Randleman at UFC 20 (7 May 1999) to win the vacant title. Rutten vacates the title to move down in weight.

5

Kevin Randleman – defeats Pete Williams at UFC 23 (19 Nov. 1999) to win the vacant UFC heavyweight title. He defends the title once, against Pedro Rizzo.

6

Randy Couture – returns to the UFC and regains his title by defeating Randleman at UFC 28 (17 Nov. 2000). He defends the title twice against Pedro Rizzo.

7

Josh Barnett – defeats Couture at UFC 36 (22 March 2002) to win the title. Barnett loses his belt after testing positive for steroids.

8

Ricco Rodriguez – defeats Couture at UFC 39 (27 Sept. 2002) to claim the UFC heavyweight title.

9

Tim Sylvia – stops Rodriguez at UFC 41 (28 Feb. 2003) to become champion. Sylvia successfully defends his title against Gan McGee, but then relinquishes his crown after testing positive for steroids.

10

Frank Mir – defeats Sylvia for the vacant title at UFC 48 (19 June 2004). Mir is seriously injured in a motorcycle accident and forced to give up his belt while he rehabilitates from his injuries.

11

Andrei Arlovski – defeats Tim Sylvia in the first round at UFC 51 (5 Feb. 2005) to claim the interim title, which is later upgraded to the full championship. Arlovski defends the title twice, against Justin Eilers and Paul Buentello.

12

Tim Sylvia – becomes only the second man to regain the heavyweight championship when he knocks out Arlovski at UFC 59 (15 April 2006). Sylvia defends the title against Arlovski and Jeff Monson.

13

Randy Couture – becomes the first man to win the heavyweight title three times when he decisions Sylvia over five rounds at UFC 68 (3 March 2007). Couture defends the title against Gabriel Gonzaga. After a period of inactivity, Minotauro Nogueira and Tim Sylvia are selected to fight for the interim title. Couture subsequently returns to active status in November of 2008.

14

Minotauro Nogueira – defeats Tim Sylvia in the third round to win the interim heavyweight championship at UFC 81 (2 Feb. 2008)

15

Frank Mir – defeats Minotauro Nogueira via TKO in the second round at UFC 92 (27 Dec. 2008) to win the interim heavyweight championship. Loses to Brock Lesnar at UFC 100.

16

Brock Lesnar – defeats Randy Couture via TKO in the second round at UFC 91 (15 Nov. 2008) to win the UFC heavyweight title. Defeats Mir via second-round TKO at UFC 100 to unify UFC heavyweight title. On hiatus due to illness, returns in July of 2010 to defeat Shane Carwin via second-round submission at UFC 116. Loses to Cain Velasquez at UFC 121.

17

Shane Carwin – defeats Frank Mir via first-round KO at UFC 111 (27 March 2010) to win interim UFC heavyweight title. Loses to Lesnar via second-round submission at UFC 116.

18

Cain Velasquez – defeats Brock Lesnar via TKO in the first round at UFC 121 (23 Oct. 2010) to win the UFC heavyweight title.

UFC HEAVYWEIGHT MOST...

SUCCESSFUL DEFENSES
Two tied with 3 (Sylvia, Couture), Brock Lesnar 2

SUCCESSFUL CONSECUTIVE DEFENSES
Four tied with 2 (Lesnar, Sylvia, Arlovski, Couture)

CHAMPIONSHIP FIGHTS
Two tied with 9 [Sylvia (5-4), Couture (6-3)], Arlovski 5 (3-2), Lesnar 4 (3-1)

CHAMPIONSHIP FIGHTS WON
Couture 6, Sylvia 5, two tied with 3 (Lesnar, Arlovski)

CHAMPIONSHIP FIGHTS LOST
Sylvia 4, Couture 3, three tied with 2 (Arlovski, Randleman, Mir)

CHAMPIONSHIP ROUNDS FOUGHT
Couture 29, Sylvia 23, Randleman 13

KNOCKOUTS IN CHAMPIONSHIP FIGHTS
Two tied with 3 (Couture, Sylvia), two tied with 2 (Lesnar, Arlovski)

SUBMISSIONS IN CHAMPIONSHIP FIGHTS
Six tied with 1 (Lesnar, Coleman, Smith, Rodriguez, Mir, Arlovski, Minotauro)

LIGHT HEAVYWEIGHT TITLE *(186 to 205 pounds)*

1 
Frank Shamrock – defeats Kevin Jackson at Ultimate Japan (21 Dec. 1997) to become the first UFC light heavyweight champion. The title at that time is called middleweight. Shamrock defends his title against Igor Zinoviev, Jeremy Horn, John Lober, and Tito Ortiz. He retires from the UFC in November of 1999.

2 
Tito Ortiz – defeats Wanderlei Silva at UFC 25 (14 April 2000) to win the vacant title. Ortiz defends his crown against Yuki Kondo, Evan Tanner, Elvis Sinosic, Vladimir Matyushenko and Ken Shamrock. After a period of inactivity, Chuck Liddell and Randy Couture are selected to fight for the interim title.

3 
Randy Couture – defeats Chuck Liddell at UFC 43 (6 June 2003) for the interim title. He defeats Ortiz at UFC 44 (26 Sept. 2003) to claim the undisputed crown.

4 
Vitor Belfort – defeats Couture at UFC 46 (31 Jan. 2004) to win the title.

5 
Randy Couture – regains the championship by defeating Belfort at UFC 49 (21 Aug. 2004).

6 
Chuck Liddell – wins the light heavyweight title by defeating Couture at UFC 52 (16 April 2005). Liddell defends his title against Jeremy Horn, Couture, Renato Sobral, and Ortiz.

7 
Quinton Jackson – wins the light heavyweight title by defeating Liddell in the first round at UFC 71 (26 May 2007). Jackson defends the title against Dan Henderson.

8 
Forrest Griffin – wins the light heavyweight title by decisioning Jackson at UFC 86 (5 July 2008).

9 
Rashad Evans – wins the light heavyweight title with a third-round TKO of Griffin at UFC 92 (27 Dec. 2008).

10 
Lyoto Machida – wins the light heavyweight title with a second-round KO of Evans at UFC 98 (23 May 2009). Defends the title against Mauricio Rua.

11 
Mauricio Rua – wins the light heavyweight title with a first-round KO of Lyoto Machida at UFC 113 (8 May 2010).

12 
Jon Jones – wins the light heavyweight title with a third-round TKO of Mauricio Rua at UFC 128 (19 March 2011).

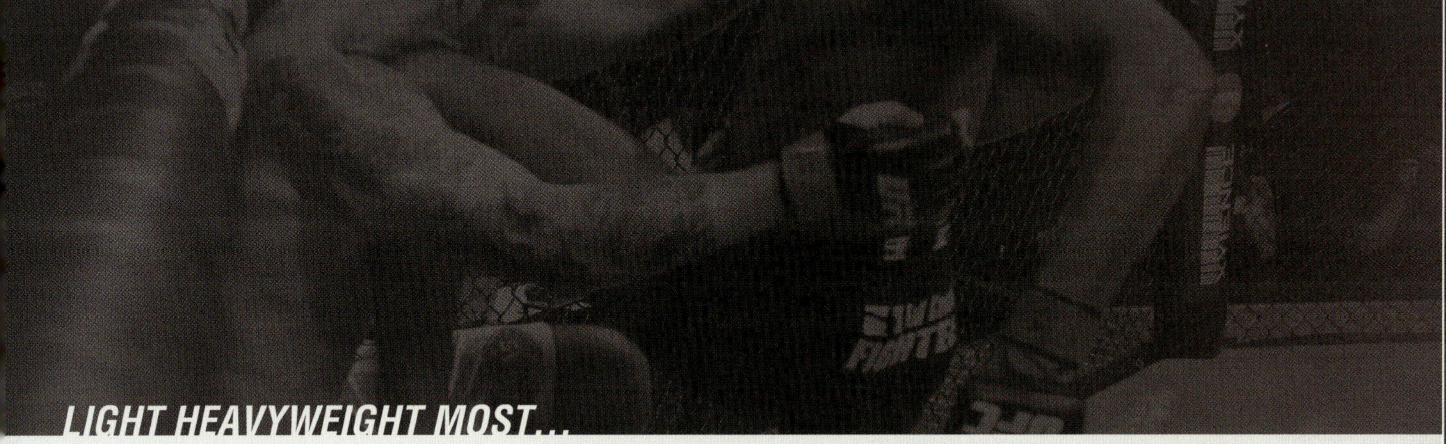

LIGHT HEAVYWEIGHT MOST...

SUCCESSFUL DEFENSES
Tito Ortiz 5

SUCCESSFUL CONSECUTIVE DEFENSES
Tito Ortiz 5

CHAMPIONSHIP FIGHTS
Ortiz 9 (6-3), Liddell 7 (5-2), Couture 6 (3-3)

CHAMPIONSHIP FIGHTS WON
Ortiz 6, two tied with 5 (Liddell, F. Shamrock)

CHAMPIONSHIP FIGHTS LOST
Two tied with 3 (Ortiz, Couture), Liddell 2

CHAMPIONSHIP ROUNDS FOUGHT
Ortiz 28, two tied at 15 (Liddell, Couture)

KNOCKOUTS IN CHAMPIONSHIP FIGHTS
Liddell 5, Ortiz 3, Couture 2

SUBMISSIONS IN CHAMPIONSHIP FIGHTS
F. Shamrock 4, Ortiz 1

MIDDLEWEIGHT TITLE *(171 to 185 pounds)*

1 

Dave Menne – defeats Gil Castillo at UFC 33 (28 Sept. 2001) to win the UFC middleweight championship.

2 

Murilo Bustamante – defeats Menne at UFC 35 (11 Jan. 2002) to win the title. Bustamante defends the title against Matt Lindland and then vacates the title as he leaves the organization.

3 

Evan Tanner – defeats David Terrell at UFC 51 (5 Feb. 2005) to win the vacant middleweight title.

4 

Rich Franklin – defeats Tanner at UFC 53 (4 June 2005) to win the title. Franklin defends the title against Nate Quarry and David Loiseau.

5 

Anderson Silva – defeats Franklin at UFC 64 (14 Oct. 2006) to win the title. Silva defeats Travis Lutter in what should have been his first title defense, but Lutter comes in overweight, rendering the bout a non-title affair. Silva has since defended the belt against Nate Marquardt, Rich Franklin, Dan Henderson, Patrick Cote, Thales Leites, Demian Maia, Chael Sonnen and Vitor Belfort.

MIDDLEWEIGHT MOST...

SUCCESSFUL DEFENSES

Anderson Silva 7

SUCCESSFUL CONSECUTIVE DEFENSES

Anderson Silva 7

CHAMPIONSHIP FIGHTS

A. Silva 8 (8-0), Franklin 5 (3-2), Three tied with 2 (Menne, Bustamante, Tanner)

CHAMPIONSHIP FIGHTS WON

A. Silva 8, Franklin 3, Bustamante 2

CHAMPIONSHIP FIGHTS LOST

Franklin 2, 10 tied with 1 (Sonnen, Menne, Tanner, Quarry, Loiseau, Terrell, Lindland, Castillo, Marquardt, Henderson, Cote, Leites, Maia)

CHAMPIONSHIP ROUNDS FOUGHT

A. Silva 24, Franklin 13, Menne 7

KNOCKOUTS IN CHAMPIONSHIP FIGHTS

A. Silva 4, Franklin 2, Tanner 1, Bustamante 1

SUBMISSIONS IN CHAMPIONSHIP FIGHTS

A. Silva 3, Bustamante 1

WELTERWEIGHT TITLE *(156 to 170 pounds)*

1 

Pat Miletich - defeats Mikey Burnett at UFC Brazil (16 Oct. 1998) to win the UFC welterweight title, which is then known as the lightweight title. Miletich defends the title against Jorge Patino, Andre Pederneiras, John Alessio, and Kenichi Yamamoto.

2 

Carlos Newton – defeats Miletich at UFC 31 (4 May 2001) to win the title.

3 

Matt Hughes – defeats Newton at UFC 34 (2 Nov. 2001) to win the title. Hughes successfully defends against Hayato Sakurai, Carlos Newton, Gil Castillo, Sean Sherk, and Frank Trigg.

4 

BJ Penn – defeats Hughes at UFC 46 (31 Jan. 2004) to win the championship. Penn subsequently leaves the organization, rendering the title vacant.

5 

Matt Hughes – regains the championship by defeating Georges St-Pierre at UFC 50 (22 Oct. 2004) to win the vacant title. Hughes defends the title against Frank Trigg and BJ Penn, and defeats Royce Gracie in a non-title bout.

6 

Georges St-Pierre – defeats Hughes at UFC 65 (18 Nov. 2006) to win the championship.

7 

Matt Serra – stops St-Pierre in the first round at UFC 69 (7 April 2007) to win the welterweight title.

8 

Georges St-Pierre – takes interim title with win over Hughes at UFC 79. Regains the undisputed title by stopping Serra in the second round at UFC 83 (19 April 2008). GSP has defended his title against Jon Fitch, BJ Penn, Thiago Alves, Dan Hardy, Josh Koscheck and Jake Shields.

WELTERWEIGHT MOST...

SUCCESSFUL DEFENSES

Matt Hughes 7, Georges St-Pierre 6, Pat Miletich 4

SUCCESSFUL CONSECUTIVE DEFENSES

Matt Hughes, Georges St-Pierre 6, Pat Miletich 4

CHAMPIONSHIP FIGHTS

Hughes 12 (9-3), St-Pierre 11 (9-2), Miletich 6 (5-1)

CHAMPIONSHIP FIGHTS WON

Hughes, St-Pierre 9, Miletich 5

CHAMPIONSHIP FIGHTS LOST

Hughes 3, three tied at 2 (St-Pierre, Newton, Trigg)

CHAMPIONSHIP ROUNDS FOUGHT

St-Pierre 37, Hughes 27, Miletich 11

KNOCKOUTS IN CHAMPIONSHIP FIGHTS

Hughes 5, St-Pierre 3, two tied at 1 (Miletich, Serra)

SUBMISSIONS IN CHAMPIONSHIP FIGHTS

Hughes 3, Miletich 2, three tied at 1 (Newton, Penn, St-Pierre)

LIGHTWEIGHT TITLE *(146 to 155 pounds)*

1 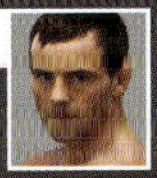

Jens Pulver – defeats Caol Uno at UFC 30 (23 Feb. 2001) to win the UFC lightweight championship. Pulver defends his title against Dennis Hallman and BJ Penn before leaving the organization and vacating the title. In 2002-03, a four-man tournament featuring BJ Penn, Caol Uno, Matt Serra, and Din Thomas is held to determine a new champion, but the title remains vacant after a five-round draw between Penn and Uno in the final match at UFC 41. The division is then used sporadically until the UFC 49 bout between Yves Edwards and Josh Thomson in 2004. The division doesn't return until UFC 58 in 2006.

2 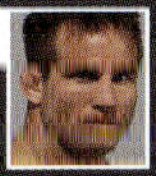

Sean Sherk – defeats Kenny Florian at UFC 64 (14 Oct. 2006) to win the vacant UFC lightweight title. Defends title against Hermes Franca but is subsequently stripped of the belt after testing positive for steroids.

3 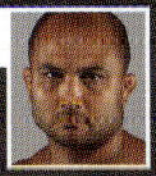

BJ Penn – defeats Joe Stevenson in the second round at UFC 80 (19 Jan. 2008) to win the vacant UFC crown. Penn defends his title against Sherk, Florian, and Diego Sanchez.

4 

Frankie Edgar – defeats BJ Penn via unanimous decision at UFC 112 (10 April 2010) to win the UFC crown. Edgar has defended the title against Penn (W5) and Maynard (Draw5)

LIGHTWEIGHT MOST...

SUCCESSFUL DEFENSES
BJ Penn 3, Edgar, Pulver 2

SUCCESSFUL CONSECUTIVE DEFENSES
BJ Penn 3, Edgar, Pulver 2

CHAMPIONSHIP FIGHTS
Penn 8 (4-3-1), three tied at 3 [Pulver (3-0), Edgar (2-0-1), Sherk (2-1)]

CHAMPIONSHIP FIGHTS WON
Penn 4, Pulver 3, three tied at 2 (Edgar, Sherk)

CHAMPIONSHIP FIGHTS LOST
Penn 3, Florian 2, Five tied with 1 (Uno, Hallman, Franca, Stevenson, Sanchez)

CHAMPIONSHIP ROUNDS FOUGHT
Penn 34, Pulver, Edgar 15, Sherk 13

KNOCKOUTS IN CHAMPIONSHIP FIGHTS
Penn 2

SUBMISSIONS IN CHAMPIONSHIP FIGHTS
Penn 2

FEATHERWEIGHT TITLE *(136 to 145 pounds)*

1 

Jose Aldo – Declared first UFC featherweight champion after WEC/UFC merger in 2010. Awarded belt before UFC 123 in November of 2010.

BANTAMWEIGHT TITLE *(126 to 135 pounds)*

1 

Dominick Cruz – WEC bantamweight champion who defeats Scott Jorgensen at WEC 53 on December 16, 2010 to win first UFC bantamweight championship.

FEATHERWEIGHT MOST...

SUCCESSFUL DEFENSES
Aldo 1

SUCCESSFUL CONSECUTIVE DEFENSES
Aldo 1

CHAMPIONSHIP FIGHTS
Aldo 1

CHAMPIONSHIP FIGHTS WON
Aldo 1

CHAMPIONSHIP FIGHTS LOST
Hominick 1

CHAMPIONSHIP ROUNDS FOUGHT
Aldo 5

BANTAMWEIGHT MOST...

CHAMPIONSHIP FIGHTS
Dominick Cruz, Scott Jorgensen 1

CHAMPIONSHIP FIGHTS WON
Dominick Cruz 1

CHAMPIONSHIP FIGHTS LOST
Scott Jorgensen 1

CHAMPIONSHIP ROUNDS FOUGHT
Dominick Cruz, Scott Jorgensen 5

THE ULTIMATE FIGHTER 1

PREMIERE DATE: JANUARY 17, 2005

THE ULTIMATE FIGHTER

THE ULTIMATE FIGHTER 1: Team Liddell vs. Team Couture

COACHES

Chuck Liddell

Randy Couture

Team Liddell	Team Couture
Bobby Southworth	Stephan Bonnar
Sam Hoger	Mike Swick
Forrest Griffin	Lodune Sincaid
Alex Schoenauer	Jason Thacker
Josh Koscheck	Nate Quarry
Diego Sanchez	Chris Leben
Kenny Florian	Alex Karalexis
Josh Rafferty	Chris Sanford
Winners	
Light Heavyweight – Forrest Griffin over Stephan Bonnar	
Middleweight – Diego Sanchez over Kenny Florian	

UFC President Dana White called it the UFC's Trojan horse, a reality show that not only entertained viewers on a weekly basis but that also introduced them to the sport of mixed martial arts and the athletes who competed in it. The Spike TV show was also a risky endeavor. If it didn't hit on all cylinders, the sport could have been in serious jeopardy.

We'll never know what that doomsday scenario would have been like though, as the first season of *The Ultimate Fighter* captivated viewers with the antics in and out of the Octagon of future standouts such as Forrest Griffin, Stephan Bonnar, Kenny Florian, Josh Koscheck, Mike Swick, Chris Leben and Diego Sanchez, all of whom were competing for a UFC contract.

Starring superstar coaches Chuck Liddell and Randy Couture, as well as UFC President Dana White and host Willa Ford, the first season saw the teams compete in various challenges to determine who would have to fight in the elimination bouts. The season made an immediate impression not only due to the fights, but to Bobby Southworth's battle with making weight, Chris Leben's feud with Southworth and Josh Koscheck, and White's unforgettable "Do you want to be a fighter?" speech. However, no reality show drama could match the drama in the light heavyweight final, as Forrest Griffin and Stephan Bonnar delivered one of the greatest fights of all-time, a three-round war that not only earned both fighters UFC contracts but that kicked off the mixed martial arts explosion.

THE ULTIMATE FIGHTER 2

PREMIERE DATE: AUGUST 22, 2005

THE ULTIMATE FIGHTER 2: Team Hughes vs. Team Franklin

COACHES

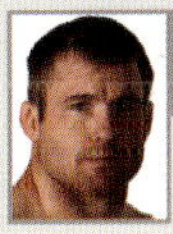

Matt Hughes

Rich Franklin

Team Hughes	Team Franklin
Joe Stevenson	Marcus Davis
Luke Cummo	Jorge Gurgel
Josh Burkman	Anthony Torres
Sammy Morgan	Melvin Guillard
Jason Von Flue (Replaced Burkman)	Keith Jardine
Mike Whitehead	Seth Petruzelli
Dan Christison	Rashad Evans
Rob MacDonald	Brad Imes
Tom Murphy	
Winners	
Heavyweight – Rashad Evans over Brad Imes	
Welterweight – Joe Stevenson over Luke Cummo	

Also appearing were Kenny Stevens, Eli Joslin, and Kerry Schall

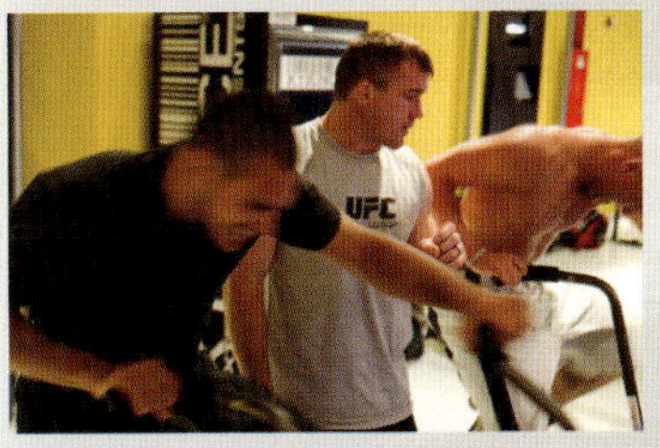

Hoping to catch lightning in a bottle, *The Ultimate Fighter 2* returned to the Spike TV airwaves four months after the groundbreaking first season. With another world-class set of competitors, the train kept rollin' with UFC welterweight champion Matt Hughes and his middleweight counterpart Rich Franklin at the helm.

This season saw the first real glimpses of what can happen to a fighter whose life was now in the reality TV fishbowl, as Eli Joslin left the show on the first episode, unable to deal with life under the bright lights. Then Kenny Stevens also left, unable to make weight for his fight.

Those who did stay were some of the best up-and-coming fighters in the game, but it was two surprises—undersized heavyweight Rashad Evans and quirky New York welterweight Luke Cummo—who stunned viewers by making it to the finals of their respective divisions. In the end though, only Evans would walk away with the season title after his war with Brad Imes, as Cummo was defeated by Joe Stevenson in the welterweight final.

THE ULTIMATE FIGHTER 3

PREMIERE DATE: APRIL 6, 2006

THE ULTIMATE FIGHTER 3: Team Ortiz vs. Team Shamrock

COACHES

Tito Ortiz

Ken Shamrock

Team Ortiz	Team Shamrock
Mike Stine	Kalib Starnes
Kendall Grove	Solomon Hutcherson
Rory Singer	Ed Herman
Danny Abbadi	Ross Pointon
Michael Bisping	Jesse Forbes
Noah Inhofer	Kristian Rothaermel
Josh Haynes	Tait Fletcher
Matt Hamill	Mike Nickels
Winners	
Light Heavyweight – Michael Bisping over Josh Haynes	
Middleweight – Kendall Grove over Ed Herman	

The first two seasons of *TUF* featured coaches who were friendly rivals (Liddell and Couture) or simply friends (Hughes and Franklin). Season three turned things upside down when former light heavyweight champion Tito Ortiz returned to the UFC fold for the first time in over a year to coach against his hated rival Ken Shamrock.

Bad blood was evident from the time the show aired in early 2006 until the men finished up their feud with back-to-back fights in the summer and fall of 2006 that ended with Ortiz victorious both times via first-round knockout.

Ortiz and Shamrock's constant sniping was the talk of the MMA world, but there were other memorable moments; a change to the rules that required each competitor to fight before earning a semifinal bid; a move from three rounds to two with a sudden-victory elimination round in the event of a tie; Ortiz' impressive coaching; and the emergence of future UFC stars Michael Bisping, Kendall Grove, Ed Herman, and Matt Hamill. But who could forget Noah Inhofer leaving the house because he couldn't make a phone call to his girlfriend?

THE ULTIMATE FIGHTER 4

PREMIERE DATE: AUGUST 17, 2006

THE ULTIMATE FIGHTER 4 THE COMEBACK

THE ULTIMATE FIGHTER 4: ***The Comeback***

COACHES

Randy Couture	Rich Franklin
Matt Hughes	Georges St-Pierre
Chuck Liddell	Mark DellaGrotte & Marc Laimon

Team No Love	Team Mojo
Travis Lutter	Pete Sell
Charles McCarthy	Scott Smith
Gideon Ray	Patrick Cote
Jorge Rivera	Edwin Dewees
Rich Clementi	Shonie Carter
Mikey Burnett	Chris Lytle
Jeremy Jackson	Matt Serra
Pete Spratt	Din Thomas
Winners	
Middleweight – Travis Lutter over Patrick Cote	
Welterweight – Matt Serra over Chris Lytle	

In a twist to the usual *Ultimate Fighter* concept of bringing the best MMA prospects together to compete for a UFC contract, *TUF4* brought in 16 UFC veterans looking for one last shot at the top. The winners of the middleweight and welterweight divisions were literally going to get skyrocketed into a title shot. It was a controversial concept among fans at the time, but one that was a brilliant move in retrospect, especially when one of the *TUF4* winners, Matt Serra, made good on the title shot by knocking out Georges St-Pierre in one of the biggest upsets in UFC history. The other winner, Travis Lutter, wasn't so lucky, and he had more than a few barbs thrown at him for not even making weight for the biggest fight of his career. The subsequent non-title loss to Anderson Silva was just the topper on a bad week.

THE ULTIMATE FIGHTER 5

PREMIERE DATE: APRIL 5, 2007

THE ULTIMATE FIGHTER 5: Team Penn vs. Team Pulver

COACHES

BJ Penn

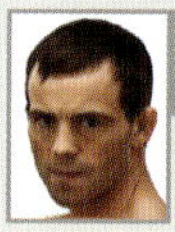

Jens Pulver

Team Penn	Team Pulver
Gray Maynard	Corey Hill
Matt Wiman	Nate Diaz
Gabe Ruediger	Brandon Melendez
Joe Lauzon	Marlon Sims
Rob Emerson	Manny Gamburyan
Andy Wang	Cole Miller
Allen Berube	Brian Geraghty
Noah Thomas	Wayne Weems
Winner	
Lightweight – Nate Diaz over Manny Gamburyan	

For years, BJ Penn seethed, hoping for the opportunity to avenge the first loss of his career to Jens Pulver. Five years after their UFC 35 bout, the two would meet again as coaches on *TUF5*. The revival of this heated feud was reason enough to tune in, but even more compelling was the fact that the field consisted of perhaps the best young talent ever assembled for the show. Gray Maynard, Matt Wiman, Joe Lauzon, Manny Gamburyan, Cole Miller and season winner Nate Diaz were on *TUF5* and are all still UFC fighters. That's an impressive lineup, even if viewers only remember the outside brawl that got Noah Thomas, Marlon Sims, and Allen Berube ousted from the house or Gabe Ruediger's battles with cake and the scale.

THE ULTIMATE FIGHTER 6

PREMIERE DATE: SEPTEMBER 10, 2007

THE ULTIMATE FIGHTER
TEAM HUGHES vs. TEAM SERRA

THE ULTIMATE FIGHTER 6: Team Hughes vs. Team Serra

COACHES

Matt Hughes

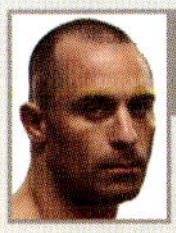

Matt Serra

Team Hughes	Team Serra
Dan Barrera	Matt Arroyo
Blake Bowman	Richie Hightower
Mac Danzig	John Kolosci
Paul Georgieff	Troy Mandaloniz
Billy Miles	Roman Mitichyan
Dorian Price	Jon Koppenhaver (replaced Roman Mitichyan)
Jared Rollins	Ben Saunders
Tommy Speer	Joe Scarola
	George Sotiropoulos
Winner	
Welterweight – Mac Danzig over Tommy Speer	

Keeping the tradition of coaches not wanting to be in the same room with each other, newly-crowned UFC welterweight champion Matt Serra battled former two-time champ Matt Hughes as coaches on *TUF6*, and you couldn't find more opposite personalities than the brash New Yorker and the no-nonsense country boy. The contrast made for compelling viewing. Beyond the coaches' rivalry and the emergence of some diamonds in the rough like George Sotiropoulos and Ben Saunders, everyone gravitated to the drama of Joe Scarola leaving the house after his loss to Mac Danzig. Thereby, severing his friendship with Serra. As for the fights, the veteran Danzig was a heavy favorite going in, and he didn't disappoint in winning the season title.

THE ULTIMATE FIGHTER 7

PREMIERE DATE: APRIL 2, 2008

THE ULTIMATE FIGHTER TEAM RAMPAGE vs. TEAM FORREST

THE ULTIMATE FIGHTER 7: Team Rampage vs. Team Forrest

COACHES

Rampage Jackson

Forrest Griffin

Team Rampage	Team Forrest
CB Dollaway	Tim Credeur
Matthew Riddle	Amir Sadollah
Patrick Schultz	Jesse Taylor
Dan Cramer	Matt Brown
Gerald Harris	Cale Yarbrough
Mike Dolce	Dante Rivera
Jeremy May	Nick Klein
Brandon Sene	Luke Zachrich
Paul Bradley	
Winner	
Middleweight – Amir Sadollah over CB Dollaway	

Change was in the air for *TUF7*, and it was a good one, as competitors weren't automatically given a spot in the house—this time they had to fight their way in, dwindling an initial pool of 32 down to 16. This made for some compelling high-stakes action and left the best possible cast to continue on for the next six weeks. With a host of top young fighters being led by Quinton "Rampage" Jackson and Forrest Griffin, the action was solid, and unknown Amir Sadollah was the surprise winner as he easily sailed to the finals and a second victory over CB Dollaway. Why two fights against the same opponent? Well, Team Forrest's Jesse Taylor's actions in Las Vegas on a night out after taping were brought to the attention of UFC President Dana White, who ousted Taylor from the final and brought Dollaway and Tim Credeur back to fight for his spot. It didn't really matter though, as it was Sadollah's time to shine.

THE ULTIMATE FIGHTER 8

PREMIERE DATE. SEPTEMBER 17, 2008

THE ULTIMATE FIGHTER
TEAM NOGUEIRA vs. TEAM MIR

THE ULTIMATE FIGHTER 8: Team Nogueira vs. Team Mir

COACHES

Minotauro Nogueira

Frank Mir

Team Nogueira	Team Mir
Rolando Delgado	Junie Browning
Efrain Escudero	Dave Kaplan
Phillipe Nover	Shane Nelson
John Polakowski	George Roop
Ryan Bader	Tom Lawlor
Jules Bruchez	Vinny Magalhaes
Kyle Kingsbury	Eliot Marshall
Shane Primm	Krzysztof Soszynski
Winners	
Light Heavyweight – Ryan Bader over Vinny Magalhaes	
Lightweight – Efrain Escudero over Phillipe Nover	

When you talk about the eighth season of *The Ultimate Fighter*, there is no shortage of standout storylines. The introduction of heavyweight legend Antonio Rodrigo "Minotauro" Nogueira to an entirely new television audience, the performances of season winners Ryan Bader and Efrain Escudero, the seemingly limitless talent of Phillipe Nover and the bizarre comments of Team Nogueira assistant coach Al Stankie are just a few. Odds are, the first thing that comes into your head will be the antics of one Junie Browning. A raw talent with an appetite for destruction, Browning polarized a nation during *TUF8* for his ability to pick fights, lose his temper and just be a lightning bolt for controversy on one of the craziest seasons in *TUF* history.

THE ULTIMATE FIGHTER 9

PREMIERE DATE: APRIL 1, 2009

THE ULTIMATE FIGHTER UNITED STATES vs. UNITED KINGDOM

THE ULTIMATE FIGHTER 9: United States vs. United Kingdom

COACHES

Dan Henderson

Michael Bisping

Team United States	Team United Kingdom
Santino DeFranco	Jeff Lawson
Jason Dent	Ross Pearson
Cameron Dollar	Martin Stapleton
Richie Whitson	Andre Winner
DaMarques Johnson	Dean Amasinger
Frank Lester	David Faulkner
Mark Miller	Nick Osipczak
Jason Pierce	James Wilks
Winners	
Welterweight – James Wilks over DaMarques Johnson	
Lightweight – Ross Pearson over Andre Winner	

Nothing gets the blood flowing like a little nation vs. nation action, and on *TUF9* Dan Henderson (United States) and Michael Bisping (United Kingdom) gladly led their nations into a little fistic battle over six weeks in Las Vegas. A tight-knit group that embraced their underdog status, Bisping's team was a destructive unit on *TUF9*. The free-wheeling US group? They were more self-destructive, never getting untracked against the battling Brits. Not surprisingly, three of the four final sports were filled by Team UK, with James Wilks and Ross Pearson winning contracts and giving Bisping bragging rights. Henderson would get the last word on "The Count" though, knocking him out in their UFC 100 bout.

THE ULTIMATE FIGHTER 10

PREMIERE DATE: SEPTEMBER 16, 2000

THE ULTIMATE FIGHTER 10: **Heavyweights**

COACHES

Rashad Evans

Rampage Jackson

Team Rashad	Team Rampage
James McSweeney	Kimbo Slice
Brendan Schaub	Abe Wagner
Justin Wren	Demico Rogers
Jon Madsen	Wes Sims
Roy Nelson	Scott Junk
Darrill Schoonover	Wes Shivers
Matt Mitrione	Marcus Jones
Mike Wessel	Zak Jensen
Winner	
Heavyweights – Roy Nelson over Brendan Schaub	

A blockbuster season in terms of media attention and ratings, *TUF10* featured streetfighting legend Kimbo Slice in his attempt to earn a UFC contract plus veteran standout (and eventual winner) Roy Nelson, and four former football players, including NFL vets Matt Mitrione and Marcus Jones and University of Colorado fullback Brendan Schaub. That could have been enough to ensure that everyone tuned in each week, but when you threw the growing rivalry between former light heavyweight champs Rampage Jackson and Rashad Evans into the mix, it was television gold. When the dust settled, Kimbo was eliminated in his first fight by Nelson, Mitrione emerged as a charismatic presence with potential, Nelson knocked out Schaub for the season title and Evans and Jackson hated each other even more at the end of the season than they did at the beginning.

THE ULTIMATE FIGHTER 11

PREMIERE DATE: MARCH 31, 2010

THE ULTIMATE FIGHTER TEAM LIDDELL VS. TEAM ORTIZ

THE ULTIMATE FIGHTER 11: Team Liddell vs. Team Ortiz

COACHES

Chuck Liddell

Tito Ortiz

Rich Franklin (replaced an injured Ortiz)

Team Liddell	Team Punishment
Kyle Noke	Nick Ring
Rich Attonito	Kyacey Uscola
Charles Blanchard	Kris McCray
Josh Bryant	Jamie Yager
Brad Tavares	James Hammortree
Court McGee	Clayton McKinney
Joseph Henle	Seth Baczynski (Replaced Chris Camozzi)
Winner	
Middleweights – Court McGee over Kris McCray	

After the fireworks of season 10, the UFC and Spike had to come up with something big for *TUF11*, and you couldn't get bigger than a reignition of the rivalry between Hall of Famer Chuck Liddell and former light heavyweight boss Tito Ortiz, with the two set to fight at the end of the season. Unfortunately, after some early fireworks, an Ortiz injury scrapped him from the fight and surgery forced his ouster from the show. Replacing him as coach late in the season was Rich Franklin, who wound up taking Ortiz' place in the Liddell fight at UFC 115 as well. In the UFC training center this time around, a wild card bout was added to the mix, allowing two fighters who had lost earlier in the competition to earn quarterfinal berths by fighting one more time. In the first season of this new addition, Kris McCray won his wild card fight and made it all the way to the finals before losing to Court McGee.

THE ULTIMATE FIGHTER 12

PREMIERE DATE: SEPTEMBER 16, 2010

THE ULTIMATE FIGHTER
TEAM GSP vs. TEAM KOSCHECK

THE ULTIMATE FIGHTER 12: Team GSP vs. Team Koscheck

COACHES

Georges St-Pierre

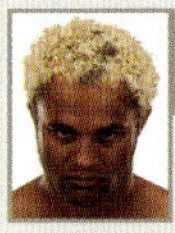
Josh Koscheck

Team GSP	Team Koscheck
Michael Johnson	Marc Stevens
Jonathan Brookins	Sevak Magakian
Spencer Paige	Sako Chivitchian
Alex Caceres	Andy Main
Kyle Watson	Nam Phan
Cody McKenzie	Aaron Wilkinson
Dane Sayers	Jeff Lentz
Winner	
Lightweights – Jonathan Brookins over Michael Johnson	

With a December 2010 showdown looming at UFC 124, what better way for old rivals Georges St-Pierre and Josh Koscheck to get reacquainted than through six weeks as coaches on *TUF12*. Surprisingly though, the expected fireworks between the standout welterweights never materialized, as St-Pierre refused to engage in Koscheck's verbal warfare, instead choosing to focus strictly on the development of his team. This was a good thing for pure fight fans, as the show turned the spotlight on the fighters, with winner Jonathan Brookins, Michael Johnson, Cody McKenzie and Nam Phan all showing particular promise when it came to the idea of them transitioning from reality television to the UFC Octagon.

THE ULTIMATE FIGHTER

WHERE ARE THEY NOW?

Not every competitor on *The Ultimate Fighter* can be a world champion like Forrest Griffin, Rashad Evans and Matt Serra or a top contender like Kenny Florian, Diego Sanchez and Michael Bisping. Some don't even cut it in the UFC. Over the course of the show's run, there have been some memorable characters who have stuck in the consciousness of fans long after their 15 minutes of fame on reality television were up. Here are a few.

NOAH INHOFER

SEASON THREE

Ah, the things we do for love. In the case of Noah Inhofer, being unable to deal with issues concerning his girlfriend while in the *TUF* house prompted him to leave the show. The decision pretty much guaranteed that he wouldn't ever make a UFC appearance, but considering his 4-5 record as of 2008, he probably wasn't going to get to the Octagon anyway. In brighter news, he did eventually marry his girlfriend.

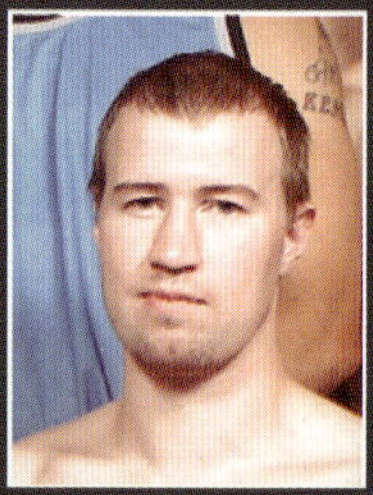

JASON THACKER

SEASON ONE

Canada's "Strange Brew," Jason Thacker, was doomed from the start, the butt of numerous jokes from his castmates on *TUF1*, the most memorable being when Chris Leben decided to relieve himself on his pillow. Thacker was simply not cut out for the show or apparently a fight career, and after being sent home from the show on the second episode, he was granted a revenge bout against Leben at the *TUF* finale but destroyed in 95 seconds. He never fought again and has faded from the public eye.

JUNIE BROWNING

SEASON EIGHT

Season eight's poster child for bad behavior, Junie Browning made previous holder of that title Chris Leben look like a choirboy. Surprisingly enough, for all of Browning's drunken antics on the show, he wasn't a bad kid. And while he had plenty of raw talent, he wasn't ready for the next level of competition in the UFC, and in his first step-up bout, he was submitted in less than two minutes by Cole Miller. He has since lost three of four bouts and hasn't competed since September of 2010.

COREY HILL
SEASON FIVE

A fighter with no professional experience but a ton of potential, Corey Hill fibbed a little bit to get on the fifth season of *TUF*. Facing perhaps the most talent-rich roster ever assembled for the show, he defeated Rob Emerson and gave a good account of himself before losing to eventual series winner Nate Diaz. He went 1-1 in his first two UFC bouts, but in the third he suffered a horrific broken leg when Dale Hartt checked one of his kicks. Amazingly, Hill returned to competition a little over a year later, so far going 2-2 on the local circuit.

MIKE DOLCE
SEASON SEVEN

It was evident that Mike Dolce probably wasn't ever going to become a world champion in mixed martial arts. But the affable Dolce did find his way to the top level of the game—not as a fighter, but as a nutritionist and conditioning coach who has helped out numerous UFC stars, including Thiago Alves, Rampage Jackson, Michael Bisping and Chael Sonnen.

TOMMY SPEER
SEASON SIX

Tommy Speer looked to be a raw clone of his coach on *TUF6*, Matt Hughes. He did his mentor proud with decision wins over Jon Koppenhaver and Ben Saunders, and he then propelled himself into the finals with a knockout of future lightweight contender George Sotiropoulos. But in the big show, Speer lost two first-rounders to Mac Danzig (in the *TUF6* finale) and Anthony Johnson and was released. After going 2-1 outside the UFC, he briefly retired, only to return six months later. He is 5-1 in his comeback.

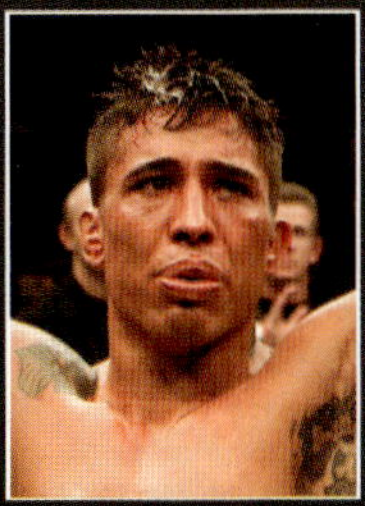

JON KOPPENHAVER
SEASON SIX

Jon Koppenhaver legally changed his name to War Machine, and that should really tell you all you need to know about this character from *TUF6*. In the Octagon he was raw but had potential and will always be remembered for his classic brawl with buddy Jared Rollins in the finale card. He was released after being submitted in less than a minute by Yoshiyuki Yoshida in 2008, and though he went 6-2 in subsequent fights, he is more remembered for his brief adult film career and his felony assault conviction. He was scheduled to be released from jail in July of 2011.

UFC® ENCYCLOPEDIA

WRITTEN BY

THOMAS GERBASI

PHOTOGRAPHS PROVIDED BY

UFC

DK/BradyGames, a division of Penguin Group (USA) Inc.
800 East 96th Street, 3rd Floor
Indianapolis, IN 46240

ISBN: 978-1-4093-8225-6
Unique ID: 001-182260-SEP/12
Printing Code: The rightmost double-digit number is the year of the book's printing; the rightmost single-digit number is the number of the book's printing. For example, 12-1 shows that the first printing of the book occurred in 2012.

First UK Edition, 2012
15 14 13 12 4 3 2 1

Printed in China by Hung Hing

BRADYGAMES STAFF

PUBLISHER
Mike Degler

EDITOR-IN-CHIEF
H. Leigh Davis

LICENSING MANAGER
Christian Sumner

TRADE AND DIGITAL PUBLISHER
Brian Saliba

CREDITS

SENIOR DEVELOPMENT EDITOR
Brian Shotton

DEVELOPMENT EDITOR
Jennifer Sims

COPY EDITOR
Heidi Newman

SENIOR BOOK DESIGNER
Keith Lowe

PRODUCTION DESIGNERS
Tracy Wehmeyer
Areva

UFC STAFF

CHIEF MARKETING OFFICER
Bryan Johnston

VP, LATIN AMERICA DIVISION
Jaime Pollack

DIRECTOR OF CREATIVE SERVICES
Heidi Noland

PHOTOGRAPHER/EDITOR
Josh Hedges

GRAPHIC DESIGNER
Rob Tonelete

DIRECTOR OF COMMUNICATIONS
Dave Sholler

WEB EDITOR
Laura Gilbert

MARKETING MANAGER
Beth Turnbull

PHOTOGRAPHY CREDITS

Al Bello
Gavin Bond
Josh Hedges
Kari Hubert
Jed Jacobsohn
Jim Kemper
Jon Kopaloff
Kevin Lynch
Donald Miralle
Susumu Nagao
Mark Nolan
Elliott Raymond
Mike Roach
Tom Szczerbowski

This encyclopedia covers the fighters and all the events from UFC 1 through UFC 130.

ACKNOWLEDGMENTS

BRADYGAMES
Mike Degler

November 2, 2001 is a date that is burned into my memory. That was the night I was invited over to a friend's house to watch my first Ultimate Fighting Championship event. I was a long-time boxing fan and wasn't sure what to expect from mixed martial arts and a cage. But after watching Matt Hughes KO slam Carlos Newton, BJ Penn's 11-second KO of Caol Uno (still my favorite UFC KO of all time), and Randy Couture fight that night, I was hooked. Ever since UFC 34, I've been on an insane campaign to introduce this awesome sport to as many friends, family, co-workers and complete strangers as possible.

The book you are holding in your hands is a culmination of hundreds of hours of work, countless meetings, a strange four days stranded in Las Vegas during an ice storm, and 3 years of dedication by the DK/BradyGames team working on our passion—the UFC. We wanted to create a book that we, as fans, would want to read from cover to cover and I truly believe we've done that. I hope you enjoy this definitive guide to the UFC as much as we enjoyed creating it.

OK, here comes my ridiculously long list of thank you's ...

Jaime P.–this book would not have been possible without you. I think the only reason you finally authorized this book to be published was to stop me from continually calling your office. Thanks for getting Dana and company on board.

Xian, KLowe, Shotton and Trace–your passion for this sport is evident on every page of this book. You guys went above and beyond on this one. Kudos!

Tom G.–every article you wrote was everything we hoped it would be. You are a great guy and a wonderful author. Someday you'll get that Tyson interview.

Heidi N. and Rob T.–thank you so much for all of your extra effort on this book. I know it wasn't easy and it was pretty frantic at the end but we did it...and it's awesome.

Josh H.–you brought this book to life by providing us with this incredible photography. Thanks for everything you did (even in the midst of having twins) to make this book so visually stunning.

Beth T.–you've been a true partner of ours since the beginning and have gone above and beyond promoting all of our UFC books. Thanks for always supporting our efforts.

Jamie, Nathan, Abigail, Lily and Natalie–I love you guys!